MW00848857

# A HISTORY OF THE JEWISH PEOPLE
# IN THE TIME OF JESUS CHRIST

# A HISTORY

## *of*

# THE JEWISH PEOPLE

## IN THE TIME OF JESUS CHRIST

### EMIL SCHÜRER, D.D., M.A.

*Being a Second and Revised Edition of a*
*"Manual of the History of New Testament Times"*

*Second Division*

THE INTERNAL CONDITION OF PALESTINE, AND OF THE
JEWISH PEOPLE, IN THE TIME OF JESUS CHRIST

*Volume I*

TRANSLATED BY

SOPHIA TAYLOR AND REV. PETER CHRISTIE

HENDRICKSON
PUBLISHERS

A HISTORY OF THE JEWISH PEOPLE IN THE TIME OF JESUS CHRIST

Hendrickson Publishers, Inc. edition

ISBN: 1-56563-049-1

reprinted from the edition originally published by
T. & T. Clark: Edinburgh, 1890

Second Printing – March 1995

*Printed in the United States of America*

Gratefully Dedicated

TO

ALBRECHT RITSCHL, D. D.

AND

CARL VON WEIZSÄCKER, D.D.

# PREFACE.

——o——

IT is a reconstruction of the *Manual of the History of New Testament Times* which here appears under another title. I believe that this new title expresses more plainly and correctly than the old title the actual contents of the book. For in fact, whether in its former or present state, it does not profess to be more than a *History of the Jewish People in the Time of Jesus Christ*, to the exclusion of the state of the heathen world. I could not decide on admitting the latter, because the selection to be made must have been an arbitrary one.

The external framework of the book has undergone but little alteration in this new revision. Most of the paragraphs remain the same. The only additions are the section on the Priesthood and the Temple worship (§ 24), and the two paragraphs on the Palestino-Jewish and the Graeco-Jewish literature (§ 32 and 33), which replace the former section on the Apocalypse. Thus the number of paragraphs is only increased by two. Within this former framework, however, the book has certainly become almost a new one. Renewed consultation of authorities and continued occupation with the subject furnished so much fresh material, that a considerable increase of extent was unavoidable. The matter of this Second Division is threefold that of the first edition, although

I have earnestly striven not to expand the form beyond the limits then observed. It is only in verbal citations from documentary authorities that I have allowed myself somewhat more liberty than in the former edition.

An apology is needed on my part for issuing the second half of the book before the first. This inversion of the natural order was not at first contemplated. I merely began operations on this second half because there was more to be done here than in the first, my purpose being to print both parts in one volume as before. The work, however, so grew under my hands as to render a division necessary. At the same time, the completion of the whole was consequently so delayed, that it seemed desirable to publish what was ready at once. This was the more possible because this half also forms a comparatively independent whole. While thus issuing this Second Division first, I can at the same time express the hope, that the First Division, which will not expand in the same proportion, may, with the needful index, follow it within the space of one year.

E. SCHÜRER.

GIESSEN, *Sept.* 1885.

# CONTENTS OF DIVISION II. VOL. I.

—— o ——

## § 22. THE STATE OF CULTURE IN GENERAL.

### I. MIXTURE OF POPULATION.  LANGUAGE.

THE *Jewish population* of Palestine experienced, during the Greek and Roman period, as well as in previous centuries, great fluctuations both in numbers and extension. From the beginning of the Hellenistic period to the rising of the Maccabees the Jewish element must be regarded as gradually receding, the Greek as triumphantly advancing. The rising of the Maccabees and its consequences produced however an important change, Judaism gaining ground thereby both intensively and extensively. It was internally consolidated and extended its boundaries in nearly every direction : to the west, by the Judaizing of the towns of Gazara, Joppa and Jamnia (see above, § 7, and below, § 23. I.) ; to the south, by the compulsory conversion of the Idumaeans under John Hyrcanus (see § 8) ; to the north, by the conversion of the Ituraeans under Aristobulus I. (see § 9) ; and in all directions by the conquests of Alexander Jannaeus. It is true that the Judaism of these Asmonean princes from John Hyrcanus onwards was not that of the scribes and Pharisees ; still they represented, though in their own fashion, the Jewish religion and nationality, as the example of the " Hellenistic Aristobulus " especially proves. Then, under Alexandra even the Pharisaic tendency again prevailed. Under the Romans and Herodians indeed the pursuit of a Graeco-Roman culture was again favoured as much as possible. But Pharisaic Judaism was now so established, both externally and internally, by the development of the last two centuries, that its state of possession could not thus be essentially encroached upon, and not till the convulsions of the wars under Vespasian and Hadrian did it again incur great losses.

For the times of Josephus we have somewhat more accurate information concerning the extension of the Jewish population in Palestine in the description he has given of the country in his *Bell. Jud.* iii. 3.[1] From this we learn—what is elsewhere confirmed—that of all the maritime towns, two only, viz. Joppa and Jamnia, which were Judaized in the Maccabaean period, contained a chiefly Jewish population. In all the other coast towns the Gentile was the prevailing element (see also § 23. I.). In the interior, on the contrary, the countries of Judaea, Galilee and Peraea had an essentially Jewish population. To these were added the regions lying to the east of the Sea of Gennesareth, viz. Gamalitis, Gaulonitis, Batanaea and Trachonitis, which had a mixed Jewish and heathen population.

The threefold division of the Jewish region into Judaea, Galilee and Peraea (עֵבֶר הַיַּרְדֵּן, גָּלִיל, יְהוּדָה) is also repeatedly

---

[1] It is evident, that Josephus intends to give in the above-mentioned passage (*Bell. Jud.* iii. 3. 1–5) a description of the Jewish country, *i.e.* of those districts of Palestine, which were entirely or chiefly inhabited by *Jews*. For all Gentile districts are excluded from the description and only mentioned to define the boundaries of the Jewish regions. He thus first describes Galilee, which is bounded on the west by the region of Ptolemais; on the east by that of Hippos, Gadara, etc. (iii. 3. 1); then Peraea, which is bounded on the north by the region of Pella, on the east by that of Gerasa, Philadelphia, etc. (iii. 3. 6). Hereupon follows a description of Samaria (iii. 3. 4), and finally one of Judaea (iii. 3. 5). The latter extends from the Jordan to Joppa (μέχρις Ἰόππης), Joppa being thus not reckoned as a part of Judaea. The Hellenistic coast towns are all excluded from the description; and Josephus only says of the Jewish territory that it was not deprived of those enjoyments, which come from the sea, because it extended *to the coast lands* (iii. 3. 5: ἀφήρηται δὲ οὐδὲ τῶν ἐκ θαλάσσης τερπνῶν ἡ Ἰουδαία, τοῖς παραλίοις κατατείνουσα). To the four provinces mentioned, Josephus adds, by way of supplement: (1) the region of Jamnia and Joppa as being the only maritime towns of which the population was chiefly Jewish (comp. § 23. I.); and (2) the provinces of Gamalitis, Gaulonitis, Batanaea and Trachonitis, in the kingdom of Agrippa, because the Jewish element here formed at least a very considerable fraction. It is of special interest to observe, that in this whole description Josephus includes *Samaria*, thus evidently regarding the *Samaritans* also as *Jews*, though as heterodox Jews.

assumed in the Mishna.[2] The central country and nucleus of the whole was Judaea, which was bounded on the north by Samaria, on the east by the Jordan and the Dead Sea, on the west by the district of the Philistine-Hellenistic cities, on the south by Arabia Petraea. In Judaea was the centre of Jewish life; it was here that the new community had first reorganized itself after the Babylonian captivity, here that the rising of the Maccabees originated, and here that the learned and educational activity of the scribes and Pharisees had its chief seat. In the north, and separated from Judaea by Samaria, was Galilee, whose boundaries were to the north the district of Tyre; to the west, that of Ptolemais; to the east, Jordan and the Lake of Gennesareth. The population of Galilee also was mainly Jewish; for the inhabitants of this district had not joined the Samaritan schism, as might have been expected from the former common history of the kingdom of Ephraim. On the contrary, the tendency adopted by Judaism in the post-exilian period had been—we no longer know how or when, but certainly during the Persian period—successfully brought to bear in this district also, and an enduring religious association thus established between the inhabitants of Judaea and Galilee. Peraea, the third of the Jewish lands, lay beyond the river Jordan, and was bounded on the north by the district of Pella, on the east by the districts of Gerasa, Philadelphia, and Heshbon, and on the south by the kingdom of Arabia Petraea. In this province also the population was an essentially Jewish one.[3] Still, neither in Galilee nor Peraea must we conceive of the Jewish element as pure and unmixed. In the shifting course of history Jews and Gentiles had here been so often, and in such a variety of ways, thrown

---

[2] *Shebiith* ix. 2; *Kethuboth* xiii. 10; *Baba bathra* iii. 2.

[3] Comp. *e.g. Antt.* xx. 1. 1 (the dispute of the Jews with the Philadelphians concerning boundaries); *Bell. Jud.* iv. 7. 4-6 (the share of the Jews of Peraea in the revolt). The Mishna too always assumes, that Peraea (עֵבֶר הַיַּרְדֵּן) is a land inhabited by Jews; see *Shebiith* ix. 2; *Bikkurim* i. 10; *Taanith* iii. 6; *Kethuboth* xiii. 10; *Baba bathra* iii. 2; *Edujoth* viii. 7; *Menachoth* viii. 3.

together, that the attainment of exclusive predominance by the Jewish element must be counted among the impossibilities. It was only in Judaea, that this was at least approximately arrived at by the energetic agency of the scribes during the course of a century.

In spite of the common religion and nationality of the three provinces, many differences of manners and customs existed between their inhabitants, and these imparted a certain independence to their inner life, quite apart from the political separation repeatedly appearing. The Mishna mentions, *e.g.*, slight differences in respect of the marriage laws between Judaea and Galilee,[4] varying customs in the intercourse between espoused persons,[5] differences of weights and coinage between Judaea and Galilee.[6] The three provinces are therefore looked upon as in certain respects " different countries."[7]

The districts east of the Lake of Gennesareth (Gamalitis, Gaulonitis, Batanaea and Trachonitis) formed a somewhat motley assemblage. The population was a mixed one of Jews and Syrians (*Bell. Jud.* iii. 5: οἰκοῦσι δὲ αὐτὴν μιγάδες 'Ιουδαῖοί τε καὶ Σύροι). But besides the settled population, numerous nomadic hosts, from whom the former had much to suffer, were wandering about in these border lands of civilisation. Very favourable to them were the caves of this district, in which they could lay up stores of water and provisions, and in case of attack find refuge, together with their flocks and herds. Hence it was very difficult to subdue them. The powerful hand of Herod however succeeded in inducing among them a certain amount of order.[8] With the view of keeping these turbulent elements permanently in check, he frequently settled foreign colonists in Trachonitis; at first, three thousand Idumaeans;[9] then a colony of warlike Jews from Babylon, to

---

[4] *Kethuboth* iv. 12.          [5] *Jebamoth* iv. 10; *Kethuboth* i. 5
[6] *Terumoth* x. 8; *Kethuboth* v. 9; *Chullin* xi. 2.
[7] *E.g.* in respect of the fundamental principle, that the wife is not bound to accompany her husband to another country (*Kethuboth* xiii. 10), in respect of the law of usucaption (*Baba bathra* iii. 2).
[8] *Antt.* xv. 10. 1.          [9] *Antt.* xvi. 9. 2.

whom he granted the privilege of immunity from taxation.[10]
His sons and grandson continued this work. Nevertheless
one of the two Agrippas had to complain in an edict of the
brutish manner of life (θηριώδης κατάστασις) of the inhabitants
and of their abode in the caves.[11] Herod's exertions for the
promotion of culture at last introduced the Greek element
into these countries. In the neighbourhood of Kanatha (see
§ 23. I.) are still found the ruins of a temple, which according
to its Greek inscriptions belongs to the period of Herod the
Great.[12] Greek inscriptions of the two Agrippas, especially of
Agrippa II., are found in larger numbers in the neighbourhood
of Hauran.[13] In the Roman period the Greek element pre-
dominated, at least externally, in these districts (see hereon
Nr. ii. 1).

The *Samaritans* also belonged in a wider sense to the
Jewish population.[14] For their character is not rightly viewed

---

[10] *Antt.* xvii. 2. 1-3. On the history of this colony, comp. also *Vita*, 11.

[11] The unfortunately very scanty fragments of this edict are given in
Le Bas et Waddington, *Inscriptions Grecques et Latines*, vol. iii. n. 2329.
Thence also in the *Zeitschrift für wissenschaftl. Theol.* 1873, p. 252.

[12] Comp. especially the inscriptions in Le Bas and Waddington, vol. iii.
n. 2364.

[13] Le Bas and Waddington, vol. iii. n. 2112, 2135, 2211, 2329, 2365,
2413b. Thence also in the *Zeitschrift für wissenschaftl. Theol.* 1873,
p. 248 sqq.

[14] Kautzsch gives in Herzog's *Real-Encycl.*, 2nd ed. xiii. 351-355, the
most complete catalogue of the copious literature on the Samaritans.
Comp. especially : Cellarius, *Collectanea historiae Samaritanae*, 1688 (also in
Ugolini, *Thes.* t. xxii.); Robinson's *Palestine*, iii. 130, 131 ; Juynboll,
*Commentarii in historiam gentis Samaritanae*, Lugd. Bat. 1846 ; Winer,
*RWB.* ii. 369 - 373 ; Lutterbeck, *Die neutestamentlichen Lehrbegriffe*,
i. 255-269 ; Herzfeld, *Gesch. des Volkes Israel*, iii. 580 sqq. ; Jost, *Gesch.
des Judenthums*, i. 44-89 ; Petermann in Herzog's *Real-Encycl.*, 1st ed.
xiii. 359-391. Hausrath, *Zeitgesch.*, 2nd ed. i. 12-23; Schrader in Schenkel's
*Bibellexicon*, v. 149-154 ; Appel, *Quaestiones de rebus Samaritanorum sub
imperio Romanorum peractis*, Gotting. 1874 ; Nutt, *A Sketch of Samaritan
History, Dogma, and Literature*, London 1874 ; Kohn, "Zur Sprache,"
"Literatur und Dogmatik des Samaritaner" (articles in the *Kunde des
Morgenlandes*, vol. v. No. iv. 1876); Kautzsch in Riehm's *Handwörter-
buch des bibl. Altertums, sub voce;* Recess, *Gesch. der heil. Schriften
Alten Testaments*, § 381, 382 ; Hamburger, *Real-Encyclopädie für Bibel und
Talmud*, div. ii. 1883, pp. 1062-1071 ; Kautzsch in Herzog's *Real-Encycl.*,

till it is regarded from the twofold point of sight—(1) of their being indeed, according to their *natural* composition, a mixed people arising from the intermingling of the former Israelitish population with Gentile elements, especially with the heathen colonists introduced by the Assyrians; and (2) of their having a *religion* essentially identical with that of Israel at an earlier stage of development. Among the colonists, whom the Assyrians had planted (2 Kings xvii. 24 sqq.) in Samaria from the provinces of Babylon, Cuthah, Ava, Hamath and Sepharvaim, those from Cuthah (כֻּתָה, כּוּת, 2 Kings xvii. 24, 30) seem to have been particularly numerous. The inhabitants of Samaria were hence subsequently called Cuthites by the Jews (Χουθαῖοι in Joseph. *Antt.* ix. 14. 3, xi. 4. 4, 7. 2, xiii. 9. 1; in Rabbinic literature כּוּתִים [14a]). We must not, however, confidently assume, that the ancient Israelitish population was entirely carried away, and the whole country peopled afresh by these heathen colonists. It is, on the contrary, certain, that a considerable percentage of the ancient population remained, and that the new population consisted of a mixture of these with the heathen immigrants. The religion of this mingled people was, according to the Bible (2 Kings xvii. 24–41), at first a mixed religion,—a combination of the heathen rites introduced by the colonists with the old Israelite worship of Jahveh upon the high places. Gradually however the Israelitish religion must have obtained a decided preponderance. For, from what we know with certainty of the religion of the Samaritans (of course leaving malicious reports out of question), it was a pure Israelitish monotheism. They acknowledged the unity of God and the authority of Moses as the greatest of the prophets; they

---

2nd ed. xiii. 340–355. Various contributions to the Samaritan literature by Heidenheim in the *deutschen Vierteljahrsschrift für engl.-theol. Forschung und Kritik*, 1861 sqq.

[14a] כּוּתִים in the Mishna in the following places: *Berachoth* vii. 1, viii. 8; *Pea* ii. 7; *Demai* iii. 4, v. 9, vi. 1, vii. 4; *Terumoth* iii. 9; *Challa* iv. 7; *Shekalim* i. 5; *Rosh hashana* ii. 2; *Kethuboth* iii. 1; *Nedarim* iii. 10; *Gittin* i. 5; *Kiddushin* iv. 3; *Ohaloth* xvii. 3; *Tohoroth* v. 8; *Nidda* iv 1, 2, vii. 3, 4, 5.

observed the Jewish rite of circumcision on the eighth day, the sanctification of the Sabbath, and the Jewish annual festivals. Nay, they even relinquished the pre-Deuteronomic standpoint of the worship of Jahveh upon high places, accepted the whole Pentateuch as the law of Israel, and consequently acknowledged the unity of the Jewish worship. It is only in the circumstance of their transferring this worship not to Jerusalem but to Gerizim that we perceive the after effect of the older standpoint. Here, according to the somewhat suspicious account of Josephus, they built in the time of Alexander the Great[15] a temple of their own ; and even after its destruction by John Hyrcanus, Gerizim continued to be their sacred mountain and the seat of their worship.[16] They did not indeed participate in the further development of Pharisaic Judaism, but rejected all that went beyond the injunctions of the Pentateuch. Nor did they accept any of the sacred writings of the Jewish canon except the Pentateuch. But for all this the right to call themselves "Israelites" cannot be denied them, so far, that is, as religion and not descent is in question.

The position of Judaism proper with regard to the Samaritans was always a hostile one: the ancient antagonism of the kingdoms of Israel and Judah was here carried on in a new form. When the Samaritans desired, in the time of Zerubbabel, to co-operate in the building of the temple at Jerusalem, they were rejected by the Jews (Ezra iv. 1) ; and "the foolish people who dwell in Sichem" are as much hated by the Son of Sirach as the Edomites and Philistines (Ecclus. l. 25, 26). The Samaritans on their side requited this disposition with like hostility.[17] The legal appointments, never-

---

[15] Josephus, *Antt.* xi. 7. 2 ; 8. 2 sqq. The history of Sanballat and his son-in-law, with which Josephus connects the building of the temple on Gerizim, happened according to Nehemiah's account in his own days (Neh. xiii. 28), about one hundred years before Alexander the Great.

[16] Destruction by John Hyrcanus, *Antt.* xiii. 9. 1. Continuance of veneration for it: John iv. 20 ; Joseph. *Antt.* xviii. 4. 1 ; *Bell. Jud.* iii. 7. 32.

[17] Neh. iv. 1 sqq. ; Luke ix. 52, 53 ; Joseph. *Antt.* xviii. 2. 2, xx. 6. 1 ; *Bell. Jud.* ii. 12. 3 ; *Rosh hashana* ii. 2.

theless, of Rabbinic Judaism with respect to the Samaritans, are, from the standpoint of Pharisaism, generally correct and just.[18] The Samaritans are never absolutely treated as "foreigners," but as a mingled people, whose Israelitish descent was not indeed proved, but always to be regarded as possible.[19] Hence their membership of "the congregation of Israel" is not denied, but only designated as doubtful.[20] Their observance of the law, e.g. with regard to tithes and the Levitical laws of purification, did not indeed correspond with Pharisaic requirements, on which account they were in many respects placed on a level with Gentiles.[21] They were never however treated as idolaters (עכו״ם), but, on the contrary, decidedly distinguished from them.[22] Their observance of the Sabbath is occasionally mentioned,[23] and it is assumed as at least possible, that they could say a genuine Israelitish grace at meals.[24] In fact they stand, so far as their observance of the law is concerned, on the same level as the Sadducees.[25]

The *language* of the Jewish population of all the districts

---

[18] A collection of Rabbinical definitions is given in the treatise כותים, in the seven small treatises published by Raphael Kirchheim (see above, § 3); the passages of the Mishna (see above, note 14a); comp. also Light-foot, *Centuria Matthaeo praemissa*, c. 56 (*Opp.* ii. 212); Hamburger, as before quoted.

[19] Compare, *on the one hand*, Shekalim i. 5 (obligatory sacrifices for the temple are to be received only from Israelites, not from Gentiles nor even from Samaritans); *on the other*, Berachoth vii. 1 (when three Israelites have eaten together, they are bound to prepare themselves formally for prayer; this also holds good if one of the three is a Samaritan); Kethuboth iii. 1 (the claim for a money compensation on account of cohabitation with an Israelitish virgin holds good in respect of a Samaritan virgin).

[20] *Kiddushin* iv. 3.

[21] Comp. in general, Demai vii. 4; Tohoroth v. 8; Nidda iv. 1, 2, vii. 3–5.

[22] *Berachoth* vii. 1; *Demai* iii. 4, v. 9, vi. 1; *Terumoth* iii. 9. The assertion, that the Samaritans worshipped the image of a dove, is a slander first appearing in the Talmud (*Jer. Aboda sara* v. fol. 44a; *Bab. Chullin* 6a; see Levy, *Neuhebr. Wörterbuch, s.v.* יון), and one, of which the Mishna as yet knows nothing.

[23] *Nedarim* iii. 10.          [24] *Berachoth* viii. 8.

[25] Comp. *Nidda* iv. 2: "The Sadducees, when they follow the customs of their fathers, are equal to the Samaritans." Epiphanius says of the Sadducees, *Haer.* 14: τὰ πάντα δὲ ἴσα Σαμαρείταις φυλάττουσιν.

here mentioned was, since the last centuries before Christ, no longer Hebrew, but Aramaic.[26] How and when the change was effected, cannot now be ascertained. At any rate, it was not the exiles, who returned from Babylon, who brought the Aramaic thence, for the post-exilian literature of the Israelites is also chiefly Hebrew. Nor was the Aramaic dialect of Palestine the Eastern (Babylonian), but the Western Aramaic. Hence it must have penetrated gradually to Palestine from the north. The period of the transition is marked by the canonical books of Ezra and Daniel (the latter about 167–165 B.C.), which are written partly in Hebrew, partly in Aramaic (Aramaic are Ezra iv. 8–6, 18, vii. 12–26 ; Dan. ii. 4–7, 28). A saying of Joses ben Joeser, about the middle of the second century before Christ, is cited in Aramaic in the Mishna,[27] also certain sayings of Hillel and other authorities.[28] That Aramaic was in the time of Christ the sole popular language of Palestine, is evident from the words mentioned in the New Testament : ἀββᾶ (Mark xiv. 36), ἀκελδαμάχ (Acts i. 19), γαββαθᾶ (John xix. 13), γολγοθᾶ (Matt. xxvii. 33), ἐφφαθά (Mark vii. 34), κορβανᾶς (Matt. xxvii. 6), μαμωνᾶς (Matt. vi. 24), μαρὰν ἀθά (1 Cor. xvi. 22), Μεσσίας = מְשִׁיחָא (John i. 41), πάσχα (Matt. xxvi. 17), ῥακά (Matt. v. 22), σατανᾶς (Matt. xvi. 23), ταλιθὰ κούμι (Mark v. 41) ; to which may be added names of persons, such as Κηφᾶς, Μάρθα, Ταβιθά,[29] and the numerous names compounded with בַּר (Barabbas, Bartholomew, Barjesus, Barjonas, Barnabas, Barsabas, Bartimæus). The words, too, of Christ upon the

---

[26] Comp. Zung, *Die gottesdienstlichen Vorträge der Juden* (1832), p. 7 sq. ; Herzfeld, *Gesch. d. Volkes Israel*, iii. 44 sqq., 58 sqq. ; Böhl, *Forschungen nach einer, Volksbibel zur Zeit Jesu* (1873), pp. 4–28 ; Delitzsch, *Ueber die palästinische Volkssprache, welche Jesu und seine Jünger geredet haben* ("*Saat auf Hoffnung*"), 1874, pp. 195–210 ; Reuss, *Gesch. der heil. Schriften Neuen Testaments*, § 40 ; the same, *Gesch. der heil. Schriften Alten Testaments*, § 416, 417 ; Kautzsch, *Grammar of Biblical Aramaic* (1884), pp. 4–12.

[27] *Edujoth* viii. 4.

[28] Hillel, *Aboth* i. 13, ii. 6 ; others, *Aboth* v. 22, 23.

[29] The accentuation in our editions is very inconsistent. Consistent accentuation would require ῥακᾰ, ταλιθᾰ, Ταβιθᾰ.

cross: 'Ελωΐ ἐλωΐ λαμὰ σαβαχθανεί (Mark xv. 34), are
Aramaic. Hebrew was so little current with the common people,
that the lessons from the Bible read in public worship had to
be translated verse by verse into the dialect of the country.[30]
Notwithstanding however this complete prevalence of
Aramaic, Hebrew still remained in use as "the sacred
language" (לְשׁוֹן הַקֹּדֶשׁ). It was read aloud in the synagogues of
Palestine both before and after the Holy Scriptures; and in
certain liturgical cases the use of Hebrew was absolutely
required.[31]   Hebrew also continued to be the language of the
learned, in which even the legal discussions of the scribes
were carried on.   Not until about the third century after
Christ do we find Aramaic in use for the last-named purpose;
and while the Mishna was still in Hebrew (second century),
the Palestinian Talmud was (fourth century) in Aramaic.
The latter is our most copious source for the knowledge of
this language of Palestine.   Some hints concerning dialectic
differences of pronunciation between Judaea and Galilee are
given in the Gospels and the Talmud.[32]

[30] *Megilla* iv. 4, 6, 10.   Comp. below, § 27.

[31] *Jebamoth* xii. 6; *Sota* vii. 2–4, viii. 1, ix. 1; *Megilla* i. 8. See especially
*Sota* vii. 2: "The following portions are delivered *in the sacred language
alone:* the section of Scripture at the offering of the first-fruits, the
formula at the Chaliza, the blessings and curses, the blessing of the priest,
the form of blessing of the high priest, the portion read by the king (at
the Feast of Tabernacles in the Sabbatic year), the formula at the killing
of a calf (on account of one found dead), and the speech of one anointed
for war when addressing the army." On the other hand, *e.g.* the Shma,
the Shmone-Esre (see on this, § 27, Appendix), grace at meals, etc., might
be said in any language (*Sota* vii. 1). All this applies to *oral* delivery.
In writing, the use of Hebrew was required for the text of the *Tefillin*
and *Mesusoth;* for all besides, even for the Scriptures, any language was
allowed, according, however, to Rabban Gamaliel, only Greek beside
Hebrew for the latter (*Megilla* i. 8). The formula for the writing of
divorcement was usually, according to R. Juda, Aramaic (*Gittin* ix. 3), but
might also be Greek (*Gittin* ix. 8).

[32] Matt. xxvi. 20, 73, and its interpreters—Buxtorf, *Lex. s.v.* גְלִיל, col. 434
sqq.; Lightfoot, *Centuria chorograph. Matthaeo praemissa,* c. 87 (*Opp.* ii.
232 sq.); Morinus, *Exercitationes biblicae* (1699), ii. 18. 2, p. 514 sqq.;
Aug. Pfeiffer, *Decas selecta exercitationum sacrarum,* pp. 206–216 (in the
Appendix to his *Dubia vexata script. sacrae,* Leipsic and Frankfort 1685);

## II. DIFFUSION OF HELLENIC CULTURE.

### 1. *Hellenism in the Non-Jewish Regions.*

The Jewish region just described was, in ancient times as well as in the Graeco-Roman period, surrounded on all sides by heathen districts. Only at Jamnia and Jóppa had the Jewish element advanced as far as the sea. Elsewhere, even to the west, it was not the sea, but the Gentile region of the Philistine and Phenician cities, that formed the boundary of the Jewish. These heathen lands were far more deeply penetrated by Hellenism, than the country of the Jews. No reaction like the rising of the Maccabees had here put a stop to it, besides which heathen polytheism was adapted in quite a different manner from Judaism for blending with Hellenism. While therefore the further advance of Hellenism was obstructed by religious barriers in the interior of Palestine, it had attained here, as in all other districts since its triumphant entry under Alexander the Great, its natural preponderance over Oriental culture. Hence, long before the commencement of the Roman period, the educated world, especially in the great cities in the west and east of Palestine, was, we may well say, completely Hellenized. It is only with the lower strata of the populations and the dwellers in rural districts, that this must not be equally assumed. Besides however the border lands, the Jewish districts in the interior of Palestine were occupied by Hellenism, especially Scythopolis (see § 23. I. Nr. 19) and the town of Samaria, where Macedonian colonists had already been planted by Alexander the Great (§ 23. I. Nr. 24), while the national Samaritans had their central point at Sichem.

The victorious penetration of Hellenistic culture is most plainly and comprehensively shown by the *religious worship.* The native religions, especially in the Philistine and Phenician cities, did indeed in many respects maintain themselves in

Wetstein, *Nov. Test.* on Matt. xxvi. 73 ; Neubauer, *Géographie du Talmud,* p. 184 sq. Further, older literature in Wolf, *Curae phil. in Nov. Test.* on Matt. xxvi. 73.

their essential character; but still in such wise, that they were transformed by and blended with Greek elements. But besides these the purely Greek worship also gained an entrance, and in many places entirely supplanted the former. Unfortunately our sources of information do not furnish us the means of separating the Greek period proper from the Roman, the best are afforded by coins, and these for the most part belong to the Roman. On the whole however the picture, which we obtain, holds good for the pre-Roman period also, nor are we entirely without direct notices of this age.

On the coins of Raphia of the times of the empire are seen especially *Apollo* and *Artemis* according to the purely Greek conception;[33] upon those of Anthedon, on the contrary, the tutelary goddess of the city is conceived of as *Astarte*.[34]

Of the worship at Gaza in the times of the Roman Empire complete information is given in the life of Porphyry, Bishop of Gaza, by Marcus Diaconus. According to this, there were in Gaza in the time of Porphyry (the end of the fourth century after Christ) eight δημόσιοι ναοί, viz. of Helios, Aphrodite, Apollo, Persephone (Kore), Hecate, Heroon, a temple of Tyche, and one of Marnas.[35] From this it appears that the purely Greek worship was the prevailing one, and this is confirmed in general by the coins, upon which other than Grecian deities also appear.[36] A temple of Apollo in

---

[33] Mionnet, *Description de médailles antiques*, v. 551 sq.; *Supplement*, viii. 376 sq. De Saulcy, *Numismatique de la Terre Sainte* (1874), pp. 237–240, pl. xii. n. 7–9. Stark, *Gaza*, p. 584.

[34] Mionnet, v. 522 sqq.; *Suppl.* viii. 364. De Saulcy, pp. 234–236, pl. xii. n. 2–4. Stark, p. 594.

[35] *Marci Diaconi Vita Porphyrii episcopi Gazensis*, ed. Haupt (Essays of the Berlin Academy, formerly known only in the Latin translation), c. 64: ἦσαν δὲ ἐν τῇ πόλει ναοὶ εἰδώλων δημόσιοι ὀκτώ, τοῦ τε Ἡλίου καὶ τῆς Ἀφροδίτης καὶ τοῦ Ἀπόλλωνος καὶ τῆς Κόρης καὶ τῆς Ἑκάτης καὶ τὸ λεγόμενον Ἡρῷον καὶ τὸ τῆς Τύχης τῆς πόλεως, ὃ ἐκάλουν Τυχαῖον, καὶ τὸ Μαρνεῖον, ὃ ἔλεγον εἶναι τοῦ Κρηταγενοῦς Διός, ὃ ἐνόμιζον εἶναι ἐνδοξότερον πάντων τῶν ἱερῶν τῶν ἀπανταχοῦ. The Marneion is also mentioned in many other passages of this work.

[36] Eckhel, *Doctr. Num.* iii. 448 sqq. Mionnet, v. 533–549; *Suppl.* viii. 371–375. De Saulcy, pp. 209–233, pl. xi. Stark, *Gaza*, pp. 583–589.

Gaza is already mentioned at the time of the destruction of the city by Alexander Jannaeus (*Antt.* xiii. 13. 3). In the Roman period only the chief deity of the city, Marnas, was, as his name (מר = Lord) implies, originally a Shemitic deity, who was however more or less disguised in a Greek garment.[37] A mixture of native and Greek worship is also found at Ascalon. A chief worship here was that of Ἀφροδίτη οὐρανίη, *i.e.* of Astarte as Queen of Heaven. She is mentioned even by Herodotus as the deity of Ascalon, and is still represented on coins of the imperial epoch chiefly as the tutelary goddess of the town.[38] With her is connected, nay probably at first identical, the *Atargatis* or *Derceto*, which was worshipped at Ascalon under a peculiar form (that of a woman with a fish's tail). Her Semitic name (עתרעתה, compounded of עתר = Astarte, and עתה) already points out that she is "merely the Syrian form of Astarte blended with another deity" (Baudissin). From this fish-form is evident, that "the fertilizing power of water" was especially honoured in her.[39] Asclepius λεοντοῦχος

[37] Comp. on Marnas besides the passages in Marcus Diaconus, Steph. Byz. *s.v.* Γάζα· ἔνθεν καὶ τὸ τοῦ Κρηταίου Διὸς παρ᾽ αὐτοῖς εἶναι, ὃν καὶ καθ᾽ ἡμᾶς ἐκάλουν Μαρνᾶν, ἑρμηνευόμενον Κρηταγενῆ. Eckhel, *Doctr. Num.* iii. 450 sq. Stark, *Gaza*, pp. 576–580. The oldest express testimony to the cult of Marnas are coins of Hadrian with the superscription Μαρνα ; see Mionnet, v. 539. De Saulcy, pp. 216–218, pl. xi. n. 4. His cult is also met with beyond Gaza. Comp. the inscription of Kanata in Le Bas and Waddington, *Inscriptions*, vol. iii. n. 2412g (Wetstein, n. 183) : Διῒ Μάρνᾳ τῷ κυρίῳ. With the worship of Marnas as Ζεὺς Κρηταγενής is also connected the later Greek legend, that Gaza was also called Μίνῳα, after Minos (Steph. Byz. *s.v.* Γάζα and *s.v.* Μίνῳα). Comp. Stark, *Gaza*, p. 580 sq.

[38] Herodotus, i. 105. The coins in Mionnet, v. 523–533 ; *Suppl.* viii. 365–370. De Saulcy, pp. 178–208, pl. ix. and x., and comp. Stark, pp. 258 sq., 590 sq. The identity of the Grecian Aphrodite with Astarte is universally acknowledged. Perhaps even the names are identical ; Aphtoreth and thence Aphroteth might, as Hommel conjectures, have arisen from Ashtoreth (Fleckeisen's *Jahrbucher für class. Philologie*, 1882, p. 176).

[39] On the worship of Derceto in Ascalon, see especially Strabo, xvi. p. 785 ; Plinius, *Hist. Nat.* v. 23. 81 ; Lucian, *De Syria dea*, c. 14 ; Ovid, *Metam.* iv. 44–46. The Semitic name upon a Palmyrian inscription and some coins (see Baudissin, and on the coins very fully Six in the

of Ascalon, to whom the Neo-Platonist Proclus composed a hymn, is, as well as these two, to be regarded as an originally Oriental deity.[40]  The genuinely Greek deities Zeus, Poseidon, Apollo, Helios, Athene, etc., appear also on the coins of Ascalon.[41]  A temple of Apollo in Ascalon is mentioned in pre-Herodian times, the grandfather of Herod having been, it is said, Hierodule there.[42]

In *Azotus,* the ancient Ashdod, there was in the pre-Maccabaean period a temple of the Philistine Dagon, who was formerly also worshipped at Gaza and Ascalon.[43]  At the conquest of Ashdod by Jonathan Maccabaeus, this temple was destroyed, and the heathen worship in general extirpated (1 Macc. x. 84, xi. 4).  Of its re-establishment at the restoration by Gabinius no particulars are known.  In any case Azotus also had in this later period a considerable number of Jewish inhabitants (see § 23. I. Nr. 5).

In the neighbouring towns of Jamnia and Joppa the Jewish element attained the preponderance after the Maccabæan age.  Joppa is nevertheless of importance to Hellenism,

*Numismatic Chronicle,* 1878, p. 103 sqq.).  With the worship of Derceto was connected the religious honour paid to the dove in Ascalon, on which comp. Philo, ed. Mang. ii. 646 (from Philo's work, *de providentia,* in Eusebius, *Praep. evang.* viii. 14. 16, ed. Gaisford; from the Armenian in Aucher, *Philonis Judaei sermones tres,* etc., p. 116).  On the literature, the article of Baudissin in Herzog's *Real-Encycl.,* 2nd ed. i. 736–740, is worthy of special mention.  To the list here given of the literature must be added the article on "Derceto the Goddess of Ascalon," in the *Journal of Sacred Literature and Biblical Record,* new series, vol. vii. 1865, pp. 1–20.  Ed. Meyer, *Zeitschr. der DMG.* 1877, p. 730 sqq.  Six, *Monnaies d'Hierapolis en Syrie* (*Numismatic Chronicle,* vol. xviii. 1878, pp. 103–131, and pl. vi.).  Rayet, *Dédicace à la déesse Atergatis* (*Bulletin de correspondance hellénique,* vol. iii. 1879, pp. 406–408).  The inscription found in Astypalia and given here runs thus: Αντιοχος και Ευπορος Αταργατειτι ανεθηκαν. Atargatis occurs only three times besides in Greek inscriptions.  *Corp. inscr. Graec.* n. 7046.  Le Bas et Waddington, *Inscriptions,* t. iii. n. 1890, 2588.

[40] Stark, *Gaza,* pp. 591–593.

[41] See the coins in Mionnet and De Saulcy, as above.  Stark, p. 589.

[42] Euseb. *Hist. eccl.* i. 6. 2 ; 7. 11.

[43] See on this temple, Baudissin in Herzog's *Real-Encycl.,* 2nd ed. iii. 460–463, and the literature there cited.

as the scene of the myth of Perseus and Andromeda; it was here on the rock of Joppa, that Andromeda was exposed to the monster and delivered by Perseus.[44] The myth retained its vitality even during the period of Jewish preponderance. In the year 58 B.C., at the splendid games given by M. Scaurus as aedile, the skeleton of the sea-monster brought to Rome from Joppa by Scaurus was exhibited.[45] The permanence of the myth in this locality is testified by Strabo, Mela, Pliny, Josephus, Pausanias, nay even by Jerome.[46] The Hellenistic legend, according to which Joppa is said to have been founded by Cepheus, the father of Andromeda, also points to it.[46a] Pliny even speaks of a worship of the Ceto there,[47] and Mela of altars with the name of Cepheus and his brother Phineus as existing at Joppa.[47a] After Joppa was destroyed as a Jewish town in the war of Vespasian, the heathen worship regained the ascendancy there.[48]

In *Caesarea*, which was first raised to a considerable city by Herod the Great, we meet first of all with that worship of *Augustus* and of *Rome*, which characterized the Roman

[44] The earliest mention of Joppa as the place of this occurrence is found in Scylax (four centuries B.C.). See Müller, *Geogr. gr. minores*, i. 79; comp. in general, Stark, p. 255 sqq., 593 sq.

[45] Plinius, *Hist. Nat.* ix. 5. 11: Beluae, cui dicebatur exposita fuisse Andromeda, ossa Romæ adportata ex oppido Judaeae Jope ostendit inter reliqua miracula in aedilitate sua M. Scaurus longitudine pedum xl., altitudine costarum Indicos elephantos excedente, spinae crassitudine sesquipedali. On Scaurus, comp. the review of the Roman Proconsols of Syria in vol. i. On the time of his aedileship, Pauly's *Encycl.* i. 1, 2nd ed. p. 372.

[46] Strabo, xvi. p. 759; Mela, 11; Plinius, v. 13. 69; Joseph. *Bell. Jud.* iii. 9. 3; Pausanias, iv. 35. 6; Hieronymus, *Comment. ad Jon.* i. 3 (*Opp.* ed. Vallarsi, vi. 394). Most make mention, that traces of Andromeda's chains were seen on the rock at Joppa.

[46a] Steph. Byz. *s.v.* Ἰόπη.

[47] Plinius, v. 13. 69: Colitur illic fabulosa Ceto. The name Ceto is indeed only a Latinizing of κῆτος (sea-monster); comp. Stark, p. 257.

[47a] Mela, i. 11: ubi Cephea regnasse eo signo accolae adfirmant, quod titulum ejus fratrisque Phinei veteres quaedam arae cum religione plurima retinent.

[48] Comp. in general the coins in Mionnet, v. 499; De Saulcy, p. 176 sq. pl. ix. n. 3, 4.

period.  Provinces, towns and princes then vied with each
other in the practice of this cult, which was indeed prudently
declined by Augustus in Rome, but looked upon with approval
and promoted in the provinces.[49]  It was self-evident that
Herod also could not remain behind in this matter.  If a
general remark of Josephus is to be taken literally, he
" founded Caesarea ($K\alpha\iota\sigma\alpha\rho\epsilon\hat{\iota}\alpha$, i.e. temples of Cæsar) in
many towns."[50]  Such are specially mentioned in Samaria,
Panias (see below) and in Caesarea.  The magnificent temple
here lay upon a hill opposite the entrance of the harbour.
Within it stood two large statues, one of Augustus after the
model of the Olympic Zeus, and one of Rome after that of
Hera of Argos, for Augustus only permitted his worship in
combination with that of Rome.[51]  With respect to the other
worships of Caesarea, the coins show a motley variety.  In
saying this we must certainly take into consideration, that

[49] Tacit. *Annal.* i. 10, Augustus is reproached nihil deorum honoribus
relictum, cum se templis et effigie numinum per flamines et sacerdotes coli
vellet.  Sueton. *Aug.* 59 : provinciarum pleraeque super templa et *aras* ludos
quoque quinquennales *paene oppidatim* constituerunt.  Only in Rome did
Augustus decline this worship (Sueton. *Aug.* 52 : in urbe quidem pertina-
cissime abstinuit hoc honore) : a temple was first erected for it there by
Tiberius (Tacit. *Annal.* vi. 45 ; Sueton. *Calig.* 21).  Among the temples to
Augustus, which have been preserved, the most celebrated is that at
Ancyra, on which comp. Perrot, *Exploration archéologique de la Galatie et
de la Bithynie*, etc. (1872), pp. 295–312, planche 13–31.  Compare in
general on the worship of the emperor, Preller, *Römische Mythologie*,
p. 770 sqq. ; Boissier, *La religion romaine d'Auguste aux Antonins* (2nd ed.
1878), i. pp. 109–186 ; Kuhn, *Die städt. und bürgerl. Verfassung des röm.
Reichs*, i. 112 ; Marquardt, *Römische Staatsverwaltung*, vol. iii. (1878) p.
144 sqq., and vol. i. (2nd ed. 1881) p. 503 sqq. ; Le Bas et Waddington,
*Inscript.* vol. iii. Illustrations to n. 885 ; Perrot as above, p. 295 ;
Marquardt, *De provinciarum Romanarum conciliis et sacerdotibus* (*Ephemeris
epigraphica*), i. 1872, pp. 200–214 ; Desjardins, *Le culte des Divi et le culte
de Rome et d'Auguste* (*Revue de philologie, de literature et d'histoire
anciennes*), nouv. serie, iii. 1879, pp. 33–63.  I am only acquainted with the
latter from Bursian's *philolog. Jahresber.* xix. 620–622.

[50] *Bell. Jud.* i. 21. 4 ; comp. *Antt.* xv. 9. 5.

[51] Sueton. *Aug.* 52 : templa . . . in nulla tamen provincia nisi communi
suo Romaeque nomine recepit.  On the temple at Caesarea, Joseph. *Bell. Jud.*
i. 21. 7 ; *Antt.* xv. 9. 6.  Philo also mentions the $\Sigma\epsilon\beta\alpha\sigma\tau\epsilon\hat{\iota}o\nu$, see *Legat. ad
Cajum*, § 38 *fin.*, ed. Mang. ii. 590, *fin.*  The remains of a temple have also

these belong for the most part to the second and third centuries, which is of importance in the case of Caesarea, because after the time of Vespasian the Roman element, in opposition to the Greek, received a considerable reinforcement in the Roman colony introduced into Caesarea by that emperor. Hence it is to be ascribed to the influence of the Roman element, that the Egyptian Serapis, who was, as is well known, highly honoured in Rome, occurs so very frequently. In general, however, we may transpose to an earlier period also the deities mentioned on the coins. We here find again Zeus, Poseidon, Apollo, Herakles, Dionysos, Athene, Nike, and of female deities chiefly Astarte, according to the view of her prevailing in Palestine.[52]

The coins of *Dora*, which are assignable to a period subsequent to Caligula, have most frequently the image of Zeus with the laurel.[53] In a narrative of Apion, which is indeed a silly fiction, Apollo is designated the *deus Dorensium*.[54] His worship, which was common in all these towns (comp. Raphia, Gaza, Ascalon, Caesarea), is to be traced to Seleucid influence. For Apollo was the ancestral God of the Seleucids, as Dionysos was that of the Ptolemies.[55]

The ancient *Ptolemais* (Akko) was in the age of the Seleucids and Ptolemies one of the most flourishing of heathen cities (see § 23. I. Nr. 11). Hence we may here assume, even without more special information, an early

been discovered in Caesarea by the recent researches of Englishmen (*The Survey of Western Palestine, Memoirs* by Conder and Kitchener, ii. 13 sqq., with plan of the town, p. 15). It must, however, remain uncertain whether they are those of the temple of Augustus.

[52] Mionnet, v. 486–497; *Suppl.* viii. 334–343. Serapis very often. Zeus, n. 53; *Suppl.* n. 43. Poseidon, n. 38. Apollo, n. 6, 12, 13; *Suppl.* n. 7, 12, 15. Herakles, n. 16. Dionysos, n. 37, 54, 56. Athene, *Suppl.* n. 37. Nike, n. 4; *Suppl.* n. 6, 8, 20. Astarte, n. 1, 2, 7, 18, 24, 51; *Suppl.* n. 9, 10, 11, 45. Still more in De Saulcy, pp. 112–141, pl. vii.

[53] Mionnet, v. 359–362; *Suppl.* viii. 258–260. De Saulcy, pp. 142–148, pl. vi. n. 6–12. Comp. also Eckhel, iii. 362 sq.

[54] Joseph. *contra Apion.* ii. 9.

[55] Stark, *Gaza*, p. 568 sqq.

penetration of the Greek worship.   Upon the autonomic coins of the town, belonging probably to the last decades before Christ (soon after Caesar), is found almost universally the image of Zeus.[56]   In the time of Claudius, Ptolemais became a Roman colony.   Upon the very numerous subsequent coins is found chiefly Tyche (Fortuna); likewise Artemis, Pluto and Persephone, Perseus with Medusa, the Egyptian Serapis and the Phrygian Cybele.[57]   The Mishna gives an account of a meeting of the famous scribe Gamaliel II. with a heathen philosopher in the bath of Aphrodite.[58]

Beside the towns on the coast, it was chiefly the districts in the *east of Palestine* which were the earliest and the most completely Hellenized.   It is probable that Alexander the Great and the Diadochoi here founded a number of Greek towns, or Hellenized towns already existing.   Hence arose in early times a series of centres of Greek culture in these parts. Their prosperity was interrupted for only a short time by the chaotic work of destruction of Alexander Jannaeus.   For Pompey already made an independent development again possible to them by separating them from the Jewish realm and combining them probably under the name of *Decapolis* into a certain sort of unity.

*Damascus* is reckoned by Pliny and Ptolemy as the chief among these cities of Decapolis.   It was an important arsenal even in the time of Alexander the Great.   Its Hellenistic character at that period is testified to by coins of Alexander, which were minted there (see § 23. I. Nr. 12). From that time onward it became increasingly a Hellenistic city.   At the partition of the great empire of the Seleucids into several portions towards the end of the second century before Christ, it even became for a while the capital of one of

---

[56] De Saulcy, pp. 154–156.

[57] Mionnet, v. 473 – 481; *Suppl.* viii. 324 – 331.   Tyche (Fortuna) frequently.   Artemis, n. 29, 39.   Pluto and Persephone, n. 37.   Perseus, *Suppl.* n. 19, 20.   Serapis, n. 16, 24, 28.   Cybele, n. 42.   Still more in De Saulcy, pp. 157–169, pl. viii.

[58] *Aboda sara* iii. 4.

these smaller kingdoms. As was consequently to be expected, the autonomic and mostly dated coins of Damascus reaching to the commencement of the Roman Empire, present us with the purely Greek deities: Artemis, Athene, Nike, Tyche, Helios, Dionysos.[59] Upon imperial coins proper the emblems and images of stated divinities are, comparatively speaking, but seldom found. Silenus, the honoured companion of Dionysus and with him Dionysos himself here occur the most frequently; especially in the third century after Christ.[60] The Hellenistic legend, which connects him with the foundation of Damascus, also points to the worship of this god.[61] Perhaps his worship both here and in other cities of Eastern Palestine is to be traced to Arabian influence. For the principal deity of the Arabians was conceived of by the Greeks as Dionysos.[62] Upon the Greek inscriptions, which have been preserved in Damascus and its neighbourhood, Zeus is more frequently mentioned.[63]

In many of the towns of Decapolis, especially in Kanatha, Gerasa, and Philadelphia, the existing magnificent ruins of temples of the Roman period still bear witness to the former splendour of the Hellenistic worship in these towns.[64] Of the special worships of the several towns, we have for the most part but deficient information. In Scythopolis, Dionysos must have been specially honoured.

[59] De Saulcy, pp. 30–33. Artemis, n. 2, 3, 7, 8, 10, 14, 21. Athene, n. 2, 8, 14, 15. Nike, n. 11, 12, 22, 23. Tyche, n. 17, 18. Helios, n. 3, 21. Dionysos, n. 24, 25. Most also in Mionnet, v. 283 sq.; *Suppl.* viii. 193 sqq.

[60] Mionnet, v. 285–297; *Suppl.* viii. 193–206. Silenus, n. 61, 62, 68, 69, 72, 77, 85; *Suppl.* n. 34, 35, 48. Dionysos, n. 80, 88. The most also in De Saulcy, pp. 35–56.

[61] Stephanus Byz. *s.v.* Δαμασκός.

[62] Herodot. iii. 8. Arrian, vii. 20. Strabo, xvi. p. 741. Origenes, *contra Cels.* v. 37. Hesych. *Lex. s.v.* Δουσάρης. Krehl, *Ueber die Religion der vorislamischen Araber*, 1863, pp. 29 sqq., 48 sqq.

[63] Le Bas et Waddington, *Inscriptions*, vol. iii. n. 1879, 2549, 2550. Ζεὺς Κεραύνιος (at Deir Kanun on the Nahr Barada). *Corp. Inscr. Graec.* 4520 = Waddington, n. 2557ᵃ.

[64] See the geographical literature mentioned in § 23. I.

For the town was also called Nysa,[65] and this is the mythological name of the place, in which Dionysos was brought up
by the nymphs.[66] The name Scythopolis was also referred
mythologically to Dionysos (see § 23. I. Nr. 19). On the
coins of *Gadara* Zeus is most frequently met with, also
Herakles, Astarte and other individual deities.[67] Artemis is
depicted on the coins of Gerasa as the $T\acute{v}\chi\eta$ $\Gamma\epsilon\rho\acute{a}\sigma\omega\nu$.[68] In
Philadelphia Herakles appears to have been the principal
divinity, $T\acute{v}\chi\eta$ $\Phi\iota\lambda\alpha\delta\epsilon\lambda\phi\acute{\epsilon}\omega\nu$, other individual gods also occurring.[69] The coins of the other cities of Decapolis are not
numerous, and offer but insufficient material.

Apart from the coast towns and the cities of Decapolis, there
are only two other cities in which especially Hellenism gained
an early footing, viz. Samaria and Panias. Alexander the Great
is said to have settled colonists in *Samaria*. In any case it
was an important Hellenistic military post in the times of the
Diadochoi (see § 33. I. Nr. 24). The town was indeed razed
to the ground by John Hyrcanus, but the Hellenist rites
must certainly have been re-established at its restoration by
Gabinius, and have attained still greater ascendancy at the

---

[65] Plinius, *Hist. Nat.* v. 18. 74 : *Scythopolim antea Nysam.* Steph. Byz.
*s.v.* Σκυθόπολις, Παλαιστίνης πόλις, ἡ Νύσσης (1. Νύσσα) Κοίλης Συρίας. On
coins chiefly Νυσ[αιων ?] Σκυθο[πολιτων].

[66] A whole number of towns claimed to be the true Nysa. See Steph.
Byz. *s.v.* (Νῦσαι πόλεις πολλαί), Pauly's *Encycl.* v. 794 sq. Pape-Benseler,
*Wörterbuch der griech. Eigennamen, s.v.*

[67] Mionnet, v. 323–328 ; *Suppl.* viii. 227–230. De Saulcy, pp. 294–303,
pl. xv.

[68] Mionnet, v. 329 ; *Suppl.* viii. 230 sq. De Saulcy, p. 384 sq., pl. xxii.
n. 1–2.

[69] Mionnet, v. 330–333. *Suppl.* viii. 232–336. De Saulcy, pp. 386–392,
pl. xxii. n. 3–9. The bust of the young Herakles is found with the superscription Ηρακλης upon a coin of Marcus Aurelius and L. Verus (see the
representation of it in De Saulcy, pl. xxii. n. 7). Upon two others (one
of Marcus Aurelius, the other of Commodus) is depicted a vehicle drawn
by four horses, with the superscription Ηρακλειον (Mionnet, n. 77, 80 ; De
Saulcy, pp. 390, 391). According to the ingenious supposition of Eckhel
(*Doctr. Num.* iii. 351), we are to understand by the latter a small statue
or *sacellum* which was on festivals carried in procession. The Τύχη
Φιλαδελφέων upon the coins of Hadrian and Antoninus Pius, see De
Saulcy, p. 389.

enlargement of the town by Herod the Great, who also here erected a magnificent temple to Augustus.[70] On the other worships some further information is furnished by coins attributable to times subsequent to Nero.[71] In *Panias*, the subsequent *Caesarea Philippi*, the Greek Pan must have been worshipped since the commencement of Hellenic times in the grotto there; for the locality is in the days of Antiochus the Great already mentioned by the name of τὸ Πάνειον (see § 23. I. Nr. 29). The continuance of his worship in later times is also abundantly testified by coins and inscriptions.[72] Herod the Great built here as well as in Caesarea Stratonis and Samaria a temple of Augustus.[73] Of other deities Zeus is most frequently found upon the coins, some appear singly ; the image of Pan is, however, by far the most prevalent.[74]

Subsequently to the second century after Christ, Hellenic worship may be proved to have existed in other towns of Palestine also, as Sepphoris, Tiberias, etc. It may however be assumed with tolerable certainty, that it found no favour in them before the Vespasian war. For till then the cities in question were chiefly inhabited by Jews, who would hardly have tolerated the public exercise of heathen worship in their midst.[75]

The case was different with the half-heathen districts of Trachonitis, Batanaea, and Auranitis, east of the Lake of Gennesareth. Here too the Hellenistic worships probably

---

[70] *Bell. Jud.* i. 21. 2 ; comp. *Antt.* xv. 8. 5.

[71] Mionnet, v. 513–516 ; *Suppl.* viii. 356–359. De Saulcy, pp. 275–281, pl. xiv. n. 4–7.

[72] The coins in Mionnet, v. 311–315, n. 10, 13, 16, 20, 23 ; *Suppl.* viii. 217–220, n. 6, 7, 8, 10. Others in De Saulcy, pp. 313–324, pl. xviii. ; comp. especially the representations of Pan with the flute in De Saulcy, pl. xviii. n. 8, 9, 10. The inscriptions in Le Bas et Waddington, *Inscr.* vol. iii. n. 1891, 1892, 1893 (= *Corp. Inscr. Graec.* n. 4538, 4537, Addenda, p. 1179).

[73] *Antt.* xv. 10. 3 ; *Bell. Jud.* i. 21. 3.

[74] See Mionnet and De Saulcy's above-named work.

[75] That there were no heathen temples in Tiberias may be indirectly inferred also from Joseph. *Vita,* 12. For only the destruction of Herod's palace adorned with images of animals is mentioned, not that of heathen temples.

first penetrated to a wider extent subsequently to the second century after Christ. But the work of Hellenization began with the appearance of Herod and his sons, who gained for culture these hitherto half-barbarous places (see above, p. 4). The worship of Hellenic deities was afterwards admitted. The inscriptions, of which a special abundance has been preserved in these regions, testify to its prevalence from the second to the fourth centuries. The same observation must however here be made as with respect to the Philistine towns, viz. that the native Arabian deities were still maintained beside the Greek gods.

Among these *Dusares*, compared by the Greeks to Dionysos, takes the first place. His worship in Roman times is testified chiefly by the games dedicated to him, the Ἄκτια Δουσάρια in *Adraa* and *Bostra*.[76] Several other Arabian gods, the names of some of whom are all that is known to us, are also mentioned upon the inscriptions.[77] The Greek deities have, however, the preponderance during this period. Among them by far the most frequently occurring is Zeus,[78] and next to him Dionysos, Kronos, Herakles.[79] Of female deities the

[76] Δουσάρης in Le Bas et Waddington, *Inscr.* vol. iii. n. 2023, 2312. The Nom. propr. Δουσάριος, n. 1916. דושרא in de Vogüé, *Syrie Centrale, Inscriptions sémitiques*, pp. 113, 120. The Ἄκτια Δουσάρια in Mionnet, v. 577–585, n. 5, 6, 18, 32, 33, 34, 36, 37. The same also in De Saulcy, pp. 375, 365, 369 sq. Comp. Tertullian, *Apolog.* 24 : Unicuique etiam provinciae et civitati suus deus est, ut Syriae Astartes, ut Arabiae Dusares. Hesych. *Lex. s.v.*: Δουσάρην τὸν Διόνυσον Ναβαταῖοι. Krehl, *Ueber die Religion der vorislamischen Araber* (1863), p. 48 sq. Waddington's illustrations to n. 2023. Mordtmann, Dusares in Epiphanius (*Ztschr. der DMG.* 1875, pp. 99–106).

[77] Θεανδρίτης or Θεάνδριος in Waddington, n. 2046, 2374ᵃ (*C. I. Gr.* 4609, *Addend.* p. 1181), 2481. See concerning him Waddington's illustrations to n. 2046. Οὐασαιάθου, Waddington, n. 2374, 2374ᵃ. קציו, Qaçiu, in de Vogüé, *Syrie Centrale, Inscr. sém.* pp. 96, 103. אלת, Allath (a female deity), de Vogüé, pp. 100, 107, 119.

[78] Waddington, n. 2116, 2140, 2211, 2288, 2289, 2290, 2292, 2339, 2340, 2390, 2412ᵈ (Wetzstein, 185), 2413ᵇ (Wetzst. 179), 2413ʲ (*C. I. Gr.* 4558), 2413ᵏ (*C. I. Gr.* 4559). Ζεὺς Τέλειος, n. 2484.

[79] Dionysos, Waddington, n. 2309. Kronos, n. 2375, 2544. Heracles, n. 2413ᶜ (Wetzst. 177), 2428.

most frequent are Athene[80] and Tyche,[81] then Aphrodite, Nike, Irene.[82] Finally, the religious syncretism of the subsequent imperial period favoured other Oriental, as well as the ancient native deities. Among these the Syrian Sun-god, who is here adored, now under his Semitic name *Aὔμου*, now under his Greek name *"Ἥλιος*, at another under both together, plays the chief part.[83] His worship so flourished in Constantine's time also, that a considerable temple could even then be erected for it in Auranitis.[84] Nay, the Christian preachers were only able to suppress it, by substituting for him the prophet *'Ηλίας*.[85] Besides the Syrian Sun-god, the worship of Marnas of Gaza and the Egyptian deities Ammon and Isis, may also be shown to have been practised.[86]

Periodical *games* were often closely connected with the religious rites. In this department also the predominance of Hellenic customs may be proved by numerous examples. But even here authorities for the Greek period, properly so called, are extremely few. We know, that Alexander the Great celebrated splendid games at Tyre.[87] The *πενταετηρικὸς*

[80] Waddington, n. 2081, 2203ᵃ (Wetzst. 16), 2216, 2308, 2410, 2453, 2461. Also with a local colouring ('Aθηνᾷ Γοζμαίη, at Kanatha), n. 2345.

[81] Waddington, n. 2127, 2176, 2413ᶠ to 2413ⁱ (= *Corp. Inscr. Graec.* n. 4554 to 4557), 2506, 2512, 2514. In the Semitic Τύχη the name of a deity is rendered by גד (see Lagarde, *Gesammelte Abhandlungen*, 1866, p. 16. Mordtmann, *Zeitschr. d. DMG.* 1877, pp. 99–101, and comp. the locality near Jerusalem mentioned in the Mishna גד יון, *Sabim* i. 5). It does not however follow that the worship of Τύχη can be traced back to the old Semitic *Gad*, the wide diffusion of which cannot be proved (comp. Baudissin in Herzog's *Real-Encycl.* 2nd ed. iv. 722 sq.). Rather is the Syrian Astarte, with which Tyche is certainly generally connected, to be thought of (so also Mordtmann).

[82] Aphrodite, Waddington, n. 2098. Nike, n. 2099, 2410, 2413ⱼ (*C. I. Gr.* 4558), 2479. Irene, n. 2526.

[83] Aὔμου, Waddington, n. 2441, 2455, 2456. "Ἥλιος, n. 2398, 2407. "Ἥλιος θεὸς Aὔμος; n. 2392, 2393, 2395.

[84] Waddington, n. 2393. [85] See Waddington on n. 2497.

[86] Marnas, Waddington, n. 2412ᵍ (Wetzst. 183). Ammon, n. 2313, 2382. Isis, n. 2527. Also upon a coin of Kanata in Mionnet, *Suppl.* viii. 225, n. 5.

[87] Arrian, ii. 24. 6; iii. 6. 1. Comp. Plutarch, *Alex.* c. 29. Droysen, *Gesch. d. Hellenismus* (2nd ed.), i. 1. 297, 325.

ἀγών held there is incidentally mentioned in the prefatory narrative of the Maccabean rising (2 Macc. iv. 18–20). On the same occasion we learn also that Antiochus Epiphanes desired to introduce the Διονύσια into Jerusalem (2 Macc. vi. 7). But it is just in the Hellenic towns of Palestine that the celebration of such solemnities during the pre-Roman period cannot be proved in detail, though from the general character of the age it must evidently be assumed.[88] Not till we come to the Roman period are authorities again abundant. The great importance of public games in imperial times is well known; not a provincial town of any consequence was without them.[89] This was especially the case with those in connection with the cult of the Imperator, the games *in honour of the emperor*, which were everywhere in vogue, even in the time of Augustus.[90] In Palestine also they were introduced by Herod into Caesarea and Jerusalem. Other games of various kinds also existed beside them. Their prevalence in the chief towns of Palestine in the second century after Christ is proved by an inscription at Aphrodisias in Caria, upon which the council and people of the Aphrodisians record the victories gained by one Aelius Aurelius Menander in several contests. Among the games here enumerated are some also which took place in Palestinian towns.[91] In a similar inscription at Laodicaea in Syria, of the

---

[88] Comp. Stark, *Gaza*, p. 594 sq.

[89] Compare on the games in the Roman period, especially Friedländer, *Darstellungen aus der Sittengesch. Roms*, vol. ii. (3rd ed. 1874) pp. 261–622. On their organization and kinds, also Marquardt, *Römische Staatsverwaltung*, vol. iii. (2nd ed. 1878) pp. 462–544 (also edited by Friedländer).

[90] Sueton. *Aug.* 59 : provinciarum pleraeque super templa et aras *ludos quoque quinquennales* paene oppidatim constituerunt.

[91] Le Bas et Waddington, vol. iii. n. 1620ᵇ. The inscription, as is proved by another pertaining to it (n. 1620ᵃ), is of the time of Marcus Aurelius. The part which interests us is as follows :—

> Δαμασκὸν β΄ ἀνδρῶν πανκράτιν,
> Βηρυτὸν ἀνδρῶν πανκράτιν,
> Τύρον ἀνδρῶν πανκράτιν,
> Καισάρειαν τὴν Στράτωνος ἀνδρῶν πανκράτιν,
> Νέαν πόλιν τῆς Σαμαρίας ἀνδρῶν πανκράτιν

beginning of the third century after Christ, the victor himself transmits to posterity the victories he obtained. Here too many towns of Palestine are mentioned as the theatres of these victories.[92] Lastly, in an anonymous *Descriptio totius orbis* of the middle of the 4th century after Christ, are enumerated the kinds of games and contests, for which the most important towns of Syria were then distinguished.[93] From these and other sources the following materials have been compiled.[94]

In Gaza a πανήγυρις 'Αδριανή was celebrated from the time of Hadrian.[95] A παγκράτιον is mentioned as held there in the inscription of Aphrodisias.[96] The *pammacarii* (= παμμάχοι or παγκρατιασταί) of Gaza were in the fourth

Σκυθόπολιν ἀνδρῶν παυκράτιν,
Γάζαν ἀνδρῶν παυκράτιν,
Καισάρειαν Πανιάδα β' ἀνδρῶν παυκράτιν, ...
Φιλαδέλφειαν τῆς 'Αραβίας ἀνδρῶν παυκράτιν.

[92] *Corp. Inscr. Graec.* n. 4472 = Le Bas et Waddington, vol. iii. n. 1839. The date of the inscription is A.D. 221. It mentions among others games at Caesarea, Ascalon and Scythopolis.

[93] This originally Greek *Descriptio totius orbis* is preserved in two Latin paraphrases, both of which are given in Müller's *Geographi Graeci minores*, ii. 513–528. One also in Riese's *Geographi Latini minores* (1878), pp. 104–126. According to the freer but more intelligible version c. 32 runs as follows: Iam nunc dicendum est quid etiam in se singulae civitates, de quibus loquimur, habeant delectabile. Habes ergo Antiochiam in ludis circensibus eminentem; similiter et Laodiciam et Tyrum et Berytum et Caesaream. Et Laodicia mittit aliis civitatibus agitatores optimos, Tyrus et Berytus mimarios, Caesarea pantomimos, Heliopolis choraulas, Gaza pammacarios, Ascalon athletas luctatores, Castabala pyctas.

[94] In enumerating the towns I follow the same order as above when treating of the worships, and in § 23. I. The further information may also be given, that the *kinds of games* were *in general* as follows: (1) in the circus (ἱππόδρομος) the chariot race; (2) in the *amphitheatre* the contests of gladiators and fights of wild beasts; (3) in the theatre plays, properly so called, to which were also added pantomimes; (4) in the stadium gymnastic games—boxing, wrestling, and running; the latter were also sometimes held in the circus (Marquardt, iii. 504 sq.). At the great annual feasts several of these games were generally combined.

[95] *Chron. pasch.*, ed. Dindorf, i. 474.

[96] The παγκράτιον is the " joint contest," which comprises both wrestling (πάλη) and boxing (πυγμή). Hence it belongs to the order of gymnastic games.

century the most famous in Syria.[97]    Jerome in his *Life of Hilarion* mentions the Circensian games there.[98]    A ταλαντιαῖος ἀγών is testified for *Ascalon* in the inscription of Laodicaea.    Its wrestlers (*athletae luctatores*, see note 93) were particularly famous.    In Caesarea a stone theatre and a large amphitheatre, the latter with a view of the sea, were built by Herod the Great ;[99] a στάδιον is mentioned of the time of Pilate ;[100] the town must also have had a circus from its commencement, since a ἵππων δρόμος was held (see below) so early as at the dedication by Herod.    Even now traces and remains of a theatre are discernible.[101]    All the four species of games having thus been from the first provided for, it follows that all four were in fact celebrated at the dedication by Herod the Great.[102]    From that time onwards they were repeated every four years in honour of the emperor.[103]    These were however of course not the only games held at Caesarea.    All the four kinds may also be pointed out singly in later times.    1. The *ludi circenses* of Caesarea were in the fourth century after Christ as famous as those of Antioch, Laodicaea, Tyre and Berytus (see note 93).    2. Titus instituted after the termina-

[97] See above, note 93.    In the text of the second Latin translation of the *Descr. totius orbis*, it is said more fully concerning Gaza : aliquando autem et Gaza habet *bonos auditores*, dicitur autem habere eam et *pammacharios*. The Latin *auditores* is undoubtedly an erroneous translation, perhaps for ἀκροαματικοί (see Stark, *Gaza*, p. 595).

[98] Hieronymus, *Vita Hilarionis*, c. 20 (Opp. ed. Vallarsi, ii. 22) : Sed et Italicus ejusdem oppidi municeps Christianus adversus Gazensem Duumvirum, Marnae idolo deditum, *circenses equos* nutriebat.

[99] *Antt.* xv. 9. 6 *fin.; Bell. Jud.* i. 21. 8.

[100] *Antt.* xviii. 3. 1 ; *Bell. Jud.* ii. 9. 3.

[101] *The Survey of Western Palestine, Memoirs* by Conder and Kitchener, ii. 13 sqq. (with plan of the town, p. 15).

[102] *Antt.* xvi. 5. 1 : κατηγγέλκει μὲν γὰρ ἀγῶνα μουσικῆς καὶ γυμνικῶν ἀθλημάτων, παρεσκευάκει δὲ πολὺ πλῆθος μονομάχων καὶ θηρίων, ἵππων τε δρόμου, etc.

[103] The games were celebrated κατὰ πενταετηρίδα (*Antt.* xvi. 5. 1) and hence called πενταετηρικοὶ ἀγῶνες (*Bell. Jud.* i. 21. 8).    According however to our mode of expression these games were held every four years.    The same formula are constantly used of all fourth yearly games, the Olympic, the Actian, etc.    See the *Lexica* and the material in the index to the *Corp. Inscr. Graec.* p. 158, *s.v.*

tion of the Jewish war gladiatorial contests and fights of wild beasts, in which hundreds of Jewish prisoners were sacrificed.[104] The Emperor Maximinus exhibited at the celebration of his birthday animals brought from India and Ethiopia.[105] 3. Games in the theatre are mentioned in the time of King Agrippa I.[106] The *pantomimi* of Caesarea were in the fourth century the most famous in Syria (see note 93). We must understand indeed of pantomimic games also, what Eusebius says of the games of Maximinus.[107] 4. A παγκράτιον is mentioned in the inscription of Aphrodisias, a boxing-match in that of Laodicaea.[108] In Ptolemais a gymnasium was built by Herod the Great.[108a]

In *Damascus* also a gymnasium and theatre were built by Herod the Great (see Josephus as before). The existence of a παγκράτιον there is testified to by the inscription of Aphrodisias, and σεβάσμια (games in honour of the emperor) are mentioned upon the coins since Macrinus.[109] Ruins of two theatres are still standing at Gadara.[110] A ναυμαχία there occurs on the coins of Marcus Aurelius.[111] *Kanatha* has besides ruins of its temple those of a small theatre, hewn out in the rock and designated on an inscription as θεατροειδὲς ᾠδεῖον.[112] In *Scythopolis* traces of a hippodrome are found, and ruins of a theatre are still standing.[113] A παγκράτιον is

---

[104] *Bell. Jud.* vii. 31.    [105] Euseb. *De Martyr. Palaest.* vi. 1–2.

[106] *Antt.* xix. 7. 4 ; 8. 2.   On the games mentioned in the last passage, as held in honour of the Emperor Claudius, see above, § 18, *s. fin.*

[107] *De Martyr. Palaest.* vi. 2 : ἀνδρῶν ἐντέχνοις τισὶ σωμασκίαις παραδόξους ψυχαγωγίας τοῖς ὁρῶσιν ἐνδεικνυμένων.   See also the note of Valesius.

[108] This πυγμή took place on the occasion of the Σεουήρειος Οἰκουμενικὸς Πυθικός (scil. ἀγών), *i.e.* of the Pythic games dedicated to the Emperor Septimius Severus.

[108a] Joseph. *Bell. Jud.* i. 21. 11.

[109] Mionnet, v. 291 sqq. ; *Suppl.* viii. 198 sqq.   De Saulcy, p. 42 sqq.

[110] See the geographical literature cited in § 23. I. note 179.

[111] See especially Eckhel, *Doctr. Num.* iii. 348 sqq., also Mionnet, v. 326, n. 38. De Saulcy, p. 299.

[112] The inscription in Le Bas et Waddington, vol. iii. n. 2341.   On the building itself, see the geographical literature cited § 23. I. note 214.

[113] See especially, *The Survey of Western Palestine, Memoirs* by Conder and Kitchener, vol. ii. p. 106 (plan of the hippodrome) and p. 107 (plan

mentioned in the inscription of Aphrodisias, and a ταλαντιαῖος ἀγών in that of Laodicaea.   Among the magnificent ruins of *Gerasa* are found those of two theatres and traces of a Naumachia (an amphitheatre erected for battles of ships).[114] *Philadelphia* too possesses the ruins of a theatre and of an Odeum (a small roofed theatre),[115] and a παγκράτιον is mentioned in the inscription of Aphrodisias.   In *Caesarea Panias* " various spectacles " (παντοίας θεωρίας), especially gladiatorial contests and wild beast fights, in which Jewish prisoners were used, were given by Titus after the termination of the Jewish war.[116]   A παγκράτιον held there is mentioned in the inscription of Aphrodisias.   On games in the Jewish towns (Jerusalem, Jericho, Tarichea, Tiberias), see the next section.

Besides the religious rites and games, there is finally a third point which shows how deeply Hellenism had penetrated in many of these towns, viz. that they produced men, who *gained a name in Greek literature*.   Among the coast towns *Ascalon* is especially prominent in this respect.   In Stephanus of Byzantium (*s.v.* ’Ασκάλων) are enumerated four Stoic philosophers: Antiochus, Sosus, Antibius, Eubius, who were natives of Ascalon.   Of these only Antiochus is elsewhere known. He was a contemporary of Lucullus and a teacher of Cicero, and therefore belongs to the first century before Christ.   His system is moreover not exactly stoic but eclectic.[117]   As grammarians of Ascalon, Ptolemaeus and Dorotheas, as historians Apollonius and Artemidorus are named by Steph. Byz.   The two latter are unknown.   Dorotheas is elsewhere quoted, but his date cannot be decided.[118]   Next to the philosopher

---

of the theatre).   The theatre is according to Conder (ii. 106) the best preserved specimen of Roman work in Western Palestine.

[114] See the geographical literature cited § 23, note 1. 253.

[115] See the literature cited § 23, note 1. 270.

[116] *Bell. Jud.* vii. 2. 1.

[117] See Pauly's *Encykl.* i. 1 (2nd ed.), p. 1141 sq., and the literature there cited, especially Zeller.   Also Hoyer, *De Antiocho Ascalonita*, Bonn 1883.

[118] See Fabricius, *Biblioth. graeca*, ed. Harles, i. 511, vi. 365, x. 719. Pauly's *Encykl.* ii. 1251.   Nicolai, *Griech. Literaturgesch.* ii. 381.

Antiochus, the grammarian Ptolemaeus is best known.[119] If he was, as stated by Stephen, Ἀριστάρχου γνώριμος, he would belong to the second century before Christ. He is probably however of a considerably later date (about the beginning of the Christian era).[120] Among the towns of Decapolis Gadara and Gerasa are especially to be mentioned as the birthplaces of distinguished men. Of Gadara was the Epicurean Philodemus, the contemporary of Cicero, numerous fragments of whose writings have become known through the rolls discovered in Herculaneum ; also the epigrammatic poet Meleager and the cynic Menippus, both probably belonging to the first century before Christ. The Greek anthology contains more than a hundred epigrams of Meleager, nay he was himself the founder of this collection. Lastly the rhetorician Theodorus, the tutor of the Emperor Tiberius, was also a Gadarene. All the four are already mentioned in combination by Strabo.[121] Of Gerasa were, according to Steph. Byz. (s.v. Γέρασα): Ariston (ῥήτωρ ἀστεῖος), Kerykos (σοφιστής) and Plato (νομικὸς ῥήτωρ), all three not otherwise known.

## 2. *Hellenism in the Jewish Region.*[121a]

In the Jewish region proper Hellenism was in its religious aspect triumphantly repulsed by the rising of the Maccabees ; it was not till after the overthrow of Jewish nationality in the wars of Vespasian and Hadrian, that an entrance for heathen

[119] See Fabricius, *Biblioth. graeca*, i. 521, vi. 156 sqq. Pauly's *Encykl.* vi. 1, 142. Nicolai, *Griech. Literaturgesch.* ii. 347. Baege, *De Ptolemaeo Ascalonita*, 1882 ; also in *Dissertationes philol. Halenses*, v. 2, 1883.

[120] Comp. on the date of Ptolemy, Baege, pp. 2–6. In Stark, *Gaza*, he is, certainly through inadvertence, transposed to the middle of the third century.

[121] Strabo, xvi. p. 759. For further particulars on all four, see the works of Fabricius (*Biblioth. graec.*), Pauly (*Encykl.*), Nicolai (*Griech. Literaturgesch.*) ; on Philodemus and Menippus in the works of Zeller and Ueberweg on the history of Greek philosophy ; on Menippus, Wildenow, *De Menippo Cynico*, Halis Sax. 1881.

[121a] Comp. in general Hamburger, *Realencyclop. für Bibel und Talmud*, 2nd Div., article " Griechenthum."

rites was forcibly obtained by the Romans. In saying this however we do not assert, that the Jewish people of those early times remained *altogether* unaffected by Hellenism. For the latter was a civilising power, which extended itself to every department of life. It fashioned in a peculiar manner the organization of the state, legislation, the administration of justice, public arrangements, art and science, trade and industry, and the customs of daily life down to fashion and ornaments, and thus impressed upon every department of life, wherever its influence reached, the stamp of the Greek mind. It is true that *Hellenistic* is not identical with *Hellenic* culture. The importance of the former on the contrary lay in the fact, that by its reception of the available elements of all foreign cultures within its reach, it became a world-culture. But this very world-culture became in its turn a peculiar whole, in which the preponderant Greek element was the ruling keynote. Into the stream of this Hellenistic culture the Jewish people was also drawn ; slowly indeed and with reluctance, but yet irresistibly, for though religious zeal was able to banish heathen worship and all connected therewith from Israel, it could not for any length of time restrain the tide of Hellenistic culture in other departments of life. Its several stages cannot indeed be any longer traced. But when we reflect that the small Jewish country was enclosed on almost every side by Hellenistic regions, with which it was compelled, even for the sake of trade, to hold continual intercourse, and when we remember, that even the rising of the Maccabees was in the main directed not against Hellenism in general, but only against the heathen religion, that the later Asmonaeans bore in every respect a Hellenistic stamp—employed foreign mercenaries, minted foreign coins, took Greek names, etc., and that some of them, *e.g.* Aristobulus I., were direct favourers of Hellenism, —when all this is considered, it may safely be assumed, that Hellenism had, notwithstanding the rising of the Maccabees, gained access in no inconsiderable measure into Palestine even before the commencement of the Roman period. Its further

diffusion was not to any considerable amount promoted by the
rule of the Romans and Herodians, who added to it that
*Latin* element, which makes itself so very apparent especially
after the first century of the Christian era. For this later
age (the first half of the second century after Christ), the
Mishna affords us copious material, plainly showing the influence of Hellenism upon every sphere of life. A multitude of
Greek and also of Latin words in the Hebrew of the Mishna
shows, how it was just Hellenistic culture which had gained
an ascendancy in Palestine also. A series of examples may
serve to substantiate this in detail also.[122]

It is chiefly of course in the department of *civil government*
and *military matters* that, together with foreign arrangements,
we find foreign terms also current. A provincial governor is
called הגמון (ἡγεμών), a province הגמוניא (ἡγεμονία), the municipal authorities of a town ארכי (ἀρχή).[123] For soldiers in
general the Latin לגיונות (legiones) is used ; an army is called
אסטרטיא (στρατία), war פולמוס (πόλεμος), pay אפסניא (ὀψώνιον),
a helmet קסדא (cassida), a shield תרים (θυρεός).[124] In matters
of jurisprudence, Jewish traditions were in general strictly
adhered to. The law, given to His people by God through

---

[122] The compilation following is for the most part the result of my own
collection. Anton Theodor Hartmann's catalogue of the Greek and Latin
words in the Mishna (*Thesauri linguae hebraicae e Mishna augendi particula*
i. (Rostochii 1825), pp. 40–47, comp. Pt. iii. (1826, p. 95)), a very careful
work, though not complete as to authorities, has furnished me with several
needed additions. Comp. also on the foreign words in the Mishna and
Talmud, Sachs, *Beitrage zur Sprach- und Alterthumsforschung aus jüdischen
Quellen*, Nos. I. and II. 1852–1854. Cassel in Ersch and Gruber's *Encycl.*,
Div. ii. vol. 27, p. 28 sq. Adolf Brull, *Fremdsprachliche Redensarten und
ausdrucklich als fremdsprachlich bezeichnete Wörter in den Talmuden und
Midraschim*, Leipzig 1869. Perles, *Etymologische Studien zur Kunde der
rabbinische Sprache und Altherthümer*, Breslau 1871. N. Brull, *Fremd-
sprachliche Wörter in den Talmuden und Midraschim* (*Jahrb. fur jüdische
Gesch. und Literatur*, i. 1874, pp. 123–220).

[123] הגמון, *Edujoth* vii. 7 ; הגמוניא, *Gittin* i. 1 ; ארכי, *Kiddushin* iv. 5.

[124] לגיונות, *Kelim* xxix. 6 ; *Ohaloth* xviii. 10 ; אסטרטיא, *Kiddushin* iv.
5 ; פולמוס, *Sota* ix. 14 ; *Para* viii. 9 ; אפסניא (not אספניא), see Levy,
*Neuhebr. Wörterbuch*, *s.v.*, *Sanhedrin* ii. 4 ; קסדא, *Shabbath* vi. 2 ; *Kelim*
xi. 8 ; תרים, *Shabbath* vi. 4 ; *Sota* viii. 1 ; *Aboth* iv. 11.

Moses, extended not only to sacred transactions, but also to
matters of civil law and the organization of the administration
of justice.     Here too then the Old Testament was in essential
points the standard.     We nevertheless meet with Greek
terms and arrangements in some particulars in these departments also.     The court of justice is indeed generally called בית
דין, but sometimes also סנהדרין (συνέδριον), the assessors פרהדרין
(πάρεδροι), the accuser קטיגור (κατήγορος), the advocate פרקליט
(παράκλητος), a deposit אפותיקי (ὑποθήκη), a testament
דיתיקי (διαθήκη), a guardian or steward אפיטרופוס (ἐπίτροπος).[125]
Nay even for a specifically Jewish legal institution, introduced in the time of Hillel, viz. the declaration before a
court of justice, that the right to call in a given loan at any
time was reserved notwithstanding the Sabbatic year, the
Greek expression פרוזבול (προσβολή) was used.[126]

Of other public institutions, *games* again come first into
notice.     Pharisaic Judaism has always repudiated the heathen
kind of games.     Philo indeed says in his work, *Quod omnis
probus liber*, that he was once present at an ἀγὼν παγ-
κρατιαστῶν, and another time at the performance of a tragedy
of Euripides.[127]     But what the cultured Alexandrian allowed
himself was no standard for the strict legal Palestinians.
Even in the period of the Maccabees the building of a
gymnasium in Jerusalem and the visiting of the same on
the part of the Jews is mentioned as a chief abomination of
the prevailing Hellenism (1 Macc. i. 14, 15; 2 Macc. iv. 9–17).
And this continued to be the standpoint of legal Judaism.[128]

---

[125] סנהדרון, *Sota* ix. 11; *Kiddushin* iv. 5; *Sanhedrin* i. 5–6; *Shebuoth*
ii. 2, *Middoth* v. 4; specially abundant in the later Targums, see Buxtorf,
*Lex. Chald.*, and Levy, *Chald. Wörterb. s.v.*—פרהדרין, *Joma* l. 1; קטינור
and פרקליט, *Aboth* iv. 11; אפותיקי, *Gittin* iv. 4; דיתיקי, *Moed katan* iii. 3;
*Baba mezia* i. 7; *Baba bathra* viii. 6; אפיטרופוס, *Shebiith* x. 6; *Bikkurim*
i. 5; *Pesachim* viii. 1; *Gittin* v. 4; *Baba kamma* iv. 4, 7; *Baba bathra* iii. 3;
*Shebuoth* vii. 8; אפיטרופא (stewardess), *Kethuboth* ix. 4, 6.

[126] פרוזבול, *Pea* iii. 6; *Shebiith* x. 3–7; *Moed katan* iii. 3; *Kethuboth*
ix. 9; *Gittin* iv. 3; *Ukzin* iii. 10.

[127] *Opp.* ed. Mangey, ii. 449 and 467.

[128] *Aboda sara* i. 7: "Neither *bears*, *lions*, nor anything from which harm

Even Josephus designates the theatre and amphitheatre as
"foreign to Jewish customs."[129]  Judaism however was
unable, in spite of this theoretic repudiation, to prevent
the pageantry of heathen games from developing in the midst
of the Holy Land during and after the Herodian period; and
we cannot assume that the mass of the Jewish population
denied themselves from visiting them.  A theatre and amphitheatre were built in Jerusalem by Herod, who instituted
there as well as at Caesarea games every four years in honour
of the emperor.[130]  The games imply the existence also of a
stadium and hippodrome, the latter indeed is once expressly
mentioned.[131]  In *Jericho* where Herod seems to have
frequently resided were a theatre, amphitheatre and hippodrome.[132]  In *Tiberias* a stadium is incidentally mentioned.[133]
Even so unimportant a town as *Tarichea* had a hippodrome.[134]

The public *baths* and public *inns* were further arrangements
showing the influence of Hellenism.  The bath indeed was
designated by a purely Hebrew expression מֶרְחָץ.  But the
name for the director of the bath, בַּלָּן (βαλανεύς), points to
its Greek origin.[135]  In the case of the public inns their Greek

to others might arise, might be sold to the heathen.  They may not be
helped in building a Basilica, a place of execution (Gradum), a Stadium or
Bema.  Comp. in general, Winer, *Realwörterb. s.v.* " Spiele " and the literature there cited.  Löw, *Die Lebensalter in der jüdischen Literatur* (1875), pp.
291–300.  Weber, *System der altsynagogalen palästin. Theologie* (1880), p.
68: Opinion was everywhere very strict "on the theatre and circus of
the heathen."  Hamburger, *Real-Encyclopädie für Bibel und Talmud*, Div.
ii. article "Theater."

[129] *Antt.* xv. 8. 1: θέατρον . . . ἀμφιθέατρον, περίοπτα μὲν ἄμφω τῇ
πολυτελείᾳ, τοῦ δὲ κατὰ τοὺς Ἰουδαίους ἔθους ἀλλότρια· χρῆσίς τε γὰρ
αὐτῶν καὶ θεαμάτων τοιούτων ἐπίδειξις οὐ παραδέδοται.  The Jews saw in
these games a φανερὰ κατάλυσις τῶν τιμωμένων παρ᾽ αὐτοῖς ἐθῶν.

[130] *Antt.* xv. 8. 1.  The games at Jerusalem, like those at Caesarea, comprised all the four kinds: gymnastic and musical games, chariot racing and
contests of wild beasts.  See the further description in Josephus as above.

[131] *Antt.* xviii. 10. 2; *Bell. Jud.* ii. 3. 1.

[132] Theatre, *Antt.* xvii. 6. 3.  Amphitheatre, *Antt.* xvii. 3. 2; *Bell.
Jud.* i. 33. 8.  Hippodrome, xvii. 6. 5; *Bell. Jud.* i. 33. 6.

[133] *Bell. Jud.* ii. 21. 6, iii. 10. 10; *Vita*, xvii. 64.

[134] *Bell. Jud.* ii. 21. 3 ; *Vita*, xxvii. 28.

[135] בַּלָּן, *Kelim* xvii. 1 ; *Sabim* iv. 2.  Compare on the baths as a heathen

name, פונדקי (πανδοκεῖον or πανδοχεῖον), already showed them
to be a product of the Hellenistic period.[136]

Architecture in general and especially in public buildings
must be regarded as emphatically a Hellenizing element.[137]
In the Hellenistic towns in the neighbourhood of Palestine
this is of course self-evident.    They all had their ναούς,
θέατρα, γυμνάσια, ἐξέδρας, στοάς, ἀγοράς, ὑδάτων εἰσαγωγάς,
βαλανεῖα, κρήνας and περίστυλα in Greek fashion.[138]    But
also in Palestine proper, the prevalence of the Greek style—
especially since the time of Herod—may be safely assumed.
When Herod built himself a splendid palace, there can be no
doubt that he adopted for it the Graeco-Roman style.[139]    The
same remark applies also to the other contemporary palaces
and monuments of Jerusalem.    In any case not only were
Stadia[140] known in Palestine,—as must be assumed from what
has been remarked about the games,—but also Basilica,[141]

institution but one permissible to Jews, especially *Aboda sara* i. 7, iii. 4.
On their diffusion and arrangements, Marquardt, *Das Privatleben der
Römer*, vol. i. (1879) p. 262 sqq. Hermann and Blümner, *Lehrb. der
griechischen Privatalterthümer* (1882), p. 210 sqq.

[136] פונדקי, *Jebamoth* xvi. 7; *Gittin* viii. 9; *Kiddushin* iv. 12; *Edujoth*
iv. 7; *Aboda sara* ii. 1. פונדקית (the hostess), *Demai* iii. 5; *Jebamoth*
xvi. 7. Foreign travellers are called אכסניא or אכסנאין (ξένοι), *Demai*
iii. 1; *Chullin* viii. 2. פונדקי not unfrequently in the Targums, see
Buxtorf, *Lex. Chald.*, and Levy, *Chald. Wörterb. s.v.* A δημόσιον or κοινὸν
πανδοχῖον occurs in two inscriptions in the Hauran, Le Bas et Waddington,
vol. iii. n. 2462, 2463. The word also occurs, as is well known, in the N. T.
(Luke x. 34). See Wetstein, *Nov. Test.* on Luke x. 34; Hermann and Blümner, *Lehrb. der griechischen Privatalterthümer*, p. 499 sqq., and the Lexicons.

[137] Comp. Winer, *RWB.*, article "Baukunst." Rüetschi in Herzog's
*Real-Encycl.*, 2nd ed. ii. 132 sqq. De Saulcy, *Histoire de l'art judaïque*,
Paris 1858. Conder, *Notes on Architecture in Palestine* (*Quarterly Statement*,
1878, pp. 29–40). Almost all the ruins that remain belong to the non-
Jewish towns of Palestine.

[138] See especially the summary of the buildings of Herod, *Bell. Jud.*
i. 21. 11. On Gaza, comp. Stark, 598 sqq. On Berytus, the buildings of
the two Agrippas, *Antt.* xix. 7. 5, xx. 9. 4. On the public buildings, which
were everywhere customary in Greek towns, see Hermann and Blümner,
*Lehrb. der griechischen Privatalterthümer* (1882), p. 132 sqq.

[139] See the description *Bell. Jud.* v. 4. 4.

[140] אצטדין (στάδιον), *Baba kamma* iv. 4; *Aboda sara* i. 7.

[141] בסילקי (βασιλική), *Aboda sara* i. 7; *Tohoroth* vi. 8.

porticoes,[142] porches,[143] Tribunes,[144] banqueting - halls [145] and other buildings after the Graeco-Roman manner. Even in the temple at Jerusalem the Grecian style of architecture was copiously adopted. It is true that in the temple proper (the ναός) Herod could not venture to forsake the old traditional forms. But in the building of the inner fore-court we see the influence of Greek models. Its gates had fore-courts (ἐξέδραι) within, between which colonnades (στοαί) ran along the inside of the walls.[146] The gate at the eastern side of the outer court had folding doors of Corinthian brass, which were more costly than those covered with gold and silver.[147] Quite in the Grecian style were the colonnades (στοαί), which surrounded the outer court on all four sides. Most of them were double (διπλαῖ),[148] but the most magnificent were those found on the south side. They were in the form of a basilikon (βασίλειος στοά); four rows of large Corinthian columns, together 162 in number, formed a three-aisled hall, the middle aisle of which was broader by a half than the two side aisles and as high again.[149] All this does not indeed prove, that the Grecian was the prevailing style for ordinary private houses, nor may this be assumed. Occasionally we

[142] איצטבא (στοά), Shekalim viii. 4; Sukka iv. 4; Ohaloth xviii. 9; Tohoroth vi. 10.

[143] אכסדרה (ἐξέδρα), Maaseroth iii. 6; Erubin viii. 4; Sota viii. 3; Tamid i. 3; Middoth i. 5; Ohaloth vi. 2. The ἐξέδρα is an open fore-court in front of the house door. See especially Ohaloth vi. 2.

[144] בימה (βῆμα), Sota vii. 8; Aboda sara i. 7.

[145] טריקלין (τρίκλινος), Erubin vi. 6; Baba bathra vi. 4; Aboth iv. 16; Middoth i. 6.

[146] The ἐξέδραι are mentioned by this name in the Mishna also (Tamid i. 3; Middoth i. 5). Comp. Bell. Jud. v. 5. 3; also v. 1. 5 fin., vi. 2. 7, 4. 1; Antt. xx. 8. 11. On the στοαί of the inner court, see Bell. Jud. v. 5. 2 fin., vi. 5. 2 (where they are decidedly distinguished from those of the outer).

[147] Bell. Jud. v. 5. 3, init. Comp. also on this gate, Bell. Jud. ii. 17. 3, vi. 5. 3. It was probably identical with the θύρα ὡραία mentioned Acts iii. 2.

[148] Bell. Jud. v. 5. 2, init.; comp. Bell. Jud. v. 3, and also Philo, De monarchia, lib. ii. § 2. The στοαί are also mentioned in the Mishna under this Greek designation (Shekalim viii. 4; Sukka iv. 4).

[149] Antt. xv. 11. 5.

see also that Phœnician and Egyptian architecture was also found in Palestine.[150]

*Plastic art* could, by reason of the Jewish repudiation of all images of men and beasts, find no entrance into Palestine ; and it was only in isolated cases, as *e.g.* when Herod the Great had a golden eagle brought into the temple, or Herod Antipas placed images of animals on his palace at Tiberias, that the Herodians allowed themselves to defy Jewish views.[151]  Grecian *music* was undoubtedly represented at the feasts at Jerusalem and elsewhere.[152]  The musical instruments of the Greeks, κίθαρις, ψαλτήριον and συμφωνία, are, as is well known, mentioned in the Book of Daniel and also in the Mishna.[153]  Of games of amusement dice, קוּבְיָא (κυβεία), were, as the name shows, introduced into Palestine by the Greeks.  They also were repudiated by the stricter Jews.[154]  In the matter of *writing* the influence

[150] Tyrian courts to houses are mentioned *Maaseroth* iii. 5 ; Tyrian and Egyptian windows, *Baba bathra* iii. 6.  The Tyrian houses were particularly large and elegant, see Strabo, xvi. p. 757, *init. ;* Joseph. *Bell. Jud.* ii. 18. 9.

[151] The eagle in the temple, *Antt.* xvii. 6. 2 ; *Bell. Jud.* i. 33. 2.  The representations of animals on the palace at Tiberias, Joseph. *Vita*, 12.  Representations of animals are also found upon the remarkable ruins of Arâk el-Emir, north-west of Heshbon, which are evidently identical with the castle of Tyrus mentioned by Josephus in the neighbourhood of Heshbon, the building of which he ascribes to one Hyrcanus of the time of Seleucus IV. (*Antt.* xii. 4. 11).  It is however questionable, whether the castle with its rude figures of animals is not older than Josephus supposes, viz. of pre-Hellenistic origin; see De Vogüé, *Le Temple de Jerusalem* (1864), pp. 37–42, pl. xxxiv., xxxv. Tuch, *Report of the Saxon Gesellsch. der Wissensch. philol.-hist. Cl.* (1865), pp. 18–36. De Saulcy, *Voyage en Terre Sainte* (1865), i. 211 sqq. The same in the *Mémoires de l'Academie des Inscr. et Belles Lettres*, vol. xxvi. 1 (1867), pp. 83–117 with pl. viii.  Duc de Luynes, *Voyage d'exploration à la mer morte*, etc., pl. 30–33.  Bädeker, *Palästina* (1875), pp. 320–322.

[152] Herod offered prizes τοῖς ἐν τῇ μουσικῇ διαγινομένοις καὶ θυμελικοῖς καλουμένοις . . . καὶ διεσπούδαστο πάντας τοὺς ἐπισημοτάτους ἐλθεῖν ἐπὶ τὴν ἄμιλλαν (*Antt.* xv. 8. 1).

[153] Dan. iii. 3, 5, 10, 15.  On the several instruments, see especially the article in Gesenius' *Thesaurus*.  סַמְפּוֹנְיָא, also *Kelim* xi. 6, xvi. 8.  On music in general among the Jews, Winer, *RWB.* ii. 120–125.  Leyrer in Herzog's *Real-Encycl.*, 2nd ed. x. 387–398.  Löw, *Die Lebensalter in der jüdischen Literatur*, p. 300 sqq.

[154] קוּבְיָא, *Shabbath* xxiii. 2 ; *Rosh hashana* i. 8 ; *Sanhedrin* iii. 3 ; *Shebuoth*

of the Greek and Roman periods is shown in the words used for pen, קלמוס, (κάλαμος), and writer, לבלר (*librarius*).[155] But it was in the department of *trade*, of *industry*, and all connected therewith, and in that of the necessaries of daily life, that the influence of Hellenism made itself the most forcibly noticeable. By their ancient commerce with the Phoenicians the coast lands of the Mediterranean had already entered into active intercourse with each other.[156] While, however, in ancient times the Phoenicians had the preponderance as givers, the Orientals now more occupied the position of receivers. At least it was the Graeco-Roman element which was now the intermediary and influential factor in the general commerce of the world. This is plainly shown in the trade and commerce of Judaeo-Palestine.[157] Already are the tech-

vii. 4. See in general Löw, *Die Lebensalter*, p. 323 sqq. Hermann and Blümner, *Griech. Privatalterthümer*, p. 511 sqq. Marquardt, *Das Privatleben der Römer*, ii. 824 sqq.

[155] קלמוס, *Shabbath* i. 3, viii. 5. לבלר, *Pea* ii. 6 ; *Shabbath* i. 3 ; *Gittin* iii. 1.

[156] On the commerce of the Phoenicians, see especially the classic work of Movers (*Die Phönicier*), the last part of which (ii. 3, 1856) is entirely devoted to this subject. On the influence thereby exerted upon Western by Eastern culture, see the literature in Hermann and Blümner, *Griechische Privatalterthümer* (1882), p. 41 sq., and in Marquardt, *Das Privatleben der Römer*, vol. ii. (1882), p. 378 sq.

[157] On Jewish commerce, see especially Herzfeld, *Handelsgeschichte der Juden des Alterthums* (1879) ; and for a short account, Winer, *RWB.* i. 458 sqq. Leyrer in Herzog's *Real-Enc.*, 2nd ed. v. 578 sqq., xiii. 513 sqq. (art. " Schiffahrt "). De Wette, *Lehrb. der hebr.-jüd. Archäologie* (Räbiger, 4th ed.), p. 390 sqq. Keil, *Handb. der bibl. Archäol.* (2nd ed. 1875) p. 599 sqq. Hamburger, *Real-Encyclopädie für Bibel und Talmud*, Div. ii. art. " Welthandel." For an acquaintance with Oriental commerce in general, in the first century after Christ, one of the most important and interesting authorities is the Περίπλους τῆς ἐρυθρᾶς θαλάσσης (probably composed by a contemporary of Pliny about 70–75 after Christ). Comp. on the Periplus, especially Schwanbeck, *Rhein. Museum*, new series, vol. vii. 1850, pp. 321–369, 481–511. Dillmann, *Monthly Report of the Berlin Academy*, 1879, pp. 413–427. Jurien de la Gravière, *Le commerce de l'Orient sous les règnes d'Auguste et de Claude* (*Revue des deux mondes*, 1883, Nov. 15, pp. 312–355). The text is given in Müller's *Geographi Graeci minores*, vol. i. 1855, pp. 257–305 (see also the Proleg., p. xcv. sqq.). The separate publication, Fabricius, *The Periplus of the Red Sea*, by an unknown traveller, in Greek and German, with critical and explanatory notes, and a complete glossary of words. Leipzig 1883 (in this work is given, pp. 1–27, the rest of the literature).

nical designations of the commercial class partly Greek. A
corn-dealer is called סיטון (σιτώνης), a sole dealer, מנפול (μονοπώλης), a retail dealer, פלטר (πρατήρ),[158] a merchant's account-
book is called פנקס (πίναξ).[159] The whole *coinage system* of
Palestine was partly the Phoenician-Hellenistic, partly the
entirely Greek or Roman.[160] Reckonings were made in Palestine in the time of the Maccabees by drachmas and talents.[161]
During the period of independence the Asmonean princes
certainly issued money of their own, coined according to a
native (Phoenician) standard, and with Hebrew inscriptions.
But the later Asmoneans already added Greek inscriptions
also. Of the Herodians only coins of Roman values with
Greek inscriptions are known. In the period of Roman
supremacy the Roman system of coins was fully carried out, nay
even the Roman *names* of coins were then more current than
the Hebrew and Greek ones, which were used simultaneously.
This is seen by the following comparison of the material
afforded by the Mishna and the New Testament.[162]    (1) The
Palestinian gold coin is the Roman *aureus* of 25 denarii, often

---

[158] סיטון, *Demai* ii. 4, v. 6; *Baba bathra* v. 10; *Kelim* xii. 1; מנפול,
*Demai* v. 4; *Aboda sara* iv. 9; on σιτώνης and μονοπώλης, see also Herzfeld, p. 135 sq. פלטר is in some places = πωλητήριον, the place of sale;
and Herzfeld (pp. 131, 132) insists on so understanding it in the two
passages quoted; but it is more probably = πρατήρ (so Hartmann, *Thes.
ling. Hebr. e Mischna aug.* p. 45).

[159] פנקס, *Shabbath* xii. 4; *Shebuoth* vii. 1. 5; *Aboth* iii. 16; *Kelim*
xvii. 17, xxiv. 7. This account-book consisted of two tablets bound together,
which could be opened and closed.

[160] On the Jewish coinage of earlier and later times, see Bertheau, *Zur
Geschichte der Israeliten* (1842), pp. 1–49. Zuckermann, *Ueber talmudische
Gewichte und Münzen*, 1862. Herzfeld, *Metrologische Voruntersuchungen zu
einer Geschichte des ibräischen resp. altjüdischen Handels*, 2 parts, 1863–1865.
The same, *Handelsgeschichte der Juden* (1879), pp. 171–185. Winer, *RWB.*
art. " Gold;" also the articles Denar, Drachme, Stater, Sekel. De Wette,
*Lehrb. der hebr.-jüdischen Archäol.* (4th ed. 1864) p. 251 sqq. The works of
De Saulcy, Madden, and others on Jewish coins; see above, § 2. Hultsch,
*Griechische und römische Metrologie* (1882), pp. 456 sqq., 602 sqq.

[161] Drachmas, 2 Macc. iv. 19, x. 20, xii. 43. Talents, 1 Macc. xi. 28,
xiii. 16, 19, xv. 31, 35; 2 Macc. iii. 11, iv. 8, 24, v. 21, viii. 10 sq. What
standard is to be assumed in this case must here be left uncertain.

[162] On the coins named in the New Testament, see Madden, *History*

mentioned in the Mishna under the name of the " gold denarius "
(דינר זהב).[163]  (2) The current silver coin was the *denarius*
(δηνάριον), which is the most frequently named of all coins in
the New Testament (Matt. xviii. 28, xx. 2 sqq., xxii. 19 ; Mark
vi. 37, xii. 15, xiv. 5 ; Luke vii. 41, x. 35, xx. 24 ; John vi. 7,
xii. 5 ; Rev. vi. 6). That this Latin designation is familiar
to the Mishna is very evident, for it is here almost more
frequently mentioned by the expression דינר than by its
Semitic equivalent זוז.[164]  The denarius being esteemed equal
in value to an Attic drachma, calculations were still made by
drachmas. Still this mode of computation was no longer
frequent.[165]  (3) Of copper coins, the two *as* piece, or *dupondius* (Hebr. פונדיון), is chiefly mentioned.[166]  Such a dupondius
is also meant in the saying of Christ, Luke xii. 6, where the
Vulgate rightly translates ἀσσαρίων δύο by *dipondio*.  (4) The
most common copper coin was the *as*, Greek ἀσσάριον (Matt.
x. 29 ; Luke xii. 6), Hebr. אסר, sometimes expressly designated

*of Jewish Coinage* (1864), pp. 232-248 ; Winer and De Wette's above-
mentioned works. On the Roman coinage, comp. especially the excellent
summary in Marquardt, *Römische Staatsverwaltung*, vol. ii. (1876), pp. 3-75.
The two chief modern works are Mommsen, *Gesch. des römischen Münz-
wesens*, 1860, and Hultsch, *Griechische und römische Metrologie*, 1882.

[163] דינר זהב, *Maaser sheni* ii. 7, iv. 9 ; *Shekalim* vi. 6 ; *Nasir* v. 2 ;
*Baba kamma* iv. 1 ; *Shebuoth* vi. 3 ; *Meila* vi. 4. On the Roman *aureus*
(called also *denarius aureus*), see Marquardt, ii. 25 sq. ; Hultsch, p. 308 sqq.
That the דינר זהב was equal to 25 denarii appears, *e.g.*, from *Kethuboth* x. 4 ;
*Baba kamma* iv. 1.

[164] דינר, *e.g.* *Pea* viii. 8 ; *Demai* ii. 5 ; *Maaser sheni* ii. 9 ; *Shekalim*
ii. 4 ; *Beza* iii. 7 ; *Kethuboth* v. 7, vi. 3, 4, x. 2 ; *Kiddushin* i. 1, ii. 2 ;
*Baba mezia* iv. 5 ; *Arachin* vi. 2, 5, and elsewhere. זוז, *Pea* viii. 8, 9 ;
*Jama* iii. 7 ; *Kethuboth* i. 5, vi. 5, ix. 8 ; *Gittin* vii. 5 ; *Kiddushin* iii. 2 ;
*Baba kamma* iv. 1, viii. 6 ; *Baba bathra* x. 2.

[165] δραχμή, Luke xv. 8 sq. ; Joseph. *Vita*, 44. In both passages, however,
drachmae of Tyrian value may be intended ; comp. below, note 172.

[166] פונדיון, *Pea* viii. 7 ; *Shebiith* viii. 4 ; *Maaser sheni* iv. 8 ; *Erubin*
viii. 2 ; *Baba mezia* iv. 5 ; *Baba bathra* v. 9 ; *Shebuoth* vi. 3 ; *Kelim*
xvii. 12 (in the last expressly named as the Italian pondion (פונדיון איטלקי).
From *Baba bathra* v. 9, it is evident that a *pondion* = two *asses*, as is also
expressly noticed in the Talmud (*jer. Kiddushin* 58d ; *bab. Kiddushin* 12a ;
Lightfoot, *Horae hebr.* on Matt. v. 26, *Opp.* ii. 288 sq.). The pondion is
therefore without doubt the Roman *dupondius*, as Guisius on *Pea* viii. 7
(in Surenhusius' *Mishna* i. 7) has remarked.

as the Italian as, אסר איטלקי.[167]   It amounted originally to one-
tenth, but after the second Punic war (B.C. 217), to only
one-sixteenth of a denarius.[168]   (5) The smallest copper coin
was the פְּרוּטָה, amounting to only the eighth of an *as*.[169]   It
was unknown to the Roman system of coinage, its name too is
Semitic.   The λεπτόν however which occurs in the New Testament (Mark xii. 42 ; Luke xii. 59, xxi. 2), and is, according
to Mark xii. 42, the half of a quadrans, is identical with it.
Coins of this size are in fact found in the period of the later
Asmoneans and single ones in the Herodian-Romish period.[170]
It is however striking, that both in the Mishna and the New
Testament reckonings are made by this smallest portion of the
*as*, and not by the *semis* (half *as*) and *quadrans* (quarter *as*),
while the latter were then coined in Palestine also, and indeed
more frequently than the λεπτόν.[171]   The mode of reckoning
seems, according to the latter, to have come down from pre-
Roman times, but to have remained in use even after the
introduction of the Roman valuation.   The coins issued in
the Phoenician towns, especially in Tyre, which were in cir-
culation in Palestine even when no more were made according
to this standard, differed in value from the Roman coins.[172]

[167] אסר איטלקי, *Kiddushin* i. 1 ; *Edujoth* iv. 7 ; *Chullin* iii. 2 ; *Mikwaoth* ix. 5.   On אסר in general, *e.g. Pea* viii. 1 ; *Shebiith* viii. 4 ; *Maaseroth* ii. 5, 6 ; *Maaser sheni* iv. 3, 8 ; *Erubin* vii. 10 ; *Baba mezia* iv. 5 ;
*Baba bathra* v. 9.

[168] Marquardt, *Römische Staatsverwaltung*, ii. 16.

[169] פְּרוּטָה, *Kiddushin* i. 1, ii. 1, 6 ; *Baba kamma* ix. 5, 6, 7 ; *Baba mezia*
iv. 78 ; *Shebuoth* vi. 1, 3 ; *Edujoth* iv. 7.   That it amounted to the eighth
of the *as* is said *Kiddushin* i. 1 ; *Edujoth* iv. 7.

[170] See Madden, *History of Jewish Coinage*, p. 301.

[171] See Madden, as above.   The *semis* and *quadrans* are not to my knowledge mentioned in the Mishna, but first occur in the Jerusalemite and
Babylonian Talmud.   In the New Testament indeed the *quadrans* (κοδράντης) is twice mentioned.   But in one passage (Mark xii. 42) the words
ὅ ἐστιν κοδράντης are only an explanation on the part of the evangelist ; in
the other (Matt. v. 26) the expression κοδράντης was probably inserted by
the evangelist in place of λεπτόν offered by his authority, and preserved by
St. Luke (xii. 59).   The authorities therefore of our Gospels mention only
the λεπτόν, as the Mishna mentions only the פרוטה.

[172] The coins of Phoenician valuation were somewhat lighter than the

That which applies to money, the medium of commerce, applies also to its *objects*. Here too we everywhere come upon the track of Greek and Roman names and matters.[173] At the same time we must not overlook the fact, that Palestine with her abundance of natural products made on her part large contributions to the commerce of the world; the produce of her soil and her industrial commodities went into all lands and were some of them world-famed.[174] But whether the

Roman; see Hultsch, *Griech. und röm. Metrologie*, p. 594 sqq. A νόμισμα Τύριον, of the value of 4 drachmae, is mentioned by Josephus, *Bell. Jud.* ii. 21. 2; comp. *Vita*, 13, *s. fin.* The δίδραχμον (Matt. xvii. 24) and the στατήρ (= 4 drachmae, Matt. xvii. 27) are coins of this valuation; for the temple tribute, as well as those generally prescribed in the A. T., were discharged according to Tyrian valuation (*Mishna Bechoroth* viii. 7; *Tosefta Kethuboth* xii. *fin.*), because this corresponded to the Hebrew; comp. Hultsch, pp. 604 sq., 471. When Josephus states the value of the νόμισμα Τύριον to have been 4 Attic drachmae, this is but an approximate valuation, for the Tyrian tetradrachmon was somewhat lighter than the Attic (Hultsch, 595 sq.).

[173] On the commercial commodities of antiquity, see especially Marquardt, *Das Privatleben der Römer*, vol. ii., Leipzig 1882 (2nd ed. of the *römischen Privatalterthümer*, vol. ii.). Karl Friedr. Hermann and H. Blümner, *Lehrb. der griechischen Privatalterthümer*, Freiburg 1882. Büchsenschütz, *Die Hauptstätten des Gewerbfleisses im klassischen Alterthums*, Leipzig 1869. On the products of Egypt in particular, Lumbroso, *Recherches sur l'économie politique de l'Egypte sous les Lagides*, Turin 1870. On the arts of the Restoration, Blümner, *Technologie und Terminologie der Gewerbe und Künste bei Griechen und Römern*, vols. i.–iii., Leipzig 1875–1884. The *Edictum Diocletiani de pretiis rerum* (1st ed.) given—(1) by Mommsen in the reports of the *Saxon Scientific Society, phil.-hist. Cl.* vol. iii. 1851, pp. 1–80, with Appendix, pp. 383–400; (2) by Waddington in Le Bas et Waddington, *Inscr.* vol. iii., *Explications*, pp. 145–191; (3) by Mommsen in *Corp. Inscr. Lat.* vol. iii. 2, pp. 801–841, is a copious source of information concerning goods. I quote from Waddington's edition.

[174] On the commercial commodities of Palestine, see Movers, *Die Phönicier*, ii. 3 (1856), pp. 200–235; Herzfeld, *Handelsgesch. der Juden*, pp. 88–117; Blümner, *Die gewerbliche Thätigkeit*, etc., pp. 24–27. A survey of the chief commodities in the fourth century after Christ is given in the *Totius orbis descriptio* in Müller, *Geographi gr. minores*, ii. 513 sqq. c. 29 · Ascalon et Gaza in negotiis eminentes et abundantes omnibus bonis mittunt omni regioni Syriae et Aegypti vinum optimum . . . c. 31: Quoniam ergo ex parte supra dictas descripsimus civitates, necessarium mihi videtur, ut etiam quidnam unaquaeque civitas proprium habeat exponamus, ut qui legit, certam eorum scientiam habere possit. Scythopolis igitur, Laodicia, Byblus, Tyrus, Berytus omni mundo linteamen emittunt; Sarepta vero,

commodities were produced in the land or introduced from abroad, they equally bore in large proportion the impress of the prevalent Hellenistic culture; the produce of the interior was regulated by its requirements, while just the objects which were the fashion in all the world were those which were imported into Palestine.[175]

A series of examples from the three departments of (1) provisions (2), clothing and (3) furniture may serve as a further illustration. Of foreign provisions, e.g., there were known in Palestine Babylonian sauce (כּוּתָּח), Median beer (שֵׁכָר), Edomite vinegar (חוֹמֶץ) and Egyptian zythos (זִיתוֹם).[176] Also other Egyptian products, viz. fish,[177] mustard, kürbis,

Caesarea, Neapolis et Lydda purpuram praestant; omnes autem fructiferae vino, oleo et frumento; Nicolaum vero palmulam invenies abundare in Palaestina regione, in loco qui dicitur Hiericho, similiter et Damasci minores palmulas, sed utiles, et pistacium et omne genus pomorum. Especially famous was the linen manufacture of Scythopolis. In the *Edictum Diocl.* c. xvii.–xviii., the linen goods of Scythopolis stand first as the most expensive. See also *Jer. Kiddushin* ii. 5: כלי פשתן הדקים הבאין מבית שאן, Movers, ii. 3, 217 sq. Herzfeld, p. 107. Marquardt, *Das Privatleben der Römer*, ii. 466. Büchsenschütz, p. 61. Blümner, *Die gewerbl. Thätigkeit*, p. 25. The Mishna too assumes, that Galilee carried on chiefly the manufacture of linen, and Judea on the contrary that of woollen goods (*Baba kamma* x. 9). Hence there was a wool-market at Jerusalem.

[175] On imported articles, see also Herzfeld, *Handelsgeschichte*, pp. 117–129.

[176] All four are mentioned, *Pesachim* iii. 1, as examples of provisions, which are prepared from kinds of grain and have gone through a process of fermentation. On the Egyptian ζῦθος (a kind of beer, Hebr. זיתום, not זיתום, see Levy, *Neuhebr. Wörterbuch, s.v.*), comp. Theophrast. *de caus. plant.* vi. 11. 2. Diodor. i. 34. Plinius, xxii. 164. Strabo, xvii. p. 824. *Digest.* xxxiii. 6, 9. *Edict. Diocletiani*, ii. 12. Buxtorf, *Lex. Chald. s.v.* Waddington's explanations to the *Edict. Diocl.* p. 154. Pauly's *Encykl. s.v. cerevisia.* Marquardt, *Privatleben der Römer*, ii. 444. Hermann and Blümner, *Griech. Privatleben*, p. 235. Hehn, *Kulturpflanzen und Hausthiere* (3rd ed. 1877), p. 136 sq. Schleusner's *Lexicon in LXX. s.v.* and the Lexicons generally. It also occurs in the Greek translations of the Old Testament Isa. xix. 10.

[177] *Machshirin* vi. 3. Pickled fish (ταρίχη), which are produced in large quantities in different places in Egypt, and formed a considerable article of exportation, are intended (Blümner, *Die gewerbl. Thätigkeit*, etc., pp. 14, 17. Lumbroso, *Recherches*, p. 133. The expositors of Num. xi. 5). A large number of places on the Egyptian coast had the name of Ταριχέαι from this branch of industry (Steph. Byz. *s.v.*). See, concerning its wide diffusion, Marquardt, *Privatleben der Römer*, ii. 420 sqq., and the chief

beans, lentils.[178] Likewise Cilician groats,[179] Bithynian cheese,[180] Greek pumpkins,[181] Greek and Roman hyssop,[182] and Spanish kolias.[183] From abroad came also, as their foreign names show, e.g. asparagus, lupines and Persian nuts.[184] Very widely diffused in Palestine was the custom of salting fish or pickling them in brine, as the name of the town Ταριχέαι on the Lake of Gennesareth and the frequent mention of brine (*muries*) in the Mishna prove.[185] The foreign origin of this custom also is evident from its foreign name.

Of materials for dress and garments of foreign origin the following are mentioned: Pelusian and Indian linen and cotton fabrics,[186]

---

work there cited, viz. Köhler, Τάριχος ou recherches sur l'histoire et les antiquités des pêcheries de la Russie méridionale (Mémoires de l'Académie imp. des sciences de St. Petersbourg, vi. serie, vol. i. 1832, pp. 347–490).

[178] Mustard (חַרְדָּל), *Kilajim* i. 2. Pumpkins (דְּלַעַת), *Kilajim* i. 2, 5. Beans (פּוֹל), *Kilajim* i. 2, ii. 11, iii. 4; *Shebiith* ii. 8, 9; *Shabbath* ix. 7; *Nedarim* vii. 1, 2. Lentils (עֲדָשִׁים), *Maaseroth* v. 8; *Kelim* xvii. 8. Egyptian lentils were known also in Rome, see Plinius, xvi. 201; Marquardt, ii. 410. Their cultivation in Egypt is of ancient date, see Hehn, *Kulturpflanzen und Hausthiere* (3rd ed.), p. 188.

[179] נרים קילקי, *Maaseroth* v. 8; *Kelim* xvii. 12; *Negaim* vi. 1.

[180] גבינה ותנייקי, *Aboda sara* ii. 4 (for thus we should here read, according to the best authorities, instead of the corrupt גבינת בית אונייקי). Bithynian cheese is also spoken of, Plinius, xi. 241: trans maria vero Bithynus fere in gloria est.

[181] דלעת יונית, *Kilajim* i. 5, ii. 11; *Orla* iii. 7; *Ohaloth* viii. 1.

[182] אזוב יון and אזוב רומי, *Negaim* xiv. 6; *Para* xi. 7. The former also *Shabbath* xiv. 3.

[183] קוליים האספנן, *Shabbath* xxii. 2; *Machshirin* vi. 3. The colias is a kind of tunny-fish (see concerning it Plinius, xxxii. 146; Marquardt, ii. 422 and the Lexicons). It was of course salted for commerce and was like the Spanish τάριχος everywhere well known (Marquardt, ii. 421; Blümner, pp. 130–135).

[184] Asparagus (אספרנוס, ἀσπάραγος), *Nedarim* vi. 10. Lupines (תורמוס, θέρμος), *Shabbath* xviii. 1; *Machshirin* iv. 6; *Tebul jom.* i. 4. Persian nuts (אפרסקי, Περσική), *Kilajim* i. 4; *Maaseroth* i. 2. In both places, as the context shows, not peaches, but Persian nuts are meant, on which comp. Marquardt, ii. 411.

[185] מורייס, *Terumoth* xi. 1; *Joma* viii. 3; *Nedarim* vi. 1; *Aboda sara* ii. 4; *Kelim* x. 5.

[186] The garments worn by the high priest on the Day of Atonement were, according to *Joma* iii. 7, made of both materials. In the morning he wore the פילוסין, in the afternoon the הנדווין (whether these were of

Cilician haircloth,[187] the *sagum* (סגום), the *dalmatica* (דלמטיקין),
the *paragandion* (פרגוד), the *stola* (אצטלית),[188] the hand-
kerchief (סודרין, σουδάριον),[189] the felt hat (פליון, πιλίον),
the felt socks (אמפליא, ἐμπίλια), the sandals (סנדל), of which
the Laodicean (סנדל לדיקי) are mentioned as a special kind.[190]

linen or cotton is not shown by these designations).   The fine *linen
of Pelusium* was famous ; see Plinius, xix. 1. 14 : Aegyptio lino minimum
firmitatis, plurimum lucri.   Quattuor ibi genera : Taniticum ac *Pelusia-
cum*, Buticum, Tentyriticum.   Movers, ii. 3. 318.   Büchsenschütz, 62 sq.
Blümner, *Die gewerbliche Thätigkeit*, p. 6 sqq., especially 16.—Indian
materials (ὀθόνιον Ἰνδικόν, ὀθόνη Ἰνδική, σινδόνες Ἰνδικαί) are *e.g.* also frequently
mentioned in the *Periplus maris Erythraei* (see above, note 157) as articles
of commerce (§ 6, 31, 41, 48, 63).   Probably cotton goods are to be understood.   See Marquardt, ii. 472 sq.   Fabricius, *Der Periplus des erythräischen
Meeres* (1883), p. 123, and Brand's article, " Ueber die antiken Namen und
die geographische Verbreitung der Baumwolle im Alterthum " (1866),
quoted in both these two works.

187 קילקי, *Kelim* xxix. 1.—*Cilicium* was a cloth made of goat's hair, and
used for very various purposes (coarse cloaks, curtains, covers, etc.).   See
Marquardt, ii. 463; Büchsenschütz, 64; Blümner, 30.   If then St. Paul was
a σκηνοποιός of Tarsus in Cilicia (Acts xviii. 3), his calling was closely
connected with the chief manufacture of his native place.   In the Mishna
קילקי is called "felt " (*Filz*), *e.g.* matted (*verfilztes*) hair on the beard,
chest, etc. (*Mikwaoth* ix. 2).

188 סגום, *Kelim* xxix. 1 ; *Mikwaoth* vii. 6.   דלמטיקין, *Kilajim* ix. 7.
פרגוד, *Shekalim* iii. 2 ; *Kelim* xxix. 1.   אצטלית, *Joma* vii. 1 ; *Gittin* vii. 5.
For particulars respecting this piece of clothing, see Marquardt, ii. 584 sq.,
563 sq., 536 sq.   Waddington, explanations to the *Edict. Dioclet.* pp. 175 sq.,
182, 174 sq.   Mommsen, *Reports of the Saxon Scientific Society, phil.-hist.
Cl.* iii. 71, 391.—The sagum was a mantle which left the arm at liberty, and
was therefore especially worn by soldiers and artisans.   The three others are
different kinds of underclothing (hence in the Armenian translation of the
Bible *paregôt* more frequently occurs for χιτών ; see Lagarde, *Gesammelte
Abhandlungen*, 1866, p. 209 sq.).   The *dalmatica* is also mentioned in
Epiphan. *Haer.*, when speaking of the garments of the scribes.

189 סודרין, *Shabbath* iii. 3 ; *Joma* vi. 8 ; *Sanhedrin* vi. 1 ; *Tamid* vii. 3 ;
*Kelim* xxix. 1.   In the New Testament, Luke xix. 20; John xi. 44, xx. 7 ;
Acts xix. 12.   Much matter concerning it is also found in Wetstein, *Nov.
Test.* on Luke xix. 20, and in the Lexicons.

190 פליון, *Kelim* xxix. 1 ; *Nidda* viii. 1.   אמפליא, *Jebamoth* xii. 1 ; *Kelim*
xxvii. 6 (comp. Marquardt, ii. 486 ; Waddington, p. 164 ; Mommsen, p. 71).
סנדל, *e.g. Shabbath* vi. 2, 5, x. 3, xv. 2 ; *Shekalim* iii. 2 ; *Beza* i. 10 ;
*Megilla* iv. 8 ; *Jebamoth* xii. 1 ; *Arachin* vi. 5.   The sandal-maker was
called סנדלר, *Jebamoth* xii. 5 ; *Kethuboth* v. 4 ; *Aboth* iv. 11 ; *Kelim* v. 5.
See on sandals in general, Marquardt, ii. 577 sq. ; Hermann and Blümner,
*Griechische Privatalterthümer*, pp. 181, 196.   סנדל לדיקי, *Kelim* xxvi. 1.

A series too of technical expressions in the department of manufactured articles testifies to the influence of Greek models. The spun thread is called נימא (νῆμα), a certain arrangement of the loom קירום (καῖρος),[191] the tanner בורסי (βυρσεύς).[192] Of raw materials, hemp (e.g. קנבום, κάνναβος, κάνναβις) was first introduced into Palestine by the Greeks.[193]

*Domestic utensils* of foreign, especially of Greek and Roman origin, are everywhere plentiful. Of Egyptian utensils, a basket, a ladder, and a rope are mentioned,[194] also a Tyrian ladder,[195] Sidonian dishes or bowls.[196] Of Greek and Roman utensils we find the bench (ספסל, *subsellium*), the arm-chair (קתדרא, καθέδρα), the curtain (וילון, *velum*), the mirror (אספקלריא, *specularia*), the Corinthian candlestick.[197] For eating and drinking, e.g. the plate (אסקוטלא, *scutella*), the bowl (פילי, φιάλη), the table-cloth (מפה, *mappa*).[198] For cases

---

Which Laodicea is meant cannot be ascertained, probably the Phrygian, which was famed for its manufactures (*Edict. Diocl.*; Marquardt, ii. 460; Büchsenschütz, p. 65; Blümner, pp. 27, 28). The Syrian Laodicea was chiefly famous for its linen manufacture (*Edict. Diocl.* xvii.–xviii.; Marquardt, ii. 466; Büchsenschütz, p. 61; Blümner, p. 26).

[191] נימא, *Erubin* x. 13; *Shekalim* viii. 5; *Kelim* xix. 1, xxix. 1; *Negaim* xi. 10. קירום, *Shabbath* xiii. 2; *Kelim* xxi. 1. Comp. on the καῖρος, especially Blümner, *Technologie und Terminologie der Gewerbe und Künste*, i. 126 sqq.

[192] בורסי, *Kethuboth* vii. 10. בורסקי (the tan-yard), *Shabbath* i. 2; *Baba bathra* ii. 9.

[193] קנבום, *Kilajim* v. 8, ix. 1, 7; *Negaim* xi. 2. On the comparatively late diffusion of hemp, see Hehn, *Kulturpflanzen u. Hausthiere* (3rd ed.), p. 168 sq.

[194] Basket (כְּפִיפָה), *Shabbath* xx. 2; *Sota* ii. 1, iii. 1; *Kelim* xxvi. 1. The reading also of *Tebul jom.* iv. 2 is certainly כפישה instead of כפיפה. Ladder (סֻלָּם), *Baba bathra* iii. 6; *Sabim* iii. 1, 3, iv. 3. Rope (חֶבֶל), *Sota* i. 6.

[195] *Baba bathra* iii. 6; *Sabim* iii. 3.

[196] *Kelim* iv. 3. קוסים, comp. the Biblical קֶסֶת. Glass vessels are certainly meant; for the making of glass vessels formed in Roman times a main branch of Sidonian industry. Plinius, *H. N.* v. 19. 76: Sidon artifex vitri. Hermann and Blümner, *Griech. Privatalterthümer*, p. 437 sq. Marquardt, *Privatleben*, ii. 726.

[197] ספסל, *Baba bathra* iv. 6; *Sanhedrin* ii. 1, *fin.*; *Kelim* ii. 3, xxii. 3; *Mikwaoth* v. 2; *Sabim* iv. 4. Comp. Marquardt, ii. 704. קתדרא, *Kethuboth* v. 5; *Kelim* iv. 3, xxii. 3; Marquardt, ii. 705. וילון, *Kelim* xx. 6, xxiv. 13. אספקלריא, *Kelim* xxx. 2. Corinthian candlesticks in the possession of King Agrippa, Joseph. *Vita*, 13.

[198] טבלא, *Shabbath* xxi. 3; *Beza* i. 8; *Moed katan* iii. 7; *Edujoth* iii. 9

of all kinds the most common designation is תיק, θήκη.[199]
Special kinds of wooden vessels are the cask or box (קופה,
cupa), the wine-barrel (פיטס, πίθος),[200] the chest (גלוסקמא,
γλωσσόκομον), the small chest (קמטרא, κάμπτρα), the casket
(קפסא, capsa), the sack (מרצוף, μαρσύπιον).[201]

The stock of Greek and Latin words in the Mishna is far
from being exhausted by the specimens quoted. They suffice
however to give a vivid impression of the full adoption of
Western manners and customs even in Palestine in the
second century after Christ. The influence of the Greek
language reached still farther. For even in cases where the
introduction of Western productions and notions is not treated
of, we meet with the use of Greek words in the Mishna. The
air is called אויר (ἀήρ),[202] the form טופס (τύπος), the sample or
pattern דוגמא (δεῖγμα),[203] an ignorant, a non-professional, or a
private individual הדיוט (ἰδιώτης), a dwarf ננס (νάννος), a
robber לסטים (λῃστής).[204]  For the notion " weak " or " ill "

(טבלא elsewhere means a marble slab in the floor, Sota ii. 2, Middoth i. 9,
iii. 3, or a tablet with pictures, Rosh hashana, ii. 8). אסקוטלא, Moed katan
ii. 7 ; Kelim xxx. 1.  פילי, Sota ii. 2 ; Marquardt, ii. 632.  מפה, Berachoth
viii. 3 ; Marquardt, ii. 469.

[199] תיק, Shabbath xvi. 1 ; Kelim xvi. 7, 8.

[200] קופה (any round hollow vessel, cask, basket, box), Pea viii. 7 ; Demai
ii. 5 ; Shabbath viii. 2, xviii. 1 ; Shekalim iii. 2 ; Kethuboth vi. 4 ; Kelim
xvi. 3 ; Ohaloth vi. 2 ; Machshirai iv. 6, vi. 3.  פיטס (more correctly
פיתם), Baba mezia iv. 12 ; Baba bathra vi. 2 ; Kelim iii. 6 ; Marquardt, ii.
45, 626 sq.  Hermann and Blümner, Privatalterthümer, p. 162.

[201] גלוסקמא, Gittin iii. 3 ; Baba mezia i. 8 ; Meila vi. 1 ; Ohaloth ix.
15.  According to the latter passage a coffin might have the form of a
γλωσσόκομον or a κάμπτρα.  The LXX. (2 Chron. xxiv. 8, 10, 11) put
γλωσσόκομον for אָרוֹן.  In the New Testament (John xii. 6, xiii. 29) γλωσσόκομον is a money-box.  See on all these meanings, Wetstein, Nov. Test. on
John xii. 6, and the Lexicons. קמטרא, Kelim xvi. 7 ; Ohaloth ix. 15. קפסא,
Kelim xvi. 7 ; Marquardt, ii. 705 sq.  מרצוף, Shabbath viii. 5 ; Kelim xx. 1.

[202] אויר, Shabbath 3 ; Chagiga i. 8 ; Kethuboth xiii. 7 ; Gittin viii. 3 ;
Kinnim ii. 1 ; Kelim i. 1, ii. 1, 8, iii. 4, and elsewhere ; Ohaloth iii. 3, iv. 1 ;
Sabim v. 9.

[203] טופס, e.g. the different shapes of the loaf (Demai v. 3, 4), or the shape
in which the loaf was baked (Menachoth xi. 1), or the holder for the
Tephillin (Kelim xvi. 7), or the formula for the bill of divorcement (Gittin
iii. 2, ix. 5). דוגמא, Shabbath x. 1, a specimen of seeds.

[204] הדיוט used very frequently in the most different relations, e.g. of a

the Greek expression אסטנים (ἀσθενής) for steep קטפרס
(καταφερής) is used.[205] The employment also of Greek and
Latin proper names is pretty frequent even among the lower
classes and the Pharisaic scribes. Not only were the aristocratic high priests, who were on friendly terms with the
Greeks, called Jason and Alexander (in the Maccabean
period), Boethus and Theophilus (in the Herodian period),
not only did the Asmonean and Herodian princes bear the
names of Alexander, Aristobulus, Antigonus, Herod, Archelaus,
Philip, Antipas, Agrippa, but among men of the common
people also, as the apostles of Christ, names such as Andrew
and Philip appear. And in the circles of the Rabbinical scribes
we find an Antigonus of Socho, a R. Dosthai (= Dositheus), a
R. Dosaben Archinos (for such and not Harkinas was the Greek
name of his father), R. Chananiah ben Antigonus, R. Tarphon
(= Tryphon), R. Papias, Symmachus. Latin names also were
early naturalized. The John Mark mentioned in the New
Testament was, according to Acts xii. 12, a Palestinian; so too
was Joseph Barsabas, whose surname was Justus (Acts i. 23).
Josephus mentions besides the well-known Justus of Tiberius,
also e.g. a Niger of Peræa.[205a]

But all that has been said does not prove that the Greek
language also was familiar to the common people of Palestine.
However large the number of Greek words which had penetrated into the Hebrew and Aramaic, an acquaintance with

layman as distinguished from a professional craftsman (*Moed katan* i. 8,
10), or of a private individual in distinction from a ruler or official
(*Nedarim* v. 5; *Sanhedrim* x. 2; *Gittin* i. 5); also of ordinary priests as
distinguished from the high priest (*Jebamoth* ii. 4, vi. 2, 3, 5, vii. 1, ix. 1,
2, 3). נכס, *Bechoroth* vii. 6, and in the proper name שמעון בן ננס, *Bikkurim*
iii. 9; *Shabbath* xvi. 5, and elsewhere; also of animals (*Para* ii. 2) and
objects (*Tamid* iii. 5; *Middoth* iii. 5). לסטים, usually in the plural
לסטים, *Berachoth* i. 3; *Pea* ii. 7, 8; *Shabbath* ii. 5; *Pesachim* iii. 7;
*Nasir* vi. 3; *Baba kamma* vi. 1, x. 2.

[205] אסטנים, *Berachoth* ii. 6; *Joma* iii. 5. קטפרס, *Ohaloth* iii. 3;
*Tohoroth* viii. 8, 9.

[205a] Compare in general, Hamburger, *Real-Encycl. für Bibel und Talmud*,
Div. ii., article " Namen."

Greek by the mass of the people is not thereby proved. In fact, it must be assumed, that the lower classes in Palestine possessed either no knowledge, or only an insufficient one of Greek. When the Apostle Paul wanted to speak to the people in Jerusalem, he made use of the Hebrew (Aramaic?) tongue (Acts xxi. 40, xxii. 2). When Titus during the siege of Jerusalem repeatedly summoned the besieged to surrender, this was always done in Aramaic, whether Titus commissioned Josephus to speak, or spoke in his own name by the help of an interpreter.[206] Thus the incidental knowledge of Greek on the part of the people was in any case by no means an adequate one. On the other hand it is probable, that a slight acquaintance with Greek was pretty widely diffused, and that the more educated classes used it without difficulty.[207] Hellenistic districts not only surrounded Palestine on almost every side, but also pushed far into the interior (Samaria, Scythopolis). Constant contact with them was inevitable. And it is not conceivable, that this should continue without the diffusion of a certain amount of knowledge of the Greek language in Palestine also. To this must be added, that the country, both before and after the Asmonean period, was under rulers, whose education was a Greek one: first under the Ptolemies and Seleucidæ, then

---

[206] Joseph. *Bell. Jud.* v. 9. 2, vi. 2. 1. Interpreter, *Bell. Jud.* vi. 6. 2. If it sometimes appears as though Titus had spoken directly to the people (*Bell. Jud.* v. 9. 2, vi. 2. 4), we see from the latter passages that this is only in appearance, and that Josephus had to interpret his speech (*Bell. Jud.* vi. 2. 5, *init.*).

[207] The question respecting the diffusion of Greek in Palestine has been much discussed both in ancient and modern times. The copious literature is recorded in Hase, *Leben Jesu*, § 29, note *b*. Credner, *Einleitung in das Neue Testament*, p. 183. Volbeding, *Index Dissertationum quibus singuli historiae N. T. etc. loci illustrantur* (Lips. 1849), p. 18. Danko, *Historia Revelationis divinae Nov. Test.* (Vindob. 1867) p. 216 sq. Of more modern times, Hug, *Einl. in die Schriften des N. T.* (4th ed. 1847) ii. 27–49. Rettig, *Ephemerides exegetico-theologicae fasc.* iii. (Gissæ 1824) pp. 1-5. Thiersch, *Versuch zur Herstellung des histor. Standpuncts* (1845), p. 48 sqq. Roberts, *Discussions on the Gospels*, Cambridge and London 1864, Macmillan & Co. (571, p. 8). Delitzsch, *Saat und Hoffnung*, 1874, p. 201 sqq.

under the Herodians and Romans; nay some even of the
Asmoneans promoted Greek civilisation. The foreign rulers
too brought with them into the country a certain amount of
elements moulded by Greek training. We know of Herod
especially, that he surrounded himself with Greek literati
(see § 15). There were foreign troops in the land; Herod
had even Thracian, German and Gallic mercenaries.[208] The
games given by Herod at Jerusalem brought not only foreign
artists, but spectators from abroad into the holy city.[209] But
the most numerous concourse of strangers took place at the
great annual Jewish festivals. The thousands of Jews, who
came on these occasions from all parts of the world to Jerusalem, were for the most part both in language and education
Hellenists. And not only Greek Jews, but actual Greeks, *i.e.*
proselytes, came at the Jewish feasts to Jerusalem to sacrifice
and worship in the temple (comp. John xii. 20 sqq.). We
must conceive of the number of such proselytes, who made
annual pilgrimages to Jerusalem, as something considerable.
Again many Jews, who had received a Greek education
abroad, took up their permanent abode at Jerusalem, and
even formed there a synagogue of their own. Hence we find
at Jerusalem in the times of the apostles a synagogue of the
Libertines, Cyrenians, Alexandrians, Cilicians, and Asiatics
(Acts vi. 9 ; comp. ix. 20), in which it is uncertain whether one
congregation or five are spoken of.[209a] In Galilee the larger
towns had probably a fraction of Greek inhabitants. We know
this for certain of Tiberias,[210] not to speak of the mainly non-
Jewish Caesarea Philippi. Together with this strong penetration of the interior of Palestine by Greek elements, there
must have been not infrequently the necessary acquaintance
with the Greek tongue. And single traces actually point to

---

[208] *Antt.* xvii. 8. 3.  [209] *Antt.* xv. 8. 1.
[209a] A synagogue of the Alexandrians at Jerusalem is also mentioned,
*Tosefta Megilla* iii., ed. Zuckermandel, pp. 224, 26 ; *Jer. Megilla* 73[d] (in
Lightfoot, *Horae* on Acts vi. 9).
[210] Joseph. *Vita*, 12.

this. For while the Asmoneans had their coins stamped with both Greek and Hebrew inscriptions, the Herodians and Romans coined even the money intended for the Jewish region proper with merely Greek inscriptions; and it is known from the gospel history that the (undoubtedly Greek) inscription upon the coins of Caesar could be read without difficulty at Jerusalem (Matt. xx. 20 sq.; Mark xii. 16; Luke xx. 24).[211] The statement of the Mishna, that even in the temple certain vessels were marked with Greek letters, is certainly supported there by only one authority (R. Tomael), while according to the prevailing tradition the letters were Hebrew.[212] When further it is determined in the Mishna that the writing of divorcement might be in the Greek language also,[213] and that the Holy Scriptures might be used in the Greek translation,[214] both these permissions may refer to the Jewish Dispersion beyond Palestine. The notice on the contrary, that at the time of the war of Titus (or more correctly Quietus) it was forbidden to any one to have his son instructed in Greek,[215] presupposes, that hitherto that which was now prohibited had taken place in the sphere of Rabbinic Judaism.[215a] Nor can the circumstance be otherwise explained, than by a certain familiarity with Greek, that in the Mishna the names of Greek letters are often used for the explanation of certain figures, e.g. כִּי for the explananation of the figure $X$, or גַּמָּא for the explanation of the figure $\Gamma$.[216]

From the commencement of the Roman supremacy the *Latin* was added to the Greek language and culture. But Latin, as in all the eastern provinces, so also in Palestine, attained no wide diffusion till the later imperial period. In the first centuries the Roman officials in their intercourse with

[211] Comp. the representation of such a denarius as Jesus probably had in His hand, in Madden's *History of Jewish Coinage*, p. 247.

[212] *Shekalim* iii. 2.  [213] *Gittin* ix. 8.

[214] *Megilla* i. 8.  [215] *Sota* ix. 14.

[215a] Comp. on the general position of Rabbinical Judaism to Greek education, Hamburger, *Real-Encycl.*, 2nd Div., art. "Griechenthum."

[216] כִּי, *Menachoth* vi. 3; *Kelim* xx. 7. גַּמָּא, *Middoth* iii. 1; *Kelim* xxviii. 7.

provincials exclusively employed the Greek language. It was only in official documents, inscriptions, and the like, that Latin was, from the time of Caesar, also adopted. Thus *e.g.* Caesar commanded the Sidonians to set up in Sidon upon a brazen tablet his decree for the appointment of the Jewish high priest Hyrcanus II. in the Greek and Roman languages (*Antt.* xiv. 10. 2). Another official decree of the same period was in like manner to be set up in the Roman and Greek tongues in the temples of Sidon, Tyre, and Ascalon (*Antt.* xiv. 10. 3). Mark Antony commanded the Tyrians to set up in a public place a decree issued by him in Greek and Latin (*Antt.* xiv. 12. 5). In the temple at Jerusalem there were placed at intervals on the enclosure (δρύφακτος), beyond which a nearer approach to the sanctuary was forbidden to Gentiles, tablets (στῆλαι) with inscriptions, which announced this prohibition partly in the Greek and partly in the Latin language (*Bell. Jud.* v. 5. 2, vi. 2. 4). The superscription also over the cross of Christ was written in Hebrew, Greek, and Latin (John xix. 20). Beyond such official use Latin had not advanced in Palestine, in the early times of the Roman supremacy.

### 3. *Position of Judaism with respect to Heathenism.*

The more vigorously and perseveringly heathenism continued to penetrate into Palestine, the more energetically did legal Judaism feel called upon to oppose it. On the whole indeed the advance of heathen culture could not, as has been shown, be prevented. But for that very reason the lines of defence against all illegality were only the more strictly and carefully drawn by the vigilance of the scribes. Extreme vigilance in this direction was indeed a vital question for Judaism. For, if it was not to succumb in the struggle for existence, in which it was engaged, it must defend itself with the utmost energy against its adversary. But the anxiety with which the struggle was carried on infinitely increased the danger which was to be guarded against, and which was in fact victoriously encountered.   For the greater the subtilty with which casuistry determined the cases, which were to be regarded as a direct or indirect pollution through heathen customs, the more frequent was the danger of incurring it. Hence the course of events placed the pious Israelite in an all but unendurable position.   He was in almost daily contact with heathenism, whether with persons or with goods and matters which sought and found entrance into Palestine in the way of trade and commerce.   And the zeal of the scribes was continually increasing the number of snares, by which an Israelite who was a strict adherent to the law might incur uncleanness through heathen practices.

Two points especially were not to be lost sight of in guarding against heathen practices — (1) heathen idolatry and (2) heathen non-observance of the Levitical law of uncleanness.   With respect to both the Pharisaism of the scribes proceeded with extreme minuteness.   (1) For the sake of avoiding even an only apparent approximation to idolatry, the Mosaic prohibition of images (Ex. xx. 4 sq.; Deut. iv. 16 sq., xxvii. 15) was applied with the most relentless consistency.[217] To suffer anything rather than the setting up of the statue of Caligula in the temple was indeed quite right.[218]   But pictorial representations in general, such as the trophies in the theatre in the time of Herod,[219] or the eagle at the gate of the temple,[220] were also repudiated.   When Pilate marched his troops into Jerusalem with the eagles of the legions, a regular tumult took place.[221]   Vitellius took his troops by an indirect course from Antioch to Petra for the sole reason of not polluting the sacred soil of Judah by the Roman eagles.[222]   And at the outbreak of the war, the first thing to be done in

---

[217] Comp. Winer, *RWB.*, art. "Bildnerei."   Rüetschi, art. "Bilder," in Herzog's *Real-Encycl.*, 2nd ed. ii. 460 sqq.   Wieseler, *Beiträge zur richtigen Würdigung der Evv.* p. 84 sqq.

[218] *Antt.* xviii. 8; *Bell. Jud.* ii. 10.                [219] *Antt.* xv. 8. 1, 2.

[220] *Antt.* xvii. 6. 2; *Bell. Jud.* i. 33. 2.

[221] *Antt.* xviii. 3. 1; *Bell. Jud.* ii. 9. 2, 3.          [222] *Antt.* xviii. 5. 3.

Tiberias was to destroy the palace of Antipas, because it was adorned with images of animals.[223] It seems indeed, that coins with the image of the emperor were circulated in Judaea (Matt. xxii. 20, and parallel passages); but the coins issued there were not, from considerate forbearance, so stamped.[224] When the famous scribe Gamaliel II. justified his visit to the baths of Aphrodite at Akko (Ptolemais) by saying, that the image of Aphrodite was there because of the baths, and not the baths because of the image of Aphrodite,[225] this was a kind of consideration by no means generally recognised as valid in the sphere of legalistic Judaism. To obviate the danger of a direct or indirect encouragement of idolatry, or any kind of contact therewith, an Israelite was forbidden to transact business with Gentiles, to lend to, or borrow anything from them, to make them payments, or receive payments from them during the three days preceding, and, according to R. Ismael, also the three days following any heathen festival,[226] while on the festival itself an Israelite was to hold no kind of intercourse in the town.[227] All objects, which might even possibly be connected with idolatrous worship, were forbidden. Thus heathen wine must not only be made no use of, because it might possibly have been offered as a libation, but it was also forbidden to derive any profit from it.[228] If wood had been taken from an idol grove all use of it was prohibited. If the stove had been heated by it, the stove must be broken to pieces, if it were still new; but if it were old, it must be let to cool. If bread had been baked with it, not only the eating, but every use of it was forbidden. If such bread were mixed with other bread, no use of it was allowed. If a weaver's

---

[223] *Vita*, 12.

[224] Ewald, *Gesch. des Volkes Israel*, v. 82 sq. Madden, *History of Jewish Coinage*, pp. 134–153. De Saulcy, *Numismatique de la Terre Sainte*, p. 69 sqq., pl. iii. and iv.

[225] *Aboda sara* iii. 4.     [226] *Aboda sara* i. 1, 2.     [227] *Aboda sara* i. 4.

[228] *Aboda sara* ii. 3 ; comp. also the Gemara (*Aboda Sara*, or the worship of idols, a tract from the Talmud, translated by Ferd. Christian Ewald, 2nd ed. 1868, p. 213 sqq., especially 221 sqq.).

shuttle were made of such wood, its use was forbidden.  If a garment had been made of the stuff woven therewith, all use of the garment was forbidden.  If this garment had been mixed among others, and these again among others, the use of all was forbidden.[229]

If all this sufficiently provided for the separation of Judaism from heathenism, it was still further inculcated by the notion, that a Gentile—as a non-observer of the laws of purification—was unclean, and that consequently all intercourse with him was defiling; that further, for the same reason, even the houses of the heathen, nay all objects touched by them,—so far as these were receptive of Levitical uncleanness,—were to be regarded as unclean.[230]  When it is said (Acts x. 28), that a Jew might have no intercourse with a heathen (ἀθέμιτόν ἐστιν ἀνδρὶ Ἰουδαίῳ κολλᾶσθαι ἢ προσέρχεσθαι ἀλλοφύλῳ), this must not indeed be misunderstood to the extent of supposing that there was an absolute prohibition of all intercourse, yet it does mean that ceremonial uncleanness was incurred by such intercourse.  All Gentile houses were as such unclean.[231]  Merely to enter them was to become unclean (John xviii. 28).  All articles belonging to Gentiles and of a kind susceptible of Levitical uncleanness, were unclean, and needed before using some kind of purification.  " If any one buys kitchen utensils of a Gentile, he must dip what is to be purified by dipping; boil what is to be boiled and heat in the fire what is to be heated; spits and gridirons are to be made red-hot; knives need only be sharpened and they are clean." [232]  Apart from this

[229] *Aboda sara* iii. 9.

[230] Comp. also on what follows, Weber, *System der altsynagogalen palä-stinischen Theologie* (1880), p. 68 sqq.

[231] *Ohaloth* xviii. 7.  Comp. Kirchner, *Die jüdische Passahfeier und Jesu letztes Mahl* (Progr. of the Duisburg Gymnasium, 1870), pp. 34–41. Delitzsch, *Talmudische Studien*, xiv.  The uncleanness of Gentile houses according to Jewish notions is testified to in the N. T. (*Zeitschr. für luth. Theol.* 1874, pp. 1–4).  Schürer on φαγεῖν τὸ πάσχα, John xviii. 28, *akademische Festschrift* (1883), p. 23 sq.

[232] *Aboda sara* v. 12.

uncleanness, which so many objects might contract by *use* on the part of Gentiles, there were lastly many heathen products, which could not be used by Jews, because in their production the Jewish laws, especially those relating to the distinction between clean and unclean, had not been observed. Partly for the former, partly for the latter reason, the most ordinary provisions, if coming from the heathen, were not to be eaten by Jews, who were only allowed to use them by buying and selling. This was especially the case with milk milked by a heathen without an Israelite seeing it, also with the bread and oil of the heathen.[233] Neither could a strictly legal Israelite at any time sit at meat at a Gentile table (Acts xi. 3 ; Gal. ii. 12). Hence Israelites travelling in foreign countries were in very evil case, and, if they wanted to be exact in their observance of the law, had to restrict themselves to vegetable raw materials, as *e.g.* certain priests, friends of Josephus, who having been brought as prisoners to Rome lived there upon nuts and figs.[234]

To all the reasons here stated, which made intercourse with the heathen and their abode in the Holy Land a heavy burden to an Israelite, who was faithful to the law, was added an entirely opposite and doctrinal view, which caused the rule of strangers in the land of Israel to be felt as a glaring contrast between the ideal and reality. For the land was the property of the chosen people. None but Israelites could be landowners therein. Even the *letting* of houses and fields to the heathen was, according to the theory of the scribes, forbidden.[235] And what with such views must have been their

---

[233] *Aboda sara* ii. 6. With respect to oil, see Joseph. *Antt.* xii. 3. 1; *Bell. Jud.* ii. 21. 2 ; *Vita*, 13. On the motives, see the Gemara (*Aboda sara*, translated by Ewald, p. 247 sqq.). Milk *e.g.* was forbidden, because there might possibly be mixed with it milk from unclean animals ; oil, because it might (at least according to one authority) have contracted uncleanness from unclean vessels. Talmudic authorities are not always clear even concerning the motives. See the discussions in the Gemara as above.

[234] Joseph. *Vita*, 3.

[235] *Aboda sara* i. 8. The letting of fields was still more strictly forbidden

feelings at finding the heathen really in possession—if not privately yet politically—of the whole land ? Under such circumstances we can understand, that the question, whether it were lawful for a faithful Israelite to pay tribute to Caesar at all, would be one of serious consideration (Matt. xxii. 15–22 ; Mark xii. 13–17 ; Luke xx. 20–26).

Thus circumstances present us with a peculiar double picture: a yielding to the influence of heathen customs together with the erection of the strongest wall of partition against them. So far as the actual purpose of the latter was a defence against heathenism in its *religious* aspect, its aim was certainly attained. In other respects, however, heathen culture was not restrained by it, but only made a burdensome oppression to Israelites.

than that of houses, since in the former case not only was the possession of the soil delivered up to Gentiles, but tithe was not paid on the produce.

## § 23. CONSTITUTION. SANHEDRIM. HIGH PRIEST.

### I. THE HELLENISTIC TOWNS

#### THE LITERATURE:

Noris, *Annus et epochae Syromacedonum in vetustis urbium Syriae nummis praesertim Mediceis expositae* (Florence 1689). I cite from the Leipsic edit. 1696.

Belley, *Suppléments aux Dissertations du Cardinal Noris sur les époques des Syro-Macédoniens*, in the *Mémoires de l'Académie des Inscriptions et Belles-Lettres*, ancient series, vols. xxvi. xxviii. xxx. xxxii. xxxv. Paris 1759–1770.

Eckhel, *Doctrina numorum veterum.* Vol. iii. Vindob. 1794.

Mionnet, *Description de médailles antiques.* Vol. v. Paris 1811. *Supplément.* Vol. viii. Paris 1837. *Recueil des planches.* Paris 1808.

De Saulcy, *Numismatique de la Terre Sainte, Description des monnaies autonomes et impériales de la Palestine et de l'Arabie Pétrée.* Paris 1874.

Droysen, *Geschichte des Hellenismus.* 2nd ed. 3 parts in 6 half vols. Gotha 1877–1878.

Stark, *Gaza und die philistäische Küste.* Jena 1852.

Kuhn, *Die städtische und bürgerliche Verfassung des römischen Reichs bis auf die Zeiten Justinians.* 2 parts. Leipzig 1864–1865.

Kuhn, *Ueber die Entstehung der Städte der Alten. Komenverfassung und Synoikismos.* Leipzig 1878 (especially pp. 422–434).

Marquardt, *Römische Staatsverwaltung.* Vol. i. (also under the title of *Handb. der röm. Alterthümer von Marquardt u. Mommsen*, vol. iv.). 2nd ed. Leipzig 1881.

Pauly's *Real-Encyclopädie der classischen Alterthumswissenschaft, unter den betr. Artikeln.*

Winer's and Schenkel's *Biblische Realwörterbucher, unter den betr. Artikeln.*

The geographical works of Reland, Raumer, Robinson, Ritter, Guérin, and others (for the titles see above, § 2).

Menke's *Bibelatlas*, maps iv. and v.

OF fundamental importance in the political life of Palestine during the Hellenic era was the independent organization of large municipal communities. This was indeed no novelty in Palestine, where from of old the large towns of the Philistine and Phoenician coasts had formed centres of political life. The entrance of Hellenism marks however a turning-point in this respect also. For, on the one hand it essentially transformed the existing communities, while on the other it founded numerous new ones and made the municipal communities in general *the basis of the political organization of the country* in a far more thorough manner than before. Wherever Hellenism penetrated—especially on the Philistine coasts and the eastern boundaries of Palestine beyond the Jordan — the country districts were grouped around single large towns as their political centres. Each of such communities formed a comparatively independent whole managing its own internal affairs, and its dependence upon the rulers of Syria consisted only in the recognition of their military supremacy, the payment of taxes, and certain other performances. At the head of such a Hellenistically organized community was a democratic senate of several hundred members, which we may probably conceive of as resembling the Athenian βουλή, *i.e.* as one changed annually, chosen from the Phylae, or as a committee chosen by lot from the people (Marquardt).[1] It formed the ruling power, not for the town only, but also for all the smaller towns and villages, which belonged to the often extensive district of the town.[2] The entire Philistinian and Phoenician coast was in this way divided into a number of municipal communities, some of which were of considerable importance. We have then briefly to consider as such the Hellenistic towns in the east and north-east of Palestine, the Hellenized towns in the interior of Palestine, such as Samaria and Scythopolis, and the towns founded by Herod and his sons, of which a considerable portion of the population was non-Jewish.

---

[1] The Senate of Gaza, *e.g.* consisted of 500 members (Joseph. *Antt.* xiii. 13. 3), that of Tiberias of 600 (*Bell. Jud.* ii. 21. 9). Comp. Kuhn, *Die städtische und bürgerliche Verfassung*, ii. 354.

[2] The furnishing of these towns with a district of greater or less extent will be shown in many cases in what follows. Compare on the Hellenistic town-constitution, F. W. Tittmann, *Darstellung der griechischen Staatsver-fassung*, Leipzig 1822. Marquardt, *Römische Staatsverwaltung*, i. 208–216 (1881). Also much matter in the *Corp. Inscr. Graec.* p. 32 sqq.

With all their independence these towns of course participated on the whole in the political fate of the rest of Palestine. In the time of the Diadochoi the government changed very frequently. Ptolemy I. three times took possession of Phoenicia and Palestine, and three times had to surrender them. It was not till about 280 B.C. that Ptolemy (II.) Philadelphus succeeded in establishing the rule of the Ptolemies over these countries for a lengthened period.[3] After that date not only Palestine proper, but also the whole of Phoenicia, as far as Eleutherus, south of Aradus, was under their dominion.[4] Their power, however, did not extend beyond Lebanon. Damascus already belonged to the Seleucidae.[5] In the years 219–217 B.C. Antiochus assumed a transitory possession of Palestine, but was obliged to give it up in consequence of the unsuccessful battle at Raphia. After the death of Ptolemy (IV.) Philopator, he however invaded Palestine a second time, and his victory at Panias (198 B.C.) was decisive in favour of the Seleucidae. From this time onward Palestine and the whole Philistinian-Phoenician coast belonged to the Syrian kingdom.[6] The supremacy of the Ptolemies, like that of the Seleucidae, found its expression chiefly in two points : in the appointment of military governors ($\sigma\tau\rho\alpha\tau\eta\gamma o\acute{\iota}$) in the regions subject to their sway, and in the imposition of regular taxes. Josephus in his account of Josephus, the farmer of taxes, and his son Hyrcanus (*Antt.* xii. 4), gives us a very vivid picture of the manner in which the system of taxation was organized in the later period of their rule, a picture which, notwithstanding its

---

[3] For particulars, see Stark, *Gaza und die philistäische Küste*, pp. 347–367. It seems probable, from an inscription of Oum el-Awamid, published by Renan (*Mission de Phénicie*, pp. 711–725), that Tyre had an era which began thirty-seven years later than that of the Seleucidae, *i.e.* 275 B.C. (see Renan as above, pp. 719–723). Its cause seems to have been the definite seizure of Phoenicia by Ptolemy II., who showed himself on that occasion the benefactor of the town. Comp. Six, *Numismatic Chronicle*, 1877, p. 192.

[4] See Stark, pp. 368, 371. Kuhn, ii. 128 sq.

[5] See below, on Damascus.

[6] Farther particulars in Stark, pp. 375–406, 425 sqq.

fictitious colouring, certainly gives a faithful reflection of the institutions.   It shows that the imposts were not collected by the authorities, but leased to great contractors, to whom their collection in the several towns was given up.[7]

Towards the end of the second century before Christ, the kingdom of the Seleucidae increasingly exhibits an image of dissolution.   The central authority was so weakened by continual revolutions, that a multitude of independent communities were founded in the border lands of the empire. During this period therefore not only did the Jews obtain and maintain their full freedom, but a *number also of the larger towns*, which had already in the wars between Syria and Egypt often played a part of their own, declared themselves independent, and as a sign of their independence began a new computation of time.   Thus Tyre had an era dating from the year 126 B.C.; Sidon a similar one from the year 111; Ascalon from 104.   In other towns individual " Tyrants " would seize upon the sovereignty.   Thus we find towards the end of the second, and in the beginning of the first century before Christ, a tyrant, Zeno Kotylas in Philadelphia, his son Theodorus in Amathus on the Jordan, Zoilus in Straton's Tower and Dora, Demetrius in Gamala.[8]   And there

[7] In illustration of Joseph. *Antt.* xii. 4, compare especially Stark, pp. 412–423, and Nussbaum, *Observationes in Flavii Josephi Antiquitates* (*Göttinger Dissertat.* 1875), pp. 15–17.   There is an internal contradiction in the narrative of Josephus.   He transposes the beginning of the renting of the taxes by Josephus, which lasted twenty-two years to the reign of Ptolemy Euergetes, who died 221 B.C. (*Antt.* xii. 4. 1; comp. 4. 6); the entire account also assumes, that Palestine was then still under the rule of the Ptolemies.   This would, as Stark states, p. 416, bring it to about the years 229–207 B.C.   On the other hand however Josephus always calls the wife of the Egyptian king, Cleopatra, while this name was first naturalized in the family of the Ptolemies by Cleopatra, the daughter of Antiochus the Great and wife of Ptolemy V.   Stark rightly finds the error to consist in the mistake as to the queen's name, and accepts the results which follow from the other dates.   The view of Nussbaum is more artificial.   It is based moreover upon the improbable assumption, that Palestine had shortly after the battle of Raphia already come again into the possession of Antiochus.

[8] Stark, p. 478 sq.   Kuhn, ii. 162.

is no lack of evidence that the Romans at their entry into Syria found there a number of independent petty princes.[9]

The strengthening of the Jewish power was in those times fatal for the towns in the neighbourhood of Palestine. Even the earlier Maccabees, and subsequently John Hyrcanus, subjected several towns. But it was especially Alexander Jannaeus who made conquests on a large scale. At the end of his rule all the coast towns from Raphia to Carmel, with the sole exception of Ascalon, almost all the towns of the country east of Jordan, and of course those also which were situated in the interior, such as Samaria and Scythopolis, as far north as the Lake of Merom,[10] were subject to the Jews.

The conquest of Syria by Pompey put an end again at a stroke to the independence of all the small towns, which had separated themselves from the empire of the Seleucidae. The only consequence to the autonomic towns was, that they now entered into the same relations of voluntary dependence towards the Romans, in which they had hitherto stood towards the Seleucidae. To those towns however, which had been subjected by the Jews, the Roman invasion had even the character of a deliverance from a hated rule. For Pompey again separated from the Jewish region all those towns which had been subjected to the Jews since the time of the Maccabees and restored to them their freedom.[11] Josephus enumerates as such " liberated " towns, which had of course to acknowledge the Roman supremacy, the following : Gaza, Azotus, Jamnia, Joppa, Straton's Tower, Dora, Samaria, Scythopolis, Hippus, Gadara, Pella, Dium.[12] The list is, however, incomplete. For besides the above-named, others also

[9] Josephus speaks quite generally of μόναρχοι (*Antt.* xiii. 16. 5). Appian. *Syr.* 50, testifies that Pompey τῶν ὑπὸ τοῖς Σελευκίδαις γενομένων ἐθνῶν τοῖς μὲν ἐπέστησεν οἰκείους βασιλέας ἢ δυνάστας, whom however Pompey certainly was not the first to create. Plinius, *Hist. Nat.* v. 23, 82, still knows in Syria of seventeen tetrarchias in regna descriptas barbaris nominibus.

[10] Joseph. *Antt.* xiii. 15. 4. See above, § 10.

[11] Compare on the Roman custom of giving their freedom to the towns of conquered regions, Kuhn, ii. 15–19.

[12] *Antt.* xiv. 4. 4 ; *Bell. Jud.* i. 7. 7.

used the Pompeian era, *i.e.* the computation since the liberation by Pompey, and many of these towns retained it till far
into the imperial period.    Those lying in the region east of
the Jordan, together with Scythopolis, then united with each
other in the "ten cities alliance," the so-called Decapolis.
The proconsul Gabinius was another benefactor to many of
these towns.    In the years 57–55 B.C. he rebuilt the towns
of Raphia, Gaza, Anthedon, Azotus, Jamnia, Apollonia, Dora,
Samaria and Scythopolis, some of which had been entirely
destroyed by the Jews.[13]    The Roman civil wars however, with
their exhaustion of the provinces and the arbitrary rule of
Antony in the East, brought bad times to these towns.    He
bestowed upon Cleopatra the entire Philistinian and Phoenician
coast, from the borders of Egypt to Eleutherus, with the sole
exception of Tyre and Sidon.[14]    Even when, after the fall of
Antony and Cleopatra, whose authority had ceased of itself, a
more quiet era had been established by Augustus, many of
these towns again changed masters.[15]    Augustus bestowed
upon Herod all the coast towns from Gaza to Straton's Tower,
with the exception of Ascalon, together with the towns of
Samaria, Hippus and Gadara in the interior.[16]    After the
death of Herod these towns again experienced different fates.
Gaza, Hippus and Gadara were placed under the immediate
government of the Roman legate of Syria (on Anthedon, see
below the section respecting it); Azotus and Jamnia with
Phasaelis, which was built by Herod, were given to his sister
Salome, while Joppa, Straton's Tower and Samaria fell with
the rest of Judaea to Archelaus.[17]    The towns belonging to

[13] *Antt.* xiv. 5. 3 ; *Bell. Jud.* i. 8. 4.

[14] *Antt.* xv. 4. 1, *fin.* ; *Bell. Jud.* i. 18. 5.

[15] The different changes of possessors subsequently to Alexander Jannaeus
are visibly represented by the numerous special maps in Menke's *Bibelatlas*,
plates iv. and v.

[16] *Antt.* xv. 7. 3 ; *Bell. Jud.* i. 20. 3.    Of the coast towns Josephus names
only Gaza, Anthedon, Joppa, and Straton's Tower.    But Azotus and Jamnia,
which after the death of Herod fell to his sister Salome, must then have
come into Herod's possession.

[17] *Antt.* xvii. 11. 4, 5 ; *Bell. Jud.* ii. 6. 4.

Salome came after her death to the Empress Livia.[18]  After
the death of Livia, they seem to have been transferred to the
private possession of her son Tiberius, on which account we
find an imperial ἐπίτροπος in his time in Jamnia.[19]  The
towns bestowed upon Archelaus, together with the rest of his
district, came after his deposition under the oversight of a
Roman procurator, then in the years 41–44 A.D. to King
Agrippa I., and were again after his death under Roman
procurators.  This frequent change of masters was however
of little more consequence to these towns, than that the taxes
had to be paid now to one now to another governor.  For
they had, on the whole, the independent management of their
own affairs, even though the supremacy of their different
masters made itself sometimes more and sometimes less
noticed.  Finally, it was of importance to the development
of their communal life that Herod and his sons refounded a
great number of towns, so especially Caesarea (= Straton's
Tower), Sebaste (= Samaria), Antipatris, Phasaelis, Caesarea
Philippi, Julias, Sepphoris, Livias, Tiberias.

The *kind of dependence* of these towns upon the Roman
power both in name and in fact differed considerably.[20]  There
were in the Roman Empire both *free* and *subject* communities.
The former (*civitates liberae*, ἐλεύθεροι) had not only their
own judicature and administration of finance, but were also
free from taxation proper and only bound to certain definitely
appointed contributions; they were αὐτόνομοι καὶ φόρων
ἀτελεῖς (Appian. *Civ.* i. 102).[21]  Again there was among
these a privileged class, the *civitates foederatae* or such as had
their freedom guaranteed by a *foedus*.  All these free cities
were indeed dependent upon Rome, but were not regarded as

[18] *Antt.* xviii. 2. 2; *Bell. Jud.* ii. 9. 1.  Azotus is not expressly named
but is certainly intended.

[19] *Antt.* xviii. 6. 3.  Comp. Marquardt, *Römische Staatsverwaltung*, ii.
248 sq.

[20] Comp. on what follows, Kuhn, ii. 14–41.  Marquardt, i. 71–86, 396.
Also Stark, *Gaza*, pp. 522–525.

[21] See especially Marquardt, i. 78 sq., 84 sq.

belonging in the strict sense to the province.  From them
must then be distinguished the subject towns (ὑπήκοοι)
properly belonging to the province, the specific difference of
which from the former consisted in their liability to taxation.
For αὐτονομία, or the privilege *suis legibus uti,* was often
conceded to them, though under the control of the Roman
proconsul.[22]    All the varieties of civic position here alluded
to were represented among the Syrian towns.   Tyre *e.g.* was
one of the privileged *civitates foederatae.*[23]   Ascalon was an
*oppidum liberum.*   But just because this is mentioned of
Ascalon as something special, the *greater* number are *not* to be
regarded *as free* communities in the technical sense of the
word.   Nor is it, according to what has just been said,
opposed to this that many of them are designated as αὐτόνομοι.
And still less does it signify, when Josephus says that
Pompey made these towns free (ἐλευθέρας).   For this means
only their liberation from Jewish sway.   Their political condition is correctly pointed out by Josephus by the expressions
προσένειμε τῇ ἐπαρχίᾳ and κατέταξεν εἰς τὴν Συριακὴν
ἐπαρχίαν.[24]   These slight political distinctions were not
indeed of much practical importance.   For the most privileged towns were taxed for certain requirements, and on the
other hand many of the subject towns, at least in Syria, had
a jurisdiction and administration of their own.   Least of all
were these distinctions paid respect to with regard to military
affairs.   It would be a great mistake to suppose, that in war
all or most of these towns were released from the obligation
of furnishing auxiliaries.   At least Josephus speaks quite
generally of the auxiliaries, which had been furnished by " the
towns " at the campaign of Cestius Gallus against Jerusalem,[25]
when in the year 4 B.C. Berytus with its district furnished

---

[22] See especially Kuhn, ii. 34 sqq.        [23] Marquardt, i. 75.

[24] *Antt.* xiv. 4. 4 ; *Bell. Jud.* i. 7. 7.

[25] *Bell. Jud.* ii. 18. 19: Πλεῖστοι δὲ καὶ ἐκ τῶν πόλεων ἐπίκουροι συνελέγησαν,
ἐμπειρίᾳ μὲν ἡττώμενοι τῶν στρατιωτῶν, ταῖς δὲ προθυμίαις καὶ τῷ κατὰ
Ἰουδαίων μίσει τὸ λεῖπον ἐν ταῖς ἐπιστήμαις ἀναπληροῦντες.

1500 auxiliaries to the army of Varus,[26] this certainly is not
a case in point, inasmuch as Berytus was then already a
Roman colony and was therefore under different legal regulations from the other towns. But we also know *e.g.* that from
A.D. 44–67 there was in Caesarea a garrison of five cohorts
and a wing of cavalry, which was formed for the most part
of Caesareans and Sebastenians (inhabitants of the towns of
Caesarea and Sebaste and their respective districts).[27] Nay we
find towards the end of the first century after Christ a *cohors
I. Tyriorum* already in Moesia.[28] So too in occupying the
towns with garrisons regard was certainly had less to political
distinctions than to military requirements. "Free" Antioch
became the chief seat of the Roman military force in Syria,
and we know of Ascalon, that though an *oppidum liberum*, it
received a Roman garrison, though but a small one.[29]

*The Roman colonies* occupied among the towns of the
Roman Empire a position of exemption from taxes.[30] There
had been such both in Palestine and Phoenicia since the time
of Augustus. The oldest were Berytus, founded by Augustus,
Ptolemais by Claudius, Caesarea by Vespasian. All the
colonies of the imperial period were military colonies, *i.e.* they
consisted of superannuated soldiers, to whom possession of
lands was awarded as payment for their services, and indeed
in such wise, that this was always done to a large number at
one place contemporaneously, thereby founding the colony.
The lands required for the purpose were in earlier times
simply taken from their possessors. Afterwards (*i.e.* after

[26] *Antt.* xvii. 10. 9 ; *Bell. Jud.* ii. 5. 1.
[27] *Antt.* xix. 9. 1, 2, xx. 6. 1 ; *Bell. Jud.* ii. 12. 5, iii. 4. 2, and especially
xx. 8. 7 : μέγα δὲ φρονοῦντες ἐπὶ τῷ τοὺς πλείστους τῶν ὑπὸ Ῥωμαίους ἐκεῖσε
στρατευομένων Καισαρεῖς εἶναι καὶ Σεβαστηνούς. Further particulars in the
*Zeitschr. für wissenschaftliche Theologie*, 1875, p. 419 sqq.
[28] *Corp. Inscr. Lat.* vol. iii. p. 863 (Diplom. xx. of the year A.D. 99).
[29] *Bell. Jud.* iii. 2. 1.
[30] See on this subject in general, Rein, art. "Colonia" in Pauly's *Real-Enc.*
ii. 504–517. Kuhn, *Die städt. und bürgerl. Verf.* i. 257 sqq. Marquardt, i.
35 sqq. 86 sqq., 92–132.

Augustus) it was customary to compensate the owners or
to give the veterans such land as was already state property.   The colonists either formed a new community beside
the older one, or themselves entered into the older community, in which case the latter received in its entirety the
Roman municipal constitution.[31]   Thus the plantation of a
colony, which had formerly been an act of cruel plunder,
gradually became an actual favour to a town.   The rights of
colonies also differed.   Those were in the most favoured
position, which had received the full *jus Italicum* and with it
exemption from poll taxes and land taxes.[32]   Herod imitated
Augustus in his system of establishing military colonies.[33]

The position of those towns, which were temporarily under
*the Herodian princes*, did not essentially differ from that of
those directly under Roman governors.   It is certainly
possible, that the Herodian princes made their power more
directly felt, but this cannot be proved.   For the security of
their sovereignty, they appointed governors of their own in
the towns; thus Herod the Great placed an ἄρχων in Idumaea
and Gaza,[34] Agrippa I. a στρατηγός in Caesarea [35] and an
ἔπαρχος in Tiberias,[36] Agrippa II. a viceroy in Caesarea
Philippi [37] and an ἔπαρχος in Gamala.[38]   Such a viceroy was
also the ἐθνάρχης of King Aretas in Damascus, 2 Cor. xi. 32.

The great independence of these towns involves the fact,
that *each had its special history*.   In following this in each
separate case, we shall begin with the towns of the Philistinian
and Phoenician coast, advancing from south to north.   Many
of these had at the commencement of the Hellenistic period a
brilliant past behind them and continued to be of prominent
importance during the whole Graeco-Roman period.

1. *Raphia*, Ῥαφία (so is it written on the coin), may still be

[31] Marquardt, i. 118 sq.          [32] Marquardt, i. 89.
[33] *Antt.* xv. 8. 5.   See below, Samaria, Geba, Heshbon.
[34] *Antt.* xv. 7. 9:              [35] *Antt.* xix. 7. 4.
[36] Joseph. *Vita*, 9 ; whether Agrippa I. or II. is spoken of is uncertain.
[37] *Vita*, 13.   Comp. Kuhn, ii. 346.          [38] *Vita*, 11.

pointed out in the ruins of *Kirbeth bir Refah,* situated according to Guérin about half a league from the sea, but upon a flat harbourless shore,[39] and therefore regarded by Pliny and Ptolemy as an inland town.[40] It was the first Syrian town after leaving Egypt.[41] Apart from the cuneiform inscriptions,[42] it is first mentioned in history in the campaign of Antigonus against Egypt, B.C. 306, when the fleet of Antigonus, under the command of his son Demetrius, was here destroyed by a storm.[43] It then became famous chiefly through the victory, which was here gained by the unwarlike Ptolemy Philopater over Antiochus the Great, and which resulted in the loss of Palestine and Phoenicia by the latter.[44] In the year 193 the marriage of Ptolemy Philopater with Cleopatra, daughter of Antiochus the Great, was celebrated here.[44a] In the beginning of the first century before Christ Raphia was conquered by Alexander Jannaeus (Joseph. *Antt.* xiii. 13. 3 ; *Bell. Jud.* i. 4. 2 ; comp. *Antt.* xiii. 15. 4), was afterwards, like the neighbouring towns, separated by Pompey from the Jewish district and was rebuilt by Gabinius (*Antt.* xiv. 5. 3 ; *Bell. Jud.* i. 8. 4). Hence the coins of Raphia, of the imperial age (from Commodus to Philip the Arabian), have an era commencing with the refoundation by Gabinius (57 B.C.).[45]

[39] Diodor. xx. 74 calls Raphia δυσπροσόρμιστον καὶ τεναγώδη.

[40] Plin. *Hist. Nat.* v. 13. 68. Ptolem. (ed. Nobbe), v. 16. 6. Comp. also, Strabo, xvi. 2. 31 ; *Itinerar. Antonini* (ed. Parthey et Pinder, 1848), p. 69. Sozomenus, *Hist. eccl.* vii. 15. Hierocles, *Synecdemus* (ed. Parthey, 1866), p. 44. Reland, *Palaestina,* p. 967 sq. Ritter, *Erdkunde,* xiv. 138 sqq., xvi. 39. Raumer, *Palästina,* p. 219. Guérin, *Judée,* ii. 233–235. Le Quien, *Oriens christianus,* iii. 630.

[41] Polyb. v. 80: Πρώτη τῶν κατὰ Κοίλην Συρίαν πόλεων ὡς πρὸς τὴν Αἴγυπτον. Joseph. *Bell. Jud.* iv. 11. 5 : ἔστι δὲ ἡ πόλις αὕτη Συρίας ἀρχή.

[42] Friedr. Delitzsch, *Wo lag das Paradies?* (1881), p. 291.

[43] Diodor. xx. 74. Droysen, *Gesch. des Hellenismus* (2nd ed.), ii. 2. 147. Stark, *Gaza,* p. 358.

[44] The battle is fully described Polyb. v. 82–86. Comp. Stark, *Gaza,* p. 382–386.

[44a] Livius, xxxv. 13.

[45] This may now be considered as certain, though Noris and Eckhel still hesitate, whether the era of Pompey or of Gabinius was to be accepted. See Noris, *Annus et epochae Syromacedonum,* v. 4. 2 (ed. Lips. p.

It seems hence to have been in the possession of the Herodian princes.

2. *Gaza, Γάζα,* Hebr. עַזָּה,[46] the ancient and important city of the Philstines, so often mentioned in the Old Testament.[47] Herodotus knows it by the name of *Κάδυτις,* and remarks, that it is not much smaller than Sardis.[47a]   Already in the times of Persian supremacy it must—as the coins testify— have been in active intercourse with Greece.[47b]   In the time of Alexander the Great it was next to Tyre the most important fortress on the Philistinian-Phoenician coast.   Alexander did not take it till after a three months' troublesome siege (332 B.C.).[48]   After that time it became more and more a Greek

515–521).   Eckhel, *Doctrina numorum,* iii. 454 sq.   Mionnet, *Description de médailles,* v. 551 sq.; *Suppl.* viii. 376 sq.; Kenner, *Die Münzsammlung des Stifts St. Florian in Ober-Oesterreich* (1871), pp. 179–182, Plate vi. n. 17–18.   De Saulcy, *Numismatique de la Terre Sainte,* pp. 237–240, pl. xii. n. 7–9.   Stark, *Gaza,* p. 515.

[46] On the Hebrew form, comp. Steph. Byz. *s.v.* Γάζα· ἐκλήθη καὶ Ἄζα· καὶ μέχρι νῦν Σύροι Ἄζαν αὐτὴν καλοῦσιν.

[47] See Reland, *Palaestina,* pp. 787–800.   Robinson's *Palestine,* ii. pp. 36–43.   Ritter, *Erdkunde,* xvi. 45–65.   Raumer, *Palästina,* pp. 192–194. Winer, *RWB. s.v.*   Arnold in Herzog's *Real-Enc.,* 1st ed. iv. 671–674. Sepp, *Jerusalem und das heilige Land,* 2nd ed. ii. 617 sqq.   Guérin, *Judée,* ii. 178–211, 219–221.   *The Survey of Western Palestine, Memoirs* by Conder and Kitchener, iii. 234 sq., 248–251, and pl. xix. of the large English chart. Gatt, *Bemerkungen über Gaza und seine Umgebung (Zeitschr. des deutschen Pal. Ver.* vii. 1–14).   For the history, see especially Stark, *Gaza.*   Also Alb. v. Hormann, *Gaza, Stadt, Umgebung und Geschichte,* 1876 (*Progr. des Knabenseminars der Diöcese Brixen zu Rothholz,* see the notice in *Zeitschr. f. die österreich. Gymnasien,* 1877, p. 142 sq.).

[47a] Herodot. ii. 159, iii. 5: Σαρδίων οὐ κολλῷ ἐλάσσονος.

[47b] Comp. on these exceedingly interesting coins the learned article of Six, *Observations sur les monnaies phéniciennes (Numismatic Chronicle,* new series, vol. xvii. 1877, pp. 177–241; on Gaza, pp. 221–239).   The coins have partly Greek, partly Phoenician inscriptions.   The name of the town (עז or עזה) is to be seen at all events on several of them.   Their most interesting feature however is, that they are coined according to an Athenian standard and with Athenian types, evidently for commerce with Greece.   It is probable, that genuine Athenian coins first came to Palestine in the period of the hegemony of Athens in the fifth century before Christ, and that henceforth others were coined after their pattern.   See Six, as above, pp. 230 sq., 234–236.

[48] The two months' duration of this siege is testified by Diodor. xvii. 48 and Josephus, *Antt.* xi. 8. 3, 4.   Comp. also Arrian, ii. 26, 27.   Curtius, iv. 6,

town.[49]   The contests of Ptolemy Lagos with the other
Diadochoi for the possession of Coelesyria of course affected
Gaza in the highest degree.   In 315 B.C. it was conquered
by Antigonus.[50]   In 312 it again fell into the hands of
Ptolemy in consequence of his victory gained at Gaza over
Demetrius the son of Antigonus.[51]   In the same year however he renounced the possession of Coelesyria, and on his
retreat had the most important fortresses, Gaza among them,
demolished.[52]   The sovereignty over these districts changed
several times during the decades next following, till at
length they were for a longer period in the possession of the
Ptolemies about 240 B.C.   In the years 218–217 Gaza, like
the rest of Syria, was temporarily in the possession of
Antiochus the Great.[53]   Twenty years later Coelesyria came
permanently under the dominion of the Seleucidae through
the victory of Antiochus the Great at Panias (198 B.C.).
Gaza also must then have been conquered after a difficult
siege, to which indeed we have only allusions in Polybius.[54]
The sway of the Seleucidae is evidenced among other things by
a coin of Demetrius I. (Soter) minted at Gaza.[55]   During the
contests in the Syrian kingdom between Demetrius II. (Nicator)
and Antiochus VI. respecting Trypho (145–143 B.C.), Gaza
refusing to join the party of Antiochus, was besieged by

and Plutarch. *Alexander*, 25.   Polyb. xvi. 40 (= ed. Hultsch, xvi. 22ª).
Droysen, *Gesch. d. Hellenismus*, 2nd ed. i. 1, 297–301.   Stark, *Gaza*, pp.
236–244.

[49] It is expressly designated a πόλις Ἑλληνίς, Joseph. *Antt.* xvii. 11. 4;
*Bell. Jud.* ii. 6. 3.

[50] Diodor. xix. 59.   Droysen, ii. 2. 11.   Stark, p. 350.

[51] Diodor. xix. 84.   On the battle, Droysen, ii. 2. 42 sqq.   Stark, pp.
351–354.

[52] Diodor. xix. 93 : κατέσκαψε τὰς ἀξιολογωτάτας τῶν κεκρατημένων πόλεων,
Ακην μὲν τῆς Φοινίκης Συρίας, Ἰόπην δὲ καὶ Σαμάρειαν καὶ Γάζαν τῆς
Συρίας.   Comp. Stark, p. 355 sq.

[53] Polyb. v. 80.   Stark, pp. 382–385.

[54] Polyb. xvi. 18, xvi. 40 (ed. Hultsch, xvi. 22ª), xxix. 6ª (ed. Hultsch,
xxix. 12).   Stark, p. 204 sq.

[55] Gardner, *Catalogue of the Greek Coins in the British Museum*, Seleucid
*kings of Syria* (1878), p. 47.

Jonathan the Maccabee in concert with him, and its environs
laid waste, whereupon it gave up its opposition and delivered
hostages to Jonathan as a pledge of its adherence to
Antiochus.[56]   With respect to the constitution of Gaza at
this time we learn incidentally, that it had a council of 500
members.[57]   About the year 96 B.C. Gaza as well as the
neighbouring cities of Raphia and Anthedon fell into the
hands of Alexander Jannaeus.   Alexander conquered it after
a siege of one year, though at last only through treachery, and
abandoned the city and its inhabitants to destruction (Joseph.
*Antt.* xiii. 13. 3; *Bell. Jud.* i. 4. 2; comp. *Antt.* xiii. 15. 4.
Stark, p. 499 sqq.).   When Pompey conquered Syria, Gaza
also—so far as its existence can be then spoken of—obtained
its freedom (*Antt.* xiv. 4. 4; *Bell. Jud.* i. 7. 7).   The newly
built town consequently began a new era from the time of
Pompey (52 B.C.).[58]   The rebuilding itself did not take place
till the time of Gabinius (*Antt.* xv. 5. 3).   Probably the
ancient Gaza was then forsaken and the new town built
somewhat farther southwards.[59]   In the year 30 B.C. Gaza

[56] 1 Macc. xi. 61, 62. Joseph. *Antt.* xiii. 5. 5.   Stark, p. 492.  No
conquest of Gaza took place in the Maccabean period.  For in the passage
1 Macc. xiii. 43–48 we must read Gazara.

[57] Joseph. *Antt.* xiii. 13. 3.

[58] On the era of Gaza, comp. Noris, *Annus et epochae Syromaced.* v. 2, 3
(ed. Lips. pp. 476–502).   Eckhel, *Doct. Num.* iii. 448–454.   Ideler, *Handb.
der Chronol.* i. 474 sq.   Stark, *Gaza*, pp. 513–515.  The coins in Mionnet, v.
535–549; *Suppl.* viii. 371-375.   De Saulcy, *Numismatique de la Terre
Sainte*, pp. 209–233, pl. xi.   The *Chronicon paschale* (ed. Dindorf, i. 352)
remarks on Olymp. 179. 4 = 61 B.C.: Ἐντεῦθεν Γαζαῖοι τοὺς ἑαυτῶν χρόνους
ἀριθμοῦσιν.   Hence Noris and Eckhel place the beginning of the era in the
year 61 B.C.   According however to Ideler and Stark, the year 62 must
according to the coins be regarded as the starting-point of the era.

[59] On the distinction between Old and New Gaza, comp. especially
Stark, pp. 352 sq., 509–513. The town near which Ptolemy Lagos conquered
Demetrius Poliorcetes, 312 B.C., is expressly called *Old Gaza* by Diodorus
and Porphyry; see Diodor. xix. 80 (τὴν παλαιὰν Γάζαν); Porphyry in the
fragment in Euseb. *Chron.* ed. Schoene, i. col. 249–250 (according to the
Armenian *veterem Gazam*, in Greek in Syncellus, Παλαίγαζαν, or as Gutschmid
reads Παλαιγαζην).   It is to just this Old Gaza that the notice of Strabo,
that Gaza was destroyed by Alexander and has since lain waste, refers;
Strabo, xvi. 2. 30, p. 759: κατεσπασμένη δ' ὑπὸ Ἀλεξάνδρου καὶ μένουσα

came under the authority of Herod the Great (*Antt.* xv. 7. 3 ; *Bell. Jud.* i. 20. 3). After his death it was again added to the province of Syria (*Antt.* xvii. 11. 4 ; *Bell. Jud.* ii. 6. 3). With this agrees the fact, that the imperial coins of Gaza do not begin till after the death of Herod the Great. The oldest known are two coins of Augustus of the years 63 and 66 aer. Gaz.[60] In the time of Claudius, Gaza is spoken of as an important city by the geographer Mela.[61] In A.D. 66 it was attacked and destroyed by the rebellious Jews (Joseph. *Bell. Jud.* ii. 18. 1). This must however have been a very partial destruction. For so strong a fortress could not have been actually destroyed by a band of insurrectionary

ἔρημος. [The remark in Acts viii. 26 : αὕτη ἐστὶν ἔρημος, is on the contrary not in point here, because αὕτη there more probably refers to ὁδός.] Strabo is indeed so far mistaken, that he seems to know nothing of New Gaza, his remark being based upon the statement of an older geographer, in whose time New Gaza did not as yet exist. The existence of a New Gaza, somewhat to the south of Old Gaza, is however chiefly evidenced by an anonymous geographical fragment (Ἀποσπασματια τινα γεωγραφικα, ed. Hudson [in the appendix to his edition of Dionysius Perieget., *Geographiae vet. scriptores Graeci minores*, vol. iv., Oxon. 1717], p. 39 : μετὰ τὰ Ῥινοκόρουρα ἡ νέα Γάζα κεῖται πόλις οὖσα καὶ αὐτὴ εἶθ᾽ ἡ ἔρημος Γάζα, εἶτα ἡ Ἀσκάλων πόλις) and by Hieronymus (*Onomast.*, ed. Lagarde, p. 125 : antiquae civitatis locum vix fundamentorum praebere vestigia, hanc autem quae nunc cernitur, in alio loco pro illa, quae conruit, aedificatam). If then the local distinction of Old and New Gaza is beyond question, we must also with Stark consider it most probable, that the foundation of New Gaza must be referred to Gabinius. For an entire destruction of Old Gaza did not, as Strabo seems to suppose, result from its conquest by Alexander the Great, but from that by Alexander Jannaeus. For the rest both Old and New Gaza lay twenty stadia inland (see on Old Gaza, Arrian, II. 26 ; on New Gaza, Sozom. *Hist. eccl.* v. 3 ; Strabo, p. 759, erroneously seven stadia, Antoninus Martyr, c. 33, mil. pass.). From both too must be distinguished the *port of Gaza*, which indeed remained the same for both, Γαζαίων λιμήν, Strabo, p. 759 ; Ptolemaeus, v. 16. 2. This port was raised to a city under the name of Κωνστάντεια by Constantine the Great (Euseb. *Vita Constantin.* iv. 38 ; Sozomenus, *Hist. eccl.* ii. 5), but lost this name again together with the rights of a city through Julian and was afterwards called again only Μαϊουμᾶς (= seaport town) ; see Sozom. *Hist. eccl.* v. 3. *Marci Diaconi Vita Porphyrii*, ed. Haupt (an article of the Berlin Acad. 1874), c. 57. Antoninus Martyr, c. 33. Reland, p. 791 sqq. Stark, p. 513. Kuhn, ii. 363. Guérin, *Judée*, ii. 219-221.

[60] Eckhel, iii. 453 sq.   Mionnet, v. 536.   De Saulcy, p. 213.

[61] Mela, i. 11 : in Palaestina est ingens et munita admodum Gaza.

Jews.  Coins too of the years 130, 132, 135 aer. Gaza.
(= A.D. 68/69, 70/71, 73/74) testify to the lasting prosperity of the city.[62]  Special tokens of favour seem to have
been bestowed upon it by Hadrian.[63]  It is called on an
inscription of the time of Gordian (A.D. 238–244) ἱερὰ καὶ
ἄσυλος καὶ αὐτόνομος.[64]  It must have subsequently become
a Roman colony.[65]  Eusebius speaks of it as a πόλις
ἐπίσημος.[66]  And this too it remained for a considerable
period.[67]  The independence of these great cities is shown
in perhaps the most striking manner by the fact, that
Gaza as well as Ascalon, Tyre and Sidon had each its own
calendar.[68]

3. *Anthedon*, Ἀνθηδών, situate on the sea, erroneously called
an inland town by Pliny,[69] was according to Sozomen only
twenty stadia from Gaza, probably in a northerly (north-
westerly) direction.[69a]  Its very name shows it to have been

[62] Mionnet, v. 537 sq. ; *Suppl.* viii. 372.  De Saulcy, p. 214.

[63] The coins of Hadrian's time have a new Hadrianic era as well as the
usual town era.  The *Chronicon paschale* (ed. Dindorf, i. 474) mentions
besides a πανήγυρις Ἀδριανή, as celebrated since the time of Hadrian.  See
Stark, p. 550.

[64] *Corp. Inscr. Graec.* n. 5892.  Comp. Stark, p. 554 sq.

[65] Le Bas et Waddington, *Inscriptions*, vol. iii. n. 1904 : Κολωνίας Γάζης.
The mention also of a *Gazensis Duumvir* by Jerome, *Vita Hilarionis*, c. 20
(Vallarsi, ii. 22), points to a Roman municipal constitution.  Comp.
Marquardt, Rom. *Staatsverwaltung*, i. 429.

[66] Euseb. *Onomast.*, ed. Lagarde, p. 242.

[67] Antoninus Martyr (about A.D. 570, *De locis sanctis*, c. 33 ; Tobler et
Molinier, *Itinera*, i. 109) : Gaza autem civitas est splendida, deliciosa,
homines in ea honestissimi, omni liberalitate decori, amatores peregrinorum.

[68] See on the whole, Ideler, *Handbuch der Chronologie*, i. 410 sq., 434 sq.,
438 sq.  On Gaza also, Noris, v. 2 (ed. Lips. p. 476 sqq.).  Stark, p. 517 sq.

[69] Plin. *Hist. Nat.* v. 13. 68 : intus Anthedon.  That it was on the coast
is however certain from the unanimous testimony of all other authors ; see
Joseph. *Antt.* xiii. 15. 4, xviii. 6. 3 ; *Bell. Jud.* i. 21. 8 ; Ptolem. v. 16. 2 ;
Steph. Byz. *s.v.;* Sozomenus, *Hist. eccl.* v. 9.  See on the subject in
general, Reland, *Palaestina*, pp. 566–568.  Raumer, *Palästina*, p. 171.
Pauly's *Real-Encycl.* i. 1. 1087 sq.  Guérin, *Judée*, ii. 215–218.  Le Quien,
*Oriens christianus*, iii. 631.

[69a] Sozomenus, v. 9.  Anthedon is according to Joseph. *Antt.* xiii. 15. 4
generally placed south of Gaza.  But the majority of the passages from
Josephus speak of it as north of Gaza (*Antt.* xv. 7. 3 ; *Bell. Jud.* i. 4. 2, 20.

founded in the Greek period. It is first mentioned in the time of Alexander Jannaeus, who conquered it about the same time as Raphia (Joseph. *Antt.* xiii. 13. 3 ; *Bell. Jud.* i. 4. 2 ; comp. *Antt.* xiii. 15. 4). Like the other coast towns it was undoubtedly retaken from the Jews by Pompey. Gabinius rebuilt it (*Antt.* xiv. 5. 3 ; *Bell. Jud.* i. 8. 4). Augustus bestowed it on Herod (*Antt.* xv. 7. 3 ; *Bell. Jud.* i. 20. 3), who again restored it and gave it the name of Agrippias or Agrippeion in honour of Agrippa (*Antt.* xiii. 13. 3 ; *Bell. Jud.* i. 4. 2, 21. 8). It is not expressly mentioned in the partition of Herod's inheritance. Hence it is uncertain whether, like its neighbour Gaza, it was united to the province of Syria, or passed like Joppa and Caesarea to Archelaus (see Stark, p. 542 sq.). In the latter case it would have shared the fate of the rest of Judaea and therefore have come, after the deposition of Archelaus, under Roman procurators and have been from A.D. 41–44 under the rule of King Agrippa. The existence of a coin of Anthedon with the name of Agrippa would give evidence of the latter, if its reading were certain.[70] At the beginning of the Jewish war Anthedon was attacked and partially devastated by the revolted Jews (*Bell. Jud.* ii. 18. 1). The name Agrippias was never naturalized ; Josephus already and all subsequent authors call it Anthedon again.[71] On coins too only this name occurs.[72]

3, ii. 18. 1) ; so too Plinius, v. 13. 68. The note of Theodosius is decisive for its lying *between Gaza and Ascalon ;* Theodosius, *De situ terrae sanctae* (ed. Gildemeister, 1882), § 18 : inter Ascalonam et Gazam civitates duae, id est Anthedon et Maioma. Rightly therefore has Gatt (*Zeitschr. des Deutschen Palästina-Vereins*, vii. 1884, pp. 5–7) identified the ruins of el-Blachije, one league north-west of Gaza, for which a native gave him the name of Teda, with Anthedon. Comp. also the remarks of Nöldeke and Gildemeister, *Zeitschr. d. DPV.* vii. 140–142.

[70] The coins in Mionnet, *Suppl.* viii. 364. Against the correctness of the reading see Madden, *Coins of the Jews* (1881), p. 134.

[71] So Plinius, Ptolemaeus, Steph. Byz., Sozomenus in the passages cited ; Hierocles, *Synecd.* p. 44 ; the Acts of the Councils in Le Quien, as above. The isolated assertion of Tzetzes (in Reland, p. 567), that the former Anthedon is " now " called Agrippias, is based upon Josephus only.

[72] Eckhel, *Doctr. Num.* iii. 443 sq. Mionnet, *Descript.* v. 522 sq. ; *Suppl.*

4. *Ascalon*, Ἀσκάλον, Hebr. אַשְׁקְלוֹן, was like Gaza an impor-
tant town of the Philistines, repeatedly mentioned in the Old
Testament and also already known to Herodotus.[73] The present
Ascalon lies close to the sea, and Ptolemy also mentions
Ascalon as a coast town.[74] But the old town must have lain
inland, if ever so little, since even in the sixth century after
Christ Ascalon and Majuma Ascalonis are distinguished.[75]
In the Persian period Ascalon belonged to the Tyrians.[76]
Coins of Alexander the Great coined at Ascalon mark the
commencement of the Hellenistic period.[76a] Like all Palestine
and Phoenicia it was in the third century before Christ under
the dominion of the Ptolemies, and had consequently to pay
them yearly tribute.[77] With Antiochus III. began its subjec-

viii. 364. De Saulcy, *Numismatique de la Terre Sainte*, pp. 234–236, pl. xii.
n. 1–4. All three indeed give also coins with the legend Ἀγριππέων. But
these do not belong to Anthedon ; see Stark, p. 515.

[73] Herodot. i. 105. See on Ascalon in general, Reland, *Palaestina*, pp.
586–596. Winer, *RWB.*, and Pauly, *Real-Enc. s.v.* Ritter, *Erdkunde*,
xvi. 70–89. Raumer, *Paläst.* p. 173 sq. Tobler, *Dritte Wanderung nach
Palästina* (1859), pp. 32–44. Sepp, *Jerusalem* (2nd ed.), ii. 599 sqq.
Guérin, *Judée*, ii. 135–149, 153–171. Guthe, *Die Ruinen Askalon's*, with a
plan (*Zeitschr. d. deutschen Palästina-Vereins*, ii. 164 sqq.). *The Survey of
Western Palestine*, *Memoirs* by Conder and Kitchener, iii. 237–247 (with
a plan), also plate xix. of the large English chart.

[74] Ptolem. v. 16. 2.

[75] Antoninus Martyr, c. 33 (in Tobler and Molinier, *Itinera*, i. 109):
Ascalonem . . . In proximo civitatis Maiuma Ascalonis. In A.D. 518 a
bishop of Ascalon and a bishop of Majuma Ascalonis are mentioned contemporaneously ; see Le Quien, *Oriens christ.* iii. 602 sq. Kuhn, ii. 363.

[76] Scylax in *Geographi graeci minores*, ed. Müller, i. 79 : Ἀσκάλων πόλις
Τυρίων καὶ βασίλεια. Movers (*Phönicier*, ii. 2. 177 sq.) insists on referring
this notice only to the harbour of Ascalon (Majuma Ascalonis) which he
considers to be a foundation of the Tyrians. But this lay in the immediate
neighbourhood of the town (see the preceding note) and could hardly have
been in the possession of any, who did not own the town itself. It is on
the contrary to be supposed, that Ascalon was, in the Persian period (to
which the statements of Scylax refer) under the rule of the Tyrians as
Joppa and Dora were under that of the Sidonians.

[76a] L. Müller, *Numismatique d'Alexandre le Grand* (1855), p. 308, planches,
n. 1472 sqq. The coins communicated by Mionnet, i. 522, *Suppl.* iii. 199,
belong, according to Müller, p. 267, to the town of Aspendos in Pamphylia.

[77] Joseph. *Antt.* xii. 4. 5 ; see above, p. 52 sq. If it is correct, that a coin
of Antiochus, coined at Ascalon, is in existence (as Mionnet, v. 8, No. 59,

tion to the Seleucidae, which is also evidenced by Ascalonian Seleucid coins from Antiochus III. to Antiochus IX.[78] Ascalon was able by prudent concessions to protect itself against the increasing power of the Jews. The Maccabaean Jonathan did indeed march twice against the town, but was on both occasions pacified by a respectful welcome on the part of the inhabitants.[79] Ascalon was also the only coast town, which remained unmolested by Alexander Jannaeus. It was able in the year 104 B.C. to attain to independence and thenceforth began a computation of time of its own, which it made use of even in the times of the Roman Empire.[80] The Romans acknowledged its independence at least formally.[81] Besides the usual era of the year 104 B.C. another of 57 B.C. occurs in several instances, which proves that Ascalon was favoured by Gabinius.[82] On some of the coins of Ascalon the heads have been taken for

states), Ascalon must at that time have been under Syrian sway. But comp. on the other side, Stark, *Gaza*, p. 476 ; Droysen, iii. 1. 274.

[78] Mionnet describes Ascalonian coins of Antiochus III. and IV., of Trypho and Antiochus VIII. (*Descript. de médailles*, v. p. 25, No. 219, pp. 38, 72, No. 625, p. 525 ; *Suppl.* viii. 366). The catalogue of the British Museum gives such of Trypho, Alexander Zebinas, Antiochus VIII. and IX. (Gardner, *Catalogue of the Greek Coins, Seleucid Kings*, 1878, pp. 68, 69, 81–88, 91) ; de Saulcy, one of Trypho (*Mélanges de Numismatique*, vol. ii. 1877, p. 82 sq.). See on the subject generally, Stark, *Gaza*, pp. 474–477.

[79] 1 Macc. x. 86 and xi. 60. Stark, *Gaza*, pp. 490 sq., 492.

[80] See on the era 104 B.C., *Chron. paschale* on Olymp. 169. 1 = 104 B.C. (ed. Dindorf, i. 346) : Ἀσκαλωνῖται τοὺς ἑαυτῶν χρόνους ἐντεῦθεν ἀριθμοῦσιν. Hieron. *Chron. ad ann. Abrah.* 2295 (in Euseb. *Chron.*, ed Schoene, ii. 185): The second year of Probus (1030 A.V.C.) = 380 aer. Ascal. Noris, *Annus et epochae*, v. 4. 1 (ed. Lips. pp. 503–515). Eckhel, *Doctr. Num.* iii. 444–447. Coins in Mionnet, *Descr.* v. 523–533 ; *Suppl.* viii. 365–370. De Saulcy, *Numismatique de la Terre Sainte*, pp. 178–208, 406, pl. ix. x. The same, *Mélanges de Numismatique*, vol. ii. 1877, pp. 148–152.

[81] Plinius, *Hist. Nat.* v. 13. 68 : oppidum Ascalo liberum. In the earlier imperial period (down to the middle of the 2nd century after Christ) Ascalon used autonomic as well as imperial coins, the former however of only the smallest kind and least value ; see de Saulcy, p. 187.

[82] The double date 56 and 102 is found on a coin of Augustus. On another (in de Saulcy, p. 189, No. 8), 55 and 102. The year 102 is according to the usual era of Ascalon 3/2 B.C. If however this, according to the second era = 55/56, then the year 1 of this latter era = 57 B.C. (not 58, as was before supposed on the strength of the coin of the year 56).

those of Cleopatra and a Ptolemy, which would point to their sovereignty or claims to sovereignty over this region.[82a] Ascalon was never in the possession of Herod and his successors, although it was indeed adorned with public buildings by Herod,[83] who seems also to have had a palace there, which after his death passed into the possession of his sister Salome.[84] The ancient enmity of the Jews and Ascalonians made the breaking out of the Jewish war in A.D. 66 fatal for both. At first Ascalon was devastated by the Jews;[85] then the Ascalonians put to death all the Jews dwelling in their city, 1500 in number;[86] finally, the Jews made a second attack upon the town, which was indeed easily repelled by the Roman garrison stationed there.[87] Ascalon long remained a flourishing Hellenistic city with celebrated religious rites and games.[88] Many individuals famous in Greek literature were natives of this town.[89]

5. *Azotus,* "Αζωτος, or Ashdod, Hebr. אַשְׁדּוֹד, like Gaza and Ascalon, an old Philistine town frequently mentioned in the Old

[82a] De Saulcy, *Note sur quelques monnaies inédites d'Ascalon* (*Revue Numismatique*, 1874, pp. 124–135). Feuardent, the same, pp. 184–194. Comp. Bursian's *philol. Jahresbericht*, vii. 467 sq.

[83] Joseph. *Bell. Jud.* i. 21. 11.

[84] Joseph. *Antt.* xvii. 11. 5 ; *Bell. Jud.* ii. 6. 3. Comp. Stark, p. 542. On the question, whether Herod was born at Ascalon, see above, § 12. De Saulcy thinks the use of certain supposed Jewish symbols (two cornucopias crossing each other with a lemon (?) in the middle) upon certain coins of Ascalon of the time of Augustus must be referred to the influence of Herod ; see his *Note sur quelques monnaies d'Ascalon*, in the *Annuaire de la Société Française de Numismatique et d'Archéologie*, iii. 253–258.

[85] Joseph. *Bell. Jud.* ii. 18. 1.    [86] Joseph. *Bell. Jud.* ii. 18. 5.

[87] Joseph. *Bell. Jud.* iii. 2. 1, 2. On the enmity of the Ascalonians to the Jews, see also Philo, ii. 576, ed. Mangey.

[88] The games are mentioned in the inscription *Corp. Inscr. Graec.* n. 4472 ; Le Bas et Waddington, *Inscriptions*, vol. iii. n. 1839 (comp. above, p. 24 sq.). Ammian. Marcellin. xiv. 8. 11 mentions Caesarea, Eleutheropolis, Neapolis, Ascalon and Gaza as the most important towns of Palestine. To this very day "the ruins of Ascalon and Kaisarieh are the most considerable on the whole coast from Ghâseh to Bêrût" (Tobler, *Dritte Wanderung*, p. 44).

[89] Steph. Byz. *s.v.* reckons four philosophers, two grammarians, and two historians of Ascalon (comp. above, p. 25) ; and the catalogue is not yet complete (see Reland, p. 594).

Testament and already known to Herodotus.[90]  Ptolemy speaks
of it as a coast town;[91] Josephus at one time as a coast, at
another as an inland town.[92]  The latter is more accurate, for it
lay, as the present Asdud does, more than a league inland, on
which account Ἄζωτος παράλιος is in Christian times distinguished from Ἄζωτος μεσόγειος.[93]  The district of Azotus
is frequently mentioned in the Books of the Maccabees; but
no certain conclusions can be drawn therefrom as to its extent.[94]
Nor are any further details of its fate under the Ptolemies and
Seleucidae known.[94a]  At the time of the rising of the Maccabees Azotus was unable to maintain itself against Jewish supremacy.  Judas already destroyed its altars and images (1 Macc.
v. 68).  Jonathan, however, devastated the city, together with its
temple of Dagon, by fire (1 Macc. x. 84, xi. 4).  At the time of
Alexander Jannaeus the city, or rather its ruins, belonged to
the Jewish region (Joseph. *Antt.* viii. 15. 4).  Pompey again
separated it from this latter, and made it a free town (*Antt.* xiv.
4. 4; *Bell. Jud.* i. 7. 7).  But the ruined city was not restored
till Gabinius (*Antt.* xiv. 5. 3; *Bell. Jud.* i. 8. 4).  It possibly
came, together with the other maritime towns, under the
dominion of Herod (B.C. 30), from whom it passed after his
death to his sister Salome (*Antt.* xvii. 8. 1, 11. 5; *Bell. Jud.*
ii. 6. 3).  Whether, like Jamnia, it fell after her death to the

[90] Herodot. ii. 157. See on the subject generally, Reland, *Palaestina*,
pp. 606–609. Winer, *RWB.*, *s.v.* Asdod. Pauly, *Real-Enc.* i. 2. 2208 sq.
Ritter, *Erdkunde*, xvi. 94–100. Raumer, *Paläst.* p. 174; Tobler, *Dritte
Wanderung*, pp. 26–32. Guérin, *Judée*, ii. 70–78; *The Survey of Western
Palestine, Memoirs* by Conder and Kitchener, ii. 409 sq., 421 sqq., also sheet
xvi. of the large English chart.

[91] Ptolem.

[92] As a coast town, *Antt.* xiii. 15. 4; as an inland town, *Antt.* xiv. 4. 4;
*Bell. Jud.* i. 7. 7; comp. Kuhn, ii. 362, 364.

[93] Hieroclis, *Synecdemus*, ed. Parthey (1866), p. 43.

[94] 1 Macc. xiv. 34, xvi. 10.

[94a] On two interesting coins of Asdod, probably of the first Diadochian
period, see Georg Hoffmann in Sallet's *Zeitschr. für Numismatik*, vol. ix.
1882, p. 96 sq. The superscription of the coins is Hebrew, but in Greek
characters. On the one is IP ΑΣΔΩΔ ΑΣΙΝΑ, *i.e.* עיר אשדוד חסינה (the
strong city of Ashdod); on the other IP ΑΣ IPOM H, *i.e.* probably the
city of Ashdod in the eighth year of Hirom (the king of the city).

Empress Livia is not quite certain, since Azotus is not expressly named (*Antt.* xviii. 2. 2 ; *Bell. Jud.* ii. 9. 1). It is probable that a considerable portion of its population was Jewish, on which account Vespasian was obliged, during the Jewish war, to place a garrison in it (*Bell. Jud.* iv. 3. 2). Coins of Azotus during the Roman period seem not to have been preserved.[95]

6. *Jamnia*, Ἰάμνεια, in the Old Testament Jabneh, יַבְנֶה (2 Chron. xxvi. 6), under which name it frequently occurs in Rabbinic literature.[96] Jamnia, like Azotus, is sometimes called a maritime, sometimes an inland town,[97] for it lay considerably inland, but had a port. Both are correctly distinguished by Pliny and Ptolemy.[98] There is express testimony that Jamnia had a district.[99] According to Strabo, it was so densely populated that Jamnia and its neighbourhood were able to furnish 40,000 fighting men.[100] In the Maccabaean period Jamnia was—at least according to the second Book of the Maccabees — attacked by Judas, and its port together with the fleet burnt.[101] The town itself however did not

---

[95] The coins with the legend Τυχὴ Ἀσωτίων, which older numismatics have referred to this town (Eckhel, iii. 448 ; Mionnet, v. 534 ; *Suppl.* viii. 370), are rightly denied to belong to it by de Saulcy (*Numism.* p. 282 sq.), even on account of the σ instead of ζ [also in the Pseudo-Aristeas Ἀσωτίων χώραν is, according to Mor. Schmid in Merx's *Archiv*, i. 275, 6, the correct reading, instead of Ἀζωτίων χώραν].

[96] Mishna, *Shekalim* i. 4 ; *Rosh hashana* ii. 8, 9, iv. 1, 2 ; *Kethuboth* iv. 6 ; *Sanhedrin* xi. 4 ; *Edujoth* ii. 4 ; *Aboth* iv. 4 ; *Bechoroth* iv. 5, vi. 8 ; *Kelim* v. 4 ; *Para* vii. 6. For the passages of the *Tosefta*, see the index to Zuckermandel's edition (1882). Neubauer, *La Géographie du Talmud*, 1868, pp. 73–76.

[97] Maritime town, *Antt.* xviii. 15. 4. Inland town, *Antt.* iv. 4. 4 ; *Bell. Jud.* i. 7. 7 ; comp. Kuhn, ii. 362 sq.

[98] Plinius, *H. N.* v. 13. 68 : Jamneae duae, altera intus. Ptolem. v. 16. 2 : Ἰαμνειτῶν λιμήν ; v. 16. 6 : Ἰάμνεια. See generally, Reland, p. 823 sq. Winer, *RWB.*, *s.v.* "Jabne." Pauly, *Real-Enc.* iv. 17. Raumer, p. 203 sq. Ritter, xvi. 125 sq. Tobler, *Dritte Wanderung*, pp. 20–25. Guérin, *Judée*, ii. 53–65. *The Survey of Western Palestine, Memoirs* by Conder and Kitchener, ii. 414, 441–433 ; also sheet xvi. of the large English chart.

[99] Joseph. *Bell. Jud.* iii. 5 : Ἰάμνεια καὶ Ἰόπη τῶν περιοίκων ἀφηγοῦνται.

[100] Strabo, xvi. p. 759. Strabo here indeed erroneously calls Jamnia a κώμη.

[101] 2 Macc. xii. 8 sq., 40 ; comp. Stark, *Gaza*, p. 487.

come into the possession of the Jews either then, or, as Josephus asserts, under Simon.[102]  It was not till Alexander Jannaeus that it formed a portion of the Jewish territory (*Antt.* xiii. 15. 4).  Pompey again separated it from the latter (*Antt.* xiv. 4. 4; *Bell. Jud.* i. 7. 7), Gabinius restored it.  Like Azotus, Jamnia must also have come into the possession of Herod, since it was left by him to his sister Salome (*Antt.* xvii. 8. 1, 11. 5; *Bell. Jud.* ii. 6. 3).  The Empress Livia received it from the latter (*Antt.* xviii. 2. 2; *Bell. Jud.* ii. 9. 1), and after her death it seems to have become a private possession of Tiberius (*Antt.* xviii. 6. 3; see above, p. 55).  The population was then a mixed one of Jews and heathen, but with a preponderance of the Jewish element.[103]  This explains the fact, that Vespasian twice found himself obliged to garrison the city,[104] and that Jamnia, after the destruction of Jerusalem, soon became a headquarter of Jewish learning.

7.  *Joppa*, Ἰόπη or Ἰόππη,[105] Hebr. יָפוֹ,[106] the present Jaffa.

[102] Joseph. *Antt.* xiii. 6. 6; *Bell. Jud.* i. 2. 2.  See, on the other hand, 1 Macc. x. 69, xv. 40.

[103] Philo, *Legat. ad Cajum*, § 30 (Mang. ii. 575): ταύτην μιγάδες οἰκοῦσιν οἱ πλείους μὲν Ἰουδαῖοι, ἕτεροι δέ τινες ἀλλόφυλοι παρεισφθαρέντες ἀπὸ τῶν πλησιοχώρων, οἱ τοῖς τρόπον τινὰ αὐθιγενέσιν ὄντες μέτοικοι, κακὰ καὶ πράγματα παρέχουσιν, ἀεί τι παραλύοντες τῶν πατρίων Ἰουδαίοις.  Philo, indeed, by here assigning the part of natives to the Jews, and that of *metoikoi* to the heathen, reverses the true order of things.  For even in the Maccabaean period Jamnia was a chiefly heathen city, nor was it till afterwards that its Jewish element increased.

[104] Joseph. *Bell. Jud.* iv. 3. 2, 8. 1.

[105] The orthography fluctuates.  In the texts of non-biblical authors the form Ἰόπη, which is required by Greek grammarians, is preferred (see Movers, *Phönicier*, ii. 2. 176, note 73.  Mendelssohn in Ritschl's *Acta societ. philol. Lips.* vol. v. p. 104) and corroborated by the usage of poets (Alexander Ephesius in *Steph. Byz.*, ed. Meineke, p. 255: Δῶρός τ᾽ ἀγχίαλός τ᾽ Ἰόπη προὔχουσα θαλάσσης, also Dionys. *Perieg.* in Müller, *Geogr. gr. min.* ii. 160: οἵτ᾽ Ἰόπην καὶ Γάζαν Ἐλαΐδα τ᾽ ἐνναίουσι).  The biblical manuscripts, on the contrary, have, as it appears, universally Ἰόππη, whether in the Old or New Testament (1 Maccabees and Acts).  Of the few coins that have been preserved some have one, some the other form.  The Greek Ἰόπη is related to יָפוֹ as Ἄκη is to עַכּוֹ.  But it might also arise from the form יָפִי (concluding with Jod), as the name is given on the inscription of Eschmunazar.  See Schlottmann, *Die Inschrift Eschmunazars* (1868), p. 150 sqq.

[106] Josh. xix. 46; Jonah i. 3; 2 Chron. ii. 15; Ezra iii. 7.  Mishna,

The special importance of Joppa is found in the fact that it was comparatively the best harbour on the coast of Palestine.[107] It was therefore at almost all periods the chief place of debarkation for the interior of Judaea, and its possession, especially on the greater development of trade and commerce in later times, was almost a vital question for the Jews.   In the Persian period, and indeed in the time of the Sidonian King Eschmunazar, Joppa was granted to the Sidonians by the "Lord of Kings," *i.e.* by the Persian monarch.[107a]   To the Greeks it was chiefly known as the scene of the myth of Perseus and Andromeda, and is mentioned as such even before the time of Alexander the Great by Scylax (see above, p. 15). In the Diadochian period it seems to have been an important arsenal.   When Antigonus wrested Coelesyria from Ptolemy Lagos, he was obliged to take Joppa as well as other places by force.[108]   And when, three years later (312 B.C.), Ptolemy Lagos found he could not hold the reconquered region against Antigonus, he had Joppa razed on his retreat as one of the more important fortresses.[109]   In the time of the Maccabees

*Nedarim* iii. 6 ; Tosefta, *Demai* i. 11 (ed. Zuckermandel, p. 46, 1). Neubauer, *La Géographie du Talmud*, p. 81 sq.

[107] Joseph. *Bell. Jud.* iii. 9. 3 indeed describes the harbour as dangerous, which it still is.  It must, however, have been *comparatively* the best. According to Diodor. i. 13, there was but one safe harbour (ἀσφαλὴ λιμένα), viz. the Pharos of Alexandria from Paraetonium in Libya to Jopa in Coelesyria.  Strabo too (xvi. p. 759) rightly gives prominence to the importance of Joppa as a port for Judaea.  See especially 1 Macc. xiv. 5.  Compare on the subject in general, Reland, pp. 864–867.  Winer, *RWB*. Pauly, *Real-Enc.*  Schenkel, *Bibellex. s.v.*  Ritter, xvi. 574–580.  Raumer, p. 204 sq. Tobler, *Topographie von Jerusalem*, ii. 576–637.  Sepp, *Jerusalem* (2nd ed.), i. 1–22.  Guérin, *Judée*, i. 1–22  Bädeker-Socin., *Palästina* (1st ed.), p. 131 sqq., with plan.  Schwarz, *Jafa und Umgebung, mit Plan* (*Zeitschr. d. deutschen Pal.-Ver.* iii. 44 sqq.).  *The Survey of Western Palestine, Memoirs* by Conder and Kitchener, ii. 254–258, 275–278 ; also sheet xiii. of the large English chart.

[107a] See the inscription of Eschmunazar, line 18–19, and Schlottmann, as above, pp. 83–147 sqq.  The text is best given in the *Corpus Inscriptionum Semiticarum*, vol. i. (1881) pp. 9–20.

[108] Diodor. xix. 59.  Comp. Droysen, *Hellenismus*, ii. 2. 11.  Stark, *Gaza*, p. 350.

[109] Diodor. xix. 93.  Comp. Droysen, ii. 2. 54.  Stark, p. 355 sq.

the efforts of the Jews were especially directed to obtain possession of this important place. It is true that Judas Maccabaeus — if the account is quite trustworthy — only destroyed the port and fleet of Joppa during a nocturnal attack (2 Macc. xii. 3–7). Jonathan however, in the year 147 or 146 B.C., made a serious assault of the town, in consequence of which the inhabitants opened the gates to him and forced the Syrian garrison to depart (1 Macc. x. 75, 76). Thenceforward the Jews remained with but slight intermission in possession of the town till the time of Pompey. From the same period also must be dated the *Judaizing of the city.* For when, a few years after its conquest by Jonathan, the inhabitants showed signs of again surrendering the town to the Syrians, Simon, the brother of Jonathan, stationed a Jewish garrison in it (1 Macc. xii. 33, 34) and compelled the heathen inhabitants to leave the town (1 Macc. xiii. 11 : ἐξέβαλε τοὺς ὄντας ἐν αὐτῇ).[110] Simon then enlarged and improved the harbour and fortified the town (1 Macc. xiv. 5, 34). When the energetic Antiochus VII. (Sidetes) endeavoured again to retrench the power of the Jews, the possession of Joppa was a main point of dispute. Even while Antiochus was contending with Trypho, he demanded from Simon the surrender of Joppa (1 Macc. xv. 28–30). The latter however declared himself only ready to pay a sum of money instead (1 Macc. xv. 35). When, some years later, in the beginning of the reign of John Hyrcanus, all Palestine was conquered and even Jerusalem besieged by Antiochus, it is probable that Joppa had already been taken by him. He was nevertheless satisfied at the conclusion of a peace with the payment of a tribute for Joppa (Joseph. *Antt.* xiii. 8. 3).[111] Thus the town continued in the possession of the Jews, and

[110] Comp. Stark, p. 493 sq. A similar procedure was observed towards Gazara.

[111] The seizure of Joppa by an Antiochus is assumed in two Roman Senatus-consultus, in the latter of which its surrender is commanded him by the Roman Senate (Joseph. *Antt.* xiii. 9. 2, xiv. 10. 22). Perhaps this

in later times even the payment of the tribute ceased.   There
is express testimony that Alexander Jannaeus possessed Joppa
(*Antt.* xiii. 15. 4).   This maritime city was however taken by
Pompey from the Jews, who were thus entirely cut off from
the sea (*Antt.* xiv. 4. 4; *Bell. Jud.* i. 7. 7).   Among the favours
bestowed by Caesar on the Jews one of the most valuable was
the restoration of Joppa (*Antt.* xiv. 10. 6).[112]   It is not quite
certain whether Herod held Joppa from the first.   At any
rate, like the other coast towns, it belonged, during the years
34–30 B.C., to Cleopatra (see above, § 15), and thenceforth to
Herod (*Antt.* xv. 7. 3 ; *Bell. Jud.* i. 20. 3).[113]   From this time
it was always united with Judaea proper, and hence passed
after Herod's death to Archelaus (*Antt.* xvii. 11. 4; *Bell. Jud.*
ii. 6. 3), and was after his deposition under Roman procurators.
At the beginning of the Jewish war, Joppa was, by reason of
its mainly Jewish population, a central seat of rebellion.
It was destroyed at the very beginning of the war by Cestius
Gallus (*Bell. Jud.* ii. 18. 10), but soon fortified again and
conquered a second time by Vespasian (*Bell. Jud.* iii. 9. 2–4).
From that time it probably again became a chiefly heathen
town.   It is shown by a coin recently discovered, that it was
also called Flavia, which leads to the inference of its refoundation in the time of Vespasian.[113a]   Notwithstanding its
close connection with Judaea, Joppa formed an independent

explains the striking leniency of Antiochus in the conditions of peace.   It
is however just questionable, whether Antiochus Sidetes is meant.

[112] For further details, see above, § 15.

[113] The Jews having been in possession of Joppa since Caesar, and it
being expressly said of Joppa, that Herod conquered it when he took
possession of his kingdom (*Antt.* xiv. 15. 1 ; *Bell. Jud.* i. 15. 3, 4), it must
be supposed that it was his from the beginning of his reign, and that he
then obtained it *again* in the year 30, after the short interregnum of
Cleopatra.   The only difficulty is, that at the enlargement of his domains
in the year 30, Joppa is named, not as a portion of the domains *again*
bestowed on Herod, but expressly as among the towns *newly* bestowed
*besides* these.

[113a] Darricarrère, *Sur une monnaie inédite de Joppe* (*Revue archéologique*,
nouv. série, vol. xliii. 1882, p. 74 sq.).   The coin is of the time of Elagabalus, and bears the inscription : Ιοππης Φλαουιας.

political community after the manner of Hellenistic towns.[114]
Of its coins few specimens have been preserved.[115]

8. *Apollonia*, Ἀπολλωνία. An Apollonia between Joppa
and Caesarea is mentioned by geographers down to the later
imperial period.[116] It occurs only twice in history : at the
time of Alexander Jannaeus, when it belonged to the Jewish
region (Joseph. *Antt.* xiii. 15. 4), and at the time of Gabinius,
who restored it (Joseph. *Bell. Jud.* i. 8. 4). According to the
statement of distance in the Peutinger table (22 *m. p.* from
Caesarea) it must have been situate where the present Arsuf
is.[117] Stark's supposition, that it is identical with Σώζουσα,
is commended by the circumstance, that in Cyrenaica also an
Apollonia and a Sozusa appear, which are probably identical.
Sozusa would thus be the town of Apollo Σωτήρ.[118] The
name Apollonia makes it probable, that it was founded by
Seleucus I. in the time of the definitive occupation of Coelesyria
by the Ptolemies.[119]

[114] This appears chiefly from the manner in which Josephus (*Bell. Jud.*
iii. 3. 5) mentions Joppa *beside* Judaea proper : μεθ᾽ ἃς Ἰάμνεια καὶ Ἰόπη
τῶν περιοίκων ἀφηγοῦνται. In *Bell. Jud.* iii. 9. 4 also, the κῶμαι and
πολίχναι τῆς Ἰόπης are mentioned.

[115] Eckhel, *Doctr. Num.* iii. 433. Mionnet, v. 499. De Saulcy, p. 176 sq.,
pl. ix. n. 3, 4. Reichardt, *Numismatic Chronicle*, 1862, p. 111 ; and *Wiener
Numismat. Monatshefte*, published by Egger, vol. iii. 1867, p. 192.
Darricarrère, as above.

[116] Plinius, *H. N.* v. 13. 69. Ptolem. v. 16. 2. *Tabula Peutinger. Segm.*
ix. *Geographus Ravennas*, ed. Pinder et Parthey (1860), pp..83 and 356.
*Guidonis Geogr.* in the above-named edition of the *Geogr. Ravenn.* p. 524.
Steph. Byz., *s.v.* Ἀπολλωνία, reckons twenty-five towns of this name,
No. 12 among them : περὶ τὴν Κοίλην Συρίαν ; No. 13 : κατὰ Ἰόπην (this
being the one now in question) ; No. 20 : Συρίας κατὰ Ἀπάμειαν.

[117] See in general, Reland, p. 573. Ritter, xvi. 590. Pauly's *Enc.* i. 2.
1308. Kuhn, ii. 362. Guérin, *Samarie*, ii. 375–382. *The Survey of Western
Palestine, Memoirs* by Conder and Kitchener, ii. 135, 137–140 (with plan) ;
also sheet x. of the large English chart. De Saulcy, *Numismatique*,
p. 110 sq., pl. vi. n. 1, 2.

[118] Σώζουσα in Hierocles, ed. Parthey, p. 44. Comp. Stark, *Gaza*, p. 452.
On Sozusa in Cyrenaica, Forbinger, *Handb.* ii. 829.

[119] Appian. *Syr.* 57 does not indeed mention our town, but speaks
of Apollonia as a Macedonian town - name transplanted into Syria by
Seleucus I. Comp. Stark, as above.

9. *Straton's Tower*, Στράτωνος πύργος, afterwards Caesarea.[120] Like Apollonia, Straton's Tower may have been a foundation of the Hellenistic period, perhaps at first a castle, so called after a general of the Ptolemies. It is however possible, that it was founded towards the end of the Persian period by a Sidonian king of the name of Straton.[121] Artemidorus, about 100 B.C., is the first geographical author by whom it is mentioned.[122] At that period too it first occurs in history, being mentioned in the time of Aristobulus I., 104 B.C. (*Antt.* xiii. 11. 2). In the beginning of the reign of Alexander Jannaeus, a "tyrant," Zoilus was master of Straton's Tower and

[120] See generally, Reland, pp. 670–678. Raumer, p. 152 sq. Winer, *RWB.*, and Schenkel's *Bibellex. s.v.* Caesarea. Pauly, *Real-Enc.* ii. 47. Kuhn, *Die städt. und bürgerl. Verfassung,* ii. 347–350. The same, *Ueber die Entstehung der Städte der Alten* (1878), pp. 423–433. Ritter, xvi. 598–607. Sepp, *Jerusalem* (2nd ed.), ii. 573 sqq. Guérin, *Samarie,* ii. 321. *The Survey of Western Palestine, Memoirs* by Conder and Kitchener, ii. 13–29 (with plans), also sheet vii. of the English chart.

[121] In Justinian's *Novelle* 103 praef. it is said of Caesarea : Καίτοι γε ἀρχαία τέ ἐστι καὶ ἀεὶ σεμνή, ἡνίκα τε αὐτὴν Στράτων ἱδρύσατο πρῶτος, ὅς ἐξ Ἑλλάδος ἀναστὰς γέγονεν αὐτῆς οἰκιστὴς ἡνίκα τε Οὐεσπασιανος . . . εἰς τὴν τῶν Καισάρων αὐτὴν ὠνόμασε προσηγορίαν. The worthlessness of this notice is shown already by the gross mistake with respect to Vespasian. As there was a *Straton's Island* on the Abyssinian coast of the Red Sea (Strabo, xvi. p. 770), Straton's Tower may have been a foundation of the Ptolemies. So Stark, *Gaza,* p. 451. To me however it seems almost more probable, that it was founded by the Sidonians. For towards the end of the Persian period they were in possession of the nearest towns both northward and southward, viz. Dora and Joppa (which see), and therefore presumably of the strip of coast also upon which Straton's Tower was built. Straton moreover was the name of one or more of the last kings of Sidon (see *Corp. Inscr. Graec.* n. 87, and also Böckh). At any rate its designation as πύργος, tower, is not usual for a town of Hellenistic foundation. Lastly, L. Müller thinks, that a coin of Alexander the Great with the letters Στ may be referred to our Straton's Tower (L. Müller, *Numismatique d'Alexandre le Grand,* p. 306, plates, n. 1466), in which case it must already have been in existence in the time of Alexander the Great, or at latest in the Diadochian period (in which also coins of Alexander were issued). All this combined favours the view, that it was already founded by the Sidonians.

[122] Artemidorus in *Steph. Byz. s.v.* Δῶρος (on Artemidorus, see Forbiger, *Handbuch der alten Geographie,* i. 246 sqq., 255 sqq. Pauly's *Enc. s.v.*). The latest geographer who knows of Straton's Tower by that name only is Strabo, xvi. p. 758.

Dora (Joseph. *Antt.* xiii. 12. 2). He was soon overthrown by
Alexander Jannaeus (*Antt.* xiii. 12. 4), and hence Straton's
Tower is named among the towns belonging to Alexander
(*Antt.* xiii. 15. 4). It obtained its freedom from Pompey
(*Antt.* xiv. 4. 4 ; *Bell. Jud.* i. 7. 7). It was bestowed upon
Herod by Augustus (*Antt.* xv. 7. 3 ; *Bell. Jud.* i. 20. 3), and
from this period dates the special importance of the town.
For it was rebuilt on the most magnificent scale by Herod,
and provided with artificial embankments and an excellent
harbour (*Antt.* xv. 9. 6, xvi. 5. 1 ; *Bell. Jud.* i. 21. 5–8).[123]
He called the town Καισάρεια in honour of the emperor, and
the harbour Σεβαστὸς λιμήν.[124] Hence on Nero's coins we
meet with Καισαρια ἡ πρὸς Σεβαστω λιμενι.[125] The designation Καισάρεια Σεβαστή occurs only once.[126] Elsewhere
the town is called in distinction from others Καισάρεια
Στράτωνος,[127] and in later times Καισάρεια τῆς Παλαιστίνης.[128]
It quickly attained to great prosperity, and remained for a
long period one of the most important towns of Palestine.[129]
After the death of Herod it passed with the rest of Judaea to

[123] Besides the above principal passages, compare also Joseph. *Antt.* xv.
8. 5. Plinius, v. 13. 69. On the time of its building, see above, § 15. On
its constitution and political position, see especially Kuhn's above-named
work.

[124] On the latter, see *Antt.* xvii. 5. 1 ; *Bell. Jud.* i. 31. 3.

[125] These coins are fully treated of by Belley in the *Mémoires de l'Académie
des Inscriptions et Belles-Lettres*, old series, vol. xxvi. 1759, pp. 440–445.
Comp. also Eckhel, iii. 428 sq. Mionnet, *Description*, v. 486 sq. De
Saulcy, *Numismatique*, p. 116 sq.

[126] Joseph. *Antt.* xvi. 5. 1. Philo, *Legat. ad Cajum*, § 38, ed. Mang. ii. 590.
The designation Αὐγοῦστα Καισάρεια occurring on an inscription (*Corp.
Inscr. Graec.* n. 4472=Le Bas et Waddington, *Inscriptions*, vol. iii. n. 1839)
is an abbreviation of colonia prima Flavia Augusta Caesarea, the official title
of Caesarea as a colony since Vespasian ; see below, p. 87, and Kuhn, ii. 349.

[127] Ptolem. v. 16. 2, viii. 20. 14. *Clement. Homil.* i. 15, 20, xiii. 7 ;
*Recogn.* i. 12. Le Bas et Waddington, *Inscriptions*, vol. iii. n. 1620[b] (Inscription of Aphrodisias in Caria of the second century after Christ, comp.
above, p. 24).

[128] Euseb. *Onomast.*, ed. Lagarde, pp. 207, 250. *De martyr. Palestinae*, i. 2.

[129] Joseph. *Bell. Jud.* iii. 9. 1. *Clement. Recogn.* i. 12. Apollonius, *Tyan.
epist.* xi. (in *Epistolographi graeci*, ed. Hercher, Paris 1873, Didot). *Totius
orbis descriptio* in Müller, *Geogr. gr. minores*, ii. 517. Ammian. xiv. p. 11.

Archelaus (*Antt.* xvii. 11. 4 ; *Bell. Jud.* ii. 6. 3). It afterwards continued on all occasions united with Judaea, and
hence came after the deposition of Archelaus under Roman
procurators, then under Agrippa I., and then again under
procurators.    Coins of Agrippa I., which were coined in
Caesarea, are still in existence.[130]    His στρατηγός in Caesarea
is incidentally mentioned (*Antt.* xix. 7. 4). It is well known
that he himself died there (see above, § 18). He was
hated by the Caesareans for his Judaizing tendencies (*Antt.*
xix. 9. 1).    The Roman procurators, both before and after the
reign of Agrippa, took up their abode at Caesarea (see above,
§ 17c).    Hence the town is called in Tacitus, *Judaeae caput*
(Tac. *Hist.* ii. 78). It was also the chief garrison for the
troops under the command of the procurators, who were for
the most part composed of natives (see above, p. 65). The
population being chiefly a heathen one (*Bell. Jud.* iii. 9. 1),
though mingled with a considerable Jewish fraction, disputes
easily occurred, and the more so that both had equal civil
rights, and had therefore to conduct the affairs of the
town in common.[130a]   Neither the Jews nor the heathen
were satisfied with this state of things. Each of these parties
claimed the exclusive government of the town. Already
towards the close of the official career of Felix there were
sanguinary contests on the subject, in consequence of which
Nero, whose adviser had been bribed by the heathen party,
deprived the Jews of their equality of right, and declared the
heathen sole governors of the town. The exasperation which
ensued gave the first inducement to the great rising of the
Jews in A.D. 66 (*Antt.* xx. 8. 7 and 9 ; *Bell. Jud.* ii. 13. 7,
14. 4, 5).    After the breaking out of the war, the Jews, as

[130] Eckhel, iii. 491, 492. Madden, *History of Jewish Coinage*, pp. 107, 109.
The same, *Coins of the Jews* (1881), pp. 133, 136. The coins with the legend
Καισαρειας ασυλου are rightly denied by Eckhel to belong to our Caesarea.

[130a] The ἄνδρες οἱ κατ᾽ ἐξοχὴν τῆς πόλεως, mentioned Acts xxv. 23, must
according to the context be regarded as heathen. This however does not
exclude Jews from a share in the government, but merely corresponds with
the preponderance of the heathen element testified to by Josephus.

the minority, fell victims to the fury of the heathen populace. It is said that all the Jewish inhabitants, 20,000 in number, were then assassinated in an hour (*Bell. Jud.* ii. 18. 1, vii. 8. 7, ed. Bekker, p. 161). Caesarea was changed by Vespasian into a Roman colony, though without the full *jus Italicum*.[131] On coins it bears the title *col(onia) prima Fl(avia) Aug(usta) Caesarensis* or *Caesarea*. To this was added after the time of Alexander Severus the title *metropolis*, or as it is more completely given on coins after Decius, *metropolis, pr. S. Pal.* (= *provinciae Syriae Palaestinae*.[132]

10. *Dora*, Δῶρα, in Polybius Δοῦρα, elsewhere also Δῶρος, in Pliny, *Dorum*,[133] Hebr. דּוֹר or דֹּאר,[134] an old Phoenician

---

[131] Plinius, *H. N.* v. 13. 69 : Stratonis turris, eadem Caesarea, ab Herode rege condita, nunc colonia prima Flavia a Vespasiano imperatore deducta. *Digest.* lib. xv. 8. 7 (from Paulus): Divus Vespasianus Caesarienses colonos fecit non adjecto, ut et juris Italici essent, sed tributum his remisit capitis ; sed divus Titus etiam solum immune factum interpretatus est. *Ibid.* lib. xv. 1. 6 (from Ulpianus): In Palaestina duae fuerunt coloniae, Caesariensis et Aelia Capitolina, sed neutra jus Italicum habet. Comp. Zumpt, *Commentationes epigr.* i. 397 sq. On the jus Italicum, see Marquardt, *Römische Staatsverwaltung*, i. 89 sqq. (1881). and the literature therein cited, p. 89, note 7, to which is to be added : Beaudouin, *Etude sur le Jus italicum*, Paris (1883). Comp. *Revue critique*, 1884, No. 6, pp. 99–101.

[132] On the coins in general, see Eckhel, iii. 428–442. Mionnet, v. 486–497 ; *Suppl.* viii. 334–343. De Saulcy, pp. 112-141, pl. vii.

[133] The form Δῶρος occurs especially in older authors, but is also preferred by Steph. Byz. Δῶρα was afterwards exclusively used. (1) Δῶρος is found in Scylax (fourth century B.C.), Apollodorus (about 140 B.C.), Alexander Ephesius (see on him Pauly's *Enc. s.v. Alex.* n. 40), Charax (the three last named in Steph. Byz. *s.v.* Δῶρος). To this series belongs also Pliny (*H. N.* v. 19. 75, *Dorum*). (2) Δῶρα or Δωρά found besides in 1 Macc., in Artemidorus (about 100 B.C.), Claudius Jolaus (both in Steph. Byz.), Josephus (constantly), on coins of Caligula, Trajan, Elagabalus (in De Saulcy), Ptolemaeus (v. 15. 5), *Clement. Recogn.* (iv. 1), Eusebius (*Onom.*, ed. Lag. p. 250), Hieronymus (the same, p. 115), Hierocles (ed. Parthey, p. 43), the lists of bishops (in Le Quien, *Oriens christ.* iii. 574 sqq.), *Geographus Ravennas* (ed. Pinder et Parthey, pp. 89, 357). To this series belong also Polybius (v. 66, Δοῦρα) and *Tab. Peuting.* (Thora). Comp. also note 136, below. The first Book of the Maccabees uses Δωρά indecl., it is elsewhere treated as a neut. plur. (Josephus usually ; Eusebius, p. 280, the lists of bishops) ; sometimes also as a fem. sing. (Joseph. *Antt.* xiii. 7. 2 ; *c. Apion.* ii. 9. *Clement. Recogn.* iv. 1).

[134] דּוֹר, Josh. xi. 2, xii. 23 ; Judg. i. 27 ; 1 Chron. vii. 29. דֹּאר, Josh.

settlement 8 or 9 miles north of Caesarea.[135]   It was known
from ancient times to the Greeks, being already mentioned
by Hecataeus of Miletus, who lived 500 years before Christ,
in his description of the earth.[136]   Nay, it is possible that it
may, during the hegemony of Athens in the Mediterranean in
the 5th century B.C., have been tributary to the Athenians.[136a]
In the time of the Sidonian King Eshmunazar it was granted
to the Sidonians by the "Lord of Kings," *i.e.* by the Persian
monarch.[137]   Hence Scylax, whose description refers to the

xvii. 11 ; 1 Kings iv. 11.   Also upon the inscription of Eshmunazar, see
below, note 137.   In the O. T. דֹּור נָפַת (Josh. xii. 23 ; 1 Kings iv. 11) or
דֹּור נָפֹות (Josh. xi. 2), properly the height or heights of Dor, and therefore
probably the hill country, which lay inland from Dor, is distinguished from
the town of Dor (see Riehm's *Wörterbuch, s.v.*).   Only the former and not
the maritime town was possessed by Solomon.   Less probable is Movers'
notion (*Phönicier*, ii. 2. 175 sq.), that Naphath-Dor is distinguished as an
inland town from Dor as a coast town.

[135] The foundation by the Phoenicians is fully described by Claudius
Jolaus in Steph. Byz. *s.v.* Δῶρος (also in Müller, *Fragm. hist. graec.* iv. 363).
Josephus also calls Dora a πόλις τῆς Φοινίκης (*Vita*, 8 ; *c. Apion.* ii. 9).
The distance from Caesarea, 8 *m. p.* according to *Tab. Peuting.*; 9 *m. p.*
according to Eusebius (*Onom.*, ed. Lag. p. 283) and Jerome (the same, pp.
115, 142).   According to Artemidorus (in Steph. Byz. *s.v.*), Dora lay ἐπὶ
χερσονησοειδοῦς τόπου.   Comp. generally, Reland, pp. 738–741 ; Raumer, p.
154 ; Winer, Schenkel, Pauly, *s.v.*; Ritter, xvi. 607–612 ; Guérin, *Samarie*,
ii. 305–315.   *The Survey of Western Palestine, Memoirs* by Conder and
Kitchener, ii. pp. 3, 7–11 ; also sheet vii. of the English chart.

[136] Hecataeus in Steph. Byz. *s.v.* Δῶρος (also in Müller, *Fragm. hist. graec.*
i. 17, n. 260) : μετὰ δὲ ἡ πάλαι Δῶρος, νῦν δὲ Δῶρα καλεῖται.   The words
cannot indeed have come down just as they stand from Hecataeus, because
they manifest a change in the usage of the language, which did not fully
take place till about 500 years later (see above, note 133).   Hence the
copy made use of by Steph. Byz. must here have had an interpolation.
On Hecataeus, see Forbiger, *Handbuch der alten Geogr.* i. 48 sqq.   C. Müller,
*Fragm. hist. graec.* t. i. Proleg. pp. ix.–xvi.   Westermann in Pauly's *Enc.*
iii. 1082 sq.

[136a] The Δῶρος tributary to the Athenians is indeed generally taken to
be a town in Caria (according to Steph. Byz. *s.v.* Δῶρος).   Such an one
however not being elsewhere known of, and the power of the Athenians
extending in any case to Cyprus, we may perhaps suppose it to have been
the Phoenician Doros.   See Ulr. Köhler, *Urkunden und Untersuchungen zur
Geschichte des Delisch-attischen Bundes* (*Transactions of the Berlin Academy*, 1869), pp. 121, 207.   Six, *Numismatic Chronicle*, 1877, p. 235.

[137] See the inscription of Eshmunazar, lines 18, 19, in the *Corp. Inscript.*

Persian period, rightly calls Dora a town of the Sidonians.[138] Although Dora was no large city,[139] it was on account of its favourable position a strong fortress. When Antiochus the Great made (219 B.C.) his first attack upon Coelesyria, he besieged Dora, but in vain.[140] Eighty years afterwards (139–138 B.C.) Trypho was here besieged by Antiochus Sidetes with a large army, but equally without result. The siege ended with the flight of Trypho.[141] On a coin of Trypho's stamped at Dora the town is called ἱε(ρὰ) κ(αὶ) ἄ(συλος).[142] Some decades afterwards we find it in the possession of the tyrant Zoilus (Joseph. Antt. xiii. 12. 2), who was afterwards overthrown by Alexander Jannaeus (Antt. xiii. 12. 4). It must therefore have subsequently belonged to the Jewish region, but was again separated from it by Pompey (Antt. xiv. 4. 4; Bell. Jud. i. 7. 7). Like many other towns, Dora also then began a new era, which it continued to use on coins of the imperial age.[143] It was restored by Gabinius (Antt. xiv. 5. 3). After Pompey

Semiticarum, vol. i. (1881) pp. 9–20; also Schlottmann, Die Inschrift Eschmunazar (1868), pp. 82 sq., 146 sqq.

[138] Scylax in Geographi graeci minores, ed. Müller, i. 79 : Δῶρος πόλις Σιδονίων. On Scylax, see e.g. Fabricius-Harles, Biblioth. gr. iv. 606 sqq. Forbiger, Handb. d. alten Geogr. i. 113 sqq., 123 sqq. Westermann in Pauly's Enc. vi. 1. 891 sq. Nicolai, Griech. Literaturgesch. i. 322 sq. Anonymi vulgo Scylacis Caryandensis periplum maris interni cum appendice, iterum rec. Fabricius, Lips. 1878.

[139] Artemidorus : πολισμάτιον. Claudius Jolaus: βραχεῖα πολίχνη (both in Steph. Byz.). Clement. Recogn. iv. 1 : breve oppidum.

[140] Polyb. v. 66.     [141] 1 Macc. xv. 11–37 ; Joseph. Antt. xiii. 7. 2.
[142] Mionnet, v. 72. Stark, p. 477.

[143] The commencement of the era cannot be strictly determined. At all events however it is that of Pompey (B.C. 63 ?), not that of Gabinius, as De Saulcy, in spite of his own objections assumes, for an era of Gabinius could not begin earlier than the autumn of 58 B.C. = 696 A.U.C. and then 175 aer. Dor., of which year coins of Trajan are in existence, would be = 870/871 A.U.C., while Trajan was already dead before the autumn of 870. See generally, Noris, iv. 5. 5 (ed. Lips. pp. 453–458). Pellerin, Recueil de médailles de peuples et de villes (3 vols. Paris 1763), ii. 216 sq. Eckhel, Doctr. Num. iii. 362 sq. Ideler, Handb. der Chronologie, i. 459. The coins in Mionnet, v. 359–362; Suppl. viii. 258–260. De Saulcy, pp. 142–148, pl. vi. n. 6–12.

it was under direct Roman government, and therefore
never belonged to Herod (whose dominions on the coast
extended no farther northward than Caesarea). It is called
on coins of the imperial period ἱερὰ ἄσυλος αὐτόνομος
ναυαρχίς.[144] The existence of a Jewish community in Dora is
evidenced by an occurrence of the time of King Agrippa I.:
a number of young people once placed a statue of the emperor
in the Jewish synagogue, and it needed energetic intervention
on the part of Petronius the governor, in a letter addressed to
the authorities of Dora (Δωριτῶν τοῖς πρώτοις), to secure to
the Jews that free exercise of their religion, which had been
pledged to them (*Antt.* xix. 6. 3). In the later imperial period,
Dora seems to have fallen into decay.[145] Christian bishops
of Dora are however mentioned down to the 7th century.[146]

11. *Ptolemais*, Πτολεμαΐς.[147] The original name of the
town was Akko, עַכּוֹ (Richter 1. 31), or, as it reads in Greek,
Ἄκη. By this name it was already known to the Greeks
in pre-Hellenistic times.[148] It was here that in the year

[144] See especially Mionnet and De Saulcy, as above.

[145] Hieronymus, *Onomast.*, ed. Lagarde, p. 115: Dora . . . nunc deserta.
*Ibid.* p. 142: Dor autem est oppidum jam desertum. The same, *Peregrinatio Paulae* (in Tobler, *Palaestinae descriptiones*, 1869, p. 13): ruinas Dor,
urbis quondam potentissimae.

[146] Le Quien, *Oriens christianus*, iii. 574–579.

[147] For a description of the situation, see Joseph. *Bell. Jud.* ii. 10. 2.
Compare in general, Reland, pp. 534–542. Pauly, *Real-Enc.* vi. 1. 243.
Winer, *s.v.* "Acco." Raumer, p. 119 sq. Ritter, xvi. 725–739. Robinson,
*Recent Scriptural Researches in Palestine*, iii. 89–101. Sepp, *Jerusalem*, ii.
513 sqq. Guérin, *Galilée*, i. 502–525. Bädeker-Socin, *Paläst.* 1st ed. p.
369 sqq. (with plan of the present Akka). *The Survey of Western Palestine*,
*Memoirs* by Conder and Kitchener, i. 145, 160–167, also sheet iii. of the
English chart. Ebers and Guthe, *Palästina*, vol. ii. p. 450.

[148] Scylax in *Geogr. gr. min.*, ed. Müller, i. 79. Isaeus, *Orat.* iv. 7.
Demosthenes, *Orat.* 52 *contra Callippum*, § 24 (where indeed the word Ἄκην
is first restored in Dindorf's edit. after the gloss in Harpocration, *Lex. s.v.*
Ἄκη, the earlier edition having Θραικην). Diodor. xv. 41, xix. 93.
Polyaen. iii. 9. 56. Cornel. Nepos, xiv. Datames, c. 5. Comp. Strabo, xvi.
p. 758. Plinius, *H. N.* v. 19. 75. Charax in Steph. Byz. *s.v.* Δῶρος.
Claudius Jolaus in Steph. Byz. *s.v.* Ἄκη. Steph. Byz. *ibid.* and *s.v.*
Πτολεμαΐς. The Lexicographers, *Etymolog. magn.*, Harpocration, Suidas
(see the passages in Reland, p. 536 sq.; also Kuhn, ii. 331). A coin of
Ακη in Mionnet, v. 473; De Saulcy, p. 154, pl. viii. n. 2; some others in

374 B.C. the army of Artaxerxes Mnemnon assembled for the campaign against Egypt.[149] Ake must have been an important town in the time of Alexander the Great. For among the coins of Alexander stamped in Phoenicia those of Ake especially are very numerous. They have the name of Alexander in Greek, that of the town in Phoenician characters (Ἀλεξάνδρου, עך, sometimes עכא), and the year of an era beginning with Alexander the Great. As elsewhere so too in Ake these coins were still issued long after the death of Alexander.[150] Ake was levelled to the ground in the year 312 by Ptolemy Lagos, when he again evacuated before Antigonus the district of Coelesyria, which he had just conquered.[151] It probably received from Ptolemy II. the

Reichardt, *Numismatic Chronicle*, 1862, p. 108; 1864, p. 187. *Wiener Numismat. Monatshefte*, published by Egger, vol. ii. 1866, p. 3. On the ancient history of Ake, comp. especially the fragment from Menander in Joseph. *Antt.* ix. 14. 2 (Ake revolts from Tyre in the time of Shalmanezar, and goes over to Shalmanezar).

[149] Diod. xv. 41. This is referred to also by Polyaen. iii. 9. 56; Cornel. Nep. xiv. 5; comp. Strabo, xvi. p. 758: Εἶθ᾽ ἡ Πτολεμαΐς ἐστι μεγάλη πόλις ἣν ῎Ακην ὠνόμαζον, πρότερον ᾗ ἐχρῶντο ὁρμητηρίῳ πρὸς τὴν Αἴγυπτον οἱ Πέρσαι.

[150] See Eckhel, iii. 408 sq. ; Mionnet, i. 520 sq. ; also *Recueil des planches*, pl. xxi. n. 1–10 ; *Suppl.* iii. 197 sq. and pl. ii. n. 1–6. Gesenius, *Scripturae linguaeque Phoeniciae monumenta*, p. 269 sq. L. Müller, *Numismatique d'Alexandre le Grand* (1855), p. 303 ; also *planches*, n. 1424–1463. Numerous copies of these coins (gold staters of Alexander, especially those of the years 23 and 24) have become known by means of a large discovery of coins at Sidon in the year 1863. See W(eckbecker) in the *Wiener Numismatischen Monatsheften*, pub. by Egger, vol. i. 1865, pp. 5–11. Waddington in the *Revue Numismatique*, 1865, pp. 3-25. Droysen, *Geschichte des Hellenismus* (2nd ed.), i. 1. 302–304. The same, *Monatsber. der Berliner Akademie*, 1877, p. 40 sqq. Weckbecker in Egger's *Wiener Numismat. Monatsheften*, i. 98, 99, tells of tetradrachmas of Ake of Alexander the Great with the years 16, 22, 31, 32, which " were brought to market in Beirut by an Armenian of Mossul at about the same time (1862–1863)." A collection of the whole material may be expected in the *Corp. Inscr. Semiticarum*. On the fact that coins were issued with the name of Alexander after his death, see L. Müller, *Numismatique d'Alexandre le Grand*, pp. 50–90. The numbers of the years on the coins of Ake are 5–46. Since the year 334 or 333 must be accepted as the starting-point, these coins were issued not only till 306, when the Diadochoi assumed the royal title, but also till about two decades afterwards. See especially, Müller, pp. 80–83.

[151] Diodor. xix. 93. Comp. above, note 52 (Gaza) and 109 (Joppa).

name of Πτολεμαΐς, which was henceforth the prevailing
one.[152]   Still its original name Akko was uninterruptedly
maintained beside the Greek one, which it subsequently supplanted.[153]   In the Seleucid period also Ptolemais figures as
one of the most important cities of the Phoenician-Philistine
coast.   The conquest of this region by Antiochus the Great
in the year 219 was much facilitated by the surrender to him
of the towns of Tyre and Ptolemais by the Phoenician general
Theodotus.[154]   Antiochus wintered in Ptolemais in 218/219.[155]
The Seleucidae after their definitive occupation of Phoenicia
specially favoured Ptolemais.   On coins, especially those of
the times of Antiochus IV. and VIII., the inhabitants are
called Ἀντιοχεῖς οἱ ἐν Πτολεμαΐδι, sometimes with the addition ἱερὰ ἄσυλος, sometimes ἱερὰ αὐτόνομος.   The bestowal of
the title " Antiochians," and with it perhaps certain privileges,
is to be regarded as a mark of favour, which was aspired after
by many other towns, e.g. Jerusalem, during the predominance
of the Hellenistic party.[156]   Seleucid coins of Antiochus V.,

---

[152] The founding and naming of the town is expressly referred to Ptolemy
in *Pseudo-Aristeas* (ed. Moritz Schmidt in Merx' *Archiv*, vol. i. p. 274):
Πτολεμαΐδα τὴν ὑπὸ τοῦ βασιλέως ἐκτισμένην.   This is also probable in itself.
Ptolemy II. was the first of the Ptolemies, who continued in possession of
Phoenicia and Coelesyria.   That he there undertook the founding of towns
is proved by the example of Philadelphia (see below).   Already in 219–217
Ptolemais is mentioned under this name in Polybius, without his pointing
out that it was then not as yet known by this name (Polyb. v. 61–62. 71).
Comp. also Droysen, iii. 2. 305.

[153] The name עכו occurs especially in Rabbinic literature, see Mishna,
*Nedarim* iii. 6; *Gittin* i. 2, vii. 7; *Aboda sara* iii. 4; *Ohaloth* xviii. 9.   The
passages of the Tosefta in the Index to Zuckermandel's ed. (1882).   Neubauer, *Géographie du Talmud*, p. 231 sq.   To this very day the town is
called Akka (Acre).

[154] Polyb. v. 61–62.   Comp. Stark, *Gaza*, p. 375 sqq.     [155] Polyb. v. 71.

[156] On the coins in question, see Eckhel, iii. 305 sq.   Mionnet, v. 37 sq., 88,
216–218.   Gardner, *Catalogue of the Greek Coins in the British Museum*,
*Seleucid Kings*, p. 41.   Even the circumstance that ἱερὰ ἄσυλος appears as
an apposition to Ἀντιοχεῖς (Ἀντιοχέων τῶν ἐν Πτολεμαΐδι ἱερᾶς ἀσύλου,
and similarly on the coins of Hippus, see below, No. 13), proves that the town
of Ptolemais and its citizens collectively, not a colony of Antiochian
merchants in Ptolemais, is intended (the latter is the view of Eckhel and
Kuhn, i. 22 ; see, on the other hand, Stark, p. 449 ; Droysen, iii. 2. 305).

Demetrius I., Alexander Balas, and Trypho, minted at
Ptolemais, are in existence.[157] The town was used as a
residence by the kings during their temporary abode in these
regions (1 Macc. x. 56–60, xi. 22, 24). It always showed
itself hostile to the Jews. Even at the beginning of the
Maccabaean rising, it was especially the towns of Ptolemais,
Tyre and Sidon, which fought against the Jews, who had
revolted from Syrian sovereignty (1 Macc. v 15 sqq.). Jonathan
was here treacherously taken prisoner by Trypho (1 Macc. xii.
45 sqq.). After the accession of Alexander Jannaeus, B.C.
104, when the Seleucidae had already lost all authority in the
southern parts of their dominions, three neighbouring powers
contended for the possession of Ptolemais. At first Alexander
Jannaeus entertained the purpose of conquering it, but was
prevented from carrying out his design by Ptolemy Lathurus,
the ruler of Cyprus, who himself took possession of the town
by force (Joseph. *Antt.* xiii. 12. 2–6). He was however soon
deprived of it by his mother Cleopatra, queen of Egypt (*Antt.*
xiii. 13. 1–2). Ptolemais seems never again to have come
under the authority of the Selucidae, nay even the still more
northward towns of Tyre and Sidon had meantime made
themselves independent. On the contrary, we still find there,
about 70 B.C., an Egyptian princess, Selene, daughter of this
Cleopatra, and widow of Antiochus Grypus, to whom she had
been given in marriage by her mother, when the latter entered
into alliance with him against Antiochus Kyzikenos, who
ruled in Coelesyria.[158] At the instance of this Selene
Ptolemais closed its gates against Tigranes, king of Armenia,
the conqueror of the Seleucid kingdom; was thereupon

---

The title Antiochians was also aspired after by the Hellenistic party in
Jerusalem; see 2 Macc. iv. 9, and Grimm (the passage should be translated,
" and to enroll the inhabitants of Jerusalem as Antiochians," or " to receive
the inhabitants of Jerusalem into the list of Antiochians "). Whether, and
what, privileges were combined therewith can hardly be ascertained.

[157] Gardner, *Catalogue of Greek Coins*, etc., pp. 44, 47, 52. A coin of
Trypho is given by De Saulcy, *Mélanges de Numism.* vol. ii. 1877, p. 82.

[158] Justin. *Hist.* xxxix. 4. 4.

conquered by Tigranes, but again liberated when Tigranes found himself obliged to retreat by reason of the attacks of the Romans upon his own kingdom (Joseph. *Antt.* xiii. 16. 4). Ptolemais seems to have experienced special favour from Caesar, when in the year 47 he was over the affairs of Syria. For there are in existence some of its coins of the imperial period with an era reaching back to Caesar.[159] Probably the coins with the legend Πτολεμαι. ἱερας καὶ ἀσυλον (or the like) belong also to this time (shortly after Caesar).[160] The Emperor Claudius settled a colony of veterans in Ptolemais. Hence the town was henceforth called *colonia Ptolemais*, though it did not possess the actual privileges of a colony.[161] At the breaking out of the Jewish war, the Jews in Ptolemais, 2000 in number, were slaughtered by the inhabitants (*Bell. Jud.* ii. 18. 5). The district of Ptolemais is mentioned by Josephus as the western boundary of Galilee (*Bell. Jud.* iii. 3. 1; comp. *Vita*, 24). The formula: Πτολεμαΐδα καὶ τὴν προσκυροῦσαν αὐτῇ, *scil.* χώραν (1 Macc. x. 39), is characteristic.

Next to the great maritime towns, the towns of the so-called *Decapolis* belong to the class of independent Hellenistic communities. The organization alluded to in this word was probably the work of Pompey. For we first meet with the term (ἡ Δεκάπολις) during the Roman period;[162] and most

---

[159] See Eckhel, iii. 425. De Saulcy, pp. 162, 164, 166. Ptolemais was not the only town which was favoured by Caesar; comp. Marquardt, i. 397.

[160] See these especially in De Saulcy, 154–156.

[161] Plinius, v. 19, 75: colonia Claudi Caesaris Ptolemais quae quondam Acce; comp. xxxvi. 26. 190. *Digest.* lib. xv. 1. 3 (from Ulpianus): Ptolemaeensium enim colonia, quae inter Phoenicien et Palaestinam sita est, nihil praeter nomen coloniae habet (also Noris, p. 427 sq.). On coins: COL. PTOL., sometimes with the numbers of the vi. ix. x. xi. legions. See in general. Noris, iv. 5. 2 (ed. Lips. pp. 424–430). Eckhel, iii. 423–425. Mionnet, v. 473–481; *Suppl.* viii. 324–331. De Saulcy, pp. 153–169. 405 sq., pl. viii. n. 2–11. The same, *Mélanges de Numismatique*, vol. ii. 1877, pp. 143–146. Zumpt, *Commentat. epigr.* i. 386. Marquardt, i. 428

[162] Matt. iv. 25; Mark v. 20, vii. 31; Plinius, *H. N.* v. 18. 74. Josephus, *Bell. Jud.* iii. 9. 7; *Vita*, 65, 74. Ptolemaeus, v. 15. 22. *Corp. Inscr. Graec.* n. 4501 (inscription of the time of Hadrian). Eusebius, *Onomast.*, ed.

of the towns of Decapolis owe their independent political
existence to Pompey.   These were the Hellenistic towns of
the country east of Jordan, which, having been subjected by
Alexander Jannaeus, were again liberated from Jewish authority by Pompey.   It is probable that they thus formed a kind
of confederacy, which originally consisted of ten towns, and
was therefore called ἡ Δεκάπολις, but retained the name
after the number was enlarged by the accession of other
towns.   For the number did not always remain the same, as
Pliny, our chief authority, remarks, *H. N.* v. 18. 74: Deca-
politana regio a numero oppidorum, in quo non omnes eadem
observant, plurimum tamen Damascum, Philadelphiam, Rha-
phanam, Scythopolim, Gadara, Hippon, Dion, Pellam, Galasam
(read: Gerasam), Canatham.   Besides Pliny, only Ptolemy
v. 15. 22–23 gives an enumeration of the several towns.
It contains all the towns mentioned by Pliny, with the exception of Raphana; and besides these, nine others (situated
chiefly in the north of Palestine in the neighbourhood of
Damascus), so that the number given by him amounts to
eighteen.   Hence we must keep to Pliny for the original
number.   To those named by him, we add only Abila and
Kanata (another town than Kanatha), both which have also
the Pompeian era.   All the towns except Scythopolis lie in
the region east of the Jordan.   The inclusion of Damascus,
lying so far to the north, is striking.   Since however it is
mentioned by both Pliny and Ptolemy, it must be retained.
In any case Decapolis, as such, continued in existence in the
second century after Christ (the time of the geographer
Ptolemy).   Its dissolution took place in the course of the third
century, in consequence of the transference of some of its
most important towns to the province of Arabia (constituted
a province A.D. 105).   The mention of Decapolis by later

Lagarde, p. 251.  Epiphanius, *Haer.* 29. 7; *de mens. et pond.* § 15.  Stephanus
Byz. *s.v.* Γέρασα (the text handed down has here τεσσαρεσκαιδεκαπόλεως,
for which however Meineke rightly reads δεκαπόλεως).  Comp. in general,
Winer, *RWB.*, *s.v.* "Decapolis."  Caspari, *Chronologisch-geographische Einleitung in das Leben Jesu Christi* (1869), pp. 83–90.

authors, as Eusebius, Epiphanius, Steph. Byz., rests therefore only on historical information. The following enumeration is in geographical order from north to south.

12. *Damascus, Δαμασκός*, Hebr. דַּמֶּשֶׂק. From the varied history of this town, we can here bring forward only such particulars as are important with respect to its constitution during the Hellenistic and Roman periods.[163]   The dominion of Alexander the Great over Damascus is evidenced not only by the narratives of authors, but by coins of Alexander issued there.[163a]   In the third century before Christ, Damascus seems to have belonged not, like Phoenicia and Palestine, to the Ptolemies, but to the Seleucidae.   It is true, that when Ptolemy II. seized Phoenicia and Palestine, B.C. 280, he must also have taken possession of Damascus.   It was however reconquered by Antiochus I. (280–262).[164]   At the great invasion of the realm of the Seleucidae by Ptolemy III., B.C. 246, in which all Syria was for some time lost to Seleucus II., Damascus seems to have been not once conquered, but only besieged.   Seleucus relieved it, when in the year 242/241 he again victoriously pressed southwards.[165]   The fact, that Damascus anciently formed part of the Seleucid dominions, is

[163] See in general, Rödiger in Ersch and Gruber's *Encycl.* sect. i. vol. 22, Div. 2, pp. 113–116.   Arnold in Herzog's *Real-Encycl.* 1st ed. iii. 259–262.   Winer, *s.v.*   Nöldeke in Schenkel's *Bibellex. s.v.*   Robinson, *Recent Scriptural Researches*, iii. 442–468.   Ritter, *Erdkunde* xvii. 2. 1332 sqq. Kremer, *Topographie von Damascus* (*Records of the Viennese Academy, phil.- hist. Cl.* vol. v. and vi. 1854–55).   Porter, *Five Years in Damascus*, 2 vols. 1855.   Sepp, *Jerusalem* (2nd ed.), ii. 358–385.   Bädeker-Socin, *Palästina in Bild und Wort*, vol. i. (1883) pp. 389–442 and 504.

[163a] Curtius, iii. 13, iv. 1.   Arrian, ii. 11. 9 sq., 15. 1.   The coins in L. Müller, *Numismatique d'Alexandre le Grand*, p. 287 sq., pl. n. 1338–1346.

[164] Polyaen. iv. 15 ; comp. Droysen, *Gesch. d. Hellenismus*, iii. 1. 256, 274. Stark, *Gaza*, pp. 366, 367.

[165] Euseb. *Chron.*, ed. Schoene, i. 251 (Armenian text according to Peter- mann's translation) : Ptolemaeus autem, qui et Triphon, partes (regiones) Syriorum occupavit : quae vero apud (ad contra) Damaskum et Orthosiam obsessio fiebat, finem accepit (accipiebat) centesimae tricesimae quartae olompiadis anno tertio, quum Seleukus eo descendisset (descenderit). Olymp. 134, 3 = 242/241 B.C.   Comp. Droysen, iii. 1. 390, 393.   Stark adopts, according to Zohrab's translation of the Armenian text, the view of an actual taking of Damascus by Ptolemy.

indirectly confirmed by the circumstance, that Polybius, when fully relating the particulars of the conquest of Phoenicia and Palestine by Antiochus the Great (v. 61–71), mentions indeed the taking of the most important Phoenician and Palestinian towns, but nowhere speaks of Damascus. When in 111 B.C. the Syrian kingdom was, in consequence of the strife between the brothers Antiochus VIII. (Grypos) and Antiochus IX. (Kyzikenos), divided, and Antiochus Kyzikenos established himself in the southern part,[166] Damascus probably became the capital of his small kingdom. At all events it was about 95–85 B.C. repeatedly the capital of a kingdom of Coelesyria separated from the kingdom of Syria, first under Demetrius Eukaerus a son of Antiochus Grypos (Joseph. *Antt.* xiii. 13. 4), then under Antiochus XII. also a son of Grypos (*Antt.* xiii. 15. 1). Antiochus XII. fell in battle against the Arabian king Aretas ; and Damascus continued henceforth under his authority (*Antt.* xiv. 15. 1, 2 ; *Bell. Jud.* i. 4. 7, 8). When Pompey penetrated into Asia, Damascus was first of all occupied by his legates (*Antt.* xiv. 2. 3 ; *Bell. Jud.* i. 6. 2). Apparently it was not restored to the Arabian king, but united to the province of Syria.[167] In the time of Cassius (44–42 B.C.) we find a Roman commander, Fabius, in Damascus (*Antt.* xiv. 11. 7, 12. 1 ; *Bell. Jud.* i. 12. 1, 2). Already in the times of Augustus and Tiberius there were Roman imperial coins of Damascus, but at the same time, as in the case of Ascalon, autonomic ones also. The Seleucid era is used on both, and this continued to be the prevailing one at Damascus.[168] There

---

[166] Euseb. *Chron.*, ed. Schoene, i. 260.

[167] Hieronymus, *Comment. in Jesaj.* c. 17 (*Opp.* ed. Vallarsi, iv. 194) : Alii aestimant de Romana captivitate praedici, quoniam et Judaeorum captus est populus, et Damascus, cui imperabat Areta, similem sustinuit servitutem. I cannot think Marquardt (i. 405) correct in adopting the notion, that the Arabian kings kept possession of Damascus in exchange for the payment of a tribute till A.D. 106.

[168] See on the coins in general, Noris ii. 2. 2 (ed. Lips. pp. 87–93). Eckhel, iii. 329–334. Mionnet, v. 283–297; *Suppl.* viii. 193–206. De Saulcy, pp. 30–56, 404, pl. ii. n. 1–10. Kremer, *Die Münzsammlung des Stifts St. Florian* (1871), pp. 167–170, table vi. n. 7, 8.

are no coins of the times of Caligula and Claudius, though there are coins from Nero onwards. With this circumstance must be combined the fact, that Damascus, when St. Paul fled from it (probably in the time of Caligula), was under a viceroy (ἐθνάρχης) of the Arabian king Aretas (2 Cor. xi. 32). Hence it then belonged temporarily to the Arabian king, whether he seized it by violence or obtained it by imperial favour. That there was a Jewish community in Damascus is already evident from the New Testament (Acts ix. 2 ; 2 Cor. xi. 32). That it was numerous may be inferred from the number of Jews slain at Damascus at the breaking out of the great war. This amounted to 10,000, or according to another statement 18,000 (the former, *Bell. Jud.* ii. 20. 2 ; the latter, *Bell. Jud.* vii. 8. 7). After Hadrian the town bore the title μητρόπολις, after Alexander Severus it was a colony (not first after Philip the Arabian, as even Eckhel supposes), both facts being witnessed to by the coins.[169] We are informed (*Antt.* xviii. 6. 3) of a dispute concerning boundaries between the Damascenes and Sidonians in the time of Tiberius, which is chiefly of interest as showing, how extensive the district pertaining to this town must have been, since it bordered upon that of Sidon.

13. *Hippus,* ῞Ιππος, is properly the name of a mountain or hill, on which stood the town of the same name.[170] Identical with it is probably the Hebrew Susitha (סוסיתא), which is frequently mentioned in Rabbinical authorities as a Gentile town of Palestine,[171] and Susije,[171a] which frequently occurs in Arabic geographers. The following statements serve to

---

[169] On the title μητρόπολις, see Eckhel, iii. 331. Kuhn, ii. 192. Marquardt, i. 430.

[170] Ptolemaeus, v. 15. 8.

[171] In the Tosefta, *Ohaloth* xviii. 4 (ed. Zuckermandel, p. 616, 23), Susitha is mentioned together with Ascalon as an example of a heathen town " girt about " by the land of Israel. It is elsewhere frequently named in conjunction with Tiberias. Comp. Lightfoot, *Centuria chronographica Matthaeo praemissa*, c. 77 ; *decas Marco praemissa*, c. 5. 1 (*Opp.* ii. 226, 413). Neubauer, *Géographie du Talmud*, pp. 238–240.

[171a] Clermont-Ganneau, *Où était Hippos de la Décapole?* (*Revue archéo-*

determine the locality. According to Pliny, it stood on the
eastern shore of the Lake of Gennesareth;[172] according to
Josephus, only 30 stadia from Tiberias;[173] according to Eusebius and Jerome, near a certain city and castle of Afeka.[174]
According to these data the ruins of el-Hösn on a hill on the
eastern shore of the Lake of Gennesareth are probably to be
regarded as marking the position of the ancient Hippus; a
village of the name of Fik, which must be identical with
the ancient Afeka, is three-quarters of a league off.[175] The
supposed identity of the name Hippos with el-Hösn (the
horse) is certainly questionable.[175a] But little is known of the
history of Hippus.[176] It received its freedom from Pompey
(Joseph. *Antt.* xiv. 4. 4; *Bell. Jud.* i. 7. 7). It was bestowed
by Augustus upon Herod (*Antt.* xv. 7. 3; *Bell. Jud.* i. 20. 3),
after whose death it was again separated from the Jewish
region (*Antt.* xvii. 11. 4; *Bell. Jud.* ii. 6. 3). On this occasion
it is expressly called a Greek city (*l.c.*). At the outbreak of
the Jewish revolt the district of Hippus as well as that of
Gadara was devastated by the Jews under the leadership of

*logique,* nouvelle série, vol. xxix. 1875, pp. 362–369). Furrer, *Zeitschr.
d. deutschen Palästina-Vereins,* ii. 74.

[172] Plinius, v. 15. 71: in lacum . . . Genesaram . . . amoenis circum-
saeptum oppidis, ab oriente Juliade et Hippo.

[173] Joseph. *Vita,* 65. The statements of Josephus are here indeed very
systematic, Hippus 30, Gadara 60, Scythopolis 120 stadia from Tiberias.
He is here following the tendency of stating distances as *low* as possible.
His figures must therefore be anything but strictly taken. Besides it is
clear also from Josephus, that the district of Hippus lay by the lake,
opposite Tarichea (*Vita,* 31) in the neighbourhood of Gadara (*Vita,* 9).

[174] Euseb. *Onomast.,* ed. Lag. p. 219. Hieron. *ibid.* p. 91.

[175] The situations of Fik and el-Hösn are already described by Burckhardt,
*Reisen in Syrien,* i. 438. That it is here that the ancient Hippus must be
sought is the view also of Raumer, p. 250. Ritter, xv. 1. 352 sq. Furrer,
*Zeitschr. d. deutschen Pal.-Vereins,* ii. 73 sq. Others identify el-Hösn with
Gamala, and find Hippus either in Fik (so Merrill, *East of the Jordan,*
1881, pp. 163–169) or in Sumra, lying far more to the south (so Guérin,
*Galilée,* i. 310–312).

[175a] Clermont-Ganneau (as above, p. 364) explains Hösn as the common
pronunciation of Hisn (fortress). The name occurs elsewhere also as an
Arabic local name in modern Palestine.

[176] Comp. besides the literature in note 175, Reland, p. 821 sq.

Justus of Tiberias (*Bell. Jud.* ii. 18. 1 ; *Vita,* 9). The inhabitants of Hippus retaliated by slaying or casting into prison all the Jews dwelling in the city (*Bell. Jud.* ii. 18. 5). In Christian times Hippus was the see of a bishop.[177] The name of the town has as yet been only once shown to exist upon coins (viz. on one of Nero's time).[177a] But coins with the legend Ἀντιοχέων τῶν πρὸς Ἵπ(πον). τῆς ἱερ(ᾶς) κ(αὶ) ἀσύλου have been rightly referred by numismatists to Hippus. They have as might be expected the Pompeian era, and on most is the image of a horse.[178]—The district of Hippus is mentioned *Vita,* 9, 31; *Bell. Jud.* iii. 3. 1. *Vita,* 9: ἐμπίπρησι τάς τε Γαδαρηνῶν καὶ Ἱππηνῶν κώμας, αἳ δὴ μεθόριοι τῆς Τιβεριάδος καὶ τῆς τῶν Σκυθοπολιτῶν γῆς ἐτύγχανον κείμεναι, is most instructive as showing, that the districts of these four towns were so extensive as to form a connected whole.

14. *Gadara,* Γαδαρά. The position of Gadara on the site of the present ruins of Om-Keis (Mkês), to the south-east of the Lake of Gennesareth, was recognised by Seetzen so early as 1806, and may now be regarded as settled.[179] The main point of connection is furnished by the warm springs for which Gadara was famous, and which are still found in this region.[180] They lie on the northern bank of the Scheriat

---

[177] Epiphan. *Haer.* 73, 26. Le Quien, *Oriens christianus,* iii. 710 sq. Hierocles, *Synecd.,* ed. Parthey, p. 44. The *Notit. episcopat.,* the same, p. 144.

[177a] The coin is given by Muret, *Revue Numismatique,* troisième série, vol. i. 1883, p. 67, and pl. ii. n. 9. It has on one side a head of Nero with the superscription Αυτ. Καισ., on the other a horse with the superscription Ιππηνων and the date ΑΛΡ (131), the latter according to the Pompeian era.

[178] Noris, iii. 9. 5 (ed. Lips. pp. 331–334). Eckhel, iii. 346 sq. Mionnet, v. 319 sq. ; *Suppl.* viii. 224. De Saulcy, pp. 344–347, pl. xix. n. 10–15.

[179] Seetzen, *Reisen durch Syrien* (ed. by Kruse, 4 vols. 1854–59), i. 368 sqq., iv. 188 sqq. Burckhardt, *Reisen in Syrien,* i. 426 sqq., 434 sqq., 537 sq. (who indeed takes Om-Keis for Gamala, but is corrected by his editor Gesenius). Buckingham, *Travels in Palestine,* 1821, pp. 414–440 (like Burckhardt). Winer, *s.v.* "Gadara." Raumer, p. 248 sq. Ritter, xv. 1. 371–384, xv. 2. 1052 sq. Sepp, *Jerusalem,* ii. 211–216. Bädeker-Socin, p. 415 sq. Guérin, *Galilée,* i. 299–308. Merrill, *East of the Jordan* (1881), pp. 145–158. For the history, Reland, pp. 773–778. Kuhn, ii. 365 sq., 371.

[180] Comp. on the situation, Euseb. *Onomast.* p. 248: Γάδαρα, πόλις ὑπὲρ

el-Mandur; on the southern bank, at about a league's distance
from the springs, are found on the lofty ridge of the hill the
ruins of the town.   Hence the Scheriat el-Mandur is identical
with the Hieromices, which according to Pliny flowed past
the town.[181]   Gadara was in the time of Antiochus the Great
already an important fortress.   It was conquered by Antiochus both at his first invasion (B.C. 218),[182] and when he
finally took possession of Palestine after his victory at
Panias, B.C. 198.[183]   It was taken by Alexander Jannaeus
after a ten months' siege (*Antt.* xiii. 13. 3 ; *Bell. Jud.* i. 4. 2).
It consequently belonged under him and his successors
to the Jewish region (*Antt.* xiii. 15. 4), but was separated
from it by Pompey (*Antt.* xiv. 4. 4; *Bell. Jud.* i. 7. 7).
On this occasion Pompey, out of regard for his freedman
Demetrius of Gadara, rebuilt the city, which had been
destroyed by the Jews (Alexander Jannaeus?).   Hence upon
the numerous coins of the town extending from Augustus to
Gordian, the Pompeian era is used.   It begins in the year

τὸν Ἰορδάνην, ἀντικρὺ Σκυθοπόλεως καὶ Τιβεριάδος πρὸς ἀνατολὰς ἐν τῷ ὄρει,
οὗ πρὸς ταῖς ὑπωρείαις τὰ τῶν θερμῶν ὑδάτων λουτρὰ παράκειται.
*Ibid.* p. 219 : Αἰμάθ . . . κώμη πλησίον Γαδάρων, ἥ ἐστιν Ἐμμαθᾶ, ἔνθα τὰ
τῶν θερμῶν ὑδάτων θερμὰ λουτρά.   On the baths, see also especially the passages
from Epiphanius, Antoninus Martyr and Eunapius (who declares them to
have been the most important after those of Baiae), in Reland, p. 775.   Also
Origenes in *Joann.* vol. vi. c. 24 (ed. Lommatzsch, i. 239): Γάδαρα γὰρ
πόλις μέν ἐστι τῆς Ἰουδαίας, περὶ ἣν τὰ διαβόητα θερμὰ τυγχάνει.   The
place where the springs are situated occurs in the Talmud under the name
חמתה.  See the passages in Levy, *Neuhebr. Wörterbuch,* ii. 69 sq.   Lightfoot,
*Centuria Matthaeo praemissa,* c. 74 (Opp. ii. 224 sq.).   Hamburger, *Real-
Encyclop. für Bibel und Talmud,* Div. ii. art. "Heilbäder."   Grätz,
*Monatschr. für Gesch. und Wissensch. des Judenth.* 1880, pp. 487–495.
[181] Plinius, v. 18. 74: Gadara Hieromice praefluente.   The form
Hieromax, which still appears in handbooks, is derived from the incorrect
reading Hieromace.   That Hieromices must be adopted as the nominative
is proved by the occurrence elsewhere of the forms Hieromicas (*Tab.
Peuting.*) and Jeromisus (*Geogr. Ravennas,* ed. Pinder et Parthey, p. 85).
The native name is Jarmuk, יַרְמוּךְ, Mishna, *Para* viii. 10, and Arabic
geographers (see Arnold in Herzog's *Real-Encycl.* 1st ed. vii. 10, xi. 20).
[182] Polyb. v. 71.   Stark, *Gaza,* p. 381.   Polybius says of Gadara on this
occasion : ἃ δοκεῖ τῶν κατ' ἐκείνους τοὺς τόπους ὀχυρότητι διαφέρειν.
[183] Polyb. xvi. 39 = Joseph. *Antt.* xii. 3. 3.   Stark, p. 403.

690 A.U.C., so that 1 *aer. Gadar.* = 64/63 B.C.[184] The
memory of its rebuilding by Pompey is also perpetuated upon
coins from Antoninus Pius to Gordianus by the legend
Πομπηιέων Γαδαρέων.[185] The notion that Gadara was the
seat of one of the five Jewish Sanhedrin established by
Gabinius is incorrect (see above, § 13). In the year 30 B.C.,
Gadara was bestowed upon Herod by Augustus (*Antt.* xv. 7.
3; *Bell. Jud.* i. 20. 3). The town was however very discon-
tented with his government. So early as the year 23–31
B.C., when M. Agrippa was staying at Mytilene, certain
Gadarenes there brought complaint against Herod (*Antt.* xv.
10. 2). Complaints were repeated when Augustus in the
year 20 personally visited Syria (*Antt.* xv. 10. 3). In both
cases those who made them were dismissed. It is quite in
accordance with this, that we find Gadarene coins of just the
year 20 B.C. (44 *aer. Gadar.*) with the image of Augustus and
the inscription Σεβαστός—Herod being desirous, by stamping
such coins at Gadara, to show his gratitude to the emperor.[186]
After the death of Herod, Gadara regained its independence
under Roman supremacy (*Antt.* xvii. 11. 4; *Bell. Jud.* ii. 6.
3). At the beginning of the Jewish revolt the district of
Gadara, like that of the neighbouring Hippus, was devastated
by the Jews under the leadership of Justus of Tiberias (*Bell.
Jud.* ii. 18. 1; *Vita,* 9). The Gadarenes, like their neigh-
bours of Hippus, avenged themselves by slaying or imprison-
ing the Jews dwelling in their town (*Bell. Jud.* ii. 18. 5).
Such of the inhabitants however as were friendly to the
Romans, not feeling themselves secure against the turbulent

[184] On the era and the coins, see Noris, iii. 9. 1 (ed. Lips. pp. 297–308).
Eckhel, iii. 348–350. Mionnet, v. 323–328; *Suppl.* viii. 227–230. De
Saulcy, pp. 294–303, pl. 15. Kenner, *Die Münzesammlung des Stifts St.
Florian* (1871), p. 171 sq., Taf. vi. n. 10.

[185] As the legend is generally abbreviated (Πο. or Πομπ. Γαδαρεων),
the reading is not quite certain. The older numismatics give for a coin of
Caracalla the reading Πομπηιτεων Γαδαρεων; De Saulcy, on the contrary (p.
302, and pl. xv. n. 9), gives Πομπηιεων Γαδαρεων, which is certainly correct.

[186] Comp. De Saulcy, p. 295. The coins in Mionnet, v. 323; *Suppl.*
viii. 227.

elements in their own city, requested and received a Roman garrison from Vespasian in the later period of the war (*Bell. Jud.* iv. 7. 3, 4).[187]   In what sense Josephus can designate Gadara as the μητρόπολις τῆς Περαίας (*Bell. Jud.* iv. 7. 3) cannot be further ascertained.[188]   On coins, especially of the time of the Antonines, it is called ἱε(ρὰ) ἄσ(υλος) α(ὐτόνομος) γ(. . .?) Κοί(λης) Συρ(ίας).[189]   According to an inscription discovered by Renan, it was during the later imperial period a Roman colony.[190]   The information of Stephanus Byz. (*s.v.*), that it was also called 'Αντιόχεια and Σελεύκεια, stands quite alone, and certainly refers only to temporary official designations, not to such as had come into common use.   There is abundant evidence that it was already in pre-Christian times a flourishing Hellenistic town.   Josephus calls it at the death of Herod a πόλις 'Ελληνίς (*Antt.* xvii. 11. 4; *Bell. Jud.* ii. 6. 3); Strabo mentions as renowned natives of Gadara, Philodemus the Epicurean, the poet Meleager, and Menippus the Cynic, who on account of his witty style was often called ὁ σπουδογέλοιος, and Theodorus the orator.[191]   Of later times must also be added Oenomaus, the cynic and the orator

---

[187] From Joseph. *Vita*, 15, it might appear as though Josephus also, as ruler of Galilee, had once taken possession of Gadara by force.   But the reading there should certainly be Γαβαρεῖς, instead of Γαδαρεῖς; comp. *Vita*, 25, 45, 47.   In *Bell. Jud.* iii. 7. 1, also Γαβαρέων must be read for Γαδαρέων. Lastly, in *Antt.* xiii. 13. 5, either the reading is corrupt or another Gadara is meant.

[188] Eckhel (iii. 349) supposes that it was the place of assembly of some association for the celebration of periodical games, in which sense the word μητρόπολις is certainly often used.

[189] See in De Saulcy especially the coins of Commodus, n. 2 (p. 301), and Elagabalus, n. 5 (p. 303).   The predicate ἱερα is also found in an epigram of Meleager, where he says of himself : ὅν θεόπαις ἤνδρωσε Τύρος, Γαδάρων θ' ἱερὰ χθών (*Anthologia palatina*, vii. 419, ed. Jacobs, vol. i. p. 431).   Gadara is also designated by Steph. Byz. as πόλις Κοίλης Συρίας.

[190] Renan, *Mission de Phénicie*, p. 191=*Corp. Inscr. Lat.* vol. iii. n. 181 (epitaph at Byblus) : col(onia) Valen(tia) Gadara.

[191] Strabo, xvi. p. 759.   Strabo indeed frequently confuses our Gadara with Gadaza=Gadara.   That the latter cannot be regarded as the native place of these men is self-evident.   The individuals in question are all known to us elsewhere (see above, p. 29).   The orator Theodorus was the tutor of the Emperor Tiberius (Sueton. *Tiber.* 57), and afterwards lived at Rhodes,

Apsines.[192] Meleager says of himself that he came of "an *Attic* race, dwelling in Assyrian Gadara." [193] The district of Gadara formed the eastern boundary of Galilee (*Bell. Jud.* iii. 3. 1). On its extent, comp. *Vita*, 9, and above, p. 100. That it reached to the Lake of Gennesareth may not only be inferred from Matt. viii. 28 (where the reading is uncertain), but also from the coins, on which a ship is often portrayed, nay once (on a coin of Marc. Aurel.) a ναυμα(χία) mentioned.[194]

15. *Abila,* Ἄβιλα. The local name Abel (אָבֵל) or Abila is very frequent in Palestine. Eusebius knows of three places of this name celebrated for the cultivation of the vine: (1) A village in South Peraea, 6 *mil. pass.* from Philadelphia; (2) A πόλις ἐπίσημος, 12 *mil. pass.* from Gadara; (3) A place between Damascus and Paneas.[195] Of these the second town on the east of Gadara is the one with which we are here concerned. Its situation, on the south bank of the Scheriat el-Mandur, was discovered, as well as that of Gadara, by Seetzen.[196] Pliny does not mention this Abila among the cities of Decapolis. Its inclusion among them is however evidenced by an inscription of the time of Hadrian.[197] An

where Tiberius frequently visited him during his exile (Pauly's *Enc.* vi. 2, 1819).

[192] Reland, p. 775.

[193] *Anthologia palatina*, vii. 417, ed. Jacobs, vol. i. p. 430 (ed. Dübner, i. 352, where however, without reason, Γαδάροις is changed into Γάδαρα):

Νᾶσος ἐμὰ θρέπτειρα Τύρος· πάτρα δέ με τεκνοῖ
Ἀτθὶς ἐν Ἀσσυρίοις ναιομένα Γαδάροις.

[194] On the latter, comp. especially Eckhel, iii. 348 sq. A ship is seen in the illustrations in De Saulcy, pl. xv. n. 9–11.

[195] Euseb. *Onomast.*, ed. Legarde, p. 225: Ἄβελ ἀμπέλων. ἔνθα ἐπολέμησεν Ἰεφθάε. γῆς υἱῶν Ἀμμών, ἥ ἐστιν εἰς ἔτι νῦν κώμη ἀμπελοφόρος Ἄβελ ἀπὸ ϛ΄ σημείων Φιλαδελφίας. καὶ ἄλλη πόλις ἐπίσημος Ἀβελὰ οἰνοφόρος καλουμένη, διεστῶσα Γαδάρων σημείοις ιβ΄ πρὸς ἀνατολάς. καὶ τρίτη τις αὐτὴ Ἀβελὰ τῆς Φοινίκης μεταξὺ Δαμασκοῦ καὶ Πανεάδος.

[196] Seetzen, *Reisen durch Syrien* (edited by Kruse), i. 371, iv. 190 sq. Comp. also Burckhardt, *Reisen in Syrien*, i. 425, 537. Raumer, p. 241. Ritter, xv. 2. 1058–1060. On the history, Reland, p. 525 sq. Kuhn, ii. 335, 371 sq.

[197] *Corp. Inscr. Graec.* n. 4501 (inscription of Palmyra of the year 445 aer. Sel. = 133–134 A.D.): Ἀγαθάγγελος Ἀβιληνὸς τῆς Δεκαπόλεος.

ʺΑβιδα by which our ʺΑβιλα is certainly intended is also placed by Ptolemy among the cities of Decapolis.[198] It first appears in history in the time of Antiochus the Great, who occupied Abila as well as its neighbour Gadara at both his first and his second conquest of Palestine, 219 and 198 B.C.[199] On the whole it seems to have frequently shared the lot of Gadara. Like the latter, Abila received its liberty through Pompey. For the coins of Abila with the Pompeian era are rightly ascribed to this town.[200] Its titles also are the same as those of Gadara: ἱ(ερὰ) ἄ(συλος) α(ὐτόνομος) γ( . . . ?) Κοί(λης) Συ(ρίας). The coins show that the town was also called Σελεύκεια, the inhabitants were called Σελευκ(εῖς) ʼΑβιληνοί.[201] In Nero's time Abila was given to Agrippa II., unless the notice of Josephus to that effect rests upon an error.[202] In the sixth century after Christ Christian bishops of Abila, who may with tolerable certainty be referred to our Abila, are mentioned.[203]

16. *Raphana*, not to be confounded with the Syrian ʽΡαφά-

[198] Ptolem. v. 15. 22. The Codex of Vatopedi also has here ʺΑβιδα; see *Géographie de Ptolémée, reproduction photolithogr. du manuscrit grec du monastère de Vatopédi* (Paris 1867), p. lvii. line 4.

[199] Polyb. v. 71 and xvi. 39 = Joseph. *Antt.* xii. 3. 3.

[200] See on these, especially Belley in the *Mémoires de l'Académie des Inscriptions et Belles-Lettres*, ancient series, vol. xxviii. 1761, pp. 557–567. Eckhel, iii. 345 sq. Mionnet, v. 318; *Suppl.* viii. 223 sq. De Saulcy, pp. 308–312, pl. xvi. n. 1–7.

[201] This is now confirmed by a coin of Faustina, jun., given by De Saulcy (p. 310, and pl. xvi. n. 2). The coins formerly known give either the abbreviated Σε. ʼΑβιληνων or (a damaged one of Faustina) . . . λευκ. Αβιλας, the former of which was completed as Σεβαστων, the latter as Λευκαδος, both erroneously, as is now shown.

[202] *Bell. Jud.* ii. 13. 2. In the parallel passage, *Antt.* xx. 8. 2, Josephus says nothing of it; and it is striking that Abila should not (like the other towns there named: Julias-Bethsaida, Tarichea, Tiberias) be connected with the rest of Agrippa's dominions. Besides *Antt.* xii. 3. 3 and *Bell. Jud.* ii. 13. 2 are the only passages in which our Abila is mentioned by Josephus. For in *Antt.* iv. 8. 1, v. 1. 1, *Bell. Jud.* iv. 7. 6, another Abila, near the Jordan, and opposite Jericho, not far from Julias-Livias, and not identical with either of the three places of the same name mentioned by Eusebius, is meant. Again, the well-known Abila Lysaniae is different. Nor is the list by any means thereby exhausted. See Winer, *RWB.*, *s.v.* " Abila."

[203] Le Quien, *Oriens christianus*, iii. 702 sq. Comp. Hierocles, *Synecd.*, ed. Parthey, p. 44. *Notit. episcopat.*, the same, p. 144.

νεια in Cassiotis, is mentioned only by Pliny (v. 18. 74).[204]
The ʿΡαφών however of the first Book of the Maccabees (v. 37
= Joseph. *Antt.* xii. 8. 4), which, according to the context of the
narrative (comp. v. 43) lay in the neighbourhood of Astaroth-
Karnaim, and therefore in Batanaea, is probably identical with
it.   Since Ptolemy has not the name of Raphana among the
towns of Decapolis, it is probable that he mentions the town
by another name; and it is at least possible, though only
possible, that Raphana is, as Quandt supposes, identical with
the *Capitolias* mentioned by Ptolemy (v. 15. 22), and so
frequently elsewhere since the second century after Christ.[205]

17. *Kanata.*   The existence of this town, as distinct from
Kanatha, has but recently been ascertained on the ground of
inscriptions by Waddington.[206]   Upon an inscription at el-Afine
(on the south-western declivity of the Hauran, to the west of

[204] On the Syrian Raphaneia, see Joseph. *Bell. Jud.* vii. 1. 3, 5. 1.   Ptolem.
v. 15. 16.   *Tab. Peuting.* Hierocles, ed. Parthey, p. 61.   Steph. Byz. *s.v.*
Eckhel, iii. 323.   Mionnet, v. 268; *Suppl.* viii. 168.   Pauly's *Encycl. s.v.*
Ritter, xvii. 1. 940 sq.

[205] Quandt, *Judäa und die Nachbarschaft im Jahrh. vor und nach der
Geburt Christi* (1873), p. 40 sq.   Capitolias was (according to *Tab. Peuting.*)
16 *m. p.* from Adraa.   Since then Raphana was in the neighbourhood of
Astaroth-Karnaim, and the latter (according to Euseb. *Onomast.*, ed. Lag.
p. 213) 6 *m. p.* distant from Adraa, Capitolias and Raphana *may* in fact
be identical.   The situation of almost all these places is indeed not yet
certainly determined.   It seems to me incorrect to seek Capitolias, as is
frequently done, to the *south*-east of Gadara.   For, according to the
*Itinerarium Antonini* (ed. Parthey et Pinder, pp. 88, 89), it lay on the direct
route from Gadara to Damascus, and therefore to the *north*-east of the
former.   With this agree also the astronomical definitions of Ptolemy
(north-east of Gadara, under the same geographical latitude as Hippus).
The roadway too given in the *Peutinger Table*, Gadara-Capitolias-Adraa-
Bostra, has therefore not a south-eastern, but a north-eastern direction.
On the whole Raumer is correct, although his more particular determination
of the locality is very problematical.   Compare on *Capitolias* in general,
Noris, iii. 9. 4 (ed. Lips. pp. 323–331).   Eckhel, 328 sq.   Mionnet, v. 281–
283; *Suppl.* viii. 192.   De Saulcy, pp. 304–307, pl. xvi. n. 9.   Reland,
p. 693 sq.   Ritter, xv. 356, 821, 1060.   Raumer, p. 246.   Seetzen, *Reisen*
(edited by Kruse), iv. 185 sqq.   Kuhn, ii. 372.   Le Quien, *Oriens christ.*
iii. 715 sq.

[206] Le Bas et Waddington, *Inscriptions grecques et latines*, vol. iii., descriptions of n. 2296, 2329, and 2412d.   Comp. also Marquardt, *Römische
Staatsverwaltung*, i. 395, note 17.

Hebran) is mentioned an ἀγωγὸς ὑδάτων εἰσφερομένων εἰς
**Κάνατα** built by Cornelius Palma, governor of Syria in the
time of Trajan.[207]   This Kanata cannot be identical with
Kanatha = Kanawat, for the latter, lying higher than el-
Afine, and being itself abundantly supplied with water, an
aqueduct from el-Afine thither is inconceivable.   The situation of Kanata is however also determined by an inscription
discovered by Wetzstein at Kerak (in the plain west-south-west
of Kanawat): Διὶ μεγίστ[ῳ] Κανατηνῶν ὁ [δῆμος].[208]   According to this Kanata is identical with the present Kerak,
to whose former Greek culture other inscriptions also bear
testimony.[209]   The few coins of Kanata, which were by former
numismatists wrongly attributed to the better known Kanatha,
prove at least that Kanata had the Pompeian era, and therefore very probably belonged to Decapolis.[210]   The coins belong
to the times of Claudius and Domitian.[211]   That Kerak was
once a town is confirmed by the mention of a βουλευτής upon
an inscription.[212]   On the other hand, another inscription of
the middle of the third century after Christ calls it a κώμη.[213]
It had thus already lost the rights of a town.   The date
on this inscription is according to the era of the province of Arabia, hence we may conclude, that at the establishment of this province (105 B.C.) it was allotted to it.

[207] Le Bas et Waddington, vol. iii. n. 2296.

[208] Wetzstein, *Ausgewählte griechische und lateinische Inschriften* (*Transactions of the Berlin Academy*, 1863, *philol.-histor. Cl.*), n. 185 = Waddington,
n. 2412d.

[209] Wetzstein, n. 183–186 = Waddington, n. 2412d–2412g.

[210] Belley in the *Mémoires de l'Académie des Inscr. et Belles-Lettres*, ancient
series, vol. xxviii. 568 sqq.   Eckhel, iii. 347.   Mionnet, v. 231 ; *Suppl.* viii.
225.   De Saulcy, p. 339 sq., pl. xxiii. n. 8, 9.   Reichardt in the *Wiener
Numismat. Zeitsch.* 1880, pp. 68–73.   De Saulcy and Reichardt were the
first to distinguish correctly the coins of Kanata and Kanatha.   Among
the older numismaticians are also other mistakes.

[211] Mionnet, *Suppl.* viii. 225, gives a coin of Maximinus, which however
does not belong to Kanata, but to Ascalon (see De Saulcy, p. 208).   De
Saulcy and Reichardt give each a coin of Elagabalus, the reading of which is
however very uncertain.

[212] Wetzstein, n. 184 = Waddington, n. 2412e.

[213] Wetzstein, n. 186 = Waddington, n. 2412f.

18. *Kanatha.* On the western declivity of the Hauran range is the place now called *Kanawat*, whose ruins are among the most important of the country east of the Jordan. Numerous inscriptions, well preserved remains of temples and other public buildings, prove that an important town once stood here; and both ruins and inscriptions point to the first centuries of the Roman imperial period. The ruins have, since Seetzen's first hasty visit, been frequently described.[214] The inscriptions have been most completely collected by Waddington.[215] It is rightly and almost universally admitted, that the Kanatha so often mentioned by ancient authors, and with which the Old Testament קְנָת (Num. xxxii. 42 ; 1 Chron. ii. 23) is probably identical, is to be sought for here.[216] The form of the name fluctuates between Κάναθα and Κάνωθα ; Κεναθηνός also occurs upon an inscription.[217] Apart from the Old Testament passages, the history of Kanatha cannot

---

[214] Seetzen, *Reisen durch Syrien* (edited by Kruse), i. 78 sqq., iv. 40, 51 sqq. Burckhardt, *Reisen in Syrien*, i. 157 sqq., 504 sq. Ritter, *Erdkunde*, xv. 2. 931–939. Porter, *Five Years in Damascus*, 1855, ii. 89–115 (with plan). Bädeker-Socin, *Palästina*, p. 433 sqq. (with plan). Merrill, *East of the Jordan* (1881), pp. 36–42. Views of the ruins in Laborde, *Voyage en Orient*, Paris (1837–1845), livraison 21, 22, 26 ; and in Rey, *Voyage dans le Haouran et aux bords de la mer morte exécuté pendant les années* 1857 et 1858, Paris. Atlas, pl. v.–viii. (pl. vi. plan).

[215] Le Bas et Waddington, *Inscriptions*, vol. iii. n. 2329–2363. Older information in *Corp. Inscr. Graec.* 4612–4615. Wetzstein, *Ausgewählte Inschriften* (*Transactions of the Berlin Academy*, 1863), n. 188–193.

[216] The identity of Kanatha with the present Kanawat is best proved in Porter's *Five Years in Damascus*, ii. 110 sqq. The statements in Eusebius and the *Tab. Peuting.* are especially convincing. Compare also for the history, Reland, pp. 681 sq., 689. Winer, *RWB.*, *s.v.* "Kenath." Raumer, p. 252. Ritter, as above. Kuhn, ii. 385 sq. Waddington's explanations on n. 2329.

[217] The form Kanatha is found in Josephus (*Bell. Jud.* i. 19. 2), Plinius (v. 18. 74), Ptolemaeus (v. 15. 23), Stephanus Byz. (*Lex. s.v.*), Eusebius (*Onomast.*, ed. Lag. p. 269) ; on coins (see the next note), inscriptions (*Corp. Inscr. Graec.* n. 4613: Καναθηνῶν ἡ πόλις; Waddington, n. 2216: Καναθηνὸς βουλευτής ; Renier, *Inscr. de l'Algérie*, n. 1534 and 1535 = *Corp. Inscr. Lat.* vol. viii. n. 2394, 2395: cohors prima Flavia Canathenorum) ; also the *Tabula Peuting.* (*Chanata*). The form Kanotha is found in Hierocles, ed. Parthey, p. 46 (Κανοθά) ; a *Notitia episcopat.*, the same, p. 92 (Κανοθάς) ; the Acts of the Council of Chalcedon in Le Quien, *Oriens christianus*, ii. 867 (gen. Κανώθας) ; an inscription in the *Bullettino dell' Instituto di corrisp. archeol.*

be traced farther back than the time of Pompey; its coins have the Pompeian era,[218] and it is reckoned by both Pliny (v. 18. 74) and Ptolemy (v. 15. 23) among the towns of Decapolis. On the coins of Commodus given by Reichardt the inhabitants are called Γαβειν(ιεῖς) Καναθ(ηνοί); the town therefore seems to have been restored by Gabinius. Herod experienced a mortifying defeat at Kanatha in a battle against the Arabians.[219] On the civic constitution of Kanatha in imperial times we get some information from inscriptions, βουλευταί being frequently mentioned,[220] and once an ἀγορανόμος.[221] A Graeco-Latin epitaph of a Syrian merchant, discovered in 1862 in the neighbourhood of Trevoux in France, is of special interest. He is designated in the Greek text as βουλευτὴς πολίτης τε Κανωθαί[ω]ν ἐ[ . . .] Συρίης, in the Latin as *decurio* Septimianus Canotha.[222] What the latter title denotes is indeed very doubtful.[223] If the Συρία of the Greek text is to be understood in the strict sense of the *province* of Syria, it follows from the combination of the two texts, that Kanatha belonged to the province of Syria down to the time of Septimius Severus.[223a] In the time of Eusebius it belonged to the province of Arabia. It is striking that Eusebius calls

1867, p. 204 (βουλευτὴς πολίτης τε Κανωθαί[ω]ν). Lastly, Κεναθηνός in Waddington, n. 2343. On the present form of the name *Kanawat*, see Wetzstein, *Reisebericht über Hauran und die Trachonen* (1860), p. 77 sq.

[218] See De Saulcy, pp. 399–401, pl. xxiii. n. 10; and especially Reichardt, *Die Münzen Kanatha's* (*Wiener Numismat. Zeitschr.* 1880, pp. 68–72).

[219] *Bell. Jud.* i. 19. 2. In the parallel passage, *Antt.* xv. 5. 1, the place is called Κανά.

[220] Waddington, n. 2216, 2339 (= Wetzstein, n. 188). *Corp. Inscr. Graec.* n. 4613 (= Waddington, n. 2331a). The last-named inscription was discovered by Seetzen, *not* in Kanawat (as is erroneously stated in the *Corp. Inscr. Graec.* and in Waddington), but in Deir el-Chlef; see Kruse in his edition of Seetzen's *Travels*, iv. 40, note.

[221] *Corp. Inscr. Graec.* 4912 = Waddington, n. 2330.

[222] The inscription is given by Henzen in the *Bullettino dell' Instituto di corrisp. archeol.* 1867, pp. 203–207.

[223] See Henzen as above, and Waddington's explanations on 2329.

[223a] So also Waddington on n. 2329, and Marquardt, i. 396. Still Marquardt is inclined, by reason of the circumstances of the garrison, to the view that Kanatha was, in the time of Caracalla, already united to the province of Arabia; see p. 433, note 3.

it a κώμη.[224]   Could it in his time have no longer had a civic constitution ? [224a]   A Christian bishop of Kanotha was present at the Councils of Ephesus (A.D. 449), Chalcedon (A.D. 451) and Constantinople (A.D. 459).[225]

19. *Scythopolis*, Σκυθόπολις, one of the most important Hellenistic towns of Palestine, the only one among the towns of Decapolis which lay westward of the Jordan.[226]   The ancient name of the town was Beth-sean, בֵּית שְׁאָן or בֵּית שָׁן, in the Septuagint and in the first Book of Maccabees (v. 52, xii. 40 sq.), Βαιθσάν.[227]   The ancient name was always maintained beside the Greek one,[228] nay at last supplanted it. To this very day the desolate ruins of Beisan in the valley of the Jordan south of the Lake of Gennesareth mark the position of the ancient city.   The name Σκυθόπολις is undoubtedly equal to Σκυθῶν πόλις, as indeed it is frequently written.[229]   The reason for this name is very obscure, probably it must be explained as by Syncellus, by the fact that a number of Scythians settled here on the occasion of their

---

[224] Euseb. *Onomast.*, ed. Lagarde, p. 269: Κανάθ. κώμη τῆς Ἀραβίας εἰς ἔτι Καναθὰ λεγομένη . . . κεῖται δὲ καὶ ἔτι καὶ νῦν ἐν Τραχῶνι πλησίον Βοστρῶν.

[224a] The statements of Eusebius are not quite trustworthy.   He calls *e.g.* Jabis at one time πόλις (p. 225), at another κώμη (p. 268).

[225] Le Quien, *Oriens christ.* ii. 867.

[226] See in general, Reland, pp. 992–998.  Winer, *s.v.* "Beth-sean."  Raumer, p. 150 sq.  Pauly's *Enc.* vi. 1. 729.  Robinson, *Palestine*, iii. 326–332.  Ritter, xv. 1. 426–435.  Kuhn, ii. 371.  Guérin, *Samarie*, i. 284–299. *The Survey of Western Palestine*, Memoirs by Conder and Kitchener, ii. 83, 101–114 (with plans) ; also sheet ix. of the large English chart.

[227] In the Old Test., Josh. xvii. 11, 16 ; Judg. i. 27 ; 1 Sam. xxxi. 10, 12 ; 2 Sam. xxi. 12 ; 1 Kings iv. 12 ; 1 Chron. vii. 29.   On the identity of Beth-sean and Scythopolis, see Joseph. *Antt.* v. 1. 22, vi. 14. 8, xii. 8. 5, xiii. 6. 1. The gloss of the LXX. on Judg. i. 27.   Euseb. *Onomast.*, ed. Lag. p. 237. Steph. Byz. (see next note).

[228] בֵּית שָׁאן in the Mishna, *Aboda sara* i. 4, iv. 12.   The adj. בֵּישָׁנִי, *Pea* viii. 1.   Comp. Neubauer, *Géographie du Talmud*, p. 174 sq.  Steph. Byz. *s.v.* Σκυθόπολις, Παλαιστίνης πόλις ἢ Νύσσης (l. Νύσσα) Κοίλης Συρίας, Σκυθῶν πόλις, πρότερον Βαίσων λεγόμενη ὑπὸ τῶν βαρβάρων.   The form Beisan is contracted from Beth-sean.

[229] Σκυθῶν πόλις, Judith iii. 11 ; 2 Macc. xii. 29 ; LXX. Judg. i. 27. Polybius, v. 70.  Aristides, ed. Dindorf, ii. 470.

great invasion of Palestine in the seventh century before
Christ.[230] On the name Nysa, which Scythopolis also bore
according to Pliny, Stephanus Byz., and which is found
upon coins, see above, p. 20. The town was perhaps
already known by its Greek name Scythopolis in the time of
Alexander the Great, or at any rate in the third century
before Christ, when it was tributary to the Ptolemies.[231] When
in 218 B.C. Antiochus the Great invaded Palestine, the town
willingly (καθ᾽ ὁμολογίαν) surrendered to him.[232] Like the
rest of Palestine however it did not come permanently under
Syrian dominion till twenty years later (198 B.C.). In the
time of the Maccabees Scythopolis is mentioned as a heathen
town, but not as one hostile to the Jews (2 Macc. xii.
29–31). Towards the end of the second century (about 107
B.C.) it came under Jewish rule, the weak Antiochus IX.
(Kyzikenos) being unable to offer effectual resistance to the
advance of John Hyrcanus, nay his general Epicrates
treacherously surrendering Scythopolis to the Jews (Joseph.
*Antt.* xiii. 10. 3 ; *Bell. Jud.* i. 2. 7 speaks otherwise).[233] Hence

[230] Syncell. ed. Dindorf, i. 405: Σκύθαι τὴν Παλαιστίνην κατέδραμον καὶ
τὴν Βασὰν (l. Βαισὰν) κατέσχον τὴν ἐξ αὐτῶν κληθεῖσαν Σκυθόπολιν. On the
invasion of the Scythians, see especially Herodotus, i. 105. Euseb. *Chron.*,
ed. Schoene, ii. 88 sq. Pliny too and his successor Solinus derive the name
from the Scythians, but indeed from those whom the god Dionysius settled
there for the protection of the grave of his nurse : Plinius, v. 18. 74:
Scythpolim, antea Nysam, a Libero Patre sepulta nutrice ibi Scythis
deductis. Solinus (ed. Mommsen), c. 36 : Liber Pater cum humo nutricem
tradidisset, condidit hoc oppidum, ut sepulturae titulum etiam urbis moenibus
ampliaret. Incolae deerant : e comitibus suis Scythas delegit, quos ut animi
firmaret ad promptam resistendi violentiam, praemium loci nomen dedit.
For another and equally mythological derivation from the Scythians, see
Malalas, ed. Dindorf, p. 140, and Cedrenus, ed. Bekker, i. 237. In general
Steph. Byz. also explains the name by Σκυθῶν πόλις (see note 228). The
derivation from Sukkoth is obviated by the fact, that the Hebrew name of
the town is not Sukkoth but Beth-sean.

[231] Joseph. *Antt.* xii. 4. 5. Comp. above, p. 53. It would be a more ancient
testimony to the use of the Greek name, if the reference of the letters Σκ on
certain coins of Alexander the Great to Scythopolis were certain. See L.
Müller, *Numismatique d'Alexandre le Grand*, p. 304, planches, n. 1429, 1464.

[232] Polyb. v. 70. Stark, *Gaza*, p. 381.

[233] On the chronology, comp. above, § 8.

we find it also in the possession of Alexander Jannaeus (*Antt.*
xiii. 15. 4).   It was again separated from the Jewish region
by Pompey (*Antt.* xiv. 5. 3, xiv. 4. 4; *Bell. Jud.* i. 7. 7),
and restored by Gabinius (*Antt.* xiv. 5. 3 ; *Bell. Jud.* i. 8. 4).
It afterwards continued to be an independent town under
Roman supremacy.   Nor did either Herod or his successors
ever possess the town.   Its membership among the cities of
Decapolis is testified by Josephus, who calls it "one of the
largest towns of Decapolis " (*Bell. Jud.* iii. 9. 7 : ἡ δέ ἐστι
μεγίστη τῆς Δεκαπόλεως).   It is not quite certain what era
it made use of.   The Pompeian era is evidently used on a
coin of Gordianus; while upon others a later one seems
adopted.   The titles of the town, especially upon the coins
of Gordianus, are ἱερὰ ἄσυλος.[234]   At the beginning of the
Jewish war, A.D. 66, the revolted Jews attacked the district
of Scythopolis (*Bell. Jud.* ii. 18. 1).   The Jewish inhabitants found themselves obliged, for the sake of safety, to fight
on the side of the heathen against their fellow-countrymen,
who were attacking the town.   The heathen inhabitants however afterwards requited this alliance by faithless treachery,
luring them into the sacred grove, and then surprising them
by night and massacring them to the number, as it is said,
of 13,000 (*Bell. Jud.* ii. 18. 3, 4, vii. 8. 7 ; *Vita,* 6).   When
Josephus says with respect to the period of the Jewish war,
that Scythopolis was then obedient to King Agrippa (*Vita,*
65, ed. Bekker, p. 341, 20 : τῆς ὑπηκόου βασιλεῖ), this is
certainly not to be understood in the sense of actual subjection, but only means, that Scythopolis was on the side of
Agrippa and the Romans.[235]   The district of Scythopolis

[234] See on the coins and the era, Belley in the *Mémoires des Inscr. et
Belles-Lettres*, ancient series, vol. xxvi. 1759, pp. 415–428.  Eckhel, iii. 438–
440.  Mionnet, v. 511 sq. ; *Suppl.* viii. 355 sq.  De Saulcy, pp. 287–290,
pl. xiv. n. 8–13.

[235] This is all that Josephus is in the context concerned with.  It is highly
improbable that Scythopolis really belonged (as Menke in his *Bibel-Atlas*
supposes) to the dominions of Agrippa, since Josephus in the passages in
which he is describing accurately the realm of Agrippa does not mention it.

must be regarded as very extensive.   At the taking of Scythopolis and Philoteria (a town of that name on the Lake of
Gennesareth of which we know nothing else) by Antiochus
the Great, in the year 218, Polybius remarks, that the district
subject to these two towns could easily furnish abundant
support for the whole army.[236]   We have also similar testimony at a later date, viz. that of Josephus (*Vita*, 9), that the
district of Scythopolis bordered on that of Gadara (see above,
p. 88).   The district of this town is also mentioned *Bell.
Jud.* iv. 8. 2.   The subsequent history of Scythopolis, which
remained for centuries an important and flourishing town,
cannot be further pursued here.   On its religious rites, games
and industry, compare above, pp. 19, 27, 41.

20. *Pella, Πέλλα.*   The district of Pella is designated by
Josephus as the northern boundary of Peraea.[237]   According
to Eusebius, the Jabesh of Scripture was only 6 *m. p.* from
Pella, on the road from this latter to Gerasa.[238]   Now as Gerasa
lies south of the present Wadi Jabis, Pella must have lain
a little to the north of it, and hence it is almost certain, that
the important ruins at Fahil, on a terrace over the Jordan valley
opposite Scythopolis in a south-easterly direction, mark the
position of the ancient Pella.[239]   That it stood here is further

[236] Polyb. v. 70: εὐθαρσῶς ἔσχε πρὸς τὰς μελλούσας ἐπιβολὰς διὰ τὸ τὴν
ὑποτεταγμένην χώραν ταῖς πόλεσι ταύταις ῥᾳδίως δύνασθαι παντὶ τ̀
στρατοπέδῳ χορηγεῖν καὶ δαψιλῆ παρασκευάζειν τὰ κατεπείγοντα πρὸς τὴν χρείαν.
[237] *Bell. Jud.* iii. 3. 3.   Peraea is here taken in its *political* meaning, *i.e.*
with the exclusion of the towns of Decapolis (comp. above, p. 2).   In a
geographical sense, it reaches much farther northward, comprising *e.g.* even
Gadara (*Bell. Jud.* iv. 7. 3).
[238] Euseb. *Onomast.*. ed. Lag. p. 225: ἡ δὲ Ἰάβις ἐπέκεινα τοῦ Ἰορδάνου νῦν
ἐστὶ μεγίστη πόλις, Πέλλης πόλεως διεστῶσα σημείοις ϛʹ ἀνιόντων ἐπὶ Γερασάν.
Similarly, p. 268 (where however Jabis is more correctly called a κώμη).
[239] Comp. Robinson's *Palestine*, iii. 320–325.   Ritter, xv. 2. 1023–1030.
Raumer, p. 254.   Guérin, *Galilée*, i. 288–292.   Merrill, *East of the Jordan*
(1881), pp. 442–447.   On the history, Reland, p. 924 sq.   Droysen,
*Hellenismus*, iii. 2. 204 sq.   Kuhn, ii. 374.   There is but slight foundation
for the objection raised by Kruse (Seetzen's *Reisen*, iv. 198 sqq.) to the
above determination of the locality.   Korb's thorough discussion of the
situation of Pella (Jahn's *Jahrb. für Philologie und Paedagogik*, 4th year,
vol. i. 1829, pp. 100–118) places the situation too far northward by partially

borne out by the fact that Pliny describes Pella as *aquis divitem*.[240]
Whether the original Semitic name was Fahil (פחלא ?), and the
name Pella chosen by the Greeks on account of its similarity
of sound, may be left uncertain.[240a] In any case the name
Pella was borrowed from the famous Macedonian town of the
same name. The latter being the birthplace of Alexander
the Great, it is not improbable that our Pella as well as the
neighbouring Dium was founded by Alexander the Great himself, as indeed the somewhat corrupt text of Stephanus Byz.
declares.[241] According to another passage of Stephanus Byz.
our Pella was also called *Βοῦτις*.[242] Pella is first mentioned
in history at the conquest of Palestine by Antiochus the
Great, B.C. 218, when after taking Atabyrion (Tabor) he

placing in the foreground the statements of Josephus, and neglecting to do
justice to the more precise statements of Eusebius.

[240] Plinius, v. 18. 74.

[240a] Tuch, *Quaestiones de Flavii Josephi libris historicis* (Lips. 1859), p. 18,
altogether regards Pella as only the Greek pronunciation for פחלא, and
scouts the idea of any connection with the name of the Macedonian town.
This is however more than improbable.

[241] Steph. Byz. ed. Meineke, *s.v.* Δῖον, πόλις . . . Κοίλης Συρίας, κτίσμα
'Αλεξάνδρου, καὶ Πέλλα. The words καὶ Πέλλα are probably the gloss of
some learned reader, who thus meant to say that Pella as well as Dium was
founded by Alexander the Great. The reading ἡ καὶ Πέλλα is an erroneous
emendation by some former editor. Comp. also Droysen, iii. 2. 204 sq.
A Syrian Pella is also mentioned among the cities founded by Seleucus I.
in Appian. *Syr.* 57, and Euseb. *Chron.*, ed. Schoene, ii. 116 sq. According
to the Latin text of Jerome: Seleucus Antiochiam Laodiciam Seleuciam
Apamiam Edessam Beroeam et Pellam urbes condidit. So also Syncell., ed.
Dindorf, i. 520, and the Armenian text of Eusebius, in which only Seleucia
is missing. By this Pella however we must probably understand the town
of Apamea on the Orontes, which was at first called by its founder
Seleucus I. Apamea, and afterwards Pella, which name was subsequently
lost (see especially Malalas, ed. Dindorf, p. 203 [according to Pausanias
Damascenus, comp. Müller, *Fragm. hist. graec.* iv. 470] ; also Strabo, xvi.
p. 752 ; Stephanus Byz. *s.v.* 'Απάμεια; in Diodor. xxi. 25, Apamea occurs
under the name of Pella, see Wesseling's note on the passage). It is true
that the lists in Appian and Eusebius mention Pella along with Apamea
as though they were two different cities. This mistake has however
arisen from the circumstance, that the change of name has been looked
upon as a second founding, and treated accordingly in the lists of founda-
tions of towns. Hence indeed our Pella (in Decapolis) is out of question.

[242] Steph. Byz. *s.v.* Πέλλα, πόλις . . . Κοίλης Συρίας, ἡ Βοῦτις λεγομένη.

turned towards the country east of the Jordan and seized Pella,
Kamus, and Gephrus.[243]   Alexander Jannaeus conquered and
destroyed the town, because its inhabitants would not adopt
" Jewish customs " (*Bell. Jud.* i. 4. 8 ; *Antt.* xiii. 15. 4).[243a]   It
was again separated from the Jewish region by Pompey (*Antt.*
xiv. 4. 4 ; *Bell. Jud.* i. 7. 7).   The fact of its having belonged
to Decapolis is attested by Eusebius and Epiphanius as well as
by Pliny and Ptolemy.[244]   The few coins which have been
preserved bear, as might be expected, the Pompeian era.[245]
When Pella is named in Josephus (*Bell. Jud.* iii. 3. 5) among
the chief places of the eleven toparchies of Judaea, this must
be ascribed either to a mistake on the part of Josephus himself or to an error in the text.   At the commencement of the
Jewish war Pella was attacked by the insurgent Jews (*Bell. Jud.*
ii. 18. 1).   During the war the Christian Church fled thither
from Jerusalem.[246]   Christian bishops of Pella are mentioned
in the fifth and sixth centuries after Christ.[247]

21. *Dium, Δῖον.*   Among the towns of this name, of which
Steph. Byz. enumerates seven, that in Macedonia at the foot
of Olympus is the best known.   Hence it is very credible,
that our Dion in Coelesyria was a foundation of Alexander the
Great.[248]   According to the astronomical definitions of Ptolemy
(v. 15. 23), Dium lay under the same degree of latitude as

[243] Polyb. v. 70.

[243a] In the last passage also our Pella is certainly intended, and not
another Moabite one.   Josephus only names Pella quite at the end of the
list after enumerating the Moabite towns, because he desires to append a
special remark concerning it.   Comp. Tuch, *Quaestiones*, etc., pp. 17–19.

[244] Plin. v. 18. 74.   Ptolem. v. 15. 23.   Euseb. *Onomast.*, ed. Lag. p. 251.
Epiphanius, *Haer.* 29. 7 ; *de mensuris et ponder.* § 15.

[245] See Belley in the *Mémoires de l'Académie des Inscr. et Belles-Lettres*,
ancient series, vol. xxviii. 568 sqq.   Eckhel, iii. 350.   Mionnet, v. 329 ;
*Suppl.* viii. 232.   De Saulcy, pp. 291–293, pl. xvi. n. 8.

[246] Euseb. *Hist. eccl.* iii. 5. 2, 3 ; Epiphanius, *Haer.* 29. 7 ; *de mensuris et
ponder.* § 15.

[247] Le Quien, *Oriens christ.* iii. 698 sq.

[248] So Steph. Byz. *s.v.* Δῖον (see above, note 241).   Stephanus remarks
ἧς τὸ ὕδωρ νοσερόν, and quotes the following epigram :—

νᾶμα τὸ Διηνὸν γλυκερὸν ποτόν, ἠνιδὲ πίης,
παύσει μὲν δίψης, εὐθὺ δὲ καὶ βιότου.

Pella, but ⅙ of a degree farther eastward. With this agree the statements of Josephus concerning Pompey's route, that the Jewish king Aristobulus accompanied Pompey on his march from Damascus against the Nabataeans as far as Dium, that here he suddenly separated from Pompey, who therefore now turned suddenly westward and came by Pella and Scythopolis to Judaea.[249] Little is known of the history of Dium.[250] It was conquered by Alexander Jannaeus (*Antt.* xiii. 15. 3), liberated by Pompey (*Antt.* xiv. 4. 4), and then belonged to Decapolis (Plin. v. 18. 74; Ptolem. v. 15. 23). The coins of Dium, with the legend *Δειηνων*, have the Pompeian era. Some of those belonging to the time of Caracalla and Geta are still in existence.[251] The *Δία* mentioned by Hierocles is certainly identical with this Dium.[252]

22. *Gerasa, Γέρασα.* The ruins of the present Dscharásch are the most important in the region east of the Jordan, and are indeed (with those of Palmyra, Baalbec and Petra) among the most important in Syria. There are still in existence considerable remains of temples, theatres and other public buildings. About one hundred columns of a long colonnade, which ran through the middle of the town, are still standing. The buildings seem from their style to belong to the second or third century after Christ.[253] Few inscriptions have as yet

---

[249] Joseph. *Antt.* xiv. 3. 3, 4 ; *Bell. Jud.* i. 6. 4, *fin.* Also Menke's *Bibel-Atlas*, sheet iv. In both passages indeed Dium first came into the text through Dindorf's emendations. The older editions have, *Antt.* xiv. 3. 3 : *εἰς Δήλιον πόλιν* ; *Bell. Jud.* i. 6. 4 : *ἀπὸ Διοσπόλεως.* As certain manuscripts have *ἀπὸ διὸς ἡλιουπόλεως* (see Cardwell's ed.) we might feel inclined to read Heliopolis in both passages. But the context makes this impossible.

[250] Comp. Reland, p. 736 sq. Raumer, p. 247. Kuhn, iii. 382 sq.

[251] See Belley in the *Mémoires de l'Académie des Inscr. et Belles-Lettres,* ancient series, vol. xxviii. 568 sqq. Eckhel, iii. 347 sq. Mionnet, v. 32; *Suppl.* viii. 26. De Saulcy, pp. 378–383, pl. xix. n. 8, 9.

[252] Hierocles, *Synecd.*, ed. Parthey, p. 45. The *Notitia episcopat.*, the same, p. 92. Also in Joseph. *Antt.* xii. 15. 3 the manuscripts have *Δίαν.*

[253] See in general, Seetzen, *Reisen,* i. 388 sq., iv. 202 sqq. Burckhardt, *Reisen,* i. 401–417, 530–536 (with plan). Buckingham, *Travels in Palestine,* 1821, pp. 353–405. Ritter, *Erdkunde,* xv. 2. 1077–1094. Bädeker-Socin, *Palästina,* p. 408 sqq. (with plan). Merrill, *East of the Jordan,* pp. 281–290. Illustrations, Laborde, *Voyage en Orient* (Paris 1837 sq.), livraison 9, 16,

been published.[254]   There can be no doubt that here was
the ancient Gerasa.[255]   The derivation of the name from
γέροντες (veterans) of Alexander the Great, who settled
here, is based only upon etymological trifling.[256]   It is
certainly possible, that the foundation of Gerasa as a
Hellenistic town may reach as far back as Alexander the
Great.   It is first mentioned in the time of Alexander
Jannaeus, when it was in the power of a certain Theodorus
(a son of the tyrant Zeno Kotylas of Philadelphia).   It was
conquered after an arduous siege by Alexander Jannaeus
towards the end of his reign.[257]   It was while still defending
the fortress Ragaba " in the district of Gerasa " that he died.[258]
Gerasa was undoubtedly liberated by Pompey, for it belonged
to Decapolis.[259]   At the outbreak of the Jewish war it was
attacked by the Jews (*Bell. Jud.* ii. 18. 1); yet the Jews
dwelling in the town were spared by the inhabitants (*Bell.
Jud.* ii. 18. 5).   The Gerasa conquered and destroyed by

34, 35.   Rey, *Voyage dans le Haouran et aux bords de la mer morte exécuté
pendant les années* 1857 and 1858 (Paris), Atlas pl. xix.-xxiii. (pl. xxi. plan).
Duc de Luynes, *Voyage d'Exploration à la mer morte à Petra et sur la rive
gauche du Jourdain,* Paris s. a. (1874), Atlas, pl. 50–57.   Also Riehm's
*Wörterb. s.v.* " Gadara."

[254] *Corp. Inscr. Graec.* n. 4661–4664.   *Corp. Inscr. Lat.* vol. iii. n.
118, 119.   Wetzstein, *Ausgewählte Inschriften (Trans. of the Berlin Acad.*
1863), n. 205–207.   Böckh, *Report of the Berlin Acad.* 1835, p. 14 sqq.   Allen,
*American Journal of Philology,* vol. iii. (Baltimore 1882), p. 206.   *Quarterly
Statement of the Palestine Exploration Fund,* 1882, p. 218 sqq.; 1883, p. 107 sq.

[255] Compare on the history, Reland, p. 806 sqq.   Pauly's *Encycl.* iii. 770.
Winer, *s.v.* "Gadara."   Raumer, p. 249 sq.   Ritter, as above.   Kuhn, ii. 370,
383.

[256] See the passages from Jamblicus and the *Etymolog. magnum* in
Droysen, *Hellenismus,* iii. 2. 202 sq.   Also Reland, p. 806.

[257] *Bell. Jud.* i. 4. 8.   In the parallel passage *Antt.* xiii. 15. 3, Ἔσσαν
stands instead of Γέρασαν.   The reading in *Bell. Jud.* is however certainly
the correct one.

[258] *Antt.* xiii. 15.5.   Ragaba can hardly be identical with the Ἐργά of Eusebius (p. 216), which lay 15 m. p. *westward* of Gerasa, and was therefore certainly under the power of Alexander Jannaeus *before* the conquest of Gerasa.

[259] Ptolem. v. 15. 23.   Steph. Byz. *s.v.* Γέρασα, πόλις τῆς Κοίλης Συρίας,
τῆς δεκαπόλεως (for such is the reading, as by Meineke, instead of the
traditional τεσσαρεσκαιδεκαπόλεως).   Plinius, v. 18. 74, names Galasa, for
which we must read Gerasa, among the cities of Decapolis.

Lucius Annius at the command of Vespasian (*Bell. Jud.* iv. 9. 1) cannot be this Gerasa, which as a Hellenistic town was certainly friendly to the Romans. The few coins of Gerasa (from Hadrian to Alexander Severus) have no era and contain no epithet of the city. They almost all have the superscription Ἄρτεμις τύχη Γεράσων.[260] On an inscription of the time of Trajan the inhabitants are called Ἀντιοχεῖς πρὸς τῷ Χρυσορόᾳ.[261] Upon another inscription, also of the Roman period, the town is called Γέρασα Ἀντιόχεια.[261a] In an ethnographic sense Gerasa must be reckoned part of Arabia,[262] but seems even in the second century after Christ to have belonged to the province of Syria and only subsequently to have been incorporated in that of Arabia.[263] In the fourth century after Christ it was one of the most important towns of this province.[264] Its district was so large,

---

[260] Eckhel, iii. 350. Mionnet, v. 329 ; *Suppl.* viii. 230 sq. De Saulcy, p. 384 sq., pl. xxii. n. 1, 2.

[261] Mommsen, *Berichte der sächsisch. Gesellsch. d. Wissensch., philol.-hist. Classe*, vol. ii. 1850, p. 223. Waddington, n. 1722. The inscription was set up in honour of A. Julius Quadratus, the imperial legate of Syria, and indeed in his native Pergamos (where the inscription was discovered). The Gerasenes designate themselves according to Waddington's completion, [Ἀντιο]χέων τῶν [πρὸς τ]ῷ Χρυσορόᾳ τῶν π[ρότ]ερον [Γε]ρασηνῶν ἡ βουλὴ καὶ ὁ δῆ[μος]. No other place in Syria is known by the name of Chrysorrhoas except the Nahr Barada near Damascus (Strabo, xvi. p. 755. Plin. v. 18. 74. Ptolem. v. 15. 9). It is self-evident that this cannot, as Mommsen strangely assumes, be intended here. On the contrary, we find that the rivulet Kerwân running through Gerasa was also called Chrysorrhoas (see Bädeker, p. 409).

[261a] *American Journal of Philology*, vol. iii. (Baltimore 1882) p. 206, communicated by Allen, from a copy by Merrill. The inscription was found in Gerasa itself. It is an epitaph consisting of four distichs on a woman of the name of Juliana from Antioch. She died in the course of her journey in Gerasa and was buried there, and it is said of her in the epitaph that she will not now return to her home in Antioch, ἀλλ᾽ ἔλαχεν γαί[η]ς [Γ]ερ[ά]σ[ης] μέρος Ἀντιοχείης. That the inscription belongs to the Roman period is shown by the name Juliana.

[262] Origenes *in Joann.* vol. vi. c. 24 (*Opp.* ed. Lommatzsch, i. 239), Γέρασα δὲ τῆς Ἀραβίας ἐστὶ πόλις.

[263] See Marquardt, *Römische Staatsverwaltung*, i. 433, note 1.

[264] Ammian. Marc. xiv. 8. 13 : Haec quoque civitates habet inter oppida quaedam ingentes *Bostram* et *Gerasam* atque *Philadelphiam* murorum

that Jerome could say, that what was formerly Gilead was now called Gerasa.[264a] Famous men of Gerasa are mentioned by Steph. Byz.[265] The names too of certain Christian bishops are well known.[266]

23. *Philadelphia,* Φιλαδέλφεια, the ancient capital of the Ammonites called in the O. T. "Rabbah of the Ammonites" (רַבַּת בְּנֵי עַמּוֹן), *i.e.* the chief city of the Ammonites, or more shortly "Rabbah" (רַבָּה).[267] In Polybius it is called Rabbat-Amana,[268] in Eusebius and Steph. Byz. Amman and Ammana.[269] The situation of the town is certainly evidenced by the ruins south of Gerasa, which to this day bear the name of Ammana. The ruins belong, like those of Kanatha, to the Roman period.[270] The town received the name of Philadelphia from Ptolemy II.

firmitate cautissimas. Comp. Euseb. *Onomast.* p. 242. Γέρασα, πόλις ἐπίσημος τῆς Ἀραβίας.

[264a] Hieronymus *in Obadjam* v. 19 (Vallarsi, vi. 381): Benjamin autem . . . cunctam possidebit Arabiam, quae prius vocabatur Galaad et nunc Gerasa nuncupatur. Comp. also Neubauer, *Géographie du Talmud,* p. 250.

[265] Steph. Byz. *s.v.* Γέρασα· ἐξ αὐτῆς Ἀρίστων ῥήτωρ ἀστεῖός ἐστιν . . . καὶ Κήρυκος σοφιστὴς καὶ Πλάτων νομικὸς ῥήτωρ. To these must also be added the Neo-Pythagorean philosopher and mathematician Nicomachus of Gerasa, second century after Christ (Fabric. *Bibl graec.,* ed. Harless, v. 629 sqq.).

[266] Epiphan. *Haer.* 73. 26. Le Quien, *Oriens christ.* ii. 859 sq.

[267] Deut. iii. 11 ; Josh. xiii. 25 ; 2 Sam. xi. 1, xii. 26–29, xvii. 27 ; Jer. xlix. 2, 3 ; Ezek. xxi. 25, xxv. 5 ; Amos i. 14; 1 Chron. xx. 1. On the identity of Rabbah of the Ammonites with Philadelphia, see below the passages from Eusebius (note 269), Steph. Byz. and Jerome (note 271).

[268] Polyb. v. 71, Ῥαββατάμανα. So too Steph. Byz. *s.v.* Ῥαββατάμ-μανα, πόλις τῆς ὀρεινῆς Ἀραβίας.

[269] Euseb. *Onomast.,* ed. Lagarde, p. 215, Ἀμμᾶν ἡ νῦν Φιλαδελφία, πόλις ἐπίσημος τῆς Ἀραβίας. *Ibid.* p. 219, Ἀμμών . . . αὕτη ἐστὶν Ἀμμᾶν ἡ καὶ Φιλαδελφία, πόλις ἐπίσημος τῆς Ἀραβίας. Comp. *ibid.* p. 288, Ῥαββά, πόλις βασιλείας Ἀμμών, αὕτη ἐστὶ Φιλαδελφία. Steph. Byz., see note 271.

[270] See in general, Seetzen, *Reisen,* i. 396 sqq., iv. 212 sqq. Burckhardt, *Reisen,* ii. 612–618. Ritter, *Erdkunde,* xv. 2. 1145–1159. De Saulcy, *Voyage en Terre Sainte,* 1865, i. 237 sqq. (with plan). Bädeker-Socin, *Palästina,* p. 318 sqq. (with plan). Merrill, *East of the Jordan,* p. 399 sqq. Conder, *Quarterly Statement,* 1882, pp. 99–112. Illustrations, Laborde, *Voyage en Orient* (Paris 1837 sqq.), livr. 28, 29. On the history, besides Ritter, the article on "Rabbath Ammon" in Winer's *Realwörterb.,* Herzog's *Real-Encycl.* (1st ed. xii. 469 sq.), Schenkel's *Bibellex.,* Riehm's *WB.* Kuhn, ii. 383 sq.

(Philadelphus), to whom consequently its Hellenization is to be referred.[271] In the time of Antiochus the Great it was a strong fortress, which in the year 218 B.C. he vainly endeavoured to take by storm, and of which he was unable to get possession, till a prisoner showed him the subterranean path, by which the inhabitants came out to draw water. This being stopped up by Antiochus, the town was forced to surrender for want of water.[272] About 135 B.C. (at the death of Simon Maccabaeus) Philadelphia was in the power of a certain Zenos Kotylas (*Antt.* xiii. 8. 1 ; *Bell. Jud.* i. 2. 4). It was not conquered by Alexander Jannaeus, though he had possession of Gerasa to the north and Esbon to the south of it. Hence Philadelphia is not named among the towns which were separated by Pompey from the Jewish region. It was however joined by him to the confederacy of Decapolis[273] and had therefore the Pompeian era.[274] It was in its neighbourhood that Herod fought against the Arabians.[275] In A.D. 44 sanguinary contests took place between the Jews

---

[271] Steph. Byz. *s.v.* Φιλαδίλφεια . . . τῆς Συρίας ἐπιφανὴς πόλις, ἡ πρότερον Ἄμμανα, εἶτ᾽ Ἀστάρτη, εἶτα Φιλαδέλφεια ἀπὸ Πτολεμαίου τοῦ Φιλαδέλφου. Hieronymus *in Ezek.* c. 25 (Vallarsi, v. 285) : Rabbath, quae hodie a rege Aegypti Ptolemaeo cognomento Philadelpho, qui Arabiam tenuit cum Judaea, Philadelphia nuncupata est. L. Müller (*Numismatique d'Alexandre le Grand*, p. 309, pl. n. 1473 sqq.) refers certain coins of Alexander the Great, with the letters Φι to our Philadelphia. Although it would not be impossible for coins with the name of Alexander to be issued in the days of Ptolemy II. (see note 150, above), yet the correctness of this explanation seems to me very questionable. Philoteria *e.g.* (Polyb. v. 70) might be intended.

[272] Polyb. v. 71. Conder found in his surveys at Amman a path, which is possibly identical with that mentioned by Polybius, see *Athenæum*, 1883, n. 2905, p. 832: *The discovery at Ammân*. Comp. also *Quarterly Statement*, 1882, p. 109.

[273] Plinius, v. 18. 74.

[274] *Chron. paschale* (ed. Dindorf, i. 351), ad Olymp. 179. 2 = 63 B.C., Φιλαδελφεῖς ἐντεῦθεν ἀριθμοῦσι τοὺς ἑαυτῶν χρόνους. The era is also frequently found upon coins. See Noris, iii. 9. 2 (ed. Lips. pp. 308–316). Eckhel, iii. 351. Mionnet, v. 330–333 ; *Suppl.* viii. 232–236. De Saulcy, pp. 386–392, pl. xxii. n. 3–9.

[275] *Bell. Jud.* i. 19. 5. In the parallel passage *Antt.* xv. 5. 4, Philadelphia is not mentioned.

of Peraea and the Philadelphians concerning the boundaries
of a village called Mia in our present text of Josephus, but
for which Zia is probably the correct reading (*Antt.* xx. 1. 1).[276]
At the outbreak of the Jewish war, Philadelphia was attacked
by the insurgent Jews (*Bell. Jud.* ii. 18. 1).   Upon an
inscription of the second century after Christ our Philadelphia is called Φιλαδέλφεια τῆς 'Αραβίας.[277]   This is
however meant only in an ethnographical sense.   For coins
down to Alexander Severus have the superscription Φιλαδελφέων, Κοίλης Συρίας.[278]   The town therefore still belonged
to the province of Syria and was probably allotted to the
province of Arabia towards the close of the third century.[279]
In the fourth century it was one of the most important towns
of this province.[280]   Josephus mentions the district of Philadelphia (Φιλαδελφηνή) as the eastern boundary of Peraea (*Bell.
Jud.* iii. 3. 3).   If the supposition be warranted, that Zia is
the correct reading in Joseph. *Antt.* xx. 1. 1, the district of
Philadelphia must have extended to about 15 *m. p.* westward
of the town, in other words, full half of the land lying between
the Jordan and the town must have belonged to the Phila-
delphian district.

*It is an undoubted fact, that all the cities hitherto described
formed independent political communities, which—at least after
the time of Pompey — were never internally blended into an
organic unity with the Jewish region, but were at most externally
united with it under the same ruler.*   Almost all of them had a
chiefly heathen population, which after the third century before

---

[276] A village of Zia lying 15 *m. p.* west of Philadelphia is mentioned by
Eusebius, *Onomast.* p. 258, καὶ ἔστι νῦν Ζία κώμη ὡς ἀπὸ ιε´ σημείων Φιλαδελφίας ἐπὶ δυσμάς.   The supposition that Zia is the correct reading in this
passage has been already expressed by Reland (p. 897), Havercamp
(on Joseph. *l.c.*) and Tuch, *Quaestiones de Fl. Josephi libris historicis*, Lips.
1859, p. 19 sq.

[277] Le Bas et Waddington, *Inscr.* vol. iii. n. 1620b; comp. above, p. 25.

[278] See Mionnet, *Suppl.* viii. 236.   De Saulcy, p. 392.

[279] Comp. Marquardt, i. 433, note 1.

[280] Ammian. Marcellin. xiv. 8. 13 (see above, note 264).   Comp. also
the passages from Eusebius (note 269).

Christ became more and more Hellenistic in its character.   It was only in Joppa and Jamnia and perhaps in Azotus, that the Jewish element obtained during and after the Maccabaean period the ascendancy.   But even these towns with their respective districts formed both before and after that time independent political units.—To the same category belonged also, as Kuhn correctly admits,[281] *the towns which were re-founded by Herod and his sons.*   It is true, that in many of these the population was mainly Jewish.   But even where this was the case, the constitution was of Hellenistic organiza-tion, as is shown especially in the case of Tiberias.   In most of them however the heathen population preponderated. Hence we must not assume, that they were organically incorporated with the Jewish realm, but that they occupied within it an independent position similar to that of the older Hellenistic towns.   Nay in Galilee, where it was indeed impregnated with heathen elements, the Jewish country seems, on the contrary, to have been subordinate to the newly built capitals—first to Sepphoris, then to Tiberias, then again to Sepphoris (see the articles concerning them). Among the towns built by Herod certainly the two most im-portant were Sebaste, *i.e.* Samaria, and Caesarea, the latter of which has been already spoken of (No. 9).   Of less importance were Gaba in Galilee and Esbon in Peraea (*Antt.* xv. 8. 5), which must also be regarded as chiefly heathen towns, for at the outbreak of the Jewish war they, like Ptolemais and Caesarea, Gerasa and Philadelphia, were attacked by the insurgent Jews (*Bell. Jud.* ii. 18. 1).   Lastly, we have to mention as towns founded by Herod, Antipatris and Phasaelis, Kypros named together with the latter being a mere castle near Jericho and not a πόλις (*Bell. Jud.* i. 21. 9 ; *Antt.* xvi. 5. 2), which also applies to the fortresses of Alexandreion, Herodeion, Hyrcania, Masada and Machaerus.   Among the sons of Herod, Archelaus founded only the village (κώμη) of Archelais.[282]   Philip, on the

---

[281] *Die städtische und bürgerliche Verfassung des röm. Reichs,* ii. 346–348.
[282] Comp. Joseph. *Antt.* xvii. 13. 1 ; *Antt.* xviii. 2. 2.   Plinius, xiii. 4,

other hand, built Caesarea = Panias and Julias = Bethsaida, and
Herod Antipas the cities of Sepphoris, Julias = Livias and
Tiberias. These ten cities still remain to be treated of:

24. *Sebaste* = Samaria.[283] The Hellenization of the town
of Samaria (Hebr. שֹׁמְרֹין) was the work of Alexander the Great.
The Samaritans had during his stay in Egypt, B.C. 332–331,
assassinated Andromachus his governor in Coelesyria. Consequently when Alexander returned from Egypt (B.C. 331), he
executed strict justice upon the offenders and planted Macedonian colonists in Samaria.[284] The *Chronicle* of Eusebius
speaks also of a refoundation by Perdiccas,[285] which could
only have taken place during his campaign against Egypt
(B.C. 321); this is however very improbable so soon after the
colonization by Alexander the Great. As in old times so
now also Samaria was an important fortress. Hence it was
levelled by Ptolemy Lagos, when in the year B.C. 312 he again
surrendered to Antigonus the land of Coelesyria, which he

---

44. Ptolem. v. 16. 7. According to the *Tabula Peutinger.*, Archelais lay
on the road from Jericho to Scythopolis 12 *m. p.* from Jericho and 24
*m. p.* from Scythopolis. See also Robinson's *Palestine*, iii. 569. Ritter,
xv. i. 457. Guérin, *Samarie*, i. 235–238. *The Survey of Western Palestine*,
*Memoirs* by Conder and Kitchener, ii. 387, 395 sq., and sheet xv. of the
chart.

[283] Compare in general, Reland, pp. 979–983. Pauly's *Encycl.* vi. 1.
727 sq. Winer, *s.v.* "Samaria." Raumer, p. 159 sq. Robinson's *Palestine*, iii.
126, 127. Ritter, *Erdkunde*, xvi. 658–666. Guérin, *Samarie*, ii. 188–210.
Bädeker-Socin, p. 354 sqq. Sepp, *Jerusalem*, ii. 66–74. *The Survey of*
*Western Palestine*, *Memoirs* by Conder and Kitchener, ii. 160 sq., 211–215
(with plan), also sheet xv. of the large English chart.

[284] Curtius, *Rufus*, iv. 8 : Oneravit hunc dolorem nuntius mortis Andro-
machi, quem praefecerat Syriae : vivum Samaritae cremaverant. Ad cujus
interitum vindicandum, quanta maxime celeritate potuit, contendit, adveni-
entique sunt traditi tanti sceleris auctores. Euseb. *Chron.*, ed. Schoene, ii.
114 (ad ann. Abr. 1680, according to the Armenian): Andromachum
regionum illorum procuratorem constituit, quem incolae urbis Samari-
tarum interfecerunt : quos Alexander ab Egipto reversus punivit : *capta*
*urbe Macedonas ut ibi habitarent collocavit.* — So too Syncell., ed.
Dindorf, i. 496 : τὴν Σαμάρειαν πόλιν ἑλὼν Ἀλέξανδρος Μακεδόνας ἐν αὐτῇ
κατῴκισεν.

[285] See below, note 287, and also Droysen, iii. 2. 204. Ewald's *Gesch. des*
*Volkes Israel*, iv. p. 293.

had shortly before conquered.[286]  Some fifteen years later (about 296 B.C.) Samaria, which had meanwhile been restored, was again destroyed by Demetrius Poliorcetes in his contest with Ptolemy Lagos.[287]  Thenceforward we are for a long time without special data for the history of the town.  Polybius indeed mentions, that Antiochus the Great in both his first and second conquest of Palestine 218 and 198 B.C. occupied the country of Samaria,[288] but the fate of the town is not further indicated.  It is of interest to find, that the country of Samaria, under the Ptolemies as well as under the Seleucidae, formed like Judaea a single province, which again was subdivided into separate νομοί.[289]  Towards the end of the second century before Christ, when the Seleucidian Epigonoi were no longer able to prevent the encroachments of the Jews, the town fell a victim to their policy of conquest; and Samaria—then a πόλις ὀχυρωτάτη—was again conquered in the reign of John Hyrcanus (B.C. 107) by his sons Antigonus and Aristobulus after a siege of a year, and entirely given up to destruction (*Antt.* xiii. 10. 2, 3 ; *Bell. Jud.* i. 2. 7).[290]  Alexander Jannaeus had possession of the town or its ruins (*Antt.* xiii. 15. 4).  It was separated from the Jewish region by Pompey and never henceforth organically combined with it (*Antt.* xiv. 4. 4 ; *Bell. Jud.* i. 7. 7).  Its rebuilding was the work of Gabinius (*Antt.* xv. 14. 3 ; *Bell. Jud.* i. 8. 4), on which account its inhabitants were for a while called Γαβινιεῖς.[291]

[286] Diodor. xix. 93.  Comp. above, note 52 (Gaza), 109 (Joppa), 151 (Ptolemais).

[287] Euseb. *Chron.*, ed. Schoene, ii. 118 (ad Olymp. 121. 1=296 B.C. according to the Armenian): Demetrius rex Asianorum, Poliorcetes appellatus, Samaritanorum urbem a Perdica constructam (s. incolis frequentatam) totam cepit.  Syncell., ed. Dindorf, i. 519 : Δημήτριος ὁ Πολιορκητὴς τὴν πόλιν Σαμαρέων ἐπόρθησεν.  So too i. 522.  Comp. Droysen, ii. 2. 243, 255.  Stark, p. 361.

[288] Polyb. v. 71. 11, xvi. 49=Joseph. *Antt.* xii. 3. 3.

[289] See in general, *Antt.* xii. 4. 1, 4 ; 1 Macc. x. 30, 38, xi. 28, 34.

[290] On the chronology, comp. above, § 8.

[291] Cedrenus, ed. Beker, i. 323: τὴν τῶν Γαβινίων (l. Γαβινιέων) πόλιν, τὴν ποτε Σαμάρειαν (Herodes) ἐπικτίσας Σεβαστὴν αὐτὴν προσηγόρευσε.  Cedrenus here indeed mistakes Herod the Great for Herod Antipas and the latter again for Herod Agrippa.

The town was bestowed upon Herod by Augustus (*Antt.* xv. 7. 3; *Bell. Jud.* i. 20. 3); and by his means it first regained prosperity. For while it had hitherto been a comparatively small though strong town, its extent was so greatly increased by Herod, that it was now twenty stadia in circumference and not inferior to the most important towns. In the city thus enlarged Herod settled six thousand colonists, composed partly of disbanded soldiers, partly of people from the neighbourhood. The colonists received excellent estates. The fortifications too were rebuilt and extended, and finally the town obtained also, by the erection of a temple to Augustus and other magnificent edifices, the splendour of modern culture.[292] Herod gave to the newly-rebuilt town the name of Σεβαστή (*Antt.* xv. 8. 5; *Bell. Jud.* i. 21. 2. Strabo, xvi. p. 860) in honour of the emperor, who had recently assumed the title of Augustus. The coins of the town bear the inscription Σεβαστηνῶν or Σεβαστηνῶν Συρ(ίας) and a special era commencing with the year of the rebuilding of the city, *i.e.* according to the usual view 25 or perhaps more correctly 27 B.C.[293] The town is also mentioned in Rabbinical literature by its new name of Sebaste (סבסטי).[294] When Josephus says, that Herod granted it "an excellent constitution," ἐξαίρετον εὐνομίαν (*Bell. Jud.* i. 21. 2), he makes indeed no great addition to our knowledge. It is however probable from other reasons, that the country of Samaria was subordinated to the town of Sebaste precisely as Galilee was to the capitals Sepphoris and Tiberias respectively and Judaea was to Jerusalem. For on the occasion of the tumults of the

[292] Considerable remains of a large colonnade running along the hill, the building of which is probably to be ascribed to Herod, are still in existence. See the literature cited in note 283.

[293] On the date of the rebuilding, see § 15. On the coins in general, Noris, v. 5 (ed. Lips. pp. 531–536). Eckhel, iii. 440. Mionnet, v. 513–516; *Suppl.* viii. 356–359. De Saulcy, pp. 275–281, pl. xiv. n. 4–7.

[294] Mishna, *Arachin* iii. 2 (the "pleasure gardens of Sebaste," פרדסוה סבסטי, are here adduced as an example of specially valuable property. See the commentary of Bartenora in Surenhusius' *Mishna*, v. 198). Neubauer, *Géographie du Talmud*, p. 171 sq.

Samaritans under Pilate a " council of Samaritans," Σαμαρέων
ἡ βουλή, is mentioned, which seems to point to a united
organization of the country (*Antt.* xviii. 4. 2).[294a]   Sebastenian
soldiers served in the army of Herod and embraced the
party of the Romans against the Jews in the conflicts which
broke out at Jerusalem after his death (*Bell. Jud.* ii. 3. 4,
4. 2, 3 ; comp. *Antt.* xvii. 10. 3).   At the partition of
Palestine after the decease of Herod, Sebaste with the rest
of Samaria fell to Archelaus (*Antt.* xvii. 11. 4 ; *Bell. Jud.*
ii. 6. 3), after whose banishment it remained for a time under
Roman procurators, was then temporarily under Agrippa, and
then again under procurators.   During this last period Sebastenian soldiers formed a main element in the Roman troops
stationed in Judaea (see above, p. 65).   At the outbreak
of the Jewish war Sebaste was attacked by the insurgent
Jews (*Bell. Jud.* ii. 18. 1).   The town of Sebaste, with its chiefly
heathen population, then remained as during the disturbances
that followed the death of Herod (*Antt.* xvii. 10. 9 ; *Bell. Jud.*
ii. 5. 1) undoubtedly on the side of the Romans, while the
native Samaritans in the district of Sichem certainly occupied a difficult position (*Bell. Jud.* iii. 7. 32).   Sebaste
became a Roman colony under Septimius Severus.[295]   But its
importance henceforth declined before the prosperity of
Neapolis = Sichem.[296]   Eusebius and Stephanus Byz. still call
Sebaste only " a small town." [297]   Its district was nevertheless

---

[294a] On the constitution and political position given by Herod to the town,
see especially Kuhn, *Ueber die Entstehung der Städte der Alten* (1878), pp.
422 sq., 428 sqq.

[295] *Digest*, lib. xv. 1. 7 (from Ulpianus): Divus quoque Severus in Sebas-
tenam civitatem coloniam deduxit.   On coins, COL. L. SEP. SEBASTE.
Comp. Eckhel, iii. 441.   Zumpt, *Commentationes epigr.* i. 432.   Kuhn, ii. 56
The coins in Mionnet and De Saulcy, as above.

[296] Ammianus Marcellinus, xiv. 8. 11, names Neapolis, but not Sebaste,
among the most important towns of Palestine.   Comp. above, note
88.

[297] Euseb. *Onomast.* p. 292: Σεβαστήν, τὴν νῦν πολίχνην τῆς Παλαιστίνης.   Steph. Byz. *s.v.* Σεβαστή . . . ἔστι δὲ καὶ ἐν τῇ Σαμαρείτιδι
πολίχνιον.

so large, that it comprised *e.g.* Dothaim, which lay 12 *m. p.* northward of the town.[298]

25. *Gaba,* Γάβα or Γαβά.  The name corresponds to the Hebrew גֶּבַע or גִּבְעָה, a hill, and is a frequent local name in Palestine.  We are here concerned only with a Gaba, which according to the decided statements of Josephus stood on Carmel, and indeed in the great plain near the district of Ptolemais and the borders of Galilee, and therefore on the north-eastern declivity of Carmel (see especially, *Bell. Jud.* iii. 3. 1, and *Vita,* 24).  Herod here settled a colony of retired knights, on which account the city was also called πόλις ἱππέων (*Bell. Jud.* iii. 3. 1 ; *Antt.* xv. 8. 5).[299]  From the manner in which the town is mentioned in the two passages, *Bell. Jud.* iii. 3. 1 ; *Vita,* 24, it is evident that it did not belong to the district of Galilee.  Its population being chiefly heathen, it was attacked by the Jews at the beginning of the Jewish insurrection (*Bell. Jud.* ii. 18. 1), while on the other hand it took an active part in the struggle against the Jews (*Vita,* 24).  This town is probably the Geba on Carmel mentioned by Pliny.[300]  Whatever other material has been adduced to the contrary by scholars with respect to Gaba, has served to complicate rather than throw light upon the questions concerning its situation and history.[301]  A Gabe 16 *m. p.* from Caesarea is mentioned by Eusebius, but the distance stated is

---

[298] Euseb. *Onomast.* p. 249 : Δωθαείμ . . . διαμένει ἐν ὁρίοις Σεβαστῆς, ἀπέχει δὲ αὐτῆς σημείοις ιβ´ ἐπὶ τὰ βόρεια μέρη.

[299] The latter passage (*Antt.* xv. 8. 5) is according to the usual text: ἔν τε τῷ μεγάλῳ πεδίῳ, τῶν ἐπιλέκτων ἱππέων περὶ αὐτὸν ἀποκληρώσας, χωρίον συνέκτισεν ἐπί τε τῇ Γαλιλαίᾳ Γάβα καλούμενον καὶ τῇ Περαίᾳ τὴν Ἐσεβωνῖτιν. According to this it might be supposed that Herod had founded *three* colonies : 1. an unknown place in the great plain ; 2. a place called Gaba in Galilee ; and 3. Esebonitis in Peraea.  The two first are, however, certainly identical ; the τε after ἐπί must be omitted, and the meaning of ἐπὶ τῇ Γαλιλαίᾳ is, as the whole context shows, "for the controlling of Galilee." This also confirms the view, that Gaba lay on the *eastern* declivity of Carmel. For the rest, the reading here, as well as in *Bell. Jud.* iii. 3. 1, fluctuates between Γαβα and Γαβαλα, but the former is preferable.

[300] Plinius, *H. N.* v. 19. 75.

[301] See in general, Reland, p. 769.  Pauly's *Encycl.* iii. 563.  Kuhn, *Die*

too short to suit the situation north-east of Carmel.[302]    Still more improbable is it, that the coins with the superscription *Κλανδι(έων) Φιλιπ(πέων) Γαβηνῶν* belong to our Gaba. These titles point rather to a Gaba, which had belonged to the Tetrarch Philip;[303] and the Gabe, mentioned by Pliny as near Caesarea Panias, may be identical with it.[304]    Lastly, which Gaba the *Γάβαι* in *Palaestina secunda*, mentioned by Hierocles, may be, must be left uncertain.[305]    Guérin thinks he has discovered one Gaba in the village of Sheikh Abreik upon a hill near Carmel, with the situation of which the statements of Josephus certainly agree.[306]

26.   *Esbon* or *Hesbon*, Hebr. חֶשְׁבּוֹן, in the LXX. and Eusebius *Ἐσεβών*, Josephus *Ἐσσεβών*, later *Ἐσβοῦς*. The town lay, according to Josephus, 20 *m. p.* east of the Jordan,

*städt. und bürgerl. Verf.* ii. 320, 350 sq.   The same, *Ueber die Entstehung der Städte der Alten*, p. 424.   Quandt, *Judäa und die Nachbarschaft im Jahrh. vor und nach der Geburt Christi* (1873), p. 120 sq.

[302] Euseb. *Onomast.*, ed. Lagarde, p. 246: *καὶ ἔστι πολίχνη Γαβὲ καλουμένη ὡς ἀπὸ σημείων ις′ τῆς Καισαρείας* et alia villa Gabatha in finibus Diocaesareae *παρακειμένη τῷ μεγάλῳ πεδίῳ τῆς Λεγεῶνος.*   The words here interpolated in Latin from Hieronymus have been omitted from the text of Eusebius through homoioteleuton.   Through their omission it came to appear, that the little town of Gabe was 16 *m. p.* from Caesarea, and yet at the same time in the great plain of Legeon (Megiddo), which is not possible. The Gabe of Eusebius seems, on the contrary, to be identical with *Jeba*, which is marked on the large English chart directly north of Caesarea on the western declivity of Carmel.   *Map of Western Palestine*, sheet viii. to the left, above; also *Memoirs*, ii. 42, where indeed this Jeba is identified with *πόλις ἱππέων.*

[303] See on the coins, Noris, iv. 5. 6 (ed. Lips. pp. 458–462).   Eckhel, iii. 344 sqq.   Mionnet, v. 316–318; *Suppl.* viii. 220–222.   De Saulcy, pp. 339–343, pl. xix. n. 1-7.   The coins have an era commencing somewhere between 693 and 696 A.U.C.

[304] Plinius, *H. N.* v. 18. 74.

[305] Hierocles, *Synecd.*, ed. Parthey, p. 44.

[306] Guérin, *Galilée*, i. 395–397.   Sheikh Abreik lies upon an isolated eminence close to Carmel, under the same degree of latitude as Nazareth. Compare *The Survey of Western Palestine*, *Memoirs* by Conder and Kitchener, i. 343–351, also the English map, sheet v.   It is certainly incorrect to seek for Gaba in the situation of the present Jebata, as Menke does in his *Bibel-Atlas*.   The latter is much too far from Carmel, in the midst of the plain; and is, on the contrary, identical with the Gabatha of Eusebius (see note 302).

opposite Jericho.[307] With this agrees exactly the situation of the present Hesbân, east of Jordan, under the same degree of latitude as the northern point of the Dead Sea, where ruins are also found.[308] Hesbon is frequently mentioned as the capital of an Amorite kingdom.[309] In Isaiah and Jeremiah, on the other hand, it appears as a Moabite town.[310] And as such it is also mentioned by Josephus even in the time of Alexander Jannaeus, by whose victories it was incorporated in the Jewish region (*Antt.* xiii. 15. 4). Its further history cannot be accurately followed. At all events it was in the possession of Herod, when he refortified it for the control of Peraea, and placed in it a military colony (*Antt.* xv. 8. 5).[311] The district of Esbon is mentioned as the eastern boundary of Peraea by Josephus, hence it did not in a political sense belong to Peraea.[312] At the outbreak of the Jewish war, it was

[307] Euseb. *Onomast.* p. 253 : Ἐσεβών . . . καλεῖται δὲ νῦν Ἐσβοῦς, ἐπίσημος πόλις τῆς Ἀραβίας, ἐν ὄρεσι τοῖς ἀντικρὺ τῆς Ἱεριχοῦς κειμένη, ὡς ἀπὸ σημείων κ΄ τοῦ Ἰορδάνου.

[308] See Seetzen, *Reisen,* i. 497, iv. 220 sqq. Burckhardt, *Reisen,* ii. 623 sq., 1063. Ritter, *Erdkunde,* xv. 2. 1176–1181. De Saulcy, *Voyage en Terre Sainte* (1865), i. 279 sqq. (with a plan of the ruins). Bädeker-Socin, *Palästina,* p. 318. On the history, Reland, p. 719 sq. Raumer, p. 262. The articles on " Hesbon," in Winer, Schenkel, Riehm, Herzog's *Real-Encycl.* 1st ed. vi. 21 sq. Kuhn, *Die städt. und bürgerl. Verfassung,* ii. 337, 386 sq.

[309] Num. xxi. 26 sqq. ; Deut. i. 4, ii. 24 sqq., iii. 2 sqq., iv. 46 ; Josh. ix. 9, xii. 2 sqq., xiii. 10, 21 ; Judg. xi. 19 sqq. Comp. also Judith v. 15.

[310] Isa. xv. 4, xvi. 8, 9 ; Jer. xlviii. 2, 34, 35, xlix. 3.

[311] Thus certainly must the passage cited be understood ; see on its tenor, note 299. The form Ἐσεβωνῖτις is the designation of the *district* of Esbon. The town itself is called Ἐσεβών or Ἐσσεβών. Σεβωνῖτις occurs for Ἐσεβωνῖτις, *Bell. Jud.* ii. 18. 1, iii. 3. 3. See the following note.

[312] Σεβωνῖτις is certainly the reading, as in *Bell. Jud.* ii. 18. 1, instead of Σιλβωνῖτις. In Menke's *Bibel-Atlas,* sheet v., Essebon is correctly placed outside Peraea ; on the other hand, it is incorrectly allotted to the Nabataean realm instead of to that of Herod the Great. It is possible that after the death of Herod it may have fallen into the hands of the Arabians, as *e.g.* Machaerus also temporarily belonged to them (*Antt.* xviii. 5. 1). The circumstance that Esbon, after the erection of Arabia to the rank of a province, belonged thereto favours this supposition. Less convincing is the mention of the Esbonitae Arabes in Plinius, v. 11. 65, since this is only said in an ethnographical sense. In any case the Σεβωνῖτις formed in the time of

attacked by the insurgent Jews (*Bell. Jud.* ii. 18. 1).   At the
creation of the province of Arabia, A.D. 105, Esbon, or as it
was now called Esbus, was probably forthwith awarded to it,
for Ptolemy already speaks of it as belonging to Arabia.[313]
The few coins as yet known are those of either Caracalla or
Elagabalus.[314]   It was an important town in the time of Eusebius,[315] and Christian bishops of Esbus (Esbundorum, 'Εσβουν-
τίων) are mentioned in the fourth and fifth centuries.[316]

27. *Antipatris*, 'Αντιπατρίς.[317]   The original name of this
town was Καφαρσαβά,[318] or Καβαρσαβά,[319] sometimes Καπερ-
σαβίνη,[320] Hebrew כפר סבא, under which name it also occurs in
Rabbinical literature.[321]   Its situation is evidenced by the
present *Kefr-Saba*, north-eastward of Joppa, the position of

Josephus a town district proper, which though perhaps subject to the
Arabians, was still distinct from the other Arabias, *Bell. Jud.* iii. 3. 3.

[313] Ptolem. v. 17. 6.   The town is here called 'Εσβουτα (so also the Codex
of Vatopedi, see *Géographie de Ptolémée, reproduction photolithographique*,
etc., Paris 1867, p. lvii. below), which however is properly the accusative
form of 'Εσβους.

[314] Eckhel, iii. 503.   Mionnet, v. 585 sq. ; *Suppl.* viii. 387.   De Saulcy,
p. 393, pl. xxiii. n. 5–7.

[315] See above, note 307.   Eusebius also frequently mentions the town elsewhere in the *Onomasticon*.   See Lagarde's Index, *s.v.* εσβουν, εσεβουν and εσεβους.

[316] Le Quien, *Oriens christianus*, ii. 863.

[317] See on the subject generally, Reland, p. 569 sq., 690.   Pauly's *Enc.*
i. 1. 1150.   Kuhn, ii. 351.   Winer, *s.v.* "Antipatris."   Raumer, p. 147.   Robinson's *Palestine*, ii. p. 242, iii. pp. 138, 139.   Ritter, xvi. 569–572.   Guérin,
*Samarie*, ii. 357–367 ; comp. ii. 132 sq.   Wilson, *Quarterly Statement*,
1874, pp. 192–196.   *The Survey of Western Palestine, Memoirs* by Conder
and Kitchener, ii. 134, 258–262 ; the English map, sheets x. and xiii.
Ebers and Guthe, *Palästina*, vol. ii. p. 452.

[318] Joseph. *Antt.* xvi. 5. 2.

[319] Joseph. *Antt.* xiii. 15. 1.   The reading here fluctuates between Καβαρ-
σαβα, Χαβαρσαβα and Χαβαρζαβα.

[320] Such is undoubtedly the reading instead of και περσαβινη in the
passage of the *Chronicon Paschale*, ed. Dindorf, i. 367 : ὁ αὐτὸς δὲ καὶ
Ἀνθηδόνα ἐπικτίσας Ἀγρίππειαν ἐκάλεσεν, ἔτι δὲ καὶ περσαβίνην εἰς ὄνομα
Ἀντιπάτρου τοῦ ἰδίου πατρός.   Comp. Reland, pp. 690, 925.   In the parallel
passage in Syncellus, ed. Dindorf, i. 595, it is said : ἔτι τε Παρσανάβαν εἰς
τιμὴν Ἀντιπάτρου τοῦ πατρὸς αὐτοῦ Ἀντιπατρίδα ὠνόμασε.

[321] Tosefta, *Nidda* 649. 35 (ed. Zuckermandel) ; *Bab. Nidda* 61ᵃ ; *Jer.
Demai* ii. 1, fol. 22ᶜ.   Hamburger, *Real-Encycl. für Bibel und Talmud*,
ii. 637, art. " Kephar Saba."

which agrees with the statements of ancient writers concerning Antipatris, that it was 150 stadia from Joppa,[322] at the entrance of the mountainous district,[323] and 26 *m. p.* south of Caesarea, on the road thence to Lydia.[324]  Herod here founded in a well-watered and well-wooded plain a new city, which he called Antipatris in honour of his father Antipater (*Antt.* xvi. 5. 2; *Bell. Jud.* i. 21. 9). The town is also mentioned in Rabbinical literature under this name, אנטיפטרס ;[325] also by Ptolemy, Eusebius, and Stephanus Byzantinus.[326]  It was much reduced in the fourth century after Christ, being spoken of in the *Itinerar. Burdig.*, not as a *civitas*, but only as a *mutatio* (stopping place), and designated by Jerome as a *semirutum opidulum.*[327]  Yet a Bishop of Antipatris still occurs in the Acts of the Council of Chalcedon, A.D. 451.[328]  Its existence in these later times is also elsewhere evidenced.[329]  Nay, so late as the eighth century after Christ it is still spoken of as a town inhabited by Christians.[330]

28. *Phasaelis, Φασαηλίς.*[331]  It was in honour of his brother Phasael that Herod founded in the Jordan valley, in a

---

[322] *Antt.* xiii. 15. 1.          [323] *Bell. Jud.* i. 4. 7.

[324] The *Itinerarium Burdigalense* (in Tobler and Molinier, *Itinera*, etc., p. 20) gives the distance from Caesarea to Antipatris at 26 *m. p.*, that from Antipatris to Lydda at 10 *m. p.* The former number agrees almost exactly with the situation of Kefr-Saba, the latter is in consequence of a clerical error too little. The general situation of Antipatris, as on the road from Caesarea to Lydda, is also elsewhere testified; see *Antt.* xxiii. 31 ; Joseph. *Bell. Jud.* ii. 19. 1, 9, iv. 8. 1. Hieronym. *Peregrinatio Paulae* (in Tobler, *Palaestinae descr.* p. 13). The reasons brought forward by Guérin, Wilson, Conder, and Mühlau (Riehm's *Wörterb.*) against the identity of Kefr-Saba and Antipatris do not seem to me decisive.

[325] Mishna, *Gittin* vii. 7 ; *Bab. Gittin* 76ᵃ. Lightfoot, *Centuria Matthaeo praemissa*, c. 58 (Opp. ii. 214). Neubauer, *Géographie du Talmud*, pp. 86–90. Hamburger, *Real-Encycl.* ii. 63, art. " Antipatris."

[326] Ptolemaeus, v. 16. 6. Eusebius, *Onomast.* pp. 245, 246. Steph. Byz. *s.v.*

[327] See the passages cited, note 324.

[328] Le Quien, *Oriens christianus*, iii. 579 sq.

[329] Hierocles, *Synecd.* (ed. Parthey) p. 43. The *Notitia episcopat.* (the same), p. 143.

[330] Theophanis, *Chronographia*, ad ann. Dom. 743 (ed. Bonnens. i. 658).

[331] See in general, Reland, p. 953 sq. Pauly's *Enc.* v. 1439. Raumer, p. 216. Robinson's *Palestine*, i. p. 569, iii. p. 293. Ritter, xv. 1. 458 sq.

hitherto untilled but fertile region, which was thus gained for
cultivation, the city of Phasaelis (*Antt.* xvi. 5. 2 ; *Bell. Jud.*
i. 21. 9).  After his death the town, with its valuable palm
plantations, came into the possession of his sister Salome
(*Antt.* xviii. 8. 1, 11. 5 ; *Bell. Jud.* ii. 6. 3) ; and after her
death into that of the Empress Livia (*Antt.* xviii. 2. 2 ; *Bell.
Jud.* ii. 9. 1).  Pliny speaks of the excellent dates obtained
from the palm trees growing there.[332]  The town is also
mentioned by Ptolemy, Stephanus Byz., and the geographers
of Ravenna.[333]  Its name has been preserved in the present
Karbet Fasail on the edge of the plain of the Jordan, in a
fertile district.  The stream flowing thence to the Jordan is
called Wadi Fasail.[334]

29. *Caesarea Panias.*[335]  Τὸ Πάνειον properly means the
grotto dedicated to Pan at the source of the Jordan.[336]  It is
first mentioned under this name by Polybius in the time of
Antiochus the Great, who there gained (198 B.C.) over the

Guérin, *Samarie*, i. 228–232.  *The Survey of Western Palestine, Memoirs*
by Conder and Kitchener, ii. 388, 392; and the large English map,
sheet xv.

[332] Plinius, *H. N.* xiii. 4. 44 : Sed ut copia ibi atque fertilitas, ita nobili-
tas in Judaea, nec in tota, sed Hiericunte maxume, quamquam laudatae et
Archelaide et *Phaselide* atque Liviade, gentis ejusdem convallibus.

[333] Ptolem. v. 16. 7.  Steph. Byz. *s.v.*  *Geographus Ravennas*, edd. Pinder
et Parthey (1860), p. 84.  The town is also mentioned in the Middle Ages
(in Burchardus and Marinus Sanutus), see the passages in Guérin, *Samarie*,
i. 231 sq.

[334] See especially the large English map, sheet xv., and the description
in Guérin and Conder, as above.

[335] See on the general subject, Reland, pp. 918–922.  Winer's *RWB.*
and Schenkel's *Bibellex. s.v.* "Caesarea."  Kuhn, ii. 334.  Robinson's
*Palestine*, iii. 397–413.  Ritter, *Erdkunde*, xv. 1. 195–207.  Guérin,
*Galilée*, ii. 308–323.  *The Survey of Western Palestine, Memoirs* by Conder
and Kitchener, i. 95, 109–113, 125–128; the large English map, sheet ii.
Ebers and Guthe, *Palästina in Bild und Wort*, i. 356–366.  Views of the
Pan-Grotto in the Duc de Luynes *Voyage d' Exploration*, etc., Atlas,
plates 62, 63.  Inscriptions, *Corp. Inscr. Graec.* n. 4537–4539.  Le Bas
et Waddington, *Inscriptions*, vol. iii. n. 1891–1894.

[336] The Paneion is described as a grotto (σπήλαιον, ἄντρον) in Joseph.
*Antt.* xv. 10. 3.  *Bell. Jud.* i. 21. 3, iii. 10. 7 : δοκεῖ μὲν Ἰορδάνου πηγὴ
τὸ Πανίον.  Steph. Byz. *s.v.* Πανία.  The mountain was called by the same
name as the grotto, Euseb. *Hist. eccl.* vii. 17 : ἐν ταῖς ὑπωρείαις τοῦ καλου-

Egyptian general Scopas the decisive victory, in consequence
of which all Palestine fell into his hands.[337]  Even this early
mention would lead us to infer a Hellenization of the place
in the third century before Christ.  In any case the population of the surrounding district, as its farther history also
shows, was chiefly non-Jewish.  In the early times of Herod
the country of Πανιάς (as it was called from the Pan-Grotto
there) belonged to a certain Zenodorus, after whose death, in
the year 20 B.C., it was given by Augustus to Herod (see
above, § 15), who built a splendid temple to Augustus in the
neighbourhood of the Pan-Grotto (*Antt.* xv. 10. 3 ; *Bell. Jud.*
i. 21. 3).  The place, which lay there, was originally called
like the country, Πανιάς or Πανεάς.[338]  It was first, however,
transformed into a considerable town by Philip the Tetrarch,
the son of Herod, who rebuilt it and called it Καισάρεια, in
honour of Augustus (*Antt.* xviii. 2. 1 ; *Bell. Jud.* ii. 9. 1).
This refoundation belongs to the early times of Philip; for
the coins of the town have an era, the commencement of
which probably dates from the year 3 B.C. (751 A.U.C.), or at
latest 2 B.C. (752 A.U.C.).[339]  After the death of Philip, his
realm was for a few years under Roman administration, then
under Agrippa I., then again under Roman procurators, and
at last, in A.D. 53, under Agrippa II., who enlarged Caesarea
and called it Νερωνιάς in honour of Nero (*Antt.* xv. 9. 4),

μένου Πανίου ὄρους (Τὸ Πάνειον is properly an adjective requiring as a
complement either ἄντρον or ὄρος.

[337] Polybius, xvi. 18, xxviii. 1.

[338] Πανιάς or Πανεάς is properly an adjective and indeed the fem. of
Πάνειος (as ἀγριάς, λευκάς, ὀρειάς are the poetic feminines of ἄγριος, λευκός,
ὄρειος).  Hence the same word serves to designate both the *country* (where
χώρα is the complement, *Antt.* xv. 10. 3, xvii. 8. 1.  *Bell. Jud.* ii. 9. 1.
Plinius, v. 18. 74 : Panias in qua Caesarea) and the *town* or village (where
πόλις or κώμη is the complement, *Antt.* xviii. 2. 1).

[339] See Noris, iv. 5. 4 (ed. Lips. pp. 442–453).  Eckhel, iii. 339–344.
Sanclemente, *De vulgaris aerae emendatione* (Rome 1793), iii. 2, p. 322 sqq.
The coins in Mionnet, v. 311–315; *Suppl.* viii. 217–220.  De Saulcy, pp. 313–
324, pl. xviii.  The addition to the *Chronicle* of Eusebius, which transposes
the foundation to the time of Tiberius, is of no value.  See below, note 390.
Also Jerome in the *Chronicle and Comment. on Matth.* xvi. 13 (see note 345).

which name is occasionally found on coins.[340]　That the town was then also chiefly a heathen one appears from Joseph. *Vita*, 13.　Hence both Titus and Vespasian passed their times of repose during the Jewish war amidst games and other festivities at this place.[341]　The name Neronias seems never to have been naturalized.　In the first century after Christ this Caesarea was, to distinguish it from others, usually called Καισάρεια ἡ Φιλίππου; [342] its official designation upon coins, especially of the second century, is Καισ(άρεια) Σεβ(αστή) ἱερ(ὰ) καὶ ἄσυ(λος) ὑπὸ Πανείω.[343]　Elsewhere it has generally been called since the second century Καισάρεια Πανιάς, which name also predominates on coins of the third.[344]　Since the fourth the name of Caesarea has been wholly lost, and the town called only Panias.[345]　This seems besides to have always remained its prevailing name among the native popu-

[340] Mionnet, v. 315. De Saulcy, pp. 316, 318. Madden, *History of Jewish Coinage*, pp. 116, 117. The same, *Coins of the Jews*, pp. 145, 146.

[341] Joseph. *Bell. Jud.* iii. 9. 7, vii. 2. 1.

[342] Matt. xvi. 13 ; Mark viii. 27. Joseph. *Antt.* xx. 9. 4 ; *Bell. Jud.* iii. 9. 7, vii. 2. 1 ; *Vita*, 13.

[343] See the literature cited in note 339, especially Mionnet and De Saulcy.

[344] Ptolem. v. 15. 21, viii. 20. 12 (Καισάρεια Πανιάς). *Corp. Inscr. Graec.* n. 4750 (upon the statue of Memnon at Thebes), and n. 4921 (at Philoe), both times Καισαρείας Πανιάδος. Le Bas et Waddington, *Inscriptions*, vol. iii. n. 1620ᵇ (at Aphrodisias in Caria in the second century after Christ)· Καισάρειαν Πανιάδα. *Tabula Peuting.* (Caesareapaneas). *Geographus Ravennas*, edd. Pinder et Parthey, p. 85. The coins in De Saulcy, pp. 317, 322 sq.

[345] Eusebius, who frequently mentions the town in the *Onomasticon*, always calls it Πανεάς only (see the Index in Lagarde's edition). And this is generally its name in ecclesiastical literature ; see Eusebius, *Hist. eccl.* vii. 17, 18. Hieron. *in Jesaj.* xlii. 1 sqq., ed. Vallarsi, iv. 507 (in confinio Caesareae Philippi, quae nunc vocatur Paneas). Idem *in Ezek.* xxvii. 19, ed. Vall. v. 317 (ubi hodie Paneas, quae quondam Caesarea Philippi vocabatur) ; Idem *in Matt.* xvi. 13, ed. Vall. vii. 121 (in honorem Tiberii (sic!) Caesaris Caesaream, quae nunc Paneas dicitur, construxit). Sozom. v. 21. Philostorg. vii. 3 (comp. also Müller, *Fragm. hist. graec.* iv. 546). Theodoret. *Quaest.* (see the passages in Reland, p. 919). Malalas, ed. Dindorf, p. 237. Glycas Theophanes (see the passages in Reland, p. 922). Photius, *Cod.* 271, *sub fin.* The Acts of the Councils (in Le Quien, *Oriens christianus*, ii. 831). Hierocles, *Synecd.*, ed. Parthey, p. 43. Theodosius, *De situ terrae sanctae*, § 13 (ed. Gildemeister 1882). On the supposed statue of Christ at Paneas, see also Gieseler, *Kirchengesch.* i. 1. 85 sq.

lation,[346] as it is also that chiefly used (in the form פנים) in Rabbinic literature.[347] When the "villages of Caesarea Philippi" (αἱ κῶμαι Καισαρείας τῆς Φιλίππου) are mentioned in the New Testament, Mark viii. 27, of course the genitive here expresses not a merely "local reference" of the villages to the town,[348] but shows that they belong and are subject to it,—in other words, that Caesarea had, like each of these towns, a district of its own which it governed.

30. *Julias*, formerly *Bethsaida*.[349] In the place of a village called Bethsaida, lying to the north of the Lake of Gennesareth, a new town was built by Philip, who called it Ἰουλιάς, in honour of Julia the daughter of Augustus (*Antt.* xviii. 2. 1; *Bell. Jud.* ii. 9. 1). Its situation eastward of the Jordan, just before the latter flows into the Lake of Gennesareth, is placed beyond doubt by the repeated and concurrent statements of Josephus.[350] The foundation of this city also must have taken place in the earlier times of Philip. For in the year 2 B.C. (752 A.U.C.) Julia had already been banished by Augustus to the island of Pandateria,[351] and it is not conceiv-

---

[346] Comp. Euseb. *H. E.* vii. 17: ἐπὶ τῆς Φιλίππου Καισαρείας, ἣν Πανεάδα Φοίνικες προσαγορεύουσι.

[347] Mishna, *Para* viii. 11; Tosefta, *Bechoroth* p. 542, 1, ed. Zuckermandel (in both passages the "Grotto of Panias," פנים מערת, is mentioned). Buxtorf, *Lex. Chald.* col. 1752. Levy, *Chald. Wörterbuch*, ii. 273 sq. Lightfoot, *Centuria Matthaeo praemissa*, c. 67 (*Opp.* ii. 220). Neubauer, *Géographie du Talmud*, pp. 236–238. The corrupted form פמים does not belong to the usage of the living language, but in the first instance to a later text. In the passages cited from the Mishna the best authorities still have פנים (so *Aruch*, *Cod. de Rossi* 138, *Cambridge University Additional*, 470. 1). In *Aruch* this form only is everywhere quoted.

[348] So Winer, *Grammatik*, § 30. 2.

[349] See in general, Reland, pp. 653 sqq., 869. Raumer, p. 122. Winer, *s.v.* "Bethsaida." Kuhn, ii. 352. Robinson, ii. pp. 405, 406, iii. pp. 358, 359. Ritter, xv. 1. 278 sqq. Guérin, *Galilée*, i. 329–338. Furrer in the *Zeitsch. of the German Pal.-Vereins*, ii. 66–70.

[350] See especially, *Bell. Jud.* iii. 10. 7; also *Antt.* xviii. 2. 1 (on the Lake of Gennesareth); *Vita*, 72 (near the Jordan); *Antt.* xx. 8. 4; *Bell. Jud.* ii. 13. 2 (in Peraea). Also Plinius, *H. N.* v. 15. 71, mentions Julias on the eastern shore of the Lake of Gennesareth.

[351] Velleius, ii. 100. Dio Cassius, lv. 10. Comp. Sueton. *Aug.* 65. Tac. *Annal.* i. 53. Pauly's *Enc.* v. 844 sq. Lewin, *Fasti sacri* (1865), n. 961.

able, that Philip should, after that date, have named a town
after her.[352]    Of its subsequent history, nothing is known but
that it was given by Nero to Agrippa II. (*Antt.* xx. 8. 4; *Bell.
Jud.* ii. 13. 2).    It is mentioned in Pliny, Ptolemy and the
geographers of Ravenna.[353]    From the manner in which
Josephus speaks of it (*Antt.* xviii. 2. 1), it might appear as
though Philip had only altered the name of the village of
Bethsaida into Julias, and thus, that the new place too was
only a κώμη.[354]    In another passage however he explicitly
distinguishes Julias from the surrounding *villages* as a πόλις,
hence the former was properly speaking a πόλις from the
time of its rebuilding.    The question as to whether the
Bethsaida of the New Testament was identical with this—a
question recently again decided in the affirmative[355]—must
here be left undiscussed.

31. *Sepphoris*, Σεπφώρις.[356]    The Semitic form of this
name fluctuates between צִפּוֹרִין and צִפּוֹרִי.    Perhaps the former
is the older, the latter the abbreviated form.[357]    With the

[352] So also Sanclemente, *De vulgaris aerae emendatione*, p. 327 sqq.
Lewin, *Fasti sacri*, n. 953.    The *Chronicle* of Eusebius erroneously places
the foundation of Julias in the time of Tiberius; see below, note 390.

[353] Plinius, v. 15. 71.    Ptolem. v. 16. 4.    *Geogr. Ravennas*, edd. Pinder
et Parthey, p. 85.

[354] *Antt.* xviii. 2. 1: κώμην δὲ Βηθσαϊδάν, πρὸς λίμνῃ δὲ τῇ Γεννησαρίτιδι,
πόλεως παρασχὼν ἀξίωμα πλήθει τε οἰκητόρων καὶ τῇ ἄλλῃ δυνάμει, 'Ιουλίᾳ
θυγατρὶ τῇ Καίσαρος ὁμώνυμον ἐκάλεσεν.

[355] Holtzmann, *Jahrb. f. prot. Theol.* 1878, p. 383 sq.    Furrer in the
*Zeitsch. of the German Päl.-Ver.* ii. 66–70.    Against this identity, see
especially Reland, Raumer and Winer, as above.

[356] See in general, Reland, pp. 999–1003.    Pauly's *Enc.* vi. 1. 1050.
Raumer, p. 139.    Kuhn, ii. 372.    Robinson's *Palestine*, iii. 111, 112.
Ritter, *Erdkunde*, xvi. 748 sq.    Guérin, *Galilée*, i. 369–376.    *The Survey of
Western Palestine, Memoirs* by Conder and Kitchener, i. 279 sq., 330–338;
also sheet v. of the English map.

[357] The place does not occur in the Old Testament, but very frequently,
on the other hand, in Rabbinical literature.    In the Mishna it is found in
the four following places: *Kiddushin* iv. 5; *Baba mezia* viii. 8; *Baba
bathra* vi. 7; *Arachin* ix. 6; very often in the Tosefta (see the Index in
Zuckermandel's edition).    Comp. also Lightfoot, *Centuria Matthaeo praemissa*, c. 82, 83 (*Opp.* ii. 229 sqq.).    Neubauer, *Géographie du Talmud*, ii.
1115.    The orthography fluctuates between צפורין (or, which is the same,
ציפורין, צפורים) and צפורי (ציפורי).    The *Cod. de Rossi* 138 has in all the

former correspond the Greek and Latin Σεπφουρίν, Saphorim, Safforine;[358] with the latter Σαπφουρεί, Sapori.[359]  Josephus constantly uses the Graecized form Σεπφώρις.  On coins the inhabitants are called Σεπφωρηνοί.[360]  The earliest mention is found in Josephus in the beginning of the reign of Alexander Jannaeus, when Ptolemy Lathurus made an unsuccessful attempt to take Sepphoris by force (*Antt.* xiii. 12. 5).  When Gabinius, about 57–55 B.C., divided the Jewish region into five "Synedria," he transferred the Synedrium for Galilee to Sepphoris (*Antt.* xiv. 5. 4; *Bell. Jud.* i. 8. 5); which shows that this town must then have been the most important town of Galilee.  It is also mentioned as a place of arms at the conquest of Palestine by Herod the Great, who was only able to take it without difficulty, because the garrison of Antigonus had evacuated the place (*Antt.* xiv. 15. 4; *Bell. Jud.* i. 16. 2).  At the insurrection, after the death of Herod, Sepphoris seems to have been a main seat of the rebellion.  Varus despatched thither a division of his army, burnt the town and sold its inhabitants as slaves (*Antt.* xvii. 10. 9; *Bell. Jud.* ii. 5. 1).  This makes a turning-point in its history; from a Jewish town adhering to the national party it now became a town friendly to the Romans, with probably a mixed population.  For Herod Antipas, to whose possession it was transferred, rebuilt it and made it "the

four places in the Mishna ציפורין ; the Cambridge manuscript too (*University Additional*, 470. 1) has throughout the plural form.  This also appears to be the prevailing form in the Jerusalemite Talmud (see the quotations in Lightfoot, as above).  Elsewhere, on the contrary, צפורי predominates, especially in the Tosefta (according to Zuckermandel's edition).

[358] Σεπφουρίν, Epiphan. *Haer.* 30. 11 (ed. Dindorf).  Saphorim, *Hierony-nus praef. in Jonam* (Vallarsi, vi. 390).  Safforine, *Hieron. Onomast.*, ed. Lagarde, p. 88.  In John xi. 54 the Greek and Latin text of the *Cod. Cantabr.* has the addition Σατφουρειν, Sapfurim, after χώραν.

[359] Σατφουρεί, Ptolem. v. 16. 4 (the Codex of Vatopedi has Σατφουρεί without the addition ἡ Σατφουρίς; see *Géographie de Ptolémée reproduction photolithographique*, etc., p. lvii.).  Sapori, *Geographus Ravennas*, edd. Pinder et Parthey, p. 85.

[360] See Eckhel, iii. 425.  Mionnet, 482.  De Saulcy, p. 325 sq., pl. xvii. n. 1–4.

ornament of all Galilee" (*Antt.* xviii. 2. 1): πρόσχημα τοῦ Γαλιλαίου παντός. But its population was—as was shown by its attitude during the great war, A.D. 66-70—no longer anti-Roman and hence no longer purely Jewish.[360a] It is perhaps this change, which is referred to in a passage of the Mishna, in which the "*ancient* government of Sepphoris" is assumed to have been a purely Jewish one.[361] At its rebuilding by Herod Antipas, Sepphoris seems to have been also raised to the rank of capital of Galilee.[362]

[360a] That it was however still *chiefly* Jewish is evident especially from *Bell. Jud.* iii. 2. 4 : προθύμους σφᾶς αὐτοὺς ὑπέσχοντο κατὰ τῶν ὁμοφύλων συμμάχους.

[361] *Kiddushin* iv. 5. It is here said, that every one is to be esteemed an Israelite of pure blood, who can prove his descent from a priest or Levite, who has actually ministered as such, or from a member of the Sanhedrim ; nay every one whose ancestors were known to have been public officials or almoners, in particular, according to Rabbi Jose, every מי שהיה החום בארכי הישנה של ציפורין. In explanation of this difficult passage we remark that חתום, properly "sealed," is here equivalent to " confirmed, acknowledged, accredited by documents " (compare the use of σφραγίζω, John iii. 33, vi. 27). The word עד, which the common text has after חתום, must according to the best MSS. be expunged. ארכי=ἀρχή. ישנה is certainly not the local name Jeshana (for which older commentators have taken it), but the adjective " old." Hence two explanations are possible. Either— 1. " Every one, who (with respect to his ancestors) was recognised *in* the old government of Sepphoris as a member thereof." It would then be assumed that all the members of the old government were Israelites of pure blood. Or 2. " Every one, who was acknowledged *by* the old government of Sepphoris," viz. as an Israelite of pure blood. *In this case also the old government of Sepphoris would be assumed to consist of purely Israelitish officials.* The first explanation seems to me to be preferable according to the context. It may certainly be questionable, *when* the ancient purely Jewish government of Sepphoris was replaced by another of mixed or heathen composition. This might have taken place in the time of Hadrian, when much may have been changed in consequence of the Jewish insurrection, at about which period also, it should be observed, Sepphoris received the new name of Diocaesarea (see below). According to all indications however, it seems to me probable, that Sepphoris so early as its rebuilding by Herod Antipas was no longer a purely Jewish town. Consider also the coins with the *image* of Trajan!

[362] Josephus says, *Antt.* xviii. 2. 1 : ἤγεν αὐτὴν αὐτοκρατορίδα. This alone tells us nothing more than that he granted it its autonomy (αὐτοκρατορίδα =αὐτόνομον). But subsequent history makes it probable, that the rest of Galilee was then already subordinated to it. The explanation of αὐτοκρα-

This rank was however afterwards bestowed by the same prince upon the newly built city of Tiberias, to which Sepphoris was subordinate.[363] It so continued until Tiberias was, in the reign of Nero, separated from Galilee and bestowed upon Agrippa II., when Sepphoris consequently again occupied the position of capital of Galilee.[364] Thus these two towns alternately assumed the same position with respect to Galilee, that Jerusalem did with respect to Judaea (see below,. § 2). Sepphoris was at that time the most important fortress in Galilee,[365] and, after Tiberias, the largest town in the province.[366] Hence, at the outbreak of the Jewish war, it was of the greatest consequence, that just this town did not participate in the insurrection, but remained from the beginning on the side of the Romans. So early as the time when Cestius Gallus marched against insurgent Jerusalem, Sepphoris took up a friendly position towards him.[367] It remained also faithful to its Romish tendencies during the winter of A.D. 66/67, when Josephus was organizing the insurrection in Galilee.[368]

τορίς as capital can hardly be conceded. Some MSS. have αὐτοκράτορι, whence Dindorf conjectures: ἀνῆκεν αὐτὴν αὐτοκράτορι, "he dedicated it to the emperor."

[363] *Vita*, 9, Justus said of Tiberias: ὡς ἡ πόλις ἐστὶν ἀεὶ τῆς Γαλιλαίας, ἄρξειεν δὲ ἐπί γε τῶν Ἡρώδου χρόνων τοῦ τετράρχου καὶ κτίστου γενομένου, βουληθέντος αὐτοῦ τὴν Σεπφωριτῶν πόλιν τῇ Τιβεριέων ὑπακούειν.

[364] *Vita*, 9 : ἄρξαι γὰρ εὐθὺς τὴν μὲν Σεπφῶριν, ἐπειδὴ Ῥωμαίοις ὑπήκουσε, τῆς Γαλιλαίας.

[365] *Bell. Jud.* ii. 18. 11 : ἡ καρτερωτάτη τῆς Γαλιλαίας πόλις Σεπφῶρις. Comp. *Bell. Jud.* iii. 2. 4. The ἀκρόπολις is mentioned *Vita*, 67. Comp. Mishna, *Arachin* ix. 6 : קצרה הישנה של ציפורין, "the old citadel of Sepphoris." Tosefta, *Shabbath*, p. 129, 27th ed. Zuckermandel, קצטרא שבציפורי.

[366] *Vita*, 65 (ed. Bekker, p. 340, 32) : τῶν ἐν τῇ Γαλιλαίᾳ πόλεων αἱ μεγίσται Σεπφῶρις καὶ Τιβεριάς. *Vita*, 45 : εἰς Σεπφῶριν, μεγίστην τῶν ἐν τῇ Γαλιλαίᾳ πόλιν. *Bell. Jud.* iii. 2. 4 : μεγίστην μὲν οὖσαν τῆς Γαλιλαίας πόλιν, ἐρυμνοτάτῳ δὲ ἐπεκτισμένην χωρίῳ. According to *Vita*, 25, Tiberias, Sepphoris and Gabara were the three largest towns of Galilee.

[367] *Bell. Jud.* ii. 18. 11.

[368] Joseph. *Vita*, 8, 22, 25, 45, 65. Two passages indeed in the *Bell. Jud.* seem to contradict this : according to *Bell. Jud.* ii. 20. 6, Josephus committed to the Sepphorites themselves the charge of fortifying their town, because he found them in other respects "ready for war" (προθύμους ἐπὶ τὸν πόλεμον), *i.e.* against the Romans ; and according to *Bell. Jud.* ii. 21. 7, Sepphoris, at the outbreak of the conflict between Josephus and the more

Josephus therefore took possession of it by force, in doing
which he was unable to prevent its being plundered by his
Galilaean troops.[369]   Cestius Gallus consequently sent a
garrison to the oppressed town, by which Josephus was repulsed, when he for the second time entered it by force.[370]
Vespasian soon after arrived in Galilee with his army, and
Sepphoris entreated and again received from him a Roman
garrison.[371]   We have but fragmentary information of the
further history of the town.   Its inhabitants are, on coins of
Trajan, still called Σεπφωρηνοί.   Soon after however it
received the name of Diocaesarea, which appears on coins
since Antoninus Pius.   Its official designation upon coins is:
Διοκαι(σάρεια) ἱερὰ ἄσ(υλος) καὶ αὐτό(νομος).[372]   The name of
Diocaesarea remained the prevailing one in Greek authors,[373]
though its original appellation continued to exist, and at last

fanatical war party, stood on the side of the latter.   The true relation
however between these two facts is seen from the more special statements
of the *Vita*. The Sepphorites alleged their readiness to attach themselves
to the cause of the revolution, solely for the purpose of keeping off from
themselves the whole revolutionary party; and fortified their city not
against, but for the Romans (see especially, *Vita*, 65).   And when in the
winter of 66/67 they had remained a long time without Roman protection,
they were obliged to tack between the two revolutionary parties, which
were mutually attacking each other, and as far as possible to take up a
friendly position towards both (see *Vita*, 25, and especially, *Vita*, 45), to
which circumstance what is said in *Bell. Jud.* ii. 21. 7 may be reduced.

[369] *Vita*, 67.

[370] *Vita*, 71.   The remark, *Vita*, 15: ὃ῀ς μὲν κατὰ κράτος ἑλὼν Σεπφω-
ρίτας, refers to this double capture of Sepphoris.

[371] *Vita*, 74; *Bell. Jud.* iii. 2. 4, 4. 1.   The former garrison sent by
Cestius Gallus had meantime either withdrawn or was now replaced or
strengthened by the troops of Vespasian.

[372] See on the coins in general, Noris, v. 6, *fin.* (ed. Lips. 562–564).
Eckhel, iii. 425 sq. Mionnet, v. 482 sq.; *Suppl.* viii. 331 sq. De Saulcy, pp.
325–330, pl. xvii. n. 1–7.   On a supposed coin of Seleucus I. (Nikator), Eckhel,
iii. 426.   Mionnet, v. 4.   On the identity of Sepphoris and Diocaesarea,
Epiphan. *Haer.* 30. 11, *fin.* Hieronymus, *Onomast.*, ed. Lagarde, p. 88. Idem,
*praefat. in Jonam* (Vallarsi, vi. 390).   Hegesippus, *De bello Jud.* i. 30. 7.

[373] Eusebius, in *Onomast.*, calls the town exclusively Διοκαισάρεια (see
the Index in Lagarde).   Compare also, beside the literature cited in the
preceding note, Socrates, *Hist. eccl.* ii. 33.   Sozom. *Hist. eccl.* iv. 7.
Theophanes, *Chronographia*, ed. Bonnens. i. 61.   Cedrenus, ed. Bekker, i.
524.   Le Quien, *Oriens christ.* iii. 714.

banished the new one.[374] The district of Diocaesarea was so extensive, that it included *e.g.* the village of Dabira on Mount Tabor.[375]

32. *Julias* or *Livias.*[376]  In the Old Testament, a place called Beth-haram (בֵּית הָרָם or בֵּית הָרָן), in the country east of the Jordan, in the realm of the Amorite kings of Hesbon, is mentioned (Josh. xiii. 27 ; Num. xxxii. 36).  In the Jerusalemite Talmud בית רמתה is stated to be the more modern name of this Beth-haram ;[377] and both Eusebius and Jerome identify the scriptural Beth-haram with the *Βηθραμφθά* or Bethramtha, which was known to them.[378]  The *Βηθαράμαθος*, where Herod the Great had a palace, which was destroyed during the insurrection after his death, is at any rate identical with the latter.[379]  It was this very Bethramphtha, which was rebuilt and fortified by Herod Antipas, and called Julias in honour of the wife of Augustus (Joseph. *Antt.* xviii. 2. 1; *Bell. Jud.* ii. 9. 1).  Eusebius and others give the name as Livias instead of Julias,[380] and the town is elsewhere frequently mentioned by this

[374] On the continued use of the name Sepphoris, see above, notes 357–359.  The place is still called Sefurije.

[375] Euseb. *Onomast.* p. 250 : Δαβειρά . . . ἐν τῷ ὄρει Θαβώρ, ἐν ὁρίοις Διοκαισαρείας, Gabatha, the present Jabata, about 7–8 *mil. pass.* from Diocaesarea, also belonged to its district.  See above, note 302.

[376] See in general, Reland, pp. 642, 874.  Pauly's *Enc.* iv. 1107. Winer, *RWB.* i. 171 (*s.v.* "Beth-haram").  Raumer, p. 260.  Ritter, xv. 538, 573, 1186.  Seetzen, *Reisen*, iv. 224 sq.  Riehm's *Wörterb. s.v.* Bethharam.  Kuhn, *Die städtische und bürgerl. Verfassung*, ii. 352 sq.  Id. *Ueber die Entstehung der Städte der Alten* (1878), p. 426.  Tuch, *Quaestiones de Flavii Josephi libris historicis* (1859), pp. 7–11.

[377] *Jer. Shebiith* 38ᵈ (on Mishna, *Shebiith* ix. 2 ; see the passage also in Reland, pp. 306–308).  Peraea is here divided into three parts, according to its physical conditions of mountain, plain, and valley (הר, שפלה and עמק).  In the mountainous part lies *e.g.* Machaerus, in the plain Hesbon, in the valley בית הרן and נמרה. בית רמתה and בית נמרין are then stated to be the more modern names of these last two places.  In the Tosefta (p. 71, 22rd ed. Zuckermandel) the two places are called בית נמרה רמתא.  Has the בית been here omitted before רמתא, or could the place have been called simply רמתא ?

[378] Euseb. *Onomast.*, ed. Lagarde, p. 234.  Hieronymus, *ibid.* p. 103.

[379] *Bell. Jud.* ii. 4. 2.  In the parallel passage, *Antt.* xvii. 10. 6, the name is corrupted.  Instead of ἐν Ἀμαθοῖς, as the traditional text has it, we must read either ἐν Ἀραμαθοῖς (with the omission of Beth, so Tuch, *Quaestiones*, etc., p. 10) or just ἐν Βηθαραμαθοῖς.

[380] Euseb. *Onomast.* p. 234 : Βηθραμφθά . . . αὕτη δέ ἐστιν ἡ νῦν καλου

name.[381]  Since the wife of Augustus was called by her own
name Livia during his lifetime, and did not bear the name
of Julia till she was admitted into the *gens Julia* by his
testament,[382] we must conclude that Livias was the older name
of the town, and that this was after the death of Augustus
altered into that of Julias ; but that this new official appellation was, as in the case of Caesarea Philippi and Neronias,
unable to banish the older and already nationalized name.
Only Josephus uses the official designation Julias.   He still
mentions the town by this name at the time of the Jewish war,
when it was occupied by Placidus, a general of Vespasian.[383]
The situation of the town is most accurately described by
Theodosius, the Palestinian pilgrim (sixth century), and after
him by Gregory of Tours : it lay beyond Jordan, opposite

μένη Λιβιάς,  Hieronymus, *ibid.* p. 103 : Bethramtha . . . ab Herode in
honorem Augusti Libias cognominata.   Euseb. *Chron.*, ed. Schoene, ii.
148 sq. : Herodes Tiberiadem condidit et *Liviadem* (according to Jerome,
also the Armenian).   *Synecd.*, ed. Dindorf, i. 605 : Ἡρώδης ἔκτισε Τιβεριάδα
εἰς ὄνομα Τιβερίου Καίσαρος, ὁ αὐτὸς Λιβιάδα.

[381] Plinius, *H. N.* xiii. 4. 44.  Ptolemaeus, v. 16. 9 (Λιβιάς according to
the Cod. of Vatopedi).  Euseb. in *Onomast.* frequently.  Hierocles, *Synecd.*,
ed. Parthey, p. 44.  The *Notitia episcopat.*, the same, p. 144.  The Acts of
the Councils (Le Quien, *Oriens christ.* iii. 655 sq.).  The *Vita S. Joannis
Silentiarii* (in the *Acta Sanctorum*, see the passage in Reland, p. 874).
*Geographus Ravennas*, ed. Pinder et Parthey, p. 84 (Liviada as nominat.).
Theodosius, *De situ terrae sanctae*, § 65, ed. Gildemeister, 1882 (Liviada
as nominat.).  Gregor. Turon. *De gloria martyr.* i. 18.  On the nominative formation Liviada, see Rönsch, *Itala und Vulgata*, p. 258 sq.

[382] On the testament of Augustus, see Tacit. *Annal.* i. 8 : Livia in
familiam Juliam nomenque Augustum adsumebatur.   The name Julia for
Livia is found in authors (see *e.g.* Tacit. *Annal.* i. 14, v. 1.  Sueton. *Calig.*
16; Dio Cassius, lvi. 46.  Plinius, *H. N.* x. 55. 154.  Joseph. frequently),
and upon coins and inscriptions.  See Pauly's *Enc.* iv. 484, 1116.
Palestinian coins of Julia, see in Madden, *History of Jewish Coinage*, pp.
141–151.  The same, *Coins of the Jews* (1881), pp. 177–182.

[383] *Bell. Jud.* iv. 7. 6, 8. 2.  The town is not elsewhere mentioned by
Josephus.  For in *Antt.* xx. 8. 4, *Bell. Jud.* ii. 13. 2, it is certainly Julias=
Bethsaida, which is intended ; and in *Antt.* xiv. 1. 4, Λιβιάς is probably
the same place, which is called Λέμβα in *Antt.* xiii. 15. 4, where it is
questionable which form is correct.  Comp. Tuch, as above, pp. 11, 14.
The Λυσιάς of Strabo, p. 763, which also lay in the same district, and is
distinct from Livias, might also be compared, since it existed in the time of
Pompey.

Jericho, 12 *m. p.* from that town, in the neighbourhood of the warm springs.[384] With this Eusebius, who places it opposite Jericho on the road to Hesbon, coincides.[385] Its cultivation of dates is as much celebrated by Theodosius as by Pliny.[386]

33. *Tiberias,* Τιβεριάς.[387] The most important work of Herod the Great was the building of a new capital on the western shore of the Lake of Gennesareth, which he called Τιβεριάς in honour of the Emperor Tiberius. It was situated in a beautiful and fertile district in the neighbourhood of celebrated warm springs (*Antt.* xviii. 2. 3 ; *Bell. Jud.* ii. 9. 1 ; compare above, § 17ᵇ).[388] Its building took place considerably after that of Sepphoris and Livias. For while Josephus mentions the building of these two cities at the very beginning of the reign of Herod Antipas, he does not speak of the building of Tiberias till the entrance of Pilate upon his office (A.D. 26); see *Antt.* xviii. 2. 1–3. This makes it probable,

---

[384] Theodosius, *De situ terrae sanctae* (ed. Gildemeister, 1882), § 65 : Civitas Liviada trans Jordanem, habens de Hiericho milia xii. . . . ibi aquae calidae sunt, ubi Moyses lavit, et in ipsis aquis calidis leprosi curantur. Gregr. Turon. *De gloria martyrum*, i. 18 : Sunt autem et ad Levidam (elsewhere Leviadem) civitatem aquae calidae . . . ubi similiter leprosi mundantur ; est autem ab Hiericho duodecim millia.

[385] Euseb. *Onomast.*, ed. Lagarde, pp. 213, 216, 233. Comp. also the passage from the *Vita S. Joannis Silentiarii* in Reland, p. 874. The data furnished are sufficient for an approximate determination of the locality, but there is as yet no certain foundation for more accurately fixing it.

[386] Plinius, *H. N.* xiii. 4. 44 (see above, note 332). Theodosius, *l.c.*: ibi habet dactulum nicolaum majorem ; also the note of Gildemeister.

[387] See in general, Reland, pp. 1036–1042. Raumer, p. 142 sq. Winer, *RWB. s.v.* Robinson's *Palestine*, ii. p. 380 sq., iii. p. 342 sq. Ritter, *Erdkunde*, xv. 315–322. Bädeker-Socin, pp. 382–387. Sepp, *Jerusalem*, ii. 188–209. Guérin, *Galilée*, i. 250–264. *The Survey of Western Palestine, Memoirs* by Conder and Kitchener, i. 361 sq., 379, 418–420 ; also sheet vi. of the large English chart.

[388] On the warm springs, see Plinius, *H. N.* v. 15. 71 : Tiberiade aquis calidis salubri. Joseph. *Antt.* xviii. 2. 3 ; *Bell. Jud.* ii. 21. 6, iv. 1. 3 ; *Vita*, 16. Mishna, *Shabbath* iii. 4, xxii. 5 ; *Negaim* ix. 1 ; *Machshirin* vi. 7. Tosefta, *Shabbath*, p. 127, 21st ed. Zuckermandel. Antoninus Martyr, c. 7 . in civitatem Tiberiadem, in qua sunt *thermae salsae*. Jakubi (9th cent.), translated in the *Zeitsch. d. deutschen Pal.- Verein*, iv. 87 sq. The present Tiberias lies about 40 minutes north of the springs ; and there is no reason for transferring the former situation of the town elsewhere. For the

that Tiberias was not built till A.D. 26 or later.[389] Eusebius
in his *Chronicle* decidedly places the building in the 14th
year of Tiberius ; but this statement is quite without chronological value.[390] Unfortunately the era of the town occurring
upon the coins of Trajan and Hadrian cannot be calculated
with certainty. It appears however, that the dates of the
coins do not contradict the conjecture arrived at from
Josephus.[391] The population of Tiberias was a very mixed

opinion of Furrer (*Zeitsch. d. DPV.* ii. 54), that the ancient Tiberias lay so
close to the springs, "that they were enclosed within the walls of the
town," rests upon a mistaken view of Joseph. *Vita,* 16 ; *Bell. Jud.* ii. 21. 6.
See on the other hand, *Antt.* xviii. 2. 3 ; *Bell. Jud.* iv. 1. 3. (The ἐν
Τιβεριάδι in the two former passages means only "in the district of Tiberias;"
thus also *e.g.* in Steph. Byz., ed. Meineke, p. 366 : Κάστνιον, ὄρος ἐν ᾿Ασπένδω
τῆς Παμφυλίας; p. 442 : ἔστι καὶ ἐν Κυζίκῳ κώμη Μέλισσα; comp. Marquardt,
*Römische Staatsverwaltung,* i. 1881, p. 16, note 5. In the Old Test. also
באשדוד=in the district of Ashdod.) The place where the springs were
was called ᾿Εμμαοῦς (*Antt.* xviii. 2. 3) or ᾿Αμμαοῦς (*Bell. Jud.* iv. 1. 3),
Hebrew חמתה, *Jer. Erubin* v. 22ᵈ below ; Tosefta, *Erubin* p. 146, 5th ed.
Zuckermandel. Comp. also Lightfoot, *Centuria Matthaeo praemissa,* c. 74
(*Opp.* ii. 244 sq.). Hamburger, *Real-Encyklop. für Bibel und Talmud,* 2nd
Div., art. "Heilbäder."

[389] So also Lewin, *Fasti sacri* (London 1866), n. 1163.

[390] Eusebius, *Chron.,* ed. Schoene, ii. 146–149 relates the building of new
towns by the sons of Herod in the following rder : Philip built Caesarea
and Julias, Herod Antipas built Tiberias and Livias. All the buildings are
placed in the time of Tiberius. Sepphoris is entirely passed over. All this
puts it beyond doubt, *that the statements of Eusebius are entirely derived
from* Joseph. *Bell. Jud.* ii. 9. 1. For the buildings are there enumerated in
exactly the same order, also after the accession of Tiberius, and with the
same omission of Sepphoris. Hence the statements of Eusebius are not
only without independent value, but are besides derived from the more
inaccurate statement of Josephus in the *Bell. Jud.,* and ignore his more
accurate account in *Antt.* xviii. 2. 1–3.

[391] On the coins and the era, see Noris, v. 6 (ed. Lips. pp. 552–564).
Sanclemente, *De vulgaris aerae emendatione,* p. 324 sq. Huber in the
*Wiener Numismatische Zeitsch.,* 1st year, 1869, pp. 404–414. De Saulcy,
pp. 333–338, pl. xvii. n. 9–14. The same, in the *Annuaire de la Société
Française de Numismatique et d'Archéol.* iii. 266–270. Among the dated coins
only those of Trajan with the date 81 and those of Hadrian with the date
101 are attested with certainty. Noris and Sanclemente assume also coins
of Trajan with the year 101, and accordingly calculate the epoch of
Tiberias to be A.D. 17 (then the year in which Hadrian succeeded Trajan,
*i.e.* A.D. 117 = 101 era of Tiberius, and A.D. 17 = 1 era of Tiberius). But the
coins with the year 101 certainly all belong to Hadrian. Other coins too

one. To obtain inhabitants for his new town Herod Antipas was obliged to settle there, partly by compulsion, a real *colluvies hominum* (see above, § 17[b]). Its attitude however during the Jewish war shows them to have been chiefly Jewish. The constitution however was one of Hellenistic organization.[392] The town had a council (βουλή) of 600 members,[393] at the head of which was an ἄρχων[394] and a committee of the δέκα πρῶτοι,[395] also

given singly by numismatists (De Saulcy gives coins of Claudius with the year 33, of Trajan with 80, and of Hadrian with 103) are also doubtful. Hence all that can with certainty be affirmed is, that the epoch of Tiberias *cannot begin earlier than* A.D. 17. The consideration, that Tiberias was probably in the possession of Agrippa II. till A.D. 100, and hence could not previously have issued imperial coins, leads somewhat farther. Under this assumption the epoch could not on account of the coins of Trajan of 81 be placed earlier than A.D 19. A still further point of contact might be obtained, if the title, which Trajan bears upon the coins of 81, could be certainly determined. For if he is on these called only *Germanicus* and not *Dacicus*, the coins in question could not have been issued later than A.D. 103 (after which year Trajan bore also the latter title), and consequently the epoch could not begin later than A.D. 22 (so Eckhel). If however in the reverse case he has just upon these coins both titles (as Reichardt asserts in Huber's above-named work, reading ΓΕΡ. Δ. instead of ΓΕΡΜ), the coins could not have been issued earlier than 103, nor the epoch begin before A.D. 22. This would be in accordance with Josephus.

[392] See on what follows, Kuhn, *Die städtische und bürgerl. Verfassung*, ii. 353. The same, *Ueber die Entstehung der Städte der Alten*, p. 427 sq.

[393] *Bell. Jud.* ii. 21. 9. Comp. in general, *Vita*, 12, 34, 55, 58, 61, 68.

[394] *Vita*, 27, 53, 54, 57; *Bell. Jud.* ii. 21. 3. One Jesus the son of Sapphias, is here throughout named as archon of Tiberias during the time of the revolt. Among his offices was that of presiding at the meeting of the council.

[395] *Vita*, 13, 57; *Bell. Jud.* ii. 21. 9 = *Vita*, 33. See especially, *Vita*, 13: τοὺς τῆς βουλῆς πρώτους δέκα. *Vita*, 57: τοὺς δέκα πρώτους Τιβεριέων. On these δέκα πρῶτοι, so frequently occurring in the Hellenistic communities, see Kuhn, i. 55; Marquardt, *Röm. Staatsverwaltung*, i. 213 sq (1881); the Index to the *Corp. Inscr. Graec.* p. 35. They were not perhaps the oldest or the most respected members of the council, but a changing committee of it with definite official functions, as the frequently occurring formula δεκα-πρωτεύσας shows (see *Corp. Inscr. Graec.* n. 2639, 2929, 2930. Add. 2930[b], 3490, 3491, 3496, 3498, 4289, 4415[b]. δεκαπρωτευκώς, n. 3418). Their chief office was the collection of taxes, for the due payment of which they were answerable with their private property, *Digest.* lib. iv. 1. 1: Munerum civilium quaedam sunt patrimonii, alia personarum. Patrimonii sunt munera rei vehicularis, item navicularis decemprimatus: ab istis enim periculo ipsorum exactiones solemnium celebrantur. *Digest.* lib. iv. 18.

Hyparchoi [396] and an Agoranomos. [397] It was also promoted to be the capital of Galilee, Sepphoris itself being
subordinated to it (see above, p. 139). The coins of
Tiberias issued in the time of Herod have simply the superscription $Τιβεριάς$. [398] After the deposition of Herod Antipas
Tiberias was transferred to the possession of Agrippa I.
A coin of his time also, with the superscription $Τιβεριέων$
is known. [399] After the death of Agrippa the town came
under the authority of the Roman procurators of Judaea.
It must at the same time have received new political
privileges or experienced some kind of favour from the
Emperor Claudius; for the inhabitants are constantly called
$Τιβεριεῖς$ $Κλαυδιεῖς$ on the coins of Trajan and Hadrian. [400]
It continued to maintain its position as capital of Galilee
till the time of Nero (Joseph. *Vita*, 9). By him, probably
in A.D. 61, it was bestowed upon Agrippa II., and thus
separated from Galilee (*Antt.* xx. 8. 4; *Bell. Jud.* ii. 13. 2;
*Vita*, 9). [401] Hence it formed part of the realm of Agrippa,
when the Jewish insurrection broke out in A.D. 66. The
attitude of the population with respect to it was a very
varying one. Some desired to remain on the side of Agrippa
and the Romans; others—and indeed the mass of those without
property—wished to join the cause of the revolution; others
again took up a position of reserve (*Vita*, 9; comp. also

26 : Mixta munera decaprotiae et icosaprotiae, ut Herennius Modestinus
. . . . decrevit : nam decaproti at icosaproti tributa exigentes et corporale
ministerium gerunt et pro omnibus defunctorum (?) fiscalia detrimenta
resarciunt. It is worthy of notice, that Josephus during his government of
Galilee delivers to the *decem primi* at Tiberias *valuables* of King Agrippa,
and makes them responsible for them, *Vita*, 13, 57.

[396] *Bell. Jud.* ii. 21. 6 : τοῖς ματὰ τὴν πόλιν ὑπάρχοις.

[397] *Antt.* xviii. 6. 2. On the office of the ἀγορανόμος, see Westermann in
Pauly's *Enc.* i. 1 (2nd ed.), pp. 582–584. Stephanus, *Thes. s.v.* The material
furnished by inscriptions in the Index to the *Corp. Inscr. Graec.* p. 32.

[398] Madden, *History of Jewish Coinage*, pp. 97, 98. The same, *Coins of
the Jews* (1881), pp. 119, 120.

[399] Madden, *History*, p. 110; *Coins of the Jews*, p. 138.

[400] See the literature cited above, especially De Saulcy.

[401] On the time, see above, § 19, Appendix 2.

*Vita*, 12, where the revolutionary party is called ἡ τῶν ναυτῶν καὶ τῶν ἀπόρων στάσις). This party had decidedly the upper hand, and the rest had consequently to submit. A chief leader of this party was Jesus the son of Sapphias, then archon of the town.[402] Still even after the triumph of the revolutionary torrent, a part of the population maintained their relations to Agrippa, and repeatedly entreated, though in vain, his support.[403] When Vespasian had subjected the greater part of Galilee and penetrated as far as Tiberias, the town ventured no resistance, but voluntarily opened its gates and begged for pardon, which was granted out of regard for Agrippa. Vespasian indeed allowed his soldiers to march into Tiberias, but spared the town and restored it to Agrippa.[404] It remained in his possession probably till his death, A.D. 100, till which period it did not again come under direct Roman rule, to which circumstance extant coins of the time of Trajan and Hadrian bear testimony.[405] Eusebius designates it as a πόλις ἐπίσημος.[406] It was in the third and fourth centuries after Christ a chief seat of Rabbinical scholarship, and is hence frequently mentioned in Talmudic literature.[407]

Of some of the last-named towns, as Antipatris, Phasaelis, Julias and Livias it cannot certainly be determined whether they really belonged to the class of independent towns with Hellenistic constitutions, since it is just as likely that, like other second-rate towns, they were incorporated in the general organization of the country. They had however to be named here, because in any case a certain proportion of the towns built by Herod and his sons belonged to the above category.

[402] Joseph. *Vita*, 12, 27, 53, 54. 57 ; *Bell. Jud.* ii. 21. 3, iii. 9. 7–8. The revolutionary attitude of the town is plainly seen throughout the whole narrative of Josephus in his *Vita*.

[403] *Bell. Jud.* ii. 21. 8–10 ; *Vita*, 32–34, 68–69, 70.

[404] *Bell. Jud.* iii. 9. 7–8.

[405] A coin of the time of Commodus has been published by Huber in the *Wiener Numismatischen Zeitschr.* Jahrg. i. 1869, p. 401 sqq.

[406] *Onomast.*, ed. Lagarde, p. 215.

[407] Neubauer, *Géographie du Talmud*, pp. 208–214. Pinner, *Compendium des jerus. und bab. Talmud* (1832), pp. 109–116.

On the other hand, it is also possible, that the number of the independent communities is not exhausted by the towns here enumerated. *Hence we cannot look upon the list we have given as a strictly defined one.* For the times of Roman imperialism a further number of independent civic communities would have to be named, which are here designedly passed over, because it was not till later (at the earliest A.D. 70) that they attained this position. This was the case especially with Nicopolis (= Emmaus), Neapolis (= Sichem), Diospolis (= Lydda), Eleutheropolis and the communities belonging to the province of Arabia, as Bostra, Adraa and others. Aelia Capitolina (= Jerusalem) too would have to be mentioned as a heathen town for the period after Hadrian. On Capitolias, comp. above, p. 106.

*Concerning the position of the Jews in these mainly heathen communities* no further material exists than what has been already communicated on the places in question. The history of Caesarea (No. 9) is the most instructive. Here heathens and Jews possessed down to Nero's time equal civic rights (ἰσοπολιτεία, *Antt.* xx. 8. 7 and 9) and hence equal eligibility to the town senate. As this of necessity entailed manifold dissensions, both parties strove to bring about an alteration of this state of things, each desiring to have the supremacy. Thus a threefold possibility existed: 1. equality, 2. exclusion of the Jews, and 3. exclusion of the heathen, from civic privileges. All three cases actually occurred. In the old Philistinian and Phoenician towns the Jews hardly possessed the privilege of citizenship. They dwelt in them indeed by thousands; but were only tolerated as inhabitants; and how strained were the relations between them and the heathen citizens, is best shown by the sanguinary persecution of the Jews in many of these towns at the outbreak of Jewish revolution, as *e.g.* in Ascalon, Ptolemais and Tyre. In other towns heathen and Jews may have been on an equality; this was especially the case in those towns, which subsequently to the Maccabaean period were mainly inhabited by Jews, as Jamnia and Joppa.

Whether heathens were excluded from civic rights in any of the hitherto named towns is very doubtful; and not probable even in Sepphoris and Tiberias. The third possibility is at all events represented by Jerusalem and in general by the towns of the strictly Jewish territory. Particulars cannot be further entered into from lack of material. It must suffice to have established the general point of sight. On the organization of the Jewish communities in these towns, see below, § 27. II. and § 31. II.–III.

## II. THE STRICTLY JEWISH TERRITORY.

### THE LITERATURE.

Selden, *De synedriis et praefecturis juridicis veterum Ebraeorum, lib.* i. *Londini* 1650, *lib.* ii. *Londini* 1653, *lib.* iii. *Londini* 1655 (reprint of the whole work, *Amstelodami* 1679). The *first* book treats of the judicial institutions of the Jews *ante legis in Sinai dationem*, the *second* of these same institutions subsequent to the giving of the law at Sinai, while the *third* is specially devoted to the consideration of the prerogatives of the supreme court (the Sanhedrim). In spite of all its critical shortcomings this learned work is still valuable on account of the rich fund of material it contains.

Saalschütz, *Das mosaische Recht*, vol. i. 1853, pp. 53–64.

Winer, *Realwörterb.*, arts. *Alter, Aelteste; Gericht; Städte.*

Schenkel's *Bibellexicon*, arts. *Aelteste* (by Schenkel); *Gerichte* (by Wittichen); *Städte* (by Furrer).

Riehm's *Handwörterb. des bibl Altertums*, arts. *Aelteste; Gerichtswesen; Dorf; Stadt.*

Arnold in Herzog's *Real-Enc.*, 1st ed. vol. xiv. p. 721 (art. *Städte*).

Leyrer in Herzog's *Real-Enc.*, 1st ed. vol. xv. p. 324 f. (art. *Synedrium*).

Kuhn, *Die städtische und bürgerl. Verfassung des römischen Reichs*, vol. ii. pp. 336–346.

Köhler, *Lehrbuch der biblischen Geschichte Alten Testaments*, vol. i. 1875, p. 350 f.

Reuss, *Gesch. der heiligen Schriften A. T.'s*, sec. cxiv.

The strictly Jewish territory—leaving Samaria out of view —consisted of the three provinces of Judaea, Galilee and Peraea, and was enclosed within such boundaries as would naturally be formed by the contiguous portions of the districts belonging to the surrounding Hellenistic towns (comp. above, § 23. I.). The Gentile element in those provinces never

formed more at the very outside than a minority of the population, while we may venture to assume that, in the towns, the
municipal councils were composed exclusively of Jews. For
there cannot be a doubt that, in Jewish towns as well, there
were civic representative bodies to whom the management of
the public affairs of the community was entrusted. So far
back even as the earliest period in the history of Israel we find
frequent mention of "the elders of the city" (זִקְנֵי הָעִיר) in the
capacity of local authorities (see in general, Deut. xix. 12,
xxi. 2 ff., xxii. 15 ff., xxv. 7 ff.; Josh. xx. 4; Judg. viii. 14;
Ruth iv. 2 ff.; 1 Sam. xi. 3, xvi. 4, xxx. 26 ff.; 1 Kings
xxi. 8, 11). Of how many members this body was composed
we are hardly ever told, but their number must have been
something considerable. In Succoth, for example, there were
as many as seventy-seven (Judg. viii. 14). Those officials
represented the community in every department of its affairs
and accordingly they were also called upon to act in the
capacity of judges (see, for example, Deut. xxii. 15). But,
besides these, "judges" (שֹׁפְטִים) and "officers" (שֹׁטְרִים) are also
specially mentioned (both classes in Deut. xvi. 18; while
in 2 Chron. xix. 5 ff. the instituting of "judges" is ascribed
to Jehoshaphat). Now seeing that the judges are expressly
mentioned along with the elders (Deut. xxi. 2; Ezra x. 14),
the two orders of officials are in any case to be regarded as
distinct, but probably only to this extent, that the judges
were those among the elders to whom the administration of
justice was specially entrusted. Similarly the "officers" are
also to be regarded as belonging to the number of the "elders,"
their special function again being to take charge of the
executive department.[408] The organization then that existed
in later times is to be assumed as having been substantially
identical with the one here in question. We further find
that the "elders" of the city are also frequently mentioned
during the Persian and Geeek era (Ezra x. 14; Judith vi. 16,
21, vii. 23 viii. 10, x. 6, xiii. 12). As regards the Roman

[408] See in particular, Knobel's notes on Ex. v. 6 and Deut. xvi. 18.

period again, we have evidence of the existence of local
tribunals at that time in such a statement, for example, as
that of Josephus, where he mentions that Albinus, actuated
by greed, liberated for a money consideration certain individuals who, for the crime of robbery, had been sentenced to
imprisonment by their respective *local courts* (βουλή).[409]
From what is here stated we can further gather that it was
the βουλή itself that discharged the judicial functions.  Still
it is quite possible that in the larger towns especially there
may have been, besides the βουλή, certain other courts of a
special kind.  Again it is the local Sanhedrims that are to be
understood as referred to when, in Matt. x. 17 = Mark
xiii. 9, it is stated that the believers would be delivered εἰς
συνέδρια; we may also regard as belonging to the same
category those courts that, in Matt. v. 22, are assumed to be
inferior in point of jurisdiction to the high court of the
Sanhedrim; and similarly with regard to the πρεσβύτεροι of
Capernaum (Luke vii. 3).  But it is in the Mishna above
all that the existence of local courts throughout the country
of the Jews is presupposed from beginning to end.[410]  As
regards the number of members of which such courts were
composed, some have been disposed to infer from the Mishna
that the most inferior ones consisted of not more than three
persons.  This however is based upon a pure misapprehension.
For the passages appealed to in support of this view do
nothing more than simply enumerate the various questions
for the deciding of which and the various causes for the trying
of which three persons were deemed sufficient.  Thus three,
for example, were considered sufficient to decide an action

---

[409] *Bell. Jud.* ii. 14. 1: καὶ τοὺς ἐπὶ λῃστείᾳ δεδεμένους ὑπὸ τῆς παρ᾽
ἑκάστοις βουλῆς ἢ τῶν προτέρων ἐπιτρόπων ἀπελύτρου τοῖς συγγενέσι.

[410] *Shebiith* x. 4: The terms of the Prosbol-formula were substantially
as follows: "I so and so declare before you THE JUDGES OF SUCH AND
SUCH A PLACE that I," etc.  *Sota* i. 3: How is the husband (of a woman
suspected of adultery) to proceed?  He is to bring her before *the local
court*, which will assign him two lawyers, etc.  *Sanhedrin* xi. 4: A criminal
of that sort is tried and executed neither by the court belonging to his own
town nor by the court at Jabne, etc.

involving money, or to pronounce judgment in cases of robbery and assault, or to award damages and such like;[411] this number was also sufficient to sentence any one to be scourged, to determine the date of the new moon, and decide as to the intercalary year;[412] also for the laying on of the hands (upon a sin-offering offered in the name of the congregation), and for breaking the heifer's neck (on the occasion of any person being found murdered). Further cases for the disposal of which only three judges were necessary were those connected with the Chaliza and the refusal of a man to marry the wife of his deceased brother (Deut. xxv. 7–9), the redemption of the produce of fruit trees during the first four years of their growth, the redemption of the second tithe the value of which had not been previously determined, the purchasing back of certain things that were holy to the Lord, and so on.[413] But nowhere is it said, that there were distinct local courts consisting of only three persons. In what sense we are to understand the statements of the Mishna above referred to may be readily seen from another passage[414] which runs thus: "Actions involving money are decided by three persons. That is to say, each of the two parties in the case chooses a judge and then both the parties or, according to another view, both the judges, choose a third to act along with them." As matter of fact the most subordinate of the local courts consisted of seven persons. For one can scarcely be far wrong in assuming that the statement of Josephus to the effect that Moses ordained that "seven men were to bear rule in every city, and that two men of the tribe of Levi were to be appointed to act as officers in every court," was intended to be regarded as a description of the state of things that existed in Josephus' own time, for there is no mention of anything of this kind in the Pentateuch.[415] This is

[411] *Sanhedrin* i. 1.

[412] *Sanhedrin* i. 2. Comp. *Rosh hashana* ii. 9, iii. 1.

[413] *Sanhedrin* i. 3.     [414] *Sanhedrin* iii. 1.

[415] *Antt.* iv. 8. 14 . ἀρχέτωσαν δὲ καθ᾽ ἑκάστην πόλιν ἄνδρες ἑπτά . . . ἑκάστῃ δὲ ἀρχῇ δύο ἄνδρες ὑπηρέται διδόσθωσαν ἐκ τῆς τῶν Λευιτῶν φυλῆς.

corroborated by the fact that Josephus himself, when on one occasion he wanted to introduce a model Jewish constitution into Galilee, established a court with seven judges in every town.[416]  No doubt from this latter circumstance one might rather infer that this organization had had no existence in Galilee previous to the revolution.  But the boast of Josephus, that he was the first to create this the ideal of a Jewish constitution, may be said to be true only to this extent, that he took steps to have it more rigidly put in force.  In the Talmud too we find "the seven leading men of the city" (שבעה טובי העיר) referred to on one occasion as forming a public board which, among other things, was entrusted with the management of the financial affairs of the community.[417]  What Josephus has stated with regard to two Levites being always appointed to act as ὑπηρέται to the local courts (see above note 415) is not without its analogies at least in the Old Testament.[418]  According to the Mishna there were certain special cases in which it was necessary to have priests as judges.[419]  In the more populous places the local courts would appear to have been composed of twenty-three members. At least we find a statement in the Mishna to the effect that an inferior Sanhedrim (סַנְהֶדְרִין קְטַנָּה) consisted of twenty-three

Again in reproducing the law with regard to restitution (Ex. xxii. 6 ff.), Josephus presupposes the existence of courts with seven judges, *Antt.* iv. 8. 38 : εἰ δὲ μηδὲν ἐπίβουλον δρῶν ὁ πιστευθεὶς ἀπολέσειεν, ἀφικόμενος ἐπὶ τοὺς ἑπτὰ κριτὰς ὀμνύτω τὸν θεόν κ.τ.λ.

[416] *Bell. Jud.* ii. 20. 5, ἑπτὰ δὲ ἐν ἑκάστῃ πόλει δικαστὰς [κατέστησεν]. Those courts of seven judges were called upon to deal only with causes of a more trifling kind, but *not* with τὰ μείζω πράγματα καὶ τὰς φονικὰς δίκας, the adjudication of which was rather reserved for the council of seventy which Josephus had established.

[417] *Megilla* xxvi.a: "Rabba said, that regulation (of the Mishna with regard to the sale of synagogues and their furniture) applies only to those cases in which *the seven leading men of the town* have not disposed of them by public sale.  But if they shall have sold them publicly," etc.  Comp. also Rhenferd's *Investigatio praefectorum et ministrorum synagogae*, ii. 25 (in Ugolini's *Thesaurus*, vol. xxi.).

[418] Deut. xxi. 5; 1 Chron. xxiii. 4, xxvi. 29. Knobel's note on Deut. xvi. 18.

[419] *Sanhedrin* i. 3.  Comp. on the subject generally of priests acting in the capacity of judges, Ezek. xliv. 24, and Smend's note on this passage.

persons, and that one of this sort was assigned to every town
with a population of at least 120 or, according to R.
Nehemiah's view, of at least 230, in order that there might
thus be a judge for every ten of the inhabitants.[420] It must
be confessed however that here too, as in so many other
instances, we have no guarantee that the actual state of
things quite corresponded with these regulations. Those
courts of twenty-three members were likewise empowered
to deal with criminal cases of a serious nature (דִּינֵי נְפָשׁוֹת),[421]
for we can also see from Matt. v. 21, 22, that the trying and
sentencing of murderers did not belong exclusively to the
jurisdiction of the supreme court of the Sanhedrim.

As in the case of the Hellenistic communes, so too within
the Jewish domain the villages were subordinate to the towns,
and the smaller towns again to the larger ones. The
distinction between a town (עִיר) and a village (חָצֵר, seldom
כְּפָר) is presupposed from beginning to end of the Old Testament itself; the former, as a rule, being an inhabited place
surrounded by a wall, and the latter one that is not so
enclosed (see in particular, Lev. xxv. 29–31); at the same
time, towns themselves are also sometimes distinguished as
walled and unwalled (Deut. iii. 5; Esth. ix. 19). Moreover,
Josephus and the New Testament uniformly distinguish
between the two notions πόλις and κώμη.[422] On one occasion
the New Testament speaks of κωμοπόλεις of Palestine
(Mark i. 38), i.e. towns which, as regards their constitution,
only enjoyed the rank of a κώμη.[423] In the Mishna there
are three conceptions of this matter, and these are uniformly

[420] Sanhedrin i. 6. Comp. Selden, De synedriis ii. 5. Winer's Realwörterb. ii. 554. Leyrer in Herzog's Real-Encycl., 1st ed. xv. p. 324 f.

[421] Sanhedrin i. 4.

[422] Comp. Winer's Realwörterb. ii. 510; also the materials to be found in
the concordances to the New Testament. For the conception of a κώμη in
the Romano-Hellenistic sense, consult Marquardt's Römische Staatsverwaltung, vol. i. (2nd ed. 1881) p. 16 f.

[423] The term κωμόπολις is also to be met with occasionally in Strabo and
the Byzantine writers; consult the Lexicons and Wetzstein's Nov. Test., note
on Mark i. 38.

distinguished from each other : that of a large city (כְּרַךְ), then
that of a city (עִיר), and lastly that of a village (כְּפָר).[424] The
distinguishing characteristic in the case of the first two would
seem to have been merely the difference in size; for even an
ordinary town (עִיר) might be enclosed by a wall, and indeed it
usually was so.[425] In the Old Testament there is already
frequent allusion to the subordination of the *villages* to the
towns. In the lists of towns given in the Book of Joshua, and
above all in the fifteenth and nineteenth chapters, we often
meet with the expression, the " cities *with their villages* "
(הֶעָרִים וְחַצְרֵיהֶן). Elsewhere we frequently read of a city and
*its daughter* (בְּנוֹתֶיהָ), Num. xxi. 25, 32, xxxii. 42 ; Josh. xv.
45–47, xvii. 11 ; Judg. xi. 26 ; Neh. xi. 25 ff. ; 1 Chron. ii.
23, v. 16, vii. 28 f., viii. 12, xviii. 1 ; 2 Chron. xiii. 19,
xxviii. 18 ; Ezek. xvi. 46 ff., xxvi. 6, xxx. 18 ; 1 Macc. v.
8, 65. And in keeping with the idea of the daughter, we
also find the term " mother " employed to designate the chief
town of a district (2 Sam. xx. 19). From all this it is, in
any case, clear that the villages were everywhere dependent
upon the cities. But it is also highly probable that this was
no less true of the smaller towns in relation to the larger ones.
For frequently it is not only to villages, but also to smaller
dependent towns that the designation " mother " is applied ;
at least in several instances is this most undoubtedly the case
(Num. xxi. 25 ; Josh. xv. 45–47 ; 1 Chron. ii. 23). And what
we thus gather from the Old Testament may be assumed to
be no less applicable to later times as well (comp. especially,
1 Macc. v. 8 : τὴν Ἰαζὴρ καὶ τὰς θυγατέρας αὐτῆς; *ibid.* v.
65 : τὴν Χεβρὼν καὶ τὰς θυγατέρας αὐτῆς). But it is in
the country on the east of the Jordan above all, and in the

---

[424] *Megilla* i. 1, ii. 3 ; *Kethuboth* xiii. 10; *Kiddushin* ii. 3 ; *Baba mezia*
iv. 6, viii. 6 ; *Arachin* vi. 5.

[425] עִיר חוֹמָה, *Arachin* ix. 3 ff. ; *Kelim* i. 7. On בְּיָך, comp. Lightfoot,
*Horae hebr.*, note on Mark i. 38 (*Opp.* ii. 437), and Levy's *Neuhebr. Wörterb.*
*s.v.* This word is, strictly speaking, Aramaic (כְּרַךְ) and frequently occurs
in the Targums in the sense of a fortification, a stronghold, a fortified
town. See Buxtorf's *Lex.* and Levy's *Chald. Wörterb.*, *s.v.*

district of Trachonitis in particular, that *capital villages* (μητροκωμίαι), *i.e.* villages holding a position corresponding to that of a capital town, were most frequently to be met with.[426] Thus Phaena, the modern Mismie, is called μητροκωμία τοῦ Τράχωνος.[427] We have another example of a μητροκωμία in the case of Borechath, the modern Breike, which is also situated within the district of Trachonitis.[428] Epiphanius mentions τὴν Βάκαθον μητροκωμίαν τῆς 'Αραβίας τῆς Φιλαδελφίας.[429] Of course those testimonies only date from somewhere between the second and the fourth centuries of our era; moreover, the population of those districts, though of a mixed character, was composed chiefly of Gentiles.

Any notices of a more special kind that we have regarding the subordination of certain provinces to some of the larger cities apply exclusively to Galilee and Judaea, and only date from the Roman period. In Galilee, *Sepphoris* was the place which Gabinius fixed upon as the seat of one of the five συνέδρια or σύνοδοι; and as the one which sat here was the only one in the province (*Antt.* xiv. 5. 4; *Bell. Jud.* i. 8. 5), Sepphoris became, in consequence, the centre of an organization that embraced the whole of Galilee. It is true the arrangement of Gabinius here referred to was of but short duration. But in later times as well, and particularly under the Idumaean dynasty, the whole of Galilee was always subordinate to some *one* capital city, whether Sepphoris on the one hand or Tiberias on the other (see above, notes 31 and 33). Here then we have an instance of a Jewish province being placed in

---

[426] See in general, Kuhn, *Die städtische und bürgerl. Verfassung des römischen Reichs,* ii. 380 ff.   Marquardt, *Römische Staatsverwaltung,* vol. i. 2nd ed. p. 427, note 1.   The Lexicons under the word μητροκωμία.

[427] *Corp. Inscr. Graec.* No. 4551 = Le Bas et Waddington, *Inscr.* t. iii. No. 2524.   The inscription dates from the time of Alexander Severus (222–235 A.D.).   On Phaena, see Raumer's *Pal.* p. 254 f.   Porter's *Five Years in Damascus,* ii. 244.   Kuhn, ii. 384.

[428] Le Bas et Waddington, vol. iii. n. 2396.

[429] Epiphanius, *Anacephal.* p. 145.

subordination to a capital city that was not of a purely Jewish character.[430]

In Judaea again it is to the division of the province into eleven or ten toparchies, vouched for both by Josephus and Pliny, that a special interest attaches. According to Josephus, Judaea was divided into the following eleven κληρουχίαι or τοπαρχίαι:—(1) Jerusalem, (2) *Gophna*, (3) *Akrabatta*, (4) *Thamna*, (5) *Lydda*, (6) *Ammaus*, (7) Pella, (8) Idumaea, (9) Engaddi, (10) *Herodeion*, (11) *Jericho*.[431] Of these, the seven printed in italics are also mentioned by Pliny, who, by adding to them the following three: *Jopica*, *Betholeptephene*, *Orine*,[432] brings up the total number of toparchies to ten. The mention of Orine instead of Jerusalem cannot be said to make any material difference. But the mention of Joppa in this instance is quite as erroneous as that of Pella by Josephus, for both of these were independent towns and did not belong to Judaea proper. Bethleptepha, on the other hand, is mentioned by Josephus in another passage, and that as being the capital of a toparchy.[433] We may therefore obtain a correct list if we adopt that of Josephus and substitute Bethleptepha for Pella.[434] In that case the toparchies would be grouped as follows:[435] in the centre, Jerusalem; to the north

---

[430] The relation is really one of *subordination*, for Josephus speaks distinctly of an ἄρχειν and ὑπακούειν ; see above, notes 363 and 364.

[431] *Bell. Jud.* iii. 3. 5: μερίζεται δὲ εἰς ἕνδεκα κληρουχίας, ὧν ἄρχει μὲν ὡς βασίλειον τὰ ʿΙεροσόλυμα, προανίσχουσα τῆς περιοίκου πάσης ὥσπερ ἡ κεφαλὴ σώματος, αἱ λοιπαὶ δὲ μετ᾽ αὐτὴν διῄρηνται τὰς τοπαρχίας. Γόφνα δευτέρα, καὶ μετ᾽ αὐτὴν Ἀκραβαττά, Θαμνὰ πρὸς ταύταις καὶ Λύδδα καὶ Ἀμμαοῦς καὶ Πέλλη καὶ Ἰδουμαία καὶ Ἐγγαδδαὶ καὶ Ἡρώδειον καὶ Ἱεριχοῦς.

[432] Pliny, *Hist. Nat.* v. 14. 70: Reliqua Judaea dividitur in toparchias X quo dicemus ordine: Hiericuntem palmetis consitam, fontibus riguam, Emmaum, Lyddam, Jopicam, Acrebitenam, Gophaniticam, Thamniticam, Betholeptephenen, Orinen, in qua fuere Hierosolyma longe clarissima urbium orientis non Iudaeae modo, Herodium cum oppido inlustri ejusdem nominis.

[433] *Bell. Jud.* iv. 8. 1: τὴν Βεθλεπτηφῶν τοπαρχίαν.

[434] Comp. Kuhn, *Die städtische und bürgerl. Verf.* ii. 339.

[435] Comp. Menke's *Bibel-Atlas*, map v.

of it, Gophna[436] and Akrabatta;[437] to the north-west, Thamna[438]

[436] According to *Tab. Peuting.* Gophna stood on the road leading from
Jerusalem to Neapolis (Sichem), sixteen miles to the north of the former,
or according to Euseb. *Onomast.* fifteen miles (ed. Lagarde, p. 300: Γοφνά
. . . ἀπέχουσα Αἰλίας σημείοις ιε΄ κατὰ τὴν ὁδὸν τὴν εἰς Νεάπολιν ἄγουσαν).
It was a place of some importance in the time of Cassius, who sold its
inhabitants as slaves (*Antt.* xiv. 11. 2; *Bell. Jud.* i. 11. 2). The Γοφνιτικὴ
τοπαρχία is also mentioned by Josephus elsewhere (*Bell. Jud.* i. 1. 5, ii.
20. 4, iv. 9. 9). Comp. besides, *Bell. Jud.* v. 2. 1, vi. 2. 2. In Ptolemaeus
v. 16. 7, it occurs in the form of Γούφνα, Hebrew גופנא (Neubauer, *Géogr.
du Talmud*, p. 157 ff.), the modern form being Dschifna, Jufna. See in
general, Raumer's *Pal.* p. 199; Robinson's *Palaest.* ii. 263, 264; Guérin's
*Judée*, iii. pp. 28–32. *The Survey of Western Palestine, Memoirs* by Conder
and Kitchener, ii. pp. 294, 323, and the accompanying maps, No. xiv.

[437] Akrabatta, still farther north than Gophna and nine miles to the
south-east of Neapolis=Sichem (Euseb. *Onomast.*, ed. Lag. p. 214: Ἀκραβ-
βείν . . . κώμη δὲ ἔστιν μόγις διεστῶσα Νέας πόλεως σημείοις θ΄). According
to Mishna, *Maaser sheni* v. 2, עקרבת was a day's journey to the north of
Jerusalem, precisely the same distance as Lydda was to the west of it,
which is as near the mark as can be. The Ἀκραβατηνὴ τοπαρχία is also of
frequent occurrence elsewhere in Josephus and Eusebius (Joseph. *Bell. Jud.*
ii. 12. 4, 20. 4, 22. 2, iii. 3. 4, iv. 9. 3–4 and 9. Euseb. *Onomast.*, ed. Lag.
pp. 214, 255, 267, 294, 295). The place is known at the present day as
Akrabeh. See in general, Raumer's *Pal.* p. 170. Robinson's *Palestine*,
iii. pp. 296, 297. Guérin's *Samarie*, ii. 3–5. *The Survey, etc., Memoirs* by
Conder and Kitchener, ii. pp. 386, 389 f.; and the accompanying map,
No. xv. Beware of confounding this with a range of hills of the same
name in the south of Judaea, Num. xxxiv. 4; Josh. xv. 3; Judg. i. 36;
Euseb. *Onomast.* p. 214; and from which the Ἀκραβαττίνη mentioned in
the first Book of the Maccabees (1 Macc. v. 3=Joseph. *Antt.* xii. 8. 1)
derives its name.

[438] Thamna is undoubtedly the ancient תִּמְנַת־סֶרַח or תִּמְנַת־חֶרֶס in
Mount Ephraim where Joshua was buried (Josh. xix. 50, xxiv. 30; Judg.
ii. 9). Eusebius frequently mentions the place as being a very large village
within the district of Diospolis=Lydda (see especially, p. 260, ed. Lag.:
Θαμνά . . . διαμένει κώμη μεγάλη ἐν ὁρίοις Διοσπόλεως), and remarks that,
in his day, people were shown Joshua's tomb at a spot near by (p. 246:
δείκνυται δὲ ἐπίσημον εἰς ἔτι νῦν αὐτοῦ τὸ μνῆμα πλησίον Θαμνὰ κώμης.
*Ibid.* p. 261: Θαμναθσαρά . . . αὕτη ἐστὶ Θαμνά . ἐν ᾗ εἰς ἔτι νῦν
δείκνυται τὸ τοῦ Ἰησοῦ μνῆμα). The place still exists, though only as
a heap of ruins, and is known by the name of Tibneh, standing in
a tolerably straight line between Akrabeh and Lydda, as was to be
expected from the order of the toparchies as given by Josephus.
Among the important tombs still to be seen at this place Guérin
believes that he has actually discovered that of Joshua. See in general,
Raumer's *Pal.* p. 165 f. De Saulcy's *Voyage en Terre Sainte* (1865), ii.
233 f. Guérin's *Samarie*, ii. pp. 89–104. *The Survey of Western Palestine*,

and Lydda;[439] to the west, Emmaus;[440] to the south-west, Bethleptepha;[441] to the south, Idumaea;[442] to the south-

*Memoirs*, etc., ii. 299 f., 274–378, with the accompanying map, No. xiv. Mühlau in Riehm's *Wörterb.* p. 1668. In the time of Cassius, Thamna shared the same fate as Gophna (*Antt.* xiv. 11. 2 ; *Bell. Jud.* i. 11. 2). The toparchy of Thamna is also mentioned elsewhere by Josephus and Eusebius (Joseph. *Bell. Jud.* ii. 20. 4, iv. 8. 1. Euseb. *Onomast.*, ed. Lagarde, pp. 219, 239). Comp. also Ptolem. v. 16. 8. We must take care to distinguish between our Thamna and another תִּמְנָה or תִּמְנָתָה situated on the border between the tribe of Dan and Judah to the west of Jerusalem and in the direction of Ashdod. This one is also existing in the present day, and is likewise known under the name of Tibneh (Josh. xv. 10, xix. 43 ; Judg. xiv. 1 ff. ; 2 Chron. xxviii. 18). And lastly, from this we must further distinguish a third one situated in the hill country of Judah (Gen. xxxviii. 12–14 ; Josh. xv. 57). Which Θαμναθά is meant in 1 Macc. ix. 50 it is impossible to determine with any certainty. See in general, Raumer, p. 224. Robinson's *Pal.* ii. pp. 239, 240. Guérin's *Judée*, ii. 30 f. *The Survey*, etc., *Memoirs*, ii. 417, maps, No. xvi.

[439] Lydda (Hebr. לֹד, afterwards Diospolis), the well-known town on the road from Joppa to Jerusalem, is also mentioned (*Bell. Jud.* ii. 20. 4) as one of the toparchies of Judaea. On one occasion Josephus characterizes it as κώμη . . . πόλεως τὸ μέγεθος οὐκ ἀποδέουσα (*Antt.* xx. 6. 2). For its history, comp. especially 1 Macc. xi. 34 ; Joseph. *Antt.* xiv. 10. 6, 11. 2 ; *Bell. Jud.* i. 11. 2, ii. 19. 1, iv. 8. 1.

[440] Emmaus or Ammaus, the Nicopolis of later times, is still existing under the name of Amwâs, and is situated to the south by south-east of Lydda. Owing to the circumstance of its standing just at the foot of the mountain range it was a place of some military importance, and is frequently mentioned as such as early as the time of the Maccabees (1 Macc. iii. 40, 57, iv. 3, ix. 50). For its later history, see especially *Antt.* xiv. 11. 2 ; *Bell. Jud.* i. 11. 2 ; *Antt.* xvii. 10. 9 ; *Bell. Jud.* ii. 5. 1, iv. 8. 1. It is also mentioned as one of the Jewish toparchies in *Bell. Jud.* ii. 20. 4. In Rabbinical Hebrew it is called אמאוס (Mishna, *Arachin* ii. 4 ; *Kerithoth* iii. 7. Lightfoot, *Chorographica Lucae praemissa*, c. 4, *Opp.* ii. 479 f. Neubauer's *Géogr. du Talmud*, pp. 100–102) ; it also occurs in Ptolemaeus, v. 16. 7, as 'Εμμαοῦς. Whether it is the same Emmaus that is intended in *Bell. Jud.* vii. 6. 6 and Luke xxiv. 13, is open to question. Comp. in general, Reland's *Palaestina*, pp. 758–760. Raumer, p. 187 f. Winer's *Realwörterb.* under this word. Arnold in Herzog's *Real-Encycl.*, 1st ed. iii. 778 f. Robinson's *Palestine*, iii. pp. 146–151. Kuhn, *Die städtische u. bürgerl. Verfassung*, ii. 356 f. Sepp's *Jerusalem*, 2nd ed. i. 40 ff. Guérin's *Judée*, i. 293–308. *The Survey of Western Palestine, Memoirs*, etc., iii. 14, 36 ff., 63–81, and the maps, No. xvii.

[441] According to *Bell. Jud.* iv. 8. 1, Bethleptepha stood between Emmaus and Idumaea, and should therefore be inserted here instead of Pella, as erroneously given in the text of Josephus.

[442] Idumaea had been Judaized by John Hyrcanus (*Antt.* xiii. 9. 1, xv.

east, Engaddi [443] and Herodeion; [444] to the east, Jericho.[445]
It may be assumed as self-evident that this division was made
chiefly for administrative reasons and, above all, with a view
to greater convenience in the *collecting of the revenue.*
Whether those districts were at the same time districts for
judicial purposes as well, it is impossible to say. In any
case it is probable that the whole organization does not date
farther back than the Roman period, for no trace of it is to
be met with previous to that time.[446] The authorities from
whom our information is derived exhibit a singular indecision
in their conceptions of the political character of the capitals
of those districts, inasmuch as at one time they are described
as πόλεις, at another as κῶμαι. It is true that here nothing
is to be made of the circumstance that Eusebius treats the

7, 9. *Bell. Jud.* i. 2. 6). Hence it was that the Idumaeans took part in
the Jewish insurrection as though they too had been Jews (*Bell. Jud.* iv.
4. 4). Elsewhere, comp. especially *Bell. Jud.* ii. 20. 4, iv. 8. 1.

[443] Engaddi, the ancient עֵין גְּדִי (Josh. xv. 62 ; 1 Sam. xxiv. 1 ff. ; Ezek.
xlvii. 10; Song of Sol. i. 14 ; 2 Chron. xx. 2), the existence of which on
the western shore of the Dead Sea is vouched for by both Josephus and
Eusebius (Joseph. *Antt.* ix. 1. 2 : Ἐγγαδδὶ πόλιν κειμένην πρὸς τῇ Ἀσφαλ-
τίτιδι λίμνῃ. Euseb. *Onomast.*, ed. Lagarde, p. 254: καὶ νῦν ἐστὶ κώμη
μεγίστη Ἰουδαίων Ἐγγαδδὶ παρακειμένη τῇ νεκρᾷ θαλάσσῃ). In *Bell. Jud.*
iv. 7. 2, Josephus calls it a πολίχνη. In Ptolemaeus, v. 16. 8, it occurs as
Ἐγγάδδα. It is known in the present day as Ain Dschidi. See in general,
Winer's *Realwörterb.* under the word. Raumer, 188 f. Robinson's *Palestine*,
i. pp. 500–508. Neubauer's *Géogr. du Talmud*, p. 160. *The Survey of Western
Palestine, Memoirs*, etc., iii. pp. 384–386, 387, and the accompanying maps,
No. xxii.

[444] Herodeion is the important fortress built by Herod the Great in the
south of Judaea, some sixty stadia from Jerusalem (*Antt.* xiv. 13. 9, xv. 9. 4 ;
*Bell. Jud.* i. 13. 8, 21. 10), the identity of which, with the modern
"Frankenberge" standing to the south-east of Bethlehem, may now be
looked upon as generally admitted. Comp. above, § 15.

[445] Jericho, the well-known city of that name near to the Jordan, was
the most important town in the east of Judaea, and for this reason it too
was chosen by Gabinius as the seat of one of the five Jewish courts or
Sanhedrims (*Antt.* xiv. 5. 4 ; *Bell. Jud.* i. 8. 5). It is also mentioned as
being one of the districts of Judaea in *Bell. Jud.* ii. 20. 4. Besides this,
comp. especially *Bell. Jud.* iv. 8. 2, 9. 1.

[446] On the division of the Roman provinces into administrative districts,
see in general Marquardt, *Römische Staatsverwaltung*, vol. i. (2nd ed. 1881)
p. 500 f.

places in question for the most part as κῶμαι, for by his time matters had undergone an essential change.[447] But Josephus himself is also somewhat undecided. For example, he speaks of Emmaus as being the μητρόπολις of the district in which it stood, and obviously therefore as that of the toparchy;[448] whereas, in speaking of Lydda, on the other hand, he calls it merely a κώμη, thus employing what would appear to be the more correct designation (see above, note 439). We are therefore bound to assume, that from the Romano-Hellenistic point of view none of the places in question were πόλεις in the strict sense of the word, that is to say, they were not civic communities with a Hellenistic constitution; while it was only in deference to Jewish and popular usage that they were spoken of as "cities." Strictly speaking, they ought rather to be called κωμοπόλεις (see above, note 423), or, viewed in their relation to their respective toparchies, μητρο-κωμίαι (see above, notes 427–429).

There was only one town in Judaea proper that, according to Romano-Hellenistic ideas, enjoyed at the same time the rank of a πόλις, and that was Jerusalem. To this latter all the rest of Judaea was subordinate, so that it ruled over it (Judaea) ὡς βασίλειον (see note 431). Consequently its relation to Judaea was similar to that in which the Hellenistic cities stood to their respective districts.[449] This among other things is implied in the style of address that is made use of in the imperial edicts issued to the Jews and which run thus: Ἱεροσολυμιτῶν ἄρχουσι βουλῇ δήμῳ, Ἰουδαίων παντὶ ἔθνει, terms precisely similar to those employed in the edicts

[447] The names of several toparchies (Ἀκραβαττηνή, Θαμνιτική) were no doubt still retained in Eusebius' day, but the constitution itself had been essentially altered by the establishment of new, independent civitates such as Diospolis, Nicopolis and others. The result of this was that Thamna, for example, ceased to be any longer the capital of a toparchy, but was now reduced to the position of a κώμη μεγάλη ἐν ὁρίοις Διοσπόλεως (see above, note 438), and so became subordinate to what was formerly known as Lydda.

[448] Bell. Jud. iv. 8. 1.

[449] Comp. Kuhn, Die städtische und bürgerl. Verfassung, ii. 342–345.

addressed to the Hellenistic communes where, in like manner, the city with its council ruled over, and therefore was regarded as representing the whole district to which it belonged.[450] It is further probable that the council (the Sanhedrim) of Jerusalem was also responsible for the collection of the taxes throughout the whole of Judaea.[451] Again there is a reminiscence of the circumstance of the " elders " exercising authority over the whole of Judaea still preserved to us in the Mishna.[452] But since the death of Herod the Great at least, the civil jurisdiction of the Sanhedrim of Jerusalem was entirely restricted to *Judaea proper.* Ever since then, Galilee and Peraea were, as regards their political relations, entirely severed from Judaea, or at all events formed independent spheres of administration, as has been pointed out above with special reference to Galilee. And least of all

---

[450] *Antt.* xx. 1. 2. Comp. besides for similar styles of address as employed in edicts, *Antt.* xiv. 10 (Σιδωνίων ἄρχουσι βουλῇ δήμῳ, 'Εφεσίων βουλῇ καὶ ἄρχουσι καὶ δήμῳ, and such like).

[451] When, after the first throes of the insurrection, it was resolved to return, for a moment, to a peaceful attitude, the magistrates and members of the council of Jerusalem distributed themselves over the villages for the purpose of collecting the arrears of the tribute (*Bell. Jud.* ii. 17. 1 : εἰς δὲ τὰς κώμας οἵ τε ἄρχοντες καὶ οἱ βουλευταὶ μερισθέντες τοὺς φόρους συνέλεγον). The sums from the different quarters were speedily gathered together and were found to amount in all to forty talents. But, immediately thereafter, Agrippa sent the ἄρχοντες and δυνατοί to Caesarea to Florus with the request that he would appoint from among them tribute collectors for the country (*ibid.* ἵνα ἐκεῖνος ἐξ αὐτῶν ἀποδείξῃ τοὺς τὴν χώραν φορολογήσοντας). Now, seeing that this took place *after* the taxes of the district, and therefore, of course, of the toparchy of Jerusalem, had been already collected, it follows that, by the term χώρα, the whole of Judaea is to be understood. It was therefore for the whole of this province that the collectors were to be appointed from among the ἄρχοντες and δυνατοί of Jerusalem. For the Roman practice of employing city councils as a medium for collecting the taxes, comp. in general, Marquardt, i. 501.

[452] *Taanith* iii. 6 : " On one occasion the elders went from Jerusalem to visit *their towns* (ירדו זקנים מירושלים לעריהם) and appointed fasts, because they found in Ascalon (באשקלון) a patch of blighted corn about the size of the mouth of an oven, etc." As Ascalon never belonged to the province of Judaea, this notice is in itself unhistorical, though it is correct in so far as it contains a reminiscence of the fact, that at one time the towns of Judaea were subject to the authority of the " elders " of Jerusalem.

can we venture to make use of the circumstance that the rebellion in Galilee was directed from Jerusalem as an argument to show, that in times of peace as well, Galilee was under the jurisdiction of the supreme court of the Sanhedrim. For the circumstances here in question are obviously of an exceptional character. It was only in earlier days, and particularly during the Asmonaean period, that the whole land of Judaea could be said to have been really one in a political sense as well (comp. below, chap. iii.). As the council of Jerusalem could scarcely have been able to attend to the administration of justice in all its details, it is antecedently probable that, besides the supreme Sanhedrim, there would be one or more inferior tribunals in Jerusalem. Of this too the Mishna has preserved a reminiscence, though it happens to be a somewhat confused one.[453]

### III. THE SUPREME SANHEDRIM IN JERUSALEM.

#### THE LITERATURE.

Selden, *De synedriis et praefecturis juridicis veterum Ebraeorum*, lib. i.–iii., Londini 1650–1655 (comp. above, p. 132).

Meuschen, *Novum Testamentum ex Talmude et antiquitatibus Hebraeorum illustratum* (Lips. 1736), pp. 1184–1199 : *Diatribe de* נשיא *seu directore Synedrii M. Hebraeorum.*

---

[453] *Sanhedrin* xi. 2 : "There were three courts of justice (בתי דינין) in Jerusalem. One held its sittings at the entrance to the temple mount (על פתח הר הבית), another at the entrance to the court of the temple (על פתח העזרה), and the third in the square chamber (בלשכת הגזית). The parties came with their causes to the one that sat at the entrance to the temple mount, and the presiding judge said : 'Thus have I and thus have my colleagues pronounced; thus have I and thus have my colleagues resolved.' If then the court had a tradition applicable to the case in question it gave a decision. But if not, the parties went to the tribunal at the entrance to the court of the temple and there restated their case. If this one again had a tradition bearing upon the case, it gave a decision. But if not, then the parties along with the members of those courts appeared before the supreme court in the square chamber, the fountainhead of law for the whole of Israel." The schematism with reference to the places at which the courts were held, is of itself sufficient to show that we are not here dealing with an authentic historical tradition.

Carpzov, *Apparatus historico-criticus antiquitatum sacri codicis* (1748), pp. 550–600.

Hartmann, *Die enge Verbindung des Alten Testaments mit dem Neuen* (1831), pp. 166–225.

Winer, *Realwörterb.* ii. 551–554, art. " Synedrium."

Sachs, *Ueber die Zeit der Entstehung des Synhedrin's* (Frankel's *Zeitschr. für die religiösen Interessen des Judenth.*, 1845, pp. 301–312).

Saalschütz, *Das mosaische Rechte*, 2nd ed. 1853, i. 49 ff., ii. 593 ff.  Also his *Archäologie der Hebräer*, vol. ii. 1856, pp. 249 ff., 271 ff., 429–458.

Levy, *Die Präsidentur im Synedrium* (Frankel's *Monatsschr. f. Gesch. und Wissensch. des Judenth.* 1855, pp. 266–274, 301–307, 339–358).

Herzfeld, *Geschichte des Volkes Israel*, vol. ii. (1855) pp. 380–396.

Jost, *Geschichte des Judenthums und seiner Secten*, vol. i. (1857) pp. 120–128, 270–281.   Comp. also pp. 403 ff., vol. ii. (1858) pp. 13 ff., 25 ff.

Geiger, *Urschrift und Uebersetzungen der Bibel* (1857), p. 114 ff.

Keil, *Handbuch der biblischen Archäologie* (2nd ed. 1875), pp. 714–717.

Leyrer, art. " Synedrium," in Herzog's *Real-Encycl.*, 1st ed. vol. xv. (1862) pp. 315–325.

Langen, *Das jüdische Synedrium und die römische Procuratur in Judäa* (*Tüb. Theol. Quartalschr.* 1862, pp. 411–463).

Grätz, *Geschichte der Juden*, vol. iii. (3rd ed. 1878) pp. 110 ff., 683–685.

De Wette, *Lehrbuch der hebräisch-jüdischen Archäologie* (4th ed. 1864), pp. 204–206.

Ewald, *Geschichte des Volkes Israel* (3rd ed. 1864–1868), iv. 217 ff., v. 56, vi. 697 ff.

Kuenen, *Over de samenstelling van het Sanhedrin* (*Verslagen en Mededeelingen der koninkl. Academie van Wetenschappen, Afdeeling Letterkunde, Deel x.*, Amsterdam 1866, pp. 131–168).   Comp. also, *De Godsdienst van Israël*, ii. (1870) pp. 512–515.

Derenbourg, *Histoire de la Palestine* (1867), pp. 83–94, 465–468.

Ginsburg, art. " Sanhedrim," in Kitto's *Cyclopaedia of Biblical Literature.*

Hausrath, *Neutestamentliche Zeitgeschichte*, vol. i. (2nd ed. 1873) pp. 63–72.

Wieseler, *Beiträge zur richtigen Würdigung der Evangelien* (1869), pp. 205–230.

Keim, *Geschichte Jesu*, iii. pp. 321 ff., 345 ff.

Wellhausen, *Die Pharisäer und die Sadducäer* (1874), pp. 26–43.

Holtzmann, art. " Synedrium," in Schenkel's *Bibellexicon*, v. 446–451.

Hoffmann (D.), *Der oberste Gerichtshof in der Stadt des Heiligthums* (*Progr. des Rabbiner-Seminares zu Berlin für* 1877–1878).   Also his *Die Präsidentur im Synedrium* (*Magazin für die Wissensch. des Judenth.* v. Jahrg. 1878, pp. 94–99).

Reuss, *Geschichte der heil. Schriften Alten Testaments* (1881), secs. ccclxxvi., ccccxcv.

Hamburger, *Real-Encyclopädie für Bibel und Talmud*, part 2, 1883, art. " Synhedrion ; " also the articles " Nassi " and " Abbethdin."

Stapfer, *Le Sanhédrin de Jérusalem au premier siècle* (*Revue de théologie et de philosophie* [Lausanne], 1884, pp. 105–119).

1. *Its history.* There is no evidence to show that, *previous to the Greek period*, there existed at Jerusalem an aristocratic council claiming to exercise either supreme, or what was substantially supreme, authority and jurisdiction over the whole Jewish nation. It is true no doubt that Rabbinical exegesis has sought to identify the Sanhedrim of later times with the council of seventy elders that, at his own request, had once been granted to Moses to assist him with its advice (Num. xi. 16), and has, in consequence, assumed that this same council continued without interruption from the days of Moses down to Talmudic times. But during the first thousand years of this period we find practically no trace whatever of its existence. For the " elders " that are sometimes mentioned as being the representatives of the people (for example in 1 Kings viii. 1, xx. 7; 2 Kings xxiii. 1; Ezek. xiv. 1, xx. 1) did not constitute a regularly organized court like the future Sanhedrim. Then again, the supreme court at Jerusalem, the existence of which is presupposed in the Deuteronomic legislation (Deut. xvii. 8 ff., xix. 16 ff.), and the institution of which the author of Chronicles ascribes to Jehoshaphat (2 Chron. xix. 8), was merely a court of justice with functions of an exclusively judicial character, and not a council *governing*, or at all events substantially governing, the country as was the Sanhedrim of the Graeco-Roman age.[453a] But further, it is, to say the least of it, uncertain whether any such court as that of the Sanhedrim existed even in the Persian era. No doubt, at that time, the *municipal* Council of Jerusalem formed the centre of the small Jewish commonwealth very much as it did at a subsequent period. And thus far we might be justified in understanding the " elders " of the Book of Ezra (Ezra v. 5, 9, vi. 7, 14, x. 8), and the חוֹרִים and סְגָנִים of the Book of Nehemiah (Neh. ii. 16, iv. 8, 13, v. 7, vii. 5), as corresponding somewhat to the future Sanhe-

---

[453a] Such certainly is the way Josephus conceives of the matter when, following the analogy of a later order of things, he speaks of the court of justice here referred to under the designation of ἡ γερουσία (*Antt.* iv. 8. 41).

drim. But judging from the whole way in which they are mentioned, it is more probable that the various orders referred to are regarded in their individual capacity and not as constituting an organized body. In any case the existence of a Jewish γερουσία earlier than the Greek period cannot be proved with any degree of certainty. The first occasion on which it is mentioned, and that under this designation, is in the time of Antiochus the Great (223–187 B.C.), so that it must, of course, have been in existence as early as the time of the Ptolemies.[454] Now seeing that, in its desire for reform everywhere and in everything, Hellenism had set itself to reorganize political institutions as well, we are bound to assume that, in all probability, it was just the new Greek rulers who would give to the Jewish γερουσία the form in which it was met with at the period now in question, whether that form were entirely an original one or whether it were simply a reorganization of a similar court that was already in existence under the Persian rule. From the circumstance of the designation γερουσία being applied to it, it is clear that, unlike the majority of Greek councils, this was not a democratic, but an *aristocratic* body.[455] This same circumstance would seem further to show that, so far as its original institution is concerned, this court dates back to an earlier period, and therefore to the time of the Persian rule. As we may well conceive, its powers would be of a tolerably large and extensive character. For the Hellenistic kings had conceded a great amount of internal freedom to municipal communities, and were on the whole satisfied if the taxes were duly paid and their own supremacy duly recognised. At the *head* of the Jewish commonwealth, and therefore of the γερουσία as well, stood the *hereditary high priest*. It was

[454] *Antt.* xii. 3. 3. For this whole matter, comp. Kuenen's admirable dissertation in the *Verslagen en Mededeelingen der koninkl. Akademie van Wetenschappen, l.c.*

[455] A γερουσία is always an *aristocratic* body. The Council of Sparta is expressly described as such, and so too with regard to councils generally in the Doric States. See Westermann in Pauly's *Real-Enc.* iii. 849 f.

this latter, in conjunction with the γερουσία over which he presided, that practically regulated the whole internal affairs of the nation.

After the Maccabaean insurrection the old high-priestly dynasty was superseded, its place being now supplied by the new *Asmonaean* line of high priests, which began with Simon, and which was likewise a hereditary one. Then again the old γερουσια must have been essentially revolutionized through its being purged of every element in it suspected of Greek sympathies and leanings. But the court itself still continued to exist and exercise its functions along with and under the Asmonaean princes and high priests; for even these latter could not venture to go so far as entirely to discard the old nobility of Jerusalem. Hence we find the γερουσία mentioned in the time of Judas (2 Macc. i. 10, iv. 44, xi. 27; the πρεσβύτεροι τοῦ λαοῦ of 1 Macc. vii. 33 being also identically the same thing), of Jonathan (1 Macc. xii. 6: ἡ γερουσία τοῦ ἔθνους; *ibid.* xi. 23: οἱ πρεσβύτεροι Ἰσραήλ; *ibid.* xii. 35: οἱ πρεσβύτεροι τοῦ λαοῦ) and of Simon (1 Macc. xiii. 36, xiv. 20, 28).[456] Its existence is likewise presupposed in the Book of Judith, which probably belongs to the period now in question (Judith iv. 8, xi. 14, xv. 8). The assumption of the title of king on the part of the Asmonaean princes, and above all the autocratic rule of an Alexander Jannaeus, indicated no doubt an advance in the direction of a pure monarchy. But, for all that, the old γερουσία still continued to assert itself as much as ever. At least in the reign of

---

[456] It is interesting in this connection to compare 1 Macc. xii. 6 with 1 Macc. xiv. 20. The matter in hand is the correspondence between the Jews and the Spartans. In the former of those passages (1 Macc. xii. 6 = Joseph. *Antt.* xiii. 5. 8) the Jews as the senders of the communication style themselves thus: Ἰωνάθαν ἀρχιερεὺς καὶ ἡ γερουσία τοῦ ἔθνους καὶ οἱ ἱερεῖς καὶ ὁ λοιπὸς δῆμος τῶν Ἰουδαίων. In the reply of the Spartans the terms of the address (1 Macc. xiv. 20) are as follows: Σίμωνι ἱερεῖ μεγάλῳ καὶ τοῖς πρεσβυτέροις καὶ τοῖς ἱερεῦσι καὶ τῷ λοιπῷ τῶν Ἰουδαίων. Observe (1) that ἡ γερουσία and οἱ πρεσβύτεροι are identically the same; (2) that in both instances the classification is of a *fourfold character:* High priest, gerousia, priests, people.

Alexandra we find τῶν Ἰουδαίων οἱ πρεσβύτεροι expressly
mentioned (*Antt.* xiii. 16. 5).[457]

It is true that, when a new order of things was introduced
by Pompey, the monarchy was abolished. But the high
priest still retained the προστασία τοῦ ἔθνους (*Antt.* xx. 10),
and therefore it may be presumed that meanwhile the position
of the γερουσία would remain essentially the same as before.[458]
The existing arrangements however were rather more seriously
disturbed by Gabinius (57–55 B.C.), when he divided the
whole of the Jewish territory into five σύνοδοι (*Bell. Jud.* i.
8. 5) or συνέδρια (*Antt.* xiv. 5. 4).[459]   Now, seeing that of
those five synedria *three* were allotted to Judaea proper (viz.
those of Jerusalem, Gazara and Jericho) it follows that the
jurisdiction of the council of Jerusalem, if it really retained
anything of its previous character at all, would extend only
to something like a third part of the province. But probably
that measure meant rather more than a mere limiting of
jurisdiction. For the five συνέδρια established by Gabinius
were not municipal councils, but—as indeed we might have
supposed from the fact that Josephus uses the term σύνοδοι
as a synonymous expression—genuine Roman *conventus juridici*, " districts for judicial purposes," into which the Romans
were in the habit of dividing every province.[460]   And, that

---

[457] Similarly in Tyre and Sidon, for example, there was a council associated with the king in the direction of affairs.  See Movers, *Die Phönizier*,
ii. 1 (1849), pp. 529–542.  Kuhn, *Die städtische und bürgerl. Verfassung*,
ii. 117.

[458] In the Psalms of Solomon, which for the most part were composed
in the time of Pompey, the author is in the habit of apostrophizing as
follows any public person or party that he happens to dislike: ἱνατὶ σὺ
κάθησαι βέβηλε ἐν συνεδρίῳ (Ps. iv. 1).  Now, as it is clear from the context
that by the term συνέδριον we are to understand a court, it is quite possible
that it is our γερουσία that is here referred to.  But, owing to the ambiguous
nature of the expression itself and the impossibility of fixing with *greater
precision* the date of the composition of the psalm, there is historically
but little to be gleaned from this passage.  Any light that is to be thrown
upon it must be derived from what we already know regarding the existing
order of things.

[459] On this comp. above, § 13.

[460] Comp. Marquardt's *Römische Staatsverwaltung*, i. (1881), p. 501.

being the case, the measure in question must have been neither more nor less than a stricter application to Judaea of the Roman system of provincial government. As things now stood the council of Jerusalem no longer exercised sole juris-diction within the circuit to which it belonged, but only in conjunction with the other communities within this same district. The arrangements of Gabinius however continued to subsist only somewhere about ten years. For they were in turn superseded by the new system of things introduced by Caesar (47 B.C.). This latter reappointed Hyrcanus II. to his former office of ἐθνάρχης of the Jews (see above, § 13); while it is distinctly evident from a circumstance that occurred about that time, that the jurisdiction of the council of Jeru-salem once more extended to Galilee as well. The circum-stance in question was the occasion on which Herod when a youth was required to appear before the συνέδριον at *Jerusalem* to answer for his doings in *Galilee* (*Antt.* xiv. 9. 3–5). Here for the first time, as frequently afterwards, the council of Jerusalem was designated by the term συνέδριον. As it is unusual elsewhere to find this expression applied to civic councils, such a use, in this instance, is somewhat strange, but probably it is to be explained by the fact that the council of Jerusalem was conceived of as being above all a court of justice (בֵּית דִּין). For it is in this sense that συνέδριον is specially used in later Greek.[461]

Kuhn (*Die städt. u. bürgerl. Verf.* ii. 336, 367) also regards the Synedria of Gabinius as identical with the *conventus juridici* of the Romans.

[461] Hesychius, *Lex.* (see word), defines συνέδριον precisely by the term δικαστήριον (a court of justice). In the Sept. version of Prov. xxii. 10 συνέδριον is given as the rendering of דִּין. Comp. also Psalms of Solomon iv. 1. In the New Testament again συνέδρια mean simply "courts of justice" (Matt. x. 17; Mark xiii. 9); similarly in the Mishna (see, in particular, *Sanhedrin* i. 5, סנהדריות לשבטים = courts for the tribes, and i. 6, סנהדרין קטנה = an inferior court of justice). Hence Steph. in his *Thes.* (see word) correctly observes: praecipue ita vocatur consessus judicum. It is true that, in itself, συνέδριον is a very comprehensive term and may be applied to every "assembly" and every corporate body, even to the Roman senate, for example (see in general, Stephanus, *Thes.*, under word, and Westermann in Pauly's *Enc.* vi. 2. 1535). It is but comparatively

Herod the Great inaugurated his reign by ordering the whole of the members of the Sanhedrim to be put to death (*Antt.* xiv. 9. 4: πάντας ἀπέκτεινε τοὺς ἐν τῷ συνεδρίῳ). Whether the πάντας here is to be understood quite literally may be left an open question. For, according to another passage, Herod is represented as having ordered the forty-five most prominent personages belonging to the party of Antigonus to be put to death (*Antt.* xv. 1. 2: ἀπέκτεινε δὲ τεσσαράκοντα πέντε τοὺς πρώτους ἐκ τῆς αἱρέσεως 'Αντιγόνου). In any case the object of this proceeding was either to get rid entirely of the old nobility, who had been somewhat hostile to his claims, or at all events so to intimidate them as to ensure their acquiescence in the rule of the new sovereign. It was of those then that were disposed to be tractable—among whom also were a good many Pharisees, who saw in Herod's despotic sway a well-merited

seldom however that it is used to denote civic councils, which as every one knows are mostly designated by the terms βουλή and γερουσία. It is more frequently employed to denote representative assemblies, composed of deputies from various constituencies. And so we have, for example, the συνέδριον of the Phoenicians which was usually convened in Tripolis (Diodor. xvi. 41), the κοινὸν συνέδριον of ancient Lycia, which was composed of representatives from twenty-three different towns (Strabo, xiv. 3. 3, p. 664 f.), and the συνέδριον κοινόν of the province of Asia (Aristides, *Orat.* xxvi., ed. Dindorf, vol. i. p. 531). Hence it is too that σύνεδροι and βουλευταί are mentioned separately as constituting two different orders of officials (see inscription at Balbura in Pisidia as given in Le Bas et Waddington's *Inscr.* vol. iii. n. 1221). Moreover, the *senatores* of the four Macedonian districts, who, according to Livy, were called σύνεδροι (Liv. xlv. 32: pronuntiatum, quod ad statum Macedoniae pertinebat, senatores, quos synedros vocant, legendos esse, quorum consilio respublica administraretur), were not municipal councillors, but deputies representing an entire *regio* (see Marquardt's *Staatsverwaltung*, i. [1881] p. 317). Now as the term in question was first heard of in Judaea in the time of Gabinius, and was thereafter currently applied to the council of Jerusalem as well, one might be inclined to suppose that it had been introduced in this quarter in connection with the Gabinian measures of reform, and that its use was still retained even after a new order of things had been established (as I have myself held, Riehm's *Wörterb.* p. 1596). But in presence of the fact, that elsewhere too, even in Hebrew itself, the term is generally used in the sense of a "court of justice," this explanation, I fear, must be abandoned as more ingenious than otherwise.

judgment of heaven—that the new Sanhedrim was now composed. For there is express evidence that such an institution
existed in the time of Herod also, inasmuch as one can hardly
understand that the "assembly" (συνέδριον) before which this
monarch successfully prosecuted his charge against the aged
Hyrcanus could be taken as referring to any other court than
our Sanhedrim (*Antt.* xv. 6. 2, *fin.*).[462]

After Herod's death Archelaus obtained only a portion of
his father's kingdom, viz. the provinces of Judaea and Samaria.
Nor can there be any doubt that, in consequence of this, the
jurisdiction of the Sanhedrim was at the same time restricted
to Judaea proper (comp. above, p. 142). This continued to
be the state of matters in the time of the *procurators* as well.
But, under their administration, the internal government of
the country was to a greater extent in the hands of the
Sanhedrim than it had been during the reign of Herod and
Archelaus. Josephus distinctly intimates as much when he
informs us that, ever since the death of Herod and Archelaus,
the form of government was that of an aristocracy under the
supreme direction of the high priests.[463] And accordingly he
regards the aristocratic council of Jerusalem as being now the
true governing body in contradistinction to the previous
monarchical rule of the Idumaean princes. So too in the
time of Christ and the apostles the συνέδριον at Jerusalem
is frequently mentioned as being the supreme Jewish
court, above all, as being the supreme Jewish court
of justice (Matt. v. 22, xxvi. 59; Mark xiv. 55, xv. 1;
Luke xxii. 66; John xi. 47; Acts iv. 15, v. 21 ff., vi. 12 ff.,
xxii. 30, xxiii. 1 ff., xxiv. 20). Sometimes again the terms

---

[462] Comp. besides, Wieseler's *Beiträge zur richtigen Würdigung der
Evangelien*, p. 215 f.

[463] *Antt.* xx. 10, *fin.*: μετὰ δὲ τὴν τούτων τελευτὴν ἀριστοκρατία μὲν ἦν ἡ
πολιτεία, τὴν δὲ προστασίαν τοῦ ἔθνους οἱ ἀρχιερεῖς ἐπεπίστευντο. Now, as
throughout the whole section it is high priests strictly so called that are in
view (and of whom only *one* was in office at a time), it follows that the
word ἀρχιερεῖς is to be taken as the categorical plural, so that the meaning
would be : the προστασία τοῦ ἔθνους was in the hands of the high priest for
the time being.

πρεσβυτέριον (Luke xxii. 66 ; Acts xxii. 5) and γερουσία
(Acts v. 21) are substituted for συνέδριον.[464]    A member of this
court, viz. Joseph of Arimathea, is described in Mark xv. 43,
Luke xxiii. 50, as a βουλευτής.    Josephus calls the supreme
court of Jerusalem a συνέδριον [465] or a βουλή,[466] or he compre-
hends the court and people under the common designation
of τὸ κοινόν.[467]    While in the Mishna again the supreme
court of justice is called בֵּית דִּין הַגָּדוֹל [468] or סַנְהֶדְרִין גְּדוֹלָה,[469] likewise סַנְהֶדְרִין שֶׁל שִׁבְעִים יָאחָד,[470] or merely סַנְהֶדְרִין.[470a]    There can
be no question that, after the destruction of Jerusalem in the
year 70 A.D., the Sanhedrim was abolished, so far at least as
its existing form was concerned.    The comparatively large
amount of self-government that had hitherto been granted to
the Jewish people could no longer be conceded to them after

[464] A singular feature about the last-mentioned passage (Acts v. 21) is the
use of such a form of designation as: τὸ συνέδριον καὶ πᾶσαν τὴν γερουσίαν
τῶν υἱῶν Ἰσραήλ.  Now, seeing that there can be no question as to the
identity of the two conceptions συνέδριον and γερουσία, only one or other of
two things is possible, either the καὶ is to be taken as explanatory, or we
must assume that the author of the Acts erroneously supposed that the
συνέδριον was of a less comprehensive character than the γερουσία ("the
Sanhedrim and all the elders of the people together").  The latter is the
more natural alternative.

[465] Thus, in addition to the passages already mentioned (Antt. xiv. 9.
3–5, xv. 6. 2, fin.), we might refer further to Antt. xx. 9. 1 ; Vita, 12, the
terms of the latter passage being: τὸ συνέδριον τῶν Ἱεροσολυμιτῶν. It
may be questioned whether it is also the supreme Sanhedrim that is
intended in Antt. xx. 9. 6 ; comp. Wieseler's Beiträge, p. 217.

[466] Bell. Jud. ii. 15. 6 : τούς τε ἀρχιερεῖς καὶ τὴν βουλήν. Bell. Jud. ii.
16. 2 : Ἰουδαίων οἵ τε ἀρχιερεῖς ἅμα τοῖς δυνατοῖς καὶ ἡ βουλή; Bell. Jud.
ii. 17. 1. οἵ τε ἄρχοντες καὶ οἱ βουλευταί.  Comp. Antt. xx. 1. 2 ; Bell.
Jud. v. 13. 1.  The place of meeting is called βουλή in Bell. Jud. v. 4. 2,
and βουλευτήριον in Bell. Jud. vi. 6. 3.

[467] Vita, 12, 13, 38, 49, 52, 60, 65, 70.

[468] Sota i. 4, ix. 1 ; Gittin vi. 7 ; Sanhedrin xi. 2. 4 ; Horajath i. 5, fin.
In most of the passages the expression שֶׁבִּירוּשָׁלַיִם is added.

[469] Sanhedrin i. 6 ; Middoth v. 4  Just as the term סנהדרין is borrowed
from the Greek, so on the Palmyra inscriptions we find the words בולא
ודמוס=ἡ βουλὴ καὶ ὁ δῆμος.

[470] Shebuoth ii. 2.

[470a] Sota ix. 11 ; Kiddushin iv. 5 ; Sanhedrin iv. 3  The term סנהדרין
(in a variety of senses) is also of frequent occurrence, especially in the later
Targums.  See Buxtorf's Lex. col. 1513 f. Levy's Chald. Wörterb. under word.

such a serious rebellion as had taken place. Hitherto, apart from the short episode in the time of Gabinius, the Roman system of provincial government had not been strictly carried out in Judaea (see above, § 17ᵉ), but now that Palestine was reduced to the position of a dependent Roman province, it was no longer exempted from the ordinary system of Roman provincial administration.[471] From all this it followed, as matter of course, that a Jewish council, invested with such extensive powers as this one had hitherto exercised, could not possibly continue any longer. It is true, no doubt, that the Jewish people lost no time in again creating for themselves a new centre in the so-called court of justice (בֵּית דִּין) at Jabne.[472] But this court was something essentially different from the old Sanhedrim, inasmuch as it was not a legislative body, but a judicial tribunal, the decisions of which had at first nothing more than a merely theoretical importance. And although this court also came ere long to acquire great power over the Jewish people through exercising over them a real jurisdiction that was partly conceded and partly usurped,[473] still Rabbinical Judaism has evidently never been able to get rid of the feeling that the old "Sanhedrim" had now become a thing of the past.[474]

[471] For the separation of Palestine from Syria and its elevation to the rank of an independent province, consult Kuhn, *Die städt. u. bürgerl. Verf.* ii. 183 f. Marquardt's *Staatsverwaltung*, i. (2nd ed. 1881) p. 419 ff.

[472] On this court at Jabne, see especially *Rosh hashana* ii. 8, 9, iv. 1, 2. *Sanhedrin* xi. 4 ; also *Bechoroth* iv. 5, vi. 8 ; *Kelim* v. 4 ; *Para* vii. 6. At a later period (in the third and fourth centuries) this centre of Rabbinical Judaism was located at Tiberias.

[473] Origen, *Epist. ad Africanum*, sec. xiv. (*Opp.* ed. Lommatzsch, vol. xvii.): Καὶ νῦν γοῦν Ῥωμαίων βασιλευόντων καὶ Ἰουδαίων τὸ δίδραχμον αὐτοῖς τελούντων, ὅσα συγχωροῦντος Καίσαρος ὁ ἐθνάρχης παρ' αὐτοῖς δύναται, ὡς μηδὲν διαφέρειν βασιλεύοντος τοῦ ἔθνους, ἴσμεν οἱ πεπειραμένοι. Γίνεται δὲ καὶ κριτήρια λεληθότως κατὰ τὸν νόμον, καὶ καταδικάζονταί τινες τὴν ἐπὶ τῷ θανάτῳ, οὔτε μετὰ τῆς πάντη εἰς τοῦτο παρρησίας, οὔτε μετὰ τοῦ γανθάνειν τὸν βασιλεύοντα. Καὶ τοῦτο ἐν τῇ χώρᾳ τοῦ ἔθνους πολὺν διατρίψαντες χρόνον μεμαθήκαμεν καὶ πεπληροφορήμεθα.

[474] *Sota* ix. 11 : " *Ever since the Sanhedrim was extinguished* (משבטלה סנהדרין) there has been no such thing as singing at the festive board, for it is written in Isa. xxiv. 9 : 'They shall not drink wine with a song,'" etc.

2. *Its composition.* In accordance with the analogy of the later Rabbinical courts of justice, Jewish tradition conceives of the supreme Sanhedrim as having been merely a collegiate body composed of scribes. This is what, down to the time of the destruction of Jerusalem, it certainly never was. On the contrary, it is certain, from the concurrent testimony of Josephus and the New Testament, that, till the very last, the head of the sacerdotal aristocracy continued to preside over the Sanhedrim. And so we see that all the vicissitudes of time had not been able to efface that original fundamental character of this court in virtue of which it was to be regarded not as an association of learned men, but as a body representative of the nobility. But, of course, it was not to be expected that the power of Pharisaism should continue to grow as it did without ultimately exerting some influence upon the composition of the Sanhedrim. The more the Pharisees grew in importance the more did the priestly aristocracy become convinced that they too would have to be allowed to have their representatives in the Sanhedrim. The first step in this direction would probably be taken some time during the reign of Alexandra, and the matter would doubtless receive no inconsiderable impetus in the time of Herod. For this monarch's high-handed treatment of the old nobility could not possibly have failed to promote the interests of Pharisaism. The Sanhedrim of the Roman period then would thus seem to have been made up of two factors: that of the priestly nobility, with its Sadducaean sympathies on the one hand, and that of the Pharisaic doctors on the other. It is moreover in the light of this fact that the various matters recorded in the traditions will require to be viewed. According to the Mishna the number of members amounted to seventy-one, clearly taking as its model the council of elders in the time of Moses (Num. xi. 16).[475] From the two statements of

---

[475] *Sanhedrin* i. 6: "The supreme Sanhedrim consisted of seventy-one members." "The Sanhedrim of seventy-one" is also mentioned in *Sheboth* i. 2. In several other passages we read of seventy-two elders (*Sebachim*

Josephus, the one in *Antt.* xiv. 9. 4 (where we are told that
Herod, on his accession to the throne, put to death *all* the
members of the Sanhedrim), and the other in *Antt.* xv. 1. 2
(where again we are informed that he put to death the forty-
five most prominent members of the party of Antigonus), one
might be disposed to infer that the number of members was
forty-five. But the πάντας in the first of those statements is
assuredly not intended to be taken literally. On the other
hand, we have a great deal that tends to bear out the view
that the number of members amounted to seventy-one.
When Josephus was planning the rising in Galilee he
appointed seventy elders to take charge of the administration
of this province.[476] In like manner the zealots in Jerusalem,
after suppressing the existing authorities, established a
tribunal composed of seventy members.[477] This then would
seem to have been regarded as the normal number of members
required to constitute a supreme court of justice among the
Jews. Consequently the traditions of the Mishna too are in
themselves perfectly probable. As to the mode in which

i. 3 ; *Jadajim* iii. 5, iv. 2). But, as a rule, these are foreign to the matter
in hand. (In all the three passages last referred to R. Simon ben Asai
appeals to traditions, which he professes to have received "from the mouth
of the seventy-two elders on the day on which they ordained R. Eleasar
ben Asariah as head of the school." Here then the matter in view is not
the supreme Sanhedrim, but the academy of Jewish scholars in the second
century of our era. Comp. besides, Selden, *De synedriis,* ii. 4. 10.) Just
as little have we to do here with the supposed seventy-two translators of
the Old Testament (six from each of the twelve tribes) ; see Pseudo-
Aristeas, ed. M. Schmidt in Merx's *Archiv,* i. 262 f.

[476] *Bell. Jud.* ii. 20. 5. When Kuenen (*Verslagen en Mededeelingen,* x.
161) seeks to invalidate the appeal to this passage by pointing to the discrepancy between it and what is said in *Vita,* 14, he may be met with the
reply that this latter passage has been purposely tampered with. The fact
of Josephus having *organized* the rising in Galilee through the appointment
of the seventy elders, has been so distorted in *Vita,* 14, as to make it
appear that, under the pretext of friendship, he took the most distinguished
of the Galilaeans "to the number of somewhere about seventy" and kept
them as hostages, and allowed the judgments he pronounced to be regulated
by their decisions.

[477] *Bell. Jud.* iv. 5. 4. Comp. in general, Hody, *De bibliorum textibus
originalibus,* pp. 126–128.

vacancies were filled up we know in reality absolutely
nothing.   But, judging from the aristocratic character of this
body, we may venture to presume that there was not a
new set of members every year, and those elected by the
voice of the people, as in the case of the democratic councils in
the Hellenistic communes, but that they held office for a longer
period, nay perhaps for life, and that new members were appointed either by the existing members themselves or by the
supreme political authorities (Herod and the Romans).   The
supplying of vacancies through co-optation is also presupposed
in the Mishna, in so far as, after its own peculiar way no doubt,
it regards the amount of Rabbinical learning possessed by the
candidate as the sole test of his eligibility.[478]   In any case we
may well believe that the *one* requirement of legal Judaism,
that none but Israelites of pure blood should be eligible
for the office of judge in a criminal court, would also be
insisted on in the case of the supreme Sanhedrim.[479]   New
members were formally admitted to take their seats through

[478] *Sanhedrin* iv. 4: " In front of them sat three rows of learned disciples
(תלמידי חכמים); each of them had his own special place.  Should it be
necessary to promote one of them to the office of judge, one of those in the
foremost row was selected.  His place was then supplied by one from the
second row, while one from the third was in turn advanced to the second.
This being done, some one was then chosen from the congregation to
supply the vacancy thus created in the third row.   But the person so
appointed did not step directly into the place occupied by the one last
promoted from the third row, but into the place that beseemed one who
was only newly admitted."

[479] That the Sanhedrim was composed exclusively of Jews is simply a
matter of course.  But the Mishna specially insists on evidence of pure
blood in the case of the *criminal judge*. *Sanhedrin* iv. 2: " Any one is qualified to act as a judge in civil causes.  But none were competent to deal with
criminal cases but priests, Levites, and *Israelites whose daughters it would be
lawful for priests to marry* " (*i.e.* those who can furnish documentary evidence of their legitimate Israelitish origin, Derenbourg, p. 453 : les Israélites
pourvus des conditions nécessaires pour contracter mariage avec le sacerdoce,
not as Geiger, *Urschrift*, p. 114, erroneously renders it: those who have
become allied by marriage to the stock of the priesthood).   From this
then it would appear that the Mishna presupposes that, in the case of
every member of the Sanhedrim, his legitimate Israelitish descent is an
admitted fact requiring no further confirmation (*Kiddushin* iv. 5).  As this
is a point in which the tendencies of the priesthood and Pharisaism coin-

the ceremony of the laying on of hands (סְמִיכָה).[480]   With regard to the different orders to which the members of the Sanhedrim belonged we have trustworthy information on that point in the concurrent testimony of the New Testament and Josephus.   Both authorities are agreed in this, that the ἀρχιερεῖς in the literal sense of the word were the leading personages among them.   In almost every instance in which the New Testament enumerates the different orders we find that the ἀρχιερεῖς are mentioned first.[481]   Sometimes οἱ ἄρχοντες is substituted for this latter as being an interchangeable expression.[482]   This is also the case in Josephus,

cided, it is, to say the least of it, probable that it was also given effect to in practice.

[480] The *verb* סָמַךְ (to lay on the hands) is already to be met with in the Mishna in the sense of to install any one as a judge (*Sanhedrin* iv. 4). This ceremony is therefore, comparatively speaking, a very ancient one, seeing that it was also observed at a very early period in the Christian Church. Of course the act of laying on of the hands was not to be understood as conferring any special charisma, but (as in the case of the victim in the Old Testament) as indicating that something was being transferred to the individual in question, that an office, a place of authority, was being committed to him on the part of the person by whom the ceremony was performed. On the later Rabbinical סְמִיכָה, see Buxtorf's *Lex. Chald.* col. 1498 f.   Selden, *De synedriis*, ii. 7.   Vitringa, *De synagoga vetere*, p. 836 ff. Carpzov's *Apparatus*, p. 577 f.   Jo. Chrph. Wolf, *Curae philol. in Nov. Test.*, note on Acts vi. 6, and the literature quoted there (being in general expositors' notes on Acts vi. 6).   Hamburger, *Real-Encycl. für Bibel und Talmud*, part ii. art. "Ordinirung."

[481] The following are the formulae that are to be met with :—I. ἀρχιερεῖς, γραμματεῖς and πρεσβύτεροι (or with the two latter in reverse order), Matt. xxviii. 41; Mark xi. 27, xiv. 43, 53, xv. 1.—II. ἀρχιερεῖς and γραμματεῖς, Matt. ii. 4, xx. 18, xxi. 15; Mark x. 33, xi. 18, xiv. 1, xv. 31; Luke xxii. 2, 66, xxiii. 10.—III. ἀρχιερεῖς and πρεσβύτεροι, Matt. xxi. 23, xxvi. 3, 47, xxvii. 1, 3, 12, 20, xxviii. 11, 12; Acts iv. 23, xxiii. 14, xxv. 15.—IV. οἱ ἀρχιερεῖς καὶ τὸ συνέδριον ὅλον, Matt. xxvi. 59; Mark xiv. 55; Acts xxii. 30. *As a rule* then, the ἀρχιερεῖς occupy *the foremost place*. The instances in which they are not mentioned first (Matt. xvi. 21; Mark viii. 31; Luke ix. 22, xx. 19), or are omitted altogether (Matt. xxvi. 57; Acts vi. 12), are extremely rare.

[482] See in particular, Acts ix. 5 and 8 (ἄρχοντες, πρεσβύτεροι and γραμματεῖς) compared with iv. 23 (ἀρχιερεῖς and πρεσβύτεροι).   Of course there are a couple of instances in which both οἱ ἀρχιερεῖς καὶ οἱ ἄρχοντες occur together (Luke xxiii. 13, xxiv. 20).

above all, who designates the supreme authorities in Jerusalem *either* by conjoining the ἀρχιερεῖς with the δυνατοῖς,
the γνωρίμοις and the βουλῇ,[483] *or* by substituting ἄρχοντες
for ἀρχιερεῖς,[484] but never by coupling the two *together at the
same time.* On the other hand, the ἀρχιερεῖς often stand
alone as being the leading personages in the Sanhedrim.[485]
And however difficult it may now be further to determine
the exact significance of this term (on this see below, under
No. iv.), there can, at all events, be no doubt whatever that
it is the most prominent representatives of the priesthood
that are here in view. We are therefore to understand that
it was always this class that played a leading part in the
conduct of affairs. But it is certain that, along with them,
the γραμματεῖς, the professional lawyers, also exercised considerable influence in the Sanhedrim. Such other members
as did not belong to one or other of the two special classes
just referred to were known simply as πρεσβύτεροι, under
which general designation both priests and laymen alike
might be included (for the two categories in question, see the
passages in the New Testament quoted in note 481). Now,
as the ἀρχιερεῖς belonged chiefly if not exclusively to the
party of the Sadducees, while the γραμματεῖς, on the other
hand, adhered not less strongly to the sect of the Pharisees,[486]
it follows from all that we have just been saying that *Sadducees and Pharisees alike* had seats in the Sanhedrim (especially
during the Romano-Herodian period with regard to which

---

[483] *Bell. Jud.* ii. 14. 8 : οἵ τε ἀρχιερεῖς καὶ δυνατοὶ τό τε γνωριμώτατον
τῆς πόλεως. *Bell. Jud.* ii. 15. 2 : οἱ δυνατοὶ σὺν τοῖς ἀρχιερεῦσι. *Bell. Jud.*
ii. 15. 3 : τούς τε ἀρχιερεῖς σὺν τοῖς γνωρίμοις. *Bell. Jud.* ii. 15. 6 : τούς τε
ἀρχιερεῖς καὶ τὴν βουλήν. *Bell. Jud.* ii. 16. 2 : οἵ τε ἀρχιερεῖς ἅμα τοῖς
δυνατοῖς καὶ ἡ βουλή. *Bell. Jud.* ii. 17. 2 : τῶν τε ἀρχιερέων καὶ τῶν
γνωρίμων. *Bell. Jud.* ii. 17. 3 : οἱ δυνατοὶ τοῖς ἀρχιερεῦσιν καὶ τοῖς τῶν
Φαρισαίων γνωρίμοις. *Bell. Jud.* ii. 17. 5 : οἱ δυνατοὶ σὺν τοῖς ἀρχιερεῦσι.
*Bell. Jud.* ii. 17. 6 : τῶν δυνατῶν καὶ τῶν ἀρχιερέων.

[484] *Bell. Jud.* ii. 16. 1 : οἱ τῶν Ἱεροσολύμων ἄρχοντες. *Bell. Jud.* ii. 17. 1 :
οἵ τε ἄρχοντες καὶ οἱ βουλευταί. *Bell. Jud.* ii. 17. 1 : τοὺς ἄρχοντας ἅμα
τοῖς δυνατοῖς. *Bell. Jud.* ii. 21. 7 : οἱ δυνατοὶ καὶ τῶν ἀρχόντων τινές

[485] For example, *Bell. Jud.* ii. 15. 3, 4, 16. 3, v. 1. 5, vi. 9. 3.

[486] Acts v. 17. Joseph. *Antt.* xx. 9. 1.

alone can we be said to have any precise information). This
is further corroborated by the express testimony of the New
Testament and Josephus.[487] During the period in question
the greatest amount of influence was already practically in
the hands of the Pharisees, with whose demands the Sadducees
were obliged, however reluctantly, to comply, " as otherwise
the people would not have tolerated them." [488] This remark
of Josephus gives us a deep insight into the actual position
of matters, from which it would seem, that though *formally*
under the leadership of the Sadducaean high priests, the Sanhedrim was by this time *practically* under the predominant
influence of Pharisaism.[489]

There is a casual notice in Josephus which may perhaps
be taken as pointing to the existence of an arrangement
peculiar to the Hellenistico-Roman period. On one occasion
when certain differences had arisen between the Jewish
authorities and Festus the procurator about some alteration
in the temple buildings, it appears that, with the concurrence
of Festus, the Jews sent "the ten foremost persons among
them and the high priest Ismael and the treasurer Helkias"
as a deputation to Nero (*Antt.* xx. 8. 11 : τοὺς πρώτους δέκα
καὶ Ἰσμάηλον τὸν ἀρχιερέα καὶ Ἑλκίαν τὸν γαζοφύλακα).
Now, if by the πρῶτοι δέκα here we are to understand not
merely the ten most distinguished persons generally, but men
holding a specific *official* position, then we are bound to
assume that they were no other than the *committee* consisting

[487] The Sadducees, Acts iv. 1 ff., v. 17, xxiii. 6 ; Joseph. *Antt.* xx. 9. 1.
The Pharisees, Acts v. 34, xxiii. 6. Comp. Joseph. *Bell. Jud.* ii. 17. 3 ;
*Vita*, 38, 39.

[488] *Antt.* xviii. 1. 4 : ὁπότε γὰρ ἐπ' ἀρχὰς παρέλθοιεν, ἀκουσίως μὲν καὶ
κατ' ἀνάγκας, προσχωροῦσι δ' οὖν οἷς ὁ Φαρισαῖος λέγει, διὰ τὸ μὴ ἂν ἄλλως
ἀνεκτοὺς γενέσθαι τοῖς πλήθεσιν.

[489] From what is here said the combination of the ἀρχιερεῖς and
Φαρισαῖοι, so frequently met with in the New Testament (Matt. xxi. 45,
xxvii. 62 ; John vii. 32, 45, xi. 47, 57, xviii. 3), is quite in keeping with
the actual state of things. A similar collocation is also to be met with
in Josephus, *Bell. Jud.* ii. 17. 3 : συνελθόντες οὖν οἱ δυνατοὶ τοῖς ἀρχιερεῦσιν
εἰς ταὐτὸ καὶ τοῖς τῶν Φαρισαίων γνωρίμοις. Comp. also, *Vita*, 38, 39.

of the δέκα πρῶτοι so often to be met with in the Hellenistic communes, and which can also be clearly shown to have had a place for example in the constitution established by Tiberias (see above, note 395). We are thus furnished with characteristic evidence of the extent to which Jewish and Hellenistico-Roman influences had become intertwined with each other in the organization of the Sanhedrim at the period in question.

As to who it was that acted as president of the Sanhedrim, this is a question in regard to which even Christian scholars down to most recent times and founding upon Jewish tradition, have entertained the most erroneous views conceivable. The later Jewish tradition, which as a rule regards the Sanhedrim in the light of a mere college of scribes, expressly presupposes that the heads of the Pharisaic schools were also the regular presidents of the Sanhedrim as well. Those heads of the schools are enumerated in the Mishna tractate *Aboth* c. i., and that with reference to earlier times, say from the middle of the second century B.C. till about the time of Christ, and are mentioned in pairs (see below, § 25); and it is asserted, though not in the tractate *Aboth*, yet in another passage in the Mishna, that the *first* of every pair had been *Nasi* (נָשִׂיא), while the *second* had been *Ab-beth-din* (אַב בֵּית דִּין), *i.e.* according to later usage in regard to those titles: president and vice-president of the Sanhedrim.[490] Further, the heads of the schools that come after the " pairs " just referred to, especially Gamaliel I. and his son Simon, are represented by the later traditions as having been presidents

---

[490] *Chagiga* ii. 2: " Jose ben Joeser affirms that there should be no laying on of hands in the case of festival sacrifices, while Jose ben Jochanan says that it is quite permissible. Josua ben Perachja decided in the negative, Nittai (or Mattai) of Arbela in the affirmative. Juda ben Tabbai in the negative, Simon ben Schetach in the affirmative. Schemaja in the affirmative, Abtaljon in the negative. Hillel and Menachem were at one in their opinion ; when Menachem withdrew and Schammai entered, Schammai pronounced in the negative, Hillel in the affirmative. Of those men the first of each pair was always a president and the second a supreme judge (הראשונים היו נשיאים ושנים להם אבית בית דין)."

of the Sanhedrim. In all this however there is, of course, nothing that is of any historical value.[491] On the contrary, according to the unanimous testimony of Josephus and the New Testament, it was always the high priest that acted as the head and president of the Sanhedrim. Speaking generally, we may say that this is only what was to be expected from the nature of the case itself. Ever since the commencement of the Greek period the high priest had uniformly acted as head of the nation as well. In like manner the Asmonaeans had also been high priests and princes, nay even kings at one and the same time. With regard to the Roman period, we have the express testimony of Josephus to the effect that the high priests were also the political heads of the nation (*Antt.* xx. 10, *fin.*: τὴν προστασίαν τοῦ ἔθνους οἱ ἀρχιερεῖς ἐπεπίστευντο). In his theoretical descriptions of the Jewish constitution this historian invariably speaks of the high priest as having been the *supreme judge* (*Apion*, ii. 23 : the high priest φυλάξει τοὺς νόμους, δικάσει περὶ τῶν ἀμφισβη-τουμένων, κολάσει τοὺς ἐλεγχθέντας ἐπ᾽ ἀδίκῳ; *Antt.* iv. 8. 14 : Moses is said to have ordained that, if the local courts were unable to decide a case, the parties were to go to Jerusalem, καὶ συνελθόντες ὅ τε ἀρχιερεὺς καὶ ὁ προφήτης καὶ ἡ γερουσία τὸ δοκοῦν ἀποφαινέσθωσαν). Even from what is here stated we are required to assume that the high priest acted the part of president in the Sanhedrim. But, besides this, we have testimony of the most explicit kind to the same effect. In a document of so early a date as the national decree declaring the combined office of high priest and sovereign to be vested by right of inheritance in the family of Simon the Maccabaean, it was ordained that nobody was to be allowed " to contradict his (Simon's) orders, or to convene an assembly in any part

---

[491] Comp. Kuenen as above, pp. 141–147 ; my article in the *Stud. u. Krit.* 1872, pp. 614–619. Wellhausen's *Pharisäer und Sadducäer*, pp. 29–43. Of the works belonging to an earlier date we would mention, in particular, Meuschen, *Nov. Test. ex Talmude illustratum*, p. 1184 f., where the fact is already recognised that the high priest always acted as president of the Sanhedrim.

of the country without his knowledge or consent." [492]   In
the few instances in which Josephus mentions the sittings of
the Sanhedrim at all, we invariably find that the high priest
occupied the position of president.   Thus in the year 47 B.C.
it was Hyrcanus II.,[493] and in the year 62 A.D. it was
Ananos the younger.[494]   Similarly in the New Testament, it is
always the ἀρχιερεύς that appears as the presiding personage
(Acts v. 17 ff., vii. 1, ix. 1, 2, xxii. 5, xxiii. 2, 4, xxiv. 1).[495]
Wherever names are mentioned we find that it is the high
priest for the time being that officiates as president.   Thus
we have Caiaphas in the time of Christ (Matt. xxvi. 3, 57),
and Ananias in the time of the Apostle Paul (Acts xxiii. 2,
xxiv. 1), both of whom, as we learn from Josephus, were the
high priests actually in office at the dates in question.   The
trial of Jesus before Annas (John xviii.) cannot be regarded
as in any way disproving this view.   For there it was merely
a question of private examination.   As little can we lay any
stress on the fact that Ananos (or Annas) the younger is
represented as being at the head of affairs [496] in the time of
the war, and that long after he had been deposed.[497]   For the
circumstance of his occupying that position then was due to
the fact of a special decree of the people having been issued
at the time at which the revolution broke out.[498]   The only
passage that might be urged in opposition to our view is Acts
iv. 6, where Annas (who was only an ex-high priest) is represented as being the president of the Sanhedrim.   But this
passage is very much in the same position as the parallel one,
Luke iii. 2.   In both Annas is mentioned *before* Caiaphas in
such a way as might lead one to suppose that the *former* was

[492] 1 Macc. xiv. 44: ἀντειπεῖν τοῖς ὑπ᾽ αὐτοῦ ῥηθησομένοις καὶ ἐπισυστρέψαι
συστροφὴν ἐν τῇ χώρᾳ ἄνευ αὐτοῦ.

[493] *Antt.* xiv. 9. 3–5.                              [494] *Antt.* xx. 9. 1.

[495] In answer to the strange view of Wieseler, that the president of the
Sanhedrim merely *as such*, even though he were not a high priest, bore the
title of ἀρχιερεύς, see *Stud. u. Krit.* 1872, pp. 623–631.

[496] *Antt.* xx. 9. 1.

[497] *Bell. Jud.* ii. 20. 3, 22. 1, iv. 3. 7–5. 2 ; *Vita*, 38, 39, 44, 60.

[498] *Bell. Jud.* ii. 20. 3.

the high priest actually in office, though in point of fact this was certainly not the case. If therefore we are not at liberty to infer from Luke iii. 2 that Annas was still in office as high priest, as little can we conclude from Acts iv. 6 that he was president of the Sanhedrim, which would be incompatible with Matt. xxvi. 57–66. We should prefer to explain the matter by saying that, in both cases, there is some inaccuracy about the narrative. That the persons who are mentioned in the Rabbinical traditions were not presidents of the Sanhedrim is further evident from the fact that, wherever those same individuals happen to be mentioned in the New Testament or by Josephus, they always appear merely as ordinary members of the court. Thus Shemaiah (Sameas) in the time of Hyrcanus II.,[499] Gamaliel I. in the time of the apostles (Acts v. 34, comp. ver. 27), and Simon ben Gamaliel in the time of the Jewish war.[500]

The Jewish tradition in question is therefore at variance with the whole of the undoubted historical facts. Not only so, but it is itself only of a very late origin, and probably does not belong to so early a period as the age of the Mishna. The *one* solitary passage in the Mishna in which it occurs (*Chagiga* ii. 2) stands there in perfect isolation. Everywhere else in this work the heads of the schools above mentioned are spoken of simply as heads of schools and nothing. more. Consequently it is extremely probable that the passage in question did not find its way into the text of the Mishna till some subsequent period.[501] Then again, it may be affirmed, unless we have been deceived on all hands, that the titles *Nasi* and *Ab-beth-din* as applied to the president and vice-president of the Sanhedrim are foreign as yet to the age of the Mishna. It is true both those *terms* are to be met with

---

[499] *Antt.* xiv. 9. 3–5.

[500] *Vita*, 38, 39.

[501] Later interpolations in the text of the Mishna may also be detected elsewhere, for example at *Aboth* v. 21. Of course the passage *Chagiga* ii. 2 already occurs in the Jerusalem Talmud, and so must be older at least than this latter.

in this work.[502]   But by *Nasi* it is always the actual *prince*
of the nation, specially the *king*, that is meant, as indeed, is
on one occasion expressly affirmed,[503] while the *Ab-beth-din*
again, if we may judge from its literal import, can hardly
have been intended to mean anything else than the *president*
of the supreme court of justice (and therefore of the Sanhedrim).   Besides this latter title, we sometimes meet with that
of *Rosh-beth-din*, and with precisely the same meaning.[504]   It
was not till the post-Mishnic age that the titles *Nasi* and
*Ab-beth-din* were, so to speak, reduced a step by being transferred to the president and vice-president respectively.[505]
Finally, the so-called מוּפְלָא, who, on the strength of a few
passages in the Talmud is also frequently mentioned by
Jewish and Christian scholars as having been a special
functionary of the court, was not so at all, but simply the
most " prominent " of its ordinary members, *i.e.* the one who
was most learned in the law.[506]

As regards the time of Christ it may be held as certain,
from all that has just been said, that the office of president
was always occupied by *the high priest for the time being*,
and that too in virtue of his being such.

3. *Its jurisdiction.*   As regards the area over which the

---

[502] נָשִׂיא, *Taanith* ii. 1 ; *Nedarim* v. 5 ; *Horajoth* ii. 5–7, iii. 1–3 and
elsewhere.   אַב בֵּית דִּין, *Taanith* ii. 1 ; *Edujoth* v. 6.

[503] *Horajoth* iii. 3.

[504] *Rosh hashana* ii. 7, iv. 4.

[505] The first Rabbinical president of the Sanhedrim to whom the title *Nasi*
is applied is R. Judah, the redactor of the Mishna, at the end of the second
century of our era (*Aboth* ii. 2).   Of the Rabbins that occupied this position
*previous* to R. Judah, there is not one that is known as yet under the
designation of *Nasi* (apart from *Chagiga* ii. 2).   We may assume therefore
that the title did not come into use till toward the close of the Mishnic
age.

[506] The expression מוּפְלָא שֶׁל בֵּית דִּין occurs only once in the Mishna, *Horajoth* i. 4.   In that passage directions are given as to what is to be done in the
event of the court having arrived at an erroneous decision in the absence
of the מוּפְלָא שֶׁל בֵּית דִּין, *i.e.* the most distinguished, most eminent member
of the collegium.   For the meaning of מוּפְלָא, comp. Buxtorf's *Lex.* col.
1729 f.   Levy's *Neuhebr. Wörterb.* under word.

jurisdiction of the supreme Sanhedrim extended, it has been already remarked above (p. 142) that its *civil* authority was restricted, in the time of Christ, to the eleven toparchies of Judaea proper. And accordingly, for this reason, it had no judicial authority over Jesus Christ so long as He remained in Galilee. It was only as soon as He entered Judaea that He came directly under its jurisdiction. In a certain sense, no doubt, the Sanhedrim exercised such jurisdiction over *every* Jewish community in the world, and in that sense over Galilee as well. Its orders were regarded as binding throughout the entire domain of orthodox Judaism. It had power, for example, to issue warrants to the congregations (synagogues) in Damascus for the apprehension of the Christians in that quarter (Acts ix. 2, xxii. 5, xxvi. 12). At the same time however the extent to which the Jewish communities were willing to yield obedience to the orders of the Sanhedrim always depended on how far they were favourably disposed toward it. It was only within the limits of Judaea proper that it exercised any direct authority. There could not possibly be a more erroneous way of defining the extent of its jurisdiction as regards the kind of causes with which it was competent to deal than to say that it was the *spiritual* or *theological* tribunal in contradistinction to the civil judicatories of the Romans. On the contrary, it would be more correct to say that it formed, in contrast to the foreign authority of Rome, that *supreme native* court which here, as almost everywhere else, the Romans had allowed to continue as before, only imposing certain restrictions with regard to competency. To this tribunal then belonged all those judicial matters and all those measures of an administrative character which either could not be competently dealt with by the inferior local courts or which the Roman procurator had not specially reserved for himself. The Sanhedrim was, above all, the final court of appeal for questions connected with the Mosaic law, but not in the sense that it was open to any one to appeal to it against the decisions of the inferior courts, but rather in so far as it was called upon to intervene in every case in which the lower courts could not agree as to their judgment.[507]   And when once it had given a decision in any case the judges of the local courts were, on pain of death, bound to acquiesce in it.[508]   In the theoretical speculations of the scribes we find the following specially laid down as cases which are to belong to the jurisdiction of the supreme court of justice: "A tribe (charged with idolatry), or a false prophet, or a high priest is only to be tried before the court of the seventy-one.   A voluntary war is only to be commenced after the decision of the court of the seventy-one has been given regarding it. There is to be no enlargement of the city (Jerusalem or the courts of the temple) till after the court of the seventy-one has decided the matter.   Superior courts for the tribes are only to be instituted when sanctioned by the court of the seventy-one.   A town that has been seduced into idolatry is only to be dealt with by the court of the seventy-one."[509] Accordingly the high priest might be tried by the Sanhedrim,[510] though the king, on the other hand, was as little amenable to its authority as he was at liberty to become one of its members.[511]   At the same time it is not difficult to perceive that all the regulations just referred to have the air of being of a purely theoretical character, that they do not represent the actual state of things, but merely the devout imaginations of the Mishnic doctors.   The facts to be gleaned from the pages of the New Testament are of a somewhat more valuable character.   We know, as matter of fact, that Jesus appeared before the Sanhedrim charged with blasphemy (Matt. xxvi. 65; John xix. 7), and that, before this same tribunal, Peter and John were brought up charged with being false prophets and deceivers of the people (Acts iv. and v.), Stephen

---

[507] *Antt.* iv. 8. 14, *fin.*; *Sanhedrin* xi. 2 (see the passage as quoted above, p. 142).                                                      [508] *Sanhedrin* xi. 2.

[509] *Sanhedrin* i. 5.   Comp. *Sanhedrin* ii. 4: "If the king is disposed to enter upon an unprovoked war, he is at liberty to do so only after the decision of the council of the seventy-one has been given."

[510] See also *Sanhedrin* i. 1.                                      [511] *Sanhedrin* ii. 2.

with being a blasphemer (Acts vi. 13 ff.), and Paul with
being guilty of transgressing the Mosaic law (Acts xxiii.).[512]
There is a special interest attaching to the question as to
how far the jurisdiction of the Sanhedrim was limited by the
authority of the Roman procurator.[513]   We accordingly proceed to observe that, inasmuch as the Roman system of provincial government was not strictly carried out in the case of
Judaea (see above, § 17ᶜ), as the simple fact of its being
administered by means of a procurator plainly shows, the Sanhedrim was still left in the enjoyment of a comparatively high
degree of independence.   Not only did it exercise civil jurisdiction, and that according to *Jewish* law (which was only a
matter of course, as otherwise a Jewish court of justice would
have been simply inconceivable), but it also enjoyed a considerable amount of criminal jurisdiction as well.   It had an
independent authority in regard to police affairs, and consequently possessed the right of ordering arrests to be made by
its own officers (Matt. xxvi. 47; Mark xiv. 43; Acts iv. 3,
v. 17, 18).[514]   It had also the power of finally disposing, on

---

[512] The series of cases being the same as in Winer's *Realwörterb.* ii. 552.

[513] On this point, comp. Bynaeus, *De morte Jesu Christi*, iii. 1. 9–14.
Deyling, *De Judaeorum jure gladii tempore Christi, ad John* xviii. 31 (*Observationes sacrae*, part ii. 1737, pp. 414–428; also in Ugolini's *Thesaurus*, vol.
xxvi.).   Iken, *De jure vitae et necis tempore mortis Servatoris apud Judaeos
non amplius superstite ad John* xviii. 31 (in his *Dissertatt. philol.-theol.* ii.
517–572).   A. Balth. v. Walther, *Juristisch-historische Betrachtungen ueber
die Geschichte vom Leiden und Sterben Jesu Christi*, etc., Breslau 1777, pp.
142–168 (this latter work I know only through the quotation from it in
Lücke's *Commentar ueber das Ev. Joh.*, ii. 736; for more of the earlier
literature, see Wolf's *Curae philol. in Nov. Test.*, note on John xviii. 31).
Winer's *Realwörterb.* ii. 553.   Leyrer in Herzog's *Real-Encycl.*, 1st ed. vol. xv.
320–322.   Döllinger's *Christenthum und Kirche in der Zeit der Grundlegung*
(2nd ed. 1868), pp. 456–460.   Langen in the *Tüb. Theol. Quartalschr.* 1862,
pp. 411–463.   On the judicial arrangements in the Roman provinces
generally see Geib, *Geschichte des römischen Criminalprocesses* (1842),
pp. 471–486.   Rudorff, *Römische Rechtsgeschichte*, vol. ii., especially pp. 12
and 345.

[514] According to Matt. xxvi. 47, Mark xiv. 43, it was by the *Jewish* police
that Jesus was arrested.   It is only in the fourth Gospel that it seems to be
implied that it was a Roman tribune (officer) with his cohort that apprehended Jesus (John xviii. 3 and 12).

its own authority, of such cases as did not involve sentence of
death (Acts iv. 5–23, v. 21–40). It was only in cases in
which such sentence of death was pronounced that the judgment required to be ratified by the authority of the procurator.
Not only is this expressly affirmed with regard to the Jews in
the Gospel of John (xviii. 31. ἡμῖν οὐκ ἔξεστιν ἀποκτεῖναι
οὐδένα), but it follows as matter of certainty, from the
account of the condemnation of Jesus as given by the Synop-
tists. Besides, a reminiscence of this fact has survived in
the Jewish traditions.[515] But it is at the same time a fact
worthy of note, that the procurator regulated his judgment in
accordance with *Jewish* law; only on this assumption could
Pilate have pronounced sentence of death in the case of Jesus.
It is true the procurator was not compelled to have any regard
to Jewish law in the matter at all, but still he was at *liberty*
to do so, and as a rule he actually did so. *There was one special
offence in regard to which the Jews had been accorded the singular privilege of proceeding even against Roman citizens according
to Jewish law.* For if on any occasion one who was not a
Jew happened to pass the barrier at the temple in Jerusalem,
beyond which only Jews could go, and thus intrude into the
inner court, he was punished with death, and that even though
he were a Roman.[516] Of course, even in this latter case, it
was necessary that the sentence of the Jewish court should
be confirmed by the Roman procurator. For we can hardly

---

[515] *Jer. Sanhedrin* i. 1 (fol. 18ᵃ) and vii. 2 (fol. 24ᵇ) : " The right of pronouncing sentences of life or death was taken from Israel (נִיטְלוּ דִינֵי
נַפְשׁוֹת מִישְׂרָאֵל) forty years before the destruction of the temple." The
date of the withdrawal here given is, of course, worthless, for it may be
assumed as certain that this did not merely occur for the first time when
Pilate was procurator, but that in fact no such right could be said to have
belonged to the Jews ever since Judaea came to be under procurators at all.

[516] *Bell. Jud.* vi. 2. 4 : Titus puts to the besieged the following question :
Did we not grant you permission to put to death any one who went beyond
the barrier, *even though he were a Roman?* (οὐχ ἡμεῖς δὲ τοὺς ὑπερβάντας ὑμῖν
ἀναιρεῖν ἐπετρέψαμεν, κἂν ᾽Ρωμαίων τις ᾖ;). On this comp. also § 24,
below. The subjecting of Roman citizens to the laws of a foreign city is
an *extraordinary concession*, which, as a rule, was made only in the case
of those communities which were recognised as *liberae*. See Khun, *Die*

venture to infer, from the terms used by Josephus in speaking
of this matter, that in this special instance, though in this
alone, the Jews had an absolute right to carry out the capital
sentence on their own authority. Nor would we be justified
in drawing any such inference from the stoning of Stephen
(Acts vii. 5 ff.). This latter is rather to be regarded either
as a case of excess of jurisdiction, or as an act of irregular
mob-justice. Still, on the other hand, it would be a mistake
to assume, as a statement in Josephus might seem to warrant
us in doing, that the Sanhedrim was not at liberty to meet at
all without the consent of the procurator.[517] But all that is
meant by the statement in question is that the high priest
had no right to hold a court of *supreme jurisdiction* in the
absence and without the consent of the procurator. As little
are we to assume that the Jewish authorities were required
to hand over every offender in the first instance to the procurator. This they no doubt did if at any time it seemed to
them to be expedient to do so,[518] but that does not necessarily
imply that they were bound to do it. We see then that the
Sanhedrim had been left in the enjoyment of a tolerably
extensive jurisdiction, the most serious restriction to it being,
of course, the fact that the Roman authorities could at any
time take the initiative themselves, and proceed independently
of the Jewish court, as they actually did in not a few instances,
as, for example, when Paul was arrested. Further, it was in
the power, not only of the procurator, but even of the tribune
of the cohorts stationed in Jerusalem, to call the Sanhedrim

*städtische und bürgerl. Verfassung*, ii. 24. Marquardt, *Römische Staatsverwaltung*, i. 75 f., and especially the decree of the Roman senate with reference to Chios passed in the year 674 A.U.C. = 80 B.C. (*Corp. Inscr. Graec.*
n. 2222): οἵ τε παρ' αὐτοῖς ὄντες Ῥωμαῖοι τοῖς Χείων ὑπακούουσιν νόμοις.
This concession then was accorded to the Jews, at least as far as the
particular case in question was concerned.

[517] *Antt.* xx. 9. 1: οὐκ ἐξὸν ἦν Ἀνάνῳ χωρὶς τῆς ἐκείνου γνώμης καθίσαι
συνέδριον.

[518] In the time of Albinus, for example, the Jewish ἄρχοντες delivered to
the procurator a certain lunatic, whose behaviour seemed to them to be of
a dangerous character (*Bell. Jud.* vii. 5. 3, ed. Bekker, p. 104, lin. 6 ff.).

together for the purpose of submitting to it any matter requiring to be investigated from the standpoint of Jewish law (Acts xx. 30 ; comp. xxiii. 15, 20, 28).

4. *The time and place of meeting.* The local courts usually sat on the *second* and *fifth* days of the week (Monday and Thursday).[519] Whether this was also the practice in the case of the supreme Sanhedrim we have no means of knowing. There were no courts held on festival days (יום טוב), much less on the Sabbath.[520] As in criminal cases a capital sentence could not be pronounced till the day following the trial, it was necessary to take care not to allow cases of this nature to be concluded on the evening preceding the Sabbath or any festival day.[521] Of course all those regulations were, in the first instance, of a purely theoretical character, and, as we know from what took place in the case of Jesus, were by no means strictly adhered to. The *place* in which the supreme Sanhedrim was in the habit of meeting (the βουλή) was situated, according to Josephus, *Bell. Jud.* v. 4. 2, close to the so-called Xystos, and that on the east side of it, in the direction of the temple mount. Now, seeing that, according to *Bell. Jud.* ii. 16. 3, there was nothing but a bridge between the Xystos and this latter, it is probable that the βουλή was to be found upon the temple mount itself, on the western side of the enclosing wall. In any case, it must have stood outside the upper part of the city, for, according to *Bell. Jud.* vi. 6. 3, we find that the Romans had destroyed the βουλευτήριον (= βουλή) before they had as yet got possession of the upper part of the city. The Mishna repeatedly mentions the לִשְׁבַּת הַגָּזִית as the place where the supreme Sanhedrim held its sittings.[522]

---

[519] *Kethuboth* i. 1.

[520] Beza (or *Jom tob*), v. 2. Comp. Oehler in Herzog's *Real-Encycl.*, 1st ed. vol. xiii. 203 (art. " Sabbath "). Bleek's *Beiträge zur Evangelien-Kritik* (1846), p. 141 ff. ; Wieseler's *Chronologische Synopse*, p. 361 ff. Kirchner, *Die jüdische Passahfeier und Jesu letztes Mahl* (Program. for the Gymnasium at Duisburg, 1870), p. 57 ff.

[521] *Sanhedrin* iv. 1, *fin.*

[522] *Sanhedrin* xi. 2 ; *Middoth* v. 4. Comp. *Pea* ii. 6 ; *Edujoth* vii. 4.

Now, seeing that its statements cannot possibly refer to any other period than that of Josephus, and considering, moreover, that by the βουλή of this historian we are undoubtedly to understand the meeting-place of the supreme Sanhedrim, we must necessarily identify the לִשְׁכַּת הַגָּזִית with the βουλή of Josephus. It may be presumed therefore that the designation לשכת הגזית was not meant to imply (as has been commonly supposed) that the hall in question was built of hewn stones (גָּזִית = hewn stones),—which could hardly be regarded as a characteristic feature,—but that it stood beside the Xystos (גָּזִי = ξυστός, as in the Sept. 1 Chron. xxii. 2 ; Amos v. 11). To distinguish it from the other לִשָׁכוֹת on the temple esplanade it was called, from its situation, " the hall beside the Xystos." It is true that the Mishna represents it as having been within the inner court.[523]   But, considering how untrustworthy and sometimes inaccurate are its statements elsewhere regarding the topography of the temple, the testimony of the Mishna cannot be supposed to invalidate the result arrived at above, especially as it happens to be corroborated by other circumstances besides.[524]   We may regard as utterly useless here the later Talmudic statement, to the effect that, forty years

---

[523] See *Middoth* v. 4 in particular ; also *Sanhedrin* xi. 2.   In the Babylonian Gemara, *Joma* xx.ᵃ, it is stated somewhat more circumstantially that the לשכת הגזית stood one half within, and the other half without the court (see the passage, for example, in Buxtorf's *Lex. Chald.* under גָּזִית).   *Pea* ii. 6 and *Edujoth* vii. 4 cannot be said to furnish any data for enabling us to determine the site of the building ; as little have we any in *Tamid* ii. *fin.*, iv. *fin.*   For although, according to the two last-mentioned passages, *the priests* were in the habit of betaking themselves to the לשכת הגזית during the intervals between the various parts of the service, for the purpose of casting the lots and of repeating the *schma*, it does not necessarily follow from this that the building was situated within the court.

[524] In the tractate *Joma* i. 1 mention is made of a לשכת פרהדרין (as we ought to read with *Cod. de Rossi* 138, instead of the לשכת פלהדרין of the printed editions), by which we are undoubtedly to understand the place in which the supreme Sanhedrim met (פרהדרין = πάρεδροι) ; and it is, to say the least of it, most in harmony with the context (comp. i. 5) to regard it as having been outside the court.   But the truth is, it is in itself somewhat unlikely that any portion of the inner court would be used for purposes other than those connected with the temple services.

before the destruction of the temple, the Sanhedrim had either removed or had been ejected (נלתה) from the *lischkath hagasith*, and that after that it held its sittings in the *chanujoth* (חנויות) or in a *chanuth* (חנות), a merchant's shop.[525] This view must be completely dismissed, for the simple reason that no trace of it is as yet to be met with in the pages of the Mishna, which, on the contrary, obviously presupposes that the Sanhedrim still held its sittings in the *lischkath hagasith* on the very eve of the destruction of the temple. As it so happens that the forty years immediately preceding the destruction of the temple are also regarded as the period during which the Sanhedrim had ceased to have the right to pronounce a capital sentence (see above, note 515), it is probable that what the Talmudic statement in question means, is that during the period just referred to the Sanhedrim was no longer at liberty, or was no longer inclined, to hold its sittings in the usual official court-house, but met in some obscure place, *i.e.* in " the merchant's shops," or, as the reading with the singular *chanuth* is perhaps to be preferred, in a " merchant's shop." For חָנוּת is the ordinary word for a shop with an arched roof, a merchant's shop.[526] As in *one* instance it is stated that the Sanhedrim subsequently removed from the *chanuth into Jerusalem*,[527] probably we are to conceive of that building as having been outside the city proper. But all further conjectures on the part of scholars as to where it stood are superfluous, for the thing itself is in the main

---

[525] *Shabbath* xv.a; *Rosh hashana* xxxi.a; *Sanhedrin* xii.a; *Aboda sara* viii.b In the edition of the Talmud now before me (Amsterdam 1644 ff.) it is only in the first-mentioned passage (*Shabbath* xv.a) that the plural *chanujoth* occurs, the singular *chanuth* being used in the other three instances. See besides the passages in Selden's *De synedriis*, ii. 15. 7–8; Wagenseil's note on *Sota* ix. 11 (in Surenhusius' *Mishna*, iii. 297); Levy's *Neuhebr. Wörterb.* ii. 80 (see under חנות).

[526] For example, see *Baba kamma* ii. 2, vi. 6; *Baba mezia* ii. 4, iv. 11; *Baba bathra* ii. 3. For the plural חנויות, see *Taanith* i. 6; *Baba mezia* viii. 6; *Aboda sara* i. 4; *Tohoroth* vi. 3. The shopkeeper or dealer was called חנוני.

[527] *Rosh hashana* xxxi.a

unhistorical.[528]   Although on the occasion on which Jesus was condemned to death (Mark xiv. 53 ff.; Matt. xxvi. 57 ff.) the Sanhedrim happened to meet in the *palace of the high priest*, we must regard this as an exception to the rule, rendered necessary by the simple fact of its having met during the night.   For at night the gates of the temple mount were shut.[529]

5. *Judicial procedure.*   This, according to the account of it given in the Mishna, was as follows.[530]   The members of the court sat in a semicircle (כַּחֲצִי גֹּרֶן עֲגוּלָה, literally, like the half of a circular threshing-floor), in order that they might be able to see each other.   In front of them stood the two clerks of the court, one on the right hand and the other on the left, whose duty it was to record the votes of those who were in favour of acquittal on the one hand, and of those who were in favour of a sentence of condemnation on the other.[531]   There also sat in front of them

[528] The above explanation of the origin of the unhistorical statement in question now appears to me to be the most probable of any.   For another see *Stud. u. Krit.* 1878, p. 625.   Even so early as in the Talmud we find nothing but a fluctuating indecision as to the motives which led the Sanhedrim to remove from the usual place of meeting ; see *Aboda sara* viii.[b], or the German translation in Ferd. Christian Ewald, *Aboda Sarah, oder der Götzendienst* (2nd ed. 1868), pp. 62–64.

[529] *Middoth* i. 1.   We have no evidence of any other meeting of the Sanhedrim ever having been held in the high priest's palace.   For in Luke xxii. 54 ff. and John xviii. 13 ff., what we have to do with is simply a preliminary investigation before the high priest.   And as for the statement with regard to the place of meeting in Matt. xxvi. 3, it is only to be regarded as a subsequent addition on the part of the evangelist, comp. Mark xiv. 1 ; Luke xxii. 2.   For a fuller discussion of the question as to where the supreme Sanhedrim held its sittings, see my article in the *Stud. u. Krit.* 1878, pp. 608–626.   See also, at p. 608 of the same, the earlier literature of the subject, in which however no decisive results have been reached owing to the uncritical way in which it has dealt with the sources.

[530] On the forms of judicial procedure in the Old Testament, see Winer's *Realwörterb.*, art. "Gericht;" Oehler's art. "Gericht und Gerichtsverwaltung bei den Hebräern," in Herzog's *Real-Enc.*, 1st ed. vol. v. pp. 57–61. Saalschütz, *Das Mosaische Recht*, ii. 593 ff.   Keil, *Handbuch der biblischen Archäologie* (2nd ed. 1875), sec. 150.   Köhler, *Lehrbuch der biblischen Geschichte*, i. 359 ff.

[531] *Sanhedrin* iv. 3.   There is also one instance in Josephus in which ὁ γραμματεὺς τῆς βουλῆς is mentioned, *Bell. Jud.* v. 13. 1.

three rows of the disciples of the learned men, each of whom
had his own special seat assigned him.[532]    The prisoner at the
bar was always required to appear in a humble attitude and
dressed in mourning.[533]   In cases involving a capital sentence,
special forms were prescribed for conducting the trial and
pronouncing the sentence.   On such occasions it was the
practice always to hear the reasons in favour of acquittal in
the first place, which being done, those in favour of a conviction might next be stated.[534]   When any one had once spoken
in favour of the accused he was not at liberty afterwards to
say anything unfavourable to him, though the converse was
permissible.[535]   Those of the student disciples who happened to
be present were also allowed to speak, though only in favour
of and not against the prisoner, while on other occasions not
involving a capital sentence they could do either the one or
the other as they thought proper.[536]   A sentence of acquittal
might be pronounced on the same day as that of the trial,
whereas a sentence of condemnation could not be pronounced till
the following day.[537]   The voting, in the course of which each
individual stood up in his turn,[538] began "at the side," מִן הַצַּד,
*i.e.* with the youngest member of the court, whereas on other
occasions it was the practice to commence with the most
distinguished member.[539]   For a sentence of acquittal a simple
majority was sufficient, while for one of condemnation again a
majority of two was required.[540]   If therefore twelve of the
twenty-three judges necessary to form a quorum voted for
acquittal and eleven for a conviction, then the prisoner was
discharged; but if, on the other hand, twelve were for a conviction and eleven for acquittal, then in that case the number

[532] *Sanhedrin* iv. 4.

[533] Joseph. *Antt.* xiv. 9. 4.   Comp. *Sacharja* 3. 3.

[534] *Sanhedrin* iv. 1.                [535] *Sanhedrin* iv. 1, v. 5.

[536] *Sanhedrin* iv. 1, v. 4.

[537] *Sanhedrin* iv. 1, v. 5.   On this ground many have sought to account
for the alleged twofold meeting of the Sanhedrim when Jesus was condemned to death.

[538] *Sanhedrin* v. 5.                 [539] *Sanhedrin* iv. 2.

[540] *Sanhedrin* iv. 1.

of the judges had to be increased by the addition of two to
their number, which was repeated if necessary until either an
acquittal was secured or the majority requisite for a conviction
was obtained.   But, of course, they had to restrict themselves
to the maximum number of seventy-one.[541]

### IV. THE HIGH PRIESTS.

#### THE LITERATURE.

Selden, *De successione in pontificatum Ebraeorum*, lib. i. cap. 11–12
(frequently printed along with Selden's other works; for example, in
the edition of the *Uxor Ebraica*, Francof. ad Od. 1673; also in Ugolini's
*Thesaurus*, vol. xii.).

Lightfoot, *Ministerium templi Hierosolymitani*, c. iv. 3 (*Opp.* ed. Roterodam.
i. 684 ff.).

Reland, *Antiquitates sacrae*, par. ii. c. 2 (ed. Lips. 1724, p. 146 f.).

Anger, *De temporum in actis apostolorum ratione* (1833), p. 93 f.

Ewald, *Geschichte des Volkes Israel*, vol. vi. 3rd ed. 1868, p. 634.

Schürer, *Die ἀρχιερεῖς im Neuen Testamente* (*Stud. u. Krit.* 1872, pp.
593–657).

Grätz, *Monatsschr. für Geschichte und Wissensch. des Judenthums*, Jahrg. 1877,
pp. 450–464, and Jahrg. 1881, pp. 49-64, 97–112.

The most distinctive feature of the Jewish constitution as it
existed during the period subsequent to the exile is this, that
the *high priest was the political head of the nation as well.*
That he was so at least from the commencement of the Greek
era down to the days of the Romano-Herodian rule is
regarded as entirely beyond dispute.   The high priests of
the pre-Maccabaean age as well as those of the Asmonaean
line were not only *priests,* but also *princes* at one and the
same time.   And although their authority was restricted on
the one hand by the Greek suzerains, and on the other by the
*gerousia,* still it was very greatly strengthened by the fact
that their high office was *hereditary and tenable for life.*   The
combination of priesthood and royalty as seen in the case of
the later Asmonaeans represented the very acme of sacerdotal
power and authority.   After the Romans came upon the

[541] *Sanhedrin* v. 5.

scene, and still more under the Herodian princes, they of course lost much of their power. The Asmonaean dynasty was overthrown, nay was extirpated altogether. The principle of inheritance and life-tenure was done away with. High priests were appointed and deposed at pleasure by Herod and the Romans alike. In addition to this, there was the steady increase of the power of Pharisaism and the Rabbinical school. But even in spite of the combined influence of all the factors we have mentioned, the high-priesthood contrived to retain a considerable share of its original power down to the time of the destruction of the temple. And even after that the high priests continued to act as presidents of the Sanhedrim, and consequently to have the chief direction of the civil affairs of the community as well. Even then there still remained a few privileged families from which the high priests continued to be almost always selected. And accordingly, although under the supreme rule of the Romans and the Herodian princes they no longer formed, it may be, a monarchical dynasty, they yet continued to exist as an influential aristocracy. As we are familiar, from political history, with the series of high priests down to the overthrow of the Asmonaeans, it will be sufficient at present merely to subjoin a list of those belonging to the Romano-Herodian period. Josephus tells us that they numbered twenty-eight in all.[542] Accordingly on collating his different notices with regard to them, we get the following twenty-eight names:—[543]

[542] *Antt.* xx. 10.

[543] A list of those high priests, based on the notices found in Josephus, has already been framed by several Greek divines, viz. (1) by Josephus the Christian in his *Hypomnesticum s. liber memorialis*, chap. ii. (first edited by Fabricius, *Codex pseudepigraphus Vet. Test.*, vol. ii., and afterwards given in Gallendi's *Biblioth. Patrum*, vol. xiv., and Migne's *Patrol. graec.*, vol. cvi.) ; (2) by Nicephorus Constantinop. in his *Chronographia compendiaria*, or rather according to De Boor, by the author of the revised version of this *Chronography* (critical edition by Credner in two programs for the University of Giessen, 1832–1838, ii. 33 f., and especially by De Boor, *Nicephori Const. opuscula*, Lips. 1880, pp. 110-112). Then Zonaras, who inserts extracts from Josephus into the first six books of his *Annals*,

(a) Appointed by Herod (37–4 B.C.):—

1. Ananel (37–36 B.C.), a native of Babylon, and belonging to an obscure priestly family, *Antt.* xv. 2. 4, 3. 1. The Rabbinical traditions represent him as having been an Egyptian.[544]

2. Aristobulus, the last of the Asmonaeans (35 B.C.), *Antt.* xv. 3. 1, 3.
Ananel for the second time (34 ff. B.C.), *Antt.* xv. 3. 3.

3. Jesus the son of Phabes, *Antt.* xv. 9. 3.[545]

4. Simon the son of Boethos, or according to other accounts, *Boethos* himself, in any case the father-in-law of Herod, he having been the father of Mariamne II. (some time between 24 and 25 B.C.), *Antt.* xv. 9. 3, xvii. 4. 2. Comp. xviii. 5. 1, xix. 6. 2. The family belonged originally to Alexandria, *Antt.* xv. 9. 3.

---

has also adopted the passages about the high priests almost entirely (*Annal.* v. 12–vi. 17). The part referring to the high priests in the time of Jesus (Joseph. *Antt.* xviii. 2. 2) is also quoted by Eusebius, *Hist. eccl.* i. 10. 5–6, and *Demonstr. evang.* viii. 2. 100; in like manner in the *Chron. paschale*, ed. Dindorf, i. 417. Of the modern lists the most correct is that of Anger, with which our own entirely agrees. For a fuller treatment of the matter, see my article in the *Stud. u. Krit.* 1872, pp. 597–607.

544 In the Mishna, *Para* iii. 5, those high priests are enumerated under whom a red heifer had been burnt (in compliance with the enactment of Num. xix.). In the post-Asmonaean age this took place under the three following:—(1) Elioenai ben ha-Kajaph, (2) Chanamel the Egyptian, (3) Ismael ben Pi-abi (אליועיני בן הקייף וחנמאל המצרי וישמעאל בן פי אבי), the orthography of the names according to *Cod. de Rossi* 138). Chanamel the Egyptian can have been no other than our *Ananel*. There can hardly be a doubt that the form of the name is just as inaccurate as is the statement to the effect that he was an Egyptian. Moreover, the chronological order is incorrect, for by the Elioenai, who is mentioned first, no other can have been intended than Elionaios the son of Kantheras, whose name occurs much farther down the list (No. 19). As for the rest, the term "Egyptian" is simply equivalent to Alexandrian, which other high priests of the time of Herod actually were, as for example the sons of Boethos (*Antt.* xv. 9. 3).

545 In Joseph. *Hypomnest.* Ἰησοῦς ὁ τοῦ Φαυβῆ, Zonaras. *Annal.* v. 16 (Bonnens. i. 433), Φάβητος, as in Josephus the Jew.

5. Matthias the son of Theophilos (5–4 B.C.), *Antt.* xvii. 4. 2, 6. 4.

6. Joseph the son of Ellem, *Antt.* xvii. 6. 4.[546]

7. Joasar the son of Boethos (4 B.C.), *Antt.* xvii. 6. 4.

(*b*) Appointed by Archelaus (4 B.C.–6 A.D.) :—

8. Eleasar the son of Boethos (4 ff.), *Antt.* xvii. 13. 1.

9. Jesus the son of Σεέ, *Antt.* xvii. 13. 1.[547]

Joasar for the second time, *Antt.* xviii. 1. 1, 2. 1.

(*c*) Appointed by Quirinus (A.D. 6) :—

10. Ananos or Hannas the son of Seth (6–15 A.D.), *Antt.* xviii. 2. 1, 2.   Comp. xx. 9. 1 ; *Bell. Jud.* v. 12. 2.   This is the high priest so well known in the New Testament, Luke iii. 2 ; John xviii. 13–24 ; Acts iv. 6.

(*d*) Appointed by Valerius Gratus (A.D. 15–26) :—

11. Ismael the son of Phabi (some time between 15 and 16 A.D.), *Antt.* xviii. 2. 2.[548]

12. Eleasar the son of Ananos (some time between 16 and 17 A.D.), *Antt.* xviii. 2. 2.

---

[546] Whether this *Joseph* should be included in the list is open to question, for he officiated only once, and that on the great day of atonement, merely as a substitute for *Matthias*, who had been prevented from doing duty himself in consequence of some Levitical defilement. But be this as it may, he was still, on this account, the actual high priest for at least a period of one day, while he is certainly included by Josephus, as otherwise the number would not have amounted to twenty-eight. His name likewise occurs in the list of Josephus the Christian (*Hypomnest.* chap. ii.). The singular incident just referred to is also frequently mentioned in the Rabbinical sources (see Selden, *De successione in pontificatum Ebr.* i. 11, ed. Francof. p. 160. Derenbourg, *Histoire de la Palestine*, p. 160, note. Grätz, *Monatsschrift*, 1881, p. 51 ff.). The high priest now in question is there known as יוסף בן אילם.

[547] In Joseph. *Antt.* xvii. 13. 1, he is called 'Ιησοῦς ὁ Σιέ or Σεέ (the manuscripts reading sometimes the one and sometimes the other) ; Joseph. *Hypomnest.* 'Ιησοῦς ὁ τοῦ Σεέ ; in Nicephorus, 'Ιησοῦς 'Ωσηέ ; in Zonaras, *Annal.* vi. 2 (ed. Bonnens. i. 472), παῖς Σεέ.

[548] The name of the father as given in Joseph. *Antt.* xviii. 2, 2 ; Euseb. *Hist. eccl.* i. 10. 5, ed. Heinichen ; and Zonaras, *Annal.* vi. 3 (ed. Bonnens. i. 477), is Φαβί ; while in Euseb. *Demonstr. ev.* viii. 2. 100, it is Φήβα ; in Joseph. *Hypomnest.* Βιαβῆ ; and in *Chron. pasch.*, ed. Dindorf, i. 417, Βαφεί.

13. Simon the son of Kamithos (somewhere about 17–18 A.D.), *Antt.* xviii. 2. 2.[549]

14. Joseph called Caiaphas (somewhere between 18 and 36 A.D.), *Antt.* xviii. 2. 2, 4. 3. Comp. Matt. xxvi. 3, 57; Luke iii. 2; John xi. 49, xviii. 13, 14, 24, 28; Acts iv. 6. According to John xviii. 13, he was the father-in-law of Hannas = Ananos.[550]

(*e*) Appointed by Vitellius (35–39 A.D.):—

15. Jonathan the son of Ananos (36–37 A.D.), *Antt.* xviii. 4. 3, 5. 3. Comp. xix. 6. 4. He was found still playing a prominent part in public life in the time of Cumanus, 50–52 A.D. (*Bell. Jud.* ii. 12. 5–6), and was ultimately assassinated at the instigation of Felix the procurator (*Bell. Jud.* ii. 13. 3; *Antt.* xx. 8. 5).

16. Theophilos the son of Ananos (37 ff. A.D.), *Antt.* xviii. 5. 3.

(*f*) Appointed by Agrippa I. (41–44 A.D.):—

17. Simon Kantheras the son of Boethos (41 ff. A.D.), *Antt.* xix. 6. 2.[551]

18. Matthias the son of Ananos, *Antt.* xix. 6. 4.

19. Elionaios the son of Kantheros, *Antt.* xix. 8. 1.[552]

---

[549] This high priest is also frequently mentioned in the Rabbinical sources (Selden, *De successione in pontificat.* pp. 161, 177, ed. Francof. Derenbourg, *Histoire*, p. 197. Grätz, *Monatsschrift* 1881, p. 53 ff.). He is there known by the name of שמעון בן קמהית. In Joseph. *Antt.*, Euseb. *Hist. eccl.*, and in Zonaras, *Annal.* vi. 3 (i. 477), the father's name is Κάμιθος, while in Euseb. *Demonstr.* it is Κάθιμος, in Joseph. *Hypomnest.* Κάθημος, and in *Chron. pasch.*, ed. Dindorf, i. 408 and 417, Καμαθεί.

[550] The surname *Caiaphas* is not = כיפא, but = קייפא or קייף; see note 544 above. Derenbourg, p. 215, note 2.

[551] See the wild combinations of every sort that have been indulged in with regard to this personage in Grätz, *Monatsschrift* 1881, pp. 97–112.

[552] According to *Antt.* xx. 1. 3, he also appears to have the surname Kantheras as well as his father. In the Mishna, *Para* iii. 5, he is known as אליועיני בן הקייף (see note 544, above). The Rabbinical tradition regards him as a son of Caiaphas. The name אֶלְיְהוֹעֵינַי (my eyes are directed to Jehovah) or אֶלְיוֹעֵינַי is also to be met with in the Old Testament (Ezra viii. 4, x. 22, 27; 1 Chron. iii. 23, iv. 36, vii. 8, xxvi. 3).

(*g*) Appointed by Herod of Chalkis (44–48 A.D.).[553]

    20. Joseph the son of Kami or Kamedes (=Kamithos), *Antt.* xx. 1. 3, 5. 2.[554]

    21. Ananias the son of Nedebaios (somewhere between 47 and 59 A.D.), *Antt.* xx. 5. 2 ; comp. xx. 6. 2 ; *Bell. Jud.* ii. 12. 6 ; Acts xxiii. 2, xxiv. 1. In consequence of his wealth he continued to be a man of great influence even after his deposition, although, at the same time, notorious for his avarice (*Antt.* xx. 9. 2–4). He was put to death by the insurgents at the commencement of the Jewish war (*Bell. Jud.* ii. 17. 6, 9).[555]

(*h*) Appointed by Agrippa II. (50–100 A.D.) :—

    22. Ismael the son of Phabi (about 59–61 A.D.), *Antt.* xx. 8. 8, 11. He is probably identical with the person of the same name whose execution at Cyrene is incidentally mentioned, *Bell. Jud.* vi. 2. 2.[556]

---

[553] It would also be somewhere about this time (about 44 A.D.) that the high priest Ismael comes in, who according to *Antt.* iii. 15. 3, was in office during the great famine in the reign of the Emperor Claudius. But as Josephus says nothing about him in the course of the narrative itself, we are probably to look upon this casual mention of him as a fault of memory on the part of the historian. Ewald (*Geschichte*, vi. 634) inserts him after *Elionaios*, while Wieseler (*Chronologie des apostol. Zeitalters*, p. 159) identifies him with this latter.

[554] The name of the father, which at one time appears as Καμεί (*Antt.* xx. 1. 3=Zonaras, *Annal.* vi. 12, *fin.*) or Κάμη (Joseph. *Hypomnest.*), at another as Κεμεδής (*Antt.* xx. 5. 2, according to the reading of Dindorf and Bekker = Zonaras, *Annal.* vi. 14), is in any case identical with Kamithos.

[555] For his avarice, comp. besides the Talmudic tradition in Derenbourg's *Histoire*, p. 233 f.

[556] It is probably this younger Ismael, son of Phabi (not the high priest of the same name who stands eleventh in the list), that is also referred to in the Rabbinical traditions regarding ישמעאל בן פיאבי פיאבי (Mishna, *Para* iii. 5 ; *Sota* ix. 15 ; in the latter passage it is also the high priest of this name that is meant, for the predicate Rabbi should, with *Cod. de Rossi*, be expunged. Tosefta. ed. Zuckermandel, pp. 182. 26, 533. 35 f., 632. 6. See in general, Derenbourg's *Histoire*, pp. 232–235). In the printed texts the father's name is frequently corrupted. The correct form is פיאבי, or divided thus פי אבי (as in *Cod. de Rossi* 138, in the one passage in which it occurs in

23. Joseph Kabi,[557] son of Simon the high priest
(61–62 A.D.), *Antt.* xx. 8. 11 ; comp. *Bell. Jud.*
vi. 2. 2.

24. Ananos the son of Ananos (62 A.D., for only three
months), *Antt.* xx. 9. 1.   He was one of those
who played a leading part during the first period
of the Jewish war, but was subsequently put to
death by the populace, *Bell. Jud.* ii. 20. 3, 22.
1–2, iv. from 3. 7 to 5. 2 ; *Vita*, 38, 39, 44, 60.[558]

25. Jesus the son of Damnaios (about 62–63 A.D.),
*Antt.* xx. 9. 1. and 4; comp. *Bell. Jud.* vi. 2. 2.

26. Jesus the son of Gamaliel (about 63–65 A.D.),
*Antt.* xx. 9. 4, 7.   In the course of the Jewish
war he is frequently mentioned along with
Ananos, whose fate he also shared, *Bell. Jud.* iv.
3. 9, 4. 3, 5. 2 ; *Vita*, 38, 41.   According to
Rabbinical tradition, his wife, Martha, was of the
house of Boethos.[559]

27. Matthias the son of Theophilos (65 ff. A.D.), *Antt.*
xx. 9. 7 ; comp. *Bell. Jud.* vi. 2. 2.[560]

the Mishna, viz. *Para* iii. 5).   There is as near an approach to this as
possible in the Greek form Φιαβι, which is found in the manuscripts in one
instance at least, viz. *Antt.* xx. 8. 8.

[557] In Joseph. *Antt.* xx. 8. 11, the surname is written Καβί ; in Zonoras,
*Annal.* vi. 17, it is Δεκαβί (*i.e.* δὲ Καβί) ; and in Joseph. *Hypomnest.*
Κάμης.   The latter would correspond to Kamithos.

[558] For combinations with respect to this high priest, see Grätz, *Monatsschr.*
1881, pp. 56–62.

[559] Mishna, *Jebamoth* vi. 4 : " If one happens to be betrothed to a widow,
and is subsequently appointed to the office of high priest, he is at liberty to
conduct her home as his bride.   Thus *Josua, son of Gamla,* was betrothed to
Martha the daughter of *Boethos*, and afterwards the king appointed him to
be high priest ; and on the back of this he conducted Martha home as his
bride."   Our Josua, son of Gamala, is probably identical again with the
Ben Gamala who, according to *Joma* iii. 9, ordered a golden urn to be
made from which to draw the lots relating to the two he-goats on the great
day of atonement.   For further Rabbinical traditions regarding this personage, see Derenbourg, p. 248 f.   As to his services in the way of promoting
education, see below, § 27, note 29.

[560] On this high priest, see also Grätz, *Monatsschr.* 1881, pp. 62–64.

(*i*) Appointed by the people during the war (67–68 A.D.):—

    28. Phannias or Phineesos the son of Samuel, and of humble origin, *Bell. Jud.* iv. 3. 8; *Antt.* xx. 10.[561]

Owing to the frequency with which those high priests were changed, the number of those who had ceased to hold office was always something considerable. But, although they no longer discharged the active functions of the office, they still continued to occupy an important and influential position, as can still be shown with regard to several of them at least.[562] We know from the New Testament, for example, what an amount of influence the elder *Ananos* or Hannas (No. 10) had even as a retired high priest. The same may be said of his son Jonathan (No. 15), who, long after he had ceased to hold office, conducted an embassy, in the year 52 A.D., to the Syrian viceroy Umidius Quadratus. This latter then sent him to Rome to answer for certain disturbances that had taken place in Judaea; and when he had got the matter settled in favour of the Jews, he took the opportunity of his being in Rome to request the emperor to send Felix as the new pro-curator. Then when Felix was found to be causing universal dissatisfaction in consequence of the way in which he was discharging the functions of his office, Jonathan took the liberty of reminding him of his duty, for doing which however he had to answer with his life.[563] Another high priest, *Ananias* the son of Nedebaios (No. 21), ruled in Jerusalem almost like a despot after he had retired from office. Then the younger *Ananos* (No. 24) and Jesus the son of Gamaliel (No. 26), although no longer exercising the functions of the high-priest-hood, were found at the head of affairs in the earlier stage of the Jewish war. From all this it is evident that, though not actually in office, those men were by no means condemned to

---

[561] This, the last of the high priests, is also known to the Rabbinical traditions; see Derenbourg, p. 269. His name in Hebrew was פינחס.

[562] For what follows, comp. *Stud. u. Krit.* 1872, p. 619 ff.

[563] The references to passages are to be found above, *passim*.

political inactivity. On the contrary, the office was such that
it imparted to the holder of it a *character indelibilis* in virtue
of which he retained, even after demitting it, a large portion
of the rights and obligations of the officiating high priest,[564]
and of course the title of ἀρχιερεύς as well, a title that, in
Josephus, is accorded to the whole of the ex-high priests.
Consequently wherever in the New Testament ἀρχιερεῖς appear
at the head of the Sanhedrim, we are to understand that
those referred to are first and foremost the ex-high priests
in question, inclusive at the same time of the one actually in
office.[565]

But sometimes we read of certain other personages who are
described as ἀρχιερεῖς, and yet their names do not appear in
the foregoing list. In the Acts (iv. 6) we have the following
enumeration : Ἄννας ὁ ἀρχιερεὺς καὶ Καϊάφας καὶ Ἰωάννης
καὶ Ἀλέξανδρος καὶ ὅσοι ἦσαν ἐκ γένους ἀρχιερατικοῦ. In a
subsequent passage (xix. 14) mention is made of a high priest
called Sceva with his seven sons. Josephus again mentions
a certain Jesus, son of Sapphias, as being τῶν ἀρχιερέων ἕνα,[566]
also one Simon ἐξ ἀρχιερέων, who was still young at the time
of the war, and consequently cannot be identical with Simon

---

[564] *Horajoth* iii. 1–4. See, in particular, iii. 4 : "Between a high priest
in office and one who has demitted it there is no more difference than
between the young oxen on the great day of atonement and the tenth of an
ephah. But both are equal to one another in respect of the service on the
great day of atonement, in respect of the law requiring them to marry a
maid ; both alike are forbidden to marry a widow, to defile themselves by
contact with the dead bodies of blood relations, to let the hair grow long,
to rend their garments, while their death (in the event of their being
murdered) has the effect of bringing back the murderer." The same points
to some extent are also found in *Megilla* i. 9 and *Makkoth* ii. 6.

[565] This is corroborated above all by the following passages, *Bell. Jud.* ii.
12. 6: τοὺς ἀρχιερεῖς Ἰωνάθην καὶ Ἀνανίαν ; *Vita*, 38 : τοὺς ἀρχιερεῖς Ἄνανον
καὶ Ἰησοῦν τὸν τοῦ Γαμαλᾶ ; *Bell. Jud.* iv. 3. 7 : ὁ γεραίτατος τῶν ἀρχιερέων
Ἄνανος. *Bell. Jud.* iv. 4. 3 : ὁ μετ' Ἄνανον γεραίτατος τῶν ἀρχιερέων Ἰησοῦς.
*Bell. Jud.* iv. 3. 9 : οἱ δοκιμώτατοι τῶν ἀρχιερέων, Γαμαλᾶ μὲν υἱὸς Ἰησοῦς,
Ἀνάνου δὲ Ἄνανος. In the last three passages the ἀρχιερεῖς must have been
high priests in the sense in which Ananos and Jesus were so, *i.e.* ex-high
priests in the strict sense of the word.

[566] *Bell. Jud.* ii. 20. 4.

Kantheras (No. 17),[567] and lastly, one Matthias, son of Boethos, τὸν ἀρχιερέα or ἐκ τῶν ἀρχιερέων.[568] Not one of those just mentioned is to be found in our list. Besides there is many a high priest known to the Rabbinical traditions whose name does not appear there.[569] This fact may perhaps be sufficiently accounted for by what we are now going to mention.

*Apropos* of the irregular appointment of Phannias to the office of high priest, Josephus remarks,[570] that the zealots, by acting as they did on this occasion, "had robbed of their importance those families from which in their order it had been the practice to select the high priests" (ἄκυρα τὰ γένη ποιήσαντες ἐξ ὧν κατὰ διαδοχὰς οἱ ἀρχιερεῖς ἀπεδείκνυντο). *The high-priesthood would therefore seem to have been vested in a few privileged families.* The truth is, one only requires to glance at the foregoing list in order to be convinced that the office was confined to only a few families. To the family of Phabi, for example, belong Nos. 3, 11, 22; to the family of Boethos, Nos. 4, 7, 8, 17, 19, 26; to the family of Ananos (or Hannas), Nos. 10, 12, 14, 15, 16, 18, 24, 27; and to the family of Kamith, Nos. 13, 20, 23. Leaving Ananel, a Babylonian of humble origin (No. 1), Aristobulus the last of the Asmonaeans (No. 2), and Phannias, the high priest of the revolution period (No. 28), out of account, there remain only five (Nos. 5, 6, 9, 21, 25) who cannot be proved to have belonged to one or other of those families, although it is still possible that they did so. Now when one considers how the high-priesthood was thus confined to a few families, and in what high estimation the office was held, it is not difficult to see that the mere fact of belonging to any one of the privileged families in question must of itself have been sufficient to confer special distinction upon a man. And hence we can understand how it should be that Josephus, in a certain passage in which he wishes to tell us particularly who of the notabilities were among those who went over to

[567] *Vita*, 39.    [568] *Bell. Jud.* iv. 9. 11, v. 13. 1, vi. 2. 2.
[569] See *Stud. u. Krit.* 1872, p. 639.    [570] *Bell. Jud.* iv. 3. 6.

the Romans, enumerates the υἱοὶ τῶν ἀρχιερέων along with
the ἀρχιερεῖς themselves.[571] In the Mishna again, we find
that on one occasion the "sons of the high priests" (בְּנֵי כֹהֲנִים
גְּדוֹלִים) are quoted as authorities on certain points of matrimonial law, and that too without mentioning their names,
seeing that the simple fact of their being high priests' sons
stamped them as men of importance and authority.[572] In
another instance, we are informed that letters with unusually
large seals had come "to the sons of the high priests" (לבני כהנים
גדולים) from distant lands,[573] from which we may again infer
that these also enjoyed a certain reputation abroad. But they
did not rest satisfied with the mere dignity of rank; so far
from that, the members of those high-priestly families also
played a prominent part in public affairs. According to Acts
iv. 6, among those who had seats and a right to speak and
vote in the Sanhedrim were ὅσοι ἦσαν ἐκ γένους ἀρχιερατικοῦ, where, from all that has been already stated, it is
certain that the γένος ἀρχιερατικόν can only refer to the
privileged families now in question. Now, if the members of
the high-priestly families occupied so distinguished a position,
it is quite conceivable that the designation ἀρχιερεῖς would
come to be used in a more comprehensive sense so as to
include them as well. That this is what actually took place
may be seen, to say nothing of all that has been previously
advanced, from the passage in Josephus mentioned above,
where after recording the fact that two high priests and eight
high priests' sons were among those who went over to the
Romans, he proceeds to include these two categories under the
common designation of ἀρχιερεῖς.[574] This will also serve to
account for the circumstance of high priests being sometimes
mentioned that are not to be found in our list.

[571] Bell. Jud. vi. 2. 2.     [572] Kethuboth xiii. 1–2.     [573] Ohaloth xvii. 5.
[574] Bell. Jud. vi. 2. 2: Ὧν ἦσαν ἀρχιερεῖς μὲν Ἰώσηπός τε καὶ Ἰησοῦς, υἱοὶ
δ' ἀρχιερέων τρεῖς μὲν Ἰσμαήλου τοῦ καρατομηθέντος ἐν Κυρήνῃ, καὶ τοῦ
Ματθίου τέσσαρες, καὶ εἷς ἑτέρου Ματθίου παῖς, διαδρὰς μετὰ τὴν τοῦ πατρὸς
ἀπώλειαν, ὃν ὁ τοῦ Γιώρα Σίμων ἀπέκτεινε σὺν τρισὶν υἱοῖς, ὡς προείρηται.
Πολλοὶ δὲ καὶ τῶν ἄλλων εὐγενῶν τοῖς ἀρχιερεῦσι συμμετεβάλοντο.

Consequently the high priests that, in the New Testament as well as in Josephus,[575] appear as leading personages would consist, in the first instance, of the high priests properly so called, *i.e.* the one actually in office and those who had previously been so, and then, of the members of those privileged families from which the high priests were taken. In the days of Roman rule they were at the head of the Sanhedrim and of the native government generally, and although the majority of them were unquestionably men of Sadducaean tendencies, yet in the actual conduct of affairs they bowed, however reluctantly, to the wishes of the Pharisees (see above, p. 154).

[575] Especially in the section, *Bell. Jud.* ii. 14–17

# § 24. THE PRIESTHOOD AND THE TEMPLE WORSHIP.

## THE LITERATURE.

Lightfoot, *Ministerium templi quale erat tempore nostri servatoris* (*Opp.* ed. Rotterdam, i. pp. 671–758).

Lundius, *Die alten jüdischen Heiligthümer, Gottesdienste und Gewohnheiten, für Augen gestellet in einer ausführlichen Beschreibung des gantzen levitischen Priesterthums, etc., itzo von neuem übersehen und in beygefügten Anmerckungen hin und wieder theils verbessert, theils vermehret durch Johan. Christophorum Wolfium*, Hamburg 1738.

Carpzov (Joh. Gottlob), *Apparatus historico criticus antiquitatum sacri codicis* (1748), pp. 64–113, 611 ff., 699 ff.

Ugolini, *Sacerdotium Hebraicum*, in his *Thesaurus Antiquitatum sacrarum*, vol. xiii. *Ibid.*, still other cognate monographs in vols. xii. and xiii.

Bähr, *Symbolik des mosaischen Cultus*, 2 vols. 1837–1839), vol. i. 2nd ed. 1874.

Winer, *Realwörterb.*, arts. "Priester," "Leviten," "Abgaben," "Erstgeburt," "Erstlinge," "Hebe," "Zehnt," "Opfer," etc.

Herzfeld, *Geschichte des Volkes Jisrael*, i. 387–424, iii. 106 ff., 162 ff.

Oehler, art. "Priesterthum," in Herzog's *Real-Enc.*, 1st ed. vol. xii. 174–187. *Ibid.* by the same, arts. "Levi," vol. viii. 347–358; "Nethinim," vol. x. 296 f.; and "Opfercultus," vol. x. 614–652. The same articles in the second edition as revised by Orelli.

De Wette, *Lehrbuch der hebräisch-jüdischen Archäol.* (4th ed. 1864), p. 268 ff.

Ewald, *Die Alterthümer des Volkes Israel*, Göttingen 1866.

Keil, *Handbuch der biblischen Archäologie* (2nd ed. 1875), pp. 166 ff., 200 ff., 357 ff., 373 ff.

Haneberg, *Die religiösen Alterthümer der Bibel* (2nd ed. 1869), pp. 356 ff., 508 ff., 599 ff.

Schenkel's *Bibellexicon*, the same articles as in Winer.

Riehm, *Handwörterbuch des biblischen Alterthums*, the articles relating to our subject.

Graf, *Zur Geschichte des Stammes Levi* (Merx' *Archiv für wissenschaftl. Erforschung des A. T.'s*, vol. i. 1869, pp. 68–106, 208–236).

Köhler, *Lehrbuch der biblischen Geschichte*, vol. i. 1875, pp. 363–454.

Wellhausen, *Geschichte Israels*, vol. i. 1878, pp. 15–174 (2nd ed., under the title: *Prolegomena zur Geschichte Israels*, 1883).

Dillmann, *Exegetisches Handbuch zu Exodus und Leviticus* (1880), pp. 455–461 and elsewhere.

Reuss, *Geschichte der heiligen Schriften Alten Testaments* (1881), sec. ccxciv.

## I. THE PRIESTHOOD AS A DISTINCT ORDER.

THE internal development of Israel subsequent to the exile

was essentially determined by the direction given to it by two equally influential classes, viz. the *priests* on the one hand and the *scribes* on the other. During the centuries immediately following the exile and till far on into the Greek era, it was, in the first instance, the influence of the *priests* that was predominant. It was they who had been instrumental in organizing the new community; it was from them that the law had emanated; and to their hands had been entrusted the direction, not only of the material, but also of the spiritual affairs of the whole body of the people. But although originally it was they who were specially versed in the law and were looked upon as its authoritative interpreters, yet by and by there gradually grew up alongside of them an independent order of doctors or men learned in the law. And the importance and influence of these latter would necessarily go on increasing in proportion as the priests grew less and less zealous for the law of their fathers on the one hand, and as the law itself came to acquire a greater value and significance in the estimation of the people on the other. This was the case more particularly after the Maccabaean wars of independence. Ever since then the *scribes* got the spiritual superintendence of the people more and more into their own hands. And so the *age of the priests* was succeeded by that of the *scribes* (comp. Reuss, *Geschichte der heiligen Schriften A. T.'s*). This however is not to be understood as implying that the priests had now lost all their influence. Politically and socially they still occupied the foremost place quite as much as ever they did. It is true the scribes had now come to be recognised as the teachers of the people. But, in virtue of their political standing, in virtue of the powerful resources at their command, and, lastly and above all, in virtue of their sacred prerogatives—for, inasmuch as they enjoyed the exclusive right of offering Israel's sacrifices to God, their intervention was necessary to the fulfilment of his religious duties in the case of every member of the community,—in virtue of all this, we say, the priests still continued to have an extraordinary significance for the life of the nation.

Now this significance of theirs was due mainly to the simple fact that they constituted a distinct order, possessing the exclusive right to offer the people's sacrifices to God. According to the legislation of the Pentateuch, which had been regarded as absolutely binding ever since the time of Ezra and Nehemiah, "*the sons of Aaron*" *were alone entitled to take part in the sacrificial worship*.[1]  The priesthood was therefore a fraternity fenced round with irremovable barriers, for they had been fixed for ever by natural descent.  No one could possibly be admitted to this order who did not belong to it by birth ; nor could any one be excluded from it whose legitimate birth entitled him to admission.  Now this order, so rigidly exclusive in its character, was in possession of the highest privilege that can well be conceived of, the privilege namely of offering to God all the sacrifices of the nation at large, and of every individual member of the community. This circumstance alone could not but be calculated to invest the priesthood with a vast amount of influence and authority, all the more that civil life was intertwined, in such an endless variety of ways, with the religious observances.[2]  But, in addition to this, there was the fact, that ever since the Deuteronomic legislation came into force in the time of Josiah

---

[1] See in particular, Ex. xxviii.–xxix. ; Lev. viii.–x. ; Num. xvi.–xviii.  I should observe here that the following view is based on the assumption that the so-called priestly code, *i.e.* the bulk of the laws in Exodus, Leviticus and Numbers, belongs to a later date than Deuteronomy and Ezekiel.  This, as it appears to me. has been clearly demonstrated by the more recent criticism of the Pentateuch.  The legislation of the priestly code evidently represents, in all its leading features, a later stage of development than Deuteronomy and Ezekiel.  The two latter books would be simply unintelligible were we to suppose that their authors wrote them with the priestly code already lying before them.

[2] There were, for example, numerous points in matrimonial law and medical jurisprudence that could only be settled by having recourse to the priests ; see Num. v. 11–31 (the procedure in the case of the woman suspected of adultery) ; Lev. xiii., xiv. ; Deut. xxiv. 8, 9 (procedure in the case of leprosy).

(about 630 B.C.), it was declared to be unlawful to offer sacrifices anywhere but in Jerusalem, *the whole worship being concentrated in its sole and only legitimate sanctuary.* Consequently all the various offerings from every quarter of the land flowed into Jerusalem and met at this one common centre of worship, the result being that the priests that officiated within it came to acquire great power and wealth. Moreover, this centralization of the worship had the additional effect of uniting all the members of the priesthood into one firmly compacted body.

From what has just been said it follows, as matter of course, that *the primary requisite in a priest was evidence of his pedigree.* On this the greatest possible stress was laid. The person who failed to produce it could claim no title whatever to the rights and privileges of the priesthood. Even so far back as the time when the first of the exiles returned under Zerubbabel, certain priestly families were debarred from the sacred office because they could not produce their genealogical registers.[3a] On the other hand, Josephus assures us, with regard to his own case, that he found his pedigree recorded "in the public archives." [3b] Consequently the family registers would appear to have had the character of public records on account of their importance for the community at large.

With the view of keeping the blood of the priestly stock as pure as possible, there were also certain regulations prescribed with regard to *marriage.* According to the law given in Lev. xxi. 7, 8, a priest was forbidden to marry a prostitute, or a deflowered maid, or a woman put away from her husband; consequently he could only choose an undefiled virgin or widow, and of course even then only such as were of Israelitish origin.[4] At the same time there was no caste-like restriction

---

[3a] Ezra ii. 61–63 = Neh. vii. 63–65.

[3b] Joseph. *Vita*, 1: τὴν μὲν οὖν τοῦ γένους ἡμῶν διαδοχήν, ὡς ἐν ταῖς δημοσίαις δέλτοις ἀναγεγραμμένην εὗρον, οὕτω παρατίθεμαι.

[4] Joseph. *contra Apion.* i. 7: δεῖ γὰρ τὸν μετέχοντα τῆς ἱερωσύνης ἐξ ὁμοεθνοῦς γυναικὸς παιδοποιεῖσθαι.

forbidding them to marry any but the daughters of priests.
Nor were these regulations in any way relaxed in later times,
for so far from that they came to be but the more sharply
defined.[5] We find, for example, that a chaluza, *i.e.* a widow
whom her brother-in-law declined to marry (according to the
law regarding levirate marriage), was also to be treated as one
"who had been put away from her husband." [6] Again a
priest was forbidden to marry a woman who had been taken
captive in war as being a person that might well be suspected
of having been violated.[7] Then, if a priest was already
without children, he was forbidden, in marrying again, to
marry a woman who was "incapable;" [8] but, in any case, he
was never to choose a female proselyte or emancipated slave ;
nor the daughter of a man who had been formerly a slave,
except in those cases in which the mother happened to be
of Israelitish extraction.[9] The regulations were still more
stringent in the case of the *high priest*. He was not allowed
to marry even a widow, but only an undefiled virgin (Lev.
xxi. 13–15). This, like the former regulations, was also
enforced and rendered yet more precise in later times.[10] In

[5] See in general, Philo, *De monarchia*, lib. ii. sec. viii.–xi. (ed. Mang.
ii. 228 f.). Joseph. *Antt.* iii. 12. 2. The Rabbinical prescriptions as given
in Selden, *De successione in pontificatum*, ii. 2, 3 ; Ibid. *Uxor Ebraica*, i. 7.
Wagenseil's note to *Sota* iv. 1 (in Surenhusius' *Mishna*, iii. 230 ff.).
Ugolini, *Thesaurus*, vol. xiii. col. 911 ff.

[6] *Sota* iv. 1, viii. 3 ; *Makkoth* iii. 1. Targum of Jonathan, Sifra and
Pesikta to Lev. xxi. 7, as given in Ugolini, *ut supra*.

[7] Joseph. *Antt.* iii. 12. 2 ; *contra Apion.* i. 7 ; *Antt.* xiii. 10. 5, *fin.*
(account of John Hyrcanus). According to *Kethuboth* ii. 9, even priests'
wives that had been found in a town captured by the enemy were debarred
from any further conjugal intercourse with their husbands, unless it could
be shown by satisfactory evidence that they had not been violated.

[8] *Jebamoth* vi. 5.

[9] Never a female proselyte or emancipated slave, *Jebamoth* vi. 5. With
regard to the daughters, see *Bikkurim* i. 5. Rabbi Elieser ben Jakob says :
"A priest is never to marry the daughter of a proselyte except when her
mother happens to be of Israel." This is no less applicable to the daughters
of emancipated slaves. Even in the tenth generation it is lawful only
where the mother is of Israelitish origin.

[10] Philo, *De monarchia*, ii. 9. Joseph. *Antt.* iii. 12. 2. *Jebamoth* vi. 4 : "A
high priest must not marry a widow, whether she has become such subse-

affirming, as he does, that the high priest could only marry a
virgin belonging to a priestly family,[11] Philo states what is
at variance at once with the text of Leviticus and the later
standpoint of the law, from both of which it is evident that
it was permissible for the high priest to marry any Israelitish
virgin, no matter to what family she might belong.  Possibly
Philo's view may have been suggested to him by the terms of
the passage in Leviticus as it stands in the Septuagint,[12] perhaps also by actual practice, or, it may be, by both combined.
The regulation in Ezekiel (xliv. 22), to the effect that a priest
was only to marry a virgin, or the widow of a priest, found
no place in the law as subsequently developed.  Considering
the great importance that was attached to the strict observance of those regulations, a priest on the occasion of his
marriage was, of course, required to furnish precise evidence
of his wife's pedigree.  Josephus has described at length the
very careful way in which this was gone about,[13] while in the

quent to her betrothal or subsequent to her actual marriage.  Nor is he at
liberty to choose as a wife a woman already perfectly marriageable.  Rabbi
Elieser and Rabbi Simon regard a marriageable woman as allowable.  Nor
is he to marry one that has been injured by an accident."  According to
Philo, *De monarchia*, ii. 9, *fin.*, the high priest was on no account to marry
one that had been previously betrothed.  Comp. Ritter's *Philo und die
Halacha* (1879), p. 72.  Lundius, *Die alten jüdischen Heiligthümer*, book
iii. chap. xix.

[11] Philo, *De monarchia*, ii. 11: προστάξας τῷ μὲν ἀρχιερεῖ μνᾶσθαι μὴ μόνον
μόνον γυναῖκα παρθένον, ἀλλὰ καὶ ἱέρειαν ἐξ ἱερέων.

[12] In the Septuagint, Lev. xxi. 13 runs thus: οὗτος γυναῖκα παρθένον ἐκ
τοῦ γένους αὐτοῦ λήψεται, there being nothing in the Hebrew text
corresponding to the words ἐκ τοῦ γένους αὐτοῦ.  Comp. Ritter's *Philo und
die Halacha*, p. 72 f.

[13] *Apion.* i. 7.  From what is there said one must necessarily assume
that surely there were a great many families that were in possession of
genealogical registers.  Comp. in addition, the copious lists in the Books of
Ezra and Nehemiah; and further, the indications of the existence of such
registers to be met with in the New Testament, Matt. i. 1 f.; Luke ii. 36,
iii. 23 ff.; Acts xiii. 21; Rom. xi. 1; Phil. iii. 5.  Also Mishna, *Jebamoth* iv. 13; *Taanith* iv. 5.  Euseb. *Hist. eccl.* i. 7=Jul. African. *Epist. ad
Aristidem* (in Routh's *Reliquiae sacrae*, ii. 228 ff., and Spitta, *Der Brief des
Julius Africanus an Aristides*, 1877).  Winer's *Realwörterb.* ii. 516-518;
Herzfeld's *Geschichte des Volkes Jisrael*, i. 378-387  Wieseler's *Beitrage zur
richtigen Wurdigung der Evangelien* (1869), p. 133 ff.  Holtzmann in

Mishna it is prescribed how far back the evidence is to extend,[14] and in what cases it may be dispensed with.[15]

Those regulations with regard to marriage are undoubtedly based upon the idea that the *priesthood is a sacred order*. The same idea has been further embodied in yet other prescriptions.   According to the law (Num. xix.), every one was defiled who came in contact with a dead body, nay who even entered a house in which such body happened to be lying; but as for the priests, they were forbidden to approach a corpse or to take part in the funeral obsequies, the prohibition being absolute in the case of the high priest, while in the case of the ordinary priests, the only exception was in favour of very near blood relations: parents, children, and brothers or sisters (Lev. xxi. 1–4, 11–12; Ezek. xliv. 25–27).   It would seem that the priest was not even at liberty to mourn for his own wife.   Or are we to understand, although it is not expressly stated, that she is intended, as matter of course, to be included among the exceptions?[16]   In

Schenkel's *Bibellex.* ii. 425–430.   Hamburger's *Real-Enc.*, 2nd part, art. "Genealogie."

[14] *Kiddushin* iv. 4: "When a priest wants to marry *the daughter of a priest*, he must go back and find evidence with regard to four generations of mothers, and therefore, strictly speaking, with regard to eight mothers. These are, her own mother and her mother's mother; the mother of her maternal grandfather and her mother again; the mother of her father and her mother; the mother of her paternal grandfather and her mother again. If, on the other hand, the woman he wants to marry be simply *a daughter of Levi or of Israel*, he must go back a step farther."

[15] *Kiddushin* iv. 5: "It is unnecessary to search back in the case of a priest who has ministered at the altar, or of a Levite who has sung in the choir, or of a member of the Sanhedrim.   As a rule, all those whose ancestors are well known to have been public officials or almoners, are at liberty to marry one belonging to a priestly family without further inquiry."

[16] According to the usual interpretation of the text of Lev. xxi. 4 as we now have it, the mourning of the priest for his wife would seem to be even expressly forbidden.   Although, in this instance, both exposition and text are exceedingly doubtful (see Dillmann's note on the passage), still the fact remains that the wife is not mentioned as one of the exceptions.   Nor is she mentioned as such either by Philo, *De monarchia*, ii. 12, or by Josephus, *Antt.* iii. 12. 2.   The Rabbinical writers, on the other hand, regard the

no case whatever was a priest to indulge in any token of grief calculated to disfigure the person, such as shaving the head or lacerating the body (Lev. xxi. 5, 6 ; comp. Ezek. xliv. 20), nor was the high priest to uncover his head and rend his garments (Lev. xxi. 10 ; comp. x. 6, 7).[16a]

Then again it was essential to the sacred character attaching to a priest, that he should be *totally free from every sort of physical defect.* If any one had a bodily defect of any kind about him, no matter though he belonged to the " sons of Aaron," he was thereby disqualified from officiating as a priest. The various kinds of defects are already enumerated with pretty considerable detail in the law as found in Leviticus (xxi. 16–23). And, as was to be expected, this too is one of those points on which a later age has exercised its ingenuity in the way of being minutely and painfully specific. It has been calculated that the number of bodily defects that disqualified a man for the office of the priesthood amount in all to 142.[17] At the same time however the priests who, for the reason now in question, were debarred from exercising any of the functions of the priesthood, were entitled to a share of the emoluments as well as the others, for they too belonged to the *ordo.*[18]

There is nothing prescribed in the law as to the *age* at which a priest was to be allowed to enter upon the duties of his office. Perhaps we may venture to assume that it must

שְׁאֵרוֹ of Lev. xxi. 2 as referring to her, while they understand xxi. 4 of the act of mourning for an illegitimate wife. See the passages from the Targum of Jonathan and Sifra in Ugolini, xiii. 929 ff. For the subject generally, consult besides, Oehler, xii. 176 f.

[16a] Comp. besides, Lundius, *Die alten jüdischen Heiligthümer,* book iii. chap. 20.

[17] Haneberg, *Die religiösen Alterthümer der Bibel,* p. 532. See in general, Philo, *De monarchia,* ii. 5. Joseph. *Antt.* iii. 12. 2. Mishna, *Bechoroth* vii. Selden, *De successione in pontificatum Ebr.* ii. 5. Carpzov, *Apparatus historico-criticus,* pp. 89–94. Ugolini, xiii. 897 ff. Haneberg, p. 531 f. Oehler, xii. 176. For parallels from heathen antiquity, see the Knobel-Dillmann *Exeget. Handb. zu Exodus und Leviticus,* p. 568.

[18] Lev. xxi. 22. Philo, *De monarchia,* ii. 13. Joseph. *Antt.* iii. 12. 2 ; *Bell. Jud.* v. 5. 7. Mishna, *Sebachim* xii. 1 ; *Menachoth* xiii. 10, *fin.*

have been the same as that at which the Levites entered upon theirs. Yet even this latter is given differently in different parts of the Old Testament.[19] The Rabbinical tradition states that a priest was duly qualified for his duties as soon as the first signs of manhood made their appearance, but that he was not actually installed till he was twenty years of age.[20]

And now when all the requirements to which we have referred were found to be satisfied, and when his fitness had been duly established to the satisfaction of the Sanhedrim,[21] the priest was set apart to his office by a special *act of consecration*. According to the leading passage in the law bearing on this matter, viz. Ex. xxix. = Lev. viii., this solemn act consisted of three parts: (1) the washing of the body with water, (2) the putting on of the sacred vestments, and (3) a series of sacrifices the offering of which was accompanied with further ceremonies of a partly special kind, viz. the anointing of various parts of the body with blood, the sprinkling of the person and the garments with oil and blood, the " filling of the hands," *i.e.* the taking of certain portions of the victims and laying them upon the hands of the priest with the view of indicating thereby his future duties and rights. In several other passages (Ex. xxviii. 41, xxx. 30, xl. 12–15 ; Lev. vii. 36, x. 7 ; Num. iii. 3) there is superadded to these the pouring of ointment upon the head, an act which, according to the leading passage on the subject, was observed, and that as a mark of distinction, solely in the case of the high priest.[22] The whole ceremony extended over *seven days* (Ex. xxix. 35 ff.; Lev. viii. 33 ff.). How it fared with this ceremony at a later period has been, so far as several of its details are

---

[19] In Num. iv. 3, 23, 30, 35, 39, 43, 47, 1 Chron. xxiii. 3, it is stated to be the thirtieth, in Num. viii. 23–26 the twenty-fifth, and in Ezra iii. 8, 1 Chron. xxiii. 24, 27, 2 Chron. xxxi. 17, the twentieth year.

[20] See the passage from Sifra ( = *Bab. Chullin* 24b) in Selden, *De successione*, ii. 4, and Ugolini, *Thes.* xiii. 927.

[21] *Middoth* v. *fin.*

[22] On this point, see Wellhausen, *Jahrb. f. deutsche Theol.* 1877, p. 412 f. Dillmann's *Exeget. Handbuch*, note on Lev. viii. 12.

concerned, a matter of some dispute.[23]  It is probable that the
pouring of oil upon the head continued to be retained as a
mark of distinction in the case of the high priest.[24]

As the priests were so numerous it was simply impossible
that they could all officiate at the same time.  It was therefore necessary to have an arrangement according to which
they could do so in regular rotation.  With a view to this
the whole body of the priests was divided into twenty-four
*families* or *courses of service*.[25]  The account of the origin and
organization of those twenty-four courses of service as given
by the Rabbinical tradition is as follows : [26] " Four courses of
service (מִשְׁמָרוֹת) came back from the exile, viz. : Jedaiah,

[23] See in general, Selden, *De successione*, ii. 8, 9.  Ugolini, *Thesaurus*, xiii.
pp. 434 ff., 476–548.  Bähr, *Symbolik des mosaischen Cultus*, ii. 165 ff.
Winer's *Realwörterb.*, art. "Priesterweihe."  Oehler in Herzog's *Real-
Encycl.*, vol. xiii. pp. 178–180.  Haneberg, pp. 526–531.  According to
some, the newly admitted priest was only required to offer the meat-offering
prescribed in Lev. vi. 12 ff.  But this is utterly incredible, and is based
upon a pure misapprehension of the Rabbinical passages, which undoubtedly
require that the newly admitted (therefore newly consecrated) priest should,
in the first instance, offer this sacrifice for himself before offering any
other.  See the passages in Ugolini, xiii. 546 f., and comp., in addition,
Frankel, *Ueber den Einfluss der palästinischen Exegese*, etc. (1851) p. 143.
No further light is thrown upon the matter by Philo, *Vita Mosis*, iii. 16–18,
and Joseph. *Antt.* iii. 8. 6, as they simply reproduce Ex. xxix.=Lev.
viii.

[24] Comp. Wellhausen, *Jahrb. f. deutsche Theol.* 1877, p. 412.  But it
would appear that, in the latter days of the temple, the high priest himself
was no longer (or not always?) anointed, for the Mishna knows of other
high priests, who in contradistinction to the anointed ones had been
introduced to their office through the ceremony of investing with the
sacred garments.  See in particular, *Horajoth* iii. 4.  But be this as it
may, there is at all events no truth in the view of Maimonides, that the
anointing had been discontinued ever since the exile.

[25] On this see Lightfoot, *Ministerium templi*, chap. vi. (*Opp.* i. pp. 691–
694).  Idem, *Harmonia evangelistarum*, note on Luke i. 5 (*Opp.* i. 258 ff.).
Idem, *Horae hebraicae*, note on Luke i. 5 (*Opp.* ii. 486 ff.).  Carpzov,
*Apparatus historico-criticus*, pp. 100–102.  Ugolini, *Thesaurus*, vol. xiii.
col. 872 ff.  Herzfeld, *Geschichte des Volkes Jisrael*, i. p. 387 ff.  Bertheau,
*Exegetisches Handbuch zu Ezra, Nehemia und Ester* (1862), pp. 228–230.
Oehler in Herzog's *Real-Encycl.*, 1st ed. vol. xii. pp. 182–186.  Haneberg,
*Die religiösen Alterthümer der Bibel*, p. 555 ff.  Graf in Merx' *Archiv*, i. p.
225 f.

[26] *Jer. Taanith* iv. fol. 68, and as being substantially to the same effect,

Harim, Pashur, and Immer. . . . . Then the prophets that
were among them arose and made twenty-four lots and put
them into an urn. And Jedaiah came and drew five lots,
which, including himself, would therefore make six. And
Harim came and drew five lots, which, including himself,
would therefore make six. And Pashur came and drew five
lots, which, including himself, would therefore make six.
And Immer came and drew five lots, which, including himself, would therefore make six. . . . . And heads of the
courses of service (רָאשֵׁי מִשְׁמָרוֹת) were appointed. And the
courses were divided into houses (בָּתֵּי אָבוֹת). And there were
courses consisting of five, six, seven, eight, or nine houses. In
a course consisting of *five* houses, three of them had to serve
one day each, while the remaining two had to serve two days
each; in a course consisting of *six* houses, five of them had
to serve one day each, while one had to serve two days;
where it consisted of *seven*, each served one day; of *eight*, six
served one day each and two served simultaneously the
remaining day; of *nine*, five served one day each and four
served simultaneously during two days." It is true that
what is here stated regarding the origin (or, according to the
Talmud, the restoration) of the twenty-four courses of service
cannot be said to possess the value of an independent tradition,
that, on the contrary, it is based merely upon inferences from
certain facts that are mentioned elsewhere. Yet it has so far
hit the mark as substantially to represent the actual state of
the case. For there returned from the exile, along with
Zerubbabel and Joshua, *four* families of priests, viz.: the
children of Jedaiah, Immer, Pashur, and Harim, numbering in
all 4289 (Ezra ii. 36–39 = Neh. vii. 39–42).[26a] Further, that

---

Tosefta, *Taanith* ii. (both passages in Hebrew and Latin being given
in Ugolini, vol. xiii. p. 876 ff.); partly also *Bab. Arachin* 12[b], comp.
Herzfeld, i. 393. In the above quotation I follow the text of *Jer. Taanith*,
only with a few abridgments here and there.

[26a] The accuracy of the alleged numbers, so far as the time of Zerubbabel
is concerned, has been questioned by Stade (*Theol. Literaturzeitung*, 1884,
218, in the notice by Smend, *Die Listen der Bücher Esra und Nehemia*,

these four families comprised the whole body of the priesthood at
the time of Ezra's arrival, and therefore some eighty years afterwards as well, is evident from Ezra x. 18–22.    But, along with
these mention is also made, as early as the time of Zerubbabel
and Joshua (Neh. xii. 1–7), of twenty-two classes of priests,
with a corresponding number of "heads" (ראשי הכהנים).    And
those same classes or divisions are also further met with in
the time of Joshua's successor, Joiakim the high priest
(Neh. xii. 12–21).[27]    It is evident therefore that the four
families were subdivided into twenty-two classes.    Then it is
substantially the same arrangement that is still to be met with
in the time of Ezra.    When this latter arrived with a fresh
band of exiles, he brought along with him two more priestly
families (Ezra viii. 2)[28] and added them to the four that were
already in the country (Ezra x. 18–22).    But we find that
shortly after, the number of classes was once more almost the
same as it had been in Zerubbabel's time, namely twenty-one,
as may be seen from the list given in Neh. x. 3–9.    However,
only fourteen of the names mentioned in this latter passage
are to be found in the two earlier lists (Neh. xii. 1–7,
12–21), all the rest being different.    Consequently the
organization of the divisions must, in the meanwhile, have
undergone certain alterations of one kind or another, as would
no doubt be deemed necessary on account of a fresh accession

---

1881).    Besides the objections advanced by this writer, there is the further
fact that, according to pseudo-Hecataeus, who belongs to the commencement of the Hellenistic period, the number of Jewish priests amounted in
all to only 1500 (Joseph. *contra Apion.* i. 22, ed. Bekker, p. 202 : καίτοι
οἱ πάντες ἱερεῖς τῶν 'Ιουδαίων, οἱ τὴν δεκάτην τῶν γινομένων λαμβάνοντες καὶ
τὰ κοινὰ διοικοῦντες, περὶ χιλίους μάλιστα καὶ πεντακοσίους εἰσίν).    May it
not be that the women and children are to be understood as included in the
above 4289 ?    So far as our purpose is concerned this question may here
be left an open one.

[27] In the second list only *one* of the names belonging to the first
(Chattusch) is wanting.    The remaining twenty-one names are all identically the same in both, as is clearly evident notwithstanding the numerous
inaccuracies of the text.    Comp. Bertheau's note on Neh. xii. 12.

[28] For the names Gershom and Daniel mentioned in this passage are the
names of priestly families ; see Bertheau's note on it.

of priestly families having been brought by Ezra, and for other reasons besides. However, under the new order of things the number of divisions remained the same as before and so continued, substantially at least, on through succeeding ages. In the time of the author of Chronicles, who traces back the arrangement that existed in his day to the time of David, the number of the divisions amounted to twenty-four (1 Chron. xxiv. 7–18). It is true that, in the catalogue of names furnished by this writer, scarcely more than a third of those in the earlier lists are to be found. That being so, we are bound to assume that, in the meanwhile, important changes must have taken place, always supposing that our author has not drawn somewhat upon his own imagination for a number of the names attributed to the time of David. Be that as it may, it is certain that, *from that point onwards, the division into twenty-four classes continued to subsist without any alteration whatever.* For we learn on the express testimony of Josephus, that it was still maintained in his own day,[29] to say nothing of the fact that some of the names of the division continued to be occasionally mentioned (Joiarib, 1 Macc. ii. 1 ; Abia, Luke i. 5).[30] It is somewhat strange that, in a passage in his *contra Apionem,*—a passage, however, that has come down to us only in a Latin version,—Josephus should be found speaking of *four* families or divisions (*tribus*) of the priests.[31] One might perhaps be disposed to think that here

---

[29] *Antt.* vii. 14. 7 : διέμεινεν οὗτος ὁ μερισμὸς ἄχρι τῆς σήμερον ἡμέρας. *Vita*, 1 : ἐμοὶ δ᾿ οὐ μόνον ἐξ ἱερέων ἐστὶ τὸ γένος, ἀλλὰ καὶ ἐκ τῆς πρώτης ἐφημερίδος τῶν εἰκοσιτεσσάρων (πολλὴ δὲ κᾶν τούτῳ διαφορά), καὶ τῶν ἐν ταύτῃ φυλῶν ἐκ τῆς ἀρίστης. Comp. besides, *Taanith* iv. 2 ; *Sukka* v. 6–8, and the commentaries thereon.

[30] *Joiarib* and *Jedaiah* are also mentioned, *Baba kamma* ix. 12. The division Joiarib is the one that is said to have been officiating when the temple was destroyed, *Bab. Taanith* 29ᵃ, in Derenbourg's *Histoire de la Palestine*, p. 291. The division or course of *Bilga* is mentioned in *Sukka* v. 8.

[31] *Contra Apion.* ii. 8 (ed. Bekker, pp. 239, 20 ff.): Licet enim sint *tribus quattuor sacerdotum,* et harum tribuum singulae habeant hominum plus quam quinque milia, fit tamen observatio particulariter per dies certos ; et his transactis alii succedentes ad sacrificia veniunt, etc.

the historian had in view the *four* families that returned with Zerubbabel. But as the context shows that he is clearly referring to the courses of service, there is nothing for it but to assume that the text has been corrupted, and that for four we ought to substitute twenty-four. Nor can it be said that this view is at once disposed of by the circumstance that Josephus alleges that the number in each division amounted to over 5000 souls. For it is probable that this number included the Levites (who were also divided into twenty-four divisions, every division of the priests having its corresponding division of Levites), and perhaps women and children as well; besides, we know only too well that one cannot depend a great deal on Josephus in the matter of numbers.

Each of the twenty-four main divisions was in turn broken up into a number of *sub-divisions*. If we may trust the Talmudic tradition quoted above (p. 182), the number of those sub-divisions ranged from five to nine for each main division. The main divisions were known either under the general designation of מַחְלְקוֹת (divisions, so 1 Chron. xxviii. 13, 21; 2 Chron. viii. 14, xxiii. 8, xxxi. 2, 15, 16), or, in so far as they were made up of the members of one family, they were called בֵּית אָבוֹת (houses of their fathers, so 1 Chron. xxiv. 4, 6), or, in so far as they had the services of the temple to attend to, they were described as מִשְׁמָרוֹת (watches, so Neh. xiii. 30; 2 Chron. xxxi. 16). As regards the sub-divisions, for our knowledge of which we are indebted solely to the testimony of post-Biblical literature, they are known by the designation of בָּתֵּי אָבוֹת. And so now it had become the regular practice to distinguish the two by calling the *main division* a מִשְׁמָר and the *sub-division* a בֵּית אָב.[32] At the same time this distinction is not necessarily involved in the signification of the words

---

[32] This distinction is specially noticeable in *Taanith* ii. 6, 7. Comp. further the passage quoted above, p. 182; also *Jer. Horajoth* iii. fol. 48[b]; and Tosefta, *Horajoth, fin.*, where it is stated that a ראש משמר is higher in point of rank than a ראש בית אב. Again, משמר is also met with in *Sukka* v. 6–8, *Taanith* iv. 2, and *Tamid* v. 1, undoubtedly in the sense of "main division," or "division for a week's service." But it is also to be similarly

themselves. For as מִשְׁמָר may mean any division for service,
so בֵית אָב, on the other hand, may mean any body composed of
the members of the same family, no matter whether they
consist of few persons or of many.[33]   Accordingly, as we have
just remarked, the author of the Book of Chronicles is still
found to be making use of בֵית אָבוֹת (in Neh. xii. 12 shortened
into אָבוֹת) as one of his expressions for denoting the main
divisions or courses.   But it would appear that somewhat later
the distinction referred to above came to be rigidly observed.
In Greek the term for one of the main divisions is πατριά or
ἐφημερία or ἐφημερίς, and for one of the sub-divisions φυλή.[34]

Then each of the divisions, the principal and subordinate
ones alike, was presided over by a *head*.   In the Old Testament the heads of the main divisions are designated שָׂרִים
(princes)[35] or רָאשִׁים (heads).[36]   At a subsequent period this
latter (רֹאשׁ הַמִּשְׁמָר) seems to have become the current designation, just as רֹאשׁ בֵּית אָב [37] came to be the one regularly employed
to denote the head of a sub-division.   Then, besides these,
we sometimes come across the term "elders" in this connection,
the זִקְנֵי כְהֻנָּה and the זִקְנֵי בֵית אָב.[38]

---

understood in *Bikkurim* iii. 12 ; *Jebamoth* xi. 7, *fin.* ; *Baba kamma* ix. 12 ;
*Temura* iii. 4, and *Para* iii. *fin.*   בֵית אָב, on the other hand, occurs in the
sense of a sub-division or a division for one day's service, in *Joma* iii. 9,
iv. 1 ; *Tamid* i. 1 ; *Middoth* i. 8.

[33] See Knobel-Dillmann, *Exegetisches Handbuch*, note on Ex. vi. 14 (p. 58).

[34] πατριά, Joseph. *Antt.* vii. 14. 7 ; ἐφημερία, Luke i. 5, 8 ; ἐφημερίς and
φυλή, Joseph. *Vita*, 1 (see the quotation given above, note 29).   We find
mention made of a φυλὴ Ἐνιαχείμ in Joseph. *Bell. Jud.* iv. 3. 8.

[35] שָׂרֵי הַכֹּהֲנִים, Ezra viii. 24, 29, x. 5 ; 2 Chron. xxxvi. 14.   שָׂרֵי קֹדֶשׁ,
1 Chron. xxiv. 5.   That those שָׂרִים are identical with the רָאשֵׁי אָבוֹת may
be seen, above all, from 1 Chron. xv. 4–12, where both expressions are
employed, as being perfectly synonymous, to denote the heads of the
Levitical divisions.

[36] רָאשִׁים לְבֵית־אָבוֹת, 1 Chron. xxiv. 4.   רָאשֵׁי הָאָבוֹת, Neh. xii. 12 ;
1 Chron. xxiv. 6.   Comp. also Neh. xi. 13, xii. 7.

[37] רֹאשׁ הַמִּשְׁמָר and רֹאשׁ בֵּית אָב, Tosefta, *Horajoth, fin.*, ed. Zuckermandel,
p. 476 ; and *Jer. Horajoth* iii. fol. 48b (the latter passage being given in
Ugolini, *Thesaurus*, xiii. 870).   רֹאשׁ הַמִּשְׁמָר also in the passage quoted
above, p. 182.   רֹאשׁ בֵּית אָב, *Joma* iii. 9, iv. 1.

[38] זִקְנֵי כְהֻנָּה, *Joma* i. 5.   זִקְנֵי בֵית אָב, *Tamid* i. 1 ; *Middoth* i. 8.

The *importance* and *influence* of the various divisions was by
no means alike.   Notwithstanding their formal equality, in so
far as they all took part in the services of the sanctuary in
regular rotation, still those divisions, from the members of
which high priests or other influential functionaries were
selected, could not fail to acquire, in consequence, a greater
amount of influence and importance.   Hence we can quite
believe that, as Josephus assures us, it was regarded as a great
advantage to belong to the first of the twenty-four classes,[39] *i.e.*
to the class Joiarib, which had the honour of contributing the
Asmonaean princes and high priests.[40]   Then we find that
within the individual classes again influential coteries were
formed.   The families living in Jerusalem would no doubt
understand how to secure for members of their own circle the
most important offices about the temple, knowing as they did
how much influence they conferred upon those who filled them.
But it was in the Roman period above all that the privileged
families from which the high priests were drawn (see p. 173,
above) were found to constitute a proud aristocracy, claiming
to occupy a rank much superior to that of the ordinary
priests.   The social difference between the one circle and the
other was so marked that, toward the close of the period just
preceding the destruction of the temple, the high priests could
even go the length of wresting the tithes from the other priests
by violence, these latter being left to starve.[41]   As a consequence of this disparity of rank, their political sympathies
were also so widely different that, at the outbreak of the revolution, the ordinary priests favoured this movement, whereas the
high priests did everything in their power to allay the storm.[42]

[39] *Vita*, 1 : πολλὴ δὲ κᾂν τούτῳ διαφορά = "there is a great advantage
also in this."

[40] One feels tempted to assume that the lists in Chronicles (1 Chron.
xxiv. 7–18) were not framed till the Asmonaean period.   For it is surely
very strange that it is precisely the class Joiarib, from which the Asmonaeans were sprung, that is here put prominently at the top, while in
the lists given in Nehemiah (xii. 1–7, 12–21) it occupies a somewhat
subordinate place.

[41] Joseph. *Antt.* xx. 8. 8, 9. 2.          [42] Joseph. *Bell. Jud.* ii. 17. 2–4.

We must be careful to distinguish between the priests properly so called and the *Levites*, a subordinate class of sacred officials.[43] It is true, no doubt, that this distinction is as yet unknown to the Book of Deuteronomy. There the Levites are all regarded as being as much entitled to share in the priestly functions as the rest, and " priests " and " Levites " are made use of simply as convertible terms (see especially, Deut. xviii. 5, xxi. 5 ; and generally, xvii. 9, 18, xviii. 1, xxiv. 8, xxvii. 9). The practice of distinguishing between the two orders is met with for the first time in Ezekiel ; and there can scarcely be a doubt that it was precisely this prophet who was the first to introduce it. According to the legislation of Deuteronomy, all places of worship outside Jerusalem were to be suppressed. At the same time the " Levites " who officiated in them, *i.e.* the priests, were not deprived of their rights as such ; all that was asked of them was that they should exercise their priestly functions exclusively in Jerusalem. This state of things however could hardly be expected to last long, In the first place it was too much to expect that the Jerusalem priests would long relish the idea of those colleagues from the provinces having the same right to officiate as themselves ; but apart from this, there was the fact that they had been guilty, to a larger extent than the priests of Jerusalem, of blending the service of strange gods with the worship of Jehovah. Consequently Ezekiel now proceeded to push the state of things brought about by the Deuteronomist to what seemed to be its legitimate result : he prohibited the Levites from beyond Jerusalem from celebrating worship altogether. This was now to be the exclusive privilege of the Levites of the house of Zadok, *i.e.* of the Jerusalem priests. Hereafter none but the sons of Zadok were " to offer the fat and the blood

[43] See in general, Winer's *Realwörterb.* ii. 20 ff.   Oehler's art. " Levi," in Herzog's *Real-Encycl.*, 1st ed. vol. viii. 347–358 (in the 2nd ed. it is revised by Orelli).   Graf, *Zur Geschichte des Stammes Levi*, in Merx' *Archiv*, vol. i. Idem, art. " Levi," in Schenkel's *Bibellexicon*, iv. 29–32.   Wellhausen, *Geschichte*, i. 123–156.   Smend, *Exeget. Handbuch zu Ezekiel*, pp. 360–362. Dillmann, *Exeget. Handbuch zu Exodus und Leviticus*, pp. 455–461.

before God," that is to say, none but these were to minister at the altar or cross the threshold of the inner sanctuary (the temple proper).    To the other Levites the more subordinate class of duties was assigned, viz. the keeping watch over the temple, the slaughtering of the victims, and such like.    An arrangement such as this had, at the same time, this further advantage, that it was now possible entirely to dispense with those Gentiles whom it had been necessary to employ for the purpose of performing the more menial services connected with the temple (see in general, Ezek. xliv. 6–16).    The order of things thus introduced by Ezekiel was the one that in all essential respects came to be permanently adopted.    The distinction which he had established between priests and the other Levites is treated in the code of the priests as one that had already come to be regularly recognised.    In this code the distinction between "the sons of Aaron," *i.e.* the priests, and the rest of the Levites, is rigidly observed.    According to its enactments it is only the former who are to enjoy the right of ministering at the altar and within the sanctuary itself (Num. xviii. 7).    The Levites, on the other hand, are merely to act as assistants to the sons of Aaron "in all the service of the tabernacle" (Num. xviii. 4).    Accordingly, what they are allowed and are called upon to do is to help the priests by performing a great many duties and services of the most varied character in connection with the temple, such as taking charge of the revenues and the sacred property, the bringing forward and preparing of all the different materials required for the celebration of worship, and others of a like nature (for more on this matter, see Part III.).    We also find that the duty of slaughtering and further preparing the victims was still assigned to them in later times precisely as it had been in that of Ezekiel.[44]    Only they were debarred from

---

[44] 2 Chron. xxix. 34, xxxv. 11.  Certainly from those passages one might infer that the Levites were called upon to assist in the slaughtering of the victims only in those instances in which a great many of them had to be dealt with.  As a rule the priests performed the act of slaughtering the

taking part in the ministrations at the altar and within the walls of the sanctuary (Num. xviii. 3 ; see in general, Num. iii. 5–13 and xviii. 1–7).

Then, like the priests, the *Levites* came to form a strictly exclusive order, the privilege of belonging to which was based upon natural descent. Their origin was now ascribed to Levi, one of the twelve patriarchs of Israel (Ex. vi. 17–25 ; Num. iii. 14–39, iv. 34–49, xxvi. 57–62 ; 1 Chron. v. 27– vi. 66, and xxiii.). Consequently in their case too as well as that of the priests it was birth that decided the claim to participation in the rights and functions of their order. The "priests" stood to them very much in the relation in which a privileged family stands to the whole stock to which it belongs. For the origin of the priestly order now came to be ascribed to Aaron, a great-grandson of Levi (Ex. vi. 17 ff.).[45]

But there is nothing that shows so plainly as just the history of the Levites itself how elastic and unsubstantial those genealogical theories were. In the post-exilic period, for example, we find that the "Levites," in the sense in which the term has been hitherto understood, were still *strictly distinguished* from the *musicians, doorkeepers* and *temple servants* (Nethinim, originally, at all events, slaves); this continues to be the case therefore not merely in the time of

victims themselves. However, the law even went so far as to allow laymen to undertake this duty. See Frankel, *Ueber den Einfluss der palästinischen Exegese auf die alexandrinische Hermeneutik* (1851), p. 134. Ritter's *Philo und die Halacha*, p. 110 ff.

[45] The genealogical derivation of the priests from Aaron is, in the first instance, merely a dogmatic postulate from which nothing whatever can be inferred with regard to the actual state of matters during the post-exilic period. Still it is undoubtedly a probable enough thing that, besides the "sons of Zadok," *i.e.* the old priestly families of Jerusalem, there were also a number of others who were not originally Jerusalem priests, who contrived to get their sacerdotal rights duly recognised. For the author of Chronicles, who traces the family of Zadok to Eleazar, Aaron's eldest son (1 Chron. vi. 4–12), derives a portion of the priests from Ithamar, another of Aaron's sons (1 Chron. xxiv. ; comp. Ezra viii. 2). These latter therefore were not Zadokites. Consequently we must assume that, *although Ezekiel's scheme was carried out in the main, still it was not so in every particular.* Comp. Wellhausen, *Die Pharisäer und die Sadducäer*, p. 48.

Zerubbabel, but also between eighty and a hundred years
later, viz. in the time of Ezra and Nehemiah (see especially
Ezra ii. 40–58 = Neh. vii. 43–60 ; further Ezra ii. 70, vii. 7,
24, x. 23, 24 ; Neh. vii. 1, 73, x. 29, 40, xii. 44–47, xiii.
5, 10). But gradually *the musicians and the doorkeepers*
came to be included among the " Levites " also. For example,
the circumstance of the musicians being now merged in the
Levites is presupposed in several remodelled portions of the
Book of Nehemiah.[46] Later on, a similar distinction seems
to have been accorded to the doorkeepers as well, for we
find the author of Chronicles taking special pains to let it
appear that both of the classes here in question belonged to
the order of the Levites, and also to show that they too were
descended from Levi.[47] The musicians again were afterwards
advanced a step higher still, in so far as, shortly before the
destruction of the temple, King Agrippa II., with the concurrence of the Sanhedrim, conferred upon them the privilege
of wearing linen robes similar to those worn by the priests.[48]

The *Levites*, like the priests, were also divided into *courses
of service*. But their history is involved in still greater obscurity
than that of the courses of the priests. Among those who
returned from exile with Zerubbabel and Joshua there were
but very few " Levites " in the stricter sense of the word, only

[46] Neh. xi. 15–19, 22, 23, xii. 8, 9, 24, 25, 27–29. Here the *musicians*
are uniformly regarded as belonging to the order of the Levites, while the
*doorkeepers*, on the other hand, are expressly excluded from it. Consequently the portions in question (Neh. xi., xii.) must have come down to
us in a revised form, representing a point of view intermediate between
the standpoint of the oldest sources of the Book of Nehemiah on the one
side, and that of the author of Chronicles on the other.

[47] On the inclusion of the *musicians* among the Levites, see 1 Chron.
xv. 16 ff., xxiii. 3–5 ; 2 Chron. xxix. 25, and elsewhere. For the doorkeepers again, see 1 Chron. ix. 26, xv. 18, 23, 24, xxiii. 3–5. Further, for
the tracing of their descent from Levi, particularly in the case of the three
families of musicians, Heman, Asaph and Ethan, see 1 Chron. vi. 16–32 ;
but for the same in the case of the doorkeepers as well, at least to
a certain extent, viz. through Obed Edom, see Graf in Merx' *Archiv*, i.
230–232. However, it is still the practice in the Chronicles as well to
distinguish between the *Nethinim* and the Levites, 1 Chron. ix. 2.

[48] Joseph. *Antt* xx. 9. 6.

seventy-four in all ; while in addition to these there were 128
singers and 139 doorkeepers (Ezra ii. 40–42, the numbers in
the corresponding passage, Neh. vii. 43–45, diverging somewhat from those just given).    Then at length when Ezra came
he managed to bring with him only thirty-eight " Levites," and
even these could be persuaded to accompany him only after
serious expostulation (Ezra viii. 15–20).    The disinclination
to return thus shown by the Levites was owing to the subordinate place that had now been assigned them.    It may be
safely assumed however that those who did return would ere
long receive considerable accessions to their ranks from those
of their order that had never left their native country.    For
there cannot be a doubt that, as the " Levites    lived scattered
all over the land, far fewer of them, comparatively speaking,
were carried into captivity than of the " priests," by whom
at that time only the priests of Jerusalem were meant.    And
hence we are enabled to account for the fact that, in the
catalogue of Levites and singers in the time of Zerubbabel
and Joshua as given in Neh. xii. 8, we find a few more
families than are to be met with in the catalogue of those
who returned with Zerubbabel (Ezra ii. 40 f. ; Neh. vii. 43 f.).[49]
In a list belonging to the time of Ezra and Nehemiah seventeen families of Levites in the stricter sense of the word are
already enumerated (Neh. x. 10–14 and Bertheau's note).
In another, probably referring, like the former, to the
time of Nehemiah as well,[50] it is only the number of the
Levites dwelling in Jerusalem that is given, inclusive of
course of the singers, and it estimates that there were 284
of them (Neh. xi. 15–18).    It is to be presumed that the
number of those who lived beyond the city, in the towns
and villages of Judaea, would be considerably larger (Neh.
xi. 20, 36).[51]    It would appear that, in the time of the author

[49] See Bertheau's note, p. 251, of his *Exeget. Handbuch* to Nehemiah.
[50] On the period to which this list refers, see Bertheau's *Exeget. Handbuch* to Chronicles, p. 99 ; to Nehemiah, p. 248.
[51] The number of *priests* living in Jerusalem is stated in this same list

of Chronicles, the division into twenty-four classes was not confined to the priests, but had been adopted in the case of the Levites as well. This writer, although including the musicians and doorkeepers among the Levites, nevertheless distinguishes between three leading groups: the Levites who did service about the temple generally, then the musicians, and lastly the doorkeepers (1 Chron. xxiii. 3–5). He then proceeds in 1 Chron. xxiii. 6–24 to give, in the case of the Levites or first group, a list of the houses of their fathers (בית אבות), which, after one or two corrections have been made, probably amount to twenty-four.[52] As for the musicians again, he expressly divides them into twenty-four classes or courses (1 Chron. xxv.). With regard to the post-Biblical period we have testimony to the effect that at that time the division now in question had been regularly established in the case of the Levites generally, so that, in fact, each class of priests had now its corresponding class or course of Levites.[53] As in the case of the priests, so also in that of

to have been 1192 (Neh. xi. 10–14), while the aggregate number then living throughout the whole land is estimated at 6000 (according to Ezra ii. 36–39 and viii. 2; comp. p. 217, above). With regard to the Levites, on the other hand, we may venture to assume that formerly the proportion of those living beyond Jerusalem to those living within it was much greater still. In any case the number of the Levites in the stricter sense of the word must have exceeded that of the singers and doorkeepers. For when the author of Chronicles tells us that in David's time there were 24,000 Levites properly so called, and 4000 singers, and 4000 doorkeepers (1 Chron. xxiii. 4, 5), we may assume that the relative proportions of those numbers must have pretty nearly corresponded with what actually existed in the writer's own day, however much the absolute numbers themselves may have been exaggerated.

[52] See Bertheau's note on the passage. To the family of Gerson are assigned nine houses of their fathers, to that of Kahat nine also, and to that of Merari probably six, if, that is to say, we supply from xxiv. 26, 27 the three missing houses of Schoham, Sakkur and Ibri, and erase from xxiii. 23 the name Mahli which occurs twice in the list.

[53] Joseph. Antt. vii. 14. 7: ἐποίησε δὲ καὶ τῆς Λευίτιδος φυλῆς εἴκοσι μέρη καὶ τέσσαρα, καὶ κληρωσαμένων κατὰ τὸν αὐτὸν ἀνέβησαν τρόπον ταῖς τῶν ἱερέων ἐφημερίσιν ἐπὶ ἡμέρας ὀκτώ. Taanith iv. 2: "The earliest prophets established twenty-four courses of service (משמרות). To each belonged a staff (מעמד) in Jerusalem, composed of priests, Levites and Israelites. As

the Levites, each of the various divisions or courses was presided over by a head (שָׂרִים or רָאשִׁים).[54]

The question as to where the priests and Levites *resided* is one with regard to which we have very little information of a reliable kind; for we must here entirely dismiss from view the legislation with reference to the forty-eight Levitical cities, which never was more than a mere theory (Num. xxxv.; Josh. xxi.). One thing however is certain, and that is, that under the new order of things that obtained subsequent to the exile, only a fraction of the priests and Levites lived in Jerusalem itself, while the rest were scattered over the towns and villages of Judaea, the majority of them being probably within a short distance of the capital and the centre of worship. In the list in Neh. xi. 10–19, to which reference has been already made, the number of priests who lived in Jerusalem is stated to have been 1192,[55] that of the Levites and musicians 284, and that of the doorkeepers 172. But the sum-total of the whole priests of the land amounted to something like five times that number, if not more (see note 51), while in the case of the other categories the proportion of those living beyond the city to those within it may have been greater still. In any case, the general fact that priests as well as Levites had their residences in the towns and villages of Judaea is confirmed by repeated and unquestionable testimony.[56] But we are left with little or no information with respect to details.[57]

soon as its turn to serve came round to a course, the priests and Levites belonging to it proceeded to Jerusalem, but the Israelites assembled in the synagogues of their different towns and there read the account of the creation."

[54] שרים, 1 Chron. xv. 4–12 ; 2 Chron. xxxv. 9.   ראשים, Neh. xii. 22, 23 ; 1 Chron. ix. 33, 34, xv. 12, xxiii. 24, xxiv. 6, 31. The divisions whose heads are here in question are, of course, separate and distinct from each other.

[55] The parallel passage, 1 Chron. ix. 10-13, puts it at a somewhat higher figure.

[56] Ezra ii. 70; Neh. vii. 73, xi. 3, 20, 36 ; 2 Chron. xxxi. 15, 19.

[57] A number of places where musicians had settled are mentioned in Neh. xii. 27–29. The Maccabees came from Modein (1 Macc. ii. 1), Zacharias the priest lived in the hill country of Judah (Luke i. 39).

## II. THE EMOLUMENTS.

The emoluments which the priests received from the people for their subsistence were, down to the time of the exile, of a very modest and rather precarious kind. But subsequent to this latter period they were augmented almost beyond measure. This fact enables us to see, in a peculiarly striking manner, what a vast increase of power and influence the priesthood had acquired through the new order of things that was introduced subsequent to the exile.[58] And this increase of power was, no doubt, the *cause* of the loftier pretensions of the order, just as, on the other hand, it was in turn also the *effect* of the augmenting of the temporalities. Nor was it ever in the power of the scribes, who came after and who in themselves were not always favourably disposed toward the priests, to do anything in the way of altering this state of matters, now that the priestly law had been for so long the acknowledged law of God. Nay, it was for this very reason that the scribes only found themselves in the position of contributing towards the yet further increase of the priests' emoluments. For proceeding as they did on the view that a man always secured for himself the divine approval in proportion to the punctuality and readiness with which he conformed to the requirements of the law, they almost invariably interpreted its prescriptions in a sense favourable to the priests. And so we have the singular spectacle of an age that had already begun to regard the priests with distrust, helping nevertheless to confirm and increase their power.

In the times previous to the exile there were as yet almost *no imposts in the strict sense* of the word at all, that is to say, none which were not connected with sacrifice, none which

According to Origen, Bethphage was a village where priests lived, *Comment. in Matt.* vol. xvi. cap. xvii. (Lommatzsch, iv. 52): ἑρμηνεύεσθαι δέ φαμεν τὴν Βηθφαγὴ μὲν οἶκον σιαγόνων, ἥτις τῶν ἱερέων ἦν χωρίον.

[58] For a correct appreciation of these matters we are indebted first and foremost to the modern criticism of the Pentateuch. See especially, Wellhausen's *Geschichte Israels*, i. 156–164.

had the character of a pure tax. Allowances to the priests were only exacted on the occasion of sacrifices being offered, and only in connection with these. The person who came to sacrifice brought the choicest portions of the produce of his fields and the first-born of his cattle to offer to Jehovah. Of this one part was consumed upon the altar, another fell to the officiating priest, but the most of it was made use of by the offerer himself, who was required to hold a sacrificial feast with it in the presence of Jehovah. It is in this sense that we are to understand the requirement already met with in *the earliest (Jehovistic) legislation,* to the effect that the best of the produce of the field and the first-born of the cattle were to be brought before Jehovah (firstlings of the field, Ex. xxii. 28, xxiii. 19, xxxiv. 26; the first-born of the cattle, Ex. xiii. 11–16, xxii. 29, xxxiv. 19, 20).[58a] The prescriptions in *Deuteronomy* bearing on this matter are perfectly plain and unequivocal. This book knows nothing whatever either of the exacting of the tithe, or of the first-born on the part of the priests. It was required no doubt that the tithe of the fruits of the field was to be separated and conveyed to Jerusalem to the sanctuary. But there it was not given to the priest, but consumed by the owner of it himself; and it was only every third year that it fell to the Levites, *i.e.* the priests, and to the poor (Deut. xiv. 22–29, xxvi. 12–15; comp. also xii. 6, 11, 17–19). It was precisely the same in the case of the firstlings of the sheep and oxen. These too, and that such of them as were males, were required to be brought to the sanctuary at Jerusalem, but they were consumed there by the owner himself in sacrificial feasts (Deut. xv. 19–23; comp. also xii. 6, 17–19, xiv. 23). Of all the things here mentioned the priests received only certain portions, that is to say, of the fruits of the field that were presented they got only the רֵאשִׁית, *i.e.* the best (Deut. xviii. 4, xxvi. 1–11),

---

[58a] The more subtle point as to whether Ex. xiii. 11–16 and xxxiv. 19, 20 belong to the Jehovist himself or were inserted by a kindred spirit, may here be left an open question. For the latter view, see Wellhausen, *Jahrbücher für deutsche Theol.* 1876, pp. 542 ff., 553 ff.; for the former, see Dillmann, *Exeget. Handbuch* to Ex. and Lev. pp. 99, 334.

while of the animals offered, they got merely the shoulder, the two cheeks and the stomach of each (Deut. xviii. 3). Beyond this there is no mention of anything else that was required to be given to the priest except a part of the fleece at the sheep-shearing (Deut. xviii. 4). As corroborative of what we have been saying we would point to the prescriptions of Ezekiel (xliv. 28–30). Although a priest himself and showing an undoubted disposition to favour rather than to discourage the pretensions of his order, still he says quite as little about a tithe and the first-born being required to be given to the priests. The claims he makes on behalf of these latter are no doubt somewhat higher than those of Deuteronomy, still, on the whole, they move on the same lines. While Deuteronomy assigns to the priests only two portions of the victims, Ezekiel requires the whole of the sin-offerings and trespass-offerings (which as yet are quite unknown to Deuteronomy) to be given to them, and similarly with regard to the meat-offerings as well (Ezek. xliv. 29); also every " dedicated thing " (xliv. 29); and lastly, the reshith, *i.e.* the best of the first-fruits, the choicest portions of offerings of every description, and of the dough in baking (xliv. 30).

But we find a considerable advance upon all the exactions we have just been referring to when we come to those contained in the *priest-code*, which, in its enumeration of the various emoluments of the priests as given in Num. xviii. 8–32, coincides in many respects with Ezekiel, only it introduces in addition what constitutes a most important innovation, the tithe and the first-born. Like Ezekiel, the priest-code also assigns the sin-offerings, the trespass-offerings and the meat-offerings, at least the greater portion of the latter, to the priests (Num. xviii. 9, 10; for fuller details, see Lev. i.-vii.). Of those sacrifices which their owners themselves were at liberty to make use of in furnishing the sacrificial feast (the so-called זִבְחֵי שְׁלָמִים), the priests were to get the breast and the right shoulder (Lev. vii. 30–34), thus obtaining considerably choicer portions than those assigned to them in Deuteronomy.

Again, as in Ezekiel so also in the priest-code, the priests
are to get everything " dedicated " (Num. xviii. 14), and the
choicest portions (the reshith) of the produce of the soil: the
oil, the wine and the wheat (Num. xviii. 12). But to the
reshith, the first-fruits, בִּכּוּרִים, are further added (Num.
xviii. 13) as an impost of a different sort; then, in the last
place, comes the most important item of all, one that considerably exceeded in value all the former ones, viz. the tithe
(Num. xviii. 20–32) and the first-born (Num. xviii. 15–18).
The tithe however belonged, in the first instance, to the
" Levites," who in turn were required to pay a tenth part of
it to the priests. With regard to the portion of the dough
that was to be given to the priests, though omitted in the
leading enumeration of the emoluments, it too is mentioned
in the priest-code, but in a different place (Num. xv. 17–21).
We find that in Nehemiah's day those enactments were already
in full force. According to Neh. x. 36–40, it was already the
practice at that time for the priests to receive the first-fruits
or bikkurim (x. 36), the choicest portions of the fruits of the
soil, which here, precisely as in the priest-code, are clearly
distinguished alike from the first-fruits and the tithe (x. 38),
then the tithe after the manner described in the priest-code
(x. 38–40), then the first-born (x. 37), and lastly, the portion
of the dough (x. 38). By the tithe here we are always to
understand the tithe of the fruits of the ground and of the
trees. But there is *one* passage in the priest-code where, in
addition to the tithe just mentioned, that of the cattle is also
exacted (Lev. xxvii. 32, 33). But it may well be presumed
that this requirement, standing there as it does in so entirely
isolated a fashion, did not originally form part of the code.[59]
It would seem that the tithe of the cattle was actually exacted
and paid in the time of the author of Chronicles; or possibly
we have only to regard it as forming part of this writer's
conceptions of what ought to be (2 Chron. xxxi. 6). In post-

[59] See Wellhausen, *Jahrb. für deutsche Theol.* 1877, p. 444; also his
*Geschichte Israels*, i. 162.

Biblical times the whole passage, Lev. xxvii. 30–33, has been understood as referring to a tithe in the sense of the one demanded by Deuteronomy.

The legal prescriptions of Deuteronomy and of the priests' code have not only been blended together so as to form one whole in a literary sense, but they would also appear to have been combined with each other in actual practice. Consequently we find that the *law in its later developments* has considerably augmented the already heavy imposts of the priest-code. With the Levites' tithe of this code there was now conjoined, and simply as " *a second tithe*," the one prescribed in Deuteronomy, and which was to be consumed by the owner himself before Jehovah. The discrepancy between the prescriptions of the code and those of Deuteronomy, with respect to the portions of the victims that were to be given to the priests, was now got rid of by regarding the former as referring exclusively to the victims offered in sacrifice, and the latter to such animals as were slaughtered for ordinary use. Of the former of these the priests, according to Lev. vii. 30–34, were to receive the breast and the right shoulder, while of the latter they were to get, according to Deut. xviii. 3, a fore-leg, the cheeks, and the stomach. Lastly, to all the imposts of the priest-code there was further added the portion of the fleece at the sheep-shearing as prescribed in Deuteronomy (xviii. 4). From this process of amalgamation there resulted the following list of the priests' emoluments, which we may venture to regard as the one that was in force in the time of Christ.[60]

[60] Philo already gives us a synopsis in his treatise, entitled *De praemiis sacerdotum et honoribus* (*Opp.* ed. Mangey, ii. 232–237) ; comp. besides, Ritter's *Philo und die Halacha*, 1879, pp. 114–126. Further, Josephus in the leading passage on the subject, *Antt.* iv. 4. 4, with which iii. 9. 1–4 (sacrificial offerings) and iv 8. 22 (firstlings) may be compared. The Rabbinical writers, according to an artificial system of reckoning, represent the various sources of the priests' emoluments as having amounted to twenty-four in all ; see Tosefta, *Challa* ii. 7–9 (ed. Zuckermandel) ; *Jer. Challa* iv. *fin.* fol. 60b ; *Bab. Baba kamma* 110b , *Chullin* 133b ; *Pesikta* in Ugolini's *Thesaurus*, vol. xiii. pp. 1122–1128. Several of the twenty-four in

(I.) Of the *victims* the following portions fell to the priests:
—(1) The *sin-offerings* in their entirety, at least as a rule,
for only two, and that of a particular sort, were required to
be burnt without the camp.[61] (2) The trespass-offerings in
their entirety also.[62] In both instances it was only the fat
that was burnt upon the altar, the flesh belonged to the
priests. (3) Of the *meat-offerings* again they got by far the
larger portion, for as a rule only a small part of it was
reserved to burn upon the altar, while the rest fell to the
priests.[63] All the sacrifices we have just mentioned were of
very frequent occurrence, particularly the meat-offerings, which
might not only be offered independently by themselves, but
which also formed a necessary accompaniment to the majority
of the animal sacrifices.[63a] To the same category we have
further to refer (4) the twelve cakes of *shewbread*, a fresh
supply of which was placed in the temple every week, while

question are already enumerated in Mishna, *Challa* iv. 9. For the Talmudic
passages, see also Reland's *Antiquitates sacrae*, ii. 4. 11, in Bernard's edition
of Josephus, note on *Antt.* iv. 4. 4, and in Havercamp's edition, note on the
same passage ; and for a German rendering of them, Saalschütz, *Das mosaische
Recht*, i. 351. Among modern writers the most complete and most correct
lists comparatively speaking are given by Saalschütz, *Das mosaische Recht*,
i. 343–353, and Haneberg, *Die religiösen Alterthümer der Bibel*, pp. 565–582.
Authentic material also in Ugolini's *Thesaurus*, vol. xiii. 1055–1129.

[61] Lev. v. 13, vi. 19, 22 f. ; Num. xviii. 9, 10 ; Ezek. xliv. 29. Joseph.
*Antt.* iii. 9. 3. *Sifra* to Lev. vi. 19 ff., in Ugolini's *Thesaurus*, vol. xiii. p.
1071 ff. For the sin- and trespass-offerings generally, see Lev. iv.-vii.
Winer's *Realwörterb.* ii. pp. 429–435.

[62] Lev. vii. 6, 7 ; Num. xviii. 9, 10 ; Ezek. xliv. 29. Joseph. *Antt.*
iii. 9. 3 ; *Sifra* to Lev. vii. 6, 7, in Ugolini's *Thesaurus*, xiii. 1078.

[63] Lev. ii. 3, 10, vi. 9–11, vii. 9, 10, 14, x. 12, 13 ; Num. xviii. 9, 10 ;
Ezek. xliv. 29. Joseph. *Antt.* iii. 9. 4: τὴν δὲ λοιπὴν οἱ ἱερεῖς πρὸς τροφὴν
λαμβάνουσιν, ἢ ἑψηθεῖσαν (ἐλαίῳ γὰρ συμπεφύραται) ἢ γενομένων ἄρτων. On
the meat-offerings generally, see Lev. ii. the whole chapter, and vi. 7–11,
also Winer's *Realwörterb.* under the word.

[63a] If we want to form some idea of the frequency of many of those
sacrifices, we have only to read the laws relating to Levitical defilement and
the mode of treating it with a view to its removal (Lev. xi.–xv. ; Num. xix.).
For example, *every woman after childbirth* had to offer a lamb as a burnt-
offering and a pigeon as a sin-offering, or in the event of her being too
poor for this, one pigeon as a burnt-offering and another as a sin-offering,
Lev. xii. 1–8 ; Luke ii. 24.

that which was taken away became the property of the priests.[64] All the four classes of offerings now mentioned were " most holy," and as such could only be consumed in a *holy place*, *i.e.* within the inner court of the temple, and exclusively by the priests themselves (and not by their relations as well).[65]

The regulations were not so stringent with regard to the two following offerings, viz. (5) the *thank-offerings* and (6) the *burnt-offerings*.    Of the former, the זִבְחֵי שְׁלָמִים, *i.e.* those offerings which were consumed by the offerers themselves, and by Luther rendered " Dankopfer," or as it should rather be " Mahlopfer," the priests received two parts of each, viz. the breast and the right shoulder.    These might be eaten in any " *clean place*," and therefore not within the sanctuary as in the previous instances, and that not by the priest alone, but by all who were connected with the priestly order as well, even by their wives and daughters.[66]    Lastly, of the burnt-offerings (6), the priests received comparatively speaking least of all, for they were entirely consumed upon the altar.    But even of these they got the skins at least, and, considering how frequently sacrifices of this sort were offered, it was certainly not without good reason that Philo estimated the amount of revenue from this source also as something very considerable.[67]

---

[64] Lev. xxiv. 5-9; for the *Sifra* to this as also the other Rabbinical passages, see Ugolini's *Thesaurus*, vol. xiii. p. 1084 ff.; see also Joseph. *Antt.* iii. 10. 7; Matt. xii. 4 ; Mark ii. 26 ; Luke vi. 4.  For the principle on which they were divided, see *Sukka* v. 7, 8 (the retiring course of service got the one half and the incoming one the other half).

[65] Num. xviii. 10 and the passages cited in the preceding notes; also Joseph. *Antt.* iv. 4. 4, *fin.*

[66] Lev. vii. 30-34, x. 14, 15.  *Sifra* to Lev. vii. 30-34, in Ugolini's *Thes.* vol. xiii. p. 1094 ff.  Philo, *De praemiis sacerdotum*, sec. iii. (ed. Mang. ii. 234): παντὸς γὰρ ἱερείου προστέτακται δύο τοῖς ἱερεῦσιν ἀπὸ δυοῖν δίδοσθαι μελῶν, βραχίονα μὲν ἀπὸ χειρὸς δεξιᾶς, ἀπὸ δὲ τοῦ στήθους ὅσον πῖον. Joseph. *Antt.* iii. 9. 2 : τὸ δὲ στῆθος καὶ τὴν κνήμην τὴν δεξιὰν τοῖς ἱερεῦσι παρασχόντες.  On the peace-offerings generally, see Lev. iii. the whole chapter, vii. 11-21, 28-34.  Winer's *Realwörterb.*, art. " Dankopfer."

[67] Lev. vii. 8 ; the *Sifra* thereto in Ugolini's *Thes.* vol. xiii. p. 1079. Mishna, *Sebachim* xii. 2-4.  Tosefta, *Sebachim* (or *Korbanoth*) xi. 7 ff. in Ugolini's *Thes.* xiii. 1080 ff.  Philo, *De praemiis sacerdotum*, sec. iv. (Mang.

II. But considerable as the amount derived from those offerings no doubt was, still it formed but the smaller portion of the sacerdotal revenues, while for the most part it was only available for the officiating priests.   The real bulk of the priests' emoluments, on the other hand, consisted strictly speaking of what was derived from *those dues that were paid independently of the sacrifices altogether,* and which consequently possessed the character of a genuine tax for the maintenance of the priesthood.   These dues were levied partly upon the produce of the soil and partly upon the offspring of the cattle, and they had to be paid partly in kind, although in some instances they might also be ransomed for their equivalent in money.   The dues derived from the *produce of the soil* were of a varied character, and had to be separated (with a view to payment) in the following order:[68] (1) The *first-fruits,* בִּכּוּרִים.   These offerings were taken from the so-called "seven kinds," *i.e.* from the principal products of the soil of Palestine as enumerated in Deuteronomy (viii. 8), viz. wheat, barley, vines, fig-trees, pomegranates, olives and honey. Those who lived in the vicinity of Jerusalem offered fresh fruits, while those living farther away brought them in a dried form.   In going up to present their offerings the people went in common procession, and according to Philo and the Mishna it was made an occasion of merry-making.   It was the practice for those living in the country to assemble in the principal towns of the districts to which they belonged and thence to go up to Zion in one merry company, marching to the music of the pipes.   At the head of the procession was led the ox that was to form the festive offering, with its horns gilded and a garland of olive branches placed upon them.   In Jerusalem the most eminent members of the priesthood came

ii. 235): Ἐφ' ἅπασι μέντοι καὶ τὰς τῶν ὁλοκαυτωμάτων, ἀμύθητα δὲ ταῦτ' ἐστί, δορὰς προστάττει τοὺς ὑπηρετοῦντας ταῖς θυσίαις ἱερεῖς λαμβάνειν, οὐ βραχεῖαν ἀλλ' ἐν τοῖς μάλιστα πολυχρήματον δωρεάν. Josephus, *Antt.* iii. 9. 1. Ritter's *Philo und die Halacha,* p. 126.   On the burnt-offerings generally, see Lev. i. 3–17.   Winer's *Realwörterb.* under the word " Brandopfer."

[68] On the order to be observed, see *Terumoth* iii. 6, 7.

to meet the procession as it approached the sanctuary. The owners of the offerings then put wreaths round the baskets containing the first-fruits and carried them on their shoulders up the temple mount as far as the court. This was done even by the most distinguished personages; it had been done even by King Agrippa himself. As soon as the procession entered the court the Levites welcomed it with the singing of the thirtieth Psalm. And now each person proceeded to hand his basket to the priest, and as he did so, repeated the confession of Deut. xxvi. 5–10, whereupon the priest took it and put it down beside the altar.[69]    (2) Then came *the so-called terumah* (תְּרוּמָה). This was distinct from the first-fruits, and in so far as the offering of these latter had always rather more of a symbolico-religious significance, it hardly could be said to have belonged to quite the same category with them. The terumah possessed the character of a pure payment in kind toward the maintenance of the priests, for Rabbinical Judaism understands it in the more restricted sense of the term (terumah in the more comprehensive sense of the word meaning every " heave " whatsoever, *i.e.* everything paid to the sanctuary) as denoting *the giving of the choicest of the fruits of the ground and of the trees* to the priests. This impost was levied not only upon the " seven kinds," but upon every species of fruit, and that whether the fruits of the ground or the fruit of trees. Here as before the most important of them were wheat, wine, and oil. The amount to be given was not regulated by any

[69] See in general, Num. xviii. 13 ; Neh. x. 36 ; also Ex. xxiii. 19, xxxiv. 26. To this matter Deut. xxvi. 1-11 was referred. Joseph. *Antt.* iv. 8. 22. In the Mishna the entire tractate *Bikkurim* is devoted to the subject of first-fruits. Comp. especially, *Bikkurim* i. 3 (regarding the " seven kinds " to be offered), and iii. 1–9 (account of the festive procession). Philo treats of this matter in his small work, *De festo cophini*, first edited by Cardinal Mai, and given in Richter's edition of Philo's works, v. 48–50 ; also in Tischendorf's *Philonea* (1868), pp. 69–71. Of the works given under the literature we would specially mention, Lundius, *Die alten jüdischen Heiligthümer*, book iii. chap. liv. Ugolini's *Thes.* vol. iii. p. 1100 ff. Winer's *Realwörterb.*, art. " Erstlinge." Saalschütz, i. 344 f. Haneberg, pp. 565–568. Grätz, *Monatsschrift für Geschichte und Wissensch. des Judenth.* 1877, p. 433 ff.

fixed measure, weight, or number,[70] but was to be, on an average, one-fiftieth of the whole yield, the person who gave one-fortieth being regarded as giving liberally, while he who gave only one-sixtieth was considered to have given somewhat stingily.[71] Whatever had once been set apart as a terumah could be lawfully made use of only by the priests.[72]   (3) After the materials of the two classes of offerings we have just mentioned had been duly separated, the largest and most important item of all now fell to be deducted, viz. the *tithe*. We know, from what the Gospels tell us, with what painful scrupulosity the prescriptions of the law in regard to this matter were observed, and how common it was to pay tithe even of the most insignificant and worthless objects, such as mint, anise, and cummin (Matt. xxiii.; Luke xi. 42). The principle laid down in the Mishna with respect to this is as follows: "Everything which may be used as food and is cultivated and grows out of the earth is liable to tithe." [73]   The

---

[70] *Terumoth* i. 7.

[71] *Terumoth* iv. 3.   Comp. Jerome's com. on Ezek. xliv. 13, 14 (*Opp.* ed. Vallarsi, v. 565): At vero primitiva quae de frugibus offerebant, non erant speciali numero definita, sed offerentium arbitrio derelicta.   Traditionemque accepimus Hebraeorum non lege praeceptam, sed magistrorum arbitrio molitam: qui plurimum, *quadragesimam partem* dabat sacerdotibus, qui minimum, *sexagesimam:* inter quadragesimam et sexagesimam licebat offerre quodcumque voluissent.

[72] See in general, Num. xviii. 12; Neh. x. 38.   The Rabbinical regulations in the tractate *Terumoth*.   Philo, *De praemiis sacerdotum*, sec. i. (Mang. ii. p. 233): προστάττει καὶ ἀπὸ τῆς ἄλλης κτήσεως ἀπάρχεσθαι, καθ' ἑκάστην μὲν ληνὸν οἶνον, καθ' ἑκάστην δὲ ἅλωνα σῖτον καὶ κριθάς.   Ὁμοίως δὲ ἐξ ἐλαιῶν ἔλαιον καὶ ἀπὸ τῶν ἄλλων ἀκροδρύων ἡμέρους καρπούς (that it is the terumah that Philo has in view here has also been correctly assumed by Richter in his *Philo und die Halacha*).   Joseph. *Antt.* iv. 4. 4: ἔτι δὲ ἀπαρχὰς τὸν λαὸν δίκαιον τῷ θεῷ πάντων τῶν ἐκ τῆς γῆς φυομένων καρπῶν ἐπιφέρειν.   Comp. also Lundius, *Die alten jüdischen Heiligthümer*, book iv. chap. xxxi.   Winer's *Realwörterb.*, art. "Erstlinge."   Saalschütz, i. 346.   Haneberg, p. 568 f.

[73] *Maaseroth* i. 1.   For details, comp. for example *Maaseroth* iv 5, 6, v. 8.   Lightfoot, *Horae hebr.*, note on Matt. xxiii. 23 (*Opp.* ii. 359).   Wetzstein, *Nov. Test.*, note on the same passage.   On the tithing of anise (ἄνηθον, שֶׁבֶת), see *Maaseroth* iv. 5; on that of cummin (κύμινον, כַּמֹּן), *Demai* ii. 1.

revenue derived from the source now in question must have been very large indeed. Yet the greater proportion of it was intended not so much for the priests as for the more subordinate class of sacred officials, viz. the *Levites*. It was to these latter, in the first instance, that the tithe had to be paid, while they had in turn to hand over a tithe of that again to the priests.[74] After separating this Levites' tithe from his produce, the owner had to deduct another one still, *the so-called second tithe*. But this, in common with several other imposts of a similar kind, was made use of by the owner himself in the way of furnishing a sacrificial feast at Jerusalem; consequently they were not for the benefit of the priests, and so do not fall to be considered here.[75]    (4) Then the last of the offerings taken

[74] See in general, Num. xviii. 20–32 ; Neh. x. 38–40.    Philo, *De caritate*, sec. x. (ed. Mang. ii. 391) ; *De praemiis sacerdot.* sec. vi. ; probably it is also the tithe that is in view in sec. ii. *init.* of the same treatise. Joseph. *Antt.* iv. 4. 3, 4.    The Rabbinical prescriptions in *Maaseroth.* Hottinger, *De decimis Judaeorum*, Lugd. Bat. 1713.    Lundius, *Die alten jüd. Heiligthümer*, book iv. chap. xxxii.    Winer's *Realwörterb.*, art. " Zehnt." Saalschütz, i. 346 f.    Haneberg, pp. 573–576.    Leyrer in Herzog's *Real-Enc.*, 1st ed. vol. xviii. 414–421.    Ritter, *Philo und die Halacha*, pp. 122–124.    Knobel-Dillmann, *Exeget. Handbuch*, note on Lev. xxvii. 30–33 (also at the same place for the instances of a similar practice among the heathen).

[75] To the category of imposts that were consumed by the owner himself at Jerusalem belong—

(1) The " *second tithe*," according to Deut. xiv. 22–26. Lev. xxvii. 30, 31 was likewise understood in this sense.    Comp. Tob. i. 7 ; Joseph. *Antt.* iv. 8. 8.    In the Mishna see the whole tractate *Maaser sheni.*    Hottinger, *De decimis Judaeorum*, pp. 146–182 (*Exercit.* vii.).    Lundius, *Die alten jüd. Heiligthümer*, iv. 33.    Winer's *Realwörterb.*, art. " Zehnt."    Saalschütz, i. pp. 169, 354–358.    Leyrer in Herzog's *Real-Enc.*, 1st ed. vol. xviii. p. 417 f. Those living at a distance from Jerusalem were allowed to convert the second tithe into money on the understanding that one-fifth of its money value was to be superadded to it (Lev. xxvii. 31 ; *Maaser sheni* iv. 3). But this money had to be spent exclusively in the purchase of such viands, beverages, and ointment as were necessary for the sacrificial feast at Jerusalem (Deut. xiv. 26 ; *Maaser sheni* ii. 1).

(2) The *tithe of the cattle.*    The only passage in the Pentateuch which requires the *cattle* to be tithed, viz. Lev. xxvii. 32, 33, was expressly understood by the later legislation in the sense of the " second tithe," and that being the case, it follows that the cattle tithe would also be devoted to the furnishing of the feasts in Jerusalem. See *Sebachim* v. 8.    Bartenora

from the products of the soil was the so-called *challah* (חַלָּה),
*i.e.* the offering from the kneaded dough (ἀπαρχὴ τοῦ

and Maimonides on *Bechoroth* ix. 1 (in Surenhusius' edition of the *Mishna*,
v. 187). At the same time, Philo would seem to include the cattle tithe
also among the priests' emoluments, *De caritate*, sec. x. (Mang. ii. 391) ;
*De praemiis sacerdotum*, sec. ii. *init.* (where the tithe is probably meant).
Comp. Ritter's *Philo und die Halacha*, p. 122 f. For a fuller account of
the matter, see Mishna, *Bechoroth* ix. 1–8 ; also *Maaser sheni* i. 2 ; *Shekalim* i. 7, iii. 1, viii. 8 ; *Rosh hashana* i. 1 ; *Chagiga* i. 4 ; *Sebachim* v. 8,
x. 3 ; *Manachoth* ix. 6 ; *Chullin* i. 7. Hottinger, *De decimis Judaeorum*,
pp. 228–253 (*Exercit.* x.). Lundius, *Die alt. jüd. Heiligth.* book iv. chap.
xxxviii.

(3) The *produce of trees and vines in the fourth year of their growth.*
According to Lev. xix. 23–25, the fruit of newly-planted trees (and vines)
was not to be gathered at all during the first three years, while in the
fourth it was to be consecrated to God, as it was not to be at the free
disposal of the owner of it till the fifth year. In later times this was taken
to mean that the produce of the fourth year was, like the second tithe, to
be consumed by the owner himself in Jerusalem. See especially, Joseph.
*Antt.* iv. 8. 19 : τῷ δὲ τετάρτῳ τρυγάτω πᾶν τὸ γενόμενον (τότε γὰρ ὥριον
εἶναι) καὶ συναγαγὼν εἰς τὴν ἱερὰν πόλιν κομιζέτω, καὶ σὺν τῇ δεκάτῃ τοῦ
ἄλλου καρποῦ μετὰ τῶν φίλων εὐωχούμενος ἀναλισκέτω καὶ μετ'
ὀρφανῶν καὶ χηρευουσῶν γυναικῶν. Comp. also Philo, *De caritate*, sec. xxi.
(Mang. ii. 402). Mishna, *Pea* vii. 6 ; *Maaser sheni* v. 1–5 ; *Orla* throughout ; *Edujoth* iv. 5. Guisius on *Pea* vii. 6 (in Surenhusius' *Mishna*, i. 68).
Hottinger, *De jure plantae quarti anni juxta praeceptum Lev.* xix. 24,
Marburg 1704. Saalschütz, i. 168 f.

(4) Then, in the last place, among the offerings that did *not* fall to the
priests were *those intended for the benefit of the poor*, viz. : (*a*) the gleanings
of the fields and what grew upon the edges of them when the corn was
reaped, Lev. xix. 9, 10, xxiii. 22 ; Deut. xxiv. 19–22. Joseph. *Antt.* iv.
8. 21. Philo, *De caritate*, sec. ix. (Mang. ii. 390). Mishna, *Pea.* (*b*) The
so-called *third tithe*, or the *tithe for the poor*. According to the terms of the
prescription (Deut. xiv. 28, 29, xxvi. 12) on which this tithe is based one
should expect that, strictly speaking, the tithe for the poor would alternate
with the second tithe. For Deuteronomy prescribes that the tithe that in
the other two years was consumed by the owner himself before Jehovah,
was in the third year to be assigned to the Levites and the poor. So too
according to the Sept. version of Deut. xxvi. 12 : (ἐν τῷ ἔτει τῷ τρίτῳ) τὸ
δεύτερον ἐπιδέκατον δώσεις τῷ Λευίτῃ καὶ τῷ προσηλύτῳ καὶ τῷ ὀρφανῷ καὶ
τῇ χήρᾳ. But it became the practice in later times to superadd the tithe
for the poor to the second tithe every third year. See Tob. i. 7, 8.
Joseph. *Antt.* iv. 8. 22. *Pea* viii. 2–9. *Demai* iv. 3, 4. *Maaser sheni*
v. 6. *Jadajim* iv. 3. *Targum of Jonathan* on Deut. xxvi. 12. Jerome's
commentary on Ezekiel xlv. 13, 14 (ed. Vallarsi, v. 565). Guisius's note
on *Pea* viii. 2 (in Surenhusius' *Mishna* i. 70). Bernard and Havercamp's
editions of Josephus, notes on *Antt.* iv. 8. 22. Hottinger, *De decimis*

φυράματος, Rom. xi. 16). According to the Mishna, offerings
of this sort required to be given in the case of dough that
happened to be made from any one of the five following kinds
of grain: wheat, barley, spelt, oats, and rye (?).[76] The offering was not to be presented in the form of flour or meal, but
required to be taken from the dough, *i.e.* as prepared for
making bread.[77] The quantity to be given was, in the case
of private individuals, one twenty-fourth part, and, in the case
of public bakers, one forty-eighth part of the whole piece.[78]

Then there was a second leading class of regular offerings,
viz. those derived *from the rearing of cattle*. These were of
three different kinds: (1) The most important of them was
that consisting of the *male first-born* of the cattle (that is to
say therefore, the first-born whenever it happened to be a
male). As far back as the earlier Jehovistic and Deuteronomist legislation we find that the male first-born of the cattle
was required to be dedicated to God, *i.e.* was to be used in
sacrifice and for sacrificial feasts (Ex. xiii. 11–16, xxii.
28, 29, xxxiv. 19, 20; Deut. xv. 19–23). This the priestly
legislation has converted into an allowance to be given to the
priests (Ex. xiii. 1, 2; Lev. xxvii. 26, 27; Num. xviii.
15–18; Neh. x. 37). Both legislations add to this the *first-
born among men* as well, for these two were regarded as,

*Judaeorum*, pp. 182–203. Lundius, *Die alt. jüd. Heiligth.*, book iv. chap.
xxxiv. Winer's *Realwörterb.*, art. "Zehnt." Leyrer in Herzog's *Real-
Encycl.*, 1st ed. vol. xviii. p. 418 f.

[76] *Challa* i. 1. There is some doubt as to the meaning of the two words
usually rendered "oats" and "rye" (שבולת שועל and שיפן); especially
with regard to שיפן = σίφων, σιφώνιον, it would certainly be more correct to
understand the word as meaning a species of oats.

[77] *Challa* ii. 5.

[78] *Challa* ii. 7. See in general, Num. xv. 17–21; Neh. x. 38; Ezek.
xliv. 30. Philo, *De praemiis sacerdotum*, sec. i. (Mang. ii. 233): Κελεύει γὰρ
τοὺς σιτοπονοῦντας ἀπὸ παντὸς στέατός τε καὶ φυράματος ἄρτον ἀφαιρεῖν
ἀπαρχὴν εἰς ἱερέων χρῆσιν. Joseph. *Antt.* iv. 4. 4: τούς τε πέττοντας τὸν
σῖτον καὶ ἀρτοποιουμένους τῶν πεμμάτων αὐτοῖς τινὰ χορηγεῖν. Mishna
tractate, *Challa*. *Sifra* to Num. xv. 17 ff. in Ugolini's *Thesaurus*, vol. xiii.
p. 1108 ff. Lundius, *Die alt. jüd. Heiligth.* book iv. chap. xxxix. Saalschütz, i. 347. Haneberg, pp. 571–573. Ritter's *Philo und die Halacha*,
p. 118.

properly speaking, belonging to God, and consequently they required to be ransomed.   Further, as a distinction had to be made between clean and unclean cattle, we accordingly have the following more specific regulations with respect to the first-born : [79] (a) the first-born of the cattle that were *clean* and suitable for sacrificial purposes, *i.e.* oxen, sheep and goats, were to be given *in natura*.   If they were free from blemish they were to be treated as sacrifices, *i.e.* the blood was to be sprinkled upon the altar and the fat consumed in the altar fires.[80]   The flesh could be eaten by all who were connected with the order of the priests, even by their wives, and that in any part of Jerusalem (Num. xviii. 17, 18 ; Neh. x. 37 ; Ex. xxii. 29, xxxiv. 19 ; Deut. xv. 19, 20).[81]   But if, on the other hand, the animals had any blemish about them, they belonged no less to the priests, only they were to be treated as unconsecrated food (Deut. xv. 21–23).[82]   (b) The first-born of *unclean* animals above all, according to Philo, those of the horse, the ass, and the camel—and here too as in every other instance only the male ones—were to be ransomed by the payment of a certain sum of money fixed by the priest with a fifth part added (Num. xviii. 15 ; Neh. x. 37 ; Lev. xxvii. 27).   An ass was to be exchanged for a sheep (Ex. xiii. 13, xxxiv. 20).   According to Josephus, the ransom would appear to have been effected by the payment of a fixed sum of one shekel and a half for each beast.   (c) The *first-born of man, i.e.* the first child that happened to be a male,

---

[79] Subsequent practice amalgamated the Jehovistic and Deuteronomic enactments with those of the priest-code, and made the latter the standard by which to interpret them.

[80] Consequently the Mishna characterizes the first-born also as "holy," but only in the second degree, קדשים קלים, like *passa* and the cattle tithe, *Sebachim* v. 8.

[81] In the passage in Deuteronomy the "thou" of xv. 20 has been understood as though it were addressed to the *priests* and not (as was the original intention of the passage) to the *Israelites*.

[82] Accordingly, in cases of this sort the flesh might be sold by the priests even to persons who did not belong to their own order and eaten by them ; see Bartenora's note on *Bechoroth* v. 1 (in Surenhusius' *Mishna*, v. 169).

required to be " ransomed " as soon as it was a month old by
the payment of five shekels (Num. xviii. 15, 16 ; comp. Num.
iii. 44 ff.; Neh. x. 37 ; Ex. xiii. 13, xxii. 28, xxxiv. 20).
It was not necessary that the boy should be presented at the
temple on the occasion of his being ransomed, as has been
supposed, for the most part on the strength of Luke ii. 22.[83]
As is expressly stated in the passages just referred to, the
shekels in question were to be those of the Tyrian standard.[84]
This tax was imposed upon poor and rich alike.[85]

(2.) *Of all the flesh that was slaughtered generally* the priests
were to receive three portions, viz. the shoulder, the two

---

[83] See, on the other hand, Löw, *Die Lebensalter in der jüdischen Literatur*
(1875), p. 110 ff.

[84] *Bechoroth* viii. 7. A shekel of the Phoenician (=the early Hebrew)
standard amounted to somewhere about 2 marks 62 pfennige of German
money (Hultsch, *Griechische und römische Metrologie*, 2nd ed. p. 420),
and consequently five shekels would be equivalent to about 13 marks.
There can be no question that, by the "ransoming," the older legislation
(Ex. xiii. 13, xxxiv. 20) does not mean a buying back for money, but
an exchanging for an animal that could be used as a sacrifice.

[85] See in general, Philo, *De praemiis sacerdotum*, sec. i. (Mang. ii. 233).
Τρίτον ἐστὶ γέρας τὰ πρωτότοκα ἀρρενικὰ καὶ πάντα τῶν χερσαίων ὅσα πρὸς
ὑπηρεσίας καὶ χρῆσιν ἀνθρώπων. Ταῦτα γὰρ κελεύει διαδίδοσθαι τοῖς ἱερωμένοις
ἀνθρώποις. Βοῶν μὲν καὶ προβάτων καὶ αἰγῶν αὐτὰ τὰ ἔκγονα, μόσχους
καὶ κριοὺς καὶ χιμάρρους, ἐπειδὴ καθαρὰ καὶ πρὸς ἐδωδὴν καὶ πρὸς θυσίας
ἐστί τε καὶ νενόμισται· λύτρα δὲ κατατιθέναι τῶν ἄλλων ἵππων καὶ ὄνων
καὶ καμήλων καὶ τῶν παραπλησίων μὴ μειοῦντας τὴν ἀξίαν. Ἔστι δὲ
καὶ ταῦτα παμπληθῆ. . . . . Τὴν δὲ τῶν πρωτοτόκων υἱῶν καθιέρωσιν,
ὡς ὑπὲρ τοῦ μήτε γονεῖς τέκνων μήτε τέκνα γονέων διαζεύγνυσθαι, τιμᾶται
τὴν ἀπαρχὴν ἀργυρίῳ ῥητῷ, προστάξας ἴσον εἰσφέρειν καὶ πένητα καὶ πλού-
σιον. Comp. also *De caritate*, sec. x. (ed. Mang. ii. 391). Joseph. *Antt.*
iv. 4. 4: τῶν τετραπόδων δὲ τῶν εἰς τὰς θυσίας νενομισμένων τὸ γεννηθὲν πρῶ-
τον, ἂν ἄρσεν ᾖ, καταθῦσαι παρασχεῖν τοῖς ἱερεῦσιν, ὥστε αὐτοὺς πανοικὶ
σιτεῖσθαι ἐν τῇ ἱερᾷ πόλει· τῶν δ' οὐ νενομισμένων ἐσθίειν παρ' αὐτοῖς κατὰ
τοὺς πατρίους νόμους τοὺς δεσπότας τῶν τικτομένων σίκλον καὶ ἥμισυ αὐτοῖς
ἀναφέρειν, ἀνθρώπου δὲ πρωτοτόκου πέντε σίκλους. Mishna tractate *Bechoroth*.
Lundius, *Die alt. jüd. Heiligthümer*, book iii. chap. xliv. Winer's *Realwörterb.*, art. "Erstgeburt." Saalschütz, i. 348 f. Haneberg, pp. 569–571.
Frankel, *Ueber den Einfluss der palästinischen Exegese*, etc., 1851, p. 98 f.
(on the Sept. rendering of Ex. xiii. 13 and xxxiv. 20). Ritter, *Philo*,
pp. 118–122 (the most exhaustive and accurate of any). Knobel-Dillmann,
*Exeget. Handbuch*, note on Ex. xiii. 1, 2. Löw, *Die Lebensalter in der jüd.
Literatur*, 1875, pp. 110–118, 390–392 (specially treating of the first-born
in the case of man).

cheeks, and the stomach.   This is the sense in which Deut. xviii. 3 was understood, and was therefore taken as referring, not to animals offered in sacrifice, but to those slaughtered for ordinary use.   According to the later interpretation of it, this prescription was also regarded as applying exclusively to such animals as were suitable for sacrifices, viz. oxen, sheep and goats.[86]

(3.) Again, a portion of the *proceeds of the sheep-shearing* had to be given to the priests, only in those cases however in which a person owned more than one sheep—according to the school of Shammai, when he owned two, according to Hillel's school, on the other hand, not unless he owned five. This offering was said to amount to five Jewish (=ten Galilaean) sela.[87]

III.   Besides the regular offerings, there also fell to the priests a considerable number of an *irregular* and *extra-ordinary* character.   To this category belonged, fundamentally at least, a large number of sacrifices offered on an almost endless variety of occasions (see p. 195 f. above); but besides

[86] See in general, besides Deut. xviii. 3, Philo, *De praemiis sacerdotum*, sec. iii. (Mang. ii. 235): Ἀπὸ δὲ τῶν ἔξω τοῦ βωμοῦ θυομένων ἕνεκα κρεωφαγίας τρία προστέτακται τῷ ἱερεῖ δίδοσθαι, βραχίονα καὶ σιαγόνα καὶ τὸ καλούμενον ἤνυστρον. Joseph. *Antt.* iv. 4. 4 : εἶναι δὲ καὶ τοῖς κατ᾽ οἶκον θύουσιν, εὐωχίας ἕνεκα τῆς αὐτῶν, ἀλλὰ μὴ θρησκείας, ἀνάγκην κομίζειν τοῖς ἱερεῦσιν ἤνυστρόν τε καὶ χελύνιον καὶ τὸν δεξιὸν βραχίονα τοῦ θύματος.   On the meaning of χελύνιον (not the breast, but the cheek), see notes on this passage in Bernard and Havercamp's editions of Josephus.   Mishna tractate *Chullin* x. and the corresponding *Gemara*, fol. 130 ff.   *Sifra* to Deut. xviii. 3 in Ugolini, vol. xiii. 1113–1115 (here too, as in Josephus, the *right* foreleg or shoulder).   Jerome, *Epist.* lxiv. *ad Fabiolam*, chap. ii. (Vallarsi, i. 355): Caeterum et alia tria, exceptis primitiis hostiarum et de privato et de macello publico, ubi non religio sed victus necessitas est, sacerdotibus membra tribuuntur, brachium, maxilla et venter.   Bernard and Havercamp's editions of Josephus, notes on *Antt.* iv. 4. 4.   Saalschütz, i. p. 350.   Haneberg, p. 576 f.   Oehler in Herzog's *Real-Encycl.*, 1st ed. vol. xii. p. 181 f.   Knobel's note on Deut. xviii. 3.   Ritter's *Philo*, p. 124 f.   Wellhausen, i. p. 158.

[87] See in general, Deut. xviii. 4.   Joseph. *Antt.* iv. 4. 4 : εἶναι δὲ ἀπαρχὰς αὐτοῖς καὶ τῆς τῶν προβάτων κουρᾶς.   Mishna, *Chullin* xi. 1, 2. *Sifra* to Deut. xviii. 4, in Ugolini, vol. xiii. p. 1113.   Philo, *De caritate*, sec. x. (Mangey, ii. 391), erroneously includes this offering among the tithes.

these they also received the following offerings: (1) *The consecration vows*, or votive offerings. These might be of a very varied character. One could dedicate oneself or some other person to the sanctuary (to the Lord). In such cases it was usual to pay a certain sum of money by way of ransom, viz. fifty shekels for a man and thirty for a woman. But one could also dedicate animals, houses, or lands to the sanctuary. If the animals happened to be such as could be offered in sacrifice, then they had to be given *in natura*. But in the case of unclean animals and in that of houses and lands, a money ransom could be paid as before, though on certain conditions specified in the law.[88] (2) A special form of con-secration vow called the *ban*, *i.e.* something irredeemably devoted to the sanctuary. Whenever anything was devoted to the sanctuary in this form (as something banned, חֵרֶם) it fell to it, *i.e.* to the priests *in natura*, whether it were in the shape of a person, cattle, or lands.[89] (3) Lastly, in those cases in which any one had appropriated or otherwise unlaw-fully got possession of anything, and in which it was no longer possible to restore the property to its rightful owner, a certain *indemnity* had to be paid, and this also fell to the priests.[90] With regard to the two things last mentioned, the

---

[88] See in general, Lev. xxvii.; Deut. xxiii. 22–24. Joseph. *Antt.* iv. 4. 4; Matt. xv. 5; Mark vii. 11. Lundius, *Die alt. jüd. Heiligthümer*, book iii. chap. xlv. Saalschütz, *Das mosaische Recht*, i. 150–153, 358–367. Winer's *Real-wörterb.* art. "Gelubde." Oehler in Herzog's *Real-Encycl.*, 1st ed. vol. iv. pp. 788–790 (art. "Gelubde bei den Hebräern"). Knobel-Dillmann, *Exeget. Handbuch*, notes on Lev. xxvii. Haneberg, *Die religiösen Alter-thümer der Bibel*, pp. 370–376. Lightfoot, *Horae hebr.*, note on Matt. xv. 5 (*Opp.* ed. Roterodamens. ii. p. 332 f.). Edzard, *Tractatus Talmudicus*, *Aboda sara* 1710, p. 294 ff. Schoettgen, *Horae hebr.*, Wolf's *Curae phil. in Nov. Test.*, and Wetzstein's *Nov. Test.*, the notes of the three last-mentioned writers on Matt. xv. 5; see in general the expositors on Matt. xv. 5 and Mark vii. 11; also "Saat auf Hoffnung," edited by Delitzsch for year 1875, pp. 37–40. On the validity of vows in the case of women, see Num. xxx.; Mishna tractate *Nedarim*.

[89] See Lev. xxvii. 28; Num. xviii. 14; Ezek. xliv. 29. Saalschütz, i. 368–373. Winer's *Realwörterb.*, art. "Bann." Lev. xxvii. 29 is not appli-cable here. See Knobel-Dillmann's note on this latter passage.

[90] Num. v. 5–8.

law distinctly states that they were to belong to the *priests*
personally, whereas the votive offering, on the other hand,
would appear to have been devoted as a rule to purposes
connected with the services of the sanctuary generally.[91]  At
the same time Josephus distinctly affirms that the ransom of
fifty or of thirty shekels to be paid in those cases in which
any one had devoted him or herself to God formed part of
the *priests'* emoluments.[92]  Further, the Rabbinical theologians
hold that, besides the cherem and the indemnity offering,
"the inherited field," consecrated as a votive offering (Lev.
xxvii. 16–21), was also to be included among the twenty-
four different kinds of offerings that fell to the priests.[93]

To what extent all the offerings to which we have referred
were contributed by the *Jews of the dispersion* as well it is no
longer possible to say with any degree of certainty in regard
to any one of them in particular.[94]  In any case a large

[91] *Shekalim* iv. 6–8: "When any one consecrates his possessions
(נְכָסִין) . . . and there happen to be cattle amongst them suitable for
sacrifice, whether males or females, then, according to Rabbi Eliesar, they
are to be sold, the males for burnt-offerings and the females for festive
offerings, to those who may be requiring them for such purposes, while the
money with the *rest of the property* was to be given to the treasury for the
support of the temple (לְבֶדֶק הַבַּיִת).  Rabbi Josua says: The males are
sacrificed as burnt-offerings, and the females are sold to such as happen to
be requiring festive offerings, while, with the money realized from the sale,
burnt-offerings are purchased and offered; the residue of the property goes
to the treasury for the maintenance of the sanctuary. . . . If any one
consecrates his possessions, and there happen to be things amongst them
suitable for the altar, such as wine, oil, birds, then, according to Rabbi
Eliesar, these are to be sold to those who are requiring offerings of this
sort, while the money thus realized is to be spent in procuring burnt-
offerings; the residue of the property goes to the treasury for the support
of the temple."

[92] Joseph. *Antt.* iv. 4. 4.

[93] Comp. the Rabbinical passages quoted in note 60, above.

[94] For material bearing upon this, see *Challa* iv. 7, 11 ; *Jadajim* iv. 3 ;
*Chullin* x. 1 (the three portions allotted to the priests at the slaughtering of
an animal to be given beyond Palestine as well).  Philo, *De monarchia*, ii. 3
(Mang. ii. 224).  *Legat. ad Cajum*, sec. xxiii. 40 (Mang. ii. pp. 568 f., 592).
Joseph. *Antt.* xvi. 6. 2–7, xviii. 9. 1.  The passages from Philo and
Josephus refer mainly, of course, to the *didrachma* tax, but not to that
alone ; see *Antt.* xviii. 9. 1: τό τε δίδραχμον . . . καὶ ὁπόσα ἄλλα

number of them was paid by those of the dispersion as well,
while the amount derived from all those sources was of so
handsome a character that the priests always had a comfort-
able provision.    As little are we any longer in a position
always to form anything like a distinct conception of the
*mode in which those offerings were paid.*  Many of them, such
as the challa and the three portions to be given on the
occasion of slaughtering an animal, were of such a nature that
they did not admit of being kept long.  Consequently to
carry these and such as these to Jerusalem for the purpose of
presenting them there would be simply impossible.  At any
rate, in all those places in which there happened to be priests,
they were given to them directly.[95]    But so far as it was
at all practicable, the *administration* of the offerings was
centralized in Jerusalem.   Thither they were conveyed and
handed over to those appointed to receive them, and from
thence again they were distributed among the priests.[96]

This central administration on the part of the priests
extended to the *tithe* as well, which in point of fact was
delivered, not to the Levites, but to the priests, in whose hands
the further disposal of it was then left.[97]

ἀναθήματα.  Hottinger, *De decimis Judaeorum,* p. 100 ff. (*Exercit.* v.).
Frankel, *Ueber den Einfluss der palästinischen Exegese auf die alexandrinische
Hermeneutik* (1851), p. 98 f.

[95] It is said in *Terumoth* ii. 4 with reference to the terumah : " *Wherever*
there happens to be *a priest,* there the terumah of the choicest portions is paid
to him ; but where there is no priest a terumah is to be paid of something
that will keep." According to *Challa* iv. 8, 9, the Challa, things banned,
the first-born, the ransom for first-born sons, the ransom for the first-born
of the ass, the shoulder, the cheeks and the stomach (on the occasion of
killing an animal for ordinary use), the portion of the fleece at the sheep-
shearing, and others, could be given to *any priest* no matter where.   Hence
it was that the terumah, for example, and the tithe, and the first-born
continued to be exacted even after the destruction of the temple, *Bikkurim*
ii. 3 ; *Shekalim* viii. 8.

[96] See especially, 2 Chron. xxxi. 11–19 ; Neh. xii. 44, xiii. 5 ; Malachi
iii. 10.   Philo, *De praemiis,* sec. iv. (Mang. ii. 235 f.) : Ὑπὲρ δὲ τοῦ μηδένα
τῶν διδόντων ὀνειδίζειν τοῖς λαμβάνουσι, κελεύει τὰς ἀπαρχὰς εἰς τὸ ἱερὸν
κομίζεσθαι, πρότερον, εἶτ' ἐνθένδε τοὺς ἱερεῖς λαμβάνειν.

[97] Comp. Joseph. *Vita,* xii. 15 ; *Antt.* xx. 8. 8, 9. 2.   Herzfeld, *Gesch. des*

Nor were *those priestly gifts made use of* merely by the priests themselves, but the *privilege of participating in the enjoyment of them was extended to those connected with them as well.* The only things that had to be partaken of exclusively by priests were those known as "most holy" (see p. 236, above). All the others might be enjoyed by the whole of the members of a priest's household—his wife, his daughters and his slaves, with the exception however of hired workmen and daughters married to other than priests. But, in every instance, only those were at liberty to participate who were in a condition of Levitical purity.[98] With regard to the priests no distinction was made, on this occasion, between those duly qualified to officiate and those debarred from doing so in consequence of some physical defect or infirmity. These latter might be allowed, when the division to which they belonged happened to be serving, to go even the length of participating in the "most holy" things themselves.[99]

All the offerings to which we have hitherto been referring only went to form the personal emoluments of the priests. From these are now further to be distinguished those imposts which were directly intended *to defray the expenses connected with public worship.* The most important of them was the

*Volkes Jisrael,* ii. 138 ff. Delitzsch, *Zeitschr. f. luth. Theol.* 1877, p. 448 f. Wellhausen, i. 171 f. Ritter's *Philo und die Halacha,* p. 123 f. In the time of Nehemiah the tithe was paid to the *Levites* precisely in accordance with what is prescribed in the priest-code, while these in turn handed over only a tenth of the tithe to the temple treasury ; at the same time the two things were done *under the supervision of the priests* (Neh. x. 38, 39). The Mishna would appear to proceed on the assumption that the correct thing was for the priests and the Levites to receive their respective shares directly from the hands of the person paying the tithe (*Maaser sheni* v. 6).

[98] Lev. xxii. 1–16. Philo, *De monarchia,* lib. ii. secs. xiii.–xv. (ed. Mangey, ii. pp. 230–233). Joseph. *Antt.* iv. 4. 4 : πάντων δὲ τῶν τοῖς ἱερεῦσι τελουμένων κοινωνεῖν διέταξε καὶ τοὺς οἰκέτας καὶ θυγατέρας καὶ γυναῖκας, ἔξω τῶν ὑπὲρ ἁμαρτημάτων ἐπιφερομένων θυσιῶν· ταύτας γὰρ ἐν τῷ ἱερῷ μόνοι δαπανῶσιν οἱ ἄρρενες τῶν ἱερέων αὐθημερόν. *Terumoth* vi. 2, vii. 2. *Sifra* to Lev. xxii. 10 ff., in Ugolini's *Thes.* vol. xiii. p. 1102 ff.

[99] Lev. xxi. 22. Philo, *De monarchia,* ii. 13. Joseph. *Antt.* iii. 12. 2; *Bell. Jud.* v. 7. *Sebachim* xii. 1 ; *Menachoth* xiii. 10, *fin.*

*half-shekel* or *didrachma-tax*.[100]   There was no tax of this description anterior to the exile, for down to that period it had been the practice for the kings to provide the public sacrifices at their own expense (Ezek. xlv. 17 ff., xlvi. 13–15, according to the Septuagint).   It was in existence however as early as the days of Nehemiah, although at that time it amounted only to a third of a shekel (Neh. x. 33, 34). The raising of it to half a shekel cannot have taken place till subsequent to Nehemiah's time.   Consequently, the passage in the Pentateuch (Ex. xxx. 11–16), in which the half-shekel tax is prescribed, must be regarded as a later modification of the terms of the priest-code, which moreover is probable for yet other reasons.[101]   The actual payment of this tax in the time of Christ is placed beyond a doubt by the unquestionable testimony of various authorities.[102]   Then again it was one that had to be paid by every male Israelite of twenty years of age or upwards, no matter whether he were rich or poor,[103] and that, in common with all sacred tribute, in money of the early Hebrew or Tyrian (Phoenician) standard.[104]

[100] Comp. Winer's *Realwörterb.*, art. "Abgaben." Saalschütz, i. pp. 291– 293.  Wieseler's *Chronologische Synopse*, p. 264 ff.  Id., *Beiträge zur richtigen Würdigung der Evangelien*, p. 108 ff.  Huschke, *Ueber den Census und die Steuer-verfassung der früheren römischen Kaiserzeit* (1847), pp. 202– 208.  Keim, *Geschichte Jesu*, ii. 599 ff.  Notes of Meyer and other expositors on Matt. xvii. 24.

[101] See Wellhausen, *Jahrb. f. deutsche Theol.* 1877, p. 412.  The passage in Exodus itself speaks only of *one special* instance in which the tax was paid, viz. on the occasion of the numbering of the people in the time of Moses (Num. i.).  But there cannot be a doubt that this was indirectly intended to furnish a legal basis on which to found the exaction of the regular half-shekel tax.  It is also in this sense that the passage has been understood so early as by the author of the Chronicles (2 Chron. xxiv. 4–10).

[102] Matt. xvii. 24; Joseph. *Antt.* xviii. 9. 1; *Bell. Jud.* vii. 6. 6.  Mishna tractate *Shekalim*.

[103] Ex. xxx. 14, 15.  Philo, *De monarchia*, ii. 3 (Mang. ii. 224): Προστέτακται γὰρ ἀνὰ πᾶν ἔτος ἀπαρχὴν εἰσφέρειν ἀπὸ εἰκοσαετοῦς ἀρξαμένους.

[104] Tosefta, *Kethuboth* xii. *fin.* : "Wherever money is mentioned in the law, it is *Syrian money* (כסף צורי) that is meant.  The specimens of Hebrew shekels that have been preserved are found really to correspond with money of the Phoenician standard.  A half-shekel therefore is equal to two

The time for payment was the month Adar (somewhere about the month of March); [105] while the mode of procedure on that occasion was to have the whole of the contributions payable by one community gathered together and then sent on to Jerusalem, there to be duly paid over in name of that community.[106]  This tax was spent mainly in defraying the expense of the daily burnt-offering, and of all the sacrifices generally that had to be offered in the name of the people, as well as for other objects of a public character.[107]  After the destruction of Jerusalem the didrachma had for a long time to be paid toward the support of the temple of *Jupiter Capitolinus* in Rome.[108]  It is true that in the reign of Nerva the *calumnia fisci Judaici* was put an end to, but the tax itself was not repealed.[109]

Over and above the half-shekel tax, and as forming a matter of regular tribute for the temple, there was, above all, the *furnishing of so much wood* every year as fuel for the altar

Tyrian drachmae, or to something like 1 mark 31 pfennige of German money.  Comp. p. 244, above.  In the time of Christ it was only the Roman standard that was in force in Palestine (1 denarius = 1 Attic drachma, both of these being somewhat heavier than the Tyrian drachma). Consequently, in paying the sacred tribute it was very often necessary to have recourse to the exchangers.

[105] *Shekalim* i. 1, 3.

[106] *Shekalim* ii. 1.   Comp. Matt. xvii. 24.

[107] Neh. x. 33, 34.   *Shekalim* iv. 1–3.

[108] Joseph. *Bell. Jud.* vii. 6. 6.   Dio Cass. lxvi. 7.   Comp. Sueton. *Domitian*, 12 : Judaicus fiscus acerbissime actus est.

[109] We have evidence of the first-mentioned fact in the shape of a coin belonging to the reign of Nerva with the words "fisci Judaici calumnia sublata" inscribed upon it (Madden's *History of Jewish Coinage*, p. 199). This cannot be taken as alluding to the repeal of the tax itself, but merely to the fact that it was no longer to be imposed in a *form* so offensive to the Jews, and therefore, of course, that it was no longer to go towards the support of heathen worship.  We find that the tax itself was still being paid subsequent to the period here in question ; comp. Appian. *Syr.* l., and especially Origen's *Epist. ad African.* sec. xiv. (ed. Lommatzsch, xvii. 44) : καὶ νῦν γοῦν ʽΡωμαίων βασιλευόντων, καὶ ᾽Ιουδαίων τὸ δίδραχμον αὐτοῖς τελούντων.  The Rabbinical writers again have decided that the payment of the half-shekel tax ceases to be binding when the temple ceases to exist (*Shekalim* viii. 8).

of burnt-offering.[110]   As early as the time of Nehemiah it was ordained that the priests, the Levites and the people were at certain periods of the year to furnish the necessary supply of wood for the altar, all of them according to the houses of their fathers, their turn being decided by lot (Neh. x. 34, xiii. 31). At a later period the " wood offering" took place, for the most part, on the 15th of the month Ab, a day which, for this very reason, came to acquire a certain festive character.[111]   However, at this same period wood was also furnished by certain families on other days besides the one just mentioned.[112]

[110] On this see Herzfeld's *Geschichte des Volkes Jisrael*, ii. 144 f.   Grätz, *Geschichte der Juden*, 3rd ed. iii. pp. 612 (note 1) and 668 (note 14). Derenbourg's *Histoire de la Palestine*, p. 109, note 2.   Hamburger, *Real-Encycl. für Bibel und Talmud*, part ii. p. 881 f., art. " Opferholzspende."

[111] *Megillath Taanith*, sec. xi. (in Derenbourg, pp. 443, 445).   Joseph. *Bell. Jud.* ii. 17. 6 : τῆς τῶν ξυλοφορίων ἑορτῆς οὔσης, ἐν ᾗ πᾶσιν ἔθος ὕλην τῷ βωμῷ προσφέρειν.   Seeing that in *Bell. Jud.* ii. 17. 7, Josephus designates the day *following* the delivery of the wood as the fifteenth of lot-casting (=Ab), it would follow from this that the delivery took place on the fourteenth of Ab.   But, according to the Rabbinical sources, there can be no doubt whatever that the fifteenth of Ab was the principal day ; see *Megillath Taanith*, sec. xi.; Mishna, *Taanith* iv. 5, iv. 8 ; in general also, *Taanith* iv. 4 ; *Megilla* i. 3 ; *Jer. Taanith* 68ᵇ, 69ᶜ; *Megilla* 70ᶜ ; *Bab. Taanith* 28ₐ–31ₐ.

[112] Mishna, *Taanith* iv. 5 : " The dates fixed for the furnishing of the wood on the part of the priests and the people were the following *nine days* :—

1. On the first of Nisan it was furnished by the family of *Arach* of the tribe of *Judah* (comp. Ezra ii. 5 ; Neh. vii. 10).
2. On the twentieth of Tammuz by the family of *David* of the tribe of *Judah* (comp. Ezra viii. 2).
3. On the fifth of Ab by the family of *Parĕosh* of the tribe of *Judah* (comp. Ezra ii. 3, viii. 3, x. 25; Neh. iii. 25, vii. 8, x. 15).
4. On the seventh of Ab by the family of *Jonadab* the Rechabite (comp. 2 Kings x. 15, 23 ; Jer. xxxv. 8 ; 1 Chron. ii. 55).
5. On the tenth of Ab by the family of *Sĕnaa* of the tribe of *Benjamin* (comp. Ezra ii. 35 ; Neh. iii. 3, vii. 38).
6. On the fifteenth of Ab by the family of *Sattu* of the tribe of *Judah* (comp. Ezra ii. 8, x. 27 ; Neh. vii. 13, x. 15).
    On this same day by The priests.
        The Levites.
        Those of unknown descent.
        The *Benê Gonbê Eli* and the *Bené Koz'ê Kezi'oth*.
7. On the twentieth of Ab by the family of *Pachath-Moab* of the tribe of *Judah* (comp. Ezra ii. 6, viii. 4, x. 30; Neh. iii. 11, vii. 11, x. 15).

Every species of wood was allowable except that of the olive and the vine.[113]

Then, in the last place, *freewill offerings* formed a copious source of wealth for the temple. We have already stated that probably the largest share of the *vows* did not fall to the priests personally, but was used to defray the expenses incurred in connection with the services of the sanctuary (see p. 247, above). But however this might be, that was certainly the case with regard to those vows that were formed for some particular purpose, as well as those other *voluntary gifts* which did not assume exactly the character of a vow.[114] Very often objects were presented that could be turned to account either in connection with the services of the temple or in the way of ornamenting it.[115] For example, to mention just a single instance, one could present so much gold in the shape of a few leaves, or grapes, or clusters of grapes, with a view to the enlargement of the golden vine that was placed over the entrance to the temple;[116] the wealthy Alabarch Alexander of Alexandria provided the gold and silver with which the gates of the court were covered;[117] nor was it uncommon for distinguished Gentiles to present gifts to the temple (on this see close of present paragraph). As a rule, however, the gifts were bestowed in the shape of money, and then even the poor widow's mite was not unwelcome (Mark xii. 41–44; Luke xxi. 1–4). In the treasury of the temple thirteen trumpet-shaped boxes were erected, and into these the money was dropped that was intended for the various purposes connected with the religious services. No fewer than six of those boxes

---

8. On the twentieth of Elul by the family of *Adin* of the tribe of *Judah* (comp. Ezra ii. 15, viii. 6; Neh. vii. 20, x. 17).

9. On the first of Tebeth by the family of *Parĕosh* for the second time."

[113] *Tamid* ii. 3. Otherwise, according to the Book of Jubilees, chap. xxi. (in Ewald's *Jahrb. der bibl. Wissensch.* iii. 19). *Testam. xii. Patriarch. Levi*, chap. ix.

[114] That at least a formal distinction was made between *vows* (נדרים) and *freewill offerings* (נדבות) may be seen from *Megilla* i. 6.

[115] See in general, Joseph. *Bell. Jud.* v. 13. 6; Mishna, *Joma* iii. 10.

[116] *Middoth* iii. 8, *fin.*        [117] Joseph. *Bell. Jud.* v. 5. 3.

were for the reception of "voluntary gifts" pure and simple, without the object for which they were intended being further specified; and the whole of these latter were expended, at least so the Mishna affirms, in the purchase of burnt-offerings (just because it was supposed that in these most benefit would, so to speak, accrue to God).[118]

### III. THE VARIOUS FUNCTIONS OF THE PRIESTHOOD.

As the priests were so numerous, their emoluments so plentiful, and their functions so varied, it was necessary that there should also be an extensive apportioning among them of the different departments of the service. As we have already pointed out in a previous section, the whole priesthood was divided into twenty-four families, each of which formed a distinct body, with presidents and elders at its head. But apart from this social organization of the entire order, there was further, the organism of the *special functions* connected with the multifarious services of the sanctuary. Of those special offices there were *two* that (at least during the last century of the temple's existence, to which period the following account is to be understood as applying) were conspicuous above all the others, and to these we will here assign the foremost place.

1. The head of the whole priesthood was the *supreme*, or as we usually designate him, the *high priest*, כהן גדול, ἀρχιερεύς.[119] The characteristic feature about the position of this distinguished functionary was the combining in one and the same person of both a *civil* and a *sacred* dignity. Not only was he

---

[118] *Shekalim* vi. 5, 6.

[119] Comp. on this functionary, Winer's *Realwörterb.* under word. Oehler's art. "Hoherpriester," in Herzog's *Real-Encycl.* (1st ed. vol. vi. pp. 198–206, 2nd ed. vi. pp. 237–245, revised by Delitzsch), and the literature quoted in both those works; also Graf's art. "Priester," in Schenkel's *Bibellex.* Wellhausen's *Gesch. Israels,* i. pp. 153–156. Riehm, *Handwörterb. des bibl. Altertums,* under word.

the supreme religious functionary, the one to whom alone pertained the privilege of performing certain acts of worship of the highest religious significance, such as, above all, the offering of the sacrifice on the great day of atonement, but he was also, at the same time, the supreme civil head of the people, the supreme head of the State, in so far, that is, as the State was not under the sway of foreign rulers. In the days of national independence the hereditary Asmonaean high priests were priests and kings at one and the same time; while, at a later period again, the high priests were, at least the presidents of the Sanhedrim, and even in all political matters, the supreme representatives of the people in their relations with the Romans (for details, see § 23. IV., above). As was to be expected, considering the distinguished social position which he held, the high priest did not officiate except on festival occasions. He was, in fact, legally bound to do so only on the great day of atonement, when he was called upon to offer before the Lord the great sin-offering of the people (Lev. xvi.); though, according to later usage, he was further required to offer the daily sacrifice during the week immediately preceding the great day of atonement.[120] Otherwise he was left perfectly free to sacrifice only when he felt disposed to do so.[121] According to the testimony of Josephus, he officiated, as a rule, every Sabbath day, and on the occasion of the new moons or other festivals in the course of the year.[122] We must beware of confounding with the sacrifices just mentioned, and which he offered as representing the people and in their name, the daily meat-offering which he required to offer purely on his own account (Lev. vi. 12–16). But on those latter occasions it was not so much required that he himself should officiate (which he seldom did) as that he

---

[120] *Joma* i. 2.  [121] *Joma* i. 2; *Tamid* vii. 3.

[122] *Bell. Jud.* v. 5. 7: ὁ δὲ ἀρχιερεὺς ἀνήει μὲν σὺν αὐτοῖς, ἀλλ' οὐκ ἀεί, ταῖς δ' ἑβδομάσι καὶ νουμηνίαις καὶ εἴ τις ἑορτὴ πάτριος ἢ πανήγυρις πάνδημος ἀγομένη δι' ἔτους. It further appears that the high-priestly functions had been actually discharged by the Asmonaean princes. See Joseph. *Antt.* xiii. 10. 3 (John Hyrcanus), xiii. 13. 5 (Alexander Jannaeus).

should defray the cost of the offerings.[123]   The somewhat
unique character of the high priest's position found further
expression in the special purity and holiness that were
expected of him (see pp. 211, 214, above), as well as in the
gorgeous official attire which he wore when exercising his
sacred functions.[124]   Only at that part of the service on the
great day of atonement at which he entered the holy of holies,
he wore a simple white dress, which however was made of
the most expensive Pelusian and Indian linen (or cotton ?).[125]

[123] Joseph. *Antt.* iii. 10. 7.   For a fuller treatment of the matter, see
chap. iv. below.

[124] The Biblical and post-Biblical sources dwell with peculiar delight upon
the splendour of this attire.   See Ex. xxviii. and xxix. ; Sirach xlv. 6–13,
l. 5 ff.   Aristeas, ed. Mor. Schmidt, in Merx' *Archiv*, i. 271. 21–272. 9 (in
Havercamp's *Josephus*, ii. 2. 113).   Philo, *Vita Mosis*, iii. 11–14 (ed. Mang.
ii. 151–155) ; *De monarchia*, ii. 5, 6 (ed. Mang. ii. 225–227).   Joseph. *Antt.*
iii. 7. 4–7, and *Bell. Jud.* v. 5. 7.   Mishna, *Joma* vii. 5.   Jerome's *Epist. ad
Fabiolam*, chap. x.–xviii. (ed. Vallarsi, i. 360–366).   Among the literature given
at the head of this section we would specially refer the reader to Joh. Braun,
*Vestitus sacerdotum Hebraeorum*, Amst. 1680.   Lundius, *Die alt. jüd. Heiligth.*
book iii. chap. iv.–viii.   Bened. Dav. Carpzov, *De pontificum Hebraeorum-
vestitu sacro* (in Ugolini's *Thes.* vol. xii., *ibid.* in vols. xii. and xiii., and other
monographs besides).   Ugolini's *Thes.* vol. xiii. pp. 163-434.   Bähr's *Symbolik des mos. Cult.* ii. 61–165.   Leyrer's art. "Kleider, heilige bei den
Hebräern," in Herzog's *Real-Encycl.*, 1st ed. vol. vii. 714–722, and the literature quoted there.   Haneberg, *Die relig. Alterthümer der Bibel*, pp. 534–555.
De Saulcy, *Revue archéologique*, new series, vol. xx. 1869, pp. 91–115.
Likewise the literature of the subject of the high priest quoted in note 119.
In the library of the University of Giessen there is a very learned work in
manuscript by Martinus Mauritii, entitled *De re vestiaria Hebraeorum*, 1685
(*Cod. Gissens.* 593-595).   During the Roman period a serious political dis-
pute arose about the custody of the high priest's dress, see Joseph. *Antt.* xv.
11. 4, xviii. 4. 3, xx. 1. 1, 2 ; further *Theol. Stud. u. Krit.* 1872, pp. 627–630.
At the conquest of Jerusalem this splendid attire fell into the hands of the
Romans (Joseph. *Bell. Jud.* vi. 8. 3).

[125] Lev. xvi. 4.   Mishna, *Joma* iii. 7 (on the materials here referred to,
comp. note 215, below).   Joseph. *Bell. Jud.* v. 5. 7 : ταύτην μὲν οὖν τὴν
ἐσθῆτα [οὐκ] ἐφόρει τὸν ἄλλον χρόνον, λιτοτέραν δ᾽ ἀνελάμβανεν ὁπότε [δὲ]
εἰσίοι εἰς τὸ ἄδυτον.   The words within brackets are here to be deleted.
The high priest wore the linen dress (בגדי לבן) only when performing
those parts of the service that had special reference to the great day of
atonement.   When performing the others however, he wore *his more
gorgeous dress* (בגדי זהב) on the great day of atonement as well as on any
other occasion.   For further particulars on this point, see *Joma* iii. 4. 6,
vii. 1. 3, 4 ; comp. besides, Joseph. *Antt.* 4. 3 (when the Romans had the

2. Next to the high priest in point of rank came the סָגָן or סֶגֶן, Aramaic סְגַן, regarding whose functions the conceptions of the Rabbinical authorities are anything but clear. They seem to think that he was simply the representative of the high priest, and that his chief function was to act as the substitute of this latter, should he happen to be disqualified for taking part in the worship in consequence of Levitical defilement; and this view has also continued to be the prevailing one among Christian scholars down to the present day.[126] But it is undoubtedly erroneous. Among all the passages in the Mishna in which the סגן is mentioned there is not one that throws any further light whatever upon his official position. All they can be said to tell us is that he stood next to the high priest in point of rank. When the high priest drew the lot, in the case of the two he-goats, on the great day of atonement, the סגן stood at his right hand, while the president of the division or course that happened to be serving (ראש בית אב) was at his left.[127] Again, when he had occasion to read a portion from the Scriptures, the president of the synagogue handed the roll to the סגן, who in turn passed it to the high priest.[128] Also when he happened to offer the daily sacrifice, the סגן was still found at his side.[129] From all this however we are not at liberty to infer that the segan (I

---

dress in their custody they allowed the Jews to have the use of it τρισὶν ἑορταῖς ἑκάστου ἔτους καὶ κατὰ τὴν νηστείαν, i.e. on the great day of atonement).

[126] See in general, Buxtorf's *Lex. Chald.* under word סגן. Selden, *De successione in pontificatum Ebraeorum*, ii. 1. Lightfoot, *Ministerium templi*, v. 1 (*Opp.* i. 687 f.). Sheringam on *Joma* iii. 9 (in Surenhusius' *Mishna*, ii. 223). Carpzov, *Apparatus historico-criticus*, p. 98 f. Vitringa, *Observationes sacrae* (1723), lib. vi. cap. xxiii. pp. 517–531. Blossius, 1711, Overkampf, 1739 (both quoted by Meusel, *Bibliotheca historica*, i. 2. 165). Quandt, *De pontificis maximi suffraganeo* (in Ugolini's *Thes.* vol. xii. pp. 963–1028). Oehler's art. "Hoherpriester," in Herzog's *Real-Encycl.*, 1st ed. vi. 204. Haneberg, *Die relig. Alterth. der Bibel*, p. 558 f. Levy, *Chald. Wörtb.* under word סגן. Idem, *Neuhebr. Wörterb.* under same word. On the סגנים in the Old Testament, consult Gesenius' *Thesaurus*, under word.

[127] *Joma* iii. 9, iv. 1.   [128] *Joma* vii. 1 ; *Sota* vii. 7–8.
[129] *Tamid* vii. 3.

prefer this Aramaic form because we are unable to say for
certain what the Hebrew form of the singular was) was
intended to act as the high priest's substitute on those
occasions on which he was prevented from officiating himself.
Such an inference would be decidedly wrong.   For what the
Mishna says with regard to this matter of the substitute is
rather to this effect: " Seven days before the great day of
atonement it is customary to appoint some other priest (כהן
אהר) to be ready to take the place of the high priest in the
event of any accident happening to the latter calculated to
interrupt the service." [130]   This would surely have been
extremely superfluous if there had been a permanent official
whose duty it was to act as the high priest's representative or
substitute.   It appears to me that we need have no difficulty
in arriving at a true and distinct conception as to what was
the real position of the segan, if we will only take due note
of the way in which the term סגנים is rendered in the Septuagint.   For we find that there it is almost invariably represented by στρατηγοί.[131]   Consequently, the סגן can have been
no other than the στρατηγὸς τοῦ ἱεροῦ, *the captain of the temple*,
whom we find frequently mentioned in the Greek sources,
both in Josephus and the New Testament.[132]   To this functionary was entrusted the chief superintendence of the
arrangements for preserving order in and around the temple.
And so when we consider the very important nature of this

[130] *Joma* i. 1.

[131] So Jer. li. 23, 28, 57; Ezek. xxiii. 6, 12, 23 ; Ezra ix. 2 (Vulgate
omits it) ; Neh. ii. 16, iv. 8, xii. 40, xiii. 11 ; Dan. iii. 2, 27, vi. 8.   In a
very few instances we have ἄρχοντες, Isa. xli. 25 ; Neh. iv. 13, v. 7, vii. 5 ;
and, on one solitary occasion, σατράπαι, Dan. ii. 48.

[132] Acts iv. 1 : ὁ στρατηγὸς τοῦ ἱεροῦ.   Similarly Acts v. 24, 26. Josephus,
*Antt.* xx. 6. 2 : Ἀνανίαν τὸν ἀρχιερέα καὶ τὸν στρατηγὸν Ἄνανον.  *Bell.
Jud.* vi. 5. 3 : οἱ τοῦ ἱεροῦ Φύλακες ἤγγειλαν τῷ στρατηγῷ.   *Antt.* xx. 9. 3 :
τὸν γραμματέα τοῦ στρατηγοῦντος Ἐλεαζάρου.  *Bell. Jud.* ii. 17. 2 :
Ἐλεάζαρος υἱὸς Ἀνανίου τοῦ ἀρχιερέως, νεανίας θρασύτατος, στρατηγῶν
τότε.   It is quite possible that, in several of the last-mentioned passages,
instead of its being the chief στρατηγός that was meant, it was rather one of
the subordinate στρατηγοί who were also among the temple officials, as will
be pointed out immediately.

office, we can quite easily understand how the priest who had the honour to hold it should have been regarded as second only to the high priest himself.

Besides the segan or στρατηγός in the singular, we also meet with the plural form סגנים or στρατηγοί. When the festive processions of the country people went up to Jerusalem with the first-fruits, it was usual for the foremost among the priests to go out to meet them, namely the פַּחוֹת and סְגָנִים and גִּזְבָּרִים.[133] The two first of those categories, the פַּחוֹת and the סְגָנִים, correspond to the οἱ ἀρχιερεῖς καὶ στρατηγοί of Luke xxii. 4, 52.[134] What we are to understand by the ἀρχιερεῖς has been already pointed out at p. 201 ff. above. But the סגנים or στρατηγοί are in any case, so far as the nature of their office is concerned, of the same order as the סגן or στρατηγός, only holding a somewhat lower rank, and therefore captains of the temple police as much as, though subordinate to, the chief στρατηγός.[134a]

In the lists of the priests that are given in several passages in the Talmud those who rank next to the *high priest* and the *segan* are the *presidents* of the courses of service, those at the head of the twenty-four leading divisions (ראש המשמר) being mentioned first, and those at the head of the sub-divisions (ראש בית אב) coming next.[135] The functions of those presidents had however no immediate reference to the worship, but to the priesthood as a corporate body, in which aspect we

---

[133] *Bikkurim* iii. 3.

[134] The פַּחוֹת and סְגָנִים are also frequently conjoined in this way in the Old Testament (Jer. li. 23, 28, 57 ; Ezek. xxiii. 6, 12, 23). In such cases the Septuagint rendering is, as a rule, ἡγεμόνες (or ἡγούμενοι) καὶ στρατηγοί, in one instance (Jer. li. 57) it is ἄρχοντες καὶ στρατηγοί. Consequently in the passage quoted from the Mishna, viz. *Bikkurim* iii. 3, as above, in which it is priests that are in question, the פַּחוֹת can scarcely be other than the ἀρχιερεῖς, for the ἄρχοντες among the priests are simply the ἀρχιερεῖς. This is corroborated by the form of expression made use of by Luke.

[134a] Possibly the סגן הכהנים, R. Chananiah, so frequently mentioned in the Mishna, was a סגן of this sort. On this personage, see § 25. IV.

[135] See especially, *Tosefta Horajoth, fin.* (ed. Zuckermandel, p. 476); *Jer. Horajoth* 48ᵇ, in Ugolini's *Thesaurus*, vol. xiii. p. 870.

have already had occasion to speak of them at p. 220 f.   The sacred functions, properly so called, which still fall to be mentioned here besides those of the high priest and the segan, are those that related partly to the *administration of the possessions and stores belonging to the sanctuary*, partly to the *superintendence of the temple police*, and partly to the religious services themselves.   All that we know with respect to those three categories is substantially as follows.[136]

I.   A very important function was that of the administration of the vast amount of property belonging to the temple. The store-chambers of the sanctuary were filled with possessions of multifarious kinds piled in masses one upon another. First there were the *utensils* employed in the sacrificial worship, which of themselves represented a handsome sum, and consisting of a whole host of gold and silver basins, cups, pots and articles of a like kind used for such purposes as catching up and sprinkling the blood, for offering the frankincense and the meat- and drink-offerings, etc.[137]   Again there were large quantities of curtains, and priests' garments, and of the materials required for making them.[138]   And there were, in particular, vast collections of natural products, viz.: flour and oil for the meat-offerings, wine for the drink-offerings, fragrant substances with which to make the frankincense, and in addition to these things, the offerings contributed for the benefit of the priests.[139]   But, above all, there were also the

---

[136] Comp. Lightfoot, *Ministerium templi*, cap. v. and vii.   Herzfeld's *Geschichte des Volkes Jisrael*, i. 387–424.   Haneberg, *Die relig. Alterth.* p. 555 ff.   Graf in Merx' *Archiv*, i. 226–232.   Also in general the literature of the subject of the *Levites* as quoted in note 43 above.

[137] See in general, Ezra i. 9–11, viii. 26, 27 ; 1 Macc. i. 21–23 ; Joseph. *Antt.* xiv. 4. 4 ; *Bell. Jud.* i. 7. 6, v. 13. 6, vi. 5. 2, vi. 8. 3 ; *Joma* iii. 10, iv. 4.   According to *Tamid* iii. 4, ninety-three gold and silver utensils were required for the daily service ; while, according to *Chagiga* iii. 8, three sets of each were kept.   For a few particulars, see Ex. xxv. 29, 38, xxvii. 3, xxxvii. 16, 23, xxxviii. 3 ; Num. iv. 7, 9, 14.

[138] *Bell. Jud.* vi. 5. 2, vi. 8. 3.

[139] Neh. xii. 44, xiii. 5, 9, 12 ; 1 Chron. ix. 20 ; *Bell. Jud.* v. 13, 6, vi. 8. 3 ; *Antt.* xiv. 4. 4 ; *Bell. Jud.* i. 7. 6.

*large sums of money* that were deposited in the store-houses of the temple, and which were of such a colossal character that they not unfrequently tempted greedy foreign potentates to plunder them, and yet it would appear that they were always speedily replaced.[140] Then, in the last place, there fall to be added to the heaps of money stored in the temple the various sums deposited there by private individuals; for it was quite common to lodge such deposits in the temple from a feeling that the sacredness of the place afforded the best possible guarantee for their security.[141] All the money and the various articles of value were kept in separate repositories (γαζοφυλάκια) in the inner court of the temple, and not only did they require to be constantly watched, but in consequence of the receiving on the one hand and giving out on the other that were continually going on, it was necessary that they should be under careful administration.[142]

The *treasurers*, to whom the administration in question was entrusted, were called γαζοφύλακες in Greek [143] and גִּזְבָּרִים in

---

[140] Attempt to plunder by *Heliodorus* (2 Macc. iii.); by *Antiochus Epiphanes* (1 Macc. i. 21–23). *Pompey* leaves the treasury intact (*Antt.* xiv. 4. 4; *Bell. Jud.* i. 7. 6); *Crassus* plunders it (*Antt.* xiv. 7. 1; *Bell. Jud.* i. 8. 8, carrying off 2000 talents); so also *Sabinus*, after the death of Herod (*Antt.* xvii. 10. 2, *fin.*; *Bell. Jud.* ii. 3. 3, *fin.*); *Pilate* (*Antt.* xviii. 3. 2; *Bell. Jud.* ii. 9. 4); *Florus* (*Bell. Jud.* ii. 14. 6). Comp. besides, on the ἱερὸ; θησαυρός in general, Matt. xxvii. 6; Joseph. *Bell. Jud.* v. 5. 1; *Antt.* xx. 9. 7.

[141] 2 Macc. iii. 10–12, 15. Joseph. *Bell. Jud.* vi. 5. 2. This was often done in the case of heathen temples as well. See in general, Winer's *Realwörterb.*, art. "Hinterlage." Grimm, *Exeget. Handb. zu den Apokryphen*, note on 2 Macc. iii. 10. Marquardt, *Römische Staatsverwaltung*, vol. iii. (1878) p. 210. Hermann and Blumner, *Lehrb. der griechischen Privatalterthümer* (1882), p. 456 f.

[142] On the γαζοφυλάκια, see especially, Joseph. *Bell. Jud.* v. 2, *fin.*, vi. 5. 2; *Antt.* xix. 6. 1; Neh. xii. 44, xiii. 5, 9, 12, 13. By the γαζοφυλάκιον mentioned in the New Testament we are not to understand a *treasure chamber* but a *treasury box* (Mark xii. 41, 43; Luke xii. 1; probably also John viii. 20). According to *Shekalim* vi. 5, there were in the temple thirteen money chests made in the form of trumpets.

[143] *Antt.* xv. 11. 4, xviii. 4. 3 (the γαζοφύλακες had the custody of the high priest's dress). *Antt.* xx. 8. 11: Ἰσμάηλον τὸν ἀρχιερέα καὶ Ἑλκίαν τὸν γαζοφύλακα (sent on an embassy to Rome). *Bell. Jud.* vi. 8. 3:

Hebrew.[144] Nor were the functions of those officials confined merely to the money in the temple, but extended to the administration of all the possessions generally, that fell under any of the categories just mentioned. They had the custody of the sacred utensils,[145] the veils, and the priests' garments;[146] they took charge of the flour for the meat-offerings and of the wine for the drink-offerings;[147] it was their duty to take delivery of things consecrated (or things presented to the temple), or to return them again on the ransom being duly paid;[148] and they also purchased wood[149] and gathered in the half-shekel tax.[150] Of course among the treasurers too there were once more gradations of rank. According to the statements of the Old Testament, it would seem as though the whole of those offices had been in the hands of the Levites.[151] This may have been actually the case so far as the more subordinate duties were concerned, but there can be no doubt whatever that the more important ones were in the hands of the priests. The fact is there is mention in Josephus of a particular occasion on which the γαζοφύλαξ (perhaps the chief one of his class) is put immediately on a level with the high priest, from his being regarded as one of the most distinguished of the temple officials.[152] We also find that elsewhere the גִּזְבָּרִים are reckoned among the higher functionaries of the

ὁ γαζοφύλαξ τοῦ ἱεροῦ Φινέας (surrenders the priests' garments to the Romans). Comp. also *Antt.* xiv. 7. 1: ὁ τῶν θησαυρῶν φύλαξ ἱερεύς, Ἐλεάζαρος ὄνομα . . . πεπιστευμένος τὴν τῶν καταπετασμάτων τοῦ ναοῦ φυλακήν (in the time of Crassus).

[144] *Pea* i. 6, *fin.*, ii. 8, *fin.*, iv. 8; *Challa* iii. 3–4; *Bikkurim* iii. 3; *Shekalim* ii. 1, v. 2, 6; *Menachoth* viii. 2, 7; *Meila* iii. 8. The term occurs in the Old Testament likewise, Ezra i. 8, vii. 21. Comp. further, Levy, *Chald. Wörterb.* under word. Idem, *Neuhebr. Wörterb.* under word.

[145] *Shekalim* v. 6; 1 Chron. ix. 28.

[146] Joseph. *Antt.* xiv. 7. 1, xv. 11. 4; xviii. 4. 3; *Bell. Jud.* vi. 8. 3.

[147] *Menachoth* viii. 2, 7.

[148] *Pea* i. 6, *fin.*, ii. 8, *fin.*, iv. 8; *Challa* iii. 3–4.

[149] *Meila* iii. 8.      [150] *Shekalim* ii. 1.

[151] 1 Chron. ix. 28, 29, xxvi. 20–28; 2 Chron. xxxi. 11–19. The predilection of the author of Chronicles for the Levites is well known. Yet in Neh. xiii. 13 it is a *priest* that is found at the head of the treasurers.

[152] *Antt.* xx. 8. 11; see note 143, above.

temple.[153]   When the Mishna affirms that there must have been at least three גִּזְבָּרִים in the temple,[154] it is certain that it can have had in view only the head treasurers and not the entire staff of officials that were required for the administration of the treasury.

It is probable that, under the category of treasury officials, we should also include the *amarkelin* (אמרכלין), who are mentioned once in the Mishna without any hint whatever being given as to the nature of their functions,[155] the consequence being that the Rabbinical writers indulge merely in empty conjectures on the point, conjectures based, to some extent, upon trivial etymological conceits.[156]   The term itself is of Persian origin, and means a "member of the chamber of accounts, or an accountant."[157]   Consequently in the Targum of Jonathan we find that in 2 Kings xii. 10 and xxii. 4, for example, the term אמרכליא is substituted for the Hebrew expression שֹׁמְרֵי הַסַּף, "keepers of the threshold," by whom the priestly treasurers are meant. We have a term in every way identical with the one now in question in the Armenian expression *hamarakar*, which in like manner denotes an official having charge of the accounts (a chief

---

[153] *Bikkurim* iii. 3 (see p. 259, above); also in the lists of the various ranks of the priests given in Tosefta, *Horajoth, fin.* (see note 135), the גזברים take precedence of the ordinary priests, while these latter again rank higher than the Levites.   In a certain Rabbinical lamentation over the degeneracy of the high priests, the גזברים are put immediately on a level with them precisely as in Josephus ("They are high priests and their sons are גזברין, and their sons-in-law אמרכלין." Tosefta, *Menachoth, fin.*; *Bab. Pesachim* 57ª. Derenbourg, *Histoire*, p. 232, note).

[154] *Shekalim* v. 2.                                   [155] *Shekalim* v. 2.

[156] In the Tosefta, *Shekalim* ii. 15 (ed. Zuckermandel, p. 177), it is affirmed that they kept the seven keys of the seven gates of the court (see also Grätz, *Monatsschrift*, 1876, p. 441).   But this is a pure conjecture founded upon a statement in the Mishna to the effect that there must have been at least seven amarkelin.   An attempt is made to explain the term etymologically by supposing it to be derived either from מר כל (lord of all), or אמר כל (he who speaks all, *i.e.* he who is entitled to order everything). See in general, Levy's *Chald. Wörterb. s.v.* Idem, *Neuhebr. Wörterb. s.v.* אמרכל and מרכל.

[157] Perles, *Etymologische Studien* (1871), p. 106. Comp. Nöldeke, *Göttinger gel. Anzeigen* (1871), 149. Idem, *Literar. Centralbl.* 1875, p. 876.

treasurer).[158]   It is true no doubt that our term also occurs
elsewhere in the Targums in the more comprehensive sense of
chiefs or heads generally.[159]   But seeing that, as a rule, the
priestly אמרכלין are mentioned along with the גזברין,[160] we may
venture to regard it as certain that they also belonged to the
same category as the treasurers.   It is possible that they were
among the subordinate officials of this department;[161] but
perhaps the distinction between the *gisbarim* and the *amarkelin* was something like this, that while to the former was
assigned the duty of receiving and taking charge of the various
treasures, the latter, on the other hand, were entrusted with
the task of distributing among the priests the gifts and
offerings that were intended for them.[162]   Besides the two
classes just mentioned, the Jerusalem Talmud mentions yet a
third, viz. the קתוליקין ($\kappa a\theta o\lambda\iota\kappa o\iota$), of whom however the Mishna
knows nothing whatever.[163]

II. For the duties connected with the *police* department,

[158] Prud'homme (*Journal Asiatique*, 16th series, vol. vii. 1866, p. 115)
renders it by *comptable ou caissier chef.*  Comp. also Levy in Geiger's *Jüd.
Zeitschrift*, v. 1867, p. 214 f.  Lagarde, *Armenische Studien* (*Abhandlungen
der Gottinger Gesellsch. der Wissench.* vol. xxii. 1877), No. 1216.

[159] Buxtorf, *Lex. Chald.*, and Levy, *Chald. Wörterb.* under word.

[160] Besides *Shekalim* v. 2, so also in the list of the ranks of the priests,
*Tosefta Horajoth, fin.*, and in the lamentation of *Tosefta Menachoth, fin.*
(see note 153, above).

[161] It is true that, in the list of the grades of the priests *Tosefta Horajoth,
fin.*, the אמרכלין rank *higher* than the גזברין.  But this can hardly be correct.
See, on the other hand, *Shekalim* v. 2 ; *Tosefta Menachoth, fin.*  In *Bikkurim*
iii. 3, the גזברין are included among the prominent members of the priesthood, while the אמרכלין again are not mentioned at all.

[162] In Chronicles (2 Chron. xxxi. 11–19) those officials whose duty it
was to *receive* the gifts for the priests are plainly distinguished from those
who were called upon to *distribute* them.  And now we find it stated in the
Mishna, *Shekalim* v. 2, that "it is usual to appoint *not fewer than three
gisbarim, and not fewer than seven amarkelim.*"  If with this we compare
what is said about the gathering in and distributing of the money for the
poor (*Pea* viii. 7 : "Two take charge of the collecting and three of the
distributing of it"), it is not unnatural to suppose that the gisbarim and
the amarkelim would stand to each other precisely in the same relation as
that in which the collectors of the money for the poor stood to the distri-
butors of it.

[163] *Jer. Shekalim* v. fol. 49a.

for which a very large staff of officials was required, it was
mostly Levites that were employed. In early times indeed,
and down even to the days of Ezra and Nehemiah, the "gate-
keepers" (שֹׁעֲרִים) did not belong as yet to the order of the
Levites, but were of a somewhat lower rank; it was the
author of the Chronicles who was the first to include these
officials also among the number of the Levites (see p. 224,
above). In the inner court the duty of keeping watch and
ward was discharged by the priests themselves. The author
of the Chronicles, and subsequently Philo and the Mishna,
have furnished us with several details regarding the organization of the department now in question.[164] We learn from
the first-mentioned authority that there were twenty-four
wards in all, under four chiefs or captains, and that they were
posted on the east, west, north and south sides of the temple
(1 Chron. xxvi. 12–18, also ix. 17, 24–27). The statements
of this writer are to be understood as applying to the temple
of Zerubbabel. But the area of the temple esplanade, or the
so-called outer court, was afterwards very much enlarged,
especially by Herod, so that it now formed a large quadrangle,
its longer side being that which extended from north to south.
Within this large square again there was an oblong quad-
rangular space enclosed by strong walls, the longer side, in
this instance, running from west to east; this was the so-
called inner court, or "the court" in the strict sense of the
word. This court was approached by a flight of steps, and at
the foot of this stair was a railing within which no Gentile
was allowed to pass. Any Gentile who ventured to pass this
boundary and set foot within the inner court was punished
with death; and the Roman authorities respected the scruples
of the Jews in regard to this matter to such an extent that
they sanctioned the execution of this sentence even in those

[164] See in general, Opitii *Commentarius de custodia templi nocturna*
(Ugolini's *Thes.* vol. ix. pp. 979–1076). Winer's *Realwörterb.* ii. 590 f.
Kneucker's art. "Tempelpolizei," in Schenkel's *Bibellex.* vol. v. p.
484 ff.

cases in which Roman citizens had been the offenders.[165]   To
this railing notices were attached at certain distances from
each other, with the prohibition and the penalty for infringing
it inscribed upon them in Greek and Latin.[166]   According to
Philo, there were keepers in his day not only at the entrances
to the inner court, but likewise at the gates of the outer one as
well, one of their principal duties being to see that the prohibition in question was rigidly complied with.   In addition
to these there were watchmen  patrolling all round  by night
and by day to make sure that nothing of an unseemly
character was going on anywhere.[167]   According to the Mishna,
there were twenty-one points at which the Levites kept watch
(at night), and three at which the priests did so.   The Levitical keepers were stationed partly at the gates and the corners
of the outer court (inside of it), and partly at the gates and
corners of the inner court (outside of it), while the priestly
guards again had charge of the inner court.[168]   It was usual

[165] See in general, Joseph. *Antt.* xv. 11. 5 ; *Bell. Jud.* v. 5. 2, vi. 2. 4 ;
*Apion.* ii. 8.  Philo, *Legat. ad Cajum*, § 31 (ed. Mang. ii. 577). Mishna,
*Middoth* ii. 3 ; *Kelim* i. 8.  It was in consequence of an alleged violation
of this prohibition on the part of the Apostle Paul, by taking Trophimus
into the inner court, that the popular tumult arose that led to the apostle's
being arrested (Acts xxi. 28).  For the judicial proceedings in such cases,
comp. further p. 188, above.

[166] One of those inscriptions was discovered and published in the year
1871 by Clermont-Ganneau.  For an account of it, see Clermont-Ganneau,
*Revue archéologique*, new series, vol. xxiii. 1872, pp. 214–234, 290–296,
pl. x.  Derenbourg, *Journal asiatique*, 6th series, vol. xx. 1872, pp. 178–195.
Piper, *Jahrb. f. deutsche Theol.* 1876, p. 51 f.  The inscription runs thus :—

ΜΗΘΕΝΑ ΑΛΛΟΓΕΝΗ ΕΙΣΠΟ
ΡΕΥΕΣΘΑΙ ΕΝΤΟΣ ΤΟΥ ΠΕ
ΡΙ ΤΟ ΙΕΡΟΝ ΤΡΥΦΑΚΤΟΥ ΚΑΙ
ΠΕΡΙΒΟΛΡΥ ΟΣ Δ ΑΝ ΛΗ
ΦΘΗ ΕΑΥΤΩΙ ΑΙΤΙΟΣ ΕΣ
ΤΑΙ ΔΙΑ ΤΟ ΕΞΑΚΟΛΟΥ
ΘΕΙΝ ΘΑΝΑΤΟΝ.

[167] Philo, *De praemiis sacerdotum*, sec. vi. (ed. Mang. ii. 236): Τούτων οἱ μὲν
ἐπὶ θύραις ἵδρυνται παρ᾽ αὐταῖς ταῖς εἰσόδοις πυλωροί· οἱ δὲ εἴσω κατὰ τὸ πρόναον
ὑπὲρ τοῦ μή τινα ὧν οὐ θέμις ἑκόντα ἢ ἄκοντα ἐπιβῆναι· οἱ δὲ ἐν κύκλῳ περινο-
στοῦσιν, ἐν μέρει διακληρωσάμενοι νύκτα καὶ ἡμέραν, ἡμεροφύλακες καὶ νυκτο-
φύλακες.

[168] *Middoth* i. 1 ; *Tamid* i. 1.

for a captain of the temple to go round at night to see that the guards were not sleeping at their posts.[169]   This captain was known under the designation of אִישׁ הַר הַבַּיִת.   Besides this official, there is also occasional mention of an אִישׁ הַבִּירָה.[170] Now, seeing that the Mishna knows of no other designation for the whole space around the temple—even in cases where it is to be distinguished from the inner court—but the expression הַר הַבַּיִת,[171] we are accordingly to understand by the אִישׁ הר הבית, a captain who had charge of the outer court, and by the אִישׁ הבירה, on the other hand, the one who had surveillance of the temple itself.   For the בִּירָה cannot possibly have been intended to refer to Fort Antonia, seeing that this latter was under the charge of a Roman φρούραρχος,[172] but only to the temple itself.[173]   The two kinds of officials now mentioned would therefore be identical with the סגנים or στρατηγοί to whom we have already had occasion to refer.

It was also part of the watchmen's duty to open and close the whole of the gates of the courts, all of which were shut during the night; and accordingly there was also an officer appointed whose special duty it was to superintend "the shutting of the gates." [174]   According to Josephus, the services of two hundred men were required every time the gates were shut,[175] and the heavy brazen gate in the east of the court took twenty men itself.[176]   Then as for the gate of the temple, we are told that when it was opened, so loud was the creaking, that it could be heard as far away as Jericho.[177]   The keys of the gates of the court were kept by the elders of the particular division of priests whose turn it was to be on watch duty within the court for the time being.[178]   When the

---

[169] *Middoth* i. 2.            [170] *Orla* ii. 12.

[171] For example, *Bikkurim* iii. 4 ; *Pesachim* v. 5–10 ; *Shekalim* vii. 2–3. *Sanhedrin* xi. 2.

[172] Joseph. *Antt.* xv. 11. 4, xviii. 4. 3.

[173] So also 1 Chron. xxix. 1, 19.   *Pesachim* iii. 8, vii. 8 ; *Sebachim* xii. 5 ; *Tamid* i. 1 ; *Middoth* i. 9 ; *Para* iii. 1.

[174] *Shekalim* v. 1.            [175] *Contra Apion.* ii. 9.

[176] *Bell. Jud.* vi. 5. 3.            [177] *Tamid* iii. 8.

[178] *Middoth* i. 8–9 ; *Tamid* i. 1.

divisions were changed, the one that retired handed them over to the one that came in to take its place.[179]   The morning sacrifice, as we know, required to be offered at daybreak, and that being the case the gates would of course have to be open some little time before; while at the Passover season they were open even so early as midnight.[180]

III. It is true the *acts of worship properly so called, i.e.* the offering of the sacrifices with all the accompanying ceremonial, devolved as a whole upon the entire priesthood, who were divided into twenty-four courses, each of which conducted the worship by turns, and that for a week at a time (on this see next paragraph).   Yet even here *special stated* officials were also necessary for certain particular functions.   We get some idea of the multifarious nature of those functions from a passage in the Mishna in which are enumerated, though in a very confused and unsystematic order, the names of those persons who at a particular period (evidently in the closing years of the temple's existence) happened to fill the most important offices in connection with the worship of the sanctuary.[181] From that passage it will be seen that there was, for example,

---

[179] *Contra Apion.* ii. 8.

[180] *Antt.* xviii. 2. 2.   Also, in the time of Pentecost, the priests who were to officiate entered the court as early as during the night.   *Bell. Jud.* vi. 5. 3.   Comp. further, *Joma* i. 8.

[181] *Shekalim* v. 1 : "The following are the officials who held appointments in the sanctuary : (1) Jochanan the son of Pinchas had charge of the seals ; (2) Achiah of the drink-offerings ; (3) Matthiah the son of Samuel of the lots ; (4) Petachiah of the money for the purchase of birds for sacrifice ; (5) Ben Achiah of the healing of the priests suffering from abdominal disorders ; (6) Nechoniah was master of the wells ; (7) Gebini a herald ; (8) Ben Gabar a chief door-shutter ; (9) Ben Bebai had charge of the scourging (? פקיע, the meaning of which is uncertain) ; (10) Ben Arsa kept the warning cymbal ; (11) Hygros, son of Levi, was conductor of the psalmody ; (12) the family of Garmu had the charge of the preparing of the shewbread ; (13) the family of Abtinas that of the preparation of the frankincense ; (14) Eleasar had the renewing (or the custody ?) of the veils ; (15) Pinchas that of the garments."   As elucidating the whole passage, comp. the Rabbinical commentaries in Surenhusius' *Mishna*, ii. p. 192 ; and especially, Herzfeld's *Gesch. des Volkes Jisrael*, i. p. 405 ff. ; also Jost, *Gesch. des Judenthums*, i. p. 151 f.

a special official " over the lots " (No. 3), on whom devolved
the duty of superintending the daily casting of the lots for
determining the particular parts of the service that were to
be apportioned to the various officiating priests.[182]   Then there
was another functionary who was " over the seals " (No. 1),
and another again " over the drink-offerings " (No. 2).   For,
with a view to simplifying matters, an arrangement had been
adopted according to which " seals " or tokens were issued
corresponding to the various kinds of drink-offerings, on
presenting which people could get the particular drink-offering
indicated upon them.   The mode of proceeding was first of
all to purchase a token from the official who was " over the
seals," then to hand this to the one who was " over the drink-
offerings," who in return would give to the person tendering
it the amount of drink-offering requisite for the particular
occasion for which it was wanted.[183]   There was a similar
arrangement for the convenience of those who wished to be
promptly supplied with birds for sacrificial purposes.   All
that was necessary was to drop the money into a box, whereupon it became the duty of the official who was " over the
winged sacrifices " (No. 4) duly to purchase with it, as speedily
as possible, the requisite offerings.[184]   Many of the offerings
were of such a nature that they required a certain amount of
skill to prepare them properly, a skill which belonged by
inheritance to particular families.   Accordingly the family of
Garmu (No. 12) had charge of the preparing of the shewbread, that of Abtinas (No. 13) had the preparing of the
frankincense.[185]   Then again the chief charge of the psalmody

[182] On the casting of the lots here in question, see *Joma* ii. 2–4 ; *Tamid*
i. 2, iii. 1, v. 2. The Matthiah, a son of Samuel, who is mentioned as having
had charge of the lots, is also mentioned in *Joma* iii. 1, *Tamid* iii. 2, where
he is introduced as vouching for the existence of certain practices in the
temple.

[183] *Shekalim* v. 3–5.

[184] The money was dropped into one of the thirteen trumpet-shaped
boxes that stood in the temple ; see note 142, above.

[185] In *Joma* iii. 11, both families are censured for having allowed strangers
to meddle with their art.   There was a chamber in the inner court that was

was entrusted to an official specially appointed for the purpose (No. 11).[186]   There was another whose duty it was to
sound a cymbal (צלצל) by way of letting the Levites know
when to commence the music (No. 10).[187]   There were besides
a temple physician (No. 5), a master of the wells (No. 6), a
herald (No. 7), whose voice was so powerful that it could be
heard as far away as Jericho.[188]   Then further, as the veils in
the temple required to be frequently renewed,[189] there was an
official appointed to see to the making of them, and to take
charge of the store in which they were kept (No. 14).   And
lastly, there was an official whose special duty it was to take
charge of the priests' garments (No. 15).[190]

A very numerous class of functionaries connected with
the worship of the sanctuary was that of *the sacred musicians*,
whose duty it was to accompany the offering of the "daily
burnt-offering" and the other solemn services with singing and
playing upon stringed instruments,[191] and who were called in
Hebrew מְשֹׁרְרִים (frequently so in Ezra and Nehemiah), and
in Greek, ψαλτῳδοί, ἱεροψάλται, ὑμνῳδοί, κιθαρισταί τε καὶ

---

named בית אבטינס after the family of Abtinas (*Joma* i. 5 ; *Tamid* i. 1 ;
*Middoth* i. 1).   In addition, comp. in general, 1 Chron. ix. 30–32, xxiii. 29.

[186] On this official, comp. further, *Joma* iii. 11.

[187] Comp. *Tamid* vii. 3.      [188] *Tamid* iii. 8.      [189] *Shekalim* viii. 5.

[190] For the priests' official garments were kept in the court (Ezek. xlii. 14).
The master of the wardrobe, Pinchas, is likewise mentioned in *Middoth* i. 4 ;
Joseph. *Bell. Jud.* vi. 8. 3.   Whether his duty was simply to take charge of
the garments, or whether he had also, when necessary, to provide new ones,
is not quite clear.

[191] On these officials and the temple music generally, compare, in addition
to the literature quoted in notes 43 and 136, Gesenius, *Thesaurus*, pp. 698,
844, 1167.   Winer's *Realwörterb.*, art. "Musik" and "Musikalische Instrumente."   Leyrer's art. "Musik bei den Hebräern," in Herzog's *Real-Encycl.*
(1st ed. vol. x. pp. 123–135 ; 2nd ed. vol. x. pp. 387–398).   Wetzstein
in Delitzsch's *Commentar zu Jesaja*, 2nd ed. pp. 702–704.   Riehm's *Handwörterb. des bibl. Altertums*, pp. 1028–1045 (with numerous illustrations).
Grätz, *Die Tempelpsalmen* (*Monatsschr.* 1878, pp. 217–222).   Idem, *Die
musikalischen Instrumente im jerusalemischen Tempel und der musikalische
Chor der Leviten* (*Monatsschr.* 1881, pp. 241–259).   Lagarde, *Erklärung
hebräischer Wörter* (*Abhandlungen der Göttinger Gesellsch. der Wissensch.* vol.
xxvi. 1880), pp. 13–27.   Stainer, *The Music of the Bible*, London (without
a date, 1879 ?) ; with 100 illustrations.

ὑμνῳδοί.[192] They formed a separate and exclusive order, to
which none were admitted but those descended from a particular family, and down even to the time of Ezra and
Nehemiah they were distinguished from the Levites, although
at a subsequent period they were included amongst them
(see above, p. 225 f.).[193]  They were divided into *three
families*, those of *Heman, Asaph* and *Ethan* or *Jeduthun*
(1 Chron. vi. 16–32, xv. 16–19, xxv. the entire chapter;
2 Chron. v. 12),[194] and the whole were sub-divided again into
twenty-four courses of service (1 Chron. xxv.).  The principal
part of their duty was to sing, playing on an instrument
being regarded merely in the light of an accompaniment to
the singing.  The musical instruments made use of for this
purpose were chiefly the *three* following :[195]—(1) The *cymbal*
(מְצִלְתַּיִם, κύμβαλα), an instrument played by striking the one
plate upon the other, and resembling the warning cymbal
(צִלְצַל), with which the signal was given for commencing the
singing.[196]  As the dual form already serves to indicate, this

[192] ψαλτῳδοί or, according to another reading, ψαλμῳδοί, Sir. xlvii. 9,
l. 18.  ἱεροψάλται, Joseph. *Antt.* xii. 3. 3, *fin.*; ὑμνῳδοί, *Antt.* xx. 9. 6;
κιθαρισταί τε καὶ ὑμνῳδοί, *Bell. Jud.* ii. 15. 4.  From this latter passage we
must beware of inferring that the players on the instruments and the
singers represent separate categories.  For the truth is, both alike
come μετὰ τῶν ὀργάνων.  "Those who play on the stringed instrument
and sing," are consequently the same persons.  Comp. 1 Chron. xv. 16,
המשררים בכלי שיר, also 1 Chron. xxiii. 5.

[193] In the Mishna too, the musicians are uniformly described as " Levites "
(לוים), *Bikkurim* iii. 4; *Sukka* v. 4; *Rosh hashana* iv. 4; *Arachin* ii. 6;
*Tamid* vii. 3–4.

[194] On the ingenious way in which those families of the musicians are
traced back to Levi, see Graf in Merx' *Archiv*, i. p. 231 f.  Only one of
those families is mentioned among the exiles that returned with Zerubbabel, viz. that of *Asaph*, Ezra ii. 41; Neh. vii. 44.

[195] See Neh. xii. 27 ; 1 Chron. xiii. 8, xv. 16–22, xv. 28, xvi. 5;
2 Chron. v. 12, xxix. 25 ; 1 Macc. iv. 54, xiii. 51.  Joseph. *Antt.* vii. 12. 3.
*Sukka* v. 4 ; *Arachin* ii. 3–6 ; *Middoth* ii. 6.

[196] Comp. p. 221, above.  In the leading passage on the musical instruments, viz. *Arachin* ii. 3–6, מצלתים are not mentioned at all, but merely
the צלצל.  Consequently one is tempted to assume that both are identically
the same.  But still the different terms undoubtedly denote different
instruments.

instrument consisted of two large shallow plates made of brass,[197] which, when struck the one upon the other, emitted a loud sound.    Of a somewhat more musical and harmonious character were (2) the נֵבֶל, νάβλα, Luther: "psalter," and (3) the כִּנּוֹר, κινύρα, Luther: "Harfe."    Both were stringed instruments, the νάβλα, according to Josephus, having twelve and the κινύρα ten strings.[198]    The νάβλα was played with the hand, whereas, according to the same authority just referred to, the κινύρα was played with the plectrum (in the earlier Biblical times the כִּנּוֹר was also played with the hand).[199]    A good deal has no doubt been written in which the nature of those instruments is fully discussed, but still no certain result has been arrived at.    According to the Mishna, the number of נְבָלִים employed in the temple choir was never fewer than *two* and never more than six, whereas with regard to the כִּנּוֹרוֹת, there required to be *nine* of them at the very least, and their number might be multiplied *ad libitum*.[200]    From all this one might venture to infer that the כִּנּוֹר was the chief, the leading instrument, while the נֵבֶל was rather intended to serve as an accompaniment to it.    Besides the three instruments just referred to, *reed pipes*, חֲלִילִים, were also introduced into the choir on the occasion of the high festivals that occurred in the course of the year (Passover, Pentecost and the feast of Tabernacles).[201]

But in addition to this, *trumpets* (חֲצוֹצְרוֹת) were in regular use, and while the playing upon the instruments hitherto mentioned was left entirely to the Levites (the traditions hesitating somewhat only with regard to the reed-pipes), the blowing with trumpets, on the other hand, was performed by priests.    This latter was also an accompaniment above all of the offering of the daily burnt-offering, and of other parts of

---

[197] 1 Chron. xv. 19.    Joseph. *Antt.* vii. 12. 3.
[198] *Antt.* vii. 12. 3.          [199] 1 Sam. xvi. 23, xviii. 10, xix. 9.
[200] *Arachin* ii. 3. 5.
[201] On the use of those last-mentioned instruments, see in particular, *Arachin* ii. 3–4.

the service as well.[202]    The dawn of the Sabbath was likewise announced by some of the priests blowing trumpets from the roof of the temple.[203]

The *services of a more menial kind* were performed, in the time of Zerubbabel, Ezra and Nehemiah, by temple slaves (נְתִינִים).[204]    It is true that נְתִינִים still continue to be mentioned in the literature of a later period,[205] but it is no longer possible to make out with certainty what the nature of their duties now was.    Instead of them we now meet with what are called "servants" (חַזָּנִים) ;[206] nay we find that, in Philo, the cleaning and sweeping of the temple are mentioned along with the duty of watching as being all of them performed by the νεωκόροι, *i.e.* the Levites.[207]    There were also a good many functions that were left to be performed by boys belonging to the families of the priests (פִּרְחֵי כְהֻנָּה).[208]

## IV. THE DAILY SERVICE.

The daily worship of the sanctuary was conducted by the twenty-four divisions of the priests (see p. 216 ff. above), each division taking its turn and officiating for a week at a time. The divisions were changed every Sabbath day, the arrange-

---

[202] See in general, Num. x. 1–10; Ezra iii. 10; Neh. xii. 35; 1 Chron. xv. 24, xvi. 6; 2 Chron. v. 12, vii. 6, xxix. 26–28; Sir. l. 16.    Joseph. *Antt.* iii. 12. 6.    *Sukka* v. 4–5; *Rosh hashana* iii. 3–4; *Tamid* vii. 3. Lundius, *Die alt. jüd. Heiligth.* book iii. chap. xlvii.

[203] Joseph. *Bell. Jud.* iv. 9. 12.    *Sukka* v. 5.

[204] Ezra ii. 43, 58, 70, vii. 7, viii. 17, 20; Neh. iii. 26, 31, vii. 46, 60, 73, x. 29, xi. 3, 21; 1 Chron. ix. 2.    Comp. Pfeffinger, *De Nethinaeis* (in Ugolini's *Thes.* vol. xiii.).    Winer's *Realwörterb.*, art. "Nethinim." Oehler, art. "Nethinim," in Herzog's *Real-Encycl.*, 1st ed. vol. x. 296 f.

[205] For example, *Jebamoth* ii. 4; *Kiddushin* iv. 1; *Makkoth* iii. 1; *Horajoth* iii. 8.

[206] *Sukka* iv. 4; *Tamid* v. 3.    Comp. further, *Sota* vii. 7–8; *Joma* vii. 1.

[207] Philo, *De praemiis sacerdotum*, sec. vi. (ed. Mangey, ii. p. 236): Ἕτεροι δὲ τὰς στοὰς καὶ τὰ ἐν ὑπαίθρῳ κοροῦντες τὸν φορυτὸν ἐκκομίζουσιν, ἐπιμελόμενοι καθαρότητος.

[208] *Joma* i. 7; *Sukka* v. 2; *Sanhedrin* ix. 6; *Tamid* i. 1; *Middoth* i. 8, iii. 8.

ment being that the retiring one should offer the morning
sacrifice and the extra Sabbath offerings (according to Num.
xxviii. 9, 10) before leaving, while the one that came in to
take its place was to offer the evening sacrifice and put the
fresh shewbread upon the table.[209]   On the occasion of the
three leading festivals of the year (Passover, Pentecost, and
the feast of Tabernacles) the whole twenty-four courses
officiated simultaneously.[210]   The attempts made by Christian
scholars to make out on chronological grounds the week
during which the course of Abia happened to serve in the
year of our Lord's birth (Luke i. 5) have no tenable historical
basis on which to rest.[211]   Every weekly division again was
broken up into somewhere between five and nine *sub-divisions,*
each of which officiated on an average for a single day the
one after the other.   If the sub-divisions happened to be
fewer than seven, then some of them required to take their
turn twice ; but if, on the other hand, there happened to be
more than seven, then on some of the days two of them

[209] See, in particular, Tosefta, *Sukka* iv. 24–25 (ed. Zuckermandel, p.
200) ; also Mishna, *Sukka* v. 7–8 ; *Tamid* v. 1.   2 Chron. xxiii. 4, 8 (where
the priestly courses of services are evidently in question ; it is otherwise in the
corresponding passage 2 Kings xi. 5, 9).   Joseph. *Antt.* vii. 14. 7 : διέταξέ
τε μίαν πατριὰν διακονεῖσθαι τῷ θεῷ ἐπὶ ἡμέρας ὀκτώ, ἀπὸ σαββάτου ἐπὶ
σάββατον.   It is probable that we ought also to understand as referring
to the changing of the weekly (and not the daily) divisions, the· passage
*contra Apion.* ii. 8 : alii succedentes ad sacrificia veniunt, et congregati in
templum mediante die a praecedentibus claves templi et ad numerum vasa
omnia percipiunt.

[210] See *Sukka* v. 6–8, and Bartenora on *Sukka* v. 6, in Surenhusius'
edition of the *Mishna,* ii. p. 279.

[211] See for such attempts, Scaliger, *De emendatione temporum* (Coloniae
Allobrog. 1629), Appendix, pp. 54–59.   Lightfoot, *Harmonia evangelistarum,*
note on Luke i. 5 (*Opp.* i. pp. 258–264).   Bengel, *Ordo temporum* (1741),
pp. 230–232.   Wieseler, *Chronologische Synopse,* pp. 140–145.   Seyffarth,
*Chronologia sacra* (1846), pp. 97–103.   Stawars, *Die Ordnung Abia in
Beziehung auf die Bestimmung des wahren Geburtsdatums Jesu* (*Tüb. Theol.
Quartalschr.* 1866, pp. 201–225).   The calculations here in question are
based partly upon purely gratuitous assumptions and partly upon a very
late and somewhat untrustworthy notice in the Talmud, to the effect that
the course of Joiarib was the one that happened to be officiating on the
day on which the temple was destroyed (*Bab. Taanith* 29[a]).

officiated at the same time (see p. 216, above).   But further,
as never more than a fraction of the priests belonging to a
sub-division were required to officiate at the regular daily
offering of the public sacrifices, it was necessary to determine
by lot those on whom the active duties of the day were to
devolve.   Like the priests, the *Levites* were also divided into
twenty-four courses of service (see p. 227 f., above), which in
like manner relieved each other every week.[212]   But lastly, in
addition to this there was an analogous *division of the people
themselves into twenty-four courses of service* (מִשְׁמָרוֹת), each of
which had to take its turn in coming before God, every day
for a whole week, by way of representing the whole body of
the people while the daily sacrifice was being offered to
Jehovah.[213]   The division actually engaged in the performance of this duty was known under the designation of מַעֲמָד,
" a station."   At the same time the case of the ordinary
Israelites differed from that of the priests and Levites in
this respect, that unlike these, the entire division did not
require to go up to Jerusalem when its turn came.   Instead
of this the persons belonging to it met together in the
synagogues in the towns in or near which they resided
and there engaged in prayer and the reading of Scripture;
probably in every instance it was merely a deputation of
them that actually went up to Jerusalem to be present at the
offering of the sacrifice.   In that case it was this deputation
that, in the strict sense of the word, constituted the מַעֲמָד,
which " stood by " while the sacrifice was being offered.[214]

---

[212] 1 Chron. ix. 25; 2 Chron. xxiii. 4, 8.   Joseph. *Antt.* vii. 14. 7.
*Taanith* iv. 2.

[213] On the whole arrangement, comp. Buxtorf's *Lex. Chald.* col. 1622 f.
(see under עמד).   Lightfoot, *Ministerium templi*, cap. vii. 3 (*Opp.* i. p.
700 f.).   Carpzov, *Apparatus historico-criticus*, p. 109 f.   Hottinger, *De
viris stationariis*, Marburg 1707 (a most exhaustive treatment of the
matter).   Herzfeld, *Gesch. des Volkes Jisrael*, vol. iii. pp. 188–200, 204–209.
Oehler in Herzog's *Real-Encycl.*, 1st ed. vol. xii. 187 (2nd ed. vol. xii. 227).
Hamburger, *Real-Encycl. für Bibel und Talmud*, vol. ii. pp. 877–880 (art.
" Opferbeistände ").

[214] See especially, *Taanith* iv. 1–4.   The principal passage, *Taanith* iv. 2,

The officiating priests wore, during the service, a special official dress, which consisted of the four following articles :—
(1) מִכְנָסִים, *i.e.* short breeches covering merely the hips and thighs, and made of byssus (probably not cotton, but fine white linen).   Then over these (2) the כֻּתֹּנֶת, a long, somewhat close-fitting coat, reaching down to the feet, with narrow sleeves, and also made of byssus.   This coat was fastened together somewhere about the breast with (3) a girdle (אַבְנֵט), which mostly consisted of byssus also, only it had ornaments of purple, scarlet and blue embroidered upon it.   It was therefore the only part of the attire that had any colour about it, all the rest being pure white.   Then the covering for the head was (4) the מִגְבָּעָה, a kind of cap or turban.[215]   Shoes

runs thus: "The early prophets instituted twenty-four courses of service (מִשְׁמָרוֹת).   There was a station (מַעֲמָד) *in Jerusalem*, consisting of priests, Levites and Israelites, to represent each course.   When the time for service came round the priests and Levites of the course went up to Jerusalem, while the Israelites belonging to that course met in the synagogues of their towns and read the account of the creation."   The terms of the passage are contradictory in so far as they seem to allege that the whole מַעֲמָד was *in Jerusalem*, while telling us, at the same time, that the Israelites merely assembled in the synagogues of their towns.   It is probable that the correct view of the matter is given in the corresponding passage in the Tosefta (ed. Zuckermandel, p. 219), where to "the Israelites belonging to that course" are added the words "who were unable to go up to Jerusalem." What is meant therefore is this, that the *whole* of the priests and Levites belonging to the same course, and who were capable of service, were *bound* to go up; while the Israelites, on the other hand, *might* stay at home if it did not happen to be convenient for them to go, though at the same time it is presupposed that some of them were expected to be actually present in Jerusalem.   Accordingly, in *Tamid* v. 6 it is assumed without more ado that the "head of the station" (רֹאשׁ הַמַּעֲמָד) was regularly present in the capital.   A similar view of the matter is taken by Herzfeld, for example, iii. p. 193, and Hamburger, ii. p. 878.   *Bikkurim* iii. 2 proceeds on the assumption that there were station-districts or circles marked off by definite boundaries and having some leading town as the centre of each.   Comp. besides, *Taanith* ii. 7.

[215] For the priests' attire, see Ezek. xliv. 17–19 ; Ex. xxviii. 40–43, xxxix. 27–29, and above all the minute description of it in Joseph. *Antt.* iii. 7. 1–3.   Philo's brief notice in *Vita Mosis*, iii. 13 (Mang. ii. 157): χιτῶνας λινοῦς, ζώνας τε καὶ περισκελῆ ; *De monarchia*, ii. 5 (Mang. ii. 225): ἡ δὲ ἐσθής ἐστι χιτὼν λινοῦς καὶ περίζωμα.   Joseph. *Antt.* xx. 9. 6: λινῆν στολήν. Aristeas, ed. M. Schmidt in Merx' *Archiv*, i. 270. 1–2: τῶν ἱερέων κεκαλυμ-

are nowhere mentioned, and it may be regarded as certain that the priests always officiated without having anything on the feet.[216]

As the white attire was a symbol of purity, so the

μένων μέχρι τῶν σφυρῶν βυσσίνοις χιτῶσιν. The literature of our subject is the same as that already referred to in connection with the high priest's dress; see note 124, above. On the question as to whether byssus is to be identified with cotton or with linen, see among others, Winer's *Realwörterb.*, art. "Baumwolle;" Dillmann's note on Ex. xxv. 4; Haneberg, *Die religiösen Alterthümer*, pp. 536-538 (who is of opinion that Rosellini has decided the question, and that in favour of cotton); and, on the other side, Marquardt, *Das Privatleben der Römer*, vol. ii. (1882) p. 464 f., and the leading work on the subject quoted there, viz. Yates' *Textrinum antiquorum, An Account of the Art of Weaving among the Ancients*, part i. London 1843; also Hehn, *Culturpflanzen und Hausthiere*, 3rd ed. p. 145. As the ancients did not always carefully distinguish between linen and cotton, it is quite possible that there were some instances in which cotton was also made use of for making the priests' attire (as witness, for example, the fine Indian fabric from which the garments were made which the high priest was in the habit of wearing on the afternoon of the great day of atonement, and which consisted of that material). On the other hand, it may be taken as certain that, as a rule, it was linen that was used. According to Mishna, *Kilajim* ix. 1, only flax (פשתים) and sheep's wool (צמר) were employed for the purpose in question, the latter being for the parti-coloured ornamentation on the girdle; see the commentaries in Surenhusius' *Mishna*, vol. i. p. 149, and Braun's *Vestitus sacerdotum Hebraeorum*, i. 6. 2, ii. 3. 4. It is with reference to this matter that it is said in Josephus, *Antt.* iv. 8. 11: μηδεὶς δ' ἐξ ὑμῶν κλωστὴν ἐξ ἐρίου καὶ λίνου στολὴν φορείτω· τοῖς γὰρ ἱερεῦσι μόνοις ταύτην ἀποδεδεῖχθαι. Consequently the priests' attire was expressly exempted from the prohibition of Lev. xix. 19; Deut. xxii. 11.

[216] See Bartenora on *Shekalim* v. 1 (in Surenhusius' *Mishna*, ii. 192). Braun's *Vestitus sacerd. Heb.* i. 3. 3 (pp. 43–47). Carpzov, *Discalceatio religiosa in loco sacro ad Ex.* iii. 5 (in Ugolini's *Thesaurus*, vol. xxix.). Ugolini's *Thesaurus*, vol. xiii. 405 ff. Winer's *Realwörterb.* ii. 271. Leyrer in Herzog's *Real-Encycl.*, 1st ed. vol. vii. p. 718. The following passage occurs in *Megilla* iv. 8 with reference to the worship of the synagogue: "He who says, I will not lead the prayers in coloured clothes, as little is he to do so in white attire. He who is unwilling to do so with sandals on, as little is he to do it barefooted." The meaning of which is simply this, that in the service of the synagogue no one is to presume to wear the dress of a priest. With regard to the priests' benediction, on the other hand, Jochanan ben Sakkai is said to have ordained, that even after the destruction of the temple it was still to be pronounced by them only with the feet bare (*Rosh hashana* 31b; *Sota* 49b. Derenbourg, *Histoire de la Palestine*, p. 305, note 3).

officiating priests required to be men characterized by
*temperance and Levitical purity.*    During the period of their
service they were prohibited from drinking wine or any
other intoxicating beverage.[217]    Nor were they allowed to
enter the court for the purpose of officiating unless they
were Levitically clean.    Nay more, even those who were so
were, in every instance, required to take a formal bath
previous to their entering upon the services of the day.[218]
But besides this, they had then to go and *wash the hands*
and *feet* in the brazen laver (כִּיּוֹר) that stood in the open
air between the temple and the altar of burnt-offering.[219]

As regards the sacrifices that were offered every day,[220]
they are to be distinguished into *two classes,* the *public* and

[217] Lev. x. 8–11; Ezek. xliv. 21.    Pseudo-Hecataeus in Josephus,
*contra Apion.* i. 22 (ed. Bekker, p. 204, 26 ff.): τὸ παράπαν οἶνον οὐ
πίνοντες ἐν τῷ ἱερῷ.  Philo, *De monarchia,* ii. 7.  Joseph. *Antt.* iii. 12. 2;
*Bell. Jud.* v. 5. 7.  Mishna, *Taanith* ii. 7.  Ugolini's *Thesaurus,* xiii. 885 ff.
(where are given *in extenso* in Hebrew and Latin the passages from the
*Jer. Taanith* 65ᵈ; Tosefta, *Taanith* ii., *Sifra* and *Pesikta* to Lev. x. 9).

[218] *Joma* iii. 3: "No priest is to be allowed to enter the court for the
purpose of officiating, *even though he be already clean,* without having
taken a bath;" comp. *Tamid* i. 2.  A bath had also to be taken above
all after every occasion of doing their needs, *Joma* iii. 2.  On the place
where the bath was to be taken, see *Tamid* i. 1; *Middoth* i. 9, *fin.*

[219] Ex. xxx. 17–21, xl. 30–32.  *Tamid* i. 4, ii. 1.  Philo, *Vita Mosis,*
iii. 15: πόδας μάλιστα καὶ χεῖρας ἀπονιπτόμενοι.  On the כִּיּוֹר itself, see
also Ex. xxxviii. 8; Sir. l. 3; *Middoth* iii. 6; *Joma* iii. 10; *Tamid* iii. 8.
Lightfoot, *Descriptio templi,* cap. xxxvii. 1 (*Opp.* i. 643 sq.).  Clemens, *De
labro aeneo,* Traject. ad Rh. 1725 (also in Ugolini's *Thes.* vol. xix.).  The
commentaries in Surenhusius' *Mishna,* ii. 223, v. 360.  Iken, *Tractatus
talmudicus de cultu quotidiano,* 1736, pp. 32–34 (full of matter).  Winer's
*Realwörterb.,* art. "Handfass."  Bähr's *Symbolik,* 2nd ed. i. pp. 583–586.
Kohler's *Lehrb. der Bibl. Geschichte,* i. p. 373 f.

[220] On the sacrificial worship generally, see Lundius, *Die alt. jüd.
Heiligth.* book iii. chap. xxxiii.-xlvi.  Bähr's *Symbolik,* ii. 187–522.
Winer's *Realwörterb.,* art. "Opfer;" and in addition, the various articles on
Brandopfer, Schuld- und Sündopfer, Dankopfer, Speisopfer, Trankopfer,
Räuchern, etc.  Oehler's art. "Opfercultus des alten Testaments," in
Herzog's *Real-Encycl.* (1st ed. x. 614–652, 2nd ed. xi. 29–61).  Thalhofer,
*Die unblutigen Opfer des mosaisch. Cult.* 1848.  Kurtz, *Der alttestamentliche
Opfercult. nach seiner Begründung und Anwendung dargestellt und erläutert,*
1862.  Kohler's *Lehrb. der Bibl. Geschichte,* i. p. 387.  Wellhausen,
*Geschichte Israels,* i. 53–84.  Dillmann's *Exeget. Handb. zu Exod. u. Levit.*

the *private* sacrifices.[221]  The former were offered in name of
the people, and were purchased with a portion of the people's
own offerings, especially the half - shekel tax ; while the
latter again were those in which only private individuals
were concerned, and which might be offered on a vast variety
of occasions, some of them being voluntary and others of them
being, for some particular reason or other, compulsory.  Both
those categories again were sub-divided into different sorts,
varying according to the particular objects for which they
were offered, though they all admit of being classified under
the three following heads :—(1) the *burnt-offerings*, the
essential characteristic of which lay in the fact that the whole
victim was consumed upon the altar ; (2) the *sin-* and the
*trespass*-offerings, in the case of which only the fat was burnt
upon the altar, while the flesh fell to the priests ; (3) the
*peace-offerings* (זִבְחֵי שְׁלָמִים), according to Luther, "thank-
offerings," in the case of which again it was only the fat that
was burnt upon the altar, while the flesh was used by the
owner of the sacrifice himself as material for a jocund
sacrificial feast.[222]  As was only natural, it was the numerous

pp, 373–387.  The dictionaries of Schenkel and Riehm, and the archaeo-
logical works of De Wette, Ewald, Keil, Haneberg and others.

[221] Philo, *De victimis*, sec. iii. (ed. Mang., ii. 238 f.) : Ἐπεὶ δὲ τῶν θυσιῶν,
αἱ μὲν εἰσιν ὑπὲρ ἅπαντος τοῦ ἔθνους, εἰ δὲ δὶ τὸ ἀληθὲς εἰπεῖν ὑπὲρ
ἅπαντος ἀνθρώπων γένους, αἱ δὲ ὑπὲρ ἑκάστου τῶν ἱερουργεῖν ἀξιούντων,
λεκτέον πρότερον περὶ τῶν κοινῶν.  Joseph. *Antt.* iii. 9. 1 : δύο μὲν γάρ εἰσιν
ἱερουργίαι· τούτων δ᾽ ἡ μὲν ὑπὸ τῶν ἰδιωτῶν, ἑτέρα δ᾽ ὑπὸ τοῦ δήμου συντε-
λούμεναι κ.τ.λ.

[222] In the leading passage on the classification of the sacrifices, viz.
Lev. i.-vii., there are, strictly speaking, *five leading kinds* of them mentioned :
(1) the burnt-offering, (2) the meat-offering, (3) the peace-offering, (4) the
sin-offering, and (5) the trespass-offering.  But the meat-offering is
certainly not to be regarded as being on a level with the animal sacrifices,
seeing that, like the drink-offering, it occurs for the most part simply as an
accompaniment of such sacrifices.  With regard to the sin- and trespass-
offerings, they are no doubt distinct, yet they are so much akin to each
other that they may well be regarded as *one species*.  Consequently in the
case of the animal sacrifices, and these are by far the most important of all,
we ought to distinguish them into three leading kinds, as Philo and
Josephus have already done (the former *De victimis*, § iv., and the latter

private offerings of so many different kinds that constituted the bulk of the sacrifices.   However, as it is with giving an account of the *regular* daily worship of the sanctuary that we are here concerned, it is only the public sacrifices that fall to be considered by us, and especially the most important of them all, *the people's daily burnt-offering.*

In order that the reader may be in a better position for understanding what is to follow, it will be well, before proceeding farther, to offer here one or two topographical observations.[223]   The *inner court*, within which the whole of the worship was celebrated, was divided by means of a wall into two divisions, a western and an eastern.   The latter was called "the court of the women," *not* however because *none* but women were admitted to it, but because women *as well* as men were allowed to enter it.[224]   The beautiful gateway in the east side of this court, with its elaborate two-leaved gate made of brass (ἡ θύρα ἡ λεγομένη ὡραία, Acts iii. 2), formed the principal entrance to it; and hence it was that beggars were in the habit of sitting here (Acts iii. 2). The western division again was reserved exclusively for male Israelites, and within it stood the *temple* proper.   Comparatively speaking, this was not a large, but a handsome edifice. The interior, which was probably almost quite dark, was divided into two divisions, the larger one being to the front,

---

*Antt.* iii. 9. 1–3).   *The whole three classes enter into public and private sacrifices alike*, although in the former the *peace-offering* (זֶבַח שְׁלָמִים) is, of course, of but rare occurrence, the only time at which it is regularly offered being Pentecost (Lev. xxiii. 19) ; otherwise we meet with it only on special occasions (see Winer's *Realwörterb.*, art. "Dankopfer").   The flesh of the public peace-offerings belonged to the priests (Lev. xxiii. 20).   On these in general, see *Pesachim* vii. 4; *Sebachim* v. 5; *Menachoth* v. 7; *Meila* ii. 5.   The *burnt-offerings* and the *sin-offerings* offered in the name of the whole body of the people were of very frequent recurrence; see the catalogue of those for festival days in Num. xxviii.–xxix.

[223] For the sources and literature connected with the temple of Herod, see § 15, above.

[224] See Joseph. *contra Apion.* ii. 8: In secundam vero porticum (by which the women's court is meant) cuncti Judaei ingrediebantur eorumque conjuges.

and the other, which was only half as large, being at the back.
The latter formed the "holy of holies," which was trodden by
human foot only once in the year, and that by the high priest
on the great day of atonement.   In the front (and therefore
eastern) division stood those three sacred articles, the punctual
ministering at which on the part of the officiating priests formed
one of the principal parts of the worship, viz. : (1) in the
middle the *golden altar of incense* (מִזְבַּח הַזָּהָב), known also as
the "*inner altar*" (מִזְבַּח הַפְּנִימִי), upon which incense had to be
offered every morning and evening ;[225] (2) to the south of the
latter the golden *candlestick* with seven branches (מְנוֹרָה),
which had to be kept constantly burning ;[226] and (3) to the

---

[225] On the daily offering of the incense, see Ex. xxx. 7, 8.   On the preparation of the incense itself, Ex. xxx. 34–38.   On the altar of incense,
Ex. xxx. 1–10, xxxvii. 25–29 ; 1 Macc. i. 21, iv. 29.   Philo, *Vita Mosis*,
iii. 9.   *De victimis offerentibus*, sec. iv.   Josephus, *Antt.* iii. 6. 8 ; *Bell. Jud.*
v. 5. 5.   Lundius, *Die alt. jüd. Heiligth.* book i. chap. xxv.-xxvii.   Monographs in Ugolini's *Thes.* vol. xi.   Winer's *Realwörterb.*, arts. "Räucheraltar"
and "Räuchern."   Thalhofer, *Die unblut. Opfer des mos. Cultes*, pp. 78–82,
131–139.   Bähr's *Symbolik*, 2nd ed. i. pp. 499–505.   Bleek, *Der Brief an die
Hebräer*, ii. 2. 479 ff., note on ix. 4.   Leyrer's arts. "Räucheraltar" and
"Räuchern," in Herzog's *Real-Encycl.*, 1st ed. vol. xii. 502–513.   The same
articles in the second edition re-written by Orelli, vol. xii. 483–489.
Delitzsch in Riehm's *Wörterb.* pp. 1255–1260.   מִזְבַּח הַזָּהָב, *Joma* v. 5, 7 ;
*Chagiga* iii. 8 ; *Sebachim* v. 2 ; *Menachoth* iii. 6, iv. 4.   מִזְבַּח הַפְּנִימִי, *Joma*
ii. 3, v. 5 ; *Sebachim* iv. 2 ; *Meila* iii. 4 ; *Tamid* iii. 6. 9, vi. 1.   Wellhausen's doubts as to the actual existence of the altar of incense (*Jahrb. f.
deutsche Theol.* 1877, p. 410 ff.) are disposed of by a unanimous testimony in
its favour from the time of the Maccabees down to Josephus and the Mishna.
On the other hand, it certainly appears as though it had been introduced at
a somewhat latish period.   It is worth noting that as yet Pseudo-
Hecataeus (in Joseph. *contra Apion.* i. 22, ed. Bekker, p. 204, 19-21)
mentions nothing else as being in the interior of the temple but the
candlestick and a golden βωμός, which latter might as readily be supposed
to refer to the table for the shewbread as to the altar of incense.

[226] On the duties connected with the candlestick, see Ex. xxvii. 20, 21,
xxx. 7, 8 ; Lev. xxiv. 1–4 ; Num. viii. 1–4 ; 2 Chron. xiii. 11.   From the
passages just quoted it would seem as though the lamps on the candlestick
were to be lighted only in the evening with a view to their burning during
the night.   So also Philo, *De victimis offerentibus*, sec. vii. *init.*  But, according
to Joseph. *Antt.* iii. 8. 3, *fin.*, on the other hand, *three* of the lamps were
kept burning during the day and the whole *seven* during the night ; while
according to the Mishna only *one* was lighted during the day and the whole

north of the altar of incense the golden *table for the shew-bread,* on which twelve fresh loaves had to be placed every Sabbath day.[227]    The front of the temple looked toward the east.    Before it and in the open air stood the *great altar of burnt-offering,* or " the altar " κατ᾽ ἐξοχήν, at which, with the exception of the burning of the incense, every act of sacrifice had to be performed.    It was a high four-square erection of large dimensions, being, according to the Mishna, thirty-two cubits square at the base (while for the sake of comparison it may be mentioned that the interior of the temple was only twenty cubits wide).    It diminished in size toward the top in such a way as to form several stages or landings round it, although on the top it still measured as much as twenty-four

seven at night (*Tamid* iii. 9, vi. 1, and the reference to those passages by Krüger, *Theol. Quartalschr.* 1857, p. 248 f.).    Comp. further, Pseudo-Hecataeus in Joseph. *contra Apion.* i. 22 : ἐπὶ τούτων φῶς ἐστιν ἀναπόσβεστον καὶ τὰς νύκτας καὶ τὰς ἡμέρας. Diodor. xxxiv. 1 (ed. Müller): τὸν δὲ ἀθάνατον λεγόμενον παρ᾽ αὐτοῖς λύχνον καὶ καιόμενον ἀδιαλείπτως ἐν τῷ ναῷ.    On the candlestick itself, see Ex. xxv. 31–40, xxxvii. 17–24; 1 Macc. i. 21, iv. 49.   Philo, *Vita Mosis,* iii. 9.   Joseph. *Antt.* iii. 6, 7; *Bell. Jud.* v. 5. 5, vii. 5. 5.   Mishna, *Menachoth* iii. 7, iv. 4, ix. 3, *fin.*; *Tamid* iii. 6, 9, vi. 1.   Lundius, *Die alt. jüd. Heiligth.* book i. chap. xxiii.   Winer's *Real-wörterb.,* art. "Leuchter."   Bähr, *Symbolik,* 2nd ed. i. 492–499.   Krüger, *Der siebenarmige Leuchter* (*Tüb. Theol. Quartalschr.* 1857, pp. 238–261). Riehm's *Wörterb.,* art. "Leuchter" (with illustrations).   On the position of the candlestick to the south of the altar of incense, see Ex. xxvi. 35, xl. 24.

[227] On the duties connected with the table of shewbread, see Lev. xxiv. 5–9.   Philo, *De victimis,* sec. iii. (ed. Mang., ii. 239 f.).   Josephus, *Antt.* iii. 10. 7.    On the table of shewbread itself, see Ex. xxv. 23–30, xxxvii. 10–16; 1 Macc. i. 22, iv. 49.   Philo, *Vita Mosis,* iii. 10.   Joseph. *Antt.* iii. 6. 6; *Bell. Jud.* v. 5. 5, vii. 5. 5.   Mishna, *Menachoth* xi. 5–7. Comp. further the description of the table alleged to have been presented to the temple by Ptolemy Philadelphus as given by Pseudo-Aristeas (Havercamp's *Joseph.* ii. 2. 109–111.   Merx' *Archiv,* i. 264–267.   Joseph. *Antt.* xii. 2. 7, 8).   Lundius, *Die alt. jüd. Heiligth.* book i. chap. xxiv. Winer's *Realwörterb.,* arts. "Schaubrode" and "Schaubrodtisch."   Bähr's *Symbolik,* 2nd ed. i. pp. 488–492.   Thalhofer, *Die unblut. Opfer des mos. Cultes,* pp. 73–78, 156–168.   Leyrer, arts. "Schaubrod" and "Schau-brodtisch," in Herzog's *Real-Encycl.,* 1st ed. vol. xiii. 467–472.   Delitzsch in Riehm's *Wörterb.* pp. 1388–1392 (with an illustration).   Strack in Herzog's *Real-Encycl.,* 2nd ed. vol. xiii. 455–458.   On the position of the table to the north of the altar of incense, see Ex. xxvi. 35, xl. 22.

cubits by twenty-four.[228] The whole structure was built of unhewn stones which no tool had ever touched.[229] Then, on the south side, there was a gradual ascent leading upward to the top of the altar, and this was likewise formed of unhewn stones. The fire upon this altar had to be kept continually burning by night as well as by day.[230] Between the temple and the altar of burnt-offering there stood, and likewise in the open air, the *brazen laver* (כִּיּוֹר) already referred to, in which the priests were required to wash their hands and feet previous to their engaging in the worship of the sanctuary. To the north of the altar, and still in the open air, was the *place* for *slaughtering the victims*, where there were rings fastened in the ground to which the animals were tied when

[228] Comp. in particular, the descriptions of it in the Mishna, *Middoth* iii. 1–4, and in Josephus, *Bell. Jud.* v. 5. 6 ; further, Pseudo-Hecataeus in Joseph. *contra Apion.* i. 22 (ed. Bekker, p. 264. 16 ff.) ; Aristeas, ed. M. Schmidt in Merx' *Archiv*, i. 269 f. (in Havercamp's *Josephus*, ii. 2. 112) ; 1 Macc. iv. 44–47.   Philo, *De victimis offerentibus*, sec. iv.   Also measurements given in Ezek. xliii. 13–17.   Monographs in Ugolini's *Thes.* vol. x. Winer's *Realwörterb.*, art. " Brandopferaltar."   Bähr's *Symbolik*, 2nd ed. i. pp. 579–582.

[229] Pseudo-Hecataeus in Josephus, *contra Apion.* i. 22 : οὐκ ἐκ τμητῶν ἀλλ᾽ ἐκ συλλέκτων ἀργῶν λίθων.   1 Macc. iv. 47.   Philo, *De victimis offerentibus*, sec. iv. : ἐκ λίθων λογάδων καὶ ἀτμήτων. Joseph. *Bell. Jud.* v. 5. 6. Mishna, *Middoth* iii. 4.   The oldest and most primitive altars were undoubtedly made merely of rough stones taken from the field, or even of simple heaps of earth ; and the Jehovistic legislation proceeds on the assumption that these were the kind that were still in ordinary use (Ex. xx. 24–26 ; comp. Deut. xxvii. 5, 6).   But we find that as early as the days of Solomon this monarch ordered a brazen altar to be erected in Jerusalem (1 Kings viii. 64, ix. 25 ; 2 Kings xvi. 14, 15 ; 2 Chron. iv. 1).   The priest-code, inasmuch as it seeks to describe the whole sanctuary as being of a portable character, accordingly represents the altar of burnt-offering as having been made of wood and covered with brass (Ex. xxvii. 1–8, xxxviii. 1–7 ; Num. xvii. 1–5).   We can scarcely think that one of this description ever existed.   The practice of post-exilic times reverted rather to a compliance with the older legal prescriptions contained in Ex. xx. 25 ; Deut. xxvii. 5, 6.   Comp. in general, Wellhausen's *Geschichte*, i. pp. 30, 38 f.

[230] Lev. vi. 6.   Philo, *De victimis offerentibus*, sec. v. *init.* (ed. Mangey, ii. 254).   Joseph. *Bell. Jud.* ii. 17. 6.   Comp. further, 2 Macc. i. 18–36, and Buxtorf, *Historia ignis sacri et coelestis sacrificia consumentis* (in Ugolini's *Thes.* vol. x.).   Lundius, *Die alt. jüd. Heiligth.* book i. chap. xxxiv.

about to be slaughtered; while there were pillars at hand on
which to hang the victims after they were killed, as well
as marble tables on which to skin them and wash the
entrails.[231]  The temple, along with the altar of burnt-
offering and the place for slaughtering, was surrounded by
an enclosure within which, as a rule, none but priests were
allowed to enter, ordinary Israelites being permitted to do so
only " when it was necessary for the purpose of the laying on
of hands, or for slaughtering, or waving " (תְּנוּפָה).[232]

Now, as regards the regular worship of the sanctuary, the
most important part of it was *the daily burnt-offering offered
in the name of the people at large*, the עֹלַת הַתָּמִיד, or simply
הַתָּמִיד, " the standing one." [233]  The practice of offering regular
daily sacrifice is, comparatively speaking, of very ancient date.
But it underwent certain modifications at different periods;
not only in so far as, previous to the exile, the kings were in
the habit of defraying the cost of the sacrifices (Ezek. xlv. 17
and xlvi. 13–15, Sept. version), whereas they were subsequently
provided at the expense of the people, but also as regards the
character and number of the sacrifices themselves.[234]  In the

[231] *Middoth* iii. 5, v. 2; *Tamid* iii. 5; *Shekalim* vi. 4.  That the
slaughtering of the burnt-offerings had to take place *to the north* of the
altar is prescribed as early as Lev. i. 11.  But it was further required that
the sin- and trespass-offerings should also be slaughtered at the very same
place (Lev. iv. 24, 29, 33, vi. 18, vii. 2, xiv. 13).  This prescription is
omitted only in the case of the peace-offerings; see Knobel-Dillmann's
note on Lev. i. 11.  For more precise information as to the places where
the victims were slaughtered, see *Sebachim* v.

[232] On this enclosure, see especially, Joseph. *Bell. Jud.* v. 5. 6; *Antt.*
xiii. 13. 5.  But according to *Kelim* i. 8, ordinary Israelites were also
allowed to enter this " court of the priests " for the purposes stated in the
text.

[233] עֹלַת הַתָּמִיד, for example, in Num. xxviii. 10, 15, 24, 31, xxix. 16, 19,
22, 25, 28, 31, 34, 38; Ezra iii. 5; Neh. x. 34.  הַתָּמִיד, for example, in
Dan. viii. 11–13, xi. 31, xii. 12; Mishna, *Pesachim* v. 1; *Joma* vii. 3;
*Taanith* iv. 6; *Menachoth* iv. 4.  It is from this that the whole tractate
bearing the title of *Tamid* derives its name.

[234] For what follows, comp. Kuenen, *De godsdienst van Israël*, ii. 270–
272.  Wellhausen's *Geschichte Israels*, i. pp. 81, 82.  Reuss, *L'histoire sainte
et la loi* (*La Bible, Ancien Testament*, part iii.), i. 202.  Smend's *Exeget.*

time of Ahaz the morning sacrifice consisted only of a burnt-offering, and the evening one of simply a meat-offering (2 Kings xvi. 15). This had become so much of an established practice that various parts of the day took their names from it. To speak for example of anything as happening at the time "when the meat-offering was presented" was equivalent to saying toward evening (1 Kings xviii. 29, 36). Not only so, but this mode of denoting the hour of the day had become so completely established that it continued in use even long after the practice had been introduced of offering a burnt-offering in the evening as well (Ezra ix. 4, 5; Dan. ix. 21).[235] It would appear that this had not been introduced as yet in Ezekiel's time. Yet in his day there must have been already an advance upon the older practice, in so far as, according to this prophet, both a burnt-offering and a meat-offering would seem to have been offered in the morning (Ezek. xlvi. 13–15). On the other hand, by the time the priest-code came to be in force it was prescribed that *both a burnt-offering and a meat-offering should be offered every morning and every evening as well*, and further, that on every occasion they should also be accompanied with a drink-offering (Ex. xxix. 38–42; Num. xxviii. 3–8). And so we find that, in the time of the author of the Chronicles, the practice thus established of offering a burnt-offering twice every day in the course of the daily service was looked upon as one of long standing (1 Chron. xvi. 40; 2 Chron. xiii. 11, xxxi. 3). This then formed the true heart and centre of the whole sacrificial system of worship. In no circumstances whatever could it be allowed to be dispensed with. We find, for example, that in the year 70 Jerusalem had for a con-

*Handbuch zu Ezekiel*, p. 381 f. The objections advanced by Dillmann, *Exeget. Handbuch zu Exod. u. Levit.* p. 313, can in no way affect what is a simple and undoubted matter of fact.

[235] In the Mishna even the expression "time of the *minchah*" (of the meat-offering) continues to be used as equivalent to the afternoon; for example, *Berachoth* iv. 1; *Pesachim* x. 1; *Rosh hashana*, iv. 4; *Megilla* iii. 6, iv. 1.

siderable time been invested by the Romans, and that, in consequence, the scarcity of food had reached a climax, but for all that the daily sacrifices continued to be regularly offered; and it was felt by the Jews to be one of the heaviest calamities that could have befallen them when, on the 17th of Tammuz, they at last found themselves in the position of having no more to offer.[236]

The following are the more specific prescriptions contained in the priest - code with regard to the *Tamid* (Ex. xxxix. 38–42; Num. xxviii. 3–8).[237] Every morning and evening alike a male lamb of a year old and without blemish was to be offered as a *burnt-offering*, and in doing so all those regulations were required to be observed that apply to burnt-offerings generally, particularly those contained in Lev. i. 10–13 and vi. 1–6. Not only so, but on every occasion a *meat-offering* and a *drink-offering* were to be offered along with the burnt-offering, as it is prescribed by the priest-code that these were to accompany all burnt-offerings without exception (Num. xv. 1–16). In cases in which the victim happened to be a lamb, the meat-offering was to consist of one-tenth of an ephah of fine flour (סֹלֶת), which was to be mixed (בְּלוּל, therefore not *baked*) with a quarter of a hin of pure oil; while the corresponding drink-offering was to consist of a quarter of a hin of wine. The time at which the morning sacrifice was to be offered was early dawn; that for the evening sacrifice again was to be, in Biblical phraseology, בֵּין הָעַרְבַּיִם, *i.e.* in the evening twilight, though at a later period it had become the practice to offer the evening sacrifice so early as the afternoon, or

---

[236] Joseph. *Bell. Jud.* vi. 2. 1; Mishna, *Taanith* iv. 6. Similarly in the days of the persecution by Antiochus Epiphanes the suppression of the *Tamid* was regarded as one of the most serious calamities possible (Dan. viii. 11–13, xi. 31, xii. 11).

[237] Comp. further, Lightfoot's *Ministerium templi*, cap. ix. (*Opp.* i. 716–722). Lundius, *Die alt. jüd. Heiligth.* book v. chap. i.–ii. Winer's *Realwörterb.*, art. " Morgen- und Abendopfer." Keil, *Handb. der bibl. Archaeol.* (2nd ed. 1875) p. 373 f. Haneberg, *Die religiösen Alterthümer*, pp. 604–609. For full details, consult the tractate *Tamid*, and comp. note 250, below.

according to our mode of reckoning, somewhere about three o'clock.[238]

It was also the regular practice to offer *the daily meat-offering of the high priest* in conjunction with the daily burnt-offering of the people. For, according to Lev. vi. 12–16, the high priest was required to offer a meat-offering every day (תָּמִיד),[239] both morning and evening, and one too which differed from that offered in the name of the people along with their burnt-offering, not only in respect of quantity, but also as regards the mode in which it was prepared. It consisted altogether of only the tenth of an ephah of fine flour, of which one half was offered in the morning and the other half in the evening; and not only was it mixed with oil, but after being so it was *baked* in a flat pan (מַחֲבַת); the cakes thus prepared were then broken into pieces, oil was poured over them, and then they were duly offered (Lev. vi. 14; comp. Lev.

---

[238] On the principal occasion on which they speak of the *Tamid*, Philo and Josephus simply reproduce the scriptural statements with regard to the times for offering it (Philo, *De victimis*, sec. iii.: Καθ᾽ ἑκάστην μὲν οὖν ἡμέραν δύο ἀμνοὺς ἀνάγειν διείρηται, τὸν μὲν ἅμα τῇ ἕῳ, τὸν δὲ δείλης ἑσπέρας. Joseph. *Antt.* iii. 10. 1: ἐκ δὲ τοῦ δημοσίου ἀναλώματος νόμος ἐστὶν ἄρνα καθ᾽ ἑκάστην ἡμέραν σφάζεσθαι τῶν αὐτοετῶν ἀρχομένης τε ἡμέρας καὶ ληγούσης). *What the actual practice was in later times* is clearly evident from *Antt.* xiv. 4. 3: δὶς τῆς ἡμέρας, πρωί τε καὶ περὶ ἐνάτην ὥραν, ἱερουργούντων ἐπὶ τοῦ βωμοῦ. This entirely accords with the statement of the Mishna (*Pesachim* v. 1), to the effect that the evening sacrifice was usually slaughtered about half-past eight and offered about half-past nine o'clock (consequently, according to our reckoning, about half-past two and half-past three o'clock in the afternoon). Comp. further, Josephus, *contra Apion.* ii. 8 (ed. Bekker, p. 239): Mane etiam aperto templo oportebat facientes traditas hostias introire et *meridie* rursus dum clauderetur templum. And hence it was also the practice to go to the temple *about the ninth hour* for devotional purposes (Acts iii. 1, x. 3, 30). See in general, Herzfeld's *Geschichte des Volkes Jisrael*, iii. 184 f.

[239] With this it is impossible to reconcile the words " in the day when he is anointed," Lev. vi. 20; one or other is a later interpolation. See Dillmann's *Exeget. Handb. zu Exod. u. Levit.* p. 442. Jewish and Christian expositors have endeavoured in various ways to dispose of the discrepancy contained in this passage. See Frankel, *Ueber den Einfluss der palästinischen Exegese auf die alexandrinische Hermeneutik* (1851), p. 143 f. Lundius, *Die alt. jüd. Heiligth.* book iii. chap. ix. Thalhofer, *Die unblut. Opfer des mos. Cultes* (1848), pp. 139-151.

ii. 5–6).[240]   Owing to the circumstance of its being made ready
in a מַחֲבַת, it was known at a later period simply as the
חֲבִיתִים, " *the baked* (the cakes), which is the designation already
given to it, directly or indirectly, by the author of the
Chronicles,[241] and subsequently by the Mishna in particular.[242]
Now as the presenting of this offering was incumbent upon
the high priest, we are, of course, justified in speaking of him
as offering a daily sacrifice.[243]   At the same time it must be
borne in mind that here the ·high priest is to be regarded as
the offerer of the sacrifice only in the same sense in which
the people is so in the case of the daily burnt-offering, *i.e.* he
causes it to be offered in his name and at his own expense,[244]
but it was by no means necessary that he himself should
officiate on the occasion.   In fact the expression used in connection with this matter in Lev. vi. 15 is not יַקְרִיב but merely

[240] On the mode of preparation, comp. further, Philo, *De victimis*, sec. xv.
Joseph. *Antt.* iii. 10. 7 ; *Menachoth* xi. 3.  Both לִישָׁה (kneading) and
אֲפִיָּה (baking) formed part of the process.  Lundius, *Die alt. jüd. Heiligth.*
book iii. chap. xxxix. pp. 56–61.  Thalhofer, *Die unblut. Opfer*, p. 151 ff.

[241] 1 Chron. ix. 31.  In this passage the Septuagint simply paraphrases the
words מַעֲשֵׂה הַחֲבִתִּים as follows : τὰ ἔργα τῆς θυσίας τοῦ τηγάνου τοῦ
μεγάλου ἱερέως.  So also Gesenius, *Thesaurus*, under חבתים.  But it is
probable that the author of the Chronicles may have had in view the baked
meat-offering generally, and not that of the high priest alone.

[242] *Tamid* i. 3, iii. 1, iv. *fin.*; *Joma* ii. 3, iii. 4 ; *Menachoth* iv. 5, xi. 3 ;
*Middoth* i. 4.

[243] Philo, *De specialibus legibus*, ii. sec. xxiii. (Mang. ii. 321): εὐχὰς δὲ
καὶ θυσίας τελῶν καθ' ἑκάστην ἡμέραν.  The well-known passage in the
Epistle to the Hebrews (vii. 27) is also to be explained on this ground ;
only it must be understood that this daily meat-offering on the part of the
high priest was not a sin-offering, as the passage in question might lead one
to suppose.  On several Talmudic passages in which, either apparently or
in reality, it is the daily offering of a sacrifice on the part of the high priest
that is in question, see Herzfeld's *Gesch. des Volkes Jisrael*, ii. p. 140 f.

[244] Joseph. *Antt.* iii. 10. 7 : θύει δ' ὁ ἱερεὺς (=the high priest) ἐκ τῶν ἰδίων
ἀναλωμάτων, καὶ δὶς ἑκάστης ἡμέρας τοῦτο ποιεῖ, ἄλευρον ἐλαίῳ μεμαγμένον
καὶ πεπηγὸς ὀπτήσει βραχείᾳ· καὶ εἷς μέν ἐστιν ἀσσάρων τοῦ ἀλεύρου, τούτου δὲ
τὸ μὲν ἥμισυ πρωΐ τὸ δ' ἕτερον δείλης ἐπιφέρει τῷ πυρί.  When a high priest
died, the meat-offering had to be furnished at the expense of the people
(according to Rabbi Juda, *Shekalim* vii. 6, at the expense of his heirs) until
his successor was installed.

יעשׂה. We learn from Josephus that the high priest officiated
as a rule on the Sabbath and on festival days (see p. 255,
above).   But on ordinary occasions the meat-offering of the
high priest, in common with the sacrifices of the people, was
offered by the priests who happened to be officiating for the
time being; and when the lots were drawn with the view of
deciding who were to take the various parts of the service for
the day, one was always drawn at the same time to determine
who was to be entrusted with the duty of presenting the חֲבִיתִין,
*i.e.* the meat-offering of the high priest.[245]   Nay more—
seeing that the law speaks of this offering as being an offering
of Aaron *and his sons* (Lev. vi. 13),—there is no reason
why it should not also be conceived of as a sacrifice which
*the priests* offered for themselves.[246]

Besides the offering of the sacrifices just referred to, the
priests in the course of the daily service were also called
upon to perform certain functions inside the temple in connection with the altar of incense and the candlestick.   On the
*former* incense had to be offered every morning and every
evening alike (Ex. xxx. 7, 8), that offered in the morning
being *previous* to the offering of the burnt-offering, and that in

[245] *Tamid* iii. 1, iv. *fin.*; *Joma* ii. 3.   It is true, no doubt, that, strictly
speaking, what is in view in the passages here referred to is not the actual
offering of the sacrifice, but the bringing of the materials of it to the ascent
leading to the top of the altar.   Still, according to *Tamid* v. 2, *Joma* ii.
4–5, there was also appointed for the actual offering (the carrying of the
sacrifice up to the altar hearth) precisely the same number of priests again
as were employed in bringing it to the foot of the altar, viz. nine, corresponding to the nine parts of which the sacrifice was composed, and among
which, even in the passages first referred to (*Tamid* iii. 1, iv. *fin.*; *Joma*
ii. 3), the חביתין are expressly mentioned.   Consequently, there can be no
doubt whatever that the actual *offering* of the חביתין also devolved, as a rule,
upon an ordinary priest.

[246] Philo, *Quis rerum div. heres.* sec. xxxvi. (Mang. i. 497): 'Αλλὰ καὶ τὰς
ἐνδελεχεῖς θυσίας ὁρᾷς εἰς ἴσα διῃρημένας, ἥν τε ὑπὲρ αὐτῶν ἀνάγουσιν οἱ
ἱερεῖς διὰ τῆς σεμιδάλεως, καὶ τὴν ὑπὲρ τοῦ ἔθνους τῶν δυοῖν ἀμνῶν, οὓς
ἀναφέρειν διείρηται.   *De victimis*, sec. xv. (ed. Mang. ii. 250): Σεμίδαλις γὰρ
ἡ ἐνδελεχὴς αὐτῶν θυσία μέτρου ἱεροῦ τὸ δέκατον καθ' ἑκάστην ἡμέραν, ου τὸ
μὲν ἥμισυ πρωΐας, τὸ δὲ ἥμισυ δείλης προσάγεται ταγηνισθὲν ἐν ἐλαίῳ, μηδενὸς
εἰς βρῶσιν ὑπολειφθέντος.

the evening, on the other hand, coming *after* it, so that the
daily burnt-offering was, as it were, girt round with the offering of incense.[247]    Then further, with regard to the *candlestick*,
it had to be attended to every morning and every evening.
In the morning the lamps were trimmed and replenished with
oil, when one or more of them (according to Josephus three)
were allowed to burn throughout the day.    In the evening
again the rest of them were lighted, for it was prescribed
that during the night the whole seven were to be burning
(see especially Ex. xxx. 7, 8 ; 2 Chron. xiii. 11 ; and in
general, p. 281, above).

Then lastly, with the view of imparting greater beauty to
the worship, it was also deemed proper to have *vocal and
instrumental music*.    When the burnt-offering was being presented the Levites broke in with singing and playing upon
their instruments, while two priests blew silver trumpets
(2 Chron. xxix. 26–28 ; Num. x. 1, 2, 10).    While this was
going on the people were also assembled in the temple for
prayer.    At the pauses in the singing the priests sounded a
fanfare with their trumpets, and as often as they did so the
people fell down and worshipped.[248]    There was a special

---

[247] Philo, *De victimis*, sec. iii. (Mangey, ii. 239) : δὶς δὲ καθ᾽ ἑκάστην
ἡμέραν ἐπιθυμιᾶται τὰ πάντων εὐωδέστατα θυμιαμάτων εἴσω τοῦ καταπετάσ-
ματος, ἀνίσχοντος ἡλίου καὶ δυομένου πρό τε τῆς ἑωθινῆς θυσίας καὶ μετὰ
τὴν ἑσπερινήν. *De victimis offerentibus*, sec. iv. (Mang. ii. 254) : οὐ γὰρ ἐφίεται
τὴν ὁλόκαυτον θυσίαν ἔξω προσαγαγεῖν, πρὶν ἔνδον περὶ βαθὺν ὄρθρον ἐπιθυ-
μιάσαι.    Still more precise is the statement of the Mishna (*Joma* iii. 5), to
the effect that " the *offering of the morning incense* took place between the
sprinkling of the blood and the offering of the various parts of the victim ;
while the corresponding *evening* one occurred between the offering of these
portions and the drink-offering."

[248] On the assembling of the people in the temple for prayer, see Luke
i. 10 ; Acts iii. 1.    For more precise information, as furnished by the
tractate *Tamid*, see below.    It is quite a mistake to suppose, as has been
done through a misapprehension of Acts ii. 15, iii. 1, x. 3, 9, 30, that the
third, sixth, and ninth hours of the day (therefore, according to our reckoning, nine, twelve, and three o'clock) were regular stated times for prayer
(so, for example, Schoettgen, *Horae hebr.* i. 418.    Winer's *Realwörterb.*
i. 398.    De Wette's note on Acts ii. 15 ; and Meyer's on Acts iii. 1).    The
actual times for prayer were rather the three following :—(1) early in the

psalm for every day of the week, the one for Sunday being
the 24th, for Monday the 48th, for Tuesday the 82nd, for
Wednesday the 94th, for Thursday the 81st, for Friday the
93rd, and for the Sabbath the 92nd.[249]
The form of the daily service in the temple which we have
just been describing, is the same as that which had been

morning, at the time of the morning sacrifice ; (2) in the afternoon, about
the ninth hour (three o'clock), at the time of the evening sacrifice; and
(3) in the evening at sunset. See *Berachoth* i. 1 ff., iv. 1. Herzfeld's
*Gesch. des Volkes Jisrael*, iii. p. 183 ff. Hamburger, *Real-Encycl. für Bibel
u. Talmud*, 2nd part, arts. "Morgengebet," "Minchagebet," "Abendgebet."
[249] *Tamid* vii. *fin.* Further, Lundius, *Die alt. jüd. Heiligth.* book iv.
chap. v. no. 25. Herzfeld's *Gesch. des Volkes Jisrael*, iii. 163 f. Grätz, *Die
Tempel psalmen (Monatsschr. f. Gesch. u. Wissens. des Judenth.* 1878, pp.
217–222). Delitzsch's *Commentar zu den Psalmen.* In the case of five of
the psalms here in question the Sept. also inserts in the title of each a correct
statement of the particular day on which it was to be sung, thus : Ps. xxiv.
(xxiii.), τῆς μιᾶς σαββάτου ; xlviii. (xlvii.), δευτέρᾳ σαββάτου ; xciv. (xciii.),
τετράδι σαββάτου ; xciii. (xcii.), εἰς τὴν ἡμέραν τοῦ προσαββάτου, ὅτε κατῴ-
κισται ἡ γῆ; xcii. (xci.), εἰς τὴν ἡμέραν τοῦ σαββάτου. As regards the
psalm for the Sabbath, the statement to the effect that it was the one
appointed for that day has forced its way even into the Masoretic text. It
has been alleged that the Jews were led to select those particular psalms
from an idea that they presented suitable parallels to the six creative days
(see *Rosh hashana* xxxi.a ; *Soferim* xviii. 1 ; the commentaries of Bartenora and Maimonides in Surenhusius' *Mishna*, vol. v. p. 310). But in the
majority of the psalms in question it is quite impossible to discover any
such parallelism. This view has obviously been suggested by the circumstance that when the "station" of Israelites assembled in the synagogue to
read a portion of the Scripture (as described at p. 275 f. above), it was so
arranged that in the course of the week the entire account of the creation
should be read through consecutively (*Taanith* iv. 3 : On the first day of
the week they read the account of the first and second days' work ; on the
second day of the week, that of the second and third days' work, and so
on). Besides the psalms for the different days of the week, many others,
of course, were used in the services of the temple on the most divers occasions. Thus, *on the high festival days*, for example, the *so-called Hallel* was
sung, *i.e.* according to the ordinary view, Ps. cxiii.-cxviii. ; at the same
time the traditions would seem to be somewhat undecided as to what we
are to understand by the Hallel ; see Buxtorf's *Lex. Chald.* col. 613–616
(under הלל). Lightfoot's *Horae hebr.*, note on Luke xiii. 35 (*Opp.* ii.
p. 538 f.). Lundius' note on *Taanith* iii. 9 (in Surenhusius' *Mishna*, ii.
p. 377). Grätz, *Monatsschr.* 1879, pp. 202 ff., 241 ff. Levy's *Neuhebr.
Wörterb.* under הלל. Hamburger, *Real-Encycl. für Bibel und Talmud*, 2nd
part, art. "Hallel."

already delineated with so much fondness by the son of Sirach (Sir. l. 11–21). A very circumstantial account of the *morning* service, founded evidently on sound tradition, is given in the Mishna in the tractate *Tamid*, the substance of which may here be subjoined by way of supplement to what we have already said.[250]

The officiating priests slept in a room in the inner court. Early in the morning, even before daybreak, the official who had charge of the lots for deciding how the different functions for the day were to be apportioned came, and, in the first place, caused a lot to be drawn to determine who was to perform the duty of removing the ashes from the altar of burnt-offering. Those who were disposed to offer themselves for this task were expected to have taken the bath prescribed by the law previous to the arrival of the above-mentioned official. The lots were then drawn, and one of those who thus presented themselves was in this way told off to perform the duty in question. This person then set to work at once while it was still dark, and with no light but that of the altar fire. The first thing he did was to wash his hands and feet in the brazen laver that stood between the temple and the altar, after which he mounted the altar and carried away the ashes with a silver pan. While this was being done, those whose duty it was to prepare the baked meat-offering (of the high priest) were also busy with their particular function.[251]  Meanwhile fresh wood was laid upon the altar, and, while this was burning, the priests, after they had all in like manner washed their hands and feet in the brazen laver, went up to the *lischkath ha-gasith* (on this see

---

[250] The tractate in question is to be found in Surenhusius' *Mishna*, vol. v. pp. 284–310; and in Ugolini's *Thes.* vol. xix. col. 1467–1502. The principal passages along with other material also in Ugolini's *Thes.* vol. xiii. 942–1055. There is a good edition of the tractate by itself (and, as in the case of those already mentioned, also furnished with a Latin translation and notes), under the title, *Tractatus Talmudicus de cultu quotidiano templi, quem versione Latina donatum et notis illustratum . . . sub praesidio Dn. Conradi Ikenii patrui sui . . . eruditorum examini subjicit auctor Conradus Iken*, Braemae 1736.

[251] *Tamid* i. 1–4.  Comp. *Joma* i. 8, ii. 1–2.

p. 191, above), where the further drawing of the lots took place.[252]

The official who had charge of this matter then caused lots to be drawn in order to determine—(1) who was to slaughter the victim ; (2) who was to sprinkle the blood upon the altar ; (3) who was to remove the ashes from the altar of incense ; (4) who was to trim the lamps on the candlestick ; further, who were to carry the various portions of the victim to the foot of the ascent to the altar, viz. who (5) was to carry the head and one of the hind legs ; (6) who the two forelegs ; (7) who the tail and the other hind leg ; (8) who the breast and the neck ; (9) who the two sides ; (10) who the entrails ; (11) who the offering of fine flour ; (12) who the baked meat-offering (of the high priest) ; and (13) who the wine for the drink-offering.[253]   The next step was to go out to see whether there was as yet any symptom of daybreak.   Then as soon as the dawn appeared in the sky they proceeded to bring a lamb from the lamb-house and the ninety-three sacred utensils from the utensil-room.   The lamb that was thus to form the victim had now some water given to it from a golden bowl, where-upon it was led away to the slaughtering place on the north side of the altar.[254]   Meanwhile the two whose duty it was to clean the altar of incense and trim the lamps proceeded to the temple, the former with a golden pail (טְנִי) and the latter with a golden bottle (כּוּז).   They opened the great door of the temple, went in, and proceeded, the one to clean the altar of incense, and the other to trim the lamps.   In the case of the latter however the arrangement was, that if the two that were farthest east were found to be still burning they were in the meantime to be left undisturbed, and only the other five were to be trimmed.   But should it so happen that the two that were farthest east were out, then *they* were, in the first place, to be trimmed and relighted before the trimming of the others was proceeded with.   And so having finished

---

[252] *Tamid* ii. 1–5.        [253] *Tamid* iii. 1 ; *Joma* ii. 3.
[254] *Tamid* iii. 2–5 ; comp. *Joma* iii. 1–2.

their task, the two priests now retired, but they left behind
them in the temple the utensils which they had been using.[255]

While the two just referred to were thus occupied within
the temple, the lamb was being slaughtered at the slaughtering
place by the priest to whose lot this duty had fallen, another
at the same time catching up the blood and sprinkling it upon
the altar.    The victim was then flayed and cut up into a
number of pieces.    The entrails were washed upon marble
tables that were at hand for the purpose.    There were whole
*six priests* appointed to carry the pieces to the altar, one piece
being borne by each priest.    Then a *seventh* carried the
offering of fine flour, an *eighth* the baked meat-offering (of the
high priest), and a *ninth* the wine for the drink-offering.    All
the things here mentioned were in the first instance laid down
on the west side of the ascent to the altar and at the foot of
it, and then seasoned with salt, whereupon the priests betook
themselves once more to the *lischkath ha-gasith* for the purpose
of repeating the schma.[256]

After they had repeated the schma, the lots were again
drawn.    In the first instance they were drawn among those
who as yet had not been called upon to offer up incense in
order to determine which one amongst them should now be
entrusted with this duty.[257]    Then another was drawn to determine who were to lay the various parts of the victim upon the
altar (which, if we are to believe Rabbi Elieser ben Jacob, was

---

[255] *Tamid* iii. 6–9. For an exposition of *Tamid* iii. 6, comp. further, Grätz,
*Monatsschr.* 1880, p. 289 ff.

[256] *Tamid* iv. 1–3. For the place where the pieces were laid down, see
also *Shekalim* viii. 8.    According to *Shekalim* vi. 4, there was a marble
table for this purpose standing on the west side of the ascent to the altar. On
the salting of the pieces, see Lev. ii. 13; Ezek. xliii. 24; Joseph. *Antt.* iii. 9. 1.

[257] The offering of the incense was regarded as the most solemn stage in
the whole sacrificial act. See Philo, *De victimis offerentibus*, sec. iv. (Mangey,
ii. 254) : "Ὅσῳ γάρ, οἶμαι, λίθων μὲν ἀμείνων χρυσός, τὰ δὲ ἐν αὐτοῖς τῶν
ἐκτὸς ἁγιώτερα, τοσούτῳ κρείττων ἡ διὰ τῶν ἐπιθυμιωμένων εὐχαριστία
τῆς διὰ τῶν ἐναίμων. Hence it was while they were offering the incense
above all that revelations were made to the priests, as for example in the
case of John Hyrcanus (Joseph. *Antt.* xiii. 10. 3) and that of Zacharias
(Luke i. 9–20).

done by the same priests who had formerly carried them to
the foot of the altar). Those on whom no lot fell upon this
occasion were now free to go away, and accordingly they took
off their official attire.[258]

The priest to whose lot the duty of offering the incense
had fallen now went and took a golden saucer (כַּף) covered
with a lid, and inside of which again there was a smaller
saucer (בָּזָךְ) containing the incense.[259] Another priest took a
silver pan (מַחְתָּה), and with it brought some live coal from the
altar of burnt-offering and then emptied it into a golden pan.[260]
This being done, both entered the temple together. The one
emptied the coals that were in his pan on to the altar of
incense, prostrated himself in an attitude of devotion, and then
withdrew. The other took the smaller saucer containing the
incense out of the larger one, then handing this latter to a
third priest, he emptied the incense out of the saucer on to
the coals upon the altar, whereupon it ascended in clouds of
smoke. This being done, he, like the other, fell down in an
attitude of devotion, and then left the temple. But, previous
to these latter having entered, the two who had charge of the
cleaning of the altar of incense and the trimming of the
lamps had also come back and entered for the second time,
the former merely to bring away his utensils (the טֶנִי), the
latter in like manner to bring away his (the כּוּז), but also for
the additional purpose of trimming the more easterly of the
two lamps that had not yet been so; the other being allowed
still to burn in order that with it the others might be lighted
in the evening. If it, too, happened to be out, then it was
trimmed like the others, and lighted with fire taken from the
altar of burnt-offering.[261]

[258] *Tamid* v. 1–3. Comp. *Joma* ii. 4–5.
[259] That the lid belonged to the כַף and not to the בוֹז may be seen from
*Tamid* vii. 2; as also from its being assumed that possibly some of the
incense might fall from the בוֹז when it was full into the כַף, *Tamid* vi. 3.
[260] *Tamid* v. 4–5. On the gold and silver pan, as well as the incense
itself, comp. further *Joma* iv. 4.
[261] *Tamid* vi. 1–3. According to this account from the Mishna, it

The five priests who had been thus occupied inside the sanctuary now proceeded with their five golden utensils in their hands to the steps in front of the temple, and there pronounced the priestly benediction over the people, in the course of which the name of God was pronounced as it spells (therefore יהוה, not אדוני).[262]

And now, at this point, the offering of the burnt-offering was proceeded with, the priests who had been appointed to this duty taking up the portions of the victim that lay at the foot of the ascent to the altar, and after placing their hands upon them, throwing them on to the altar.[263] In those cases in which the high priest officiated, he caused the pieces to be given to him by the ordinary priests, and then placing his hands upon them he threw them on to the altar. And now, in the last place, the two meat-offerings (that of the people and that of the high priest) and the drink-offering were presented. When the priest was bending forward to pour out the drink-offering a signal was given to the Levites to proceed with the music. They accordingly broke in with the singing of the psalm, and at every pause in the music two priests blew with silver trumpets, and every time they blew the people all fell down and prayed.[264]

appears that only *one* of the seven lamps of the candlestick was kept burning during the day, and that the middle one of the three on the east side. According, on the other hand, to what must be regarded as the more important testimony of Josephus, it was usual to have three lamps burning in the day-time; see p. 281, above. On the whole controversy as to which and how many lamps burnt during the day, see also Iken, *Tractatus Talmudicus de cultu quotidiano templi* (1736), pp. 73–76, 107 f.

[262] *Tamid* vii. 2.

[263] The throwing required a special dexterity on the part of the priests, a dexterity of which Pseudo-Aristeas already speaks in terms of admiration (Havercamp's *Josephus*, ii. 2. 112; Merx' *Archiv*, i. 271).

[264] *Tamid* vii. 3. Towards the close this tractate becomes somewhat less detailed. It only describes the mode of offering the sacrifice in those cases in which the high priest himself officiated. Besides, the offering of the two meat-offerings is not expressly mentioned. That we have inserted them in their proper place it is impossible to doubt, if we may judge from the order in which they are introduced elsewhere ( *Tamid* iii. 1, iv. *fin.*). Consequently, the meat-offering of the high priest was *not* offered before that

The *evening* service was exactly similar to the morning one, which has just been described. The only difference was that in the former the incense was offered *after* the burnt-offering instead of before it, while in the evening again the lamps were not trimmed, but simply lighted (see p. 290 f. above).

Those two daily public sacrifices formed the substratum of the entire worship of the temple. They were also offered, and that in the manner we have described, on *every Sabbath and every festival day*. But with the view of distinguishing them above ordinary occasions, it was the practice on those days to add further public offerings to the ordinary tamid. The addition on the Sabbath consisted of two male lambs of a year old, which were offered as a burnt - offering along with two-tenths of an ephah of fine flour as a meat-offering, and a corresponding amount of wine as a drink-offering. Consequently the sacrifices offered at a single service on the Sabbath would be exactly equivalent to the daily morning and evening sacrifices put together.[265] On *festival days* again the additional offerings were on a still more extensive scale. On the occasion of the *feast of the Passover*, for example, there were offered as a burnt-offering, and that *daily* during the whole seven days over which the festival extended, two young bullocks, a ram, and seven lambs, along with the corresponding meat- and drink-offerings, and in addition to all this, a he-goat as a sin-offering (Num. xxviii. 16–25); and on the *feast of Weeks* again, which lasted

of the people, as Heb. vii. 27 might lead us to suppose, but *after* it. See also Lundius, *Die alt. jüd. Heiligth.* book iii. chap. xxxix. no. 58.

[265] Num. xxviii. 9, 10. Philo, *De victimis*, sec. iii. (Mang. ii. 239) : Ταῖς δὲ ἑβδόμαις διπλασιάζει τὸν τῶν ἱερείων ἀριθμόν. Joseph. *Antt.* iii. 10. 1. κατὰ δὲ ἑβδόμην ἡμέραν, ἥτις σάββατα καλεῖται, δύο σφάζουσι, τὸν αὐτὸν τρόπον ἱερουργοῦντες. The prescriptions in Ezek. xlvi. 4, 5 are essentially different from this. But the main difference between pre- and post-exilic times, as regards both the festival sacrifices and the tamid alike, lay in this, that *previous to the exile the king* was called upon to defray the cost of them, whereas *after the exile* they were provided at the expense of the *people themselves*. See in particular, Ezek. xlv. 17 ; and in general, Ezek. xlv. 18, xlvi. 15. For an account of the form of worship observed on the Sabbath, see Lundius, *Die alt. jüd. Heiligth.* book v. chap. v.

only one day, there were offered the same sacrifices as on
each of the seven days of the feast of the Passover (Num.
xxviii. 26–31). Then on the occasion of the *feast of Tabernacles*, which, as being the festival that took place when the
harvest was over, would naturally be celebrated with special
tokens of thankfulness, the number of sacrifices was much
greater still.    On the first day of this feast there were offered,
as a burnt-offering, thirteen young bullocks, two rams, and
fourteen lambs, along with the corresponding meat- and drink-
offerings, and over and above all this a he-goat as a sin-
offering; while on each of the six following festival days, all
those sacrifices were repeated, with this difference, that every
day there was one bullock fewer than on the preceding day
(Num. xxix. 12–34). Similar supplementary sacrifices and
offerings, at one time on a larger at another on a smaller
scale, were also prescribed for the other festivals (the new
moon, the new year, and the great day of atonement) that
occurred in the course of the year (see in general, Num.
xxviii.–xxix.).    Then to those sacrifices which merely
served to indicate in a general way the festive character of
the occasions on which they were offered, there were further
added those special ones that had reference to the peculiar
significance of the feast (on this see Lev. xvi. and xxiii.).

But copious as those *public sacrifices* no doubt were, they
still seem but few when compared with the multitudes of
*private* offerings and sacrifices that were offered.    It was the
vast number of these latter—so vast in fact as to be well-nigh
inconceivable—that gave its peculiar stamp to the worship at
Jerusalem. Here day after day whole crowds of victims
were slaughtered and whole masses of flesh burnt ; and when
any of the high festivals came round, there was such a host
of sacrifices to dispose of that it was scarcely possible to attend
to them all notwithstanding the fact that there were thousands
of priests officiating on the occasion.[266]    But the people of

[266] Aristeas (in Havercamp's *Josephus*, ii. 2. 112. Merx' *Archiv*, i. 270.
5, 6): Πολλαὶ γὰρ μυριάδες κτηνῶν προσάγονται κατὰ τὰς τῶν ἑορτῶν

Israel saw in the punctilious observance of this worship the principal means of securing for themselves the favour of their God.

---

# APPENDIX.

## PARTICIPATION OF GENTILES IN THE WORSHIP AT JERUSALEM.

Considering the wall of rigid separation which, as regards matters of religion, the Jews had erected between themselves and the Gentiles, it would not readily occur to one that these latter were also permitted to take part in the worship at Jerusalem. And yet that such was the case is a fact as well authenticated as any fact could be. Nor are we thinking here of the large body of *proselytes, i.e.* of those Gentiles who, to some extent, professed their adherence to the *faith* of Israel, and who on this account testified their reverence for Israel's God by sacrificing to Him. No, we have in view such as were real Gentiles, and who, in sacrificing at Jerusalem, would by no means care to acknowledge that in so doing they were professing their belief in the *superstitio Judaica.* There is however but one way of understanding this singular fact, and that is by reflecting how formal and superficial the connection often is, in practical life, between *faith* and *worship,*—a connection that originally was of so very intimate a character,— and also how this was peculiarly the case at the period now in question. The presenting of a sacrifice with a view to its being offered in some famous sanctuary was very often nothing more than an expression, on the part of the offerer, of a cosmopolitan piety, nay, in many instances a mere act of

---

ἡμέρας. Philo, *Vita Mosis*, iii. 19, *init.*: Πολλῶν δὲ κατὰ τὸ ἀναγκαῖον ἀναγομένων θυσιῶν καθ᾿ ἑκάστην ἡμέραν, καὶ διαφερόντως ἐν πανηγύρεσι καὶ ἑορταῖς ὑπέρ τε ἰδίᾳ ἑκάστου καὶ κοινῇ ὑπὲρ ἁπάντων διὰ μυρίας καὶ οὐχὶ τὰς αὐτὰς αἰτίας κ.τ.λ. Comp. the numbers given in 1 Kings viii. 63 ; 1 Chron. xxix. 21 ; 2 Chron. xxix. 32 f., xxx. 24, xxxv. 7-9.

courtesy toward a particular people or a particular city, and
not in the least intended to be regarded as indicating the
man's religious creed. And if this was a thing that occurred
in the case of famous sanctuaries elsewhere, why should it not
take place at Jerusalem as well ? There was no reason why
the Jewish people and their priests should discountenance an
act intended to do honour to their God, even though it were
purely an act of politeness. As for the offering of the
sacrifice, that was really the priests' affair ; it was for them to
see that this was gone about in proper and due form. And if
the sacrifice were provided, there did not seem to be any
particular reason for caring at whose expense it was so. In
any case the Jew was not called upon, through any religious
scruple, to decline a gift of this nature even from one who did
not otherwise yield obedience to the law. And accordingly
we find the Old Testament itself proceeding on the assumption
that a sacrifice might be legitimately offered even by a Gentile
(בֶּן נֵכָר).[267] And so the Judaism of later times has also
carefully specified what kinds of sacrifices might be accepted
from a Gentile and what might not : for example, all were to
be accepted that were offered in consequence of a vow or as
freewill offerings (all נְדָרִים and נְדָבוֹת); while, on the other
hand, those of an obligatory character, such as sin-offerings,
trespass-offerings, and those presented by those who had issues,
and by women after child-birth and such like, could not be
offered by Gentiles.[268] The offerings therefore which these
latter were permitted to present were burnt-offerings, meat-
offerings, and drink-offerings.[269] Hence it is, that in enumerating the special legal prescriptions relating to offerings, there

---

[267] Lev. xxii. 25 and Dillmann's note. It is here stated that it would be
*unlawful* to take blemished animals for victims even from a Gentile, which
presupposes, of course, that, generally speaking, Gentiles might lawfully
present sacrifices.               [268] *Shekalim* i. 5.

[269] Thank- or peace-offerings they were debarred from presenting, for the
simple reason that they would not possess the Levitical purity required of
those who, in this instance, partook of the flesh of the victims at the
sacrificial feast (Lev. vii. 20, 21).

is frequently a reference, at the same time, to the sacrifices of the Gentiles as well.[270]

The general fact, that sacrifices were offered by and in the name of Gentiles, is one that is vouched for in the most explicit way possible by Josephus, who informs us that on the occasion of the breaking out of the revolution in the year 6 A.D., precisely one of the first things done was to pass a resolution declaring that it was no longer lawful to take sacrifices from Gentiles.[271] By way of protesting against such a proceeding, the opposite conservative party took care to point out that " all their forefathers had been in the habit of receiving sacrifices at the hands of Gentiles ; " and that if the Jews were to be the only people among whom a foreigner was not to be allowed to sacrifice, then Jerusalem would incur the reproach of being an ungodly city.[272] History records at least several remarkable instances of the matter now in question. When we are told, for example, that *Alexander the Great* once sacrificed at Jerusalem,[273] the truth of this fact no doubt depends on how far it is historically true that this monarch ever visited that city at all. But be this as it may, the simple fact of such a thing being even recorded goes to prove that Judaism looked upon such a proceeding as perfectly legitimate and proper. Then *Ptolemaeus III.* is likewise alleged to have offered sacrifices at Jerusalem.[274] Again, *Antiochus VII.* (*Sidetes*), while he was at open feud with the Jews and was in the very act of besieging Jerusalem, went so far as, on the occasion of the feast of Tabernacles, to send sacrifices into the city, presumably with the view of disposing the God of the enemy in his favour, while the Jews on their part cordially

[270] *Shekalim* vii. 6 ; *Sebachim* iv. 5 ; *Menachoth* v. 3, 5, 6, vi. 1, ix. 8. Comp. further, Hamburger's *Real-Encycl. für Bibel u. Talmud*, 2nd part, art. " Opfer der Heiden."

[271] *Bell. Jud.* ii. 17. 2–4.

[272] *Bell. Jud.* ii. 17. 4: ὅτι πάντες οἱ πρόγονοι τὰς ἀπὸ τῶν ἀλλογενῶν θυσίας ἀπεδέχοντο. *Bell. Jud.* ii. 17. 3: καταψηφίσασθαι τῆς πόλεως ἀσέβειαν, εἰ παρὰ μόνοις Ἰουδαίοις οὔτε θύσει τις ἀλλότριος οὔτε προσκυνήσει.

[273] Joseph. *Antt.* xi. 8. 5.     [274] Joseph. *contra Apion.* ii. 5, *init.*

welcomed the sacrifices as a token of the king's sympathy
with their faith.[275]  Further, when *Marcus Agrippa*, the distinguished patron of Herod, came to Jerusalem in the year
15 B.C., he there sacrificed a hecatomb, consequently a burnt-
offering consisting of no fewer than a hundred oxen.[276]  Once
more, Josephus tells us with regard to *Vitellius*, that he came
to Jerusalem at the Passover season in the year 37 A.D., for
the purpose of offering sacrifice to God.[277]  How frequent
such acts of courtesy or cosmopolitan piety were may be
further seen from the circumstance that Augustus expressly
commended his grandson Caius Caesar, because on his way
from Egypt to Syria he did not stay to worship in Jerusalem.[278]  Tertullian is therefore perfectly justified in saying
that once upon a time the Romans had even honoured the
God of the Jews by offering Him sacrifice, and their temple
by bestowing presents upon it.[279]  Nor are we to suppose that
it is merely proselytes that are in view when Josephus
describes the altar at Jerusalem as "the altar venerated by
all Greeks and barbarians," [280] and says of the place on which
the temple stood, that it "is adored by the whole world, and
for its renown is honoured among strangers at the ends of the
earth." [281]

In the class of sacrifices offered for and in the name of
Gentiles should also be included *the sacrifice for the Gentile
authorities*.  As previous to the exile the Israelitish kings
were in the habit of defraying the cost of the public sacrifices,

[275] *Antt.* xiii. 8. 2.
[276] *Antt.* xvi. 2. 1.  Sacrifices on so large a scale as this were nothing
unusual in the temple at Jerusalem. See Ezra vi. 17. Philo, *Legat. ad
Cajum*, sec. xlv. (Mang. ii. 598).  *Orac. Sibyll.* iii. 576, 626.
[277] *Antt.* xviii. 5. 3.
[278] Sueton. *August.* cap. xciii.: Gajum nepotem, quod Judaeam prae-
tervehens apud Hierosolyma non supplicasset, conlaudavit.
[279] Tertullian, *Apologet.* cap. xxvi.: Cujus (Judaeae) et deum victimis et
templum donis et gentem foederibus aliquamdiu Romani honorastis.
[280] *Bell. Jud.* v. 1. 3: τὸν Ἕλλησι πᾶσι καὶ βαρβάροις σεβάσμιον βωμόν.
[281] *Bell. Jud.* iv. 4. 3 (ed. Bekker, v. 315. 2–4): ὁ δὲ ὑπὸ τῆς οἰκουμένης
προσκυνούμενος χῶρος καὶ τοῖς ἀπὸ περάτων γῆς ἀλλοφύλοις ἀκοῇ τετιμημένος.

so Cyrus in like manner is said to have given orders that whatever means and materials might be required for this purpose should be furnished out of the royal exchequer, at the same time however with the view of prayer being offered "for the life of the king and his sons" (Ezra vi. 10). The fact of a sacrifice being specially offered in behalf of the sovereign (ὁλοκαύτωσις προσφερομένη ὑπὲρ τοῦ βασιλέως) is further confirmed by still more explicit testimony belonging to the time of the Maccabaean movement (1 Macc. vii. 33). Consequently we see that even then, at a time when a great proportion of the people was waging war with the king of Syria, the priests were still conscientiously offering the sacrifice that, as we may venture to suppose, had been founded by the Syrian kings themselves. In the Roman period again this sacrifice, offered on behalf of the Gentile authorities, was precisely the only possible form under which Judaism could furnish something like an equivalent for that worship of the emperor and of Rome that went on throughout all the other provinces. We learn indeed from the explicit testimony of Philo, that *Augustus himself* ordained that, in all time coming, two lambs and a bullock were to be sacrificed every day at the *emperor's* expense.[282] It was to this sacrifice offered "*in behalf of the emperor and the Roman people*" that the Jews expressly pointed in the time of Caligula, when their loyalty happened to be called in question in consequence of their having opposed the erection of the emperor's statue in the temple.[283] And we are further informed that it continued to

---

[282] Philo, *Leg. ad Cajum*, sec. xxiii. (ed. Mang. ii. 569) : προστάξας καὶ δι' αἰῶνος ἀνάγεσθαι θυσίας ἐνδελεχεῖς ὁλοκαύτους καθ' ἑκάστην ἡμέραν ἐκ τῶν ἰδίων προσόδων, ἀπαρχὴν τῷ ὑψίστῳ θεῷ, αἳ καὶ μέχρι τοῦ νῦν ἐπιτελοῦνται καὶ εἰς ἅπαν ἐπιτελεσθήσονται. He also uses terms almost identical with these in sec. xl., ed. Mang. ii. 592, where however he adds the remark, that ἄρνες εἰσὶ δύο καὶ ταῦρος τὰ ἱερεῖα, οἷς Καῖσαρ ἐφήδρυνε [l. ἐφήδυνε] τὸν βωμόν.

[283] Joseph. *Bell. Jud.* ii. 10. 4 : Ἰουδαῖοι περὶ μὲν Καίσαρος καὶ τοῦ δήμου τῶν Ῥωμαίων δὶς τῆς ἡμέρας θύειν ἔφασαν. From the conclusion of this sentence we see that, like the public sacrifices, the daily sacrifice for the emperor was also offered partly in the *morning* and partly in the *evening*.

be regularly offered down till the time when the revolution broke out in the year 66 A.D.[284]    Then we have it, on the authority of Philo, that it was not merely a sacrifice *for* the emperor, but one that had been also instituted *by* him ; a step which, in spite of his strong antipathy to Judaism, Augustus would probably deem it prudent to take from political considerations.    It is true, no doubt, that Josephus affirms that the expenses connected with the sacrifice now in question were defrayed by the Jewish people themselves.[285]    Possibly however this historian himself was not at the time aware that the money to pay for the sacrifice came actually from the emperor. At the same time it would appear that, on special occasions, very large sacrifices were offered in behalf of the emperor at the public expense ; as, for example, in the time of Caligula, when a hecatomb was offered on each of three different occasions, first on the occasion of that emperor's accession to the throne, then on that of his recovery from a serious illness, and lastly at the commencement of his campaign in Germany.[286]

Besides offering sacrifices, it was also very common for Gentiles to bestow gifts upon the temple at Jerusalem. Pseudo-Aristeas, for example, gives a very minute account of the splendid presents which Ptolemaeus Philadelphus gave to

---

[284] *Bell. Jud.* ii. 17. 2–4.

[285] Joseph. *contra Apion.* ii. 6, *fin.* : Facimus autem pro eis (scil. imperatoribus et populo Romano) continua sacrificia ; et non solum quotidianis diebus ex impensa communi omnium Judaeorum talia celebramus, verum quum nullas alias hostias ex communi neque pro filiis peragamus, solis imperatoribus hunc honorem praecipuum pariter exhibemus, quem hominum nulli persolvimus.

[286] Philo, *Legat. ad Cajum*, sec. xlv. (ed. Mang. ii. 598).    Sacrifice and prayer in behalf of the Gentile authorities is recommended generally in Jer. xxix. 7 ; Bar. i. 10, 11.    *Aboth* iii. 2 : " Rabbi Chananiah, president of the priests, said : Pray for the welfare of the higher authorities " (מלכות meaning here the Gentile authorities).    For the *Christian* practice, comp. 1 Tim. ii. 1, 2.    *Clemens Romanus*, lxi. ; and in addition, the material collected by Harnack (*Patrum apostol. opp.* i. 1, ed. 2, 1876, p. 103 f.).    Mangold, *De ecclesia primaeva pro Caesaribus ac magistratibus Romanis preces fundente*, 1881.

the temple on the occasion of his requesting the Jewish high priest to send him a number of persons who would be sufficiently competent to take part in a translation of the Old Testament into Greek, the articles presented being twenty golden and thirty silver cups, five goblets, and a golden table of elaborate workmanship.[287] Although this story may belong to the realm of the legendary, still it may be regarded as faithfully reflecting the practice of the time. For, apart from this, we have it vouched for elsewhere over and over again that the Ptolemies frequently gave presents to the temple of Jerusalem.[288] Nor was it different in the Roman period. When *Sosius*, in conjunction with Herod, had suceeded in conquering Jerusalem, he presented a golden crown.[289] *Marcus Agrippa* too, on the occasion of his visit to Jerusalem to which we have already referred, presented gifts for the further embellishment of the temple.[290] Among the vessels of the temple which John of Gischala caused to be melted during the siege were the wine goblets (ἀκρατοφόροι) that had been presented by *Augustus* and his consort.[291] Altogether it was not in the least unusual for Romans to dedicate gifts to the temple.[292] And so, strange to say, in this way even the exclusive temple of Jerusalem became in a certain sense cosmopolitan ; it too received the homage of the whole world in common with the more celebrated sanctuaries of heathendom.

[287] Pseudo-Aristeas in Havercamp's edition of *Josephus*, ii. 2. 108–111 (also in Merx' *Archiv*, i. 262–269) ; in the citation as given in *Antt.* xiii. 3. 4 ; *contra Apion.* ii. 5, *init.*

[288] 2 Macc. iii. 2, v. 16. Joseph. *Antt.* xiii. 3. 4 ; *contra Apion.* ii. 5, *init.*

[289] *Antt.* xiv. 16. 4.

[290] Philo, *Legat. ad Cajum*, sec. xxxvii., ed. Mang. ii. 589.

[291] *Bell. Jud.* v. 13. 6. Comp. Philo, *Legat. ad Cajum*, sec. xxiii., ed. Mang. ii. 569.

[292] *Bell. Jud.* iv. 3. 10 (Bekker, v. 305. 20 f.). Comp. ii. 17. 3.

# § 25. SCRIBISM.

## I. CANONICAL DIGNITY OF HOLY SCRIPTURE.[1]

THE fact most essentially conclusive for the religious life of the Jewish people during the period under consideration is, that the law, which regulated not only the priestly service but the whole life of the people in their religious, moral and social relations, was acknowledged as given by God Himself. Its every requirement was a requirement of God from His people, its most scrupulous observance was therefore a religious duty, nay the supreme and in truth the sole religious duty. The whole piety of the Israelite consisted in obeying with fear and trembling, with all the zeal of an anxious conscience, the law given him by God in all its particulars. Hence the specific character of Israelitish piety during this period depends on the acknowledgment of this dignity of the law.

The age of this acknowledgment may be determined almost to the day and hour. It dates from that important occurrence, whose epoch-making importance is duly brought forward in the Book of Nehemiah, the reading of the law by Ezra, and the solemn engagement of the people to observe it (Neh. viii.–x.). The law, which was then read, was the Pentateuch in essentially the same form as we now have it. Isolated passages may have been subsequently interpolated, but with respect to the main substance, these need not be taken account of. Henceforward then *the law given by God through Moses was acknowledged by the people as the binding rule of life, i.e. as canonical.* For it is in the very nature of the

[1] See the literature on the history of the Old Test. canon in Strack, art. "Kanon des A. T.," in Herzog's *Real-Encycl.* vol. vii. 2nd ed. (1880) p. 450 sq. ; and in Schmiedel, art. "Kanon," in Ersch and Gruber's *Allgem. Encyclopädie,* § 2, vol. xxxii. (1882) p. 335 sq.

law that its acceptance *eo ipso* involves the acknowledgment
of its binding and normative dignity.[2]   Hence this acknowledgment was from that time onwards a self-evident assumption to every Israelite.   It was the condition without which
no one was a member of the chosen people, or could have a
share in the promises given to them.   " He who asserts that
the Thorah is not from heaven (אין תורה מן השמים), has no part in
the future world." [2a]   It is however in the nature of the thing
that this notion should, as time went on, be held with increasing strictness and severity.   While its original meaning was
only that the *commands* of the law were in their entirety and
in their details the commands of God, the assumption of a
divine origin was gradually referred to the entire Pentateuch
according to its whole wording.   " He who says that Moses
wrote even one verse of his own knowledge (מִפִּי עַצְמוֹ) is a
denier and despiser of the word of God." [3]   The whole Pentateuch was thus now regarded as dictated by God, as prompted
by the Spirit of God.[4]   Even the last eight verses of Deuteronomy, in which the death of Moses is related, were said to
have been written by Moses himself by means of divine
revelation.[5]   Nay at last, the view of a divine dictation was
no longer sufficient.   The complete book of the law was
declared to have been handed to Moses by God, and it was
only disputed, whether God delivered the whole Thorah to
Moses at once or by volumes (מְגִלָּה מְגִלָּה).[6]

After the law and as an addition to it, certain other writings
of Israelite antiquity, *the writings of the prophets and works on
the older* (pre-exilian) *history of Israel,* attained to similar

[2] Comp. Wellhausen, *Geschichte Israels,* i. 2 sq., 425 sq.
[2a] *Sanhedrin* x. 1.
[3] *Bab. Sanhedrin* 99[a].
[4] See in general, Joh. Delitzsch, *De inspiratione scripturae sacrae quid
statuerint patres apostolici et apologetae secundi saeculi* (Lips. 1872), pp. 4–8,
14–17.
[5] *Baba bathra* 15[a] (lat. in Marx, *Traditio rabbinorum veterrima de librorum
Vet. Test. ordine atque origine,* Lips. 1884, p. 23).   Philo, *Vita Mosis,* iii.
39 (ed. Mang. ii. 179).   Joseph. *Antt.* iv. 8. 48.
[6] *Gittin* 60[a].

authority. They were for a long time respected and used as
a valuable legacy of antiquity, before their canonization was
thought of. Gradually however they appeared beside the
law as a second class of " sacred Scriptures," and the longer
their combination with the law became customary, the more
was its specific, *i.e.* its legally binding dignity, and therefore
its canonical validity, transferred to them. They too were
regarded as documents in which the will of God was revealed
in a manner absolutely binding. Lastly, at a still later stage
there was added to this body of the " prophets " (נביאים) *a third
collection* of " writings " (כְּתוּבִים), which gradually entered into
the same category of canonical Scriptures. The origin of these
two collections is quite veiled in obscurity. The most ancient
testimony to the collocation of *both* collections with the Thorah
is the prologue to the Book of Wisdom (second century B.C.).⁷
We cannot, however, determine from it that the third collection was then already concluded; on the other hand, it is very
probable that in the time of Josephus the canon had already
assumed a lasting form, and indeed the same which it has to
this day. Josephus expressly says, that there were among
the Jews only twenty-two books acknowledged divine (βιβλία
. . . θεῖα πεπιστευμένα); that all the others were not
esteemed of equal credit (πίστεως οὐχ ὁμοίας ἠξίωται). He
does not, indeed, separately enumerate them, but it is very
probable that he means by them the collected writings of the
present canon, and these only. For the Fathers, especially
Origen and Jerome, expressly say, that the Jews were accustomed so to count the books of the present canon as to make
their number twenty-two.⁸ It was only with respect to cer-

⁷ Prologue to Wisdom : Πολλῶν καὶ μεγάλων ἡμῖν διὰ τοῦ νόμου καὶ τῶν
προφητῶν καὶ τῶν ἄλλων τῶν κατ' αὐτοὺς ἠκολουθηκότων δεδομένων, ὑπὲρ ὧν
δέον ἐστὶν ἐπαινεῖν τὸν Ἰσραὴλ παιδείας καὶ σοφίας κ.τ.λ.

⁸ Joseph. *contra Apion.* i. 8 : Οὐ γὰρ μυριάδες βιβλίων εἰσὶ παρ' ἡμῖν ἀσυμ-
φώνων καὶ μαχομένων, δύο δὲ μόνα πρὸς τοῖς εἴκοσι βιβλία, τοῦ παντὸς
ἔχοντα χρόνου τὴν ἀναγραφήν, τὰ δικαίως θεῖα πεπιστευμένα. Καὶ τούτων
πέντε μέν ἐστι τὰ Μωϋσέως, ἃ τούς τε νόμους περιέχει καὶ τὴν τῆς ἀνθρωπογο-
νίας παράδοσιν μέχρι τῆς αὐτοῦ τελευτῆς. Οὗτος ὁ χρόνος ἀπολείπει τρισχιλίων

tain books, especially the Song of Solomon and the Book of
Ecclesiastes, that opinion was not yet quite decided in the first
century after Christ. Yet in respect of these also the prevailing view was already that they " defile the hands," *i.e.* are
to be regarded as canonical books.[9] It cannot be proved of

ὀλίγου ἐτῶν. Ἀπὸ δὲ τῆς Μωϋσέως τελευτῆς μέχρι τῆς Ἀρταξέρξου τοῦ μετὰ
Ξέρξην Περσῶν βασιλέως ἀρχῆς οἱ μετὰ Μωϋσῆν προφῆται τὰ κατ᾽ αὐτοὺς
πραχθέντα συνέγραψαν ἐν τρισὶ καὶ δέκα βιβλίοις. Αἱ δὲ λοιπαὶ τέσσαρες
ὕμνους εἰς τὸν θεὸν καὶ τοῖς ἀνθρώποις ὑποθήκας τοῦ βίου περιέχουσιν. Ἀπὸ
δὲ Ἀρταξέρξου μέχρι τοῦ καθ᾽ ἡμᾶς χρόνου γέγραπται μὲν ἕκαστα, πίστεως δὲ
οὐχ ὁμοίας ἠξίωται τοῖς πρὸ αὐτῶν διὰ τὸ μὴ γενέσθαι τὴν τῶν προφητῶν ἀκριβῆ
διαδοχήν. Jerome in his *Prologus galeatus to the Books of Samuel* (*Opp.* ed.
Vallarsi, ix. 455 sq.; see the passage, *e.g.* in Gfrörer, *Jahrh. des Heils*, i.
237 sq., and in the introductions of De Wette, Bleek and others) gives the
following enumeration *as that customary among the Jews:* (1–5) Pentateuch;
(6) Joshua; (7) Judges and Ruth; (8) Samuel; (9) Kings; (10) Isaiah;
(11) Jeremiah and Lamentations; (12) Ezekiel; (13) twelve minor prophets; (14) Job; (15) Psalms; (16) Proverbs; (17) Ecclesiastes;
(18) Song of Solomon; (19) Daniel; (20) Chronicles; (21) Ezra and
Nehemiah; (22) Esther. The same enumeration, but in a somewhat different order (and with the omission of the twelve minor prophets, which
must however be an oversight of the transcriber), is given by Origen in
Eusebius' *Hist.Eccl.* vi. 25 (in which the designation Ἀμμεσφεκωδείμ for
the Book of Numbers, which is generally left unexplained, is nothing else
than חוֹמֶשׁ פְּקוּדִים, *Joma* vii. 1; *Sota* vii. 7; *Menachoth* iv. 3). It can
consequently be hardly doubtful, that Josephus also takes this enumeration
for granted, and intends by his $5+13+4=22$ books our present canon.
The four books containing " hymns of praise to God and rules of life for
men," are the Psalms and the three Books of Solomon. That 1 Chron. and
2 Chron. formed, as early as the time of Christ, the closing books of the
canon, may be inferred from Matt. xxiii. 35=Luke xi. 51, where the slaying of Zachariah is mentioned as the last murder of a prophet. Chronologically viewed the death of Urijah, Jer. xxvi. 20-23, was later, but according
to the order of the canon the assassination related in 2 Chronicles is
certainly the last.

[9] *Jadajim* iii. 5: " All holy Scriptures, even the *Song of Solomon and
Ecclesiastes*, defile the hands." R. Judah says: The Song of Solomon defiles
the hands, but Ecclesiastes is doubtful. R. Joses says: Ecclesiastes does not
defile the hands, and the Song of Solomon is doubtful. R. Simon says:
Ecclesiastes is among the points on which the school of Shammai decides
in a manner to lighten, the school of Hillel in a manner to aggravate difficulty. R. Simon ben Asai said: I have received it as the tradition of the
seventy-two elders, that on the day that R. Eleazar ben Asariah was named
president, it was decided that the Song of Solomon and Ecclesiastes defile
the hands. R. Akiba said: No, no. Never has any one in Israel affirmed
that the Song of Solomon did not defile the hands. For no day in the

other books than those of our present canon, that they were ever reckoned canonical by the Palestinian Jews, although the Book of Wisdom was so highly esteemed that it was some- times cited " in a manner only customary in the case of passages of Scripture." [10] It was only the Hellenistic Jews who combined a whole series of other books with those of the Hebrew canon. But then they had no definite completion of the canon at all.

Notwithstanding the combination of the *Nebiim* and *Kethu-*

history of the world was ever of so great importance as that on which the Song of Solomon appeared in Israel. For all other scriptures are holy, but the Song of Solomon the holiest of all. If there was any dispute, it was respecting Ecclesiastes. R. Johanan, son of Joshua, the son of R. Akiba's father-in-law, said: As ben Asai has declared, so was it disputed and so decided. *Edujoth* v. 3: R. Simon (according to R. Ismael) says: In three cases the school of Shammai decided in a manner to lighten, the school of Hillel to aggravate difficulties. According to the school of Shammai, Ecclesiastes does not defile the hands ; the school of Hillel says : It defiles the hands, etc. Hieronymus, *Comment. in Ecclesiast.* xii. 13 (*Opp.* ed. Vallarsi, iii. 496) : " Aiunt Hebraei quum inter caetera scripta Salomonis quae antiquata sunt nec in memoria duraverunt et *hic liber obli- terandus videretur* eo quod vauas Dei assereret creaturas et totum putaret esse pro nihilo et cibum et potum et delicias transeuntes praeferret omnibus, ex hoc uno capitulo meruisse auctoritatem, ut in divinorum voluminum numero poneretur." See in general, Bleek, *Theol. Stud. und Kritik.* 1853, p. 321 sq. Delitzsch, *Zeitsch. für luth. Theol.* 1854, pp. 280-283. Strack, art. "Kanon des A. T.'s," in Herzog's *Real-Encycl.*, 2nd ed. vii. 429 sq. Weber, *System der altsynagogalen paläst. Theologie*, p. 81.

[10] S. Zunz, *Die gottesdienstlichen Vorträge der Juden*, p. 101 sq. Against the canonical authority of the Book of Wisdom, see Strack in Herzog's *Real- Encycl.* vii. 430 sq. It is quite a mistake to think we have a right to infer with Movers (*Loci quidam historiae canonis Vet. Test. illustrati*, 1842, p. 14 sq.), and after him with Bleek (*Stud. u. Krit.* 1853, p. 323), from those passages in Josephus (*Antt.* Preface, § 3, x. 10. 6, xxii. 11. 2 ; *contra Apion.* i. 1. 10) in which he states generally that the Holy Scriptures (τὰ ἱερὰ γράμ- ματα, αἱ ἱεραὶ βίβλοι) were his authorities for his whole history, that he also regarded such of his authorities as did not belong to the Hebrew canon as " holy Scriptures." For these were chiefly heathen authorities. Geiger too can scarcely be right when he insists on regarding as among such "holy scriptures," which according to *Shabbath* xvi. 1 might not be read on the Sabbath day, the apocryphal books (*Zeitschr.* 1867, pp. 98–102). For by these are probably meant, as Jewish expositors also declare, the Kethubim (of these only the five Megilloth were used in the public worship of the synagogues, and these only on special occasions during the year). See Kisch, *Monatsschr. für Gesch. und Wissensch. des Judenth.* 1880, p. 543 sqq.

*bim* with the Thorah, they were never placed quite on a level
with it. The Thorah always occupied a higher position as
to its religious estimation. In it was deposited and fully
contained the original revelation of the Divine will. In the
*prophets* and the other sacred writings this will of God was
*only further delivered.* Hence these are designated as the
" tradition " (קַבָּלָה, Aramaean אִשְׁלְמְתָּא), and cited as such.[1]
On account of its higher value it was decided that a book
of the law might be purchased by the sale of the Holy
Scriptures, but not Holy Scriptures by the sale of a book of
the law.[12] In general, however, the *Nebiim* and *Kethubim*
participate in the properties of the Thorah. They are all
" Holy Scriptures " (כִּתְבֵי הַקֹּדֶשׁ) ;[13] with respect to them all it
is determined, that contact with them defiles the hands (so that
they may not be touched inconsiderately, but with reverent
awe).[14] They are all cited by essentially the same formulas.
For although special formulas are sometimes used for the
Thorah, yet the formula, which most frequently occurs, שֶׁנֶּאֱמַר,
" for it is said," is applied without distinction to the Thorah
and the other Scriptures ;[15] as also in the sphere of Hellenism
(comp. the N. T.), the formula γέγραπται and the like.[16] Nay

[11] In the Mishna, *Taanith* ii. 1, a passage from Joel is cited with the
formula : " in the tradition he says " (בקבלה הוא אומר). Comp. in general,
Zunz, *Die gottesdienstlichen Vorträge der Juden*, p. 44. Herzfeld, *Gesch. des
Volkes Jisrael*, iii. 18 sq. Joh. Delitzsch, *De inspiratione scripturae sacrae*,
p. 7 sq. Taylor, *Sayings of the Jewish Fathers* (Cambridge 1877), p. 120 sq.
[12] *Megilla* iii. 1.
[13] *Shabbath* xvi. 1 ; *Erubin* x. 3 ; *Baba bathra* i. 6, *fin.* ; *Sanhedrin* x. 6 ;
*Para* x. 3 ; *Jadajim* iii. 2, 5, iv. 5, 6.
[14] *Edujoth* v. 3 ; *Kelim* xv. 6 ; *Jadajim* iii. 2, 4, 5, iv. 5, 6.
[15] So *e.g.* to adduce citations from the Kethubim only : *Berachoth* vii. 3
(Ps. lxviii. 27), *Berachoth* ix. 5 (Ruth ii. 4), *Pea* viii. 9 (Prov. xi. 27), *Shabbath* ix. 2 (Prov. xxx. 19), *Shabbath* ix. 4 (Ps. cix. 18), *Rosh hashana* i. 2
(Ps. xxxiii. 15). In these the quotation is always introduced by the formula
שנאמר. But this very formula is also by far the most frequent in quotations from the Nebiim and the Thorah. Comp. the list of scriptural quota-
tations in Pinner, *Uebersetzung des Tractates Berachoth* (1842), Introd.
fol. 21b.
[16] See in general on the formulas of citation, Surenhusius, βίβλος καταλλαγῆς (Amstelodami 1713), pp. 1–36. Döpke, *Hermeneutik der neutestament-*

the Nebiim and Kethubim are sometimes quoted as "the law" (νόμος).[17] And there is perhaps nothing more characteristic of the full appreciation of their value on the part of the Jews, than the fact that *they too are not first of all to Jewish conviction* didactic or consolatory works, not books of edification or history, but also "law," the substance of God's claims upon His people.

## II. THE SCRIBES AND THEIR LABOURS IN GENERAL.

### THE LITERATURE.

Ursinus, *Antiquitates Hebraicae scholastico-academicae.* Hafniae 1702 (also in Ugolini's *Thesaurus*, vol. xxi.).

Hartmann, *Die enge Verbindung des Alten Testaments mit dem Neuen* (1831), pp. 384–413.

Gfrörer, *Das Jahrhundert des Heils*, i. (1838) pp. 109–214.

Winer, *RWB*. ii. 425–428 (art. "Schriftgelehrte").

Jost, *Das geschichtliche Verhältniss der Rabbinen zu ihren Gemeinden* (*Zeitschr. für die historische theologie* (1850), pp. 351–377).

Levysohn, *Einiges über die hebräischen und aramäischen Benennungen für Schule, Schüler und Lehrer* (Franke's *Monatsschr. für Gesch. und Wissensch. des Judenth.* (1858), pp. 384–389).

Leyrer, art. "Schriftgelehrt," in Herzog's *Real-Encycl.*, 1st ed. vol. xiii. (1860) pp. 731–741.

Klöpper, art. "Schriftgelehrte," in Schenkel's *Bibellexicon*, vol. v. pp. 247–255.

Ginsburg, art. "Scribes," in Kitto's *Cyclopaedia of Biblical Literature*.

Plumptre, art. "Scribes," in Smith's *Dictionary of the Bible*.

Weber, *System der altsynagogalen palästinischen Theologie* (1880), pp. 121–143.

Hamburger, *Real-Encycl. für Bibel und Talmud*, Div. ii., arts. "Gelehrter," "Lehrhaus," "Rabban," "Schüler," "Sopherim," "Talmudlehrer," "Talmudschulen," "Unterhalt," "Unterricht."

Strack, art. "Schriftgelehrte," in Herzog's *Real-Encycl.*, 2nd ed. xiii. (1884) pp. 696–698.

---

*lichen Schriftsteller* (1829), pp. 60–69. Pinner, *Uebersetzung des Tractates Berachoth*, Introd. fol. 21a, 22a. Joh. Delitzsch, *De inspiratione scripturae sacrae*, p. 4 sq. Comp. also Strack, *Prolegomena critica in Vet. Test.* (1873), p. 60 sqq.

[17] Rom. iii. 19; 1 Cor. xiv. 21; John x. 34, xii. 34, xv. 25.

With the existence of a law is naturally involved the
necessity of its *scientific study, and of a professional acquaintance
with it.* Such necessity exists at least in proportion as this
law is comprehensive and complicated. An acquaintance with
its details, a certainty in the application of its several enactments to everyday life, can then only be attained by its being
made a matter of professional occupation. In the time of
Ezra, and indeed long after, this was chiefly the *concern of the
priests.* Ezra himself was at the same time both priest and
scribe (סוֹפֵר). The most important element of the Pentateuch was written in the interest of the priestly cultus.
Hence the priests were at first the teachers and guardians of
the law. Gradually however this was changed. The higher
the law rose in the estimation of the people, the more did its
study and exposition become an independent business. It
was the law of God, and every individual of the nation had
the same interest as the priests in knowing and obeying it.
Hence *non-priestly Israelites* more and more occupied themselves with its scientific study. An independent class of
" biblical scholars or scribes," *i.e.* of men who made acquaintance with the law a profession, was formed beside the priests.
And when in the time of Hellenism the priests, at least those
of the higher strata, often applied themselves to heathen
culture, and more or less neglected the law of their fathers,
the scribes ever appeared in a relative contrast to the priests.
It was no longer the priests, but the scribes, who were the
zealous guardians of the law. Hence they were also from
that time onwards the *real teachers of the people,* over whose
spiritual life they bore complete sway.

In the time of the New Testament we find this process
fully completed; the scribes then formed a firmly compacted
class in undisputed possession of a spiritual supremacy over
the people. They are usually called in the New Testament
γραμματεῖς, *i.e.* " learned in Scripture," " the learned," corresponding to the Hebrew סוֹפְרִים, which in itself means nothing
more than *homines literati* (men professionally occupied with

the Scriptures).[18] That such occupation should concern itself chiefly with the law was self-evident. Besides this general designation, we also meet with the more special one νομικοί, *i.e.* "the learned in the law," "jurists" (Matt. xxii. 35 ; Luke vii. 30, x. 25, xi. 45 sq., 52, xiv. 3) ;[19] and inasmuch as they not only knew, but taught the law, they were likewise called νομοδιδάσκαλοι, "teachers of the law" (Luke v. 17 ; Acts v. 34). Josephus calls them πατρίων ἐξηγηταὶ νόμων,[20] or in Graecized fashion σοφισταί,[21] also ἱερογραμματεῖς.[22] In the Mishna the expression סוֹפְרִים is only used of the scribes of former times, who in the times of the Mishna had already become an authority.[23] Contemporary scribes are

---

[18] סוֹפֵר is any one professionally employed about books, *e.g.* also a *writer* (*Shabbath* xii. 5 ; *Nedarim* ix. 2 ; *Gittin* iii. 1, vii. 2, viii. 8, ix. 8 ; *Baba mezia* v. 11 ; *Sanhedrin* iv. 3, v. 5) or a *bookbinder* (*Pesachim* iii. 1). On its use in the Old Testament, see Gesenius' *Thesaurus*, p. 966. When it is said in the Talmud, that the scribes were called סופרים because they counted the letters of the Thorah (*Kiddushin* 30ᵃ, in Wunsche, *Neue Beiträge zur Erlauterung der Evangelien*, 1878, p. 13. 179), this is of course only a worthless etymological trifling.

[19] νομικός is in later Greek the proper technical expression for a "jurist," *juris peritus.* Thus especially of Roman jurists in Strabo, p. 539 : οἱ παρὰ Ῥωμαίοις νομικοί, also in the *Edictum Diocletiani*, see Rudorff, *Römische Rechtsgeschichte*, ii. 54. It is not accidentally that the expression is so frequently found in St. Luke. He purposes thereby to make clear to his Roman readers the character of the Jewish scribes.

[20] *Antt.* xvii. 6, 2. Comp. xviii. 3. 5.

[21] *Bell. Jud.* i. 33. 2, ii. 17. 8, 9.

[22] *Bell. Jud.* vi. 5. 3.

[23] See *Orla* iii. 9 ; *Jebamoth* ii. 4, ix. 3 (*Sota* ix. 15) ; *Sanhedrin* xi. 3 ; *Kelim* xiii. 7 ; *Para* xi. 4–6 ; *Tohoroth* iv. 7, 11 ; *Tebul jom* iv. 6 ; *Jedajim* iii. 2. In all these passages, with the exception of that in *Sota* ix. 15, which does not belong to the original text of the Mishna, "the ordinances of the scribes (דברי סופרים)" are spoken of as distinct from the prescriptions of the Thorah, and in such wise that the former also are regarded as having been for a long period authoritative. Apart from these passages the expression סופרים only occurs in the Mishna in the sense stated above, note 18. On the other hand, in *Shemoneh Esreh*, in the 13th *Beracha*, God is entreated to let His mercy dispose of " the righteous, the pious, and the elders of Israel and the rest of the scribes " (פליטת סופרים), which latter are consequently assumed to be still existing. The Greek γραμματεύς is still found in Jewish epitaphs in Rome of the date of the later emperors (2nd to 4th century after Christ) ; see Garrucci, *Cimitero degli antichi Ebrei scoperto recentemente in Vigna Randanini* (1862), pp. 42, 46, 47, 54, 55, 59, 61.

always called חֲכָמִים in the Mishna. The extraordinary respect
paid to these "scholars" on the part of the people was
expressed by the titles of honour bestowed upon them. The
most usual was the appellation רַבִּי, "my master;" Greek,
ῥαββί (Matt. iii. 7 and elsewhere).[24] From this respectful
*address* the *title* Rabbi was gradually formed, the suffix losing
its pronominal signification with the frequent use of the
address, and רַבִּי being also used as a title (Rabbi Joshua,
Rabbi Eliezer, Rabbi Akiba).[25] This use cannot be proved
before the time of Christ. Hillel and Shammai were never
called Rabbis, nor is ῥαββί found in the New Testament
except as an actual *address*. The word does not seem to have
been used as a title till after the time of Christ. רַבָּן, or as
the word is also pronounced רַבּוֹן, is an enhanced form of רַב.
The first form seems to belong more to the Hebrew, the
second to the Aramaean usage.[26] Hence רַבָּן is found in the

Garrucci, *Dissertazioni archeologische*, vol. ii. (1865), p. 165, no. 20, 21, p.
182, no. 21.

[24] רַב means simply "master," in opposition, *e.g.*, to slave (*Sukka* ii. 9 ;
*Gittin* iv. 4, 5 ; *Edujoth* i. 13 ; *Aboth* i. 3). The mode of address רַבִּי, "my
master," is found in the Mishna, *e.g. Pesachim* vi. 2 ; *Rosh hashana* ii. 9,
*fin.; Nedarim* ix. 5 ; *Baba kamma* viii. 6. Also with the plural suffix
רַבֵּינוּ, "our master," *Berachoth* ii. 5, 7. This predicate having been bestowed
upon the scribes in their teaching capacity, רַב gradually acquired the
meaning of "teacher." It seems to have been already thus used in a
saying attributed to Joshua ben Perachiah, *Aboth* i. 6. In the time of the
Mishna this meaning was, at all events, quite common ; see *Rosh hashana*
ii. 9, *fin.; Baba mezia* ii. 11 ; *Edujoth* i. 3, viii. 7 ; *Aboth* iv. 12 ; *Kerithoth*
vi. 9, *fin.; Jadajim* iv. 3, *fin.* Comp. John i. 39.

[25] Like *Monsieur*. Comp. on the title of Rabbi generally, Seruppii
*Dissert. de titulo Rabbi* (in Ugolini's *Thesaurus*, vol. xxi.). Lightfoot and
Wetzstein on Matt. xxiii. 7. Buxtorf, *De abbreviaturis hebraicis*, pp. 172–177.
Carpzov, *Apparatus historico-criticus*, p. 137 sqq. Winer, *RWB.* ii. 296 sq.
Pressel in Herzog's *Real-Enc.*, 1st ed. xii. 471 sq. Grätz, *Gesch. der Juden*,
iv. 431. Ewald, *Gesch. des Volkes Israel*, v. 305. Steiner in Schenkel's
*Bibellex.* v. 29 sq. Riehm's *Wörterb. s.v.* Hamburger, *Real-Enc.*, Div. ii.
art. "Rabban." The Lexica to the New Testament, *s.v. ῥαββί.*

[26] Both forms appear in the Targums (see Buxtorf, *Lex. Chald. s.v.*
Levy, *Chald. Wörterb. s.v.*), and on the other hand רַבָּן almost always in
the Hebrew. Of the form רבון only one example is known to me in the
Mishna, viz. in *Taanith* iii. 8, where it is used with reference to God. On

Mishna as the title of four prominent scribes of the period of
the Mishna (about A.D. 40–150),[27] and in the New Testament,
on the other hand, ῥαββουνί (רַבּוֹן or רַבּוּן) as a respectful
address to Christ (Mark x. 51 ; John xx. 16).[28]  In the Greek
of the New Testament Rabbi is represented by κύριε (Matt.
viii. 2, 6, 8, 21, 25 and frequently) or διδάσκαλε (Matt. viii. 9
and frequently) ; in St. Luke also by ἐπιστάτα (Luke v. 5, viii.
24, 45, ix. 33, 49, xvii. 13).   Πατήρ and καθηγητής (Matt.
xxiii. 9, 10) are also mentioned as other names of honour given
to scribes.   The latter is probably equal to מוֹרֶה, " teacher." [29]
The former answers to the Aramaic אַבָּא, which also occurs
in the Mishna and Tosefta as the title of several Rabbis.[30]

the meaning of רבן *Aruch* says (*s.v.* אבי, see the passage, *e.g.* in Buxtorf,
*De abbreviaturis*, p. 176) : גדול מרב רבי ונדול מרבי רבן, "greater than
Rab is Rabbi, and greater than Rabbi is Rabban."

[27] These four are—(1) Rabban Gamaliel I., (2) Rabban Johanan ben
Sakkai, (3) Rabban Gamaliel II., (4) Rabban Simon ben Gamaliel II.   To
all these the title רבן is as a rule ascribed in the best MSS. of the Mishna
(*e.g. Cod. de Rossi* 138).   Rabban Gamaliel III., son of R. Judah ha-Nasi,
also occurs once in the Mishna (*Aboth* ii. 2).   Of two others, to whom this
title is usually applied (Simon the son of Hillel, and Simon the son of
Gamaliel I.), the former does not occur in the Mishna at all, the latter, at
least in the chief passage, *Aboth* i. 17, not under this title.   He is however
probably intended by Rabban Simon ben Gamaliel, mentioned *Kerithoth*
i. 7.

[28] The opinion formerly expressed by Delitzsch, that the form רבון is only
used with reference to God (*Zeitschr. f. luth. Theol.* 1876, pp. 409, 606), has
been since withdrawn by himself as erroneous from consideration of the
usual diction of the Targum (*Zeitschr. f. luth. Theol.* 1878, p. 7).   That
the form רבון is pronounced *ribbon* by modern Jews, as also רבי, *ribbi*, is
quite irrelevant.   The shortening of *a* into *i* is confessedly very frequent in
Hebrew, but in this case of very recent date.   In the Middle Ages it was
probably still pronounced רַבּוֹן, as the *Cod. de Rossi* 138 prints the passage
*Taanith* iii. 8.   Comp. also Delitzsch, *Zeitschr. f. luth. Theol.* 1876, p. 606.
It is only for the Aramaean that the pronunciation *ribbon* is well evidenced.
See Berliner's *Ausgabe des Onkelos, e.g.* Gen. xix. 2, xlii. 30; Ex. xxi.
4–8, xxiii. 17.

[29] See Wünsche, *Neue Beitrage zur Erlauterung der Evangelien* (1878),
p. 279 sq.

[30] Abba Saul is the most frequently mentioned among these, *Pea* viii. 5 ;
*Kilajim* ii. 3 ; *Shabbath* xxiii. 3 ; *Shekalim* iv. 2 ; *Beza* iii. 8 ; *Aboth* ii. 8 ;
*Middoth* ii. 5, v. 4 and elsewhere.   Comp. also Abba Gurjan (*Kiddushin* iv.
14) ; Abba Joses ben Chanan (*Middoth* ii. 6.   Tosefta, ed. Zuckermandel,

The Rabbis required from their pupils the most absolute reverence, surpassing even the honour felt for parents. "Let thine esteem for thy friend border upon thy respect for thy teacher, and respect for thy teacher on reverence for God." [31] "Respect for a teacher should exceed respect for a father, for both father and son owe respect to a teacher." [32] "If a man's father and teacher have lost anything, the teacher's loss has the precedence (i.e. he must first be assisted in recovering it). For his father only brought him into this world. His teacher, who taught him wisdom, brings him into the life of the world to come. But if his father is himself a teacher, then his father's loss has precedence. If a man's father and his teacher are carrying burdens, he must first help his teacher and afterwards his father. If his father and his teacher are in captivity, he must first ransom his teacher and afterwards his father. But if his father be himself a scholar, the father has precedence." [33] The Rabbis in general everywhere claimed the first rank. "They loved the uppermost rooms at feasts, and the chief seats in the synagogues and greetings in the markets, and to be called of men Rabbi, Rabbi" (Matt. xxiii. 6, 7; Mark xii. 38, 39; Luke xi. 43, xx. 46).

All the labours of the scribes, whether educational or judicial, were to be *gratuitous*. R. Zadok said: Make the knowledge of the law neither a crown wherewith to make a show, nor a spade wherewith to dig. Hillel used to say: He who uses the crown (of the law) for external aims fades away.[34] That the judge might not receive presents was already prescribed in the Old Testament (Ex. xxiii. 8; Deut. xvi. 9). Hence it is also said in the Mishna: "If any one

pp. 154. 18, 199. 22, 233. 22, 655. 31); Abba Joses ben Dosai (*Tosefta* 23. 4, 217. 19, 360. 16, etc.); Abba Judan (*Tosefta* 259. 18, 616. 31). Others in Zuckermandel's *Index to the Tosefta*, p. xxxi.

[31] *Aboth* iv. 12.      [32] *Kerithoth* vi. 9, *fin.*

[33] *Baba mezia* ii. 11. Comp. also Gfrörer, *Das Jahrhundert des Heils*, i. 144 sq. Weber, *System der altsynagogalen paläst. Theologie*, p. 121 sq.

[34] *Aboth* iv. 5, i. 13. Comp. also Gfrörer, *Das Jahrh. des Heils*, i. 156–160.

receives payment for a judicial decision, his sentence is not valid."[35] The Rabbis were therefore left to other sources for obtaining a livelihood. Some were persons of property, others practised some trade as well as the study of the law. The combination of some secular business with the study of the law is especially recommended by Rabban Gamaliel III., son of R. Judah ha-Nasi. "For exertion in both keeps from sin. The study of the law without employment in business must at last be interrupted, and brings transgression after it."[36] It is known that St. Paul, even when a preacher of the gospel, practised a trade (Acts xviii. 3 ; 1 Thess. ii. 9 ; 2 Thess. iii. 8). And we are told the like of many Rabbis.[37] In such a case their occupation with the law was of course esteemed the more important, and they were cautioned against over-estimation of their secular business. The son of Sirach already warns against a one-sided devotion to handicraft, and extols the blessing of scriptural wisdom (Wisd. xxxviii. 24–39, 11). R. Meir said : Give yourselves less to trade and occupy yourselves more with the law ;[38] and Hillel : He who devotes himself too much to trade will not grow wise.[39]

The principle of non-remuneration was strictly carried out only in their *judicial* labours, but hardly in their employment as *teachers*. Even in the Gospel, notwithstanding the express admonition to the disciples, δωρεὰν ἐλάβετε, δωρεὰν δότε (Matt. x. 8), it is also said that a labourer is worthy of his hire (Matt. x. 10 ; Luke x. 7), to which saying St. Paul expressly refers (1 Cor. ix. 15) when he claims as his right—although he but exceptionally used it—a maintenance from those to whom he preached the gospel (1 Cor. ix. 3–18 ; 2 Cor. xi.

---

[35] *Bechoroth* iv. 6.    [36] *Aboth* ii. 2.

[37] Comp. Hartmann, *Die enge Verbindung des Alten Testaments mit dem Neuen*, p. 410 sq. Gfrörer, *Das Jahrh. des Heils*, i. 160–163. Delitzsch, *Handwerkerleben zur Zeit Jesu* (2nd ed. 1875), pp. 71–83 ; *Lehrstand und Handwerk in Verbindung*. Hamburger, *Real - Enc.*, Div. ii. p. 288 (art. "Gelehrter") and p. 1241 (art. "Unterhalt"). Seligmann Meyer, *Arbeit und Handwerk im Talmud* (1878), pp. 23–36.

[38] *Aboth* iv. 10.    [39] *Aboth* ii. 5.

8, 9 ; Phil. iv. 10-18. Comp. also Gal. vi. 6). If such was the view of the times, it may be supposed that the Jewish teachers of the law also did not always impart their instruction gratuitously, nay the very exhortations quoted above, not to practise instruction in the law for the sake of selfish interest, lead us to infer that absence of remuneration was not the general rule. In Christ's censures of the scribes and Pharisees their covetousness is a special object of reproof (Mark xii. 40 ; Luke xx. 47, xvi. 14). Hence, even if their instruction was given gratuitously, they certainly knew how to compensate themselves in some other way. The moral testimony borne to them by Christ was by no means of the best : " All their works they do to be seen of men : they make broad their phylacteries and enlarge the borders of their garments (Matt. xxiii. 5), and love to go in long garments " (Mark xii. 38 ; Luke xx. 46).

The headquarters of the operations of the scribes was of course Judaea until A.D. 70. But we should be mistaken if we expected to find them there only. Wherever zeal for the law of the fathers was active they were indispensable. Hence we meet with them in Galilee also (Luke v. 17), nay in the distant Dispersion ; for γραμματεῖς are frequently mentioned in Jewish epitaphs in Rome of the later imperial period (see above, note 23), and the Babylonian scribes of the fifth and sixth centuries were the authors of the Talmud, the chief work of Rabbinic Judaism.

After the separation of the *Pharisaic* and *Sadducaean* tendencies the scribes in general adhered to the former. For this was nothing else but the party, that acknowledged as an authoritative rule of life the maxims, which had in the course of time been developed by the scribes, and sought to carry them strictly out. Inasmuch however as the " scribes " were merely " men learned in the law," there must have been also Sadducaean scribes. For it is not conceivable that the Sadducees, who acknowledged the written law as binding, should have had among them none who made it their profession to study it. In fact those passages of the New Testament, which speak of scribes who were of the Pharisees (Mark ii. 16 ; Luke v. 30 ; Acts xxiii. 9), point also to the existence of Sadducaean scribes.

The professional employment of the scribes referred, if not exclusively, yet first and chiefly, to *the law,* and therefore to the *administration of justice.* They were in the first instance *Jurists,* and their task was in this respect a threefold one : (1) *the more careful theoretical development of the law itself;* (2) *the teaching of it to* their pupils; (3) *its practical administration,* that is, the *pronunciation of legal decisions* as learned assessors in courts of justice.[40]

1. *First the theoretic development of the law itself.* This indeed was immovably fixed as to its principles in the Thorah itself. But no codex of law goes into such detail as to be in no need of exposition, while some of the appointments of the Mosaic law are expressed in very general terms. Here then was a wide field for the labours of the scribes. They had always to develop with careful casuistry the general precepts given in the Thorah, that so a guarantee might exist, that the tendency of the precepts of the law had been really apprehended according to their full extent and meaning. In those points for which the written law made no direct provision a compensation had to be created, either by the establishment of a precedent, or by inference from other already valid legal decisions. By the diligence with which this occupation was carried on during the last centuries before the Christian era, Jewish law became gradually an extensive and complicated science ; and this law not being fixed in writing, but propagated by oral tradition, very assiduous study was required to obtain even a general acquaintance with it. An acquaintance however with what was binding was but the foundation and prerequisite for the professional labours of the scribes. Their special province was to develop what was already

[40] This threefold "power of the wise " is also correctly distinguished by Weber (*System der altsynagogalen palästinischen Theologie,* pp. 130–143).

binding by continuous methodical labours into more and more subtle casuistic details. For all casuistry is by its very nature endless.[41]

The object of all these labours being to settle a system of law binding on all, the work could not be performed in an isolated manner by individual scribes. It was necessary that constant mutual communication should be going on among them for the purpose of arriving, upon the ground of a common understanding, at some generally acknowledged results. *Hence the whole process of systematizing the law was carried on in the form of oral discussions of the scribes among each other.* The acknowledged authorities not merely gathered about them pupils, whom they instructed in the law, but also debated legal questions among themselves, nay discussed the entire matter of the law in common disputations. Of this method of giving structure to the law, the Mishna everywhere testifies.[41a] To make this possible, it was needful that the heads at least of the body of scribes should dwell together at certain central localities. Many indeed would be scattered about the country for the purposes of giving instruction and pronouncing judicial decisions. But the majority of those authorities, who were mainly of creative genius, must have been concentrated at some one central point—till A.D. 70 at Jerusalem, and afterwards at other places (Jabne, Tiberias).

The law thus theoretically developed by scholars was certainly, in the first place, only a theory. In many points it also remained such, the actual historical and political circumstances not allowing of its being carried into practice.[41b] In general however the labours of the scribes stood in an active relation to actual life; and in proportion as their

---

[41] See further details in No. 3: Halachah and Haggadah.

[41a] Compare *e.g. Pea* vi. 6; *Kilajim* iii. 7, vi. 4; *Terumoth* v. 4; *Maaser sheni* ii. 2; *Shabbath* viii. 7; *Pesachim* vi. 2, 5; *Kerithoth* iii. 10; *Machshirin* vi. 8; *Jadajim* iv. 3.

[41b] For an instructive example of the kind, see *Jadajim* iv. 3–4. Comp. also the purely theoretical definitions as to the composition of the tribes, *Sanhedrin* i. 5; *Horajoth* i. 5.

credit increased, did *their theory become valid law.* In the last
century before the destruction of Jerusalem the Pharisaic
scribes bore already such absolute spiritual sway, that the
great Sanhedrim, notwithstanding its mixed composition of
Pharisees and Sadducees, adhered in practice to the law
developed by the Pharisees (see above, p. 179). Many
matters were besides of such a nature as not to need any
formal legislation. For the godly would observe religious
institutions, not on account of formal legislation, but by
reason of a voluntary subjection to an authority which they
acknowledged as legitimate.[42] Hence the maxims developed
by the scribes were recognised as binding in practice also,
so soon as the schools were agreed about them. The *scribes*
were in fact, though not upon the ground of formal appointment, *legislators.* This applies in a very special manner to
the time *after the destruction of the temple.* There then no
longer existed a *civil* court of justice like the former Sanhedrim.
The Rabbinical scribes, with their purely spiritual authority,
were now the only influential factors for laying down a rule.
They had formerly been the *actual* establishers of law, they
now were more and more acknowledged as deciding authorities.
*Their judgment sufficed to determine what was valid law.* As
soon then as doubt arose concerning any point, or it was
questioned whether this or that course of action should be
embraced, it was customary to bring the matter "before the
learned," who then pronounced an authoritative decision.[43]
And so great was the authority of these teachers of the law,
that the judgment of even one respected teacher sufficed to
decide a question.[44] New dogmas, *i.e.* new rules legally valid,

---

[42] The priests too almost always followed the theory of the scribes.
They are but exceptional cases in which the Mishna has to report a differ-
ence between the practice of the priests and the theory of the Rabbis ; see
*Shekalim* i. 3–4 ; *Joma* vi. 3 ; *Sebachim* xii. 4.

[43] " *The matter came before the learned* (חכמים) *and they decided thus and
thus,*" is a formula of frequent occurrence. See *e.g. Kilajim* iv. 9 ; *Edujoth*
vii. 3 ; *Bechoroth* v 3.

[44] In this manner are doubtful cases decided, *e.g.*, by Rabban Johanan

sometimes even differing from what had hitherto been customary, were laid down, without even such special occasion.[45] In such cases however it was always assumed that the decision of the individual agreed with the decision of the majority of all the teachers of the law, and was accepted by them (see No. 3). Hence it might happen that the decision of a single teacher would be subsequently corrected by the majority,[46] or that even an eminent teacher would be obliged to subordinate his own view to those of a " court " of teachers.[47]

The legislative power of the Rabbis was a thing so self-evident in the time of the Mishna, that it is often without further ceremony assumed also for the time before the destruction of Jerusalem. It is said quite naturally that Hillel decreed this or that,[48] or that Gamaliel I. enacted this or that.[49] And yet not Hillel or Gamaliel I., but the great Sanhedrim of Jerusalem, was then the ultimate resort for decision. For thence proceeded, as is said in the Mishna itself, " the law for all Israel." [50] The truth in this representation is, that in any case the great teachers of the law were already the deciding authorities.

2. The second chief task of the scribes was to *teach the law.* The ideal of legal Judaism was properly, that every Israelite should have a professional acquaintance with the law. If this were unattainable, then the greatest possible number was

ben Sakkai (*Shabbath* xvi. 7, xxii. 3), Rabban Gamaliel II. (*Kelim* v. 4), R. Akiba (*Kilajim* vii. 5 ; *Terumoth* iv. 13 ; *Jebamoth* xii. 5 ; *Nidda* viii. 3).

[45] So *e.g.* by Rabban Johanan ben Sakkai (*Sukka* iii. 12 ; *Rosh hashana* iv. 1, 3, 4 ; *Sota* ix. 9 ; *Menachoth* x. 5) and by R. Akiba (*Maaser sheni* v. 8 ; *Nasir* vi. 1 ; *Sanhedrin* iii. 4).

[46] Thus was a decision of Nahum the Median subsequently corrected by " the learned," *Nasir* v. 4.

[47] *E.g.* R. Joshua had to agree to a decision of Rabban *Gamaliel II. and his court, Rosh hashana* ii. 9.

[48] *Shebiith* x. 3 ; *Gittin* iv. 3 ; *Arachin* ix. 4. Everywhere with the formula הִתְקִין, " he decreed."

[49] *Rosh hashana* ii. 5 ; *Gittin* iv. 2-3. Equally with the formula הִתְקִין.

[50] *Sanhedrin* xi. 2.

to be raised to this ideal elevation. " Bring up many scholars " is said to have been already a motto of the men of the Great Synagogue.[51] Hence the more famous Rabbis often assembled about them in great numbers, youths desirous of instruction,[52] for the purpose of making them thoroughly acquainted with the much ramified and copious " oral law." The pupils were called תַּלְמִידִים, or more fully תַּלְמִידֵי חֲכָמִים.[53] The instruction consisted of an indefatigable continuous exercise of the memory. For the object being that the pupils should remember with accuracy the entire matter with its thousands upon thousands of minutiae, and the oral law being never committed to writing, the instruction could not be confined to a single statement. The teacher was obliged to repeat his matter again and again with his pupils. Hence in Rabbinic diction " to repeat " (שָׁנָה = δευτεροῦν) means exactly the same as " to teach " (whence also מִשְׁנָה = teaching).[54] This repetition was not however performed by the teacher only delivering his matter. The whole proceeding was, on the contrary, disputational. The teacher brought before his pupils several legal questions for their decision and let them answer them or answered them himself. The pupils were also allowed to propose questions to the teacher.[55] This form of catechetical lecture has left its mark upon the style of the Mishna, the question being frequently started how this or that subject is to be under-

[51] *Aboth* i. 1.     [52] Joseph. *Bell. Jud.* xxxiii. 2.

[53] *Pesachim* iv. 5 ; *Joma* i. 6 ; *Sukka* ii. 1 ; *Chagiga* i. 8 ; *Nedarim* x. 4 ; *Sota* i. 3 ; *Sanhedrin* iv. 4, xi. 2 ; *Makkoth* ii. 5 ; *Aboth* v. 12 ; *Horajoth* iii. 8 ; *Negaim* xii. 5. Pupils *e.g.* of Rabban Johanan ben Sakkai (*Aboth* ii. 8), of Rabban Gamaliel II. (*Berachoth* ii. 5–7), of R. Ismael (*Erubin* ii. 6), R. Akiba (*Nidda* viii. 3), pupils of the school of Shammai (*Orla* ii. 5, 12), are severally mentioned. The appellation חָבֵר for one who has finished his study of the law, but has not yet obtained any publicly acknowledged position, belongs to the later Middle Ages. In the Mishna the word has quite another meaning. See § 26.

[54] Comp. Hieronymus, *Epist.* 121 *ad Algasiam*, quaest. x. (*Opp.* ed. Vallarsi, i. 884 sq.) : Doctores eorum σοφοί hoc est sapientes vocantur. Et si quando certis diebus traditiones suas exponunt discipulis suis, solent dicere : οἱ σοφοὶ δευτερῶσιν, id est sapientes docent traditiones.

[55] See Lightfoot and Wetzstein on Luke ii. 46.

stood for the purpose of giving a decision.[56] All knowledge
of the law being strictly traditional, a pupil had only two
duties. One was to keep everything faithfully in memory.
R. Dosthai said in the name of R. Meir: He who forgets a
tenet of his instruction in the law, to him the Scripture
imputes the wilful forfeiture of his life.[57] The second duty
was never to teach anything otherwise than it had been
delivered to him. Even in expression he was to confine himself to the words of his teacher: "Every one is bound to
teach with the expressions of his teacher," חַיָּב אָדָם לוֹמַר בִּלְשׁוֹן
רַבּוֹ.[58] It was the highest praise of a pupil to be "like a well
lined with lime, which loses not one drop."[59]

For these theoretical studies of the law, whether the
disputations of the scribes with each other or instruction
properly so called, there were in the period of the Mishna,
and probably also so early as the times of the New Test.,
special localities, the so-called "houses of teaching" (Heb.
בֵּית הַמִּדְרָשׁ, plur. בָּתֵּי מִדְרָשׁוֹת).[60] They are often mentioned in
conjunction with the synagogues as places, which in legal
respects enjoyed certain privileges.[61] In Jabne a locality
which was called "the vineyard" (כֶּרֶם) is mentioned as a
place of meeting of the learned, from which however we
cannot infer, that כֶּרֶם was in general a poetic term for a

[56] E.g. Berachoth i. 1–2; Pea iv. 10, vi. 8, vii. 3, 4, viii. 1; Kilajim ii. 2,
iv. 1, 2, 3, vi. 1, 5; Shebiith i. 1, 2, 5, ii. 1, iii. 1, 2, iv. 4. The question
is very frequently introduced by כֵּיצַד (=how?): Berachoth vi. 1, vii. 3;
Demai v. 1; Terumoth iv. 9; Maaser sheni iv. 4, v. 4; Challa ii. 8; Orla
ii. 2, iii. 8; Bikkurim iii. 1, 2; Erubin v. 1, viii. 1.
[57] Aboth iii. 8.        [58] Edujoth i. 3.
[59] Aboth ii. 8. Comp. also Gfrörer, Das Jahrh. des Heils, i. 168–173.
[60] Berachoth iv. 2; Demai ii. 3, vii. 5; *Terumoth xi. 10; Shabbath xvi. 1,
xviii. 1; *Pesachim iv. 4; Beza iii. 5; Aboth v. 14; Menachoth x. 9;
Jadajim iv. 3, 4. In the passages marked * the plural form occurs. On
other designations of the house of teaching, see Vitringa, De synagoga
vetere, p. 133 sqq.
[61] Terumoth xi. 10; Pesachim iv. 4. It is evident from both passages,
that the houses of teaching were distinct from the synagogues. On the high
estimation in which these houses of teaching were held, see also Hamburger,
Real-Encycl. ii. 675–677, art. "Lehrhaus."

house of teaching.[62]  In Jerusalem indeed the catechetical lectures were held "in the temple" ($\dot{\epsilon}\nu$ $\tau\hat{\omega}$ $\dot{\iota}\epsilon\rho\hat{\omega}$, Luke ii. 46; Matt. xxi. 23, xxvi. 55; Mark xiv. 49; Luke xx. 37; John xviii. 20), i.e. in the colonnades or some other space of the outer court.  The pupils sat on the ground during the instruction (בְּקַרְקַע) of the teacher, who was on an elevated place (hence Acts xxii. 3: $\pi\alpha\rho\dot{\alpha}$ $\tauο\dot{\upsilon}ς$ $\pi\dot{ο}δας$ $\Gamma\alpha\mu\alpha\lambda\iota\dot{\eta}\lambda$; comp. also Luke ii. 46).[63]

3. A third duty, which equally belonged to the calling of the scribes, was *passing sentence* in the court of justice. Their acquaintance with the law being a professional one, their votes could not but be of influential importance. It is true that at least during the period under consideration, a special and scholarly acquaintance with the law was by no means essential to the office of a judge.  Any one might be a judge, who was appointed such through the confidence of his fellow-citizens.  And it may be supposed, that the small local courts were for the most part lay courts. It was nevertheless in the nature of things, that confidence should be placed in a judge in proportion as he was distinguished for a thorough and accurate knowledge of the

[62] *Kethuboth* iv. 6; *Edujoth* ii. 4.  According to the connection of the two passages, כרם was a place where the learned were accustomed to assemble in Jabne (R. Eleasar and R. Ismael delivered this and that *before the learned in the vineyard at Jabne*).  It is probable that an actual vineyard with a house or court, which served as a place of meeting, is intended. The traditional explanation tries indeed to deduce the appellation from the circumstance, that in the house of teaching the תַּלְמִידִים sat in rows like vine plants (so already *Jer. Berachoth* iv. fol. 7d in Levy, *Neuhebr. Wörterb.* ii. 408, and after this the commentators of the Mishna, see Surenhusius' edition iii. 70, iv. 332).  See, on the contrary, Derenbourg, *Histoire de la Palestine*, p. 380, note 3.

[63] According to later Talmudic tradition, the sitting on the ground on the part of scholars was not customary till after the death of Gamaliel I.; in earlier times they used to stand (*Megilla* 21a, in Lightfoot, *Horae hebraicae on Luke* ii. 46).  The whole tradition however is merely an explanation of *Sota* ix. 15: "Since Rabban Gamaliel the elder died, reverence for the law has disappeared."  See, on the other hand, beside Luke ii. 46, *Aboth* i. 4, according to which Joses ben Joeser already said, one ought to let oneself be covered with dust at the *feet of the wise*.

law. So far then as men learned in the law were to be found, it is self-evident that such would be called to the office of judge. With respect to the great Sanhedrim at Jerusalem, it is expressly testified in the New Testament, that γραμματεῖς also were among those who were its members (comp. above, p. 177 sq.). After the fall of the Jewish State, A.D. 70, the authority of the Rabbis increased in independent importance in this respect also. Being now recognised as independent *legislators*, they were also regarded as independent *judges*. Their sentences were voluntarily acquiesced in, whether they gave judgment collectively or individually. Thus it is *e.g.* related, that R. Akiba once condemned a man to 400 sus (denarii) as compensation for uncovering his head to a woman in the street.[64]

This threefold activity of the scribes as men learned in the law formed their chief and special calling. But the Holy Scriptures are something besides law. Even in the Pentateuch *narrative* occupies a wide space, while the contents of other books are almost exclusively either *historical* or *didactic*. This fact always remained, customary as it was to look upon the whole chiefly from the view-point of law. These Scriptures then being also deeply studied, it was impossible not to let history be spoken of as history and religious edification as such. What however was common in the treatment of these Scriptures and those of the law was, that they too were dealt with as *a sacred text, a sacred standard*, which was not only to be deeply studied, but which had also to be subjected to a complete *elaboration*. As the law was more and more developed, so also was the sacred history and the religious instruction further developed, and that always in connection with the text of Scripture, which just in its quality of a sacred text silently invited to such deep investigation. In such development the notions of subsequent times had, of course, a very important influence in modifying results. History and dogma were not merely further

[64] *Baba kamma* viii. 8.

developed, but fashioned according to the views of after times.
This gave rise to what is usually called the Haggadah.[65]  It is
true that it did not belong to the special province of teachers
of the law to occupy themselves therewith.  But since the
manipulation of the law and that of the historical religious
and ethical contents of the sacred text arose from a kindred
exigency, it was a natural result, that both should be effected
by the same persons.  As a rule the learned occupied themselves with both, though some distinguished themselves more
in the former and others more in the latter department.

In their double quality of men learned in the law and
learned in the " Haggadah," the scribes were also qualified
above others for *delivering lectures and exhortations in the
synagogues.*  These were not indeed confined to appointed
persons.  Any one capable of so doing might stand up to
teach in the synagogue at the invitation of the ruler (see
§ 27).  But as in courts of justice the learned doctors of the
law were preferred to the laity, so too in the synagogue their
natural superiority asserted itself.

To the juristic and haggadic elaboration of Holy Scripture,
was added a third kind of occupation therewith, viz. *the care
of the text of Scripture as such.*  The higher the authority of
the sacred text, the more urgent was the necessity for its conscientious and unadulterated preservation.  From this necessity
originated all those observations and critical notes subsequently
comprised under the name of the Massora (the computation
of verses, words and letters, orthographical notes, critical
remarks on the text, and such like).  This work however was
mainly the labour of a later period.  During that with which
we are occupied its first beginnings had at most been made.[66]

[65] For further particulars, see No. 3.

[66] Comp. on the Massora, Strack in Herzog's *Real-Encycl.*, 2nd ed. ix.
388–394. Reuss, *Gesch. der heiligen Schriften A. T.' s*, § 581, and the literature cited by both; also Hamburger, *Real-Encycl.* ii. 1211–1220 (art. " Text
der Bibel "). Only isolated remarks, which perhaps belong to the subject,
are found in the Mishna, *Pesachim* ix. 2 (that a point stands over the ה in
רחקה, Num. ix. 10); *Sota* v. 5 (that the לא in Job xiii. 15 may mean

III. HALACHAH AND HAGGADAH.

The Literature.

Surenhusius, Βίβλος καταλλαγῆς in quo secundum veterum theologorum *Hebraeorum formulas allegandi et modos interpretandi conciliantur loca ex V. in N. T. allegata* (Amstelodami 1713), especially pp. 57–88.

Wachner, *Antiquitates Ebraeorum*, vol. i. 1743, p. 353 sqq.

Döpke, *Hermeneutik der neutestamentlichen Schriftsteller*, part i. 1829.

Hartmann, *Die enge Verbindung des Alten Testaments mit dem Neuen* (1831), pp. 384–731.

Zunz, *Die gottesdienstlichen Vorträge der Juden, historisch entwickelt*, Berlin 1832.

Hirschfeld, *Der Geist der talmudischen Auslegung der Bibel.* Erster Thl. *Halachische, Exegese* 1840. The same, *Der Geist der ersten Schriftauslegungen oder die hagadische Exegese*, 1847.

Frankel, *Vorstudien zu der Septuaginta* (Leipzig 1841), pp. 163–203, especially pp. 179–191. The same, *Ueber den Einfluss der palästinischen Exegese auf die alexandrinische Hermeneutik*, Leipzig 1851 (354, p. 8). The same, *Ueber palästinische und alexandrinischen Schriftforschung*, Breslau 1854 (42, p. 4).

Welte, *Geist und Werth der altrabbinischen Schriftauslegung* (*Tüb. Theol. Quartalschrift*, 1842, pp. 19–58).

Reuss, *Gesch. der heil. Schriften Neuen Testaments*, § 502–505 (*über die Auslegung des A. T. bei den Juden*).

Diestel, *Gesch. des Alten Testamentes in der christlichen Kirche* (1869), pp. 6–14.

Herzfeld, *Geschichte des Volkes Jisrael*, iii. 137 ff., 226–263.

Jost, *Geschichte des Judenthums und seiner*, Secten i. 90 ff., 227–288.

Geiger, *Urschrift und Uebersetzungen der Bibel in ihrer Abhängigkeit von der inneren Entwickelung des Judenthums*, Leipzig 1857.

Pressel, " Rabbinismus," in Herzog's *Real-Encycl.*, 1st ed. vol. xii. (1860), pp. 470–487.

Hausrath, *Neutestamentl. Zeitgeschichte*, 2nd ed. i. 80–113.

Freudenthal, *Hellenistische Studien* (1875), pp. 66–77 (on the influence of Hellenism upon the Palestinian Midrash, see also Geiger, *Jüd. Zeitschr.* xi. 1875, p. 227 sqq.).

Siegfried, *Philo von Alexandria* (1875), p. 142 sqq. (on the mutual influence of the Palestinian and Alexandrian theology and exegesis).

Bacher, *Die Agada der babylonischen Amoräer*, 1878.

Bacher, *Die Agada der Tannaiten* (Grätz' *Monatsschrift für Gesch. und Wissensch. des Judenth.* 1882–1884). Also separately under the title,

"him" or "not"). When R. Akiba says, *Aboth* iii. 13, that the מָסֹרֶת is "a fence about the Thorah," מסרת means not the critico-textual, but the Halachic tradition ; see Strack, p. 388.

*Die Agada der Tannaiten,* vol. i. From Hillel to Akiba, Strasbourg 1884.

Weber, *System der altsynagogalen palästin. Theologie* (1880), especially pp. 88–121.

Reuss, *Gesch. der heiligen Schriften Alten Testaments* (1881), § 411–415, 582–584.

Hamburger, *Real-Enc. für Bibel und Talmud,* Div. ii. (1883) art. "Agada" (pp. 19–27), "Allegorie" (pp. 50–53), "Exegese" (pp. 181–212), "Geheimlehre" (pp. 257–278), "Halacha" (pp. 338–353), "Kabbala" (pp. 557–603), "Mystik" (pp. 816–819), "Rabbinismus" (pp. 944–956), "Recht" (pp. 969–980).

## 1. *The Halachah.*

The *theoretical* labours of the scribes were, as has been already remarked in the preceding section, of a twofold kind, —1. the development and establishment of the law, and 2. the manipulation of the historical and didactic portions of the Holy Scriptures. The former developed a *law of custom* beside the written Thorah, called in Rabbinical language the Halachah (הֲלָכָה, properly that which is current and customary). The latter produced an abundant variety of historical and didactic notions, usually comprised under the name of the Haggadah or Agadah (הַגָּדָה or אֲגָדָה, properly narrative, legend). The origin, nature and contents of both have now to be more fully discussed.

Their common foundation is the investigation or exposition of the Biblical text, Hebr. דָּרַשׁ.[67] By investigation however

---

[67] דָּרַשׁ is found in the Mishna in the following constructions :—1. To *investigate, to explain a passage or portion of Scripture,* the accusative object being either expressed or to be mentally supplied. *Berachoth* i. 5; *Pesachim* x. 4, *fin.; Shekalim* i. 4, v. 1; *Joma* i. 6; *Megilla* ii. 2; *Sota* v. 1, 2, 3, 4, 5, ix. 15; *Sanhedrin* xi. 2. 2. with בְּ in the same sense "to give explanations of a passage," *Chagiga* ii. 1. 3. "To find or discover a doctrine by investigation," *e.g.* אֶת זוֹ דָּרַשׁ מִן, "he discovered this from such and such a passage" (*Joma* viii. 9), or without מִן (*Jebamoth* x. 3; *Chullin* v. 5), or in the combination זֶה מִדְרָשׁ דָּרַשׁ, "Such or such a one gave this explanation" (*Shekalim* vi. 6; *Kethuboth* iv. 6). The substantive formed from דרש is מִדְרָשׁ, investigation, explanation, elaboration (*Shekalim* vi. 6; *Kethuboth* iv. 6; *Nedarim* iv. 3; *Aboth* i. 17); also in the combination בית המדרש, see above, note 60. It is already found 2 Chron. xiii. 22, 24, 26.

was not meant historical exegesis in the modern sense, but the search after new information upon the foundation of the existing text. The inquiry was not merely what the text in question according to the tenor of its words might say, but also what knowledge might be obtained from it by logical inference, by combination with other passages, by allegorical exegesis and the like. The kind and method of investigation was different in the treatment of the law and in that of the historical and dogmatico-ethic portions, and comparatively stricter in the former than in the latter.

The *Halachic Midrash* (*i.e.* the exegetic development of passages of the law) had first of all to regard only the extent and range of the several commands. It had to ask: to what cases in actual life the precept in question applied, what consequences it in general entailed, and what was to be done, that it might be strictly and accurately observed according to its full extent. Hence the commandments were split and split again into the subtlest casuistic details, and care was taken by the most comprehensive precautionary measures, that no kind of accidental circumstance should occur in observing them, which might be regarded as an infringement of their absolutely accurate fulfilment. The legal task was not, however, exhausted by this analysis of the existing text. There were also many *difficulties* to solve, some arising from internal contradictions in the legal code itself, some from the incongruity of certain legal requirements with the actual circumstances of life; others, and these the most numerous, from the incompleteness of the written law. To all such questions scholars had to seek for an answer; it was their business to obviate existing discrepancies by establishing an authoritative explanation; to point out how, when the observance of a precept was either impossible, difficult, or inconvenient, by reason of the actual relations of life, a compromise might nevertheless be made with the letter of its requirements; and lastly, to find for all those cases of actual occurrence, which were not directly regulated by the written law, some legal

direction when the need for such should arise. This last
department especially furnished an inexhaustible source of
labour for juristic discussion. Again and again did questions arise concerning which the written or hitherto
appointed law gave no direct answer, and to reply to
which became therefore a matter of juristic discussion.
For answering such questions two means were actually
at their disposal, viz. inference from already recognised
dogmas and the establishment of an already existing tradition. The latter, so far as it could be determined, was of
itself decisive.

Scientific exegesis (Midrash) was thus by no means the
only source for the formation of a legal code. A considerable portion of what subsequently became valid law had on the
whole no point of connection with the Thorah, but was at first
only *manner and custom.* This or that had been done thus or
thus, and so imperceptibly custom grew into a *law of custom.*
When anything in the legal sphere had been so long usual
that it could be said, it has always been thus, it was law by
custom. It was then by no means necessary that its deduction from the Thorah should be proved; ancient tradition was
as such already binding. And the recognised teachers of the
law were enjoined and competent to confirm this law of
custom.

From these two sources there grew up in the course of
time a multitude of legal decisions by the side of, and of equal
authority with, the written Thorah. These were all comprised
under the common notion of the *Halachah, i.e.* the *law of custom.*
For what was discovered by scientific investigation was, when
it obtained validity, also law by custom, הֲלָכָה.[68] Hence valid

---

[68] This comprehensive notion of the הֲלָכָה appears from the following
passages: *Pea* ii. 6, iv. 1, 2 ; *Orla* iii. 9 ; *Shabbath* i. 4 ; *Chagiga* i. 8 ;
*Jebamoth* viii. 3 ; *Nedarim* iv. 3 ; *Edujoth* i. 5, viii. 7 ; *Aboth* iii. 11, 18,
v. 8 ; *Kerithoth* iii. 9 ; *Jadajim* iv. 3, *fin.* " Jewish custom," דַּת יְהוּדִית
(*Kethuboth* vii. 6), is synonymous with דֶּרֶךְ אֶרֶץ (*Kiddushin* i. 10), and
as only designating the conventional, must not be confounded with the
Halachah.

law now included two main categories, the written Thorah
and the Halachah,[69] which, till at least towards the close of the
period with which we are occupied, was propagated only orally.
*Within the Halachah* there are again *different categories:*
(1) single Halachoth (traditional enactments) decidedly traced
back to Moses;[70] (2) the great body or Halachah proper;
(3) certain enactments which are designated as the " *appointments of the scribes* " (דִּבְרֵי סוֹפְרִים).[71] All three categories are of
legal obligation. But their authority nevertheless differs
in degree according to the above sequence, those of the first
class being highest, and those of the third relatively lowest.
For while the Halachah in general was regarded as having been
at all times valid, there was with regard to the דִּבְרֵי סוֹפְרִים the
conviction, that they were first introduced by the successors
of Ezra, viz. by the סוֹפְרִים.[72] There was in general, in the
period of the Mishna, a perfect consciousness that many traditional ordinances had no kind of foundation in the Thorah,
and that others were connected with it by the slightest of
ties.[73] Nevertheless the law of custom was quite as binding

---

[69] תּוֹרָה or מִקְרָא (writing) and הֲלָכָה are distinguished, *e.g.* in *Orla* iii. 9 ;
*Chagiga* i. 8 ; *Nedarim* iv. 3. So too are מִקְרָא and מִשְׁנָה (the teaching
of the law), *Kiddushin* i. 10.

[70] Such הֲלָכוֹת לְמֹשֶׁה מִסִּינַי are mentioned in the Mishna in three passages:
*Pea* ii. 6 ; *Edujoth* viii. 7 ; *Jadajim* iv. 3, *fin.* There are altogether from
fifty to sixty in the Rabbinical-Talmudic literature.

[71] *Orla* iii. 9 ; *Jebamoth* ii. 4, ix. 3 ; *Sanhedrin* xi. 3 ; *Para* xi. 4-6 ;
*Tohoroth* iv. 7 ; *Jadajim* iii. 2. Comp. also *Kelim* xiii. 7 ; *Tebul jom* iv. 6.

[72] That the דברי סופרים had *relatively* less authority than the Halachah
simply, is evident from *Orla* iii. 9 (where it is quite unjustifiable to supplement הֲלָכָה by למשה מסיני). On the recent date of the דברי סופרים, comp.
especially *Kelim* xiii. 7 ; *Tebul jom* iv. 6 : דְּבָר חָדָשׁ חִדְּשׁוּ סוֹפְרִים.

[73] Compare especially the remarkable passage, *Chagiga* i. 8: " Release
from a vow is a dogma which hovers, as it were, in the air, for there is
nothing in Scripture on which it can be founded. The laws concerning
the Sabbath, the festival sacrifices, and the defrauding (of sacred things
by misuse), are like mountains hanging by a hair, for there are few passages of Scripture and many laws of custom (הֲלָכוֹת) concerning them. On
the other hand, the civil laws (דִּינִין), the laws of ritual, the laws concerning
uncleanness and incest, are entirely founded on Scripture, and form the
essential contents of the (written) Thorah."

as the written Thorah; [74] nay, it was even decided that opposition to the דברי סופרים was a heavier transgression than
opposition to the decrees of the Thorah; [75] because the former,
being the authentic exposition and completion of the latter,
were therefore in fact the ultimate authority.

It was in the nature of the Halachah that it never could be
a thing *finished and concluded*. The two sources, whence it
arose, were continually flowing onwards. New enactments were
always being evolved by successive scientific exegesis (Midrash),
and new customs might always arise as usage differed. Both,
when they had attained prescriptive right, became Halachah, the
extent of which might thus be enlarged *ad infinitum*. But at
each stage of development *a distinction was always made
between what was already valid and what was only discovered
by the scientific inferences of the Rabbis*, between הֲלָכָה and דִּין
(to judge). Only the former was legally binding, the latter
in and of itself not as yet so. [76] Not till *the majority* of the
learned had decided in their favour were such tenets binding
and henceforth admitted into the Halachah. For the majority
of those distinguished for learning was the *decisive tribunal*. [77]
Hence the דִּבְרֵי חֲכָמִים were also to be kept as binding. [78] It is
self-evident however, that this principle applies only to such
cases as were not decided by an already valid Halachah. For
concerning any matter for which a Halachah is in existence
this must be unconditionally obeyed, though ninety-nine
should be against and only one for it. [79] By the help of this
principle of the majority the great difficulty which arose
through the separation of the schools of Hillel and Shammai
was overcome (see No. 4). So long as the differences between
the two were not reconciled, the conscientious Israelite must

---

[74] Comp. especially, *Aboth* iii. 11, v. 8.

[75] *Sanhedrin* xi. 3: חֹמֶר בְּדִבְרֵי סוֹפְרִים מִבְּדִבְרֵי תוֹרָה.

[76] See especially, *Jebamoth* viii. 3; *Kerithoth* iii. 9. The הלכות and
מדרש are therefore distinguished from each other as two kinds of subjects
of instruction. *Nedarim* iv. 3.

[77] *Shabbath* i. 4 sqq.; *Edujoth* i. 4–6, v. 7; *Mickwaoth* iv. 1; *Jadajim*
iv. 1, 3.        [78] *Negaim* ix. 3, xi. 7.        [79] *Pea* iv. 1–2.

have been in great perplexity which to adhere to. The
majority here too gave the final decision, whether it was that
the schools themselves compared numbers, and that one was
outvoted by the other,[80] or that subsequent scholars settled
differences by their final decision.[81]

The strictness with which the unchangeableness of the
Halachah was in general proclaimed might induce one to suppose, that what was once valid must remain unaltered. But
there is no rule without exception, nor was this so. Nor
indeed are the cases few in which laws or customs were
afterwards *altered*, whether on purely theoretical grounds, or
on account of altered circumstances, or because the old custom
entailed inconvenience.[82]

Widely as the Halachah differed from the written Thorah
the fiction was still kept up, that it was in reality nothing else
than an exposition and more precise statement of the Thorah
itself. *The Thorah was still formally esteemed as the supreme
rule from which all legal axioms must be derived.*[83] Certainly
the Halacha had its independent authority, and was binding,
even if no scriptural proof was adduced. Hence, though its
validity did not depend upon success in finding a scriptural
proof, it formed part of the business of the scribes to confirm the maxim of the Halachah by the Scriptures.[84] More

---

[80] A few cases are mentioned in which the school of Hillel was outvoted
by the school of Shammai, *Shabbath* i. 4 sqq.; *Mikwaoth* iv. 1.

[81] As a rule the Mishna, after mentioning the differences of the two
schools, states the decision of " scholars."

[82] Such innovations were *e.g.* introduced by Hillel (*Shebiith* x. 3; *Gittin*
iv. 3; *Arachin* ix. 4), Rabban Gamaliel (*Rosh hashana* ii. 5; *Gittin* iv. 2-3),
Rabban Johanan ben Sakkai (*Sukka* iii. 12; *Rosh hashana* iv. 1, 3, 4;
*Sota* ix. 9; *Menachoth* x. 5), R. Akiba (*Maaser sheni* v. 8; *Nasir* vi. 1;
*Challa* iv. 7; *Bikkurim* iii. 7; *Shekalim* vii. 5; *Joma* ii. 2; *Kethuboth* v. 3;
*Nedarim* xi. 12; *Gittin* v. 6; *Edujoth* vii. 2; *Tebul jom* iv. 5).

[83] This holds good notwithstanding the admission mentioned in note 73.
See especially, Weber, p. 96 sqq.

[84] That this supplementary learned confirmation of the Halachah often
referred to passages of Scripture entirely different to those from which the
Halachic maxims really arose, is seen, *e.g.* in the classic passage *Shabbath*
ix. 1-4.

absolute was the demand for satisfactory confirmation in the
case of newly advanced or disputed maxims. These could
only obtain recognition by methodical Midrash, *i.e.* by being
deduced in a convincing manner from passages of Scripture,
or from other already acknowledged propositions. The *method
of demonstration* which was in such cases applied, was one
which, though it indeed appears somewhat strange to us, has
its rules and laws. A distinction was made between the proof
proper (רְאָיָה) and the mere reference (זֵכֶר).[85] *Hillel* is said to
have laid down for the proof proper *seven rules,* which may
be called a kind of Rabbinical logic.[86] These seven rules
are as follows: (1) קַל וָחוֹמֶר, "light and heavy," *i.e.* the inference *a minori ad majus;*[87] (2) גְּזֵרָה שָׁוָה, "an equal decision,"
*i.e.* an inference from the similar, *ex analogia;*[88] (3) בִּנְיַן אָב
מִכָּתוּב אֶחָד, "a main proposition from *one* passage of Scripture,"
*i.e.* a deduction of a main enactment of the law from a
single passage of Scripture; (4) בִּנְיַן אָב מִשְּׁנֵי כְתוּבִים, "a main
proposition from two passages of Scripture;" (5) כְּלָל וּפְרָט
וּפְרָט וּכְלָל, "general and particular," and "particular and
general," *i.e.* a more precise statement of the general by the
particular, and of the particular by the general;[89] (6) כַּיּוֹצֵא בוֹ

[85] *Shabbath* viii. 7, ix. 4; *Sanhedrin* viii. 2. Comp. Weber, p. 115 sqq.

[86] They are found in the Tosefta, *Sanhedrin* vii. *fin.* (ed. Zuckermandel,
p. 427), in the *Aboth de-Rabbi Nathan* c. 37, and at the close of the introduction to the *Sifra* (Ugolini, *Thesaurus,* vol. xiv. 595). The text of the
*Sifra* is, at least according to the edition of Ugolini, defective. The correct
reading is found from the almost verbally identical texts of the two other
authorities. Comp. Hillel and his seven rules of interpretation in the *Monatsschr. für Gesch. und Wissensch. des Judenth.* 1851–52, pp. 156–162.

[87] Examples in *Berachoth* ix. 5; *Shebiith* vii. 2; *Beza* v. 2; *Jebamoth*
viii. 3; *Nasir* vii. 4; *Sota* vi. 3; *Baba bathra* ix. 7; *Sanhedrin* vi. 5;
*Edujoth* vi. 2; *Aboth* i. 5; *Sebachim* xii. 3; *Chullin* ii. 7, xii. 3; *Bechoroth* i. 1; *Kerithoth* iii. 7, 8, 9, 10; *Negaim* xii. 5; *Machshirin* vi. 8.

[88] *E.g. Beza* i. 6: "Challah and gifts are presents due to the priests, and
so is the Terumah. As then the latter may not be brought to the priest on
a holy day, so neither may the former." Another example in *Arachin* iv. *fin.*
In both passages the expression גְּזֵרָה שָׁוָה is used.

[89] In the thirteen Middoth of R. Ismael this figure is specified in eight
different manners, *e.g.* by the formula כְּלָל וּפְרָט וּכְלָל—"general and particular and general"—*i.e.* a more precise statement of two general expres-

בְּמָקוֹם אַחֵר, " by the similar in another passage," *i.e.* a more precise statement of a passage by the help of another; (7) דָּבָר הַלָּמֵד מֵעִנְיָנוֹ, " a thing which is learned from its connection," a more precise statement from the context. These seven rules were subsequently increased to thirteen, the fifth being specified in eight different manners, and the sixth omitted. The laying down of these thirteen Middoth is ascribed to R. Ismael. Their value for the correct interpretation of the law was so highly esteemed on the part of Rabbinic Judaism, that every orthodox Israelite recited them daily as an integral element of his morning devotions.[90]

The *matter* which formed the subject of juristic investigation on the part of the scribes was in effect furnished by the Thorah itself. The precepts concerning the priestly sacrifices and religious usages in general occupy the largest space therein. For the peculiarity of the Jewish law is, that it is pre-eminently a *law of ritual*. It seeks in the first place to establish by law in what manner God desires to be honoured, what sacrifices are to be offered to Him, what festivals are to be kept in His honour, how His priests are to be maintained, and what religious rites in general are to be observed. All other matters occupy but a small space in comparison with this. The motive whence all the zealous labours of the scribes arose corresponded with this content of the law: it was the desire to make sure by an accurate expression of the law, that none of the claims of God should be violated in even the slightest particular, but that all should be most conscientiously observed to their fullest extent. The endeavours of

sions by a particular one intervening, as *e.g.* Deut. xiv. 26, where the general expression, "whatever thy soul desireth," used at the beginning and end, is limited by the words "oxen, sheep, wine, intoxicating drink, which stand between.

[90] Hence they are found in every Jewish Siddur (Book of Prayers), as well as in the introduction to the *Sifra*. Comp. Waehner, *Antiquitates Ebraeorum*, i. 422–523. Pinner's translation of the treatise, *Berachoth*, Introd. fol. 17ᵇ–20ᵃ. Pressel in Herzog's *Real-Encycl.*, ed. 1, xv. 651 sq. Weber, *System der altsynagogalen paläst. Theol.* pp. 106–115.

the scribes were therefore directed chiefly to the development of (1) the precepts concerning sacrifices, the various kinds of sacrifice, the occasions on which it was to be offered, the manner of offering, and all connected therewith, *i.e.* of the entire sacrificial ritual; (2) the precepts concerning the celebration of holy seasons, especially of the Sabbath and the annual festivals—Passover, Pentecost, Tabernacles, the Day of Atonement, the New Year; (3) the precepts concerning tribute for the temple and priesthood—first-fruits, heave-offerings, tithes, the first-born, the half-shekel tribute, vows and freewill offerings and whatever related to them—their redemption, valuation, embezzlement, etc.; and lastly (4) the various other religious appointments, among which *the precepts concerning clean and unclean* occupy by far the largest space. The appointments of the law in this last respect were an inexhaustible source for the exercise of the most minute and conscientious acuteness on the part of the scribes. The statutes by which it was determined, under what circumstances uncleanness was incurred, and by what means it might be obviated, were truly endless and incalculable. Such religious decrees however by no means formed the exclusive matter of the labours of the scribes. For the law of Moses contains also the principles of a criminal and civil law; and the practical requirements of life offered occasion enough for the further development of these materials also. Of course the materials in question were not all equally elaborated. The laws concerning marriage were the most completely developed, partly because the marriage law gave more opportunity, and partly because this subject was the most closely connected with religion. The other departments of civil life are not treated with quite the same fulness in the Mishna (in the treatises *Baba kamma, Baba mezia,* and *Baba bathra*), and still less is the criminal law worked out (in the treatises *Sanhedrin* and *Makkoth*). The department of public law is as good as completely ignored. It is true that the Thorah furnished but extremely little opportunity for its development, and that such labour as was expended on it would have been utterly useless by reason of political circumstances.[91]

## 2. *The Haggada.*

The *Haggadic Midrash, i.e.* the elaboration of the historical and didactic portions of Holy Scripture, is of an entirely different kind from the Halachic Midrash. While in the latter the treatment is pre-eminently a development and carrying on of what is actually given in the text, the Haggadic treatment does not take for the most part its content from the text, but interpolates it therein. It is an amplification and remodelling of what was originally given, according to the views and necessities of later times. It is true, that here also the given text forms the point of departure, and that a similar treatment to that employed in passages from the law takes place in the first instance. The history is worked up by combining the different statements in the text with each other, completing one by another, settling the chronology, etc. Or the religious and ethical parts are manipulated by formulating dogmatic propositions from isolated prophetic utterances, by bringing these into relation to each other, and thus obtaining a kind of dogmatic system. But this stricter kind of treatment is overgrown by the much freer kind, which deals in a perfectly unrestrained manner with the text, and supplements it by additions of the most arbitrary and manifold kind. In other words, the treatment is Midrash in its stricter sense in only the smaller portion, and is on the contrary and for the most part a free completion by means of אֲגָדוֹת, *i.e.* legends.[91a]

[91] The survey of the contents of the Mishna (see § 3) furnishes proof of what is stated above.

[91a] Just as the *Halachah* was developed from *Midrash* in the province of law, was the Haggadah developed from Midrash in the other books of Scripture, only the relation was in the latter case a much looser one. The אֲגָדוֹת are mentioned as an independent subject of instruction beside מדרש and הלכות in *Nedarim* iv. 3.

A canonical book of the Old Testament, viz. the Book of Chronicles, furnishes a very instructive example of the *historical* Midrash. A comparison of its narrative with the parallel portions of the older historical books (Kings and Samuel) will strike even the cursory observer with the fact that the chronicler has enlarged the history of the Jewish kings by a whole class of narratives, of which the older documents have as good as nothing, viz. by *narratives of the merit acquired,* not only by David, but by many other pious kings *through their maintenance of, and more abundant provision for, the priestly ritual.* The chronicler is especially solicitous to tell of the conscientious care of these kings for the institutions of public worship. In the older documents scarcely anything is found of these narratives which run through the whole of Chronicles. It may be said that their absence in the books of Kings and Samuel is no proof of their non-historical nature, and that the chronicler obtained them from other sources. But the peculiarity is, that the very institutions for the maintenance of which these kings are said to have been distinguished, belong in general to the post-exilian period, as may, at least in the main points, be still proved (see § 24). Evidently then the chronicler dealt with the older history from a stated point of sight, which appeared to him very essential ; and as public worship was the most important matter in his own eyes, the theocratic kings could not but have been distinguished by their interest in it. At the same time he pursues the practical object of pointing out the just claims and high value of these institutions by showing the attention, which the most illustrious kings devoted to them. The notion that this was any adulteration of the history, was probably one which never occurred to him. He thought he was improving it by treating it according to the needs of his age. His work, or rather the larger work from which our Books of Chronicles are probably but an extract, is therefore, properly speaking, an *historical Midrash,* as indeed it is expressly designated

(מִדְרָשׁ) by its editor and abbreviator (2 Chron. xiii. 22, xxiv. 27).[92]

The method of dealing with the sacred history here described continued its exuberant growth to later ages and went on striking out ever bolder paths. The higher the credit and importance of the sacred history rose in the ideas of the people, the more thorough was the labour bestowed upon it, and the more urgent was the impulse to give more accuracy, more copious elaboration of details, and to surround the whole with a more complete and brighter halo. Especially were the histories of the patriarchs and the great lawgiver more and more adorned in this fashion. The *Hellenistic* Jews were particularly active in this manner of working up history. Nay, one might almost have supposed that it had originated with them, but that the Books of Chronicles furnish proof to the contrary, and that the whole method of this Midrash so entirely corresponds with the spirit of Rabbinical scholarship. The *literature*, in which the remains of this Haggadic treatment of history are still preserved is comparatively copious and varied. We find such in the works of the Hellenists Demetrius, Eupolemus, Artapanus (see concerning them, § 33); in Philo and Josephus,[93] in the so-called Apocalypses, and generally in the pseudepigraphic literature;[94] much also in the Targums and Talmud, but most in the Midrashim proper, which are *ex professo* devoted to the treatment of the sacred text (see above, § 3). Among these the oldest is the so-called Book of Jubilees, which may rank as the specially classic model of this Haggadic treatment of Scripture. The whole text of the canonical Book of Genesis is here reproduced in such wise,

---

[92] Comp. Wellhausen, *Geschichte Israels*, i. 236 sq.

[93] On Josephus, see Zunz, *Die gottesdienstlichen Vorträge der Juden*, p. 120. On Philo's contact with the Palestinian Midrash, see Siegfried, *Philo von Alexandria*, pp. 142–159.

[94] Comp. especially, Fabricius, *Codex pseudepigraphus Veteris Testamenti* (2 vols. 1713–1723), whose work is so arranged that the literary remains relating to each Scripture character are placed together, according to their chronological order.

that not only are the particulars of the history chronologically fixed, but also enlarged throughout in contents, and remodelled according to the taste of after times. By way of illustrating this branch of labour on the part of the scribes, the following few specimens are given.[95]

*The history of the creation, e.g.,* is completed in the following manner: "Ten things were created in the twilight on the evening before the Sabbath—1. the abyss of the earth (for Korah and his company); 2. the opening of the well (Miriam's); 3. the mouth of the ass (Balaam's); 4. the rainbow; 5. the manna in the wilderness; 6. the rod of Moses; 7. the shamir, a worm which spits stones; 8. alphabetic writing; 9. the writing of the tables of the law; 10. the stone tables. Some reckon with these: the evil spirits, the grave of Moses, and our father Abraham's ram; and others the first tongs for the preparation of future tongs.[96] A copious circle of legends, with which we are acquainted by means of their deposits and continuations in later Jewish literature, was formed concerning the life of Adam.[97] Enoch, who was miraculously translated to heaven by God, seemed especially adapted for revealing heavenly mysteries to men. Hence a book of such revelations was ascribed to him towards the end of the second century before Christ (see § 32). Later legends praise his piety and describe his ascension to heaven.[98] The Hellenist Eupolemus (or whoever else may be the author of the fragment in question) designates him as the inventor of astrology.[99] It is self-evident that Abraham, the ancestor of Israel, was a subject of special interest for this kind of

[95] Compare in general, Hartmann, *Die enge Verbindung,* etc., pp. 464–514. Herzfeld, *Gesch. d. Volkes Jisrael,* iii. 490–502. Ewald, *Gesch. des Volkes Israel,* i. 286 sqq.

[96] *Aboth* v. 6.

[97] Fabricius, *Codex pseudepigr.* i. 1–24, ii. 1–13. Hort, art. "Adam, books of," in Smith's *Dictionary of Christian Biography,* vol. i. (1877), pp. 34–39. Dillmann in Herzog's *Real-Enc.,* 2nd ed. xii. 366 sq.

[98] Hamburger, *Real-Enc. für Bibel und Talmud,* Div. ii. art. "Henochsage."

[99] Euseb. *Praep. evang.* ix. 17.

historical treatment. Hellenists and Palestinians took equal
pains with it. A Hellenistic Jew, probably as early as the third
century before Christ, wrote, under the name of Hecataeus
of Abdera, a book concerning Abraham.[100] According to
Artabanus, Abraham instructed Pharethothes, king of Egypt,
in astrology.[101] He was in the eyes of Rabbinic Judaism a
model of Pharisaic piety and a fulfiller of the whole law, even
before it was given.[102] He victoriously withstood—it is com-
puted—ten temptations.[103] In consequence of his righteous
behaviour, he received the reward of all the ten preceding
generations, which they had lost by their sin.[104] *Moses* the
great lawgiver *and his age* are surrounded with the brightest
halo. The Hellenists, in works designed for heathen readers,
represent him as the father of all science and culture. He
was, according to Eupolemus, the inventor of alphabetical
writing, which first came from him to the Phoenicians, and
from them to the Greeks. Artabanus tells us that the
Egyptians owed to him their whole civilisation.[105] It is therefore something less, when it is only said in the Acts, that he
was learned in all the wisdom of the Egyptians (Acts vii.
22), though even this goes beyond the Old Testament. The
history of his life and work is dressed up in the most varied
manner in Hellenistic and Rabbinic legends, as may be seen
even from the representations of Philo and Josephus.[106] The
names of the Egyptian sorcerers, who were conquered by

[100] Joseph. *Antt.* i. 7. 2. Clemens Alex. *Strom.* v. 14. 113.

[101] Euseb. *Praep. evang.* ix. 18. Comp. also on Abraham as an astro-
loger, Joseph. *Antt.* i. 7. 1. Fabricius, *Codex pseudepigr.* i. 350-378.

[102] *Kiddushin* iv. 14, *fin.* Comp. *Nedarim* iii. 11, *s. fin.*

[103] *Aboth* v. 3. Book of Jubilees in Ewald's *Jahrb.* iii. 15 ; *Aboth de-
Rabbi Nathan*, c. 33; *Pirke de-Rabbi Elieser*, c. 26-31; *Targum Jer.* on
Gen. xxii. 1. Fabricius, i. 398-400. Beer, *Leben Abrahams*, pp. 190-192.
The interpreter of *Aboth* v. 3 (Surenhusius' *Mishna*, iv. 465. Taylor,
*Sayings of the Jewish Fathers*, p. 94).

[104] *Aboth* v. 2. Comp. generally, Beer, *Leben Abraham's nach Auffassung
der jüdischen Sage*, Leipzig 1859.

[105] Eupolemus, *Euseb. Praep. evang.* ix. 26 = Clemens Alex. *Strom.* i.
23. 153. Artabanus, *Euseb. Praep. evang.* ix. 27.

[106] Philo, *Vita Mosis.* Joseph. *Antt.* ii.-iv. Compare generally, Fabri-

Moses and Aaron, are known (2 Tim. iii. 8). In the march
through the wilderness, the Israelites were not merely once
miraculously provided with water from a rock, but a rock
pouring forth water accompanied them during their whole
wandering in the wilderness (1 Cor. x. 4). The law was not
given to Moses by God Himself, but reached him by the
means of angels (Acts vii. 53 ; Gal. iii. 19 ; Heb. ii. 2). It
was part of the perfection of his revelation to have been
written in seventy languages on stones set up upon Mount
Ebal (Deut. xxvii. 2 sqq.).[107] The two unlucky days in the
history of Israel being Tammus 17 and Ab 9, the unfortunate
events of the Mosaic age must of course have taken place on
one of these two days; on Tammus 17 the tables of the law
were broken, and on Ab 9 it was ordained that the generation
of Moses should not enter the land of Canaan.[108] The strange
circumstances at the death of Moses also furnished abundant
material for the formation of legends (Deut. xxxiv.).[109] It is
known that Michael the Archangel contended with Satan for
his body (Jude 9). The history too of the post-Mosaic period
was manipulated by historical Midrash in the same manner as
the primitive history of Israel. To give only a few examples
from the New Testament. In 1 Chronicles and Ruth there
occurs in the list of David's ancestors a certain Salma or
Salmon, the father of Boaz (1 Chron. ii. 11 ; Ruth iv. 20 sq.).
The historical Midrash knows, that this Salmon had Rahab for
his wife (Matt. i. 5).[110] The drought and famine in the days
of Elijah lasted, according to the historic Midrash, three and a

cius, *Codex pseudepigr.* i. 825–868, ii. 111–130. Beer, *Leben Moses nach
Auffassung der jüdischen Sage*, Leipzig 1863.

[107] *Sota* vii. 5, with reference to Deut. xxvii. 8, בַּאֵר הֵיטֵב, "plainly
engraven (therefore intelligibly to all)." The seventy languages correspond
with the seventy nations of Gen. x.; see Targum Jonathan on Gen. xi. 7–8 ;
Deut. xxxii. 8; *Pirke de-Rabbi Elieser*, c. 24, in Wagenseil on *Sota* vii. 5,
in Surenhusius' *Mishna*, iii. 263.

[108] *Taanith* iv. 6, also the passages of the Gemara in Lundius, in Surenhusius' *Mishna*, ii. 382.

[109] Comp. already Joseph. *Antt.* iv. 8. 48.

[110] According to another Midrash, Rahab was the wife of Joshua.

half years, *i.e.* half of a week of years (Luke iv. 25 ; Jas. v. 17).[111] The author of the Epistle to the Hebrews mentions among the martyrs of the Old Testament those who were sawn asunder (Heb. xi. 37). He means Isaiah, of whom the Jewish legend says that this was the manner of his death.[112]

As in the case of the sacred history, so also in that of the religious and ethical matter of the Scriptures, the manipulation was of two kinds. On the one hand there was a dealing by combination, by inference and the like, with what was actually given ; on the other there was also a free completion by the varied formations of creative religious speculation. And the two imperceptibly encroached one upon the other. Not a few of the doctrinal notions and ideas of after times actually arose from the circumstance, that the existing text of Scripture had been made a subject of "investigation," and therefore from reflection upon data, from learned inferences and combinations founded thereupon. Imagination freely employing itself was however a far more fertile source of new formations. And what was obtained in the one way was constantly blended with what was arrived at in the other. With the results of investigation were combined the voluntary images of fancy, nay the former as a rule always followed, either consciously or unconsciously, the same lines, the same tendency and direction as the latter. And when the free creations of speculation had gained a settled form, they

[111] So too *Jalkut Shimoni* in Surenhusius, Βίβλος καταλλαγῆς, p. 681 sq. On the Elijah legends in general, comp. S. K., *Der Prophet Elia in der Legende* (*Monatsschr. f. Gesch. und Wissensch. des Judenth.* 1863, pp. 241–255, 281–296). Hamburger, *Real-Enc. für Bibel und Talmud*, Div. i.

[112] *Ascensio Isajae* (ed. Dillmann, 1877), c. v. 1 ; *Jebamoth* 49b. Justin, *Dial. c. Tryph.* c. 120. Tertullian, *de patientia*, c. 14 ; *scorpiace*, c. 8. Hippolyt. *de Christo et Antichristo*, c. 30. Origenes, *epist. ad African.* c. 9 ; *comment. ad Matt.* xiii. 57 and xxiii. 37 (*Opp.* ed. Lommatzsch, iii. 49, iv. 238 sq.) ; *Commodian. carmen apologet.* v. 509 sq. (ed. Ludwig) ; Hieronymus, *comment. ad Isaiam*, c. 57, *fin.* (*Opp.* ed. Vallarsi, iv. 666). Other patristic passages in Fabricius, *Codex pseudepigr.* i. 1088 sq. Wetzstein and Bleek on Heb. xi. 37, and in Otto's note on Justin. *Tryph.* 120.

were in their turn deduced from Scripture by scholastic Midrash.

These theological labours, which were always investigating old, and incessantly creating new material, were extended over the entire religious and ethical department. *It was owing to them that the whole circle of religious ideas in Israel had received in the times of Christ on the one hand a fanciful, on the other a scholastic character.* For the religious development was no longer determined and directed by the actual religious productivity of the prophets, but in part by the action of an unbridled imagination, not truly religious though dealing with religious objects, and in part by the scholastic reflection of the learned. Both these ruled and directed the development, in proportion as really religious life lost in inward strength.

It was in entire consistency with this tendency of the whole development, that special preference was shown for dealing with such *objects* as lay more at the circumference than in the centre of religious life, with the temporally and locally transcendent, with the *future* and the *heavenly* world. For the weaker the power of genuine religion, the more would fancy and reflection move from the centre to the circumference, and the more would such objects be detached from their central point and acquire an independent value and interest. The grace and glory of God were no longer seen in the present earthly world, but only in the future and heavenly world. Hence on the one side eschatology, on the other mythological theosophy, were cultivated with the greatest zeal. A copious abundance of notions concerning the realization of the salvation of Israel in a future period of the world's history was the growth of scientific investigation and unfettered religious fancy. The conditions, the premises and the accompanying circumstances, under which the means and forces by which this salvation would be realized, were stated, and most especially was it declared wherein it would consist and how surpassing would be its glory; in a word, Messianic dogma was more and more carefully cultivated and extensively developed. So too was there much solicitous occupation with the heavenly world: the nature and attributes of God, heaven as his dwelling - place, the angels as His servants, the whole fulness and glory of the heavenly world; such were the objects to which learned reflection and inventive fancy applied themselves with special predilection. Philosophic problems were also discussed: how the revelation of God in the world was conceivable, how an influence of God upon the world was possible without His being Himself drawn down into the finite, how far there was room for evil in a world created and governed by God, and the like. Two portions of Holy Scripture in particular gave much scope for the development of theosophic speculation, these were the history of the creation (מַעֲשֵׂה בְרֵאשִׁית) and the " chariot " of Ezekiel (מֶרְכָּבָה), i.e. the introductory vision of Ezekiel, chap. i. In the explanation of these two portions, profound mysteries which, according to the view of scholars, ought to form an esoteric doctrine, were dealt with. " The history of the creation might not be explained before two, and the chariot not even before one, unless he were a scholar and could judge of it from his own knowledge." [113] In these thus carefully guarded expositions of the history of the creation and of the chariot, we have the beginnings of those strange fancies concerning the creation and the spiritual world, which reached their climax in the so-called Kabbala of the Middle Ages.

The exposition and further development of the law was a process under comparatively strict regulations, but an almost unbridled caprice prevailed in the province of religious speculation. *Rules and method*, except in a very figurative sense, were here out of question. One thing especially, which made the development of the law so continuous and consequent, viz. the principle of a strict adherence to tradition, was here absent. The manipulator of the religious and ethical matter was not bound, like the interpreter of the law, to a strict

[113] *Chagiga* ii. 1. Comp. also *Megilla* iv. 10. Further particulars in Herzfeld, iii. 410–424.

adherence to tradition. He might give his imagination free play, so long as its products would on the whole admit of being inserted in the frame of Jewish views. A certain tradition was indeed formed in this sphere also, but it was not binding. Religious *faith* was comparatively free, while *action* was all the more strictly shackled. With the absence more-over of the principle of tradition in this department all rules in general ceased. For there was really but one *rule* for the "investigator," viz. the right of making anything of a passage, which his wit and understanding enabled him. If neverthe-less certain "rules" are laid down even for Haggadic interpre-tation, it was only that caprice here became methodical. A number of such rules for Haggadic exposition are met with among the thirty-two *Middoth* (hermeneutical principles) of R. Joses ha-Gelili, the age of which cannot indeed be more particularly determined.[114] Later Judaism discovered that there is a fourfold meaning of Scripture, which is indicated in the word פר״דס (Paradise), viz. 1. פְּשָׁט, the simple or literal meaning; 2. רֶמֶז (suggestion), the meaning arbitrarily imported into it; 3. דְּרוֹשׁ (investigation), the meaning deduced by investigation; and 4. סוֹד (mystery), the theosophistic mean-ing.[115]

It would be a superfluous task to give examples in illustra-tion of this kind of exegetical method, since we are sufficiently acquainted with it from the New Testament and the whole body of ancient Christian literature. For together with Holy

---

[114] See the 22 Middoth, *e.g.* in Waehner, *Antiquitates Ebraeorum*, i. 396–421. Pinner, translation of the treatise *Berachoth*, Introd. fol 20a–21a. Pressel in Herzog's *Real-Enc.*, 1st ed. xv. 658 sq. On the historical litera-ture, comp. also Zunz, *Die gottesdienstlichen Vorträge der Juden*, p. 86. Fürst, *Bibliotheca Judaica*, ii. 108.

[115] The initials of these four words produce the word פר״דס. I am unable to say how ancient this distinction of a fourfold meaning may be. Compare on this subject, Waehner, *Antiquitates Ebraeorum*, i. 353–357. Döpke, *Hermeneutik der neutestamentlichen Schriftsteller*, pp. 135 – 137. Deutsch, *Der Talmud* (1869), p. 16 sq. The distinction between רמז and דרוש is essentially the same as that between זָכָר and רְאָיָה, see note 85, above.

Scripture itself, its own mode of exegetical treatment was transferred by Judaism to the Christian Church. In saying this however it must also be remarked, that the exegetic method practised in the New Testament, when compared with the usual Jewish method, is distinguished from it by its great enlightenment. The apostles and the Christian authors in general were preserved from the extravagances of Jewish exegesis by the regulative norm of the gospel. And yet who would now justify such treatment of Old Testament passages, as are found *e.g.* in Gal. iii. 16, iv. 22–25 ; Rom. x. 6-8 ; Matt. xxii. 31–32 ? Jewish exegesis however, from which such a regulator was absent, degenerated into the most capricious puerilities.[116] From its standpoint, *e.g.* the transposition of words into numbers, or of numbers into words, for the purpose of obtaining the most astonishing disclosures, was by no means strange, and quite in accordance with its spirit.[117]

With the comparatively great freedom allowed to development in the sphere of religious notions, it is not to be wondered, that *foreign influences* also made themselves felt with more or less power. Palestine had already been for a long time open to the general intercourse of the world. So early as the foundation of the great world-powers of the Assyrians,

---

[116] Comp. generally the literature mentioned p. 269, especially Döpke, pp. 88–188. Hartmann, pp. 534–699. Gfrörer, *Das Jahrhundert des Heils*, i. 244 sqq. Hirschfeld, 1847. Welte in the *Tübinger Quartalschrift*, 1842. Hausrath, i. 97 sqq. Hamburger's article in the *Real-Enc. für Bibel und Talmud*, Div. ii. On Philo's allegorical exposition of Scripture, see especially Gfrörer, *Philo*, i. 68–113. Zeller, *Die Philosophie der Griechen*, iii. (3rd ed.), pp. 346–352. Siegfried, *Philo*, p. 160 sqq.

[117] In an appendix to the Mishna, the statement, *e.g.*, that God will give to every righteous man 310 worlds as his inheritance, is proved by Prov. viii. 21 : להנחיל אהבי יש ; because יש stands for 310 (*Ukzin* iii. 12 ; the passage is missing in the Cambridge MS. edited by Lowe). On the other hand, the author of the Epistle of Barnabas, who herein entirely follows the paths of Jewish exegesis, proves from the 318 servants of Abraham that Abraham had already in spirit beheld the cross of Jesus, because the number 18 = *IH* means the name Jesus, and the number 300 = *T* means the cross. *Barnab.* c. 9.

Chaldaeans and Persians, influences of the most varied kind had passed over the land. When it lay for two centuries under Persian supremacy, it would indeed have been very surprising if this fact had left behind it no kind of trace in the sphere of Israelitish intellectual life. Nor could it, with all its struggles for intellectual isolation, have possibly withdrawn itself entirely from the supremacy of the Greek spirit. Hence it cannot be denied that on the one hand Babylonian, on the other Greek influences are especially discernible in the development of Israel's religious notions. The amount of this influence may indeed be disputed. A careful investigation of details, especially in respect of the influence of Parseeism, has not as yet been made. This influence may perhaps have to be reduced to a comparatively small proportion. The fact however, that both Babylonian and Greek influences asserted themselves, is undeniable.[118] At first sight indeed it seems strange, nay enigmatical, considering the high wall of partition which Judaism erected in respect of religion between itself and heathenism. There is however no need of appealing, in explanation to the circumstance, that such influences were felt at a time when this wall of partition was as yet no unscaleable one, for they continued to be exerted in later times also;[119] nor to the fact, that no wall of partition is strong enough to resist the power of intellectual influences. The deepest reason that can be offered in explanation is, on the contrary, that legal Judaism itself laid the chief stress upon correctness of *action,* and that comparatively free play was therefore permitted in the sphere of religious *notions.*

[118] Compare with respect to Parseeism the certainly candid judgment of Lücke, *Einleitung in die Offenbarung Johannes* (2nd ed.), p. 55 sq. : " The influence of the ancient Persian religion upon the development of Jewish religious notions . . . is an indisputable fact." On the influence of Hellenism upon the Palestinian Midrash, see Freudenthal, *Hellenistischen Studien* (1875), pp. 66–77. Siegfried, *Philo,* p. 283 sqq.

[119] Angelology was far more strongly under the influence of Parseeism at the period of the Babylonian Talmud than previously. Comp. Kohut, *Ueber die jüdische Angelologie und Dämonologie,* 1866. The influences of Hellenism upon the Palestinian Midrash, pointed out by Freudenthal and

## IV. THE MOST FAMOUS SCRIBES.

### THE LITERATURE.

The older Hebrew works on the Mishna teachers in Wolf, *Biblioth. Hebr.* ii. 805 sq. Fürst, *Biblioth. Judaica*, ii. 48 sq.

Ottho, *Historia doctorum misnicorum qua opera etiam synedrii magni Hierosolymitani praesides et vice-praesides recensentur.* Oxonii 1672 (frequently reprinted, *e.g.* also in Wolf's *Biblioth. Hebr.* vol. iv., and in Ugolini's *Thesaurus*, vol. xxi.).

Joh. Chrph. Wolf, *Bibliotheca Hebraea*, ii. 805–865 (gives an alphabetical catalogue of the scholars mentioned in the Mishna).

Herzfeld, *Geschichte des Volkes Jisrael*, iii. 226–263. The same, *Chronologische Ansetzung der Schriftgelehrten von Antigonus von Socho bis auf R. Akiba* (*Monatsschr. für Gesch. und Wissensch. des Judenth.* 1854, pp. 221–229, 273–277).

Kämpf, *Genealogisches und Chronologisches bezuglich der Patriarchen aus dem Hillel'schen Hause bis auf R. Jehuda ha-Nasi, den Redacteur der Mischnah* (*Monatsschr. f. Gesch. und Wissensch. des Judenth.* 1853, pp. 201–207, 231–236; 1854, pp. 39–42, 98–107).

Jost, *Geschichte des Judenthums und seiner Secten*, vols. i. ii.

Grätz, *Geschichte der Juden*, vols. iii. iv.

Derenbourg, *Essai sur l'histoire et la géographie de la Palestine d'après les Thalmuds et les autres sources rabbiniques.* P. i.: *Histoire de la Palestine depuis Cyrus jusqu'à Adrien.* Paris 1867.

The works, written in Hebrew, of Frankel (1859), Brüll (1876) and Weiss (1871–1876). For further details concerning them, see the literature on the Mishna, § 3.

Friedländer, *Geschichtsbilder aus der Zeit der Tanaiten und Armoräer*, Brunn 1879 (a careless performance, see *Theol. Litztg.* 1880, p. 433).

Hamburger, *Real-Encyclopädie für Bibel und Talmud*, Div. ii., the several articles.

Bacher, *Die Agada der Tanaiten* (*Monatsschr. für Gesch. und Wissensch. des Judenth.* 1882–1884). Also separately, *Die Agada der Tanaiten*, vol. i. 1884.

It is not till the period of the Mishna, *i.e.* about 70 A.D., that we have any detailed information concerning individual scribes. Of those who lived before this time, our knowledge is extremely scanty. This too is almost the case in respect of Hillel and Shammai, the famous heads of schools; for, setting aside what is purely legendary, our information concerning Siegfried, generally belong to a period when the religious seclusion had long been a very strict one.

them is comparatively small and unimportant. The names
and order of the most celebrated heads of schools since about
the second century after Christ have been handed down to
us chiefly by the 1st chapter of the treatise *Aboth* (or *Pirke
Aboth*), in which is enumerated the unbroken succession of
individuals, who were from Moses till the time of the
destruction of Jerusalem the depositaries of the traditions of
the law. The whole chapter runs as follows :—[120]

1. *Moses* received the law upon Sinai, and delivered it to
Joshua; he to the elders; the elders to the prophets; and
the prophets delivered it to the men of *the Great Assembly.*
These laid down three rules: Be careful in pronouncing judgment! bring up many pupils! and make a fence about the
law! 2. *Simon the Just* was one of the last of the Great
Assembly. He said: The world subsists by three things—
by the law, the worship of God, and benevolence. 3. *Antigonus of Socho* received the tradition from Simon the Just.
He said: Be not like servants who serve their master for the
sake of reward, but be like those who do service without
respect to recompense; and live always in the fear of God.

4. *Joses ben Joeser* of Zereda and *Joses ben Johanan* of
Jerusalem received the tradition from them. Joses ben Joeser
said: Let thy house be a place of meeting for the wise, dust
thyself with the dust of their feet, and drink eagerly of their
teaching. 5. Joses ben Johanan of Jerusalem said: Let thy
house be always open (to guests), and let the poor be thy
household. Avoid superfluous chatter with women. It is
unbecoming with one's own wife, much more with the wife of
another. Hence the wise also say: He who carries on useless conversation with a woman, brings misfortune upon

[120] The following translation is for the most part taken from the edition
of the Mishna which has lately appeared under the management of Jost;
but partly corrected according to the careful explanation of Cahn (*Pirke
Aboth*, 1875). Comp. also for the exposition the editions of Surenhusius
(*Mishna*, vol. iv.), P. Ewald (*Pirke Aboth*, 1825), Taylor (*Sayings of the
Jewish Fathers*, Cambridge 1877), and Strack (*Die Sprüche der Väter*,
1882).

himself, is hindered from occupation with the law, and at last inherits hell.

6. *Joshua ben Perachiah* and *Nithai of Arbela* received the tradition from these. The former said: Procure a companion (in study), and judge all men according to the favourable side. 7. Nithai of Arbela said: Depart from a bad neighbour; associate not with the ungodly; and think not that punishment will fail.

8. *Judah ben Tabbai* and *Simon ben Shetach* received the tradition from these. The former said: Make not thyself (as judge) an advocate. When both sides stand before thee, look upon both as in the wrong. But when they are dismissed and have received sentence, regard both as justified. 9. Simon ben Shetach said: Test the witnesses well, but be cautious in examination, lest they thereby learn to speak falsehood.

10. *Shemaiah* and *Abtalion* received from them. Shemaiah taught: Love work, hate authority, and do not press thyself upon the great. 11. Abtalion said: Ye wise, be cautious in your teaching, lest ye be guilty of error, and err towards a place of bad water. For your scholars, who come after you, will drink of it, die, and the name of God be thereby dishonoured.

12. *Hillel* and *Shammai* received from these. Hillel said: Be a disciple of Aaron, a lover of peace, a maker of peace, love men, and draw them to the law. 13. He was accustomed also to say: He who will make himself a great name, forfeits his own. He who does not increase his knowledge diminishes it, but he who seeks no instruction is guilty of death. He who uses the crown (of the law) (for external purposes) perishes. 14. The same said: Unless I (work) for myself, who will do so for me? And if I do so for myself alone, what am I? And if not now, when else? 15. Shammai said: Make the study of the law a decided occupation; promise little and do much; and receive every one with kindness.

16. Rabban *Gamaliel* said: Appoint yourself a teacher, you

thus avoid the doubtful; and do not too often tithe according to mere chance.

17. His son *Simon* said: "I have grown up from early youth among wise men, and have found nothing more profitable for men than silence. Study is not the chief thing, but practice. He who speaks much only brings sin to pass."

18. Rabban *Simon ben Gamaliel* said: The world subsists by three things—by the administration of justice, by truth, and by unanimity. (Thus also it is said, Zech. viii. 16: "Let peace and truth judge in your gates.")[121]

So far the Mishna. Among the authorities here specified, those which chiefly interest us are "the men of the great assembly," or of the *great synagogue* (אַנְשֵׁי כְנֶסֶת הַגְּדוֹלָה). They appear here as the depositaries of the tradition of the law between the last prophets and the first scribes known by name. Later Jewish tradition ascribes to them all kinds of legal enactments.[122] Very recent, indeed really modern, is, on the other hand, the opinion, that they also composed the canon of the Old Testament.[123] As no authorities tell us who they really were, there has been the more opportunity for the most varying hypotheses concerning them.[124] The correct one, that they

---

[121] The bracketed words are wanting in the best manuscripts, *e.g.* Berolin. MSS. fol. 567 (see Cahn, *Pirke Aboth*, p. 62), and *Cambridge University Additional*, 470. 1 (see Taylor, *Sayings of the Jewish Fathers*, p. 4).

[122] See Rau, *De synagoga magna*, pp. 6–24. Herzfeld, *Gesch. des Volkes Jisrael*, iii. 244 sq. Kuenen, *Over de mannen der groote synagoge*, pp. 2–6. Taylor, *Sayings of the Jewish Fathers*, p. 124 sq. D. Hoffmann in the *Magazin für die Wissenschaft des Judenth.* x. 1883, p. 45 sqq.

[123] This opinion became current chiefly through Elias Levita (sixteenth century), and was transferred from him to Christian theology. See Strack in Herzog's *Real-Enc.*, 2nd ed. vii. 416 sq. (art. "Kanon des Alten Testaments").

[124] See Hartmann, *Die enge Verbindung des Alten Testaments mit dem Neuen*, pp. 120–166. The Introductions to the Old Testament, *e.g.* De Wette-Schrader, § 13. Heidenheim, *Untersuchungen über die Synagoga magna* (*Studien und Kritik*. 1853, pp. 286–300). Herzfeld, *Gesch. des Volkes Jisrael*, ii. 22–24, 380 sqq., iii. 244 sq., 270 sq. Jost, *Gesch. des Judenth.* i. 41–43, 91, 95 sq. Grätz, *Die grosse Versammlung* (*Monatsschr. f. Gesch. und Wissensch. des Judenthums*, 1857, pp. 31–37, 61–70). Leyrer in Herzog's *Real-Enc.*, 1st ed. xv. 296–299. Derenbourg, *Histoire de la*

never existed at all in the form which Jewish tradition represents, was already advocated by older Protestant criticism,[125]
though it was reserved for the conclusive investigation of
Kuenen to fully dissipate the obscurity resting upon this
subject. The only historical foundation for the idea is the
narrative in Neh. viii.–x., that in Ezra's time the law was
solemnly accepted by a great assembly of the people. This
" great assembly" was in fact of eminent importance to the
maintenance of the law. But after the notion of a great
assembly had been once fixed as an essential court of appeal
for the maintenance of the law, an utterly non-historical
conception was gradually combined therewith in tradition.
Instead of an assembly of the people receiving the law, a
college of individuals transmitting the law was conceived of,
and this notion served to fill up the gap between the latest
prophets and those scribes to whom the memory of subsequent
times still extended.[126]

Together with the notion of the great synagogue may be
dismissed also the statement, that *Simon the Just* was one of
its latest members. This Simon is, on the contrary, no other
than the high priest Simon I. in the beginning of the third
century before Christ, who, according to Josephus, obtained
the surname ὁ δίκαιος.[127] Undoubtedly this name was con-

*Palestine*, pp. 29-40. Ginsburg in Kitto's *Cyclopaedia*, iii. 909 sqq. Neteler,
*Tüb. Theol. Quartalschr.* 1875, pp. 490-499. Bloch, *Studien zur Geschichte
der Sammlung der althebräischen Literatur* (1876), pp. 100-132. Ham-
burger, *Real-Enc. für Bibel und Talmud*, Div. ii. pp. 318-323. Montet,
*Essai sur les origines des partis saducéen et pharisien* (1883), pp. 91-97. D.
Hoffmann, *Ueber " die Männer der grossen Versammlung "* (*Magazin für
die Wissenschaft des Judenthums*, 10th year, 1883, pp. 45-61). Strack in
Herzog's *Real-Enc.*, 2nd ed. xv. 95 sq.

[125] Joh. Eberh. Rau, *Diatribe de synagoga magna*, Traj. ad Rh. 1726.
Aurivillius, *Dissertationes ad sacras literas et philologiam orientalem pertinentes*
(ed. Michaelis, 1790), pp. 139-160.

[126] See Kuenen, *Over de mannen der groote synagoge*, Amsterdam 1876
(separate reprint, *Verslagen en Mededeelingen der koninklijke Akademie van
Wetenschappen, Afdeeling Letterkunde*, 2de Reeks, Deel vi.). Comp. *Theol.
Litztg.* 1877, p. 100.

[127] Joseph. *Antt.* xii. 2. 4.

ferred on him by the Pharisaic party on account of his strict
legal tendencies, while most of the high priests of the Greek
period left much to be desired in this respect. It was on
this very account also that he was stamped by Jewish tradition as a vehicle of the tradition of the law.[128]

The most ancient scribe of whom tradition has preserved
at least the name is *Antigonus of Socho*. Little more than
his name is however known of him.[129] The information too
given in the Mishna of the subsequent scribes down to the
time of Christ is extremely scanty and uncertain, as is indeed
evident from the externally systematic grouping of them in
five pairs. For there could hardly be historical foundation
for such a fact as that in each generation only a pair of
scholars should have specially distinguished themselves. It
is likely that just *ten names* were known, and that these were
formed into five pairs of contemporaries, after the analogy
of the last and most famous pair, Hillel and Shammai.[130] In
such a state of affairs, of course, only the most general out-
lines of the chronology can be determined. The comparatively
most certain points are the following.[131] Simon ben Shetach
was a contemporary of Alexander Jannaeus and Alexandra, and
therefore lived about 90–70 B.C.[132] Hence the first pair must

[128] He is also mentioned in *Para* iii. 5 as one of the high priests under
whom a red heifer was burnt. Comp. in general, Wolf, *Biblioth. Hebr.* ii.
864. Fürst's *Literaturbl. des Orients*, 1845, p. 33 sqq. Herzfeld, ii. 189 sqq.,
377 (who in opposition to Josephus maintains that Simon II., the high
priest at the close of the third century, is Simon the Just). Grätz, *Simon
der Gerechte und seine Zeit* (*Monatsschrift*, 1857, pp. 45–56). Hamburger,
*Real-Enc.*, Div. ii. pp. 1115–1119. Montet, *Essai sur les origines*, etc.
pp. 135–139.

[129] Comp. also Wolf, *Biblioth. Hebr.* ii. 813 sqq. Fürst's *Literaturbl. des
Orients*, 1845, p. 36 sq. Hamburger, *Real-Enc. s.v.* In the *Aboth de-Rabbi
Nathan*, c. 5, two disciples, Zadok and Boethos, are ascribed to Antigonus,
and the Sadducees and Boethosees traced to them.

[130] Hence these ten are in Rabbinical literature sometimes simply called
" the pairs " (זוגות), *e.g. Pea* ii. 6.

[131] Comp. on the chronology, Zunz, *Die gottesdienstlichen Vorträge der
Juden*, p. 37, and Herzfeld in the *Monatsschrift f. Gesch. und Wissenschaft
des Judenth.* 1854.

[132] With this agrees the statement in *Taanith* iii. 8, that Simon ben Shetach

be placed two generations earlier, viz. about 150 B.C. Hillel is said, according to Talmudic tradition, to have lived 100 years before the destruction of Jerusalem, and thus to have flourished about the time of Herod the Great.[133] His supposed grandson, Gamaliel I., is mentioned in the Acts (v. 34, xxii. 3), about 30–40 A.D.[134] It has been already stated (p. 180 sq.) that subsequent tradition makes the whole five pairs *presidents and vice-presidents of the Sanhedrim,* and the utter erroneousness of this assertion is there pointed out. They were in fact nothing more than heads of schools.

The first pair, Joses ben Joeser and Joses ben Johanan, is only mentioned, besides the chief passage in the treatise *Aboth,* a few times more in the Mishna,[135] and still less frequently do we meet with the second pair, Joshua ben Perachiah and Nithai of Arbela.[136] Of the third pair only Simon ben Shetach has a somewhat tangible form, though what is related of him is for the most part of a legendary character.[137] There is no

was a contemporary of the Onias so famed for his power in prayer, and whose death is related by Josephus, *Antt.* xiv. 2. 1, as taking place about 65 B.C.

[133] *Shabbath* 15ª. Hieronymus *ad Jesaj.* 11 sqq. (*Opp.* ed. Vallarsi, iv. 123): Sammai et Hellel non multo prius quam Dominus nasceretur orti sunt Judaea.

[134] *Bell. Jud.* iv. 3. 9 ; *Vita,* 38, 39, 44, 60.

[135] Both besides *Aboth* i. 4, 5 only in *Chagiga* ii. 2 ; *Sota* ix. 9. Joses ben Joeser also in *Chagiga* ii. 7 ; *Edujoth* viii. 4. According to *Chagiga* ii. 7, Joses ben Joeser was a priest, and indeed a pious one (חָסִיד) amongst the priesthood. The information in *Sota* ix. 9, that since the death of Joses ben Joeser and Joses ben Johanan, there had been no more אֶשְׁכּוֹלוֹת, is obscure. Since the Mishna itself here refers to Micah vii. 1, it is probable that אֶשְׁכּוֹלוֹת is to be taken in its usual signification (grapes), as a figurative designation of men who could afford mental refreshment. Others desire to take it like σχολαί. Comp. Herzfeld, iii. 246–249. Derenbourg, pp. 65, 75, 456 sqq.

[136] The two only in *Aboth* i. 6, 7 and *Chagiga* ii. 2. Instead of Nithai (נתאי or נתיי) there is good testimony in both passages (*Cod. de Rossi* 138, *Cambridge University Additional,* 470. 1, also the Jerusalem Talmud, *Chagiga* ii. 2) for מתאי or מתיי, *i.e.* Matthew, which is perhaps preferable. The native place of Nithai (אַרְבֵּל) is the present Irbid, north-west of Tiberias, where ruins of an ancient synagogue, the building of which is of course ascribed by tradition to Nithai, are still found (see § 27, note 89a). Comp. Herzfeld, iii. 251 sq. Derenbourg, p. 93 sq.

[137] On his relations with Alexander Jannaeus and Alexandra, see above,

mention of any of them in Josephus. On the other hand, he seems to speak of the fourth pair, Shemaiah and Abtalion, under the names Σαμέας and Πωλίων. He tells us that when, in the year 47 B.C., the youthful Herod was accused before the Sanhedrim on account of his acts in Galilee, and all owners of property were silent through cowardly fear, that a certain *Sameas* alone raised his voice, and prophesied to his colleagues that they would yet all perish through Herod. His prophecy was fulfilled ten years later, when Herod, after his conquest of Jerusalem in the year 37, had all his former accusers executed.[138] Only the Pharisee Pollio and his disciple Sameas (Πωλίων ὁ Φαρισαῖος καὶ Σαμέας ὁ τούτου μαθητής) were spared, nay highly honoured by him, because during the siege by Herod they had given counsel, that the king should be admitted into the town. The Sameas here mentioned is expressly identified by Josephus with the former.[139] Lastly, Pollio and Sameas are mentioned by Josephus, and again in the same order, in a third passage. Unfortunately however we obtain no entire certainty as to time. For he informs us that the followers of Pollio and Sameas (οἱ περὶ Πωλίωνα τὸν Φαρισαῖον καὶ Σαμέαν) refused the oath of allegiance demanded of them by Herod, and were not punished on this account, " obtaining indulgence for the sake of Pollio" (ἐντροπῆς διὰ τὸν Πωλίωνα τυχόντες).[140] Josephus relates this among the events of the eighteenth year of Herod (= 20–19 B.C.). It cannot however be quite certainly determined from the context, whether this occurrence really took place in that year. Now the two names Σαμέας and Πωλίων so strikingly coincide with שְׁמַעְיָה and אַבְטַלְיוֹן, that the view of their being identical is very obvious.[141] The

§ 10. Comp. beside *Aboth* i. 8–9, *Chagiga* ii. 2, also *Taanith* iii. 8, *Sanhedrin* vi. 4. Landau in the *Monatsschr. f. Gesch. und Wissensch. des Judenth.* 1853, pp. 107–122, 177–180. Herzfeld, iii. 251 sq. Grätz, *Gesch. der Juden*, vol. iii. 3rd ed. pp. 665–669 (note 14). Derenbourg, pp. 96–111.

[138] *Antt.* xiv. 9. 4.     [139] *Antt.* xv. 1. 1.     [140] *Antt.* xv. 10. 4.

[141] The name שְׁמַעְיָה, which also frequently occurs in the Old Testament, especially in Nehemiah and Chronicles, is rendered in the LXX. by Σαμαία,

chronology too would about agree. The only thing that
causes hesitation is, that Sameas is called the disciple of Pollio,
while elsewhere Shemaiah stands before Abtalion.  Hence
we might feel tempted to identify Sameas with Shammai,[142]
but that it would then be strange, that Josephus should mention him twice in connection with Abtalion, and not with his
contemporary Hillel.  If however by reason of this connection we take Hillel and Shammai to be meant by Pollio and
Sameas,[143] there is against this identification, first the difference of the names Pollio and Hillel, and then the designation
of Sameas as the disciple of Pollio, while Shammai was certainly no disciple of Hillel.  All things considered, the connection of Sameas and Pollio with Shemaiah and Abtalion
seems not only the more obvious, but the more probable.[144]

Hillel and Shammai are by far the most renowned among
the five pairs.[145]  An entire school of scribes, who separated,
if not in principle, yet in a multitude of legal decisions, in

Σαμαίας, Σαμείας and Σεμείας. The name Πωλίων is not indeed identical
with Abtalion, but, on the contrary, like the Latin Pollio. It is well known
however, that besides their Hebrew, the Jews often bore like-sounding
Greek or Latin names (Jesus and Jason, Saul and Paulus, etc.).

[142] שמאי or שמיי (probably only an abbreviation of שמעיה, see Derenbourg, p. 95) may very well be rendered by Σαμέας in Greek, as ינאי by
Ἰαννέας in Antt. xiii. 12. 1.

[143] So e.g. Arnold in Herzog's Real-Enc., 1st. ed. vi. 97.

[144] Comp. on both, beside Aboth i. 10, 11 and Chagiga ii. 2, also Edujoth
i. 3, v. 6. Landau in the Monatsschrift für Gesch. und Wissensch. des
Judenth. 1858, pp. 317–329. Herzfeld, iii. 253 sqq. Grätz, Gesch. der Juden,
3rd ed. iii. 671 sq. (note 17). Derenbourg, pp. 116–118, 149 sq., 463 sq.
Hamburger, Real-Enc., Div. ii. p. 1113 sq. (art. "Semaja").

[145] On both, especially on Hillel, see Biesenthal in Fürst's Literaturbl.
des Orients, 1848, Nos. 43–46. Kämpf in the same, 1849, Nos. 10–38.
Arnold in Herzog's Real-Enc., 1st ed. 96–98 (and the older literature
there cited). Herzfeld, iii. 257 sqq. Grätz, iii. 222 sqq. Jost, i. 255–270.
Ewald, Jahrb. der bibl. Wissenschaft, vol. x. pp. 56–83. Gesch. des Volkes
Isr. vol. v. 12–48. Geiger, Das Judenthum und seine Gesch. i. 99–107.
Delitzsch, Jesu und Hillel, 1866 (2nd ed. 1867). Keim, Gesch. Jesu, i.
268–272. Derenbourg, pp. 176–192. Strack in Herzog's Real-Enc.,
2nd ed. vi. 113–115. Hamburger, Real-Enc. ii. 401–412. Bacher,
Monatsschr. f. Gesch. und Wissensch. des Judenth. 1882, pp. 100–110.
Goitein, Magazin für die Wissensch. des Judenth. 11th year, 1884, pp. 1–16,
49–87.

two different directions, adhered to each of them. This circumstance certainly makes it evident, that both are of eminent importance in the history of Jewish law. Both indeed manifestly laboured with special zeal and ingenuity to give a more subtle completeness to the law, but it must not therefore be supposed, that their personal life and acts stand out in the clear light of history. What we know of them with certainty is comparatively very little. In the Mishna, the only trustworthy authority, they are each mentioned barely a dozen times.[146] And what we know of them from later sources bears almost always the impress of the legendary. Hillel, called " the elder," הַזָּקֵן,[147] to distinguish him from others, is said to have sprung from the family of David,[148] and to have immigrated from Babylon to Palestine. Being poor he was obliged to hire himself as a day-labourer to earn a living for himself and his family and to meet the expenses of instruction. His zeal for study was so great that on one occasion, not being able to pay the entrance-fee into the Beth-ha-Midrash, he climbed up to the window to listen to the instruction. As this happened in winter, he was frozen with cold, and was found in this position by his astonished teachers and colleagues.[149] Tradition tells strange things of the learning he acquired by such zeal. He understood all tongues, and even the language of the mountains, hills, valleys, trees, plants, of wild and tame animals and of daemons.[150] At all events he was the most celebrated jurist of his age, but he was no more president of the Sanhedrim than was any other learned

---

[146] Hillel is mentioned in the Mishna only in the following passages : *Shebiith* x. 3 ; *Chagiga* ii. 2 ; *Gittin* iv. 3 ; *Baba mezia* v. 9 ; *Edujoth* i. 1–4 ; *Aboth* i. 12–14, ii. 4–7, iv. 5, v. 17 ; *Arachin* ix. 4 ; *Nidda* i. 1. Shammai only in the following : *Maaser sheni* ii. 4, 9 ; *Orla* ii. 5 ; *Sukka* ii. 8 ; *Chagiga* ii. 2 ; *Edujoth* i. 1–4, 10, 11 ; *Aboth* i. 12, 15, v. 17 ; *Kelim* xxii. 4 ; *Nidda* i. 1.

[147] *Shebiith* x. 3 ; *Arachin* ix. 4.

[148] *Jer. Taanith* iv. 2, fol. 68ᵃ ; *Bereshith rabba* c. 98, on Gen. xlix. 10 (see *Bereshith rabba*, translated by Wünsche, pp. 485, 557).

[149] Delitzsch, *Jesus und Hillel*, pp. 9–11.

[150] Delitzsch, *Jesus und Hillel*, p. 8.

scribe of the time. The leading features of his character were the gentleness and kindness of which singular proofs are related.[151] It is manifested in the first of the maxims given above: " Be a disciple of Aaron, a lover and maker of peace, love men and attract them to the law." Shammai, noted for sternness, and also called " the elder," הַזָּקֵן, was the antipodes of the gentle Hillel.[152] The following example of his rigorous zeal for the literal observance of the law is given in the Mishna. When his daughter-in-law brought forth a child on the feast of Tabernacles, he had the ceiling broken through and the roof over the bed covered with boughs, that the new-born child also might keep the feast according to the precept of the law.[153]

The tendencies of their respective schools correspond with the mildness of Hillel and the strictness of Shammai. The school of Hillel decided legal questions in a mitigated, that of Shammai in an aggravated sense.[154] As they are however only minutiae on which the difference turns, it will not be worth while to follow the contrast into further details.[155]

[151] See Delitzsch, p. 31 sq.   [152] *Orla* ii. 5; *Sukka* ii. 8.
[153] *Sukka* ii. 8.   [154] *Edujoth* iv. 1–12, v. 1–5.
[155] For the sake of those who may desire to go farther into the subject I here give *all those passages in the Mishna in which differences between the two schools are mentioned.* *Berachoth* i. 3, viii. 1–8; *Pea* iii. 1, vi. 1, 2, 5, vii. 6; *Demai* i. 3, vi. 6; *Kilajim* ii. 6, iv. 1, 5, vi. 1; *Shebüith* i. 1, iv. 2, 4, 10, v. 4, 8, viii. 3; *Terumoth* i. 4, v. 4; *Maaseroth* iv. 2; *Maaser sheni* ii. 3, 4, 7, 8, 9, iii. 6, 7, 9, 13, iv. 8, v. 3, 6, 7; *Challa* i. 6; *Orla* ii. 4; *Shabbath* i. 4–9, iii. 1, xxi. 3; *Erubin* i. 2, vi. 4, 6, viii. 6; *Pesachim* i. 1, iv. 5, viii. 8, x. 2, 6; *Shekalim* ii. 3, viii. 6; *Sukka* i. 1, 7, ii. 7, iii. 5, 9; *Beza* i. 1–9, ii. 1–5; *Rosh hashana* i. 1; *Chagiga* i. 1–3, ii. 3, 4; *Jebamoth* i. 4, iii. 1, 5, iv. 3, vi. 6, xiii. 1, xv. 2, 3; *Kethuboth* v. 6, viii. 1, 6; *Nedarim* iii. 2, 4; *Nasir* ii. 1, 2, iii. 6, 7, v. 1, 2, 3, 5; *Sota* iv. 2; *Gittin* iv. 5, viii. 4, 8, 9, ix. 10; *Kiddushin* i. 1; *Baba mezia* iii. 12; *Baba bathra* ix. 8, 9; *Edujoth* i. 7–14, iv. 1–12, v. 1–5; *Sebachim* iv. 1; *Chullin* i. 2, viii. 1, xi. 2; *Bechoroth* v. 2; *Kerithoth* i. 6; *Kelim* ix. 2, xi. 3, xiv. 2, xviii. 1, xx. 2, 6, xxii. 4, xxvi. 6, xxviii. 4, xxix. 8; *Ohaloth* ii. 3, v. 1–4, vii. 3, xi. 1, 3–6, 8, xiii. 1, 4, xv. 8, xviii. 1, 4, 8; *Para* xii. 10; *Tohoroth* ix. 1, 5, 7, x. 4; *Mikwaoth* i. 5, iv. 1, v. 6, x. 6; *Nidda* ii. 4, 6, iv. 3, v. 9, x. 1, 4, 6–8; *Machshirin* i. 2–4, iv. 4, 5, v. 9; *Sabim* i. 1–2; *Tebul jom* i. 1; *Jadajim* iii. 5; *Ukzin* iii. 6, 8, 11; בֵּית שַׁמָּאי only: *Berachoth* vi. 5; *Demai* iii. 1; *Kilajim* viii. 5; *Terumoth* iv. 3; *Orla* ii. 5, 12; *Beza* ii. 6;

Some examples may suffice. The command to prepare no
food on the Sabbath was extended to laying-hens, and hence
it was debated, whether and under what conditions an egg
laid upon a holy day might or might not be eaten.[156]   Or it
was discussed, whether fringes (Zizith) were needful or not to
a square linen night-dress;[157] or whether on a holy day a
ladder might be carried from one pigeon-house to another, or
might only be slanted from one hole to another.[158]   Of ideas
of reformation, which Jewish self-love would so willingly
have us believe in, there is not, as we see, a single word.   In
practice the milder school of Hillel gained in the course of
years the upper hand, though in many points it voluntarily
relinquished its own view and assented to those of the school
of Shammai,[159] while in others neither the opinion of Hillel
nor that of Shammai was subsequently followed.[160]

An enactment, contrary indeed to the law, but authorized
by the state of things, and certainly of salutary results, is
connected with the name of Hillel. The legal appointment
of a release of all debts every seventh year (Deut. xv. 1–11)
entailed the evil consequence, " that people hesitated to lend
each other money," although the law itself warned against
backwardness in lending on account of this institution (Deut.
xv. 9).   In order then to do away with this evil, the so-called
Prosbol (פְּרוֹזְבּוֹל = προσβολή), i.e. the delivery of a declaration,

---

*Edujoth* iii. 10 ; *Mikwaoth* iv. 5. This list of passages shows that the
differences relate chiefly to the matters treated of in the first, second, third
and fifth parts of the Mishna, *i.e.* (1) religious dues, (2) the Sabbaths and
holy days, (3) the marriage laws, and (4) the laws of purification, and
scarcely at all to those treated of in the fourth and fifth parts (civil and
criminal law and the laws of sacrifice). The latter, which do not affect the
religious acts of private individuals, but either purely civil or sacerdotal
transactions, were not discussed with equal zeal in the schools. The civil
and criminal law did not on the whole excite the same interest as religious
decrees. It is however probable that the sacrificial laws had already been
dealt with by the more ancient priestly scribes, and lay outside the direct
sphere of Rabbinical authority.

[156] *Beza* i. 1 ; *Edujoth* iv. 1.   Delitzsch, p. 21 sq.
[157] *Edujoth* iv. 10.          [158] *Beza* i. 3.          [159] *Edujoth* i. 12–14.
[160] *E.g. Edujoth* i. 1–3.   Comp. the passages cited in note 155.

or as we should say a registered declaration, was introduced by Hillel's influence.[161] It was, that is to say, allowed to a creditor to make in court a declaration to the following effect :

מוֹסֵר אֲנִי לָכֶם אִישׁ פְּלוֹנִי וּפְלוֹנִי הַדַּיָּנִים שֶׁבְּמָקוֹם שֶׁכָּל חוֹב שֶׁיֵּשׁ לִי, שֶׁאֶגְבֶּנּוּ כָּל זְמָן שֶׁאֶרְצֶה, "I so and so *deliver* [162] to you the judges of such and such a place (the declaration), that I may at any time I choose demand the payment of all my outstanding debts." Such a reservation made before a court secured the creditor even during the Sabbath year, and he needed not to be backward in lending money on its account. Thus credit was again laid upon a more solid foundation.[163]

A Simon, said also to be the father of Gamaliel I., is generally named by both Jewish and Christian scholars as the son of Hillel. The existence of this Simon, and with him the whole genealogical relation, is however very questionable.[164] We do not reach a really historical personage till Gamaliel I., רַבָּן גַּמְלִיאֵל הַזָּקֵן, as he is called in the Mishna, in distinction from

---

[161] According to others פרוזבול = πρὸς βουλήν, which is however very improbable.

[162] מסר, "to deliver" (whence also מְסוֹרָה, tradition), answers to the Greek word προσβάλλειν.

[163] Comp. on the Prosbol especially, *Shebiith* x. 3–7 (the formula will be found *Shebiith* x. 4) ; the institution by Hillel, *Shebiith* x. 3 ; *Gittin* iv. 3 ; generally : *Pea* iii. 6 ; *Moed katan* iii. 3 ; *Kethuboth* ix. 9 ; *Ukzin* iii. 10. Such Prosbol declarations are indeed to be understood by the συμβόλαια τῶν δεδανεικότων, which, according to Joseph. *Bell. Jud.*, were deposited among the archives at Jerusalem. Literature : Buxtorf, *Lex. Chald.* col. 1806 sq. Guisius in Surenhusius' *Mishna*, i. 196. Jost, *Gesch. des Judenth.* i. 265 sq. Hamburger, *Real-Enc.* ii. 939 sq. (art. "Prosbol"). Levy, *Neuhebr. Wörterb. s.v.* פרוזבול.

[164] He is not mentioned in the Mishna at all. His name first occurs in the Babylonian Talmud, and there not as the son of Hillel, but only as holder of the dignity of Nasi between Hillel and Gamaliel I. The whole passage (*Shabbath* 15ª, below) is as follows : הלל ושמעון גמליאל והמעון נהגו נשיאותן לפני הבית מאה שנה. "Hillel and Simon, Gamaliel and Simon held the dignity of Nasi, during the time of the existence of the temple, for a hundred years," *i.e.* during the last hundred years before the destruction of the temple. Considering the worthlessness of this late Talmudic information, B. Lebrecht *e.g.* is quite justified in disputing the existence of this Simon altogether (Geiger's *Jüdische Zeitschr. für Wissensch. und Leben*, xi. 1875, p. 278, note). For older views of him, see Wolf, *Biblioth. Hebr.* ii. 861 sq.

Gamaliel II.[165] It was at his feet that the Apostle Paul sat (Acts xxii. 3); and it was he who once gave counsel in the Sanhedrim to release the accused apostles, since their work, if it were of man, would come to nought, while if it were of God, it was in vain to oppose it (Acts v. 34–39). Christian tradition has in consequence of this represented him as being a Christian,[166] while Jewish tradition glorifies him as one of the most celebrated teachers. " Since Rabban Gamaliel the elder died there has been no more reverence for the law (כְּבוֹד הַתּוֹרָה) ; and purity and abstinence (טָהֳרָה וּפְרִישׁוּת) died out at the same time."[167] That he was as little the president of the Sanhedrim

---

[165] *Orla* ii. 12; *Rosh hashana* ii. 5; *Jebamoth* xvi. 7; *Sota* ix. 15; *Gittin* iv. 2–3. In all these passages he is expressly called "the elder" (הַזָּקֵן). Independently of *Aboth* i. 16, this elder Gamaliel is probably meant also in *Pea* ii. 6 and *Shekalim* vi. 1. In other passages this is doubtful. In particular the famous jurist Slav Tabi (טָבִי) was not in the service of the elder, but of the younger Gamaliel (*Berachoth* ii. 7; *Pesachim* vii. 2; *Sukka* ii. 1). Comp. in general, Graunii, *Historia Gamalielis*, Viteb. 1687. Wolf, *Biblioth. Hebraea*, ii. 821 sq. The same, *Curae philol. in Nov. Test.* on Acts v. 34. Palmer, *Paulus und Gamaliel*, Giessen 1806. Winer, *RWB.* i. 389. Pressel in Herzog's *Real-Enc.*, 1st ed. 656 sq. Grätz, *Gesch. der Juden*, 3rd ed. iii. 373 sqq. Jost, *Gesch. des Judenth.* i. 281 sqq., 423. Ewald, *Gesch. des Volkes Israel*, vi. p. 256 sq. Derenbourg, *Histoire de la Palestine*, pp. 239–246. Schenkel in the *Bibellex.* ii. 328–330. Hamburger, *Real-Enc.*, Div. ii. art. " Gamaliel I."

[166] *Clement. Recogn.* i. 65 sqq. Comp. also the narrative of the presbyter Lucianus of Jerusalem on the finding of the bones of the martyr Stephen (in Latin in Surius, *Vitae Sanctorum*, iv. 502 sqq. (3 August); Baronius, *Annal. ad ann.* 415, and in the Benedictine edition of Augustine, vol. vii. Appendix), according to which the bones of Nicodemus, Gamaliel and his son Abiba, who all here figure as Christians, were found at the same time as those of Stephen. This legend of Lucianus, which was already known to Gennadius, *Vitae*, 46, 47 (see also Fabricius, *Biblioth. graeca*, ed. Harles, x. 327), was drawn upon by the presbyter Eustratius of Constantinople, 6th century, in his book on the state of the dead, cap. 23 (published in Greek by Leo Allatius 1655; see Fabricius, *Bibl. gr.* x. 725, xi. 623). Lastly, Photius gives extracts from Eustratius in his *Bibliotheca cod.* 171. On a monument of the three saints, Gamaliel, Abibas and Nicodemus at Pisa, see Wagenseil on *Sota* ix. 15 (in Surenhusius' *Mishna*, iii. 314 sq.). Comp. also Thilo, *Cod. apocr.* p. 501; Nilles, *Kalendarium Manuale* (1879), p. 232, and the literature there cited.

[167] *Sota* ix. 15. כְּבוֹד הַתּוֹרָה means "reverence for the law;" see Wagenseil in Surenhusius' *Mishna*, iii. 312, n. 13, 315, n. 20. Comp.

as Hillel was, appears from Acts v. 34 sqq., where he figures as a simple member of it. Much confusion concerning him has arisen, especially among Christian scholars, by attributing to him matters which apply to Gamaliel II., *e.g.* labours at Jabne and elsewhere.

His son Simon also enjoyed extraordinary fame as a scribe.[168] Josephus says of him:[169] Ὁ δὲ Σίμων οὗτος ἦν πόλεως μὲν Ἱεροσολύμων, γένους δὲ σφόδρα λαμπροῦ, τῆς δὲ Φαρισαίων αἱρέσεως, οἳ περὶ τὰ πάτρια νόμιμα δοκοῦσι τῶν ἄλλων ἀκριβείᾳ διαφέρειν. Ἦν δ᾽ οὗτος ἀνὴρ πλήρης συνέσεώς τε καὶ λογισμοῦ, δυνάμενός τε πράγματα κακῶς κείμενα φρονήσει τῇ ἑαυτοῦ διορθώσασθαι. He lived at the time of the Jewish war, and during its first period (A.D. 66–68) took a prominent part in the conduct of affairs. Still neither was he at any time president of the Sanhedrim.

Of profound importance to the further development of scribism was the fall of Jerusalem and the destruction of the hitherto relative independence of the Jewish common-wealth. The ancient Sanhedrin, at the head of which had stood the Sadducean high priests, now for ever retired from the stage. The Pharisaic teachers of the law, who during the last century before the destruction of the temple had already actually exercised very great influence, became the sole leaders of the people. Hence the direct result of the political fall was an increase of Rabbinical power and an exaltation of Rabbinical studies. Henceforth our authorities became more copious,—the first codification of Jewish law having been undertaken by men directly connected with the generation which survived the fall of the city.

*Nedarim* ix. 1: כבוד אביו = "respect towards his father." So too *Aboth* iv. 12. The sense thus is, that no one any longer had such reverence for the law as Rabban Gamaliel the elder.
[168] Comp. Joseph. *Bell. Jud.* iv. 3. 9; *Vita*, 38, 39, 44, 60. Jost, i. 446 sqq. Derenbourg, pp. 270–272, 474 sq. Hamburger, *Real-Enc.* ii. 1121. By the Rabban Simon ben Gamaliel, so frequently mentioned in the Mishna, is generally intended the son of Gamaliel II. So especially in *Aboth* i. 18; *Kerithoth* i. 7 alone, besides *Aboth* i. 17, refers perhaps to Simon the son of Gamaliel I.
[169] *Vita*, 38.

*Jamnia* or Jabne, which had since the Maccabaean period been chiefly inhabited by Jews, became after the destruction of the holy city a chief seat of these studies. The most distinguished of those scholars, who survived the fall of Jerusalem, seem to have settled here.[170] Lydda or Lud is besides mentioned as an abode of eminent scribes.[171] Later on, perhaps subsequent to the middle of the second century after Christ, Tiberias became a centre of scribism.

The most important scribe in the decade after the destruction of Jerusalem was Rabban Johanan ben Sakkai.[172] The period of his activity is evident from the circumstance, that he altered several legal enactments or customs "after the temple was destroyed."[173] His place of residence seems to have been chiefly Jabne.[174] But Berur Chail (ברור חיל) is also mentioned as a scene of his labours.[175] And he must likewise have temporarily sojourned in Arab (ערב), where various legal questions were propounded for his decision.[176] Among

---

[170] See in general, *Shekalim* i. 4; *Rosh hashana* ii. 8–9, iv. 1–2; *Kethuboth* iv. 6; *Sanhedrin* xi. 4; *Edujoth* ii. 4; *Aboth* iv. 4; *Bechoroth* iv. 5, vi. 8; *Kelim* v. 4; *Para* vii. 6.

[171] *Rosh hashana* i. 6; *Taanith* iii. 9; *Baba mezia* iv. 3; *Jadajim* iv. 3.

[172] See concerning him the Hebrew works of Frankel, Brüll and Weiss (titles above, § 3), also Jost, *Gesch. des Judenthums und seiner Sekten*, ii. 13 sqq. Landau, *Monatsschr. für Gesch. und Wissensch. des Judenth.* 1851–52, pp. 163–176. Grätz, *Gesch. der Juden*, iv. 10 sqq. Derenbourg, *Histoire de la Palestine*, pp. 266 sq., 276–288, 302–318. Hamburger, *Real-Enc.*, Div. ii. pp. 464–473. Bacher, *Monatsschr. für Gesch. und Wissensch. des Judenth.* 1882, pp. 145–165. Spitz, *Rabban Johanan ben Sakkai, Rector der Hochschule zu Jabneh*, Dissertation, Leipzig 1883. He is mentioned in the Mishna in the following passages: *Shabbath* xvi. 7, xxii. 3; *Shekalim* i. 4; *Sukka* ii. 5, iii. 12; *Rosh hashana* iv. 1, 3; *Kethuboth* xiii. 1–2; *Sota* v. 2, 5, ix. 9, 15; *Edujoth* viii. 3, 7; *Aboth* ii. 8–9; *Menachoth* x. 5; *Kelim* ii. 2, xvii. 16; *Jadajim* v. 3, 6. Only as בי זכאי, *Sanhedrin* v. 2. For the passages in the Tosefta, see the index to Zuckermandel's edition.

[173] *Sukka* iii. 12; *Rosh hashana* iv. 1, 3, 4; *Menachoth* x. 5.

[174] *Shekalim* i. 4; *Rosh hashana* iv. 1.

[175] *Sanhedrin* 32b; Tosefta, *Maaseroth*, 82. 13 (comp. *Jer. Demai* iii. 1, fol. 23b; *Jer. Maaseroth* ii. 3, fol. 49d). Derenbourg, 307. Many, as *e.g.* B. Derenbourg, are of opinion that Johanan ben Sakkai was driven from Jabne by Gamaliel II. and retired to Berur Chail.

[176] *Shabbath* xvi. 7, xxii. 3. Arab is a small town in Galilee not far from Sepphoris. See Derenbourg, *Histoire*, p. 318, note 3.

his legal innovations perhaps the most prominent is his doing away with the water of bitterness to be drunk by one accused of adultery.[177] How closely connected he still was with matters as they were before the destruction of Jerusalem, is seen by the fact of his disputing concerning legal questions with Sadducees,[178] who soon after it disappear from history. He is also the vehicle of ancient traditions which are referred to Moses himself.[179] Legend tells us of him what Josephus tells us of himself, viz. that he predicted to Vespasian his future elevation to the imperial dignity.[180] R. Elieser ben Hyrkanos, R. Joshua ben Chananiah, R. Joses the priest, R. Simon ben Nathanael and R. Eleasar ben Arach are named in the Mishna as his five disciples.[181] The best known and most eminent are the two first named, R. Elieser and R. Joshua.

R. Zadok, or as his name would be more correctly pronounced, R. Zadduk,[182] was about contemporary with Rabban Johanan ben Sakkai. He is said to have lived before the destruction of the temple, and also to have held intercourse with Gamaliel II., Joshua and Elieser.[183] He is in fact often mentioned in conjunction with them in the Mishna.[184] In

---

[177] *Sota* ix. 9. Nine decrees (תקנות) introduced by him are enumerated in the Talmud, *Rosh hashana* 31ᵇ ; *Sota* 40ᵃ. Derenbourg, p. 304 sq.

[178] *Jadajim* iv. 6.

[179] *Edujoth* viii. 7 ; *Jadajim* iv. 3, *fin.* Comp. above, p. 272.

[180] *Midrash rabba* on Lam. 1, 5. Derenbourg, p. 282 sq. ; Wünsche, *Der Midrash Echa rabbati* (1881), p. 66 sqq.

[181] *Aboth* ii. 8-9. The abbreviation R means Rabbi, while the higher title Rabban is generally written in full.

[182] See concerning him, Derenbourg, pp. 342-344. Bacher, *Monatsschr. für Gesch. und Wissensch. des Judenth.* 1882, pp. 208-211. In the Mishna, *Terumoth* x. 9 ; *Pesachim* vii. 2 ; *Sukka* ii. 5 ; *Nedarim* ix. 1 ; *Edujoth* iii. 8, vii. 1-4 ; *Aboth* iv. 5 ; *Bechoroth* i. 6 ; *Kelim* xii. 4-5 ; *Mikwaoth* v. 5. On *Shabbath* xx. 2, xxiv. 5, comp. note 185. For the passages in the Tosefta, see the index to Zuckermandel's edition. The pronunciation Zadduk is pointed according to the *Cod. de Rossi* 138. Comp. Σαδδούκ in the LXX. in Ezekiel, Ezra and Nehemiah.

[183] Proofs of both in Derenbourg and Bacher's above-named works.

[184] With Gamaliel II., *Pesachim* vii. 2 ; with Joshua, *Edujoth* vii. 1= *Bechoroth* i. 6 ; with Elieser, *Nedarim* ix. 1.

certain passages, according to which the date of his life would have to be considerably postponed, a subsequent R. Zadok is probably intended.[185]

To the first decades after the destruction of the temple belongs also a distinguished priestly scribe, R. Chananiah, "president of the priests" (סגן הכהנים).[186] He relates what his father had done, and what he had himself seen in the temple,[187] and appears in the Mishna almost entirely as a narrator of the details of the priestly ritual.[188] It is characteristic of him as an eminent priest, that he exhorts to prayer for the welfare of the heathen authorities.[189]

R. Elieser ben Jacob[190] also belongs to the first generation after the destruction of the temple. For it is very probable that a former scribe of the same name must be distinguished from the considerably later R. Elieser ben Jacob so frequently quoted in the Mishna. He flourished not long after the destruction of the temple,[191] in which his uncle had ministered as a Levite,[192] and he is frequently quoted as an authority in the treatise *Middoth ;*[193] nay, subsequent tradition

---

[185] So *Shabbath* xx. 2, xxiv. 5. Comp. Bacher, *Monatsschr.* 1882, p. 215. If we acknowledge the existence of this subsequent R. Zadok, the question of course arises, whether other passages must not also be referred to him.

[186] See Derenbourg, pp. 368–370. Hamburger, *Real-Enc.* ii. 131, and Bacher, *Monatsschr.* 1882, pp. 216–219. His name according to the best authorities is not Chanina but Chananiah (so *Cod. de Rossi* 138, and the Cambridge MS. edited by Lowe). On the office of a priestly סגן, see above, p. 259.

[187] *Sebachim* ix. 3, xii. 4.

[188] See in general, *Pesachim* i. 6 ; *Shekalim* iv. 4, vi. 1 ; *Edujoth* ii. 1–3 ; *Aboth* iii. 2 ; *Sebachim* ix. 3, xii. 4 ; *Menachoth* x. 1 ; *Negaim* i. 4 ; *Para* iii. 1.

[189] *Aboth* iii. 2.

[190] Derenbourg, p. 374 sq. Bacher, *Monatsschr.* 1882, pp. 228–233.

[191] So also Derenbourg, 375, n. 2, and Bacher, 228. The younger Elieser ben Jacob was a contemporary of R. Simon about A.D. 150 (*Para* ix. 2), and narrates in the name of Chananiah ben Chakinai, who again narrates in that of R. Akiba (*Kilajim* iv. 8. Tosefta, *Negaim* 617. 38 ; *Tohoroth* 672. 15, ed. Zuckermandel).

[192] *Middoth* i. 2.

[193] *Middoth* i. 2, 9, ii. 5, 6, v. 4. Comp. *Shekalim* vi. 3.

even ascribes to him the composition of the whole treatise.[194]
It can no longer be decided in particular cases which passages
are to be attributed to him and which to R. Elieser ben
Jacob the younger. Perhaps the statements on circumstances
of ritual may be referred to the elder.[195]

Rabban Gamaliel II., son of Simon and grandson of Gamaliel I., the most renowned scholar of the turn of the century
(about A.D. 90–110), lived only a few decades later than
Johanan ben Sakkai.[196] The tribunal at Jabne, of which he
was the head, was in his days generally acknowledged as the
chief authority in Israel.[197] The most famous scholars were
here assembled about him, and in this respected circle Gamaliel was reckoned the decisive authority.[198] Among the
scholars in close intercourse with him, R. Joshua, about his
equal in age, and R. Akiba, his junior, were the most
eminent.[199] On the other hand, Gamaliel does not seem to
have entered into close relations with his famous contem-

[194] *Joma* 16ₐ. Derenbourg, 374, n. 1.

[195] *E.g.* the statements concerning the marriages of priests (*Bikkurim* i. 5 ;
*Kiddushin* iv. 7), the sacrificial rites (*Menachoth* v. 6, ix. 3 ; *Tamid* v. 2),
the first-born of cattle (*Bechoroth* iii. 1), the sacred singers (*Arachin* ii. 6),
the offerings of proselytes (*Kerithoth* ii. 1).

[196] See concerning him the Hebrew works of Frankel, Brüll and Weiss,
also Jost, *Gesch. des Judenth.* ii. 25 sqq. Landau, *Monatsschr. für Gesch.
und Wissensch. des Judenth.* 1851–52, pp. 283–295, 323–335. Grätz,
*Geschichte der Juden,* iv. 30 sqq., 423 sq. Derenbourg, pp. 306–313, 319–
346. Hamburger, *Real-Enc.* ii. 237–250. Bacher, *Monatsschr.* 1882, pp.
245–267. The chronology results from the fact that his younger contemporary Akiba played a part in the Barkochba war.

[197] *Rosh hashana* ii. 8–9 ; *Kelim* v. 4. Comp. Derenbourg, pp. 319–322.
He seems to have sojourned but temporarily at Kefar-Othnai, where we
only once (*Gittin* i. 5) meet with Gamaliel.

[198] Hence when once during a protracted absence of Gamaliel it had to
be decided, whether the year was to be a leap year, this was only done with
the reservation that Gamaliel should agree to it (*Edujoth* vii. 7). Comp.
also for the authoritative position of Gamaliel, the formula " Rabban Gamaliel and the elders " (*Maaser sheni* v. 9 ; *Shabbath* xvi. 8 ; *Erubin* x. 10).

[199] On the mutual relations of Gamaliel, Joshua and Akiba, comp. especially,
*Maaser sheni* v. 9 ; *Erubin* iv. 1 ; *Rosh hashana* ii. 8–9 ; *Maaser sheni* ii. 7 ;
*Sukka* iii. 9 ; *Kerithoth* iii. 7–9 ; *Negaim* vii. 4. Gamaliel and Joshua,
*Jadajim* iv. 4. Gamaliel and Akiba, *Rosh hashana* i. 6 ; *Jebamoth* xvi. 7.

porary R. Elieser ben Hyrcanus. At least there is no trace of this in the Mishna, while subsequent tradition on the contrary relates that Elieser was excommunicated by Gamaliel (see below). Gamaliel once undertook in conjunction with R. Joshua, R. Akiba and the equally renowned R. Eleasar ben Asariah, a sea voyage to Rome, which obtained a certain celebrity in Rabbinical literature.[200] He is said to have been on one occasion removed by the seventy-two elders from the presidential dignity on account of his too autocratic dealings, and R. Eleasar ben Asariah to have been appointed to replace him. Gamaliel was however, on showing contrition, soon reinstated in his office, which Eleasar voluntarily vacated.[201] The elevation of Eleasar by the seventy-two elders to the headship of the school is at any rate evidenced by the Mishna.[202] In his legal decisions Gamaliel followed the school of Hillel; it is mentioned as an exception, that in three things he decided in an aggravated sense, according to the school of Shammai.[203] In general he is characterized as much by legal strictness on the one hand,[204] as on the other by a certain amount of worldly conformity, nay of candour of judgment.[205]

The two most celebrated contemporaries of Gamaliel were R. Joshua ben Chananiah and R. Elieser ben Hyrcanus, both pupils of Johanan ben Sakkai.[206] We frequently find them disputing with each other on legal questions, and Akiba the

---

[200] *Erubin* iv. 1–2; *Maaser sheni* v. 9; *Shabbath* xvi. 8. Grätz, *Monatsschr. f. Gesch. und Wissensch. des Judenth.* 1851–52, pp. 192–202. Derenbourg, pp. 334–340. Renan, *Les évangiles* (1877), p. 307 sqq. Bacher, *Monatsschr.* 1882, p. 251 sqq.

[201] *Jer. Berachoth* iv. 1, fol. 7[cd]; *Bab. Berachoth* 27[b] (in German in Pinner, *Talmud Babli Tractat Berachoth*, 1842, in Latin in Surenhusius' *Mishna*, ii. 337, iii. 247). Jost, *Gesch. des Judenth.* ii. 28 sqq. Grätz, *Gesch. der Juden*, iv. 35 sqq. Derenbourg, pp. 327–329.

[202] *Sebachim* i. 3; *Jadajim* iii. 5, iv. 2.

[203] *Beza* ii. 6; *Edujoth* iii. 10.     [204] *Berachoth* ii. 5–6.

[205] Comp. beside the journey to Rome, his intercourse with the governor (hegemôn) of Syria (*Edujoth* vii. 7) and his visit to the bath of Aphrodite at Akko, although there was there a statue of the heathen goddess (*Aboda sara* iii. 4).

[206] *Aboth* ii. 8. Comp. *Edujoth* viii. 7; *Jadajim* iv. 3, *fin.*

younger taking part in these discussions.[207] With Gamaliel
however Joshua only, and not Elieser, seems to have been in
familiar intercourse. According to later tradition this would
be explained by the fact that Elieser was excommunicated by
Gamaliel.[208] R. Joshua was descended from a Levitical
family.[209] He was of a gentle and yielding disposition, and
hence submitted to the unbending Gamaliel.[210] "Since the
death of R. Joshua, there is no longer any kind-heartedness
(טוֹבָה) in the world."[211] His motto was, " Envy, evil desire and
hatred bring a man out of the world.[212] Pekiin or Bekiin
(בקיען ,עקיען), is named as the place of his labours.[213] His
close relations with Gamaliel however lead to the conclusion
that he also resided partly at Jabne. Tradition relates of
him, among other things, that he had various conversations
with the Emperor Hadrian on religious subjects.[214] In contrast with the yielding Joshua, Elieser was of a firm, unbending
character, and a very strict adherent to tradition, over which,
by reason of his faithful memory and extensive scholarship,
he had more influence than any other.[215] His teacher

[207] On the mutual relations of Joshua, Elieser and Akiba, comp.
especially *Pesachim* vi. 2 ; *Jebamoth* viii. 4 ; *Nedarim* x. 6 ; *Nasir* vii. 4 ;
*Edujoth* ii. 7. On Joshua and Elieser, *Pesachim* vi. 5 ; *Taanith* i. 1 ;
*Sebachim* vii. 4, viii. 10 ; *Nasir* vii. 4. On Joshua and Akiba, *Pesachim* ix. 6 ;
*Sanhedrin* vii. 11. On Elieser and Akiba, *Pea* vii. 7 ; *Kerithoth* iii. 10 ;
*Shebiith* viii. 9–10.

[208] *Jer. Moed Katan* iii. 1, fol. 81ᵈ ; *Bab. Baba mezia* 59ᵇ ; Jost, *Gesch.
des Judenth.* ii. 35. Grätz, *Gesch. der Juden*, iv. 47. Derenbourg, 324 sq.

[209] This appears from *Maaser sheni* v. 9. Comp. on Joshua, the
Hebrew works of Frankel, Brüll and Weiss ; also Grätz, *Gesch. der Juden*,
iv. 50 sqq., 426 sq. Derenbourg, pp. 319 sqq., 416 sqq. Hamburger, *Real-
Enc.* ii. 510–520. Bacher, *Monatsschr.* 1882, pp. 340–359, 433–464, 481–496.

[210] *Rosh hashana* ii. 8–9. Derenbourg, 325–327.

[211] *Sota* ix. 15.

[212] *Aboth* ii. 11: עין הרע ויצר הרע ושנאת הבריות.

[213] פקיען, *Sanhedrin* 32 ; Tosefta, *Sota* 307, 8. בקיען, *Jer. Chagiga*
i. 1. Derenbourg, 307.

[214] Bacher, *Monatsschr.* 1882, pp. 461 sqq., 481 sqq.

[215] See the Hebrew works of Frankel, Brüll and Weiss ; also Gratz,
*Gesch. der Juden*, iv. 43 sq., 425 sq. Derenbourg, 319 sqq., 366 sqq.
Hamburger, ii. 162–168. Bacher, *Monatsschr.* 1882, pp. 289–315, 337–359,
433–445.

Johanan ben Sakkai boasted of him, that he was like a well coated with lime, which does not loose a single drop.[216] He was not to be moved by any reasons or representations from what he knew as tradition. Hence his strained relations with Gamaliel, although he is said to have been his brother-in-law.[217] His dwelling-place was Lydda.[218] The strange opinion of a modern scholar, that he was inclined to Christianity, nay was secretly a Christian,[219] rests upon a legend which really proves the contrary. Elieser is at one time brought before a heathen tribunal, and looks upon this as a just punishment of God for his having been pleased with the ingenious solution of a legal question, which a Jewish Christian had communicated to him as having been derived from Jesus.[220]

R. Eleasar ben Asariah,[221] a rich and eminent priest, whose genealogy is traced back to Ezra, also occupies an honourable position together with those last mentioned.[222] His wealth was so great, that it was said that after his death there was no longer any wealth among the learned.[223] His relations with Gamaliel, Joshua and Akiba, his journey with them to Rome, his elevation by the seventy-two elders to the office of president, and his voluntary relinquishment of this position have been already spoken of. It is evident even from

[216] *Aboth* ii. 8. 　　　　[217] *Shabbath* 116ᵃ. Derenbourg, 323.

[218] *Jadajim* iv. 3 ; *Sanhedrin* 32ᵇ. Derenbourg, 307.

[219] Toetterman, R. Eliezer ben Hyrcanos sive de vi qua doctrina Christiana primis seculis illustrissimos quosdam Judaeorum attraxit, Lipsiae 1877. Comp. *Theol. Litztg.* 1877, pp. 687–689.

[220] There are two versions of this legend : (1) *Aboda sara* 16ᵇ in German in Ewald's *Aboda sarah oder der Götzendienst*, 1868, pp. 120–122 ; (2) *Midrash rabba* on Eccles. i. 8 in German in Wünsche, *Der Midrasch Koheleth*, 1880, p. 14 sq. See in general, Jost, ii. 41 sq. Grätz, iv. 47 sq. Derenbourg, 357–360. Bacher, *Monatsschr.* 1882, p. 301.

[221] See concerning him, Derenbourg, 327 sqq. Hamburger, ii. 156–158. Bacher, *Monatsschr.* 1883, pp. 6–27. According to the best authorities, his name is not Elieser but Eleasar (in the *Cod. de Rossi* 138, and in the Cambridge MS. generally, לעזר).

[222] Bacher, *Monatsschr.* 1883, p. 7. That he was a priest is clear from *Maaser sheni* v. 9.

[223] *Sota* ix. 15.

these personal circumstances that he must have laboured in Jabne, a fact also testified elsewhere.[224] He was also in personal relation with R. Ishmael and R. Tarphon, the contemporaries of Akiba.[225]

R. Dosa ben Archinos (or Harkinos) was another contemporary of Gamaliel and Joshua.[226] Of him it is especially stated, that he induced Joshua to submit to Gamaliel.[227]

Among the later men of this generation is also Eleasar ben Zadok, son of the already mentioned R. Zadok.[228] The son was, as well as the father, intimately acquainted with Gamaliel, and hence gives information concerning his enactments and the legal customs of his house.[229]

R. Ishmael occupies an independent position among the scribes of the time.[230] We find him indeed occasionally in Jabne.[231] He was also intimate with his renowned contemporaries R. Joshua, Eleasar ben Asariah, Tarphon, and

---

[224] *Kethuboth* iv. 6. Some sentences of Eleasar in *Aboth* iii. 17.

[225] A disputation between him, Tarphon, Ishmael and Joshua is given *Jadajim* iv. 3. Eleasar and Ishmael in Tosefta, *Berachoth* 1, lin. 15, ed. Zuckermandel. Eleasar and Akiba, Tosefta, *Berachoth* i. 12; *Shabbath* 113. 23.

[226] See Derenbourg, 368 sq., 370 sq. Hamburger, ii. 155. His name is, in *Cod. de Rossi* 138, ארכינס, elsewhere generally הרכינס, but is in any case not like Hyrcanus, but Archinos.

[227] *Rosh hashana* ii. 8–9. Comp. also *Erubin* iii. 9; *Kethuboth* xiii. 1–2; *Edujoth* iii. 1–6; *Aboth* iii. 10; *Chullin* xi. 2; *Ohaloth* iii. 1; *Negaim* i. 4.

[228] See concerning him, Derenbourg, pp. 342–344. Bacher, *Monatsschr.* 1082, pp. 211–215. As in the case of R. Zadok, so probably in that of Eleasar ben Zadok, we must distinguish between two scribes of the same name, an older and a younger (so Frankel, *Darke hamishna*, pp. 98, 178; Bacher, *Monatsschr.* 1882, p. 215; otherwise Derenbourg, p. 262, n. 2, 344, n. 4). The younger relates in the name of R. Meir (*Kilajim* vii. 2), and therefore did not live till the middle of the second century. The name of both is according to the best authority not Elieser but Eleasar (*Cod. de Rossi* 138, and the Cambridge MS. have chiefly לעזר).

[229] Tosefta, *Challa* 99. 9; *Shabbath* iii. 15; *Jom. tob.* 202. 28, 204. 15–16; *Kiddushin* 336. 13 (ed. Zuckermandel).

[230] See concerning him, Grätz, *Gesch. der Juden*, iv. 60 sqq., 427 sqq. Derenbourg, pp. 386–395; Hamburger, ii. 526–529. Bacher, *Monatsschr.* 1883, pp. 63 sqq., 116 sqq., 209 sqq. On the school of Ishmael, D. Hoffmann, *Magazin für die Wissensch. des Judenth.* xi. 1884, pp. 17–30.

[231] *Edujoth* ii. 4.

Akiba.[232] His usual dwelling was however in the south of Palestine on the borders of Edom, in the village of Kephar-Asis (כפר עזין), where Joshua once visited him.[233] He seems, judging from his age, to have stood in nearer relation to Tarphon and Akiba than to Joshua; he questioned Joshua, and went " behind him" (like a pupil), while he was on equal terms with Tarphon and Akiba.[234] It would be of special interest, if his father really did, as tradition asserts, also exercise the functions of high priest. The matter is however more than questionable, and only so far probable that he was of priestly descent.[234a] In the history of the Halachah, Ishmael represents a special tendency: in opposition to the artificial and arbitrary exegesis of Akiba, he adhered more to the simple and literal meaning of Scripture, but this must be understood in only a very comparative sense.[235] The laying down of the *thirteen Middoth*, or exegetic rules for Halachic exegesis, is ascribed to him.[236] A large portion of the exegetic material contained in two of the oldest Midrashim (*Mechilta* on Exodus, and *Sifre* on Numbers and Deuteronomy) comes from him and his disciples, even if these are not, as tradition asserts, the exclusive production of his school.[237] According to the legend, Ishmael,

[232] Joshua and Ishmael, *Kilajim* vi. 4; *Aboda sara* ii. 5; Tosefta, *Para* 638. 35. Akiba and Ishmael, *Edujoth* ii. 6; *Mikwaoth* vii. 1. On a disputation between Tarphon, Eleasar ben Asariah, Ishmael and Joshua, see *Jadajim* iv. 3. But that Joshua and Ishmael *e.g.* did not live in the same place is seen from *Kilajim* vi. 4; Tosefta, *Bechoroth* 536. 24. The same is evident with respect to Akiba from *Erubin* i. 2; Tosefta, *Sabim* 677. 6 (pupils of Ishmael are reporting to Akiba the instruction of the former).

[233] On the borders of Edom, *Kethuboth* v. 8; in Kephar-Asis, *Kilajim* vi. 4; on Kephar-Asis, comp. *The Survey of Western Palestine, Memoirs* by Kitchener and Conder, iii. 315, 348–350. *Mikwaoth* vii. 1, according to which people of Medaba, the well-known Moabite town, relate concerning his teaching, points to labours in Peraea.

[234] Compare the passages cited in note 232. With respect to Joshua, *Aboda sara* ii. 5; Tosefta, *Para* 638. 35. Bacher, *Monatsschr.* 1883, p. 64.

[234a] Derenbourg, p. 387 sq.

[235] Comp. briefly, Hamburger, p. 528. Bacher, *Monatsschr.* 1883, p. 73 sq.

[236] See above, p. 336; and Derenbourg, pp. 389–391.

[237] The tradition is reduced to its true proportion *e.g.* in Bacher, *Monatsschr.* 1883, p. 66 sq. Comp. also on the two Midrashim, § 3, above.

like most of his contemporaries, is said to have died as a martyr in the Barkochba war.[238]

Among those scribes who also had intercourse with Gamaliel, Joshua and Elieser, but stood more or less in a relation of discipleship to them, by far the most celebrated was R. Akiba ben Joseph.[239] He flourished about A.D. 110–135. His relations with Gamaliel, Joshua and Elieser have already been spoken of (notes 199, 200, 207). He surpassed them all in influence and reputation. None gathered about him so large a number of pupils;[240] none was so glorified by tradition. It is scarcely possible however to pluck the historically true from the garland of myths. Not even the place of his labours is known with certainty; from the Mishna it seems to have been Lydda,[241] while the Babylonian Talmud names Bene-Barak (בני ברק).[242] Such sentences of his as have been handed down are not only characteristic of his rigidly legal stand-point, but also show that he made dogmatic and philosophic questions the subjects of study.[243] Like the ancient Zealots, he combined national patriotism with religious zeal. Hence he hailed the political hero Barkochba as the Messiah,[244] and is said to have suffered martyrdom as one of the most eminent sacrifices for the national cause.[245] Of his exegetic method it can only be said, that it is an exaggeration and degeneration of that which prevailed among the Rabbis in general, " it is

---

[238] Grätz, iv. 175. Derenbourg, p. 436.

[239] See concerning him the Hebrew works of Frankel, Brüll and Weiss; also Jost, *Gesch. des Judenth.* ii. 59 sqq. Landau, *Monatsschr. für Gesch. und Wissensch. des Judenth.* 1854, pp. 45–51, 81–93, 130–148. Grätz, *Gesch. der Juden,* iv. 53 sqq.; Ewald's *Gesch. des Volkes Israel,* vii. 376 sqq. Derenbourg, pp. 329–331, 395 sqq., 418 sqq. Hamburger, ii. 32–43. Bacher, *Monatsschr.* 1883, pp. 254 sqq., 297 sqq., 347 sqq., 419 sqq., 433 sqq. Gastfreund, *Biographie des Tanaiten Rabi Akiba* (in Hebrew), Lemberg 1871.

[240] Derenbourg, p. 395 sq.          [241] *Rosh hashana* i. 6.

[242] *Sanhedrin* 32b; Derenbourg, pp. 307, 395.

[243] The sentences, *Aboth* iii. 13–16. Among them, iii. 15, is the saying הכל צפוי והרשות נתונה, "Everything is watched (by God), but freedom is granted (to men)."

[244] Derenbourg, p. 425 sq.

[245] Grätz, iv. 176, 177. Derenbourg, p. 436. Bacher, 1883, p. 256.

the art of deducing heaps of Halachoth from every jot of the law." [246] To attain this, the principle was acted on, that no word of the text was superfluous, that even the slightest, the most apparently superfluous elements of the text contain the most important truths.[247] It is of much more value than these exegetical tricks, and of real epoch-making importance in the history of Jewish law, that in the time of Akiba, and probably *under his direction*, the *Halachah*, which had hitherto been only orally propagated, was for the *first time codified*. The various materials were arranged according to the point of view of their actual matter, and what was current law was recorded in writing together with adductions of the divergent views of all the more eminent scribes. This work forms the foundation of the Mishna of R. Judah ha-Nasi, which has been preserved to us.[248]

R. Tarphon, a priestly scribe, who is said to have been very much in earnest about his priestly duties and privileges, so far as this was possible after the destruction of the temple, was a contemporary of Akiba.[249] He lived at Lydda,[250] and was chiefly in intercourse with Akiba,[251] but took part in a

[246] Bacher, *Monatsschr.* 1883, p. 254 sq.

[247] Thus *e.g.* the particle את is said to indicate, that besides the object *mentioned*, something else is also intended together with it. In the account of the creation את השמים is used, because the sun, moon and stars are also meant (Wünsche, *Bereshith rabba*, p. 6 sq.). Comp. Derenbourg, p. 397. The proselyte Aquila tried to be faithful to this exegetical principle by translating in his Greek version of the Bible σὺν τὸν οὐρανὸν καὶ σὺν τὴν γῆν, at which Jerome vents his just scorn (*Epist.* 57 *ad Pammachium*, c. 11, *Opp.* de Vallarsi, i. 316). Comp. also, on Aquila as a disciple of Akiba, Hieronymus, *Comment. in Jes.* viii. 11 sqq. (Vallarsi, iv. 122): Akibas quem magistrum Aquilae proselyti autumant. Grätz, *Gesch. der Juden*, iv. 437.

[248] That an older work of the time of Akiba is the foundation of our present Mishna, may be inferred almost with certainty from its contents. That the work in question was edited by Akiba himself may also be accepted as probable from the testimony of Epiphanius (*haer.* 33. 9). For further particulars, see § 3. Comp. also Derenbourg, pp. 399–401.

[249] See in general, Derenbourg, pp. 376–383. Hamburger, ii. 1196 sq. Bacher, *Monatsschr.* 1883, pp. 497–507.

[250] *Taanith* iii. 9 ; *Baba mezia* iv. 3.

[251] *Terumoth* iv. 5, ix. 2 ; *Nasir* vi. 6 ; *Bechoroth* iv. 4 ; *Kerithoth* v. 2–3. Tosefta, *Mikwaoth*, 654. 4, 660. 33.

disputation with Eleasar ben Asariah, Ishmael and Joshua.[252] Subsequent tradition makes him, like all the scribes of his time, a martyr in the Barkochba war.[253] As this is however of just the same value as the Christian tradition, which makes all the apostles martyrs, he may very well be identical with that Trypho with whom Justin met, and who said of himself that he had fled from Palestine on account of the war.[254] It is peculiar that hard words against the Gospels and against the Christian faith should have been reported exactly of him.[255]

Beside R. Tarphon there remain to be mentioned as contemporaries of R. Akiba, R. Johanan ben Nuri, who lived also in the time of Gamaliel II., Joshua and Elieser, but is most frequently spoken of as in intercourse with Akiba;[256] R. Simon ben Asai, or merely Ben Asai, who is famed for

---

[252] *Jadajim* iv. 3.  [253] Grätz, iv. 179. Derenbourg, p. 436.

[254] Justin. *Dial. c. Tryphone*, c. 1 : εἰμὶ δὲ Ἑβραῖος ἐκ περιτομῆς, φυγὼν τὸν νῦν γενόμενον πόλεμον, ἐν τῇ Ἑλλάδι καὶ τῇ Κορίνθῳ τὰ πολλὰ διάγων. The names טרפון and Τρύφων are identical, for it cannot be proved that the former is a genuine Semitic name, although, according to its form, this is possible. The time too exactly agrees. Hence the identity of R. Tarphon with Justin's Trypho has been accepted by many scholars. See Wolf, *Bibliotheca Hebraea*, ii. 837.

[255] He said that the Gospels ought to be burned although they contained the name of God (*Shabbath* 116a ; Derenbourg, p. 379 sq. ; Bacher, 1883, p. 506). On account of the great interest of R. Tarphon to Christian theologians, I here give *all the passages of the Mishna in which he is named: Berachoth* i. 3, vi. 8 ; *Pea* iii. 6 ; *Kilajim* v. 8 ; *Terumoth* iv. 5, ix. 2 ; *Maaseroth* iii. 9 ; *Maaser sheni* ii. 4, 9 ; *Shabbath* ii. 2 ; *Erubin* iv. 4 ; *Pesachim* x. 6 ; *Sukka* iii. 4 ; *Beza* iii. 5 ; *Taanith* iii. 9 ; *Jebamoth* xv. 6–7 ; *Kethuboth* v. 2, vii. 6, ix. 2, 3 ; *Nedarim* vi. 6 ; *Nasir* v. 5, vi. 6 ; *Kiddushin* iii. 13 ; *Baba kamma* ii. 5 ; *Baba mezia* ii. 7, iv. 3 ; *Makkoth* i. 10 ; *Edujoth* i. 10 ; *Aboth* ii. 15–16 ; *Sebachim* x. 8, xi. 7 ; *Menachoth* xii. 5 ; *Bechoroth* ii. 6–9, iv. 4 ; *Kerithoth* v. 2–3 ; *Kelim* xi. 4, 7, xxv. 7 ; *Ohaloth* xiii. 3, xvi. 1 ; *Para* i. 3 ; *Mikwaoth* x. 5 ; *Machshirin* v. 4 ; *Jadajim* iv. 3. For the passages in the Tosefta, see the index to Zuckermandel's edition.

[256] In the time of Gamaliel, *Rosh hashana* 148. In the time of Joshua, Tosefta, *Taanith* 217. 14. In the time of Elieser, Tosefta, *Orla* 45. 1. *Kelim* 575. 18, 20. In association with Akiba, *Rosh hashana* iv. 5 ; *Bechoroth* vi. 6 ; *Temura* i. 1 ; *Ukzin* iii. 5. Tosefta, *Pesachim* 155. 27. Comp. in general, Hamburger, ii. 490 sq. Bacher, *Monatsschr.* 1883, p. 537 sq.

being specially indefatigable in study;[257] R. Johanan ben Beroka, who was an associate of Joshua and Johanan ben Nuri;[258] R. Joses the Galilean, who is mentioned as the contemporary of Eleasar ben Asariah, Tarphon and Akiba;[259] R. Simon ben Nannos, or only Ben Nannos, also a contemporary of Tarphon and Akiba.[260]

To the same period belongs also Abba Saul, who indeed gives an account even of a saying of Johanan ben Sakkai, and is repeatedly quoted as an authority concerning the arrangements of the temple, but cannot have been of earlier date than Akiba, since he frequently reports his sayings also.[261] Also R. Judah ben Bethera, who is mentioned on the one hand as

[257] Contemporaries of Akiba, *Shekalim* iv. 6; *Joma* ii. 3; *Taanith* iv. 4; *Baba bathra* ix. 10. It was said of him: "Since the death of Ben Asai there are no longer any indefatigable students" (*Sota* ix. 15: שְׁקְדָנִים, properly, waking ones, *i.e.* untiringly studying ones). Some sentences of his in *Aboth* iv. 2–3. Comp. in general, Hamburger, ii. 1119–1121. Bacher, *Monatsschr.* 1884, pp. 173–187, 225 sq.

[258] With Joshua, Tosefta, *Sota* 307. 7. With Johanan ben Nuri, Tosefta *Terumoth* 38. 15. In the Mishna, Johanan ben Beroka is mentioned, *Erubin* viii. 2, x. 15; *Pesachim* vii. 9; *Jebamoth* vi. 6; *Kethuboth* ii. 1; *Baba kamma* x. 2; *Baba bathra* viii. 5; *Shebuoth* vii. 7; *Aboth* iv. 4; *Bechoroth* viii. 10; *Kelim* xvii. 11. Comp. also Bacher, *Monatsschr.* 1884, p. 208 sq.

[259] With these three, *Jer. Gittin* ix. 1 (Derenbourg, p. 368). With Akiba and Tarphon, Tosefta, *Mikwaoth* 660. 32. He relates also in the name of Johanan ben Nuri, Tosefta, *Orla* 45. 1. See in general, Hamburger, ii. 499–502. Bacher, *Monatsschr.* 1883, pp. 507–513, 529–536.

[260] See especially Tosefta, *Mikwaoth* 660. 33. We find him associated with Ishmael, *Baba bathra* x. 8. He is mentioned by his full name Simon ben Nannos (νάννος=dwarf), *Bikkurim* iii. 9; *Shabbath* xvi. 5; *Erubin* ix. 15; *Baba bathra* x. 8; *Menachoth* iv. 3. Only as Ben Nannos, *Kethuboth* x. 5; *Gittin* viii. 10; *Baba bathra* vii. 3, x. 8; *Shabbath* vii. 5.

[261] On a saying of Johanan ben Sakkai, *Aboth* ii. 8. On the arrangements of the temple, *Middoth* ii. 5; also *Menachoth* viii. 3, xi. 5. On sayings of Akiba, Tosefta, *Kilajim* 79. 9; *Sanhedrin* 433. 27. Comp. also *Pea* viii. 5; *Kilajim* ii. 3; *Shabbath* xxiii. 3; *Shekalim* iv. 2; *Beza* iii. 8; *Kethuboth* vii. 6; *Nedarim* vi. 5; *Gittin* v. 4; *Kiddushin* iv. 2; *Baba mezia* iv. 12, vi. 7; *Baba bathra* ii. 7, 13; *Sanhedrin* x. 1; *Makkoth* ii. 2. Lewy, *Ueber einige Fragmente des Mischna des Abba Saul*, Berlin 1876 (comp. *Magazin für die Wissensch. des Judenth.* iv. 1877, pp. 114–120; *Monatsschr. für Gesch. und Wissensch. des Judenth.* 1878, pp. 187–192, 227–235).

a contemporary of Elieser, on the other as a contemporary of R. Meir, and who must consequently have flourished in the period between the two, *i.e.* in the time of Akiba.[262]

R. Judah, R. Joses, R. Meir and R. Simon, men of the next generation, are more frequently mentioned in the Mishna than all those hitherto named. Their labours however, having taken place in the middle of the second century, fall outside the limits of the period here dealt with.

[262] Contemporary of Elieser, *Negaim* ix. 3, xi. 7. Contemporary of Meir, Tosefta, *Nasir* 290. 14. Comp. also on the chronology, *Pea* iii. 6 ; *Pesachim* iii. 3 ; *Edujoth* viii. 3 ; *Kelim* ii. 4 ; *Ohaloth* xi. 7. Tosefta, *Jebamoth* 255. 28. See in general, Bacher, *Monatsschr.* 1884, pp. 76-81.